THE RECEPTION OF ASYLUM SEEKERS UNDER INTERNATIONAL LAW

Increasingly, European states are using policy on the reception of asylum seekers as an instrument of immigration control, eg by deterring the lodging of asylum applications, preventing integration into their societies and exercising a large degree of control over asylum seekers in order to facilitate expulsion. The European Union is currently engaged in a process of developing minimum conditions for the reception of asylum seekers, as part of a Common European Asylum System. This book critically examines the outcomes of the negotiation process on these minimum standards—Directive 2003/9/EC and Directive 2013/33/EU—in relation to international refugee law, international social security law and international human rights law. It presents a comprehensive analysis of state obligations that stem from these different fields of law with regard to asylum seekers' access to the labour market and social security benefits and compares them to the minimum standards developed in the European Union. To this end, it offers an in-depth study into the notion of non-discrimination on the basis of nationality in the field of social security and a detailed analysis of recent developments in the case law of the European Court of Human Rights on positive obligations in the socioeconomic sphere. It takes into account both the special characteristics of international legal obligations for states in the socioeconomic sphere and the legal consequences of the tentative legal status of asylum seekers. In addition, this book particularly examines how the instrumental use of social policy relates to international law.

Volume 51 in the series Studies in International Law

Studies in International Law

Recent titles in this series

Promises of States under International Law
Christian Eckart

Multilevel Regulation of Military and Security Contractors: The Interplay between International, European and Domestic Norms
Edited by Christine Bakker and Mirko Sossai

Europe and Extraterritorial Asylum
Maarten den Heijer

The Practice of International and National Courts and the (De)Fragmentation of International Law
Edited by Ole Kristian Fauchald and André Nollkaemper

The Politics of International Criminal Justice: A Spotlight on Germany
Ronen Steinke

Fighting Corruption in Public Procurement: A Comparative Analysis of Disqualification or Debarment Measures
Sope Williams-Elegbe

The Interception of Vessels on the High Seas: Contemporary Challenges to the Legal Order of the Oceans
Efthymios Papastavridis

Integration at the Border: The Dutch Act on Integration Abroad and International Immigration Law
Karin de Vries

An Equitable Framework for Humanitarian Intervention
Ciarán Burke

Democratic Statehood in International Law: The Emergence of New States in Post-Cold War Practice
Jure Vidmar

International Law and the Construction of the Liberal Peace
Russell Buchan

The OIC, the UN, and Counter-Terrorism Law-Making: Conflicting or Cooperative Legal Orders?
Katja Samuel

Statelessness: The Enigma of the International Community
William E Conklin

For the complete list of titles in this series, see 'Studies in International Law' link at www.hartpub.co.uk/books/series.asp

The Reception of Asylum Seekers under International Law

Between Sovereignty and Equality

Lieneke Slingenberg

• HART •
PUBLISHING
OXFORD AND PORTLAND, OREGON
2016

Published in the United Kingdom by Hart Publishing Ltd
16C Worcester Place, Oxford, OX1 2JW
Telephone: +44 (0)1865 517530
Fax: +44 (0)1865 510710
E-mail: mail@hartpub.co.uk
Website: http://www.hartpub.co.uk

Published in North America (US and Canada) by
Hart Publishing
c/o International Specialized Book Services
920 NE 58th Avenue, Suite 300
Portland, OR 97213-3786
USA
Tel: +1 503 287 3093 or toll-free: (1) 800 944 6190
Fax: +1 503 280 8832
E-mail: orders@isbs.com
Website: http://www.isbs.com

First published in hardback 2014
Paperback edition, 2016

Hart Publishing is an imprint of Bloomsbury Publishing plc.

British Library Cataloguing in Publication Data
Data Available

ISBN: HB: 978-1-84946-482-6
PB: 978-1-50990-925-4

Typeset by Compuscript Ltd, Shannon
Printed and bound in Great Britain by
Lightning Source UK Ltd

Acknowledgements

This book is based on my PhD thesis. I would like to thank my supervisors Gijs Vonk, Thomas Spijkerboer and Sarah van Walsum. I was very lucky to have three excellent supervisors, who complemented each other very well. The frequent discussions we had and the critical comments they gave, each from their own perspective, have significantly improved the manuscript. I would like to thank Professor H Battjes, Professor LS Bosniak, Professor MB Dembour, Professor JC Hathaway and Professor P Schoukens for their willingness to be a member of the thesis committee and for their valuable comments on the manuscript. Others have read smaller pieces of the manuscript and have provided insightful comments. I thank Juan Amaya Castro, Gareth Davies, Lisanne Groen, Klaus Kapuy, Marcelle Reneman, Karin de Vries, and Jorg Werner for this. Thanks are also due to Anne de Hingh for her editorial assistance.

This research formed part of the Cross-Border Welfare State research project, led by Gijs Vonk and funded by Instituut Gak. It was a pleasure to be part of a larger research group and I thank all the members of this group for the good and inspiring cooperation. I am grateful to Instituut Gak for making this research possible.

The joy in writing this book was for a large part caused by the stimulating working environment at the Department of Constitutional and Administrative Law and the Migration Law Research Group of the Faculty of Law of VU University Amsterdam. I would therefore like to express my gratitude to all (former) colleagues of this department and research group for the many conversations over coffee, fundamental and less fundamental discussions, interesting seminars, case law meetings, daily lunches, Friday afternoon drinks, and so on, which were helpful for my research and/or provided the necessary distraction from it.

Finally I would like to thank Jorg Werner for his support and his encouragement throughout this project. Our numerous discussions about research methods, case law and philosophy of law have been instrumental in the writing of this book. Above all, I am grateful for his patience with all my worries about the completion of this book and his ability, together with our daughter Aline and our son Iwan, to put this book into the proper perspective.

I dedicate this book to my parents.

Amsterdam, 27 November 2013

Table of Contents

Table of Cases

Court of Justice of the European Union

1

Introduction

1.1 RECEPTION OF ASYLUM SEEKERS IN THE EUROPEAN UNION

THIS BOOK IS about the reception of asylum seekers in the European Union. Asylum seekers form a special category of aliens.[1] They are outside their country of nationality and apply to another country for protection, invoking (one of the) various prohibitions of *refoulement* that have been laid down in international law. Pending the determination of their application for protection, it has to be examined whether a prohibition of *refoulement* actually applies and, consequently, whether or not they are able to be returned to their country of nationality or origin. During this determination, asylum seekers may not be expelled, even though they might not have fulfilled legal requirements for entering and/or staying in the country in which they apply for protection. The duration of this period is highly variable; it may last for several weeks or for several years.[2] Asylum seekers therefore find themselves in a state of legal limbo; they might not be able or are not willing to invoke the protection of their country of nationality or origin, while it has not yet been determined whether they qualify for international protection.[3]

Since asylum seekers usually arrive without means in the host country, they are often dependent on the possibility to work and/or on the eligibility for public benefits in order to meet their basic needs during the time in which their applications are being examined. In many European countries, asylum seekers' access to the labour market and public benefits has been subject to change during the last decades. As from the mid-1980s, EU Member States were confronted with increasing numbers of asylum applications. In 1992 the number of asylum applications lodged in the

1 Eg Gibney: '[A]sylum seekers raise a unique set of practical and moral issues' (Gibney 2004, p 9).

2 Bank 2000, p 287.

3 Fox O'Mahony and Sweeney have termed this 'double displacement' (Fox O'Mahony and Sweeney 2010).

European Union reached a peak at 672,385.[4] One general reaction to this increase in asylum applications has been the restriction of asylum seekers' access to the labour market and/or their eligibility for public benefits. Many states introduced separate welfare schemes for asylum seekers providing benefits in kind, whereas other states only provided general welfare benefits for a limited period of time or at a limited level.[5] In addition, states introduced dispersal policies for asylum seekers, housing them in accommodation centres throughout the country.[6] The literature suggests that by implementing such restrictive measures, states have mainly tried to deter potential asylum seekers and to facilitate expulsion of rejected asylum seekers by impeding social integration.[7] In this way, these authors argue, social law was used as an instrument of immigration control and exclusion from general welfare schemes and from the labour market was introduced as an alternative for closure at the border.[8]

In the early 2000s, the reception of asylum seekers became a European Community affair. In 1991 already, the European Commission called for the approximation and harmonization of reception conditions for asylum seekers in the Member States, in order to 'prevent any diversion of the flow of asylum seekers towards the Member State with the most generous arrangements'.[9] Under the Treaty of Amsterdam, concluded in 1997, Member States of the European Union transferred powers over asylum to the European Community. The Treaty of Amsterdam provided that the Council should adopt within five years after the entry into force of the Treaty of Amsterdam measures on asylum, including 'minimum standards on the reception of asylum seekers in Member States'.[10] In 2003 the Council adopted a directive on minimum standards for the reception

[4] P Juchno, 'Asylum applications in the European Union' 2007, available at: www.epp.eurostat.ec.europa.eu/portal/page/portal/product_details/publication?p_product_code=KS-SF-07-110. In 2012, 331,975 asylum applications were lodged in the EU (source: Eurostat). As some Member States produce statistics based on cases, the number of individuals per counted application may vary and is in many cases greater than 1. In addition, asylum application statistics for some countries may include repeat applications and appeals. The number of asylum applications mentioned above therefore does not correspond to the actual number of persons arriving in a certain year in Europe and applying for international protection.

[5] Bank 2000; Minderhoud 1999; Schuster 2000.

[6] Bank 2000; Robinson, Andersson and Musterd 2003; Schuster 2000.

[7] Eg Bank 2000; Bloch and Schuster 2002; Bouckaert 2007; Geddes 2000; Liedtke 2002; Mabbett and Bolderson 2002; Minderhoud 1999; Morris 2010; Sawyer and Turpin 2005; Schuster 2000. More generally, Tazreiter identifies withdrawal or limiting social and economic rights as a general form of deterrence in asylum policy (Tazreiter 2004, p 53).

[8] *Cf* Bosniak 2004, p 332. See also Geddes 2000, p 145.

[9] Communication from the Commission to the Council and the European Parliament on the right of asylum, Brussels 11 October 1991, SEC(91) 1857 final, p 7.

[10] Art 63(1)(b) of the Treaty establishing the European Community (TEC).

of asylum seekers (Directive 2003/9).[11] The Treaty of Lisbon, adopted in 2009, provided the basis for the adoption by the European Parliament and the Council of measures for a Common European Asylum System compromising 'standards concerning the conditions for the reception of applicants for asylum or subsidiary protection'.[12] In 2013, a recast of Directive 2003/9 was adopted: Directive 2013/33/EU of the European Parliament and of the Council laying down standards for the reception of applicants for international protection (recast)[13] (Directive 2013/33, together, the Directives are also referred to as the EU Reception Conditions Directives). Member States should implement Directive 2013/33 into their national laws before 21 July 2015.

Both Directives have to be in accordance with relevant international law. According to their legal basis in the treaty,[14] the Directives should be in accordance with the Refugee Convention and other relevant treaties. The preambles of the Directives refer to the 'full and inclusive application' of the Refugee Convention and to Member States' 'obligations under instruments of international law to which they are party'.[15] Such explicit references to international law are not common in primary or secondary Union law. They make international law a direct standard of review for the EU Reception Conditions Directives.[16] The standards ultimately laid down in the Directives have, however, been criticized from an international law point of view.[17]

The aim of this study is to investigate in depth which obligations for EU Member States stem from 'relevant treaties' of international refugee law, international social security law and international human rights law with regard to the reception of asylum seekers and to compare them with the minimum standards laid down in the EU Reception Conditions Directives. When examining which obligations stem from international law with regard to the reception of asylum seekers, two different questions need to be addressed. It should be examined whether international law does in fact contain any binding obligations for states with regard to social and economic policy. Further, it should be examined if it makes a difference that

11 Council Directive 2003/9/EC of 27 January 2003 laying down minimum standards for the reception of asylum seekers, [2003] OJ L31/18.

12 Art 78(2)(f) of the Treaty on the Functioning of the European Union (TFEU).

13 [2013] OJ L180/96.

14 Arts 63(1) of the TEC and 78(1) of the TFEU.

15 See recitals 2 and 6 of the preamble to Directive 2003/9 and recitals 3 and 10 of the preamble to Directive 2013/33.

16 Battjes 2006, pp 97–105; Reneman 2012, pp 61–62. This seems also to be the approach of the Court of Justice of the European Union (see, eg, CJEU 2 March 2010, Joined Cases C-175/08, C-176/08, C-178/08 and C-179/08 *Salahadin Abdulla* [2010] ECR I-1493, para 53).

17 See, eg, Battjes 2006, pp 496–507; Guild 2004; Ippolito 2013; UNHCR 2003. On the other hand, Bank has argued that international law imposes very few limitations on states' discretion in designing reception policies (Bank 2000).

it concerns state obligations with regard to aliens in general and asylum seekers in particular. What difference does the alienage of asylum seekers make with regard to the existence, scope and content of state obligations in the socioeconomic sphere? It will turn out that this latter question is a very important, and sometimes even decisive, aspect of the examination of state obligations for asylum seekers under international law.

The general approach, research questions and outline of the book will be further discussed below in sections 1.3 and 1.4. Section 1.5 will explain the terminology used in this book and section 1.6 will discuss the sources used for this study. Finally, section 1.7 will discuss the method of interpretation to be applied. First, however, some attention will be paid to the more theoretical debate on the rights of aliens.

1.2 SOVEREIGNTY AND EQUALITY

It is important to stress at the outset that the aim in this section is not to offer a comprehensive study of the large literature on the tension between the sovereignty of the state and the ideal of equal human rights with regard to the position of aliens. The more limited aim of this section is to give a rough sketch of a number of analytical concepts presented in this literature, with which the results of this study can be analysed and explained. For this purpose, this section will mainly draw upon the work of Linda Bosniak, as her work is particularly elucidating with respect to the themes in this book.

It is generally acknowledged that the tension existing in liberal democratic states between sovereignty, on the one hand, and the ideal of human rights, on the other hand, comes to the fore with regard to immigration issues.[18] This is caused by the fact that immigration control is generally seen as a crucial and fundamental aspect of state sovereignty.[19] Benhabib has provided convincing arguments for the importance attached to the interest of immigration control. In her view, a certain degree of closure is required for the legitimacy of democratic governance, which is one of the cornerstones of current liberal democratic states. The core of democratic governance is the ideal of public autonomy, which can be summarized in the principle that those who are subject to the law should also be its authors. Such a principle can only function properly if those in whose name the laws have been enacted are clearly demarcated from those upon whom the laws are not binding. Hence, a circumscribed people upon a given territory is crucial for the sake of maintaining democratic legitimacy,

[18] Benhabib 2004; Gibney 2004; Morris 2010, p 24 with further references; Noll 2000, pp 73–96.

[19] Benhabib 2004; Bosniak 2004, p 329.

according to Benhabib.[20] Another important liberal value and foundation of democratic constitutional states is the observance of individual human rights as recognition of inherent dignity and equal rights of all human beings.[21] Human rights by definition accrue to people on the basis of their personhood; not on their membership to a particular state. Accordingly, in Benhabib's words: 'There is thus an irresolvable contradiction (...) between the expansive and inclusionary principles of moral and political universalism, as anchored in universal human rights, and the particularistic and exclusionary conceptions of democratic closure'.[22] As Morris notes, much of the theorizing around the phenomenon of asylum tends to weigh these two principles against each other and tries to find a balance.[23]

Bosniak has identified two different regulatory domains in the migration context in which these two principles meet and compete.[24] I will call these domains the 'border domain' and the 'material rights domain'.[25] The border domain concerns the admission and expulsion of aliens into and from the national territory, hence the more 'traditional' instrument of immigration control. In this domain, the principle of sovereignty usually prevails over the principle of universal human rights. Even though exceptions should sometimes be made on the basis of human rights, states are generally free to decide who to admit and who to expel. In other words, the main rule in this domain can be summarized as: no, unless. ... Aliens do not have a right to enter or remain in the country, unless refusal of entrance or expulsion would be in violation with human rights norms.[26]

The second regulatory domain, which I have called the 'material rights domain', concerns the general, ie non-immigration-related treatment of aliens who are present on the territory. This domain concerns the rights of aliens that are not related to permission to enter, stay or reside in the territory, such as employment, social security and education rights

[20] Benhabib 2004.

[21] See also Habermas 1996, p 99.

[22] Benhabib 2004, p 19.

[23] Morris 2010, p 24 with further references.

[24] Bosniak 2004, p 329.

[25] These domains could also be referred to as the domain of 'immigration law' and the domain of 'immigrant or aliens law' (Martin 2001, p 88).

[26] Bosniak 2004, p 329. See also the Human Rights Committee in General Comment no 15 on the position of aliens under the Covenant: 'The Covenant does not recognize the right of aliens to enter or reside in the territory of a state party. It is in principle a matter for the State to decide who it will admit to its territory'. Also the ECtHR generally states in immigration cases that 'as a matter of well-established international law and subject to its treaty obligations, a State has the right to control the entry of non-nationals into its territory' (for the first time in *Abdulaziz, Cabales and Balkandali v United Kingdom* app nos 9214/80; 9473/81; 9474/81 (ECtHR, 28 May 1985), para 67). With reference to this case law of the ECtHR, the European Committee on Social Rights has adopted the same position (*Defence for Children v the Netherlands* complaint no 47/2008 (European Committee of Social Rights, 20 October 2009), para 41).

('material rights'). This book will focus completely on this second domain. In this domain, the relation between the principles of state sovereignty and human rights is more complex. No straightforward main rule can be identified in this field.[27] Bosniak argues that the main question in this domain is in fact a jurisdictional one: Where does the regulatory regime of the border legitimately begin and end?[28] Or stated differently: '[H]ow far does sovereignty reach before it must give way to equality'?[29] Bosniak discerned two broad models for answering this question, and, accordingly, for finding a proper balance between the principles of sovereign self-determination and equal universal human rights. She calls these models, inspired by the theories of Walzer,[30] the sphere separation model and the sphere convergence model.[31]

Under the 'sphere separation model', the state's interest in immigration control, or the sphere of membership regulation, must remain more or less confined to the border. The state's immigration power may only be exercised legitimately as regards decisions on entrance and expulsion made at the border. To structure an immigrant's status within the national territory according to the state's border-regulative interests or imperatives would be illegitimate under the sphere separation model. In other words, immigration status is relevant for decisions made at the border, but it may not be the decisive factor with regard to decisions made about the treatment of aliens within the border. Hence, this model implies that social law cannot be used as an instrument of immigration control. In the words of Owen Fiss: 'Admission laws can be enforced by fences at the borders, deportation proceedings, or criminal sanctions, not, I maintain, by imposing social disabilities'.[32] In short, under the separation model, national society may be 'hard on the outside', but must be 'soft on the inside'.

27 Bosniak 2004.

28 Bosniak 2006, p 76.

29 Ibid, p 39.

30 In his book *Spheres of Justice*, Walzer advocates a system of 'complex equality'. In such a system, different social goods, such as money, security and welfare, and political power, should be distributed in their own sphere on the basis of their own distributive principles. Justice exists if dominance between the different spheres is prevented; a certain social good should not be distributed on the basis of the possession of another social good. In other words: 'no citizen's standing in one sphere or with regard to one social good can be undercut by his standing in some other sphere, with regard to some other good' (Walzer 1983, p 19). He formulates therefore the following 'open-ended distributive principle': No social good x should be distributed to men and women who possess some other good y merely because they possess y and without regard to the meaning of x' (Walzer 1983, p 20).

31 Bosniak 2006. The same distinction has been made by Legomsky, albeit less elaborated. He distinguishes between the 'dichotomous, or bipolar, model' and the 'continuum model' (Legomsky 1995, p 1463). In the same vein, Noll distinguishes between divisible and bundled jurisdiction (Noll 2010).

32 Fiss 1998. With the term 'Social disabilities', Fiss refers to exclusion from the labour market, exclusion from education and exclusion from welfare benefits. See for other adherents of this line of reasoning: Bosniak 2006, pp 124–29 with further references.

Under the 'sphere convergence model', the interest of immigration control or the immigration status continues to play a legitimate and even decisive role in defining the position of aliens who are physically present on the territory. Under this model, the national community is envisioned as a series of concentric circles or as a continuum, with nationals in the innermost circle or at the ultimate edge enjoying full benefits and burdens of membership and those farther away possessing progressively few claims on the community. According to Michael Perry:

> [The] proposition that the members of a political community may appropriately decide whether, to what extent, and under what conditions persons who are not members may enter the territory of the political community and share its resources and largesse (...) necessarily entails the view that a person, in some respects at least, is more deserving by virtue of his status as a citizen than a person who is not a citizen.[33]

Hence, under this model, material rights are characterized as membership rights.[34] For persons who are not full members yet, their legal status or the state's immigration power may affect the content and scope of their material rights. In other words, the regulatory domain of the border may, to a certain extent, converge with the 'material rights domain'.

Adherents of this model disagree, however, about the basis for an accretion of rights. For some proponents rights should increase through a change in legal status,[35] sometimes combined with the length of legal residence and the degree of integration,[36] while others argue that rights should accrue through the mere passage of time.[37] Still others have identified other facts of 'social reality' that should have significance for the level of rights. Martin, for example, distinguishes between three different categories of non-admitted aliens as regards membership levels: entrants without inspection, parolees and applicants at the border. He argues that applicants at the border have the lowest claim to membership rights as they will not have established any community connection yet. Entrants without inspection deserve a higher rank as they might have established significant social ties in the (local) community, particularly when they remain for a lengthy period. 'Such connections then deserve some weight in deciding on the exact protections owed to them in light of this complex relationship they hold to our polity and society'.[38] Parolees have not

33 Michael Perry, cited in Bosniak 2006, p 76.

34 Da Lomba argues that states do indeed characterize the right to health care as a membership right (Da Lomba 2011).

35 Legomsky 1995.

36 Hailbronner 2008, p 12.

37 See, eg, Carens 2005.

38 Martin 2001, p 99. Martin recognizes that there are also sound arguments to place entrants without inspection below applicants at the border, as they failed to respect elemental

been formally admitted but are released from detention and allowed a certain freedom to move at large in the territory during their procedure for admission. They have the strongest claims of these three categories of aliens, according to Martin, as their social ties established in the community 'will have occurred with a form of deliberate permission from the US government, following an opportunity for screening'.[39] While Martin treats all applicants for admission the same, Aleinikoff argues that asylum seekers should 'occupy some circle closer to the centre than that occupied by other applicants for entry'. According to Aleinikoff, the fact that an asylum seeker might not have a political community to return to should count in establishing his constitutional position.[40]

While Bosniak distinguishes between the separation and the convergence model, she does not wish to overstate the distinction between these two models and notes that adherents of the convergence model also argue for some insulation from the border regime for aliens present on the territory, while separation proponents usually allow some convergence (eg with regard to political rights). In addition, she argues that complete separation between the border regime and the material rights regime cannot, as a matter of fact, be achieved. For aliens, the exclusionary territorial border is always, to some extent and in some form, present on the territorial inner area as well.[41]

Nevertheless, the jurisdictional dispute between the border regime and the material rights regime and the two possible solutions to this dispute are valuable concepts with which the results of this study can be analysed and explained. In answering the question which state obligations stem from international law as regards the reception of asylum seekers, this study will shed light on how this jurisdictional dispute is dealt with under contemporary international law. As has been stated above, it will indeed become evident that this question is a relevant and often decisive aspect of establishing which state obligations result from international law as regards the reception of asylum seekers. Should the regulatory domain of the border with its emphasis on the interest of immigration control remain confined to the border, as a result of which asylum seekers

border procedures and simply established their presence on the territory in defiance with the law. Applicants at the border have at least attempted to establish their community membership on the right footing and have provided the authorities with the possibility to apply their immigration policy (Martin 2001, pp 97–98). Nevertheless, he finds that more weight should be attached to de facto community ties.

39 Martin 2001, pp 99–100. Martin acknowledges that according parolees a lower status can be justified on pragmatic grounds. If parole is applied only in order to avoid needless confinement, providing them with more rights might prompt some curtailments of the use of parole.

40 Aleinikoff 1983, pp 257–58.

41 Bosniak 2006, pp 122–40.

are entitled to equal treatment with nationals as regards their material rights (separation model)? Or does the state's immigration power have some bearing on the normative content of state obligations as regards asylum seekers' material rights under international law? (convergence model.) If so, to what extent? It will turn out that in establishing relevant state obligations for asylum seekers under international law, both elements of the separation model and elements of the convergence model will frequently pass in review.

In order to avoid repetition, the results of the present study will primarily be analysed in the light of these theoretical concepts in the concluding chapters to Part II (chapter seven) and Part III (chapter thirteen) and, most elaborately, in chapter 14. However, throughout the book, references to these concepts will be made in a more ad hoc way.

1.3 AIM AND GENERAL APPROACH

In view of the above, the aim of this study is twofold. First of all, it aims to identify and describe the international legal framework with regard to the social rights of asylum seekers in Europe and to assess the minimum standards adopted within the European Union on the reception of asylum seekers for compatibility with this framework. Secondly, on a more abstract level, it aims to examine to what extent the immigration power of the state may converge with the field of social policy under current international law. Does the state's immigration power have some bearing on the normative content of state obligations with regard to asylum seekers' social rights under international law? And if so, to what extent?

This study applies a positivist, systematic legal approach and understands law as an argumentative discipline.[42] It tries to offer a convincing argument on the meaning of the relevant law, without necessarily endorsing the outcome or merely describing the law from an outside perspective.[43] Without denying the close relationship between law, politics and morality, it conceives law as an autonomous system that can be analysed as such.

Especially in the field of human rights research, it is important to make one's specific perspective on human rights explicit. Dembour has convincingly shown that when people talk about human rights, they are not necessarily talking about the same thing. She has detected four different 'schools' in human rights research. In brief, she presents them as 'natural scholars' who conceive of human rights as *given*, 'deliberative scholars' who conceive of human rights as *agreed*, 'protest scholars' who conceive of human rights as *fought for*, and 'discourse scholars' who

[42] MacCormick 2005, p 14–15.
[43] *Cf* Hart in his postscript (Hart 1994, p 242–44).

conceive of human rights as *talked about*.[44] While acknowledging that the different schools overlap and that the model does not always reflect the complexity of arguments made about human rights in reality, she submits that the distinction in four schools helps to clarify intellectual and moral positions, which enables an understanding of the reasons for and implications of arguments made by a particular author.[45] The approach adopted in this study shows most similarity to the 'deliberative school' identified by Dembour, in that it views human rights as legal standards and not as moral principles, and, consequently, acknowledges the limited scope of human rights. In addition, it does not presume outcomes in advance and certain outcomes may be found unreasonable on moral grounds.[46]

The distinction between legal rules on the one hand and moral and political rules on the other hand is often made on the basis of the source from which the rules result. In this view, in order to qualify as international law, a rule has to derive from one of the accepted sources of international law.[47] This view is adopted in this book as well. The question of which sources of international law are accepted, will be discussed in section 1.6.1. In order to offer a convincing argument on the meaning of the legal rules found in these sources, it is important to identify the relevant and acceptable forms of legal argument.[48] Which forms of legal arguments or, put differently, methods of interpretation will be applied in this study will be explained in section 1.7.

The next section will list the research questions for this study, discuss more specific delimitations and explain the outline of the book.

1.4 RESEARCH QUESTIONS, DELIMITATIONS AND OUTLINE OF THE BOOK

The main question of this book can be formulated as follows:

Which state obligations for EU Member States stem from international refugee law, international social security law and international human rights law with regard to the social security of asylum seekers and their access to wage earning employment and how do these obligations relate to the standards laid down in Directive 2003/9 and Directive 2013/33 (the EU Reception Conditions Directives)?

The choice to focus on the social security of asylum seekers and their access to the labour market has been prompted by the wish to concentrate

44 Dembour 2006 pp 232–71.
45 Dembour and Kelly 2011, pp 18–22.
46 Ibid, p 15.
47 Nollkaemper 2005, p 16; Hathaway 2005, p 15; Jennings and Watts 1992, p 23.
48 See Patterson who states that the best way of understanding truth in law is in the use of forms of legal arguments. '[L]aw has its own argumentative grammar, and it is through the use of this grammar that the truth of legal propositions is shown' (Patterson 1999, p 73).

on asylum seekers' ability to generate income and on the protection against the absence or loss of (enough) income. Other aspects addressed by the EU Reception Conditions Directives, such as access to education, entitlement to information and documentation, detention and protection of family unity, will not form part of the object of inquiry of this study. The term 'wage-earning employment' implies that self-employment does not fall under the scope of this study, either.

This study will discuss and assess provisions of both Directive 2003/9 and Directive 2013/33, as Directive 2003/9 will remain effective until 20 July 2015 and as Directive 2013/33 does not apply to the United Kingdom, as a result of which Directive 2003/9 will continue to apply for the United Kingdom even after 20 July 2015.

The main question can be divided in a number of sub-questions. First of all, which standards concerning access to employment and social security are laid down in the EU Reception Conditions Directives has to be examined. For the evaluation of these standards under international law, it is necessary to pay attention to the rationale and official justifications brought forward for their inclusion. Consequently, not only should the standards laid down in the Directives be described and analysed, but it should also be examined which reasons have been put forward by Member States for including these standards.

In order to further a better understanding of the choices made by the European legislator, it is helpful to examine national developments as regards the reception of asylum seekers as well. Obviously, the Directives did not appear out of the blue, but are for a large part based on pre-existing national rules and practices. In order to gain a better understanding of the background of the provisions of the Directives, it is therefore important to have some insight into the development of the social rights of asylum seekers at the national level.

These issues will be examined in Part I. This part will argue that there is a strong convergence between the sphere of asylum policy and the sphere of asylum seekers' material rights in the EU, which manifests itself in the background, legal basis and negotiating history of the EU Reception Conditions Directives and in the actual provisions laid down in these Directives.

With regard to the subsequent examination of relevant state obligations under international law a distinction will be made between two kinds of provisions: provisions on equal treatment and non-discrimination, on the one hand, and other provisions with relevance to social security and access to employment, on the other hand.[49] Part II will systematically

[49] This distinction reflects the distinction that was made under international aliens law. Before the rise of international human rights law after the Second World War, individuals were not yet considered to be subjects of international law. The treatment of aliens was mainly dealt with within the doctrine of diplomatic protection and state responsibility. Under this

examine equal treatment and non-discrimination provisions of international refugee law, international social security law and international human rights law as to their relevance for asylum seekers' access to social security schemes and access to wage-earning employment. It will be examined whether and to what extent asylum seekers are entitled to equal treatment with nationals in these fields.

This part will argue that Member States are not required under current international law to provide asylum seekers with access to their labour markets on an equal footing with nationals. With regard to social security schemes, however, Member States are obligated under international law to grant equal treatment to asylum seekers as compared to nationals if asylum seekers fulfil certain conditions with regard to legal status and/or community ties. This part will examine in detail the meaning of the different conditions used in international law with regard to legal status of aliens in general and refugees in particular.

Finally, Part III of the book will investigate whether any obligations for EU Member States as regards the social security of asylum seekers and access to the labour market stem from international law *not* devoted to equal treatment and non-discrimination. In other words, this part of the book will examine provisions of international law other than provisions on equal treatment and non-discrimination with possible relevance for asylum seekers' social security and access to the labour market. It will be examined whether international law contains positive obligations or obligations to provide asylum seekers with social security benefits or access to the labour market, besides the (possible) obligation to grant complete equal treatment with nationals. Part III will therefore examine whether such other kinds of obligations for EU Member States stem from international law and what the scope and content of such obligations is.

This part will argue that, under certain circumstances, Member States can be responsible under international law for preventing asylum seekers from becoming destitute. In addition, this part will argue that this responsibility may extend under international law, if the degree of state control exercised over asylum seekers increases. Finally, this part will show that international law does contain some obligations for Member States with regard to the access to wage-earning employment.

doctrine, an injury to a citizen is an injury to his state (Brownlie 2003, p 497). If an alien was injured by acts contrary to international law, the host state incurred responsibility and the state of nationality of the alien was permitted to seek redress through diplomatic protection (Lillich 1984, pp 8–14). The question as to which acts were contrary to international law has been answered in two different ways. Under the theory of national treatment, aliens were entitled to equal treatment with nationals. If aliens were granted equality of treatment, state responsibility and the right to diplomatic protection did not arise. Opponents of this theory held that there is an 'international minimum standard' for the protection of aliens that must be upheld irrespective of how the state treats its own nationals. Under this theory, a state that failed to guarantee this minimum standard to aliens incurred international liability (Brownlie 2003, pp 500–05; Lillich 1984, pp 14–17; Shaw 2003, pp 733–37).

The final chapter will contain conclusions. Besides answering the main question of this study, the final chapter will also reflect on the state obligations identified under international law and list a number of relevant factors for their existence. Further, it will reflect upon the more abstract question as to the extent to which international law allows for a convergence of the regulatory domain of the border or the state's immigration power with the domain of aliens' material rights. This study will show that it is possible to identify binding state obligations resulting from international law with regard to employment and social security in general, but that the alienage of asylum seekers is often decisive for the content and scope of these obligations with regard to asylum seekers. Hence, even though human rights generally accrue to 'everybody', this study will show that in order for human beings to receive full protection of international law, a number of additional factors have to be met. The final chapter will elaborate on these relevant factors. Taking these factors into account, this study will argue that international law does set a number of limits on and attaches some consequences to the large degree of convergence between the state's immigration power and the field of social security and employment as manifested in the EU Reception Conditions Directives. The final chapter will provide guidance with regard to the interpretation of the EU Reception Conditions Directives in order to ensure compliance with international law. In addition, it will show that with regard to a number of issues conciliatory interpretation is not possible, as a result of which some provisions of the EU Reception Conditions Directives fall short of Member States' obligations under international law.

This study was concluded on 1 August 2013. Later developments have only been taken into account in exceptional cases.

1.5 TERMINOLOGY

This section will explain the meaning attached to the terms 'asylum seeker' and 'social security' for the purpose of this study.

1.5.1 Asylum Seeker

For the purpose of this book, 'asylum seeker' is defined as a person who is outside his country of nationality or is stateless and who applies for protection in or at the border of another country, until a final decision on that application has been made.

Some terms need further specification. 'Application for protection' is understood broadly. A person is considered to be an asylum seeker as from the moment he has made his intention to apply for protection known to the authorities, irrespective of whether he has officially lodged his application yet. In addition, it is implied by the concept of *seeking* asylum that it has not been established yet that the person concerned meets the relevant criteria. Furthermore, the basis on which the application has been lodged is irrelevant. The application can be lodged on the basis of the Refugee Convention, on the basis of another prohibition of *refoulement* stemming from international law, for example Article 3 of the European Convention on Human Rights, or on the basis of a domestic title for protection. The decisive criterion is that the person concerned applies for protection from some kind of danger abroad, or, more formally, for protection from subjection to human rights violations abroad.[50]

'Final decision' has a specific meaning as well for the purposes of this research. If an asylum application has been granted, a 'final decision' has been taken, and the person concerned is no longer an asylum seeker. The term 'final decision' also includes the granting of 'temporary protection' within the meaning of Directive 2001/55/EC.[51] If an asylum application is rejected, this decision is only 'final' for the purpose of this research if no domestic or international possibility of review is available, either because the period in which to lodge an application for review has expired, or because the person concerned has decided not to make use of the possibility. This means that in this book persons whose asylum application has been rejected in the final instance at the domestic level and who have lodged a complaint with, for example, the European Court of Human Rights or the Human Rights Committee also fall under the scope of the term 'asylum seeker'.

The requirement that persons need to be outside their country of nationality and apply in or at the border of another country means that persons who apply from abroad, for example at embassies or during a process of resettlement, do not fall within the scope of this research. This book only addresses persons who already find themselves in or at the border of the host state, without it being established that they are eligible for protection by that state.

1.5.2 Social Security

The term 'social security' has a wide variety of meanings.[52] It is therefore important to adopt a working definition for the purposes of this book.

[50] Battjes 2006, pp 6 and 8.

[51] Council Directive 2001/55/EC of 20 July 2001 on minimum standards for giving temporary protection in the event of a mass influx of displaced persons and on measures promoting a balance of efforts between Member States in receiving such persons and bearing the consequences thereof. [2001] OJ L212/12.

[52] Noordam and Vonk 2011, pp 1–3; Pieters 2006, pp 1–2.

The International Labour Organization has defined the concept of 'social security' as:

> [A]ll measures providing benefits, whether in cash or in kind, to secure protection, inter alia, from
>
> (a) lack of work-related income (or insufficient income) caused by sickness, disability, maternity, employment injury, unemployment, old age, or death of a family member;
> (b) lack of access or unaffordable access to health care;
> (c) insufficient family support, particularly for children and adult dependants;
> (d) general poverty and social exclusion.[53]

This definition is suitable for the purposes of this book. The list of social risks against which social security should provide protection under this definition are the same as the contingencies mentioned in ILO Convention no 102 on Minimum Standards of Social Security, complemented with the social condition of 'need' or 'destitution'.[54] A difference between this latter condition and the risks mentioned in ILO Convention no 102 is that the cause of the loss or absence of income is not relevant. It is important to note that social security in the definition adopted here is not limited to cash benefits, but includes benefits in kind as well. The in-kind support provided to asylum seekers in many EU Member States therefore falls under this definition of social security.

As the ILO report notes, access to social security is a public responsibility, and is typically provided through public institutions, financed either by contributions or general taxes.[55] According to this report:

> What distinguishes social security from other social arrangements is that: (1) benefits are provided to beneficiaries without any simultaneous reciprocal obligation (thus it does not, for example, represent remuneration for work or other services delivered); and (2) that it is not based on an individual agreement between the protected person and provider (as, for example, a life insurance contract) but that the agreement applies to a wider group of people and so has a collective character.[56]

In international social security law, a distinction is generally made between contributory and non-contributory social security schemes and between social insurance and social assistance schemes. Contributory benefits

[53] International Labour Organization, *World Social Security Report 2010/11. Providing Coverage in Times of Crisis and Beyond*, Geneva 2010, p 13.
[54] See the definition adopted by Noordam and Vonk 2011, pp 3–5.
[55] International Labour Organization, *World Social Security Report 2010/11* (n 53), p 14. See also Noordam and Vonk 2011, pp 5–6.
[56] International Labour Organization (n 53), p 14. The same approach is adopted by Pieters (Pieters 2006, pp 4–5).

are benefits the grant of which depends on direct financial participation by the persons protected or their employer or on a qualifying period of occupational activity. Hence, the financing of such benefits is primarily employment-based. Non-contributory benefits are benefits the grant of which does not depend on direct financial participation by the persons protected or their employer or on a qualifying period of occupational activity. Such benefits are primarily residence-based. The distinction between social insurance and social assistance schemes lies essentially in the cause of the loss or absence of income. Social assistance provides protection against need or poverty and does not require that there is a link between the reason for that need and a recognized social risk. Social insurance schemes, on the other hand, do require a link between the reason for the shortage of income and one of the recognized social risks. These terms will be further explained in chapter five.

Social assistance schemes can be subdivided into general and categorical schemes. General schemes have a general scope of application, whereas categorical schemes only apply to persons who belong to a certain group of people needing social assistance.[57] Support provided to asylum seekers in kind, under a separate scheme, can be seen as a categorical social assistance scheme. Throughout this book, the terms 'material reception benefits' or 'minimum subsistence benefits' will also be used to refer to such (categorical) social assistance schemes.

1.6 SOURCES

1.6.1 Sources of International Law

Although there is no explicit authoritative document in the international legal order that exhaustively enumerates the international sources of law, Article 38(1) of the Statute of the International Court of Justice is generally regarded as providing an authoritative list.[58] This article states:

> The Court, whose function is to decide in accordance with international law such disputes as are submitted to it, shall apply:
>
> a. international conventions, whether general or particular, establishing rules expressly recognized by the contesting states;
> b. international custom, as evidence of a general practice accepted as law;
> c. the general principles of law recognized by civilized nations;

[57] Pieters 2006, pp 26 and 97.

[58] Brownlie 2003, p 5; Nollkaemper 2005, pp 53–54; Jennings and Watts 1992, p 24; Shaw 2003, p 66; Wallace 2002, p 8.

d. (…), judicial decisions and the teachings of the most highly qualified publicists of the various nations, as subsidiary means for the determination of rules of law.

The first source mentioned in this article, international conventions, is often considered to be the most important source of international law.[59] Section 1.6.2 below will list the specific conventions used for this study.

With regard to international custom, Article 38(1) refers to 'evidence of a general practice accepted as law'. This means that a 'general recognition among States of a certain practice as obligatory is needed'.[60] Two elements can be deduced from this: 1) state practice and 2) the conviction that such practice reflects law (*opinio juris*).[61] In order to gain the status of customary international law, state practice must be 'both extensive and virtually uniform'.[62] With regard to the requirement of *opinio juris*, the International Court of Justice has held:

> Not only must the acts concerned amount to a settled practice, but they must also be such, or be carried out in such a way, as to be evidence of a belief that this practice is rendered obligatory by the existence of a rule of law requiring it. The need for such a belief, i.e., the existence of a subjective element, is implicit in the very notion of the *opinio juris sive necessitatis*. The States concerned must therefore feel that they are conforming to what amounts to a legal obligation. The frequency, or even habitual character of the acts is not in itself enough.[63]

In the legal doctrine, a number of human rights are identified as customary international law. These include: freedom from slavery, genocide, racial discrimination and torture.[64] Some authors also mention freedom from gender discrimination,[65] murder or enforced disappearance of

[59] Shaw 2003, p 89; Nollkaemper 2005, p 67.

[60] JL Brierly, *The Law of Nations*, cited in Brownlie 2003, p 6.

[61] Cassese 2005, p 119.

[62] *North Sea Continental Shelf* ICJ Reports 1969 (International Court of Justice, 20 February 1969), p 3, para 74.

[63] Ibid, para 77.

[64] Brownlie 2003, pp 537–38; Cassese 2005, pp 370–71; Hannum 1996, pp 340–51; Shaw 2003, pp 256–57. Hathaway is of the opinion that, in light of non-conforming state practice, only the right to freedom from systematic racial discrimination forms part of customary international law (Hathaway 2005, pp 36–39). I do not follow this view, since for a rule to become customary law, it is sufficient for a majority of states to engage in a consistent practice. Universal participation in the formation of a customary rule is not required (Brownlie 2003, pp 7–8; Cassese 2005, p 123). In addition, the non-conforming state practice Hathaway is referring to, such as genocide in Bosnia and Rwanda and the existence of 'not less than 27 million' slaves in the world, has been followed by widespread protest and accordingly 'have been treated as breaches of that rule, not as indications of the recognition of a new rule' (*Military and Paramilitary Activities in and against Nicaragua (Nicaragua v United States of America)* ICJ Reports 1986 (International Court of Justice, 27 June 1986), p 14, para 186).

[65] Cassese 2005, p 370.

individuals,[66] prolonged arbitrary detention,[67] the right to a fair trial[68] and the prohibition of *refoulement*[69] as forming part of customary international law. However, the absence of consensus on the status of these rights might lead to the conclusion that the necessary general state practice and/or *opinion juris* is lacking. It is therefore assumed that in any case the right to freedom from slavery, genocide, racial discrimination and torture have acquired the quality of customary law. Accordingly, they are binding upon all states of the world. However, these rights are laid down in widespread ratified human rights conventions (such as the International Covenant on Civil and Political Rights (ICCPR)) as well. The fact that they have gained the status of international customary law therefore does not have much added value. Accordingly, no separate attention will be paid to international custom in this study.

The same conclusion applies to the third source of international law mentioned in Article 38(1) of the Statute of the International Court of Justice: the general principles of law. This source was inserted in Article 38(1) to close the gap in the case of an apparent absence of relevant legal rules.[70] There is no universally agreed definition of general principles of law and it is not clear whether it refers to principles of the international legal order or to principles appearing in municipal systems.[71] It is clear, however, that in order for general principles to acquire any authority, very strong international consensus is required. The International Court of Justice has used this source only sparingly.[72]

Judicial decisions and 'the teachings of the most highly qualified publicists of the various nations' are included in Article 38(1) as subsidiary means for the determination of rules of law. As Brownlie observes, 'the practical significance of the label "subsidiary means" in Article 38(1)(d) is not to be exaggerated. A coherent body of jurisprudence will naturally have important consequences for the law'.[73] Nevertheless, judicial decisions cannot be regarded as formal sources of law, since the task of judges is to apply existing law and not to make law.[74] This means that these sources can be used as authoritative evidence of the state of the law[75] and serve as a method of interpretation. Consequently, these sources will be discussed further in section 1.7.3.

66 Brownlie 2003, p 537.
67 Brownlie 2003, p 537; Hannum 1996, p 345.
68 Hannum 1996, pp 345–46.
69 Battjes 2006, p 13; Hannum 1996, p 346 with further references.
70 Shaw 2003, p 93.
71 Wallace 2002, pp 22–23; Shaw 2003, pp 93–94.
72 Jennings and Watts 1992, p 37.
73 Brownlie 2003, p 19. See also Shaw 2003, p 103.
74 Jennings and Watts 1992, p 41.
75 Brownlie 2003, p 19.

1.6.2 International Refugee Law, International Social Security Law and International Human Rights Law

The research in this book is limited to sources of international refugee law, international social security law and international human rights law that are considered relevant for the issue of the access of asylum seekers to social security and employment. This subsection will list the specific international conventions used as sources for this study. Given the large amount of social security and, especially, human rights conventions, it is necessary to restrict the research to a number of general treaties.

First, two general remarks will be made about the scope of the study. This study will only address instruments with possible relevance for *all* asylum seekers in Europe. Accordingly, instruments or provisions that apply to only a subset of asylum seekers, such as women, children, disabled asylum seekers or older asylum seekers, fall outside the scope of this book. This approach resembles the approach adopted by Hathaway in his study on the rights of refugees under international law.[76] As Hathaway notes, this does not reflect the view that more specialized instruments applicable to members of other internationally protected groups, such as the Convention on the Rights of the Child or the Convention on the Elimination of all Forms of Discrimination against Woman, are not of real importance. To the contrary, especially the Convention on the Rights of the Child seems to be becoming more and more important for the rights of non-national children. This is clearly reflected in case law of the European Court of Human Rights and the European Court of Justice.[77] Nevertheless, the goal of this study is to examine which state obligations stem from international law as regards asylum seekers on the sole basis that they fall within this category of aliens. An advantage of this approach is that by doing so, the consequences of the special legal situation in which asylum seekers find themselves come to the fore, regardless of their specific identity or circumstances.[78]

A second general remark is that the research in this book will not be limited to conventions that have been ratified by *all* EU Member States, but will also include (social security) conventions that have been ratified by only a number of EU Member States. While these treaties might not be 'relevant treaties' within the meaning of Article 78(1) of the TFEU and therefore not direct instruments of review for the EU Reception Conditions Directives,[79] they may be relevant sources for the interpretation of other instruments of international law discussed in this study (see

[76] Hathaway 2005.
[77] See, eg, Reneman 2011.
[78] Hathaway 2005, p 8.
[79] Battjes 2006, p 97.

section 1.7.2). Given the evident relevance of international social security conventions for this study's research question, these conventions are therefore included.

The instruments of international law dealt with under the heading of international refugee law in this book are the 1951 Refugee Convention and the 1967 Refugee Protocol. Even though these instruments can also be seen as forming part of human rights law,[80] they will be examined separately in this study.

As regards international social security law, conventions on social security adopted within the framework of the International Labour Organization (ILO) and within the framework of the Council of Europe (CoE) will be addressed. The research will be limited to conventions that are wide in scope (applying to different kind of social security benefits) and which have been ratified by relatively many EU Member States. Accordingly, at the ILO level, Convention no 102 on Social Security (Minimum Standards), Convention no 97 on Migration for Employment and Convention no 118 on Equality of Treatment will be discussed. The instruments on social security adopted within the framework of the CoE to be addressed by the study are: the European Interim Agreements on Social Security, the European Convention on Social Security and the European Convention on Social and Medical Assistance (ECSMA).

The examination of international human rights law is also conducted at the UN and CoE level. The investigation is limited to the International Covenant on Economic, Social and Cultural Rights (ICESCR), the European Convention on Human Rights (ECHR) and the European Social Charter (revised) (ESC). No separate attention will be paid to the International Covenant on Civil and Political Rights, as it is assumed that this convention has only limited impact on the issues at stake here in addition to the obligations arising from the ECHR.[81]

1.6.3 The Charter of Fundamental Rights of the European Union

With the entry into force of the Lisbon Treaty in December 2009, the Charter of Fundamental Rights of the European Union (CFR or the Charter) became a legally binding instrument.[82] The CFR applies to the institutions, bodies,

[80] Hathaway 2005, pp 4–5.

[81] *Cf* Koch, who also argues that although the Human Rights Committee has adopted a similar integrated or holistic approach to the ECtHR with respect to the relevance of social demands, judgments from the ECtHR are 'far more developed and much more comprehensive, and unlike *views* from the HRC the judgments of the ECtHR are binding on the Contracting States' (Koch 2009, p 10).

[82] TEU, Art 6(1).

offices and agencies of the Union and to the Member States when they are implementing Union law.[83] Secondary Union law, such as the European Reception Conditions Directives, has therefore to be in accordance with the CFR.[84] The preambles to the European Reception Conditions Directives frequently refer to the CFR.[85] It is therefore at first sight a very relevant instrument of review for these Directives.

Case law of the Court of Justice of the European Union (CJEU)[86] on the scope and meaning of Charter provisions is still scarce, especially with regard to the provisions with possible relevance for the research question in this book (eg Articles 15 on the right to engage in work; 21 on non-discrimination; 34 on social security and social assistance; and 35 on health care).[87]

The CFR itself contains, however, a few instructions for interpretation. The preamble to the Charter makes clear that its provisions are to a large extent based on pre-existing standards of international law.[88] Article 52(3) of the CFR provides that

> [i]n so far as this Charter contains rights which correspond to rights guaranteed by the Convention for the Protection of Human Rights and Fundamental Freedoms, the meaning and scope of those rights shall be the same as those laid down by the said Convention.

This article also stipulates that this provision shall not prevent Union law from providing more extensive protection.[89] Hence, the ECHR functions as a minimum standard of review for the interpretation of the Charter.

[83] CFR, Art 51.

[84] Ie directives have to be interpreted in conformity with the CFR and the validity of provisions of directives can be tested against the CFR. See, eg, the *Test Achats* case in which the CJEU declared a provision of a directive invalid because of incompatibility with provisions of the CFR (CJEU 1 March 2011, Case C-236/09 [2011] ECR I-773).

[85] See recital 5 of the preamble to Directive 2003/9 and recital 35 of the preamble to Directive 2013/33.

[86] The abbreviation CJEU is used to refer to the European Court of Justice (pre-Lisbon) and to the Court of Justice of the European Union (after Lisbon).

[87] While the CJEU frequently refers to provisions of the CFR, these provisions do not often function as the decisive standard for deciding cases. According to de Burca, the CJEU has, between December 2009 and the end of 2012, made reference to provisions of the CFR in at least 122 judgments. In only 27 of these 122 judgments, did the CJEU engage substantially with arguments based on Charter provisions (de Búrca 2013, p 169).

[88] The preamble to the CFR states that it is necessary to strengthen the protection of fundamental rights 'by making those rights more visible in a charter'. In addition, the preamble states that the Charter seeks to 'reaffirm' the rights as they result from a large number of sources, such as the international obligations common to the Member States and, in particular, the ECHR. Barkhuysen and Bos observe that the Charter brings together all human rights already laid down in the ECHR, ESC and the UN human rights conventions in one document. It does contain a few novelties, connected to advancing technological and social developments, such as a prohibition of the reproductive cloning of human beings and the protection of personal data (Barhkuysen and Bos 2011, p 7).

[89] Remarkably, this latter sentence refers to *Union law* and not to the Charter.

More generally, on the basis of Article 53 of the CFR, the same is true for human rights recognized in international law and by international agreements to which all the Member States are party.

In addition, Article 52(7) of the CFR provides that the explanations to the Charter should be given due regard. This is also emphasized in Article 6(1) of the TEU, as the explanations 'set out the sources of those [the Charter's] provisions'. These explanations were prepared under the authority of the Praesidium of the Convention which drafted the Charter and have been updated under the responsibility of the Praesidium of the European Convention.[90] Hence, it has been explicitly laid down in primary Union law that the intention of the drafters should be taken into account when interpreting the Charter. The explanations frequently refer to the ECHR and the ESC as relevant sources of Charter provisions.

The foregoing makes clear that instruments of international law, in particular the ECHR and the ESC, are very important sources of inspiration for the interpretation of the CFR.

For the purpose of this study, the text of relevant Charter provisions will be described and analysed in the introductory chapters to Part II and Part III. It will turn out that the text of these provisions does not contain indications that the protection offered is more far-reaching than the protection offered by similar provisions laid down in other instruments of international law. Consequently, in the absence (so far) of a body of case law of the CJEU indicating that the provisions of the CFR do indeed contain more far-reaching obligations for the Member States than those resulting from pre-existing standards of international law with regard to the issues relevant in this study, the attention paid to the CFR in this book will be rather marginal. The conclusions of this study might, however, serve as a relevant resource for the interpretation of the CFR.

1.7 METHOD OF INTERPRETATION

1.7.1 Introduction

This section will examine which methods and rules of interpretation arise from accepted sources of international law and, accordingly, will determine a methodology of interpretation that will be applied in this book. A distinction can be made between, on the one hand, rules of interpretation, such as the rules laid down in the Vienna Convention on the Law of Treaties, and, on the other hand, authoritative interpretations by various organs. These organs have to apply the rules of interpretation as well;

[90] Explanations relating to the Charter of Fundamental Rights (2007/C 303/02).

however, owing to their authority, a deviation from their interpretation needs explicit argumentation.[91] Consequently, they function as a valuable supplement to the interpretation rules. Examples of such authoritative interpretations include the already-mentioned judicial decisions and 'teachings of the most highly qualified publicists of the various nations', mentioned in Article 38 of the Statute of the International Court of Justice as subsidiary means for the determination of rules of law. This section will first examine the rules of interpretation. Then, the legal value of various forms of authoritative interpretations will be discussed.

1.7.2 Rules of Interpretation

The rules on interpretation of international treaties are laid down in Articles 31, 32 and 33 of the Vienna Convention on the Law of Treaties (hereafter Vienna Convention). According to the International Court of Justice, these rules reflect customary law.[92] This means that these rules are binding upon all states in the world. This section will provide a brief overview of the relevant rules.[93]

Article 31 of the Vienna Convention reads as follows:

General rule of interpretation

1. A treaty shall be interpreted in good faith in accordance with the ordinary meaning to be given to the terms of the treaty in their context and in the light of its object and purpose.
2. The context for the purpose of the interpretation of a treaty shall comprise, in addition to the text, including its preamble and annexes:
   (a) any agreement relating to the treaty which was made between all the parties in connection with the conclusion of the treaty;
   (b) any instrument which was made by one or more parties in connection with the conclusion of the treaty and accepted by the other parties as an instrument related to the treaty.
3. There shall be taken into account, together with the context:
   (a) any subsequent agreement between the parties regarding the interpretation of the treaty or the application of its provisions;

[91] Battjes 2006, pp 19–23.

[92] See, eg, *Territorial Dispute (Libyan Arab Jamahiriya v Chad)* ICJ Reports 1994 (International Court of Justice, 3 February 1994), p 6, para 41; *La Grand Case (Germany v United States of America)* ICJ Reports 2001 (International Court of Justice, 27 June 2001), p 466, paras 99 and 101; *Sovereignty over Pulau Ligitan and Pulau Sipadan (Indonesia v Malaysia)* ICJ Reports 2002 (International Court of Justice, 17 December 2002), p 625, para 37.

[93] See for a more extensive discussion of these rules, eg, Aust 2007; Brownlie 2003; Sinclair 1984.

(b) any subsequent practice in the application of the treaty which establishes the agreement of the parties regarding its interpretation;
(c) any relevant rules of international law applicable in the relations between the parties.
4. A special meaning shall be given to a term if it is established that the parties so intended.

This article thus includes literal ('ordinary meaning'), systematic ('in their context') and teleological ('in the light of its object and purpose') interpretation methods.[94] Although some authors argue that Article 31 confirms the primacy of the text and others argue that the object and purpose should be determinative,[95] the position that there is no hierarchy in these different methods and that all elements of Article 31 are equally important has gained most support.[96] Indeed, the singular noun in 'general rule' indicates that there is only one rule, with different elements.[97] This means that all aspects of a treaty—the wording used in the text of the treaty, its preamble and its annexes, the internal harmony between the different provisions, the aim of the treaty and the intention of the parties—must be taken into account.

The duty to interpret treaties 'in good faith' is often held to imply a principle of effectiveness.[98] According to this principle, 'provisions are to be interpreted so as to give them their fullest weight and effect consistent with the normal sense of the words and with other parts of the text, and in such a way that a reason and a meaning can be attributed to every part of the text'.[99] In the *Territorial Dispute* case, the International Court of Justice called the principle of effectiveness 'one of the fundamental principles of interpretation of treaties, consistently upheld by international jurisprudence'.[100] Especially in the field of human rights, the International Court of Justice has adopted a value-oriented approach based on this interpretation principle.[101] In the case law of the European Court of Human Rights too, the principle of effectiveness plays a central

[94] Cassese 2005, p 179.
[95] See, eg, Vanneste 2010, pp 221–25.
[96] McAdam, 'Interpretation of the 1951 Convention' in Zimmermann 2011, p 83; Aust 2007, p 243; Battjes 2006, p 16; Vanneste 2010, pp 225–26 with further references. Vanneste argues that the approach of the ECtHR (and the Inter-American Court of Human Rights) endorses the view that this article should be understood as favouring such a 'holistic approach' (Vanneste 2010, p 345).
[97] Brownlie 2003, p 603; ILC, *Draft Articles on the Law of Treaties with Commentary*, Yearbook 1966, vol II, pp 219–20.
[98] Brownlie 2003, p 606; Hathaway 2005, p 62.
[99] Fitzmaurice 1986, p 50.
[100] *Territorial dispute (Libyan Arab Jamahiriya v Chad)* (n 90), p 6, para 51. See also *Fisheries Jurisdiction (Spain v Canada), Jurisdiction of the Court, Judgment* ICJ Reports 1998 (International Court of Justice, 4 December 1998), p 432, para 52.
[101] Shaw 2003, pp 842–44; Zyberi 2008, p 31.

role.[102] The principle has its limits, however. In the *Interpretation of Peace Treaties* case, the Court held that the rule of effectiveness 'cannot justify the Court in attributing to the provisions (…) a meaning which, as stated above, would be contrary to their letter and spirit'.[103]

Article 31(3)(a) and (b) indicates that subsequent agreements between the parties and subsequent practice in the application of the treaty must be taken into account. Obviously, an agreement 'regarding the interpretation of the treaty or the application of its provisions' can only be reached with all the parties to a convention. Nevertheless, the agreement does not have to be a legally binding document in order to be of value for interpretation.[104] Subsequent practice needs only to be taken into account if the practice is consistent and is common to, or accepted by all parties.[105]

Article 31(3)(c) contains the principle of 'systematic integration' within the international legal system.[106] This principle means that a treaty should be interpreted against the background of other relevant and applicable rules of international law.[107] The International Court of Justice has made clear that treaties have to be interpreted within the framework of the entire legal system prevailing at the time of interpretation.[108] Hence, it is not the rules of international law in force at the time of the conclusion of the treaty, but the contemporary international legal system that has to be taken into account.[109] In addition, with reference to Article 31(3)(c) of the Vienna Convention, the European Court of Human Rights has observed that in searching for common ground among the norms of international law, it does not distinguish between sources of law according to whether or not they have been signed or ratified by a certain state.[110] For the Court '[i]t will be sufficient … that the relevant international instruments denote a continuous evolution in the norms and principles applied in international law … and show, in a precise area, that there is common ground in modern societies'.[111] The rule of systematic integration also has its limits.

[102] Merrills 1993, p 113. The Court generally holds: 'Since the Convention is first and foremost a system for the protection of human rights, the Court must interpret and apply it in a manner which renders its rights practical and effective, not theoretical and illusory' (see, eg, *Demir and Baykara v Turkey* app no 34503/97 (ECtHR, 12 November 2008), para 66).

[103] *Interpretation of Peace Treaties (second phase),* Advisory Opinion ICJ Reports 1950 (International Court of Justice, 18 July 1950), p 229.

[104] Aust 2007, p 240.

[105] Aust 2007, p 241; Brownlie 2003, p 605.

[106] McLachlan 2005.

[107] See also *Demir and Baykara v Turkey* (n 102), para 76.

[108] *Legal Consequences for States of the Continued Presence of South Africa in Namibia (South West Africa) notwithstanding Security Council Resolution 276 (1970), Advisory Opinion* ICJ Reports 1971 (International Court of Justice, 21 June 1971), p 16, para 53.

[109] Battjes 2006, p 19.

[110] *Demir and Baykara v Turkey* (n 102), para 78.

[111] Ibid, para 86.

Clear conflicts of different norms of international law cannot be resolved by reference to this interpretation rule.[112]

Pursuant to Article 31(4) it is only allowed to give a 'special meaning' to a term in a convention if it is established that the parties so intended.

Article 32 of the Vienna Convention contains supplementary means of interpretation. According to this article:

> Recourse may be had to supplementary means of interpretation, including the preparatory work of the treaty and the circumstances of its conclusion, in order to confirm the meaning resulting from the application of article 31, or to determine the meaning when the interpretation according to article 31 leaves the meaning ambiguous or obscure, or leads to a result which is manifestly absurd or unreasonable.

So, if no satisfactory result has been reached by applying Article 31, or if the result of applying Article 31 needs to be confirmed, recourse may be had to supplementary means of interpretation, such as the preparatory work of the treaty. It has often been mentioned that preparatory work should be used with care, since the records of conference proceedings may be confusing, incomplete or inconclusive and circumstances may have changed over time.[113] Aust concludes with regard to preparatory work: '[t]heir investigation is time-consuming, their usefulness often being marginal and very seldom decisive'.[114] Accordingly, preparatory work will be used with the required caution and only as a subsidiary method of interpretation.[115]

Paragraph 4 of Article 33 of the Vienna Convention deals with differences in meaning between various authentic texts of treaties. According to this provision

> when a comparison of the authentic texts discloses a difference of meaning which the application of articles 31 and 32 does not remove, the meaning which best reconciles the texts, having regard to the object and purpose of the treaty, shall be adopted.

112 McLachlan 2005. In such cases, other rules exist for resolving the conflict, such as *lex specialis* and *jus cogens* (McLachlan 2005, pp 285–86).

113 Aust 2007, pp 244 and 246–47; Battjes 2006, pp 17–18; Brownlie 2003, p 606; Sinclair 1984, p 142.

114 Aust 2007, p 247.

115 Hathaway states that 'there appears to be neither theory nor practice to justify the view that the designation of a treaty's preparatory work as a supplementary means of interpretation requires that it be relegated to an inherently subordinate or inferior place in a comprehensive, interactive process of treaty interpretation' (Hathaway 2005, p 59). Nonetheless, as Sinclair explains, the fact that international tribunals in practice regularly assess preparatory work is probably caused by the fact that disputes about the interpretation of treaty provisions often reach the stage of international adjudication *because* the text is ambiguous or obscure in the sense of Art 32 of the Vienna Convention. Moreover, counsel for the parties in these disputes will often seek to derive support for their interpretation from an analysis of the preparatory work, as a result of which international tribunals are called upon to assess the significance of it (Sinclair 1984, p 142).

1.7.3 Authoritative Interpretations

This section will discuss the various authoritative interpretations of treaties that are available and the legal value to be attached to them. The most attention will be paid to the value of views and decisions of treaty-monitoring bodies for the interpretation of treaties, as this is most contested.

Judicial Decisions

Article 38(d) of the Statute of the International Court of Justice designates judicial decisions as subsidiary means for the determination of rules of law. The adjective 'judicial' means that the decision has to be taken by a court or tribunal of competent jurisdiction.[116] Obviously, judgments from international courts, such as the International Court of Justice or the European Court of Human Rights, function as very authoritative interpretations of international law.[117] Besides judgments from international courts, Article 38(d) applies to decisions from national courts as well. Generally, decisions from national courts will, however, provide merely evidence of the existence of a customary rule or of state practice.[118] Accordingly, judgments of national courts will be used sparingly in this book and primarily as evidence of state practice, not as authoritative interpretations. In addition, owing to the practical difficulty in examining decisions from all national courts in the world, national judicial decisions will mainly be used to falsify interpretations derived from applying other interpretation methods.

Legal Doctrine

'Teachings of the most highly qualified publicists of the various nations' are mentioned in Article 38(d) of the Statute of the International Court of Justice as subsidiary means for the determination of rules of law as well. Hence, texts from scholarly writers are also relevant for interpretation. However, as Schwarzenberger states very clearly: 'Comparatively speaking, no other element in this hierarchy [hierarchy in law-determining agencies] deserves to be treated with so much reserve as writers on international law'.[119] Since the risk of subjectively coloured judgements

[116] 'Judicial decision' can be defined as the '[a]pplication by a court or tribunal exercising judicial authority of competent jurisdiction of the law to a state of facts proved, or admitted to be true, and a declaration of the consequences which follow' (Black's Law Dictionary, 6th edn, 1990) or as 'the determination by a court of competent jurisdiction on matters submitted to it' (WordNet, wordnet.princeton.edu).

[117] Brownlie 2003, p 19; Shaw 2003, p 103.

[118] Brownlie 2003, p 22; Jennings and Watts 1992, pp 41–42; Shaw 2003, p 105.

[119] Schwarzenberger 1957, p 36.

is obviously large and individual writers often reflect national and other prejudices,[120] publications of academics will be used with the requisite caution. In the absence of relevant judicial decisions, legal doctrine sometimes functions as a good starting point for interpretation,[121] but these writings have always to be assessed as to their observance of the interpretation rules and the quality of their reasoning.[122]

Views and Decisions of Treaty-monitoring Bodies

For almost all treaties that will be examined in this book, monitoring bodies have been established to supervise states' compliance with the obligations laid down in the treaties. The European Convention on Human Rights is the only treaty that has established a court with the power of issuing binding decisions.[123] As has been stated above, the decisions of such a court have an important legal value for the interpretation of the convention.

The monitoring bodies that have been established to examine compliance with the other treaties do not have the power to issue binding decisions.[124] Nevertheless, the views and decisions of treaty-monitoring bodies do have particular significance for interpretation. Different arguments have been put forward for the relevance of the opinions of treaty-monitoring bodies for legal interpretation. It has been argued that (some of) their decisions are 'judicial decisions' in the sense of Article 38(1)(d) of the Statute of the International Court of Justice, as they fulfil the criteria established by the European Court of Human Rights (ECtHR) for 'tribunals'.[125] Other arguments for the relevance for interpretation is that the output of treaty-monitoring bodies should be taken into account as 'subsequent practice' in the sense of Article 31(3)(b) of the Vienna Convention[126] or as part of states' obligation to act in good faith.[127] Finally, the fact that states have accepted their monitoring power by becoming a party to

[120] Brownlie 2003, pp 23–24.

[121] '[T]he more the field is covered by decided cases the less becomes the authority of commentators and jurists' (Lord Summer quoted in Schwarzenberger 1957, p 37).

[122] See Schwarzenberger, who assesses the hierarchy of 'law-determining agencies' by subjecting them to a 'threefold scrutiny which ought to take into account the degree of its generic and individual independence, its international outlook and its technical standards' whereby he states that '[t]he degree of skill and technical qualification attained by the element concerned is obviously of the highest importance' (Schwarzenberger 1957, p 30).

[123] ECHR, Art 46.

[124] Battjes 2006, pp 20–23; Churchill and Khaliq 2004, pp 437–40; Cullen 2009, p 75; Mechlem 2009; Sepúlveda 2003, pp 87–88.

[125] Rieter 2010, p 810.

[126] Mechlem 2009, p 920; Nu berger 2007, p 47.

[127] Human Rights Committee, General Comment no 33 on the Obligations of States Parties under the Optional Protocol to the International Covenant on Civil and Political Rights, para 15.

the treaty is a relevant factor for giving weight to the interpretations of treaty-monitoring bodies.[128]

As the output of monitoring bodies is non-binding, its authority hinges on the body's legal standing and, particularly, the persuasiveness and coherence of its reasoning.[129] The quality of the reasoning of relevant views and decisions will be examined, especially in the light of the interpretation rules of the Vienna Convention, in the chapters in which they come up for discussion. Here, some general remarks will be made about the legal standing of various committees.

Under the Refugee Convention, there is no specific monitoring body,[130] but the Office of the United Nations High Commissioner for Refugees (UNHCR) has been given the duty of supervising the application of the provisions of the convention.[131] The UNHCR was established by a General Assembly resolution of 1949.[132] Pursuant to the Statute of the UNHCR,[133] an Advisory Committee on Refugees was established by the Economic and Social Council. This 'Executive Committee' consists of representatives of the Member States of the UN. Its conclusions could therefore be taken into account as evidence of 'subsequent agreement between the parties' in the sense of Article 31(3)(a) of the Vienna Convention.[134]

The International Covenant on Economic, Social and Cultural Rights (ICESCR) does not provide for a monitoring body, but leaves oversight to the Economic and Social Council of the United Nations.[135] By a resolution from the Economic and Social Council, the Committee on Economic, Social and Cultural Rights (Com ESCR) was established for the purpose

[128] Battjes 2006, p 19. Craven mentions that also the endorsement of the Annual Report of the Committee on Economic, Social and Cultural Rights by the UN General Assembly gives considerable weight to the committee's interpretation (Craven 1995, p 92).

[129] Battjes 2006, pp 19–23; Mechlem 2009; Sepúlveda 2003, pp 87–111; Schwarzenberger 1957, p 30.

[130] Settlement of disputes between parties relating to interpretation or application of the convention is referred to the International Court of Justice (Art 38 RC).

[131] RC, Art 35.

[132] Resolution 319 (IV) of 3 December 1949 of the United Nations General Assembly.

[133] This statute was adopted by the General Assembly on 14 December 1950 as Annex to Resolution 428 (V).

[134] Battjes 2006, p 20; Hathaway 2005, pp 54–55. Not all states parties to the Refugee Convention are members of the Executive Committee at any given moment and not all members of the Executive Committee are members of the Refugee Convention. However, all states parties to the convention are invited to observe and to comment upon draft proposals. As Hathaway observes: 'While this process is no doubt imperfect, it is difficult to imagine in practical terms how subsequent agreement among 145 state parties to the Refugee Convention could more fairly be generated' (Hathaway 2005, pp 54–55, fn 146). The *Handbook on Procedures and Criteria for determining Refugee Status under the 1951 Convention and the 1967 Protocol relating to the Status of Refugees* has been requested by the Executive Committee, but has not been adopted by this committee (Battjes 2006, p 20). Consequently, this handbook is not evidence of subsequent agreement between the states parties.

[135] See ICESCR, Arts 16 to 21.

of assisting the Council.[136] This resolution provides that the committee has 18 members 'who shall be experts with recognized competence in the field of human rights', who serve in their personal capacity and who shall be elected for a term of four years. On the basis of this resolution, the committee has the competence to submit to the Economic and Social Council a summary of its considerations of the reports submitted by states parties to the ICESCR and to make suggestions and recommendations of a general nature. Since the committee is a subsidiary organ of the Economic and Social Council, the interests of states parties to the covenant are represented only in so far they are taken up by the Economic and Social Council. As Craven notes, the committee differs quite significantly from other (UN) human rights committees in this regard.[137] On 5 May 2013, the Optional Protocol to the ICESCR entered into force. This protocol provides the committee with the competence to receive and consider individual complaints and to transmit its views to the parties concerned. State parties to this Optional Protocol explicitly recognize this competence of the committee.[138] The protocol provides that states parties should give due consideration to the views of the committee and should submit to the committee within six months a written response, including information on any action taken.[139] At the time of writing, the Optional Protocol has been ratified by three EU Member States.[140]

The European Social Charter establishes a 'Committee of Experts' to examine the reports submitted by states parties.[141] As from 1998 this committee has been called the European Committee of Social Rights (ECSR). The members of the committee are elected by the Committee of Ministers 'from a list of independent experts of the highest integrity and of recognised competence in international social questions, nominated by the Contracting Parties'.[142] They are elected for a term of six years.[143] On the basis of the Additional Protocol to the European Social Charter Providing for a System of Collective Complaints, the committee is competent to consider collective complaints about unsatisfactory application of the Charter lodged by organizations of employers, trade unions or non-governmental organizations. The protocol provides that the committee is to examine the

[136] ECOSOC Resolution 1985/17 of 28 May 1985.

[137] Craven 1995, p 50.

[138] Art 1 of the Optional Protocol to the International Covenant on Economic, Social and Cultural Rights.

[139] Ibid, Art 9.

[140] The Optional Protocol to the International Covenant on Economic, Social and Cultural Rights has been ratified by the following EU Member States: Portugal, Slovakia and Spain. see treaties.un.org/Pages/ViewDetails.aspx?mtdsg_no=IV-3-a&chapter=4&lang=en_.

[141] ESC, Art 24.

[142] ESC, Art 25(1).

[143] ESC, Art 25(2).

complaint and present its conclusions as to whether or not the contracting party concerned has ensured the satisfactory application of the Charter.[144] On the basis of this report, the Committee of Ministers of the Council of Europe must adopt a resolution. If the ECSR finds that the Charter has not been applied in a satisfactory manner, the Committee of Ministers should adopt a recommendation addressed to the contracting party concerned.[145] This additional protocol has been ratified by 12 countries, including 10 EU Member States.[146]

The annual report that each ILO member state has to submit on the measures which it has taken to give effect to the provisions of ILO conventions to which it is a party[147] are examined by the Committee of Experts on the Application of Conventions and Recommendations. This committee was established by the Governing Body of the ILO in accordance with a resolution adopted by the International Labour Conference in 1926.[148] However, just like the Refugee Convention, the ILO Constitution provides that any question or dispute relating to the interpretation of the Constitution or of any convention should be referred to the International Court of Justice.[149]

In brief, the legal standing of the various monitoring bodies differs significantly. Some bodies, such as the European Committee on Social Rights, are established by the treaty itself, and therefore with the consent of all state parties to the treaties. The treaty concerned also contains important safeguards as regard independence and impartibility. Other bodies, such as the Committee on Economic, Social and Cultural Rights and the ILO Committee of Experts, have merely been established as subsidiary organs in order to assist the organ that has been assigned with the task of supervising state reports. The Refugee Convention does not provide for a specific monitoring process, but the UNHCR has been assigned the general task of supervising the application of the convention by the treaty itself. For these latter bodies, the authority of their views hinges even more on the quality of the reasoning.[150]

With the exception of the UNHCR, all bodies typically carry out two or three main functions: 1) they formulate 'concluding observations' (Com ESCR), 'conclusions' (ECSR) or 'observations' (ILO Committee of Experts)

144 Art 8 of the Additional Protocol.
145 Art 9 of the Additional Protocol.
146 The additional protocol has been ratified by the following EU Member States: Belgium, Cyprus, Finland, France, Greece, Ireland, Italy, the Netherlands, Portugal and Sweden. See conventions.coe.int/Treaty/Commun/ChercheSig.asp?NT=158&CM=7&DF=01/07/2011&CL=ENG.
147 ILO Constitution, Art 22.
148 International Labour Conference, eighth session, vol I, Geneva 1926, app VII, p 429.
149 ILO Constitution, Art 37(1).
150 See also Sepúlveda 2003, p 90.

on state reports; 2) they develop 'General comments' (Com ESCR), 'statements of interpretation' (ECSR) or 'General surveys' (ILO Committee of Experts) which contain more general statements of understanding based on the examination of different state reports; and 3) they adopt views on individual complaints (Com ESCR) or on collective complaints (ECSR). This book will only examine the latter two forms of output from the monitoring bodies. The concluding observations and conclusions are rather country specific and their jurisprudential impact has been described as marginal and exceptional.[151]

1.7.4 Summary

In brief, (provisions of) treaties will be interpreted using the literal, systematic and teleological interpretation rules. In addition, they will be interpreted in the light of the entire contemporary international legal system. Only if no satisfactory result has been reached by applying these rules, or if the result of applying them needs to be confirmed, will supplementary means of interpretation be applied, such as the preparatory work of the treaty. Further, judicial decisions, in particular from international courts, serve as important authoritative interpretations. The authority of non-binding views and decisions of treaty-monitoring bodies is dependent on the body's legal standing and on the quality of the reasoning. The legal doctrine and domestic case law will be used cautiously mainly in order to falsify interpretations derived from applying other interpretation methods.

[151] Mechlem 2009, p 923 with further references.

Part I

Reception of Asylum Seekers in the European Union

2

EU Directives on Reception Conditions for Asylum Seekers

2.1 INTRODUCTION

ON 27 JANUARY 2003, after a legislative process of more than two years, the Council of the European Union adopted Directive 2003/9/EC laying down minimum standards for the reception of asylum seekers (hereafter Directive 2003/9).[1] This directive contains provisions on information and documentation, freedom of movement, family unity, schooling and education for minors, employment, the level and kind of benefits, accommodation, access to health care, reduction and withdrawal of reception conditions, provisions for asylum seekers with special needs,[2] the right to appeal, and the organization of the reception system. On 26 June 2013, a recast of this directive was adopted by the European Parliament and the Council: Directive 2013/33/EU laying down standards for the reception of applicants for international protection (recast) (hereafter Directive 2013/33).[3]

This chapter will discuss these two Directives. Besides a short description of the background, purpose and personal scope of both Directives, this chapter will focus on the provisions of the Directives dealing with social security benefits for asylum seekers and access to the labour market, as well as the provisions on reduction and withdrawal of these benefits. It will be seen that the Directives only contain (minimum) standards regarding protection against general poverty and lack of (affordable) access to health care; they do not address protection against the occurrence of other social risks.

Throughout this chapter, attention will be paid to reasons that have been put forward by the Member States and the Commission for including or excluding certain provisions in the Directives. The reason for this

[1] Council Directive 2003/9/EC of 27 January 2003 laying down minimum standards for the reception of asylum seekers, [2003] OJ L31/18.

[2] Such as (unaccompanied) minors and victims of torture and violence.

[3] Directive 2013/33/EU of the European Parliament and of the Council of 26 June 2013 laying down standards for the reception of applicants for international protection (recast), [2013] OJ L180/96.

is that in testing the norms of the Directives against international human rights law, the official reasons put forward by the legislator are relevant, as the question needs to be answered whether these reasons provide a sound basis for restricting human rights norms.

First, section 2.2 will pay attention to a number of general features of the reception of asylum seekers in EU Member States before the adoption of Directive 2003/9.

2.2 BACKGROUND: RECEPTION OF ASYLUM SEEKERS IN EU MEMBER STATES PRIOR TO DIRECTIVE 2003/9/EC

This section will provide a short overview of the reception of asylum seekers in a number of traditional EU Member States before the coming into force of Directive 2003/9. This background information can help to better understand the provisions of the directive, as it is likely that existing national law and practices have had a large impact on the content of these provisions.[4]

While all (at the time 15) EU Member States had rules on the reception of asylum seekers prior to the agreement of Directive 2003/9, the content of these rules differed greatly, eg as regards the conditions under which rights and benefits are granted to asylum seekers and the level and mode of provision.[5] Nevertheless, this section will identify, on the basis of secondary sources, a number of general tendencies in the policy on the reception of asylum seekers in different EU Member States in the years preceding the adoption of Directive 2003/9.

In general, it has been observed that all Member States had exclusionary aspects to their rules on the reception of asylum seekers.[6] As main reasons for restrictive reception policies, deterring potential asylum seekers as well as impeding the integration of asylum seekers has been mentioned in official government documents and scholarly literature.[7] While the specific form and content of such exclusionary and restrictive measures differed from state to state, a number of common features will be discussed below.

In the course of the 1990s, many Western European states excluded asylum seekers from general social assistance schemes and introduced separate welfare schemes for asylum seekers. Under these separate schemes,

[4] *Cf* Bank 2000, p 258; Rosenberger and König 2011, p 2.
[5] See, eg, UNHCR 2000.
[6] Mabbett and Bolderson 2002, p 205. See also Bank 2000, p 259.
[7] Bank 2000, p 286–87; Bloch and Schuster 2002, p 401, Liedtke 2002, p 494, Minderhoud 1999, p 146; Rosenberger and König 2011, p 1.

most benefits were generally granted in kind. The Netherlands was one of the first countries to introduce such a separate scheme. Confronted with the arrival of increasing numbers of, especially Tamil, asylum seekers in the course of the 1980s, the Government decided to promulgate a special regulation on the basis of which asylum seekers could no longer apply for social assistance benefits and received accommodation in reception centres, food and clothing in kind. At first, this regulation applied only to Tamil asylum seekers, but as from 1987, all asylum seekers fell under this scheme. An important goal of this special regulation as put forward by the Government was, besides ameliorating the poor housing situation of asylum seekers in the large cities, to deter potential asylum seekers. Eligibility for general social assistance schemes was seen by the Government as a possible pull factor for asylum seekers.[8]

In Germany too, a special welfare scheme for asylum seekers had been issued. This happened in 1993. Under this scheme, asylum seekers were initially entitled to benefits in kind during the first year of their stay. Only in exceptional situations, asylum seekers were eligible for a financial benefit, but the amount of this benefit was 20 per cent lower than the amount of regular social assistance benefits. In 1997, the period during which asylum seekers were, in general, only entitled to benefits in kind was extended from one year to three years. During this three-year period, accommodation, food, clothing and sanitary items were provided in kind or through vouchers that were valid in certain shops only. After three years, asylum seekers became eligible for the same social assistance benefits as nationals.[9]

The special scheme for asylum seekers in Austria was the Federal care act for asylum seekers (*Bundesbetreuungsgesetz)* which was adopted in 1991. Under this Act, asylum seekers could receive housing, subsistence and basic medical care. The Act did not, however, contain a legal entitlement to this assistance for asylum seekers; their eligibility was dependent on their co-operation in establishing their identity and in assessing their need for assistance. Owing to its discretionary character, only about 30 per cent of all asylum seekers in Austria received support under this scheme.[10] The stated aim for this discretionary power was to prevent the federal scheme from becoming a pull factor for asylum seekers.[11]

In the United Kingdom, a separate scheme for asylum seekers was only introduced in 1999, with the passage of the Immigration and Asylum Act 1999. Before the coming into force of this Act, asylum seekers (as from 1996 only 'at port asylum seekers', see below) could claim and receive

[8] Jansen 2006, p 124, de Jong 1990, p 123, Minderhoud 1999, pp 133–34.
[9] Bank 2000, pp 279–82; Liedtke 2002, p 486–87; Minderhoud 1999, pp 141–42.
[10] Bank 2000, pp 276–77; UNHCR 2000, pp 38–39, Rosenberger König, 2011, p 7.
[11] Bank 2000, p 277.

'urgent payments' as 'persons from abroad', the value of which was 90 per cent of the general social assistance benefits. Under the Immigration and Asylum Act 1999, a separate parallel welfare system was set up, run by the central agency National Asylum Support Service (NASS). All asylum seekers who were destitute according to a set of criteria were eligible for support. It was not mandatory for NASS to actually provide this support; support could be removed when destitution was deemed to have ceased. NASS support has therefore been described as 'highly conditional'.[12] Support provided by NASS included vouchers worth 70 per cent of basic income support, a small amount of cash and, if desired, accommodation in designated areas. Since the set-up of this separate system, eligibility for general social assistance benefits was withdrawn for all asylum seekers.[13]

Belgium also knew a separate and in kind support system for asylum seekers, but this applied only during the first stage of the asylum procedure of about three to four months, in which the admissibility of the asylum application was examined. During this stage, asylum seekers generally received housing in accommodation centres, material support and a small amount of pocket money. Once their application had been declared admissible, asylum seekers had (limited) access to regular social assistance benefits. They had to leave the accommodation centre and were assigned to a specific Public Social Assistance Centre (*Openbaar Centrum voor Maatschappelijk Welzijn*). The assigned Public Social Assistance Centre provided needy asylum seekers with a kind of social assistance called social services (*maatschappelijke dienstverlening*).[14] The possibility to deny asylum seekers *maatschappelijke dienstverlening* during the admissibility stage and to offer in kind support instead was laid down in the relevant legislation in 1992. Until 2001, owing to a shortage of capacity in accommodation centres, asylum seekers could also directly be referred to a Public Social Assistance Centre during the admissibility stage. In 2001, the relevant legislation changed and living in an accommodation centre became mandatory for asylum seekers during the admissibility stage.[15]

A common feature of these special schemes for asylum seekers was the aspect of dispersal coupled with the exercise of control over the place of residence of asylum seekers. The UNHCR noted in 2000 that 'the practice of dispersing asylum seekers, and making the receipt of assistance dependent on accepting the allocated accommodation, is becoming more common'.[16] Boswell noticed in 2001 that Germany, the Netherlands, Belgium, Denmark and the United Kingdom had all introduced some

[12] Dwyer and Brown 2005, p 370.
[13] Bolderson 2007, pp 132–37; Dwyer and Brown 2005, p 370; Sales 2002, pp 464–65.
[14] Bank 2000, p 277; Minderhoud 1999, p 143.
[15] Bouckaert 2007, pp 535–42.
[16] UNHCR 2000, p 27. See also Mabbett and Bolderson 2002, p 205.

form of dispersal. While the different policies varied in the degree of compulsion involved, most of them involved a substantial form of state control over movement and residence.[17] Dispersal policies were generally aimed at distributing costs, easing social tensions, deterrence of potential asylum seekers and control over asylum seekers' residence and movement.[18]

Another common aspect of these separate schemes was the provision of a level and kind of social assistance inferior to that granted to nationals.[19] As has been mentioned above, asylum seekers were generally granted social assistance (partly) in kind, whereas under general social assistance schemes in Europe, assistance is usually granted as financial benefits. In addition, the level of assistance granted to asylum seekers is often (explicitly or implicitly) lower than the level of social assistance granted to nationals.[20]

In many countries, certain categories of asylum seekers have been excluded from the special assistance scheme. In the Netherlands for example, asylum seekers on behalf of whom a request was filed to another state to take charge of the asylum application under the Dublin Convention as well as asylum seekers who had lodged a second or further asylum application were denied benefits under the special scheme between 1998 and 2002/2005 respectively. The reason for this exclusion was twofold. This exclusion primarily aimed to help solve the shortage of capacity in the accommodation centres. Besides, however, this exclusion also aimed to deter potential asylum seekers to travel to the Netherlands or to lodge a new asylum application.[21] In the United Kingdom, between 1996 and 1999, asylum seekers who did not apply for asylum at the port of entry immediately on arrival were denied access to social assistance benefits

[17] Boswell 2001, p 1. According to Schuster, dispersal is most developed in the United Kingdom, Sweden, the Netherlands, Germany and Ireland (Schuster 2005, p 615).

[18] Boswell 2001, p 13–14; Jansen 2006, pp 123–27.

[19] Bank 2000, p 286.

[20] In Germany, the financial benefit for asylum seekers was 20% lower than the general social assistance benefit (Bank 2000, p 280, Minderhoud 1999, p 141. Liedtke 2002, p 486). Until 1999, asylum seekers in the United Kingdom were eligible for a financial benefit worth 90% of the general social assistance level and as from 1999, asylum seekers received vouchers worth 70% of the basic income level (Bolderson 2007, pp 132–37; Dwyer and Brown 2005, p 370, Sales 2002, p 464–65). Also in France, the assistance granted to asylum seekers was 'well below what was generally granted to persons in need' (Bank 2000, p 278). See for the more implicit difference between the benefits for asylum seekers and the benefits under the general social assistance scheme in the Netherlands: Franssen, Larsson and Slingenberg 2007, pp 410–11. See also the table on all 15 EU Member States in the study of the European Commission of 2001: 'Study on the legal framework and administrative practices in the Member States of the European Communities regarding reception conditions for persons seeking international protection. Final Report Part A: Comparative Analysis of Reception Conditions for Persons seeking protection in the Member States of the European Union', p 42.

[21] Pluymen 2008, pp 147–49.

(so-called 'in-country applicants', as opposed to 'at port applicants'). As from 2002, asylum seekers who did not claim for asylum 'as soon as reasonably practicable' after arrival in the United Kingdom were not eligible for support.[22] The purpose of this exclusion was, again, deterrence of potential asylum seekers and preventing misuse of the asylum procedure and welfare benefits for asylum seekers.[23]

Exclusion was also common with regard to access to the labour market.[24] Asylum seekers were either denied all access to the labour market or only granted access under certain (sometimes rather stringent) conditions. In most Member States that did grant access, this access was not granted during the first few months of the asylum procedure.[25] In Germany for example, asylum seekers had access to the labour market after three months before 1997. Between 1997 and 2001, asylum seekers were denied any kind of access to the labour market. After 2001, access was granted after one year.[26] In the Netherlands, asylum seekers did not have access to the labour market until 1998. As from 1998, asylum seekers could be granted a work permit for a maximum of 12 weeks a year if they had been living in an asylum seekers' reception centre for more than six months, provided that the work for which the permit would be issued had a temporary character. As from 2002, this latter condition no longer applied.[27]

2.3 DIRECTIVE 2003/9/EC

2.3.1 Introduction

This section will elaborate on the provisions of Directive 2003/9, which will remain effective until 20 July 2015. Since the United Kingdom has opted out of the recast of this directive, Directive 2003/9 will continue to apply for the United Kingdom. After a short description of the realization,

[22] Bolderson 2007. Both cases of withdrawal of support have been successfully challenged in court. The complete denial of any kind of support to asylum seekers was found to be in violation of the 'law of humanity' (Court of Appeal in *R v Secretary of State for Social Security, ex p Joint Council for the Welfare of Immigrants; R v Secretary of State for Social Security, ex p B* [1996] 4 All ER 385 (CA)) or, under certain circumstances, with Art 3 of the ECHR (House of Lords in *R v Secretary of State for the Home Department, ex p Adam, ex p Limbuela and ex p Tesema* [2005] UKHL 66 (HL)). The distinction between 'port' and 'in-country' applicants as such was not challenged in court, however.

[23] Mabbett and Bolderson 2002, p 205; Minderhoud 1999, pp 136–37.

[24] Bank 2000, p 286; Mabbett and Bolderson 2002, p 205.

[25] See the report of the European Commission (n 20), pp 86–90.

[26] Liedtke 2002, p 491.

[27] Klaver and Tromp 2004, pp 7–8. Owing to these restrictive conditions, asylum seekers scarcely made use of the possibility to (legally) work. In 2000, work permits were issued to 13% of all asylum seekers aged 18–64 living in reception centres (Klaver and Tromp 2004).

purpose and personal scope of this directive, this section will examine in detail the provisions of the directive dealing with social security benefits for asylum seekers and access to the labour market, as well as the provisions on reduction and withdrawal of these benefits. The directive only contains minimum standards as regards protection against general poverty and lack of (affordable) access to health care; it does not address protection against the occurrence of other social risks. Within the Common European Asylum System, access to social insurance benefits (as distinguished from social assistance benefits) is only addressed by the Qualification Directive, which applies to persons whose application for asylum has been granted.[28] This section will therefore examine the provisions of Directive 2003/9 on 'material reception conditions' (housing, food and clothing), on health care, on access to the labour market and on the reduction and withdrawal of reception benefits. First, the final text of the provisions will be discussed. Next, it will be considered to what extent this text differs from the text of the Commission's proposal for the directive. Attention is paid to these differences as this will reveal on which standards the Member States were not willing to agree.

2.3.2 Realization of Directive 2003/9

In as early as 1991, the Commission of the European Communities devoted attention to the social rights of asylum seekers. In a discussion paper attached to a communication to the Council and the European Parliament, the Commission considered that the lengthening of procedures, as a result of the 'ever-swelling influx of asylum seekers', has the effect of attracting even more asylum seekers 'who, while their case is being considered, enjoy a legal status which carries with it various social security benefits'. In addition, the Commission considered that it is difficult to expel applicants who, during these long procedures, have become 'socially and economically integrated'.[29] The Commission noted that there were marked differences in the material situation of asylum seekers among the Member States, in particular the position regarding access to employment, the right to social assistance and

[28] See Art 26(5) of Council Directive 2004/83/EC of 29 April 2004 on minimum standards for the qualification and status of third country nationals or stateless persons as refugees or as persons who otherwise need international protection and the content of the protection granted, [2004] OJ L304/12 (Qualification Directive). Art 28 of this directive addresses social assistance benefits.

[29] Discussion paper on the right of asylum, attached to Communication from the Commission to the Council and the European Parliament on the right of asylum, Brussels 11 October 1991, SEC(91)1857 final, p 5.

housing conditions.[30] In order to 'prevent any diversion of the flow of asylum seekers towards the Member State with the most generous arrangements', the Commission recommended harmonizing the treatment extended to asylum seekers while their application is being examined.[31] The call for approximation of reception policies for asylum seekers was repeated by the Commission in a communication to the Council and the European Parliament of 1994.[32] However, despite a joint action on conditions for the reception of asylum seekers tabled by the Spanish Presidency in 1995,[33] no measures relating specifically to reception conditions were adopted at the time. The need to adopt such measures became more urgent with the coming into force of the Treaty of Amsterdam on 1 May 1999. Since then, Article 63(1)(b) of the Treaty establishing the European Community (TEC) provided that the Council should, within a period of five years after the entry into force of the Treaty of Amsterdam, adopt measures on asylum, including minimum standards on the reception of asylum seekers in Member States. According to Article 63(1)(b), such measures should be in accordance with the Geneva Convention of 28 July 1951 and the Protocol of 31 January 1967 relating to the Status of Refugees and other relevant treaties. In the conclusions of its meeting in Tampere in 1999, the European Council agreed 'to work towards establishing a Common European Asylum System, based on the full and inclusive application of the Geneva Convention'.[34] As one of the elements to be included in the short term in this system, 'common minimum conditions of reception of asylum seekers' were mentioned.

In June 2000, the French delegation presented a discussion paper on reception conditions for asylum seekers, which can be seen as the effective starting point for Directive 2003/9.[35] During its meeting on 30 November and 1 December 2000, the Council adopted conclusions on the conditions for the reception of asylum seekers containing guidelines for the future Community instrument on this issue.[36] These conclusions reveal that no consensus yet existed on the personal scope of the instrument; the

[30] Ibid, p 7.

[31] Communication from the Commission to the Council and the European Parliament on the right of asylum, Brussels 11 October 1991, SEC(91)1857 final, p 7.

[32] Communication from the Commission to the Council and the European Parliament on Immigration and Asylum Policies, Brussels 23 February 1994, COM(94)23 final, p 24.

[33] Handoll 2004, p 116; Rogers 2002, p 216.

[34] Tampere European Council 15 and 16 October 1999, Presidency Conclusions, available at: www.consilium.europa.eu/uedocs/cms_data/docs/pressdata/en/ec/00200-r1.en9.htm.

[35] Handoll 2004, p 120. See Note from the French Delegation to the Asylum Working Party on Conditions for the Reception of Asylum Seekers, Brussels 23 June 2000, Council Document 9703/00 ASILE 28.

[36] Council Document 13865/00 (Presse 457).

freedom of movement of asylum seekers; and the access of asylum seekers to the labour market.

On 3 April 2001, the Commission presented its proposal for a Council Directive laying down minimum standards on the reception of applicants for asylum in Member States. This proposal was based on a study on the current law and practice in the Member States regarding reception conditions for asylum seekers, the above-mentioned Council conclusions, a study by the UNHCR, and bilateral consultations with Member States, the UNHCR and relevant non-governmental organizations.[37] The asylum working party of the Council started to examine the proposal in July 2001.[38] On 27 January 2003, Directive 2003/9 was formally adopted by the Council. The directive entered into force on its publication on 6 February 2003. The implementation deadline for the Member States was 6 February 2005. The directive does not apply to Denmark and Ireland.

Directive 2003/9 forms part of the Common European Asylum System. The other constituents of the Common European Asylum System are:

— Council Directive 2001/55/EC of 20 July 2001 on minimum standards for giving temporary protection in the event of a mass influx of displaced persons and on measures promoting a balance of efforts between Member States in receiving such persons and bearing the consequences thereof (Temporary Protection Directive);[39]
— Council Directive 2004/83/EC of 29 April 2004 on minimum standards for the qualification and status of third country nationals or stateless persons as refugees or as persons who otherwise need international protection and the content of the protection granted (Qualification Directive);[40]
— Council Directive 2005/85/EC of 1 December 2005 on minimum standards on procedures in Member States for granting and withdrawing refugee status (Procedures Directive);[41] and
— Council Regulation 2003/343/EC of 18 February 2003 establishing the criteria and mechanisms for determining the Member State

[37] See explanatory memorandum to Commission, Proposal for a Council Directive laying down minimum standards on the reception of applicants for asylum in Member States, Brussels 3 April 2001, COM(2001) 181 final.

[38] Handoll 2004, p 123.

[39] Council Directive 2001/55/EC of 20 July 2001 on minimum standards for giving temporary protection in the event of a mass influx of displaced persons and on measures promoting a balance of efforts between Member States in receiving such persons and bearing the consequences thereof, [2001] OJ L212/12.

[40] Council Directive 2004/83/EC of 29 April 2004 on minimum standards for the qualification and status of third country nationals or stateless persons as refugees or as persons who otherwise need international protection and the content of the protection granted, [2004] OJ L304/12.

[41] Council Directive 2005/85/EC of 1 December 2005 on minimum standards on procedures in Member States for granting and withdrawing refugee status, [2005] OJ L326/13.

responsible for examining an asylum application lodged in one of the Member States by a third-country national (Dublin Regulation).[42]

The background and treaty basis of Directive 2003/9 shows that in the EU context rules on asylum seekers' access to the labour market and social security form part of asylum policy. This could have been different. In 1987 the European Court of Justice ruled that the access of third-country nationals to the labour market and other issues related to the employment and working conditions of third-country nationals must be held to fall within the field of social policy, since 'the employment situation and, more generally, the improvement of living and working conditions within the Community are liable to be affected by the policy pursued by the Member States with regard to workers from non-member countries'.[43]

2.3.3 Object and Purpose

The purpose of Directive 2003/9 is to lay down minimum standards for the reception of asylum seekers in the Member States.[44] According to the preamble, these minimum standards should 'normally' suffice to ensure asylum seekers a dignified standard of living and comparable living conditions in all Member States.[45]

The text of the preamble therefore suggests that the purpose of the directive is twofold. First, the directive aims to secure asylum seekers generally a dignified standard of living.[46] The preamble states in this regard that the directive respects the fundamental rights and observes the principles recognized in particular by the Charter of Fundamental Rights of the European Union. According to this recital, the directive seeks in particular to ensure full respect for human dignity and to promote the application of Articles 1 and 18 of the said Charter.[47] In addition, the preamble states that with respect to the treatment of persons falling within the scope of this directive, Member States are bound by obligations

[42] Council Regulation 2003/343/EC of 18 February 2003 establishing the criteria and mechanisms for determining the Member State responsible for examining an asylum application lodged in one of the Member States by a third-country national, [2003] OJ L50/1.

[43] CJEU 9 July 1987, Joined Cases 281, 283 to 285 and 287/85 *Germany and others v Commission* [1987] ECR 3203. Apparently, the Court of Justice applied the 'sphere separation model' in this judgment (see s 1.2).

[44] Directive 2003/9, art 1.

[45] Recital 7 of the preamble.

[46] The word 'normally' may indicate that the minimum standards occasionally allow for an undignified standard of living (Battjes 2006, p 204; Handoll 2007, pp 206–07).

[47] Recital 5 of the preamble. Arts 1 and 18 of the Charter of Fundamental Rights of the European Union concern respect and protection for human dignity and the right to asylum, respectively.

under instruments of international law to which they are party and which prohibit discrimination.[48] Secondly, the directive aims to ensure comparable living conditions for asylum seekers in all Member States. This harmonization of reception conditions should help to limit the secondary movements of asylum seekers influenced by the variety of conditions for their reception.[49] According to Peek, the reduction of secondary movements can be assumed to be the most decisive factor for the adoption of the directive.[50] The limitation of secondary movements is a purpose that (almost) all instruments of the Common European Asylum System, to which the preamble of the directive also refers, have in common.[51] Accordingly, just as the background and treaty basis of the directive, the object and purpose as reflected in the preamble show that the directive falls in the context of asylum policy.[52] This is most clearly reflected in recital 4 of the preamble, which states that the 'establishment of minimum standards for the reception of asylum seekers is a further step towards a European asylum policy'.

The directive lays down 'minimum' standards. 'It is in the very nature of minimum standards that Member States have the power to introduce or maintain more favourable provisions for third-country nationals and stateless persons who ask for international protection from a Member State'.[53] The introduction or maintaining of more favourable provisions would, however, counteract the purpose of harmonization of reception conditions. Consequently, as Handoll notes, the minimum standards of the directive risk becoming 'the' standards.[54]

2.3.4 Personal Scope

According to Article 3(1), Directive 2003/9 applies

> to all third country nationals and stateless persons who make an application for asylum at the border or in the territory of a Member State as long as they are allowed to remain on the territory as asylum seekers, as well as to family members, if they are covered by such application for asylum according to the national law.

48 Recital 6 of the preamble.

49 Recital 8 of the preamble.

50 Peek 2010, p 887. In support of this statement, he refers to Meyer, who took part in the negotiations as representative of the German Ministry of Justice.

51 The purpose of limiting secondary movements can be found in recital 9 of the preamble to the Temporary Protection Directive; recital 7 of the preamble to the Qualification Directive; and recital 6 of the preamble to the Procedures Directive.

52 *Cf* Handoll 2004, p 125.

53 Recital 15 of the preamble.

54 Handoll 2004, p 116.

'Application for asylum' is defined in the directive as 'the application made by a third-country national or a stateless person which can be understood as a request for international protection from a Member State, under the Geneva Convention'.[55] This definition is supplemented with the presumption that any application for international protection is an application for asylum, unless a third-country national or a stateless person explicitly requests another kind of protection that can be applied for separately.[56] This means that only if a Member State has a separate procedure for applications for protection on other grounds than the Geneva Convention *and* the applicant applies for such protection explicitly, has no 'application for asylum' been made. 'Asylum seeker' is defined in the directive as a 'third-country national or a stateless person who has made an application for asylum in respect of which a final decision has not yet been taken'.[57]

Hence, in order to fall under the scope of Directive 2003/9, three important conditions have to be fulfilled:

1. a request for international protection must have been made/lodged;
2. no final decision must have been taken on this request; and
3. the asylum seeker must be allowed to remain on the territory.

The directive does not contain provisions on the meaning of these conditions. However, as the Tampere conclusions made clear, the directive on minimum standards for the reception of asylum seekers should not be seen as an independent instrument, but as part of a system, of an organized body of law.[58] This aim of a Common European Asylum System has been repeated in the preamble to the directive.[59] As a result, the provisions of Directive 2003/9 should be read and interpreted in conjunction with the other elements of the Common European Asylum System.[60]

Lodging or Making an Asylum Application

According to the English-language version, Directive 2003/9 applies to third-country nationals and stateless persons who *make* an application for asylum. Article 6 of this version of the directive, on the right to documentation, contains a time limit of three days after an application is *lodged*. This might indicate that in order to fall under the personal scope of the directive, it suffices to *make* an application for asylum; it is not necessary

[55] The Convention of 28 July 1951 relating to the Status of Refugees, as amended by the New York Protocol of 31 January 1967 (Directive 2003/9, Art 2(a)).
[56] Directive 2003/9, Art 2(b).
[57] Directive 2003, Art 2(c).
[58] *Cf* Battjes 2006, pp 30–31 and 195.
[59] See recitals 1–3 of the preamble to Directive 2003/9.
[60] See also CJEU 27 September 2012, Case C-179/11 *Cimade and GISTI*, eg para 47.

to officially *lodge* the application in conformity with national law. Other language versions of the directive, however, do not distinguish between making and lodging an application in Articles 3 and 6 and indicate that the application must have been *lodged* in order to fall under the personal scope of the directive.[61]

The difference between making and lodging an application is particularly relevant in Member States where asylum applications have to be made in person. When asylum applications can be made in writing, the lodging of an application is less dependent on action by the authorities, and therefore usually coincides with making the application. Article 6(1) of the Procedures Directive states that Member States may require that applications for asylum be *made* in person and/or at a designated place. Arguably, persons who do not fulfil such a national requirement have not made an 'application for asylum' in the sense of EU asylum law.[62] Article 4(2) of the Dublin Regulation stipulates that 'an application for asylum shall be deemed to have been *lodged* once a form submitted by the applicant for asylum or a report prepared by the authorities has reached the competent authorities of the Member State concerned' (emphasis added). This article continues by stating that where 'an application is not made in writing, the time elapsing between the statement of intention and the preparation of a report should be as short as possible'. Hence, these two articles indicate that Member States may require making an application for asylum in person and/or at a designated place. Once a statement of intent has been made in person and/or at the designated place, the asylum application has been *made*. This application has been *lodged* once an official report on this statement has reached the authorities. The period between *making* and *lodging* an asylum application must be as short as possible.

The English-language version of the directive indicates that an asylum seeker falls under the personal scope of the directive once he has stated his intention to apply for asylum, if necessary in person and/or at a designated place. Other versions indicate that asylum seekers only fall under the personal scope of the directive once the application has been lodged, ie when an official report on the application has been prepared and received by the competent authorities.[63] On this point, no uniform interpretation is therefore possible on the basis of the text. In that case, the directive must be interpreted by reference to the purpose and its general

[61] Eg, the Dutch-language version uses the word *indienen* in both articles and the French version uses *qui déposent* in Art 3(1) and *le dépôt de leur demande* in Art 6(1).

[62] *Cf* Spijkerboer 2010, p 10.

[63] On the basis of the Dutch-language version, Larsson for example concludes that an asylum seeker should have lodged his application in order to fall under the personal scope of the directive (Larsson 2011, pp 62–63).

scheme.[64] A reading in conformity with the purpose of the directive might indicate that lodging an asylum application in the sense of Article 4(2) of the Dublin Regulation is not necessary in order to fall under the personal scope, as this would make it possible for EU Member States to unilaterally postpone or even withhold the application of the directive, which runs counter to the purpose of harmonizing reception conditions.[65]

In the first judgment on Directive 2003/9 CJEU ruled that it is not necessary in order to fall under the directive's personal scope to submit[66] the application to the authorities of the Member State responsible for the examination of that application under the Dublin Regulation.[67] The Dublin Regulation contains rules in order to identify the Member State responsible for the examination of an asylum application. According to the CJEU, Directive 2003/9 applies as soon as an application for asylum is first submitted to a Member State; not only once it is submitted to the authorities of the Member State *responsible* for the examination of that application.

No Final Decision

The directive does not contain a definition of the term 'final decision'. Article 2(d) of the Procedures Directive defines 'final decision' as

> a decision on whether the third country national or stateless person be granted refugee status by virtue of Directive 2004/83/EC and which is no longer subject to a remedy within the framework of Chapter V of this Directive irrespective of whether such remedy has the effect of allowing applicants to remain in the Member States concerned pending its outcome.

Chapter V of the Procedures Directive deals with appeals procedures and contains the right to an effective remedy. According to Article 39(1) of this chapter, asylum seekers have the right to an effective remedy before a court or tribunal against decisions taken on their application for asylum. This chapter does not contain a right to a remedy in two instances. A restrictive reading of the term 'final decision' would therefore be that

[64] See, eg, CJEU 21 November 1974, Case 6/74 *Moulijn v Commission* [1974] ECR 1287, paras 10–11.

[65] Spijkerboer 2010, p 11. As Spijkerboer argues, to require the official lodging of an asylum application in order to fall under the personal scope of the directive would make it possible for Member States to first examine the well-foundedness of the application, and only thereafter allow the asylum seeker to lodge the application, which will be rejected immediately thereupon. The asylum seeker will in that way not fall under the scope of the directive, which runs counter to the effectiveness of the directive and its purpose of harmonizing reception conditions.

[66] The CJEU did not clarify the difference (if any) between 'lodging' and 'making' an application.

[67] *Cimade and GISTI* (n 60).

a final decision has been taken if a court or tribunal, of first instance, has reviewed the decision of the authorities on the application for asylum or if the asylum seeker has not made use of the possibility to appeal this decision. In this reading, asylum seekers who appeal to a higher national court or authority do not fall under the scope of the directive. A wider reading of the term 'final decision' is also possible. In that case 'a remedy within the framework of Chapter V' of the Procedures Directive should be understood more broadly and 'final decision' would mean a non-appealable decision. In that case, a decision on the asylum application should only be considered to be 'final' if all domestic remedies have been exhausted. This latter interpretation would solve problems of interpretation when the higher court refers back to the court of first instance. Since international courts or committees are clearly not remedies within the framework of the Procedures Directive, and no 'appeal' can be lodged against national decisions with these bodies, asylum seekers who have exhausted domestic remedies and who lodge a complaint with an international court or committee have received a 'final decision' on their asylum application and, consequently, do not fall under the personal scope of the directive.

In the context of 'Dublin' procedures, when a Member State calls upon another Member State to take charge of or to take back an asylum seeker, the CJEU has ruled that only the actual transfer of the asylum seeker by the requesting Member State brings an end to the examination of the application for asylum and should therefore be seen as the 'final decision' as meant in Directive 2003/9. The CJEU based this interpretation on the general scheme and purpose of Directive 2003/9 and on the observance of human rights.[68] This wide interpretation by the CJEU seems to be an indication for a wide interpretation of the personal scope of Directive 2003/9 in general.

Allowed to Remain on the Territory

A final important condition in order to fall under the scope of the directive is to be allowed to remain on the territory. Again, the directive does not contain further provisions on this condition. According to Article 2(k) of the Procedures Directive, 'remain in the Member State' means to remain in the territory, including at the border or in transit zones, of the Member State in which the application for asylum has been made or is being examined. Hence, the border and the transit zone of an airport must be considered to form part of a Member State's territory. The question remains, however, as to when an asylum seeker is 'allowed' to remain on

[68] Ibid, paras 51–58.

the territory. The Procedures Directive shows that it is not completely left to the Member States to decide on this question.

Pursuant to Article 7(1) of the Procedures Directive, an asylum seeker is allowed to remain in the Member State until the determining authority has made a decision in accordance with the procedures at first instance set out in Chapter III. Chapter III of the Procedures Directive contains rules and guarantees for different kind of procedures and applications, such as accelerated procedures, inadmissible and unfounded applications, subsequent applications and border procedures. Accordingly, asylum seekers are allowed to remain on the territory, and fall under the personal scope of Directive 2003/9, in all these situations, until a decision in first instance has been taken. Article 7(2) contains two important exceptions to this rule, however. Member States can make an exception to the right to remain on the territory if they decide not to further examine a subsequent application, in accordance with the procedural guarantees of Articles 32 and 34 of the Procedures Directive; or if they will surrender or extradite the asylum seeker. The CJEU confirmed in *Arslan* that an asylum seeker has the right to remain in the territory of the Member State concerned 'at least until his application has been rejected at first instance'.[69]

With regard to the appeal phase, the relevant rules are less clear. According to Article 39(3) of the Procedures Directive, the Member States should provide for rules in accordance with their international obligations dealing with a) the question of whether the appeal has the effect of allowing the asylum seeker to remain in the Member State pending its outcome; and b) the possibility of a legal remedy or protective measures where the appeal does not have the effect of allowing the asylum seeker to remain in the Member State pending its outcome. This article further states that Member States may also provide for an *ex officio* remedy. Hence, it is left to the Member States to decide, in accordance with their international obligations, whether asylum seekers are allowed to remain pending the outcome of their appeal. If asylum seekers are not allowed to remain pending the outcome of the appeal, then Member States should provide for rules on the possibility of a legal remedy or protective measures. This can also be an *ex officio* remedy. In *Arslan,* the CJEU observed that:

> Article 39(3) of Directive 2005/85 grants each Member State *the possibility* of extending the right established by Article 7(1) of the directive by providing that lodging an appeal against the decision of the responsible authority at first instance has the effect of allowing asylum applicants to remain on the territory of that State pending the outcome of that remedy.[70]

[69] CJEU 30 May 2013, C-534/11 *Arslan*, para 48.
[70] Ibid, para 47 (emphasis added).

This means that domestic law decides whether asylum seekers are allowed to remain pending the outcome of their appeal and, consequently, whether they fall under the personal scope of Directive 2003/9. This domestic law must, however, be in accordance with the international obligations of the Member State. According to case law of the European Court on Human Rights, Article 13 of the European Convention on Human Rights (ECHR) requires in the case of an arguable claim that expulsion violates Article 3 of the ECHR, a remedy with automatic, de jure suspensive effect. As a remedy must be effective in practice as well as in law in order to fulfil the requirements of Article 13 of the ECHR, it is not enough that a court can order a stay of execution; the suspensive effect must be an automatic consequence of lodging an appeal.[71] Accordingly, if domestic law must be in accordance with international obligations, it should provide for an appeal with automatic suspensive effect for asylum seekers who have an arguable claim that expulsion violates Article 3 of the ECHR. As the condition 'to be allowed to remain on the territory' seems to be a mere factual criterion, since no *lawful* or *legal* presence is required, it can be assumed that asylum seekers whose appeal has suspensive effect fulfil this condition.[72] Arguably, then, asylum seekers who have an arguable claim that expulsion violates Article 3 of the ECHR, are, on the basis of the international obligations of the Member States, allowed to remain on the territory pending the outcome of their appeal, and, consequently, fall under the personal scope of Directive 2003/9.

Again, the CJEU judgment in the *Cimade and GISTI* case[73] seems to indicate a wide interpretation of the condition to be allowed to remain on the territory. One of the questions in this case was when the obligation to provide reception benefits to an asylum seeker in respect of whom a Member State calls upon another Member State to take charge of him or to take him back under the Dublin Regulation (a 'Dublin claimant') ceases. In answering this question, the CJEU does not pay attention to the question whether such an asylum seeker is allowed to stay on the territory.[74]

[71] See, eg, *Gebremedhin v France* app no 25389/05 (ECtHR, 26 April 2007), para 66; *Abdolkhani and Karimnia v Turkey* app no 30471/08 (ECtHR, 22 September 2009), paras 108 and 116.

[72] Also if a legal obligation to leave the territory still exists, but is temporarily not enforced because of this suspensive effect. Peek argues that asylum seekers whose obligation to leave the country is not enforced and who are therefore only factually allowed to remain on the territory do not fall under the scope of the directive (Peek 2010, pp 897–98). In my view, however, *as long as no final decision on their asylum application has been taken*, asylum seekers whose obligation to leave the country is explicitly not enforced fulfil the mere factual criterion of the directive.

[73] *Cimade and GISTI* (n 60).

[74] The CJEU does pay attention to this condition when answering the question whether the obligation to provide benefits to such asylum seekers actually exist, see ibid, paras 46–49.

After establishing that only the actual transfer to another Member State is a 'final decision', it simply holds:

> In addition, further to the general scheme and purpose of Directive 2003/9 and the observance of fundamental rights, in particular the requirements of Article 1 of the Charter, under which human dignity must be respected and protected, the asylum seeker may not, […], be deprived—even for a temporary period of time after the making of the application for asylum and before being actually transferred to another Member State—of the protection of the minimum standards laid down by that directive.[75]

Hence it seems that in particular for 'Dublin claimants', the CJEU is of the opinion that they are always allowed to remain on the territory pending the entire examination of this request.

In brief, under the Procedures Directive, asylum seekers are allowed to remain on the territory until the authorities have decided in first instance on their asylum application, unless they submit a subsequent application that the authorities do not examine further[76] or they will be extradited or surrendered and they are not allowed to remain for those reasons under domestic law. The question whether asylum seekers are allowed to remain, and, consequently, fall under the personal scope of the directive pending appeal is left to domestic law by the Procedures Directive. However, arguably, asylum seekers who have an arguable claim that expulsion violates Article 3 ECHR should be allowed to remain on the basis of Article 13 of the ECHR and therefore fall under the personal scope of Directive 2003/9. In addition, according to the CJEU 'Dublin claimants' fall under the personal scope of Directive 2003/9 pending the entire procedure on establishing the Member State responsible for examining their asylum application. Arguably therefore, they should be considered to be allowed to remain on the territory pending this period.

[75] Ibid, para 56.

[76] The CJEU holds that 'the personal scope of Directive 2003/9 encompasses any asylum seeker who has lodged an application for asylum for the first time with a Member State' (ibid, para 52). The Court seems therefore to be of the opinion that asylum seekers who lodge a subsequent asylum application do not fall under the personal scope of Directive 2003/9. This is not supported by the text of Directive 2003/9 in combination with the Procedures Directive. These directives suggest that asylum seekers who lodge a subsequent application are only not allowed to remain on the territory, and, therefore, excluded from the personal scope of Directive 2003/9, if the authorities decide not to deal with this application in accordance with certain rules. In addition, Art 16 of Directive 2003/9 gives Member States the possibility to deny reception benefits to asylum seekers who have already lodged an application in the same Member State. The inclusion of this ground in Art 16 confirms in my view that asylum seekers who lodge a subsequent application can fall under the directive's personal scope.

Concluding Remarks

Asylum seekers fall under the scope of Directive 2003/9 as from the moment that they have submitted their asylum application. Arguably, they already fall under the personal scope as from the moment they make their intention to apply for asylum known to the authorities, if necessary in person and/or at a designated place. They fall under the scope of the directive until the competent authorities have decided on their application in first instance, unless they are not allowed to remain on the territory because they have submitted a subsequent application that the authorities do not examine further or they will be extradited or surrendered. If their asylum application has been rejected and they lodge an appeal against this rejection, they fall under the personal scope of the directive if they are allowed to remain on the territory pursuant to domestic law. This domestic law should, however, be in accordance with the international obligations, as a result of which asylum seekers with an arguable claim that expulsion violates Article 3 of the ECHR, should be allowed to remain on the territory pending the appeal, by virtue of Article 13 of the ECHR. In addition, the CJEU judgment in the *Cimade and GISTI* case suggests that the condition of being allowed to remain on the territory should be interpreted widely.

Hence, the stage of the asylum procedure is decisive for the question whether asylum seekers fall under the scope of the directive. A number of categories of 'asylum seekers', as defined in section 1.5.1, do not fall under the personal scope of Directive 2003/9. First of all, two categories of asylum seekers do not fall under the personal scope of the directive pending the examination of their application by the determining authorities if they are, under domestic law, not allowed to remain on the territory pending this examination. This concerns asylum seekers whose subsequent asylum application will not be further examined in accordance with the Procedures Directive and asylum seekers who will be extradited or surrendered. A second category of asylum seeker falling outside the scope of the directive concerns asylum seekers who lodge an appeal against the rejection of their asylum application and, under domestic law, are not allowed to remain on the territory pending the appeal. Arguably, however, asylum seekers who have an arguable claim based on Article 3 of the ECHR should be allowed to remain on the territory pursuant to Article 13 of the ECHR. Finally, asylum seekers who lodge a complaint to an international court or committee that their expulsion violates a human rights provision do not fall under the scope of the directive. The same might be true for asylum seekers who lodge a further (domestic) appeal against a decision of a court in first instance that the appeal is unfounded.

2.3.5 Material Reception Conditions

Text of the Directive

According to Article 2(j) of the directive, 'material reception conditions' means 'the reception conditions that include housing, food and clothing, provided in kind, or as financial allowances or in vouchers, and a daily expenses allowance'. Asylum seekers have an enforceable right to these kinds of reception conditions, as Member States should 'ensure' that material reception conditions are available when the application for asylum is made.[77] Article 13(5) explicitly reiterates the possibility for Member States to provide material reception conditions in kind, or in the form of financial allowances or vouchers[78] or in a combination of these provisions.[79] As Peek argues, the possibility to provide reception conditions in kind or in vouchers reveals that the directive envisions a separate support scheme for asylum seekers, as provision of benefits in kind or in vouchers is rather uncommon in general social assistance schemes for nationals.[80]

As to the level of the material reception conditions, the directive states rather vaguely that these conditions should 'ensure a standard of living adequate for the health of applicants and capable of ensuring their subsistence'.[81] As this provision allows for wide interpretation, it can be interpreted as a very minimalist standard, requiring only vital basic needs to be met.[82] The provision of material reception conditions may be made subject to the condition that asylum seekers do not have sufficient means to reach this standard of living.[83] In addition, if asylum seekers have sufficient

[77] Directive 2003/9, Art 13(1).

[78] The possibility to provide asylum seekers with vouchers has been criticized by the European Parliament, the Economic and Social Committee and the UNHCR for more or less the same reasons, namely that it causes difficulties for asylum seekers and it unnecessarily distinguishes them from the rest of the population (in the words of the Economic and Social Committee). See *European Parliament, Report on the proposal for a Council directive laying down minimum standards on the reception of applicants for asylum in Member States* 15 April 2002, A5-0112/2002 Final, p 32; Opinion of the Economic and Social Committee on the 'Proposal for a Council Directive laying down minimum standards on the reception of applicants for asylum in Member States', [2002] OJ C 48/63, para 4.4.2.2; UNHCR 2003, comment to Art 13(5).

[79] A Commission report on the application of the directive reveals that the majority of Member States provide accommodation, food and clothing in kind (Commission, *Report from the Commission to the Council and to the European Parliament on the Application of Directive 20039/EC of 27 January 2003 laying down Minimum Standards for the Reception of Asylum Seekers*, COM(2007) 745 final, p 5).

[80] Peek 2010, p 934.

[81] Directive 2003/9, Art 13(2).

[82] *Cf* McAdam 2007, pp 249–50; Handoll 2007, p 217; Peek 2010, p 934. Such a minimalist interpretation raises the question, however, whether this is in conformity with the directive's objective to ensure asylum seekers a dignified standard of living.

[83] Directive 2003/9, Art 13(3).

resources, for example if they have been working for a reasonable period of time, Member States may require them to cover or contribute to the cost of the material reception conditions or they may ask for a refund afterwards.[84]

The provision of housing in kind is more elaborately regulated in the directive. If housing is provided in kind, it should take one or a combination of the following forms:

1. premises used for the purpose of housing applicants during the examination of an application for asylum lodged at the border;
2. accommodation centres which guarantee an adequate standard of living; or
3. private houses, flats, hotels or other premises adapted for housing applicants.[85]

Member States should ensure that transfers of asylum seekers from one housing facility to another only take place when necessary.[86]

'Accommodation centres' are defined in Article 2(l) of the directive as 'any place used for the collective housing of asylum seekers'. The directive contains some specific guarantees for this kind of housing, as the directive explicitly states that these centres should guarantee an adequate standard of living[87] and that persons working in these centres should be adequately trained.[88]

The directive further contains some rules regarding the freedom of movement in relation to accommodation of asylum seekers. Besides confinement to a particular place (ie detention) when it proves necessary, Member States may decide on the residence of the asylum seeker

[84] Directive 2003/9, Art 13(4). As Peek observes, it can be problematic to oblige asylum seekers to pay for accommodation in assigned collective accommodation centres, while they have no possibility to choose alternative accommodation (Peek 2010, p 935).

[85] Directive 2003/9, Art 14(1). The Commission report on the application of the directive shows that collective housing is the most common form of accommodation for asylum seekers in the Member States (*Commission report* (n 79), p 5).

[86] Directive 2003/9, Art 14(4).

[87] It is remarkable that this provision explicitly states that accommodation centres should guarantee an adequate standard of living, since Art 13(2) of Directive 2003/9 already provides that the material reception conditions should ensure a standard of living adequate for the health of applicants and capable of ensuring their subsistence. Furthermore, this addition seems to imply that the other two forms of housing do not necessarily have to guarantee an adequate standard of living.

[88] Directive 2003/9, Art 14(5). According to the Economic and Social Committee, 'the period spent in reception centres should be as short as possible—especially since reception centres often resemble detention centres—before people are moved to alternative, normal accommodation' (Opinion of the Economic and Social Committee (n 78) para 4.4.1). Also the Committee on Employment and Social Affairs of the European Parliament was of the opinion that '[a]ccommodation centres often resemble detention centres, and do nothing to advance social integration for applicants for asylum or their contact with the host country'. For those reasons, the Committee found it necessary 'to reduce the stay in such centres to the minimum and to grant access as soon as possible to normal housing' (European Parliament Report (n 78), p 83).

for reasons of public interest, public order or, when necessary, for the swift processing and effective monitoring of his or her application.[89] In addition, Member States are allowed to make provision of the material reception conditions subject to actual residence by the asylum seeker in a specific place.[90] There should be a possibility for granting temporary permission to leave this place of residence.[91]

Exceptionally, Member States may deviate from these guarantees for the provision of housing in kind, but only for a reasonable period which must be as short as possible. Basic needs should in any case be covered. Deviation is only possible when:

— an initial assessment of the specific needs of the applicant is required;
— material reception conditions are not available in a certain geographical area;
— housing capacities normally available are temporarily exhausted; or
— the asylum seeker is in detention or confined to border posts.[92]

This means that if one of these situations applies, it is possible to house asylum seekers in facilities that are not adapted or specifically intended for the housing of asylum seekers.[93]

As regards material reception conditions (and health care), the directive further contains the general principle that Member States should take into account the specific situation of vulnerable persons found to have special needs.[94] Neither 'vulnerable persons' nor 'special needs' has been defined by the directive, but a number of examples of 'vulnerable persons' have been listed: (unaccompanied) minors, disabled people, elderly people, pregnant women, single parents with minor children and persons who have been subjected to torture, rape or other serious forms of psychological, physical or sexual violence.[95]

[89] Directive 2003/9, Art 7(2).

[90] Directive 2003/9, Art 7(4). According to this article, such a decision may be of a general nature. This article specifically speaks of 'material reception conditions'. Consequently, the provision of health care may not be subject to the actual residence of an asylum seeker at a designated place.

[91] Directive 2003/9, Art 7(5).

[92] Directive 2003/9, Art 14(8).

[93] From the discussion in the Asylum Working Party of the Council, it follows that delegations of some Member States have proposed this provision in order to make it possible to house asylum seekers for limited periods of time, eg, in castles, boats or camp sites (Council Document 11541/01 ASILE 43, p 26).

[94] Directive 2003/9, Art 17.

[95] Directive 2003/9, Art 17(1).

Differences from the Commission Proposal

The provisions discussed above differ on some important points from the text of the proposal of the Commission. As to the level of the material reception conditions, the Commission proposed to lay down that these conditions should ensure 'a standard of living adequate for the health and the well being of applicants and their accompanying family members as well as the protection of their fundamental rights',[96] which can be seen as a more sympathetic level for asylum seekers.[97] This formulation was, however, considered to be too vague and not well suited to the content of a directive by the Member States.[98] An important guarantee laid down in the Commission proposal concerns the provision that Member States should ensure that the standard of living is determined with regard to the length of the asylum procedure.[99] Although this link between reception conditions and the length of the procedure was very much welcomed by the UNHCR,[100] most Member States did not consider it appropriate to link the level of benefits to the duration of the procedure.[101] As regards transfers of asylum seekers from one housing facility to the other, the Commission proposal stated that this should take place only when necessary in relation to the examination of the application or for security reasons.[102] Delegations of the Member States already agreed, however, during the first meeting in which the Commission proposal was examined to delete this extra guarantee.[103] Finally, the Commission proposal only provided for detention of asylum seekers, under certain circumstances, and for limiting the freedom of movement of asylum seekers to a specific area of their territory, not for deciding on the particular place of residence or for subjecting the provision of material reception conditions to actual residence in a particular place.[104]

[96] Art 15(2) of the Proposal for a Council Directive laying down minimum standards on the reception of applicants for asylum in Member States, COM(2001) 181 final.

[97] Handoll 2004, p 144; Peek 2010, p 933. The UNHCR would have preferred the language of the Commission in the final text of the directive, see UNHCR 2003, comment on Art 13(1) and (2).

[98] Council Document 11320/01 ASILE 39, p 25; Council Document 6906/02 ASILE 13, p 15.

[99] Art 15(2) of the Commission proposal (n 96). According to the Explanatory Memorandum, it is assumed that 'the longer the procedure the more the needs that must be addressed to ensure the well being of the applicant increase'. European Parliament proposed to delete this provision, since 'the reception conditions must at all times be such as to ensure that human rights are respected, irrespective of the length of the procedure' (European Parliament Report (n 78), p 32).

[100] See comments of the UNHCR on the Commission proposal, Council Document 11347/01 ASILE 40, p 4.

[101] Council Document 11320/01 ASILE 39, p 25.

[102] Art 16(4) of the Commission proposal (n 96).

[103] Council Document 11320/01 ASILE 39, p 29.

[104] Art 7 of the Commission proposal (n 96).

2.3.6 Health Care

Text of the Directive

Article 15(1) of the directive stipulates that the Member States should 'ensure that applicants receive the necessary health care which shall include, at least, emergency care and the essential treatment of illness'. For applicants who have special needs, the Member States should provide necessary medical or other assistance, according to Article 15(2). 'Special needs' is not further defined in the directive, or in other instruments of the Common European Asylum System, as a result of which the second paragraph of Article 15 is rather vague.

Hence, under the directive asylum seekers are not entitled to the same kind of health care as nationals, but only to emergency care and the essential treatment of illness. The directive does not determine who should decide which care is 'emergency care' and which treatment of illness is 'essential'. It is left to the Member States to set up a system for this.

Differences from the Commission Proposal

The rather short provision on health care in the directive differs significantly from the more extensive and detailed provisions on health care in the proposal of the Commission. Most importantly, the Commission proposal makes a distinction in the level of health care that should be provided to asylum seekers between different kinds of asylum procedures. During the regular procedure in first instance and the regular appeal procedure,[105] the proposal stated that Member States should ensure that asylum seekers have access to 'primary health care provided by a general practitioner, psychological care and health care that cannot be postponed'.[106] During admissibility and accelerated procedures and during the procedure to decide on their right to legally enter the territory, Member States should ensure that asylum seekers have access to 'emergency health and psychological care and health care that cannot be postponed'.[107] The proposal stated that if no decision has been taken within 65 working days after the asylum application is lodged or notice

[105] Provided that the appeal has suspensive effect or that the applicants have obtained a decision allowing them to remain at the border or on the territory during the examination of the appeal.

[106] Art 20(1) of the Commission proposal (n 96). According to the explanatory memorandum to the proposal, the assessment of care that cannot be postponed 'should be done by the doctor together with the authority that will pay for it'.

[107] Art 21(1) of the Commission proposal (n 96). According to the explanatory memorandum to the proposal, these kinds of care were at that time given to asylum seekers in all Member States. This standard thus confirms an existing practice.

of appeal is given, asylum seekers are entitled to the same health care as during regular procedures.[108] This distinction between different kinds of asylum procedures disappeared in the final text of the directive, as well as the entitlement of asylum seekers to primary health care provided by a general practitioner and the specific reference to psychological care. Some Member States had problems with the expression 'primary health care', as this term might have different meanings in the various Member States.[109] The terminology of 'emergency care and essential treatment of illness' has been proposed in Council, as this terminology was also used in the Temporary Protection Directive.[110] In particular, Germany stated several times that the distinction in the level of health care between different kinds of procedures should be deleted, as the real needs of asylum seekers must be taken into account, which are not dependent on the kind of procedure.[111] In the end, all asylum seekers receive the same treatment with respect to access to health care, albeit at a lower level than provided for in the Commission proposal for the regular procedure. Notably, the level of health care that asylum seekers are entitled to under the directive is more or less the same as the level of health care that the Commission found suitable for only a few months.

A further difference between the text of the directive and the Commission proposal is that the latter stipulated that Member States should lay down the conditions of access to health care that prevents aggravation of existing illness.[112] The directive does not contain a provision on this issue.

2.3.7 Access to the Labour Market

Text of the Directive

The possibility for asylum seekers to legally enter the labour market was one of the areas causing quite some controversy among the Member States. As a result of the great diversity on this issue prevailing at the time of adoption of the directive in the Member States, it was difficult to arrive at consensus in this area.[113] Consequently, the provision on access to the labour market in the directive gives considerable latitude to the Member States and permits restrictive application.[114]

108 Art 21(4) and (5) of the Commission proposal (n 96).
109 Council Document 11541/01 ASILE 43, p 33.
110 Ibid.
111 Council Document 11320/01 ASILE 39, p 34; Council Document 11541/01 ASILE 43, p 35.
112 Art 20(3) and 21(3) of the Commission proposal (n 96).
113 Handoll 2004, p 141; Rogers 2002, p 227.
114 *Cf* UNHCR 2003, comment to Art 11.

According to Article 11 of the directive, Member States should determine a period of time, starting from the date on which an application for asylum was lodged, during which an applicant may *not* have access to the labour market. The wording of this provision does not leave open the possibility for Member States to waive a waiting period before access to the labour market is granted. On this aspect, Member States are therefore not allowed to introduce or retain more favourable provisions.[115] If a decision at first instance has not been taken within one year of the presentation of an application for asylum and this delay cannot be attributed to the applicant, Member States should *decide the conditions* for granting access to the labour market for the applicant. In deciding these conditions, Member States may give priority to EU citizens and nationals of states parties to the Agreement on the European Economic Area and also to legally resident third-country nationals, for reasons of labour market policies. The only clear guarantee for asylum seekers in this article is that if access to the labour market is granted, it cannot be withdrawn during appeals procedures, provided that the appeal has suspensive effect, until a negative decision on the appeal is notified.

Hence, Member States are allowed under the directive to ban access to the labour market for one year as from the lodging of an asylum application. After that year, asylum seekers should get access to the labour market, but this access can be subject to (all kinds of) conditions set by the Member States[116] and Member States may give priority to certain categories of other aliens in their territory. This possibility in particular of giving priority to other groups of aliens may render the access of asylum

[115] Peek 2010, p 928. Art 4 of Directive 2003/9 allows Member States to introduce or retain more favourable provisions, but only 'insofar as these provisions are compatible with this Directive'. See in this regard the judgment of the CJEU in the case of *B and D* (CJEU 9 November 2010, Case C-57/09 and C-101/09 [2010] ECR I-10979). This case is about the Qualification Directive which contains a similar clause on more favourable provisions in Art 3. Art 12(2) of the Qualification Directive contains the grounds on which a person 'is excluded' from being a refugee. The Bundesverwaltungsgericht asked the CJEU whether it is compatible with Directive 2004/83, for the purposes of Art 3 of that directive, for a Member State to recognize that a person excluded from refugee status pursuant to Art 12(2) of the directive has a right of asylum under its constitutional law. The Court held that the reservation in Art 3 precludes Member States from introducing or maintaining provisions granting refugee status to persons who are excluded from that status pursuant to Art 12(2) of the Qualification Directive. Member States are only allowed to introduce or maintain more favourable provisions in this regard if the national provisions provide for a clear distinction between national protection and protection under the Qualification Directive. The other kind of (national) protection may not 'entail a risk of confusion with refugee status within the meaning of the directive' according to the Court (paras 113–21).

[116] According to the Commission, Member States 'can decide the kind of work asylum applicants may apply for, the amount of time per month or per year they are allowed to work, the skills they should have, etc.' and remain therefore 'in full control of the internal labour market' (explanatory memorandum to the Commission proposal (n 96), p 14).

seekers to the labour market a rather theoretical possibility.[117] If, however, a negative decision at first instance has been taken on the asylum application *within* one year after the lodging of the application, Member States are not bound to grant the asylum seeker access to the labour market. Consequently, even if the asylum seeker lodges an appeal against the rejection of his application, which might have suspensive effect, he may still be banned from the labour market, irrespective of the length of the appeal procedure. On the other hand, if the decision at first instance was taken *after* one year of the lodging of the application, access to the labour market may not be withdrawn pending the appeal procedure, provided that the appeal has suspensive effect.[118]

Differences from the Commission Proposal

The text of the directive differs to a great extent from the text of the Commission proposal, even though this proposal did not provide for a far-reaching harmonization.[119] The most important difference is that the Commission proposed to ban access to the labour market for a maximum of six months, instead of one year.[120] In addition, the Commission proposal stipulated that access to the labour market should be granted six months after the asylum application had been lodged, regardless of whether a decision at first instance on the application had yet been taken or not. During the first examination of the Commission proposal in the Asylum Working Party, a lot of Member States had reservations on the issue of access to the labour market. Some Member States expressed their concern that granting access to employment would bring about an increase in asylum applications by immigrants looking for work or that asylum seekers might delay procedures in order to obtain access to employment.[121] After a discussion in the Strategic Committee on Immigration, Frontiers and Asylum, most Member States agreed that Member States should be obliged to allow

[117] Peek 2010, p 930.

[118] If the appeal does not have suspensive effect, but the asylum seekers is nevertheless allowed to remain on the territory pending the appeal pursuant to a court decision, access to the labour market may apparently be withdrawn. See in this regard the text of the Commission proposal, which added 'or a decision has been obtained allowing the applicant to remain in the member state in which the application has been lodged or is being examined for the time an appeal against a negative decision is examined' (Art 13(2) of the Commission proposal (n 96)). It seems that this phrase has been deleted in order 'to improve readability' (Council Document 11320/01 ASILE 39, p 22).

[119] Peek 2010, p 927.

[120] Art 13(1) of the Commission proposal (n 96). It is remarkable in this regard that the European Parliament proposed allowing asylum seekers access to the labour market 'as soon as possible but within four months after their application has been lodged' (*European Parliament report* (n 78) p 28).

[121] Council Document 11320/01 ASILE 39, p 21.

access to employment not later than one year after the date of filing the asylum application.[122] The Luxembourg delegation expressed concern, however, that this might create the situation in which asylum seekers who had appealed against an initial decision refusing asylum, before the end of this one-year period, might obtain prolonged access to employment.[123] The Presidency proposed thereupon to state that Member States should grant access to the labour market *if a decision in first instance* has not been taken one year after the presentation of an application for asylum.[124]

Another important difference between the final text and the Commission proposal is that under the Commission proposal, Member States were not explicitly allowed to give priority to EU citizens, nationals of states parties to the Agreement on the European Economic Area and legally resident third-country nationals. The possibility of priority for EU citizens was proposed by some Member States with reference to a similar provision in the Temporary Protection Directive.[125]

A less important, and more textual, difference between the final text and the text of the Commission proposal is that the latter contained the phrase 'Member States shall authorise access to the labour market for the applicant subject to the conditions laid down by the Member States'. At Germany's request, this phrase was ultimately replaced by the phrase 'Member States shall decide the conditions for granting access to the labour market for the applicant'.[126]

2.3.8 Reduction and Withdrawal of Reception Conditions

Text of the Directive

The directive contains an exhaustive list of grounds for reducing or withdrawing reception conditions. Article 16 of the directive mentions six grounds. Three grounds concern the behaviour of the asylum seeker in the asylum procedure. Reception conditions may be reduced, withdrawn or refused:

— if the asylum seeker does not comply with reporting duties or with requests to provide information or to appear for personal interviews concerning the asylum procedure during a reasonable period laid down in national law;

[122] Council Document 5791/02 ASILE 5, p 1.
[123] Ibid, p 2.
[124] Council Document 6467/02 ASILE 11, p 13.
[125] Council Document 11320/01 ASILE 39, p 21.
[126] See Council Document 14658/02 ASILE 70, p 16; Council Document 14658/02 ASILE 70 ADD 1, p 2; and Council Document 15398/02 ASILE 78, p 15.

— if the asylum seeker has failed to demonstrate that the asylum claim was made as soon as reasonably practicable after arrival in that Member State; or
— if the asylum seeker has already lodged an asylum application in the same Member State.

Two other grounds for reduction or withdrawal relate to the behaviour of the asylum seeker in accommodation centres or other housing premises:

— if the asylum seeker abandons the place of residence determined by the competent authority without informing it or, if requested, without permission;[127] or
— in the case of a serious breach of the rules of the accommodation centres or seriously violent behaviour.

Finally, reception conditions may be reduced or withdrawn if the asylum seeker has concealed financial resources.

The directive contains a number of safeguards for asylum seekers in the case of reduction, withdrawal or refusal of reception conditions. First of all, the directive stipulates that decisions for reduction, withdrawal or refusal of reception conditions or sanctions should be taken individually, objectively and impartially and reasons should be given. Such decisions should be based on the particular situation of the person concerned, especially with regard to vulnerable persons such as (unaccompanied) minors, disabled people, elderly people, pregnant women, single parents with minor children and persons who have been subjected to torture, rape or other serious forms of psychological, physical or sexual violence, and the principle of proportionality should be taken into account.[128] This means that decisions for reduction, withdrawal or refusal of reception conditions should be taken on a case-by-case basis; it is not possible to categorically exclude certain asylum seekers from reception conditions. Only the decision to make provision of material reception conditions subject to actual residence of an asylum seeker at a specific place may be of general nature.[129] Secondly, Member States should under all circumstances ensure access to emergency health care.[130] Thirdly, material reception conditions may only be reduced or withdrawn if a negative decision has

[127] According to Art 7(4) of Directive 2003/9, only the provision of 'material reception conditions' may be made subject to actual residence of the asylum seeker at a specific designated place. The difference between this and the possibility to reduce or withdraw all kinds of reception conditions seems to be that the safeguards provided in Art 16(4) do not apply in the former case. The decision under Art 7(4) may be of general nature.

[128] Directive 2003/9, Art 16(4) in conjunction with Art 17.

[129] Directive 2003/9, Art 7(4). This article also states, rather contradictorily, that this decision should be taken individually.

[130] Directive 2003/9, Art16(4).

been taken.[131] The meaning of the wording 'negative decision' is rather unclear, but in view of the context of Article 16, it can be assumed that a negative decision on the grating of reception conditions is meant, and not a negative decision on the asylum application.[132] Finally, Member States should ensure that negative decisions relating to the granting of benefits under the directive may be the subject of an appeal before, at least in the last instance, a judicial body.[133]

In a statement to the Council minutes, the Council confirms in relation to the application of Article 16(2) on refusal of reception conditions if the asylum seeker has failed to demonstrate that the asylum claim was made as soon as reasonably practicable and of Article 16(4) on the conditions for taking of decisions that Member States will in all cases:

— comply with their international obligations on human dignity, including the European Convention on Human Rights, and in particular the obligations under Article 3 to ensure that no one is subject to inhuman or degrading treatment;
— take account of the situation of the person concerned, and in particular the general principle provided for in Article 17 regarding the specific situation of vulnerable persons in providing access to material benefits including food and housing; and
— ensure that as a minimum access to emergency healthcare is guaranteed under all circumstances.[134]

Differences from the Commission Proposal

Some grounds for reduction or withdrawal in the directive were absent in the proposal of the Commission and the Commission proposal contained grounds that are not included in the final text of the directive. The Commission proposal contained the possibility of reducing or withdrawing reception conditions if an asylum seeker is regarded as a threat to national security or if there are serious grounds for believing that the asylum seeker has committed a war crime or a crime against humanity or that Article 1(F) of the Geneva Convention may apply with respect to the asylum seeker.[135] In addition, under the proposal Member States were allowed to reduce material reception conditions when an asylum seeker prevents minors under his care from attending school or single classes in ordinary school programmes.[136] The Commission proposal did not contain the possibility of

131 Directive 2003/9, Art 16(5).
132 See also Larsson 2011, p 71 and Peek 2010, p 947.
133 Directive 2003/9, Art 21(1).
134 Council Document 15444/02 ASILE 80, p 3.
135 Art 22(1)(d) of the Commission proposal (n 96).
136 Art 22(3) of the Commission proposal (n 96).

reducing, withdrawing or refusing reception conditions on the ground that an asylum application has already been lodged in the same Member State and that an asylum seeker has failed to demonstrate that the asylum claim was made as soon as reasonably practicable after arrival. The latter ground was proposed by the United Kingdom in a late stage of the discussion of the directive,[137] since the United Kingdom was intending to implement an internal policy according to which reception conditions would be refused on this ground.[138] The Netherlands tried to introduce the possibility to refuse reception conditions where another Member State can be held responsible for processing the application for asylum, but failed in this attempt.[139]

Another difference from the final text of the directive is that under the Commission proposal, emergency health care and *health care that cannot be postponed* could not be reduced or withdrawn. During the discussion in the Council, food and housing were also included in this provision, but this was then deleted.[140]

Finally, the Commission proposal set a period of 30 days during which the asylum seeker had disappeared or had neglected reporting duties or requests to provide information or to appear for personal interviews before reception conditions could be reduced or withdrawn. A large number of Member States found this 30-day period to be excessive and preferred not to specify any period.[141] Ultimately, the directive speaks of a 'reasonable period laid down in national law'.

2.4 DIRECTIVE 2013/33/EU

2.4.1 Introduction

This section will discuss the provisions of Directive 2013/33 dealing with social security benefits for asylum seekers and access to the labour market, as well as the provisions on reduction and withdrawal of these benefits. The same order of discussion as in the foregoing section will be used. The

[137] Council Document 14658/02 ASILE 70, annex 1, p 23.

[138] Vincenzi 2004, p 165–66. This policy was found to violate Art 3 of the ECHR under certain individual circumstances by the House of Lords (*R v Secretary of State for the Home Department, ex p* Adam [2005] UKHL 66 (HL)).

[139] See, among other documents, Council Document 7802/02 ASILE 19, p 19, Council Document 8090/02 ASILE 21, p 14. Ultimately, the Netherlands supported the objective of reaching as soon as possible an agreement on the draft regulation on the determination of the Member State responsible for examining an asylum application lodged in one of the Member States by a third-country national. In this respect, the Netherlands put special emphasis on a substantive shortening of the procedure provided for in this draft regulation (Council Document 9097/02 ASILE 27, p 3).

[140] See, among other documents, Council Document 6906/02 ASILE 13, p 21; Council Document 7307/02 ASILE 16, p 20.

[141] Council Document 11320/01 ASILE 39, p 38.

discussion will focus mainly on the relevant differences between Directive 2013/33 and Directive 2003/9. It will turn out that no major changes have been laid down in Directive 2013/33 as compared to the 2003 Directive with regard to social benefits and access to the labour market. The (minor) changes that have been agreed upon will be discussed below. Again, in order to show on which standards the Member States and/or Parliament were not willing to agree, attention will be paid to differences between the final text of Directive 2013/33 and the text of the Commission proposal for the recast.

2.4.2 Realization of Directive 2013/33

Since the entry into force of the Treaty of Lisbon on 1 December 2009 Article 63(1) of the TEC has been replaced by Article 78 of the Treaty on the Functioning of the European Union (TFEU). Paragraph 1 of the latter article provides:

> The Union shall develop a common policy on asylum, subsidiary protection and temporary protection with a view to offering appropriate status to any third-country national requiring international protection and ensuring compliance with the principle of non-refoulement. This policy must be in accordance with the Geneva Convention of 28 July 1951 and the Protocol of 31 January 1967 relating to the status of refugees, and other relevant treaties.

The second paragraph provides that measures for a Common European Asylum System must be adopted comprising 'standards concerning the conditions for the reception of applicants for asylum or subsidiary protection'.

This article therefore no longer refers to minimum standards on the reception of asylum seekers, but rather to common standards. This is in line with the Tampere conclusions of the European Council of 1999, which provided for two phases for the development of the Common European Asylum System. In the short term, minimum and general standards should be adopted in a number of fields, whereas in the longer term, 'Community rules should lead to a common asylum procedure and a uniform status for those who are granted asylum valid throughout the Union'. This aim has been reconfirmed in the 'European Pact on Immigration and Asylum', adopted by Council of 2008, which called on the Commission to present proposals for establishing, in 2012 at the latest, a single asylum procedure comprising common guarantees.[142]

[142] Council of the European Union, *European Pact on Immigration and Asylum*, 24 September 2008, 13440/08, ASIM 72.

In June 2007 the Commission issued a Green Paper on the future Common European Asylum System.[143] This paper aimed to identify what options were possible under the current EU legal framework for shaping the second stage of the construction of the Common European Asylum System. The goals in this second stage were to achieve both a higher common standard of protection and greater equality in protection across the EU and to ensure a higher degree of solidarity between EU Member States. In order to reach these goals, existing gaps in the current asylum *acquis* had to be filled and legislative harmonization based on high standards had to be pursued.[144] With regard to Directive 2003/9, the Commission noted that ensuring a high level of harmonization with regard to reception conditions of asylum seekers is crucial if secondary movements are to be avoided. However, the wide margin of discretion left to Member States by several key provisions of this directive resulted in negating the desired harmonization effect. The Commission mentioned as examples of areas where wide divergences exist the access of asylum seekers to the labour market, the standards of reception and access to health care.[145] In addition, this wide margin of manoeuvre has led to the establishment of low reception standards, according to the Commission. The Commission emphasises that:

> [L]ow standards concerning the level of social rights granted to asylum seekers raise strong concerns about respect for fundamental rights; (...) the wide margin of discretion granted to Member States in implementing its provisions could lead to policies that might be perceived as not being fully in line with fundamental rights established by the EU Charter of Fundamental Rights as well as the International Covenant on Economic, Social and Cultural Rights, the UN Convention on the Rights of the Child, and the UN Convention Against Torture.[146]

After reflection and debate with all relevant stakeholders on the basis of the Green Paper, the Commission issued a policy plan on asylum in June 2008.[147] In this communication, the Commission launched its proposal to amend Directive 2003/9 in order to (amongst others) cover persons seeking subsidiary protection, ensure greater equality and improved standards of treatment with regard to the level and form of material reception

[143] COM(2007) 301 final.
[144] Ibid, pp 2–3.
[145] Ibid, pp 4–5.
[146] Commission, Commission Staff Working Document accompanying the Proposal for a Directive of the European Parliament and of the Council laying down minimum standards for the reception of asylum seekers. Impact assessment, SEC(2008) 2944, p 7.
[147] Communication from the Commission to the European Parliament, the Council, the European Economic and Social Committee and the Committee of Regions. Policy plan on asylum. An integrated approach to protection across the EU, COM(2008) 360 final.

conditions and to provide for simplified and more harmonized access to the labour market, ensuring that actual access to employment is not hindered by additional unnecessary administrative restrictions.[148]

The proposal for a recast of Directive 2003/9 was issued by the Commission in December 2008.[149] It contained a number of important amendments in the areas discussed above.[150] In May 2009, the European Parliament adopted its position on the proposal which approved most of the proposed amendments.[151] The Council documents on this proposal reveal, however, that the proposed changes encountered opposition from a significant number of Member States and no agreement was reached on this proposal. Delegations wanted 'a better balance between, on the one hand, high standards of reception conditions for applicants for international protection and, on the other hand, the administrative and financial implications for Member States'.[152]

In order to 'boost up the work towards achieving a true Common European Asylum System', the Commission therefore presented a modified proposal for a recast of Directive 2003/9 in June 2011.[153] The Commission put forward that this modified proposal granted Member States more flexibility and latitude and better ensured that Member States have the tools to address cases where reception rules are abused and/or become pull factors. At the same time, the modified proposal maintained high standards of treatment in line with fundamental rights, according to the Commission.

After more than one year of negotiations between the European Parliament and the Council, the position of the Council at first reading on the recast of Directive 2003/9 was published on 7 June 2013.[154] By resolution of 12 June 2013, Parliament approved the Council position. Directive

[148] Ibid, p 4.

[149] Commission, Proposal for a Directive of the European Parliament and of the Council laying down minimum standards for the reception of asylum seekers (recast), COM(2008) 815 final.

[150] It also contained elaborate provisions on the detention of asylum seekers, but this issue will not be discussed in this book.

[151] EP-PE_TC1-COD(2008)0244.

[152] Council Document 6394/1/12 REV 1, ASILE 24, p 1.

[153] European Commission, Amended proposal for a Directive of the European Parliament and of the Council laying down minimum standards for the reception of asylum seekers (recast), COM(2011) 320 final.

[154] Position (EU) no 6/2013 of the Council at first reading with a view to the adoption of a Directive of the European Parliament and of the Council laying down standards for the reception of applicants for international protection (recast), adopted by the Council on 6 June 2013 (2013/C 197). On the basis of the amended proposal of the Commission, the European Parliament and the Council had conducted negotiations with a view to concluding an agreement at the stage of the Council's position at first reading. Political agreement was confirmed by the Council at its meeting on 25 and 26 October 2012 (Council Document 14112/1/12 REV 1, ASILE 116).

2013/33 was formally adopted on 26 June 2013 and entered into force upon its publication on 29 June 2013. Member States should implement this directive into their national laws before 21 July 2015. The directive does not apply to the United Kingdom, Ireland and Denmark. For the United Kingdom, Directive 2003/9 will therefore continue to apply.

With the exception of the Temporary Protection Directive, all other instruments of the Common European Asylum System have been revised as well. The new instruments are:

— Directive 2011/95/EU on standards for the qualification of third-country nationals or stateless persons as beneficiaries of international protection, for a uniform status for refugees or for persons eligible for subsidiary protection, and for the content of the protection granted (Qualification Directive (recast));[155]
— Directive 2013/32/EU on common procedures for granting and withdrawing international protection (Procedures Directive (recast));[156] and
— Regulation (EU) No 604/2013 establishing the criteria and mechanisms for determining the Member State responsible for examining an application for international protection lodged in one of the Member States by a third-country national or a stateless person (Dublin Regulation (recast)).[157]

2.4.3 Object and Purpose

Article 1 of Directive 2013/33 states that the purpose of this directive is 'to lay down standards for the reception of applicants for international protection ("applicants") in Member States'. According to the preamble, these standards should suffice to ensure applicants a dignified standard of living and comparable living conditions in all Member States.[158] Hence, the twofold character of the directive's purpose is still manifest in the preamble.[159] Reference is no longer made to 'minimum' standards, but

[155] Directive 2011/95/EU of the European Parliament and of the Council of 13 December 2011 on standards for the qualification of third-country nationals or stateless persons as beneficiaries of international protection, for a uniform status for refugees or for persons eligible for subsidiary protection, and for the content of the protection granted, [2011] OJ L337/9.

[156] Directive 2013/32/EU of the European Parliament and of the Council of 26 June 2013 on common procedures for granting and withdrawing international protection (Procedures Directive (recast)), [2013] OJ L180/60.

[157] Regulation (EU) No 604/2013 of the European Parliament and of the Council of 26 June 2013 establishing the criteria and mechanisms for determining the Member State responsible for examining an application for international protection lodged in one of the Member States by a third-country national or a stateless person, [2013] OJ L180/31.

[158] Recital 11 of Directive 2013/33. Note that the word 'normally' before the word 'suffice' has been deleted in Directive 2013/33; see n 46.

[159] See s 2.3.3.

the possibility for Member States to introduce or retain more favourable provisions in the field of reception conditions still exists.[160]

The preamble to Directive 2013/33 shows that the directive is based on the same underlying principles as Directive 2003/9. At the same time, the preamble states that the goal of this directive is to ensure 'improved' reception conditions for applicants.[161] The following sections will examine to what extent an improvement has been established with regard to material reception conditions, health care and access to the labour market. First, section 2.4.4 will pay attention to the directive's personal scope.

2.4.4 Personal Scope

The same conditions have to be fulfilled in order to fall under the personal scope of Directive 2013/33 as under Directive 2003/9:

1. an application for international protection must have been made/lodged;[162]
2. no final decision must have been taken on this application; and
3. the applicant must be allowed to remain on the territory.[163]

The meaning of these conditions has been discussed in section 2.3.4 above. Nevertheless, there are a number of differences in personal scope between Directive 2013/33 and 2003/9. An important difference from Directive 2003/9 concerns the definition of application for protection. Article 2(a) of Directive 2013/33 defines it as 'an application for international protection as defined in Article 2(h) of Directive 2011/95/EU'. This means that also applicants for subsidiary protection (next to applicants for refugee status) within the meaning of Directive 2011/95/EU (the Qualification Directive (recast)) are explicitly included in the personal scope of Directive 2013/33. This widens the personal scope of Directive 2013/33 and improves the

[160] Directive 2013/33, Art 4.

[161] Recital 7 of the preamble to Directive 2013/33.

[162] Also in Directive 2013/33, a difference exists between different language versions. The English-language version refers in Art 3 to persons who 'make' an application, whereas the Dutch-language version refer to persons who *indienen* an application. This difference does not exist in the Procedures Directive (recast), where the terms in Art 3 are 'made' and *worden gedaan* respectively. The recast of the Procedures Directive further indicates that persons who have 'made' an application for asylum should be able to 'lodge' their application as soon as possible (Art 6(2)) As from which moment in time Directive 2013/33 applies remains, therefore, rather unclear. See further s 2.3.4.

[163] See Arts 3 of Directive 2003/9 and of Directive 2013/33. This latter condition is also explicitly mentioned in the preamble to Directive 2013/33. Recital 8 holds: 'In order to ensure equal treatment of applicants throughout the Union, this Directive should apply during all stages and types of procedures concerning applications for international protection, in all locations and facilities hosting applicants and *for as long as they are allowed to remain on the territory of the Member States as applicants*' (emphasis added).

consistency within the current EU asylum *acquis*.[164] Another difference from Directive 2003/9 is that Article 3 of Directive 2013/33 explicitly refers to applications made in the territorial waters or in the transit zone of Member States. Such applications also fall under the Directive's personal scope.

More important differences in personal scope between Directive 2003/9 and Directive 2013/33 result from the recast of the Procedures Directive (Directive 2013/32/EU). As has been discussed in section 2.3.4, the meaning of the phrase 'allowed to remain on the territory' can be explained with reference to the Procedures Directive. Article 9(1) of the Procedures Directive (recast) still contains a right to remain on the territory until a decision on the asylum application in first instance has been made. In the recast of the Procedures Directive, the exception to this main rule is, however, laid down in a more detailed provision than in the original version. Article 9(2) of the recast version states that Member States may make an exception where they will surrender or extradite an asylum seeker or where an asylum seeker makes a subsequent application referred to in Article 41. Article 41(1) stipulates that Member States may make an exception from the right to remain on the territory where an asylum seeker:

a. has lodged a first subsequent application, which is not further examined pursuant to Article 40(5), merely in order to delay or frustrate the enforcement of a decision which would result in his or her imminent removal from that Member State; or
b. makes another subsequent application in the same Member State, following a final decision considering a first subsequent application inadmissible pursuant to Article 40(5) or after a final decision to reject that application as unfounded.

In addition, this article provides that Member States may make such an exception only where the determining authority considers that a return decision will not lead to direct or indirect *refoulement* in violation of that Member State's international and Union obligations.

A subsequent decision that is not further examined will be considered inadmissible pursuant to Article 40(5). Since an inadmissibility decision is a decision in first instance, the end of the right to remain on the territory seems to follow directly from Article 9(1) of the Procedures Directive (recast). Article 41(1)(a) seems therefore to be rather superfluous.[165] The exception mentioned in Article 41(1)(b) is of more relevance. This

[164] See recital 13 of the preamble to Directive 2013/33.

[165] As Art 9(1) only obliges Member States to allow asylum seekers to remain on the territory 'until the determining authority has made a decision in accordance with the procedures at first instance set out in Chapter III'. An inadmissibility decision on the basis of Art 40 is such a decision.

provision stipulates that Member States may deny the right to remain to asylum seekers who make a further subsequent application, following a subsequent application that has been declared inadmissible or unfounded, irrespective of whether that further subsequent application will be further examined or not. In the original version of the Procedures Directive (Directive 2005/85/EC), an exception was only possible if a subsequent application will not be further examined, regardless of whether this was the first or the second subsequent application. In this regard, the recast of the Procedures Directive reduces the personal scope of Directive 2013/33 as compared to Directive 2003/9.

On the other hand, the recast of the Procedures Directive also brings about a broadening of the personal scope of Directive 2013/33 as compared to Directive 2003/9, with regard to asylum seekers who lodge an appeal against the rejection of their application. On the basis of Article 46(5–8) of the Procedures Directive (recast), asylum seekers who lodge an appeal against the rejection of their application have the right to remain on the territory pending the outcome of the remedy or, in certain specified cases, until a court or tribunal has ruled whether or not the applicant may remain on the territory pending this period. This latter rule applies for example when an application is declared inadmissible or manifestly unfounded in an accelerated asylum procedure. This means that in any case, all asylum seekers who lodge an appeal must be allowed to remain on the territory until a court or tribunal has considered, at least, their request to stay on the territory pending the outcome of their appeal. During this period, they therefore fall under the personal scope of Directive 2013/33. Although it could be argued that this was already the case under Directive 2003/9, as a result of case law of the ECtHR (see section 2.3.4), this has now been explicitly laid down in the EU asylum *acquis*.

All this means that, just as with regard to Directive 2003/9, a number of categories of 'asylum seekers' as defined for the purpose of this book in section 1.5.1 do not fall under the personal scope of Directive 2013/33. First of all, Member States may choose to exclude two categories of asylum seekers from the right to remain on their territory pending the procedure in first instance, and, consequently, from the personal scope of Directive 2013/33. These two categories are asylum seekers who lodge a further subsequent application and asylum seekers who will be surrendered or extradited. Secondly, a court or tribunal may rule on (and, hence, may deny) the right to remain on the territory during the appeal stage in certain specified circumstances.[166] Finally, asylum seekers who lodge a complaint with an international court or committee, or, arguably, who lodge a further domestic appeal against the rejection of their application

[166] See Art 47(6) and (7) of the Procedures Directive (recast).

do not fall under the personal scope of Directive 2013/33, since they have already received a 'final decision' on their application.[167]

2.4.5 Material Reception Conditions

Text of the Directive

With regard to material reception conditions, Directive 2013/33 contains no major differences with Directive 2003/9. Member States are still required to provide asylum seekers with housing, food, clothing and a daily expenses allowance as soon as they make their application and Member States may still choose to provide these benefits in kind, in vouchers, as financial allowances or in a combination of the three.[168] If Member States provide housing in kind, it should take one or a combination of the following forms:

a. premises used for the purpose of housing applicants during the examination of an application for international protection made at the border or in transit zones;
b. accommodation centres which guarantee an adequate standard of living;
c. private houses, flats, hotels or other premises adapted for housing applicants.[169]

Member States may still decide on the residence of the asylum seeker for reasons of public interest, public order or, when necessary, for the swift processing and effective monitoring of the asylum application and Member States may still make the provision of material reception conditions subject to actual residence by the asylum seeker in a specific place.[170]

As regards the level of material reception conditions, Directive 2013/33 does contain a few changes as compared to Directive 2003/9. Article 17(2) of Directive 2013/33 states:

> Member States shall ensure that material reception conditions provide an adequate standard of living for applicants, which guarantees their subsistence and protects their physical and mental health.

Hence, this obligation for Member States has been formulated somewhat more strongly as compared to this obligation laid down in Directive 2003/9, as it states that material reception conditions should 'guarantee' asylum seekers' subsistence (instead of 'capable of ensuring') and should

[167] See s 2.3.4 above.
[168] Directive 2013/33, Art 2(g) in conjunction with Art 17(1).
[169] Directive 2013/33, Art 18(1).
[170] Directive 2013/33, Art 7.

'protect their physical and mental health' (instead of 'adequate for the health').

Article 17(5) of Directive 2013/33 holds:

> Where Member States provide material reception conditions in the form of financial allowances or vouchers, the amount thereof shall be determined on the basis of the level(s) established by the Member State concerned either by law or by the practice to ensure adequate standards of living for nationals. Member States may grant less favourable treatment to applicants compared with nationals in this respect, in particular where material support is partially provided in kind or where those level(s), applied for nationals, aim to ensure a standard of living higher than that prescribed for applicants under this Directive.

Accordingly, Directive 2013/33 explicitly stipulates that Member States do not have to provide asylum seekers with equal treatment with nationals as regard minimum subsistence benefits.[171] As a result of the many negotiations on this topic, the obligation that does result from this article is rather unclear. It seems that Member States are at least required to explain and justify the level of material reception conditions provided to asylum seekers on the basis of objective standards.

Differences from the Commission Proposal

As regards the level of material reception conditions provided in the form of financial allowances or vouchers, agreement was difficult to reach during the negotiation process.[172] The Commission initially proposed to stipulate that in calculating the amount of assistance to be granted to asylum seekers, Member States should ensure that the total value of material reception conditions is equivalent to the amount of social assistance granted to nationals. Any differences in this respect would have to be duly justified.[173] In this way, the principle of non-discrimination would be reinforced, according to the Commission.[174]

The European Parliament adopted in first reading an amendment to delete the safeguard that in calculating the amount of assistance to be granted to asylum seekers, Member States should ensure that the total value of material reception conditions is equivalent to the amount of social assistance granted to nationals.[175] In the Council as well, this

[171] See the Council's Presidency about this article: 'there is no obligation on the Member State to give asylum seekers the same level of social welfare assistance as nationals' (Council Document 6942/12, ASILE 34, p 3).

[172] See, eg, Council Document 6394/1/12 REV 1, ASILE 24, p 4.

[173] Art 17(5) of the Commission proposal (recast) (n 149).

[174] Explanatory memorandum to the Commission proposal (recast) (n 149), p 8.

[175] Outcome of the European Parliament's first reading, Council Document 9333/09 ASILE 30, p 11.

safeguard met strong resistance.[176] Initially, the Presidency suggested as a compromise text to lay down that Member States should 'take into consideration the amount of social assistance granted to nationals eligible for such assistance'.[177] Later on, the compromise suggestion drafted by the Presidency ran: 'Member States shall ensure provisions on material reception conditions … taking into consideration the level of costs or living in the Member State concerned'.[178] In the amended proposal, the Commission proposed to lay down the following rule:

> Where Member States provide material reception conditions in the form of financial allowances and vouchers, the amount thereof shall be determined on the basis of the point(s) of reference established by the Member State concerned either by law or practice to ensure adequate standards of living for nationals, such as the minimum level of social welfare assistance. Member States may grant less favourable treatment to asylum applicants compared to nationals in this respect, where it is duly justified.[179]

The Commission explained that in this way, the modified proposal allows flexibility and does not aim to establish a single EU point of reference but allows the application of different national benchmarks in this respect, provided that they are measurable and can facilitate the monitoring of the level of support provided to applicants.[180] According to the Commission, the provision now allows Member States to apply less favourable standards for applicants vis-à-vis nationals when duly justified. The Commission provided two examples:

> [F]or example when some level of support is provided in kind and it is therefore deducted from financial assistance or when the level of support provided to nationals goes beyond what is necessary to ensure 'standards of living which guarantee their subsistence and protect their physical and mental health' and therefore asylum applicants are only granted a percentage of this national support.[181]

During the debate in Council, compromise suggestions drafted by the Presidency proposed to include the examples mentioned by the Commission in the text of the article.[182] In addition, the Presidency proposed to delete the obligation to 'duly justify' a difference in treatment between asylum seekers and nationals, as some delegations were concerned that the text of the provision could still imply equal treatment

176 Council Document 17519/11 ASILE 126, p 2.
177 Council Document 8366/09 ASILE 20, pp 24–25.
178 Council Document 11837/09 ASILE 50, p 24.
179 Art 17(5) of the amended Commission proposal (recast) (n 153).
180 Explanatory memorandum to the amended Commission proposal (recast) (n 153), p 7.
181 European Commission, Detailed Explanation of the Amended proposal, COM(2011) 320 final ANNEX, p 5.
182 Council Documents 13102/11 ASILE 67 and 15254/11 ASILE 85, p 38.

between asylum seekers and nationals.[183] This has in the end been adopted.

2.4.6 Health Care

Text of the Directive

Article 19(1) of Directive 2013/33 stipulates that Member States should ensure that applicants receive the necessary health care which shall include, at least, emergency care and essential treatment of illnesses and of serious mental disorders. Hence, the only difference with Directive 2003/9 is the reference to serious mental disorders. Also with regard to asylum seekers with special needs, the only difference between Directive 2013/33 and Directive 2003/9 is a reference in Directive 2013/33 to 'appropriate mental health care where needed'.[184] The adverbs 'serious' and 'appropriate' (just as the adjectives 'emergency' and 'essential') make the obligation for Member States not very clear as it leaves Member States a rather significant discretionary power in deciding which mental disorder is 'serious' or which mental health care is 'appropriate'.[185]

Differences from the Commission Proposal

With regard to the access to health care, the Commission initially proposed to add that Member States should ensure that asylum seekers receive essential treatment of mental disorders. Asylum seekers with special needs should receive appropriate mental health care under the same conditions as nationals, according to the Commission.[186] The reference to equal treatment with nationals met with strong reservations in the Council and the European Parliament.[187] The amended proposal therefore only added essential treatment of post-traumatic disorders to the article on health care laid down in the directive.[188] During the negotiations between Parliament and Council, the reference to 'post-traumatic disorders' has been substituted with 'serious mental disorders'.[189]

[183] Council Document 7709/12, ASILE 48, pp 3–4.

[184] Directive 2013/33, Art 19(2).

[185] The drafting history of Directive 2013/33 shows that the European Parliament wanted to include a reference to 'mental disorders' in Art 19(1), whereas the Council did not want to change anything in this article. The compromise has been to include a reference to 'serious mental disorders' (Council Document 12090, ASILE 100, p 133).

[186] Art 19(1) and (2) of the Commission proposal (recast) (n 149).

[187] Explanatory memorandum to the amended Commission proposal (recast) (n 153), p 7.

[188] Art 19(1) of the amended Commission proposal (recast) (n 153).

[189] According to the Commission, this substitution does not restrict the scope of the provision (Communication from the Commission to the European Parliament pursuant to

2.4.7 Access to the Labour Market

Text of the Directive

Article 15(1) of Directive 2013/33 holds:

> Member States shall ensure that applicants have access to the labour market no later than 9 months from the date when the application for international protection was lodged if a first instance decision by the competent authority has not been taken and the delay cannot be attributed to the applicant.

Hence, asylum seekers should have access to the labour market after nine months, but only if a first instance decision has not yet been taken. If the authorities reject the application within nine months (or if a delay can be attributed to the asylum seeker), Member States may deny asylum seekers access to the labour market pending possible appeal procedures. This article therefore still allows Member States, under certain conditions, to deny access to the labour market pending the entire asylum procedure. On the other hand, it does allow Member States to grant access to the labour market earlier than after nine months as well.[190]

Article 15(2) of Directive 2013/33 stipulates that Member States may decide the conditions for granting access to the labour market. This means that Member States may, for example, require a work permit, or decide on the length of time an asylum seeker is allowed to work. This article however also contains the safeguard that Member States should ensure that asylum seekers have *effective* access to the labour market. Finally, Article 15(2) lays down that, for reasons of labour market policies, Member States may give priority to Union citizens and nationals of states parties to the Agreement on the European Economic Area, and to legally resident third-country nationals. Accordingly, Member States may give priority to a large group of non-nationals when granting access to the labour market, as a result of which this access for asylum seekers might not be very effective after all.

The third paragraph of Article 15 prescribes that *if* an asylum seeker has access to the labour market, this shall not be withdrawn during appeals procedures, where an appeal against a negative decision has suspensive effect, until such time as a negative decision on the appeal is notified.

Art 294(6) of the Treaty on the Functioning of the European Union concerning the Position of the Council on the adoption of a Directive of the European Parliament and of the Council laying down standards for the reception of asylum seekers, COM/2013/0415 final).

[190] This is an important difference from Directive 2003/9, see s 2.3.7 above.

Differences from the Commission Proposal

Access to the labour market has been one of the key issues pending the negotiations between the Parliament and the Council. The Commission initially proposed to lay down that Member States should ensure access to the labour market no later than six months following the lodging of the asylum application.[191] The Commission proposed to grant access to the labour market after six months, regardless of whether a decision at first instance on the application had yet been taken or not during these six months. In addition, the proposal stated that in deciding the conditions for granting access to the labour market, Member States may not unduly restrict this access.[192] The possibility for Member States to give priority to other aliens in granting access to the labour market had disappeared in the Commission proposal.[193]

While the European Parliament did not amend these proposals,[194] the Council could not agree with them. In a compromise suggestion drafted by the Presidency, it was suggested to lay down that Member States should ensure that asylum seekers have access to the labour market no later than 12 months after the date when the asylum application was lodged.[195] The same compromise suggestion also deleted the safeguard that Member States may not unduly restrict access to the labour market in deciding the conditions for granting this access and reinstalled the possibility for Member States to give priority to other (legally residing) aliens over asylum seekers.

The amended Commission proposal still referred to the six-month period after which access to the labour market should be ensured. However, it also contained the possibility for Member States to extend this time limit with another six months, in conformity with the Procedures Directive (recast).[196] Instead of the safeguard that Member States may not unduly restrict access to the labour market, the Commission proposal stated that in deciding conditions for entering the labour market,

[191] Art 15(1) of the Commission proposal (recast) (n 149).

[192] Art 15(2) of the Commission proposal (recast) (n 149).

[193] The Commission indicated that this provision should be deleted from the Reception Conditions Directive 'in order to avoid confusion with the principle of EU preference and other relevant EU law' (Council Document 14178/11, ASILE 75, p 42).

[194] European Parliament legislative resolution of 7 May 2009 on the proposal for a directive of the European Parliament and of the Council laying down minimum standards for the reception of asylum seekers (recast) (COM(2008)0815—C6-0477/2008 2008/0244(COD)).

[195] Council Document 15195/09 ASILE 84, p 25.

[196] Such an extension would therefore be possible if there was a large number of simultaneous requests for international protection and if the delay could clearly be attributed to the failure of the applicant to comply with certain obligations (European Commission, Detailed Explanation of the Amended proposal, COM(2011) 320 final ANNEX, pp 4–5).

Member States should ensure that asylum seekers have effective access to the labour market. The amended proposal still deleted the possibility for Member States to give priority to other aliens over asylum seekers as regards access to the labour market.[197]

In reaction to the amended proposal, the German, French and United Kingdom delegations brought forward in a joint contribution that access to the labour market should not be authorized after six months, but after a year. 'Otherwise, we will be adding a new element that makes claiming asylum more attractive, and will encourage the integration of asylum seekers making their eventual removal more difficult if their claim is ultimately rejected'.[198] Some Member States have also proposed again including the condition that a first instance decision has not yet been taken, 'so as to avoid access to the labour market becoming a pull factor'.[199]

Eventually, a compromise was reached in allowing asylum seekers access to the labour market after nine months. According to the Council:

> Allowing access three months earlier is based on two counter-balancing considerations: on the one hand, the considerations that earlier access makes applicants economically independent sooner—thereby lowering the risk of exploitation on the black market and decreasing the need for public support—and that earlier access allows them to integrate more effectively in the host society; on the other hand, the consideration that earlier access possibly makes it attractive for economic migrants who do not qualify for international protection to attempt to exploit the asylum system.[200]

Most of the restricting conditions that the Commission had proposed to delete (such as that access will only be granted if no first instance decision has been taken during the nine-month waiting period and the possibility to give priority to other non-nationals) have eventually been kept.

[197] Art 15 of the amended Commission proposal (recast) (n 153).

[198] Council Document 12168/11, ASILE 54, p 3.

[199] Council Document 14178/11, ASILE 75, p 40. The Netherlands adopted the position that access to the labour market should be withdrawn as soon as a first negative decision has been taken on the asylum application. The reason being that to be in (legal) employment contributes to one's integration into the host society, which is not desirable if the chances of getting a residence permit are slim (*Kamerstukken I*, 2010/11, 22 112, no EV, p 9).

[200] Statement of the council's reasons, Council Position (EU) no 6/2013 of the Council at first reading, with a view to the adoption of a Directive of the European Parliament and of the Council laying down standards for the reception of applicants for international protection (recast), p 24.

2.4.8 Reduction and Withdrawal of Reception Conditions

Text of the Directive

Article 20 of Directive 2013/33 contains a limited number of grounds for reducing or, 'in exceptional and duly justified cases' withdrawal of material reception conditions. Material reception benefits may be reduced or withdrawn if an asylum seeker:

— abandons the place of residence determined by the competent authority without informing it or, if requested, without permission;
— does not comply with reporting duties or with requests to provide information or to appear for personal interviews concerning the asylum procedure during a reasonable period laid down in national law;
— has lodged a subsequent application; or
— has concealed financial resources and has therefore unduly benefited from material reception conditions.[201]

These grounds are the same as the grounds for reduction or withdrawal laid down in Directive 2003/9, but the safeguard that withdrawal is only possible in exceptional and duly justified cases is new. Another difference from Directive 2003/9 is that Article 20 of Directive 2013/33 only applies to material reception conditions (and, consequently, not to health care, education, access to the labour market etc), whereas Article 16 of Directive 2003/9 applies to all reception conditions.

Article 20(2) of Directive 2013/33 stipulates that Member States may *reduce* (and, therefore, not withdraw) material reception conditions when they can establish that the asylum seeker, for no justifiable reason, has not lodged an application for international protection as soon as reasonably practicable after arrival in that Member State. Under Directive 2003/9, also complete withdrawal is possible in such cases. Finally, Member States may determine sanctions applicable to serious breaches of the rules of the accommodation centres as well as to seriously violent behaviour.[202] Arguably, this latter rule leaves open the possibility for Member States to *withdraw* material reception benefits in case of serious breaches of the rules of accommodation centres and of seriously violent behaviour.

Article 20(5) and (6) contains a number of procedural safeguards in cases of reduction or withdrawal. They are similar to the ones laid down in Directive 2003/9 and stipulate that decisions on reduction or withdrawal should be taken individually, objectively and impartially and that reasons should be given. In addition, such decisions should be based on the particular situation of the person concerned and the principle of

[201] Directive 2013/33, Art 20(1) and (3).
[202] Directive 2013/33, Art 20(4).

proportionality should be taken into account. An important and new safeguard laid down in this article is that Member States should under all circumstances 'ensure a dignified standard of living for all applicants'.[203] This phrase begs the question how this safeguard relates to the possibility to entirely withdraw all material reception benefits. Arguably, Member States are required to examine whether the asylum seeker has alternative ways to provide for his basic needs (eg work, relatives, friends, church) before all material reception benefits may be withdrawn.

Differences from the Commission Proposal

The Commission initially proposed to introduce a number of important amendments in the provision on reducing and withdrawal reception conditions. First of all, the Commission proposed to delete the possibility for Member States to entirely withdraw reception conditions in a number of situations.[204] Withdrawal was only possible under the Commission proposal if the asylum seeker has concealed financial resources or in the case of serious breaches of the rules of accommodation centres or seriously violent behaviour. In addition, the Commission proposed to add that Member States should under all circumstances ensure subsistence.[205] Finally, the Commission proposed to delete the possibility to refuse reception conditions in cases where an asylum seeker has failed to demonstrate that the asylum claim was made as soon as possible after arrival.

The European Parliament did not amend these proposals in its first reading,[206] but the Council could not agree with them. Compromise suggestions of the Council Presidency reinstated the possibility to 'withdraw' reception conditions in a number of circumstances and deleted the safeguard that Member States should under all circumstances ensure subsistence.[207] The amended Commission proposal adopted the Council's position.[208] Eventually, a compromise was reached between the European

[203] Member States should also under all circumstances ensure access to health care in accordance with Art 19, but since Art 20 only applies to material reception benefits (see definition in Art 2(g)), this safeguard seems to be superfluous.

[204] Ie in the situation that the asylum seeker abandons, without informing the competent authority or without permission, the place of residence, does not comply with reporting duties or with requests to provide information or to appear for a personal interview, or has already lodged an application in the same Member State (Art 20(1) of the Commission proposal (recast) (n 149)).

[205] Art 20(4) of the Commission proposal (recast) (149). In addition, the Commission proposed to add 'essential treatment of illness or mental disorder' to this provision.

[206] European Parliament legislative resolution of 7 May 2009 on the proposal for a directive of the European Parliament and of the Council laying down minimum standards for the reception of asylum seekers (recast) (COM(2008)0815—C6-0477/2008 2008/0244(COD)).

[207] Council Document 8366/09 ASILE 20, pp 28 and 30.

[208] Art 20 of the amended Commission proposal (recast) (n 153).

Parliament and the Council by stipulating that withdrawal is only possible in exceptional and duly justified cases and by obliging Member States to ensure under all circumstances a dignified standard of living for all asylum seekers.

2.5 CONCLUDING REMARKS

Directives 2003/9 and 2013/33 on the reception of asylum seekers form part of the Common European Asylum System, which arose in the context of an 'ever-swelling influx of asylum seekers'. The background and legal basis of both Directives clearly indicate that they form an integral part of EU immigration and asylum policy and not, as the Court of Justice ruled in 1987, of general social policy. Hence, under EU law, the sphere of asylum seekers' material rights is not separated from the sphere of immigration control, but, to the contrary, these spheres are explicitly and strongly converged. The fact that the Directives form part of asylum policy is reflected in their personal scope, which is dependent on the stage of the asylum procedure and on whether the asylum seeker is allowed to remain on the territory, and in the possibility for Member States to reduce or withdraw reception conditions based on the behaviour of the asylum seeker in the asylum procedure.

Both Directives aim to reduce secondary movements of asylum seekers between Member States and to ensure asylum seekers a dignified standard of living. The discussions in the Council and the amendments made to the Commission proposals reveal, however, that the Member States also, or mainly, tried to prevent possible abuse of their reception systems, for example by immigrants looking for work, to prevent generous reception conditions from becoming a pull factor for asylum seekers and to facilitate the expulsion of asylum seekers whose application has been rejected. This purpose of deterrence and preventing integration was also apparent in national practice predating the Directives. For this reason, the final text of the Directives is considerably less generous than the proposals issued by the Commission.[209]

Nevertheless, since the coming into force of Directive 2003/9, Member States have been obliged to provide asylum seekers who fall under the Directive's personal scope with some kind of housing, food, clothing ('material reception conditions') and health care. As the directive contains an exhaustive list of grounds for reduction or withdrawal of reception benefits, EU Member States are no longer free to deny assistance to categories of asylum seekers of their own choosing. In addition, asylum

[209] *Cf* Handoll 2007, p 226.

seekers who have not yet received a decision in first instance on their asylum application within a year can no longer be completely denied any kind of access to the labour market.

One of the goals of the recast of Directive 2003/9 was to ensure improved reception conditions for asylum seekers in the EU. Section 2.4 shows, however, that the differences between Directive 2003/9 and Directive 2013/33 are, owing to difficult negotiations, rather modest. Differences include the extension of the personal scope to applicants for subsidiary protection, a reduction in the time limit for access to the labour market from 12 to nine months and a number of limiting conditions for withdrawing material reception conditions.

With regard to other aspects, Directive 2013/33 is very similar to Directive 2003/9 and leaves a wide margin of discretion for the Member States. Member States may, for example, still choose to provide material reception conditions in kind, in vouchers, as financial allowances or in a combination of these three forms. In addition, also Directive 2013/33 does not contain a time limit for provision of benefits in kind. Accordingly, this directive still allows Member States to accommodate asylum seekers in collective reception centres during the entire asylum procedure. With regard to access to the labour market, Member States are allowed to ban access for nine months following the lodging of the asylum application and to set all kinds of requirements and restrictions for accessing the labour market after that year. Moreover, if a decision in first instance has been taken within nine months, Member States are not bound to grant access to the labour market during the remainder of the asylum procedure.

In addition, both Directives allow Member States in various ways to exercise a large amount of control over asylum seekers with regard to the provision of reception benefits. First, the mode of provision may have monitoring and control built in, where Member States are allowed to accommodate asylum seekers in large-scale reception centres, to make the provision of material reception conditions subject to the actual residence of an asylum seeker in such a centre and to reduce or withdraw reception conditions if the place of residence has been abandoned without permission or when the asylum seeker does not comply with reporting duties. Secondly, the Directives permit Member States to make the enjoyment of material reception conditions subject to the behaviour of asylum seekers in the asylum procedure, as a result of which Member States are able to influence and control this behaviour.

A noticeable element of Directive 2013/33 is the provision that Member States may provide asylum seekers with less favourable treatment compared to nationals with regard to the amount of material reception conditions. The initial proposal by the Commission to prescribe that the total value of material reception conditions should be equivalent to the amount of social assistance granted to nationals, in order to 'reinforce the principle of non-discrimination', has eventually led to exactly the opposite: an explicit approval of unequal treatment.

With regard to Directive 2003/9, the Commission stated that the wide margin of discretion left for the Member States has led to the adoption (or maintenance) of low reception standards. The Commission argued that these low standards concerning the level of social rights granted to asylum seekers raised strong concerns about respect for fundamental rights. Since Directive 2013/33 does not contain major differences compared to Directive 2003/9, such concerns might still exist. In this book it will be examined whether these concerns are indeed well-founded.

Part II

Equality of Treatment?

3

Introduction to Part II

3.1 INTRODUCTION

AS PART I shows, the EU Reception Conditions Directives do not require Member States to grant asylum seekers access to general social security schemes. Instead, the Directives allow for the provision of housing, food and clothing in kind or in vouchers, which is rather uncommon in general social assistance schemes for nationals. In addition, the value of these material reception benefits does not necessarily have to be equivalent to the amount of social assistance granted to nationals. Directive 2013/33 even explicitly states that Member States may grant asylum seekers less favourable treatment compared with nationals in this respect. The initial proposal of the Commission to stipulate that Member States should ensure that the total value of material reception conditions is equivalent to the amount of social assistance granted to nationals, met too much resistance in the European Parliament and the Council. With regard to health care, the Directives provide that Member States should at least provide asylum seekers with emergency care and essential treatment of illness (and, in Directive 2013/33, of serious mental disorders). The Directives contain no provisions on protection against the occurrence of other social risks. This means that the Directives permit the unequal treatment of asylum seekers with nationals as regards social security benefits. The same is true with respect to access to the labour market. The Directives allow Member States to deny asylum seekers access to the labour market for (at least) one year or nine months and to subject asylum seekers to all kinds of conditions for entering the labour market after that period. The discussions in the Council and the background of the Directives reveal that by allowing this unequal treatment, Member States mainly tried to prevent possible abuse of their reception systems; to prevent generous reception conditions from becoming a pull factor for asylum seekers; and to facilitate the expulsion of asylum seekers whose application has been rejected.

This part of the study will examine how this unequal treatment between nationals and asylum seekers with respect to social security and employment relates to various norms of equal treatment and non-discrimination laid down in international refugee law, international social security law and international human rights law. It tries to answer the question whether asylum seekers can derive a right to equal treatment with nationals in the field of social security and access to employment from these different instruments of international law. Relevant questions in this regard are whether asylum seekers fall under the personal scope of the various instruments' norms; if so, whether these instruments allow for justifications for unequal treatment; and if so, whether immigration control is a legitimate aim for unequal treatment and how strictly possible justifications should be reviewed.

First of all, this chapter deals with some general aspects of the principle of equal treatment and the consequences for the scope and the methodology of the research. Section 3.2 deals with the empty character of the principle of equal treatment. Section 3.3 explains the difference between open and closed models of equal treatment provisions. On the basis of various kinds of distinctions made in legal doctrine as regards the principle of equal treatment, section 3.4 will provide a further demarcation of the scope of the research in this part of the book. In addition, section 3.5 will explain the scope of the research regarding the discrimination ground. This section will also examine the difference between indirect and direct discrimination and the consequences of this distinction for the investigation. This is an important issue, as the ground on which the difference of treatment can be based determines the applicability of certain provisions on equal treatment and, to a large extent, the strictness of the judicial review. Relevant articles from the EU Charter of Fundamental Rights for this part of the book will be discussed in section 3.6. The structure of this part of the book will be further explained in section 3.7.

3.2 THE EMPTY CHARACTER OF THE PRINCIPLE OF EQUAL TREATMENT

Most authors, referring to Aristotle, define the principle of equal treatment as a principle requiring that equals be treated equally and unequals be treated unequally in proportion to the inequality.[1] This maxim, while often seen as a fundamental legal principle,[2] is a complicated legal concept.[3] This has to do with the fact that two situations or persons are never entirely the same. Any two people or things are distinguishable in some

[1] See, eg, Arnardóttir 2003, pp 8–9; Gerards 2002, p 9; Schiek, Waddington and Bell 2007, p 26–27; Tobler 2005, p 19; Vierdag 1973, p 7; Westen 1982, pp 542–43.

[2] Or 'a central element in the idea of justice' (Hart 1994, p 159).

[3] Or even 'one of the most complex legal principles' (Van Dijk et al 2006, p 1034).

way, be it the age, the place etc. At the same time, every two people or things are alike in some respects.[4] The question therefore is which differences and similarities are relevant from a legal point of view. The principle of equal treatment, however, does not answer this question, nor the question what constitutes equal treatment.[5] Consequently, this principle can be adapted to many value systems and is generally called an empty or indeterminate principle.[6] As Hart states clearly, the principle

> is by itself incomplete and, until supplemented, cannot afford any determinate guide to conduct. This is so because any set of human beings will resemble each other in some respects and differ from each other in others and, until it is established what resemblance and differences are relevant, 'Treat like cases alike' must remain an empty form.[7]

Hence, this means that the principle of equal treatment needs to be interpreted and construed to become functional in legal contexts.[8] We must know when, for the purposes in hand, cases are to be regarded as alike and what differences are legally relevant.[9]

3.3 OPEN AND CLOSED MODELS

The principle of equal treatment has been laid down in many international conventions. The codification in legal documents has not always solved the indeterminate character of the principle. Some treaty provisions on equal treatment are narrowly formulated. They prohibit unequal treatment on certain specific grounds in some specific areas and lay down a limited number of exceptions and exclusions to this prohibition.[10] In legal doctrine, this is called the 'closed model'.[11] As this part of the book will show, provisions in ILO and Council of Europe social security conventions often fit this model. These provisions generally prescribe equal treatment between nationals and non-nationals in the field of social security, and lay down a number of qualifications and exceptions to this general rule. Hence, these provisions make clear that 'for the purposes

[4] Westen 1982, p 544.
[5] Arnardóttir 2003, p 9; Gerards 2002, p 9.
[6] Schiek, Waddington and Bell 2007, p 27; Westen 1982, p 547. *Cf* Vierdag who states that the 'judgment whether aspects of equality or aspects of inequality prevail is a value judgment, a matter of choice, of will' (Vierdag 1973, p 10).
[7] Hart 1994, p 159.
[8] Arnardóttir 2003, p 10.
[9] Hart 1994, p 159; Davies 2003, p 9.
[10] It is possible to make a distinction between exceptions and exclusions, where exceptions refer to specific circumstances identified in law under which acts that would otherwise be unlawful discrimination will not be so treated and where exclusions refer to the personal and material scope of non-discrimination provisions (Bell 2007, pp 270–71).
[11] Gerards 2002, pp 16–17; Heringa 1999, pp 27–28; Tobler 2005, pp 50–52.

in hand' (social security), nationals and non-nationals are to be regarded as alike and nationality is not a relevant difference. With regard to provisions of the closed model, the principle of equal treatment has therefore been construed and interpreted in order to get a specific meaning and is no longer (entirely) indeterminate. However, other treaty provisions on equal treatment fit the so-called 'open model'. These provisions are broadly formulated and do not provide an exhaustive enumeration of prohibited grounds of discrimination or specify exceptions to the prohibition of discrimination. Non-discrimination provisions in general human rights conventions, such as the International Covenant on Economic, Social and Cultural Rights or the European Convention on Human Rights generally fit this model. Obviously, this broad formulation does not mean that no exceptions are possible to the general rule of equal treatment,[12] but it means that provisions of the open model are still rather 'empty' norms and have to be applied and interpreted in order to acquire specific meaning and become functional in legal contexts.

The different characteristics of equal treatment provisions have consequences for the methodology of the research. Particularly where provisions of the open model are concerned, the question whether certain distinctions violate the principle of equal treatment will only be answered by examining different authoritative interpretations of courts and treaty-monitoring bodies. With regard to provisions of the closed model, these interpretations are less necessary in order to answer this question, as more can be learned from the text of the treaties themselves.

3.4 A FURTHER DEMARCATION OF THE SCOPE OF THE RESEARCH

In legal doctrine, a number of relevant distinctions have been made regarding the principle of equal treatment. On the basis of these distinctions, the scope of the research in this part of the study can be further clarified.

A first distinction that has been made in legal doctrine is the distinction between unequal treatment at the 'law application level' (before the law), and unequal treatment at the 'law creation level' (in the law). Equality *before* the law means the equal application of the rules to all to whom the rules in question are addressed. It does not relate to a legal classification

[12] This would lead to 'absurd results' as making distinctions is inevitable in legislation (Gerards 2002, p 1; Vierdag 1973, p 9). See *Case relating to certain aspects of the laws on the use of languages in education in Belgium* app no 1474/62 et al (ECtHR, 23 July 1968): 'One would, in effect, be led to judge as contrary to the Convention every one of the many legal or administrative provisions which do not secure to everyone complete equality of treatment in the enjoyment of the rights and freedoms recognised' (para 10).

as such; it merely requires equal treatment within the classification. Equality *in* the law is concerned with the character of the classifications themselves.[13] As Vierdag explains, equality of 'social conditions' can only be brought about at the law creation level, since at the law application level, the principle of equal treatment preserves unequal treatment that has been established in the legislation.[14]

Another distinction that has often been made in legal doctrine is that between formal and material or substantive equality.[15] Although different definitions of these terms are used, 'formal equality' can be defined as equality as to treatment, while 'material' or 'substantive equality' can be defined as equality as to final result.[16] In other words: material equality aims at de facto equality and focuses on the factual effects of distinctions in social reality, while formal equality focuses on the distinction itself, irrespective of social reality.[17] The distinction between these two concepts of equality can also be described with reference to the 'Aristotelian' definition of the principle of equal treatment. Formal equality then refers to the first part of the maxim (equals are treated equally) and material equality refers to the second part of the maxim (unequals are treated unequally in proportion to the inequality).[18]

A final distinction that needs to be mentioned here is the distinction between equality and non-discrimination. According to the explanatory report to Protocol no 12 to the European Convention on Human Rights:

> the non-discrimination and equality principles are closely intertwined. For example, the principle of equality requires that equal situations are treated equally and unequal situations differently. Failure to do so will amount to discrimination unless an objective and reasonable justification exists.

The term 'discrimination' is used in this sense, which corresponds with the conventional legal use of this term, in this study as well. Hence, it only refers to unjustified distinctions, and is therefore an exclusively negative term.[19]

On the basis of these distinctions, the scope of the research in this part of the book can be further demarcated. The research in this part of the book will be restricted to the question whether the *formal* difference of treatment of asylum seekers in the field of social security and

[13] Gerards 2002, p 2; Tobler 2005, pp 17–19; Vierdag 1973, pp 16–17.
[14] Vierdag 1973, p 18.
[15] Sometimes equality before the law is referred to as formal equality and equality in the law as material equality (Arnardóttir 2003, p 18; Vierdag 1973, p 16).
[16] Vierdag 1973, p 14. See also Schiek, Waddington and Bell 2007, p 28.
[17] Gerards 2002, p 12; Holtmaat 2000, pp 253–55; Schiek, Waddington and Bell 2007, pp 26–27.
[18] Gerards 2002, p 12; Tobler 2005, pp 25–26.
[19] *Cf* Vierdag 1973, p 60–61.

employment, as laid down *in the law,* violates norms on equal treatment and non-discrimination as laid down in various international conventions. This chapter will therefore not examine how cases of de facto inequality, or factual effects of distinctions in social reality, relate to international law. It will, for example, not examine the question whether the *factual* difficulties that asylum seekers may experience in receiving social benefits violates the prohibition of discrimination if asylum seekers are treated the same as nationals *in the law.*

3.5 GROUND OF DISCRIMINATION

Another demarcation of the scope of the research concerns the ground of discrimination. The research will be limited to the question how the exclusion of asylum seekers from social security schemes relates to the prohibition of non-discrimination on the grounds of nationality and immigration status.[20]

Treaty provisions of the open model usually contain a list of prohibited grounds of discrimination. These lists often include race, colour, sex, language, religion, political or other opinion, national or social origin, property and birth. Most of these lists use the words: 'on any ground such as' or 'other status' and are therefore not exhaustive. This means that all situations of unequal treatment are covered by these provisions, regardless of the ground on which it is based. Accordingly, unequal treatment between nationals and aliens in general or asylum seekers in particular is usually covered by these non-discrimination provisions. Nevertheless, the ground on which the unequal treatment is based can still be relevant,

[20] This study will therefore not examine the question how this exclusion relates to the prohibition of (indirect) discrimination on the grounds of national or ethnic origin and race. Although nationality and national origin are partly overlapping concepts (if 'national origin' refers to people who are born in another nation state, see Gerards 2007, p 57), 'nationality' refers to the legal concept of citizenship of a certain nation state, while 'national origin' is a more sociological, cultural and historical concept referring to certain national characteristics, irrespective of the individual's nationality (Gerards 2007, p 57; Vierdag 1973, pp 100–01). Due to the sensitive character of the term, 'race' is often defined as a broad legal concept covering different forms of discrimination encompassing a variety of biological, cultural and historical group characteristics (Gerards 2007, pp 41–44). Since asylum seekers primarily originate from a select number of (usually called non-Western) countries, it might be possible to argue that the exclusion of asylum seekers based on their legal status of asylum seeker amounts to indirect discrimination on the ground of national origin or race (see, eg, the Dutch Supreme Court, which held that asylum seekers belong to a race since they distinguish themselves by their skin colour, national or ethnic origin and/or geographic or cultural origin (Hoge Raad 13 June 2000, ECLI: NL:HR:2000:AA6191); for a different opinion, see opinion 1998-57 of the Dutch Equal Treatment Commission). This question will not be examined any further in this study. See de Vries 2013a for an analysis of whether exclusion of people from so-called non-Western countries amounts to indirect discrimination on the ground of racial or ethnic origin.

as this ground usually determines to a large extent the strictness of the judicial review applied by courts.[21] Treaty provisions of the closed model do not contain a non-exhaustive enumeration of prohibited grounds of discrimination. Consequently, it is necessary to examine whether unequal treatment between nationals and asylum seekers as regards social security benefits can be classified under one of the prohibited grounds of discrimination mentioned in the text of these provisions.

Part I shows that the EU Reception Conditions Directives (explicitly) allow for the exclusion of asylum seekers from general social security schemes. In national legislation, such an exclusion is often based on asylum seekers' legal status under national immigration law (on the unlawfulness of their presence or residence) combined with the absence of a residence permit and/or work permit or on their specific status as an asylum seeker.[22] In none of the treaty provisions on equal treatment is 'alienage' or 'immigration status' specifically listed as a prohibited ground of discrimination. An important question is therefore whether distinctions based on the lawfulness of the presence or residence or on the possession of a residence or work permit qualify as discrimination on the basis of nationality, since, as this part of the study will show, this ground is often explicitly recognized as forbidden or as requiring a strict level of review in the field of social security.[23]

In this regard, it is necessary to make a distinction between direct and indirect discrimination. The concept of direct discrimination refers to (unjustified) distinctions explicitly based on a prohibited ground, whereas the concept of indirect discrimination refers to (unjustified) distinctions explicitly based on another, neutral, ground, that have a disproportionate effect or impact upon a group that is protected by an explicit prohibition of discrimination.[24] The classic example of indirect discrimination is a distinction made between persons who work full-time and persons who work part-time. The number of working hours is a neutral criterion and usually not a forbidden ground of discrimination. However, since in present society (far) more women perform part-time work than man, this distinction, if it cannot be justified, qualifies as indirect discrimination on the basis of (the usually forbidden ground of) sex. Especially with regard to equal treatment provisions of the 'closed model' the distinction between direct and indirect discrimination is relevant. Without the concept of indirect

21 Arnardóttir 2003; Gerards 2007, p 33.

22 Minderhoud 1999.

23 See, eg, Art 24 of the Refugee Convention; Art 68 of ILO Convention no 102 on Social Security (Minimum Standards); ILO Convention no 118 on Equality of Treatment (Social Security); and case law of the European Court on Human Rights (eg, in the *Gaygusuz* case, see further section 6.3).

24 Tobler 2005, pp 56–57.

discrimination, distinctions based on a neutral criterion that have an unreasonable effect cannot be dealt with under such provisions. At first sight, with regard to non-discrimination provisions that do not use an exhaustive enumeration of prohibited grounds, there is no need for the use of the concept of indirect discrimination; any equality of treatment will be covered by such provisions. Nevertheless, the concept may be useful since, for example, the European Court on Human Rights applies a more strict scrutiny as regards a number of specific prohibited grounds of discrimination.[25]

It is generally assumed that the possibilities to justify indirect distinctions are broader than the possibilities to justify distinctions directly based on a prohibited ground.[26] As regards non-discrimination provisions of the closed model, the general theory is that with regard to direct distinctions, only exceptions and exclusions expressly mentioned in the provisions apply, whereas with regard to indirect distinctions, an additional and open category of objective justifications applies.[27]

With regard to non-discrimination provisions of the closed model, the question therefore is whether distinctions between nationals and asylum seekers in social security schemes or with regard to access to the labour market based on the immigration status of asylum seekers qualifies as direct or indirect discrimination on the ground of nationality. In the former case, justifications for the difference in treatment might only apply if the text of the non-discrimination provision allows for exceptions, while in the latter case, (any kind of) objective justifications might be brought forward to justify the difference in treatment. With regard to non-discrimination provisions of the open model this question is also relevant, since the strict level of scrutiny as applied to some prohibited grounds of discrimination possibly only applies with respect to discrimination that is directly based on these grounds.[28]

Distinctions based on the kind of immigration status in social security schemes and on access to employment involve a distinction between a group of persons that is not eligible for social security benefits or employment based on their immigration status (only aliens) and a group of persons that is eligible for social security benefits or employment (nationals and aliens with a secure residence status). As nationals by definition cannot have an insecure immigration status, it is obvious that such distinctions

[25] Gerards 2004a, p 12. See further section 6.3.

[26] Arnardóttir 2003, pp 124–25; Gerards 2004b, p 181.

[27] Bell 2007, p 269; Tobler 2005, p 316. Examination of case law of the EU Court of Justice shows, however, that this dividing line is not as strict in practice as it is in theory. In a number of cases the Court has for example accepted extra-textual justification for direct discrimination as well (Tobler 2005, p 330).

[28] *Cf* the case comment of Pennings in *AB* 1999/393. See further section 6.3.

have a disproportionate effect upon non-nationals. Consequently, such distinctions qualify in any case as indirect distinctions on the ground of nationality. A more difficult question to answer is whether such distinctions should actually qualify as direct distinctions on the ground of nationality, as a result of which a higher level of protection applies.

An important question in this regard is whether for direct discrimination, it is necessary to base a distinction on a ground that entirely correlates with the prohibited ground of discrimination, or whether it suffices that the distinction exclusively (and not merely predominantly) applies to the group that is protected by an explicit prohibition of discrimination. According to some authors, distinctions that exclusively exclude persons of one group *or* exclusively benefit persons of one group, in other words distinctions that are not capable of excluding members of both groups, should already be understood as leading to direct discrimination.[29] Let me explain this by the example of pregnancy discrimination. Only women can become subject to, for example, refusal of employment on the ground of pregnancy. Distinctions based on pregnancy therefore exclusively (and not only predominantly) apply to women and such distinctions are not capable of excluding both men and women. According to the European Court of Justice, a refusal of employment based on pregnancy therefore amounts to direct discrimination on the ground of sex.[30]

Others argue that incapability of making a distinction excluding members of both groups is not sufficient to qualify as a direct distinction. They argue, for example, that a distinction based on pregnancy does not correlate exactly with the ground of sex, since not every women is pregnant. Distinctions based on pregnancy distinguish between pregnant persons (all female) and non-pregnant persons (both male and female). Pregnancy therefore does not correlate perfectly with the ground of sex, and distinctions based on pregnancy therefore merely amount to indirect discrimination on the ground of sex.[31] Otherwise, an employer who prefers a non-pregnant women over a pregnant one would be guilty of direct sex discrimination, which would be, according to Davies, a 'result doing violence to both language and logic'.[32]

[29] Tobler 2005, pp 315–16 and 427 and, *a contrario*, Nickless and Siedl 2004, p 23.

[30] CJEU 8 November 1990, Case C-177/88 *Elisabeth Johanna Pacifica Dekker v Stichting Vormingscentrum voor Jong Volwassenen (VJV-Centrum) Plus* [1990] ECR I-3941.

[31] Davies 2011, p 11.

[32] Ibid. According to Davies, even though it would be possible to include pregnancy discrimination within the definition of direct discrimination, this is not a desirable choice because of these problems of coherence and language.

The situation of pregnancy discrimination shows a close connection to distinctions based on immigration status.[33] Distinctions based on immigration status exclusively apply to non-nationals, but it could be argued that they do not correlate exactly with distinctions based on the ground of nationality. This argument would be that whereas distinctions based on immigration status favour all persons of one group (nationals), they do not exclude all persons of the other group (non-nationals) since some categories of non-nationals are in possession of the required immigration status. Hence, it could be argued that such distinctions are not directly based on nationality.[34]

In my opinion, even if it is necessary in order for there to be direct discrimination to make a distinction based on a ground that entirely correlates to the forbidden ground of discrimination, distinctions based on immigration status could nevertheless be treated as distinctions directly based on nationality. The argument then is that whereas distinctions based on immigration status or on possession of employment authorization do not necessarily *exclude* all non-nationals, they do in fact *disadvantage* all non-nationals in another way.

Nationals by definition have the right to reside permanently and to work in the country. Non-nationals do not have that right automatically. They have to fulfil certain criteria in order to acquire the right to (permanently) reside or work in the country, such as being economically active or self-sufficient under EU law; having protected family life with a national or admitted alien; being a refugee or entitled to supplementary protection under EU asylum law, etc. Even though certain or many non-nationals might fulfil the requirements and might therefore be eligible for the benefit concerned (just like the non-pregnant woman), this eligibility is for all non-nationals *conditional* upon the fulfilment of an additional criterion, whereas for nationals, the fulfilment of this criterion is necessarily and automatically linked to their nationality. Such conditionality therefore disadvantages all non-nationals as compared to nationals.

[33] See also the Opinion of Advocate General Sharpston in the *Bressol* case (Case C-73/08, Opinion delivered on 25 June 2009).

[34] This is, for example, the approach of the Dutch Equal Treatment Commission with regard to telecom businesses that require a secure immigration status when offering mobile telephone contracts (view no 1996-60, 2001-26 and 2007-170) or employers who refuse to hire an alien with a temporary residence permit (view no 1997-117). The Commission argues in these views that not all aliens are by definition excluded through the requirements concerned. According to Gerards, however, such situations should be seen as distinctions based directly on the ground of nationality. The Commission only chooses to consider this as a form of indirect discrimination in order to be able to apply the open justification test meant for cases of indirect discrimination (Gerards 2002, p 586, fn 272; Gerards 2008a, pp 579–80 and Gerards 2011, pp 149–50).

Hence, it is in my opinion perfectly possible to treat requirements laid down in general rules as regards immigration status or possession of a residence or work permit as amounting to a difference of treatment based directly on the ground of nationality.[35] Not only are such requirements not capable of excluding nationals, as a result of which they should, according to some authors, already be characterized as distinctions directly based on the ground of nationality. But it is in my view even possible to argue that such distinctions correlate *exactly* with distinctions based on nationality, since they affect and disadvantage all aliens as compared to nationals by making rights conditional for all non-nationals and are based on a criterion which is inherently attached to (the absence of) nationality.[36] Accordingly, statements that distinctions based on immigration status do *not* amount to distinctions directly based on nationality use a very strict definition of the concept of disadvantage by

[35] *Cf* the Opinion of Advocate General Sharpston in the *Bressol* case (n 33). Regarding a right to reside criterion in Belgian legislation, she observed that all Belgian nationals *automatically* enjoy the right to remain permanently in Belgium, whereas non-Belgians do not automatically have such a right and must meet certain additional conditions to acquire such a right. Therefore, she argued that 'the category of those receiving a certain advantage (those *automatically* having a right to remain permanently in Belgium) … therefore coincides exactly with the category of persons distinguished only on the basis of a prohibited classification (nationality, in this case those possessing Belgian nationality). The category of those suffering a corresponding disadvantage (those *not automatically* having such a right) coincides exactly with the category of persons distinguished only on the basis of a prohibited classification (nationality, in this case those not possessing Belgian nationality)' (point 66). She concludes that the right to reside requirement discriminates directly on the ground of nationality (point 76). The Court did not pay separate attention to this right to reside criterion and treated the case as a difference of treatment between residents and non-residents (CJEU 13 April 2010, Case C-73/08 *Bressol* [2010] ECR I-2735). In the *Martinez Sala* case, the Court of Justice did, however, conclude that for a Member State to require a national of another Member State who wishes to receive a benefit to produce a document which is constitutive of the right to the benefit and which is issued by its own authorities, when its own nationals are not required to produce any document of that kind, amounts to unequal treatment directly based on nationality (CJEU 12 May 1998, Case C-85/96 *Martinez Salah* [1998] ECR I-2691, paras 54 and 64). Also the UK Supreme Court seems to be of the opinion that requirements as to the right to reside amount to direct discrimination on the ground of nationality. In the case of *Patmalniece (FC) v Secretary of State for Work and Pensions* [2011] UKSC 11 (HL), Lord Hope held that the right to reside requirement is a test which no UK national could fail to meet and puts non-nationals at a disadvantage, which is due entirely to their nationality. Such a requirement would therefore be 'without doubt' directly discriminatory on the grounds of nationality (para 26). Eventually, the Supreme Court found itself forced to treat the case as one of indirect discrimination, on the basis of the *Bressol* judgment of the Court of Justice. According to Lord Hope, the right to reside requirement formed part of a composite test and not all UK nationals would be able to meet this composite test, either. However, Lord Walker held, 'the correlation between British nationality and the right to reside in Great Britain is so strong that the issue of justification must in my view be scrutinised with some rigour' (para 73).

[36] *Cf* Bell who argues that the 'challenge for the law is how to uncover direct discrimination where this is kept covert and hidden' (Bell 2007, p 237).

equating it with exclusion. Such statements therefore in my view need explicit foundation.

3.6 RELEVANT CHARTER PROVISIONS

Title III of the EU Charter of Fundamental Rights is devoted to equality. For the purpose of this book, Article 21 is most relevant. This article is also explicitly mentioned in the preamble to Directive 2013/33 as one of the Charter articles the application of which the Directive seeks to promote.[37] Paragraph 2 of Article 21 is concerned with discrimination on the ground of nationality. According to this article, any discrimination on grounds of nationality is prohibited 'within the scope of application of the Treaties and without prejudice to any of their specific provisions'. This provision copies the text of Article 18 of the TFEU (ex Article 12 of the TEC). Since the EU Reception Conditions Directives have their legal basis in the Treaties, and therefore fall within the scope of application of the EU Treaties, it could be argued that the prohibition of discrimination on grounds of nationality applies to all measures related to the reception of asylum seekers.[38] Generally, however, it is assumed that the prohibition of discrimination on grounds of nationality laid down in Article 18 of the TFEU (ex Article 12 of the TEC) has a limited personal scope: it only applies to EU citizens and not to persons who do not have the nationality of an EU Member State (third-country nationals).[39] This interpretation is also endorsed by the EU Court of Justice.[40] The EU Court of Justice has, until now, not ruled on the application of Article 21(2) of the CFR to third-country nationals, but it is likely that the same interpretation applies to this article.[41] This means, therefore, that, as it stands, the prohibition of discrimination on grounds of nationality laid down in the Charter does not apply to asylum seekers.

Arguably, distinctions between nationals and asylum seekers based on the specific (immigration) status of asylum seekers could also fall under the scope of Article 21(1) of the CFR which applies to discrimination 'based on any ground'.[42] While Article 21(2) implicates that nationality

[37] Recital 35 of the preamble to Directive 2013/33. It is noticeable that the term 'promote' is used here and not, eg, 'ensure'.

[38] See, eg, Boeles 2005; Hublet 2009.

[39] Bell 2003, p 98–99; De Vries 2013a, p 296 with further references.

[40] CJEU 4 June 2009, Joined Cases C-22/08 and C-23/08 *Vatsouras and Koupatantze* [2009] ECR I-4584, para 52; CJEU 13 June 2013, C-45/12 *Hadj Ahmed*, paras 39–41.

[41] CFR, Art 52(2) states in general that rights recognized by the Charter for which provision is made in the Treaties should be exercised under the conditions and within the limits defined by those Treaties. According to the explanations to the Charter, Art 21(2) corresponds to the first paragraph of Art 18 of the TFEU and must be applied in compliance with that Article. See for arguments to the contrary de Vries 2013b, pp 255–56.

[42] *Cf* de Vries 2013a, p 296.

discrimination does not fall under the scope of Article 21(1), it could be argued, if the limited understanding of nationality discrimination is endorsed (see section 3.5 above), that discrimination based on immigration status does. In that case, it is likely that Article 14 of the ECHR will be used as a source of inspiration for the interpretation of Article 21(1) of the CFR. Both provisions are provisions of the open model (see section 3.3) and do not set out an exhaustive list of forbidden grounds of discrimination. The explanations to Article 21(1) of the CFR refer to Article 14 of the ECHR and state that, in so far as it corresponds to Article 14 of the ECHR, Article 21(1) of the CFR applies in compliance with it. In the absence of indications to the contrary, it is submitted here that Article 21(1) of the CFR does not provide more or different protection against discrimination based on immigration status than Article 14 of the ECHR.

3.7 STRUCTURE OF PART II

This chapter has discussed a number of characteristics of the principle of equal treatment that have implications for the methodology of the research or that can clarify the scope of the research. In addition, an important preliminary question has been answered: whether distinctions based on immigration status or possession of employment authorization can amount to distinctions directly based on nationality. Finally, it has been examined whether the EU Charter of Fundamental Rights contains relevant articles in this respect. The next chapter will examine whether asylum seekers should be treated the same as nationals as regards eligibility for social security benefits and access to employment under international refugee law. Chapter five will examine this question with respect to international social security co-ordination law. In this chapter, social security and migrant workers conventions realized within the framework of the International Labour Organization and within the framework of the Council of Europe will be discussed. Chapter six examines whether the difference of treatment of asylum seekers in social security schemes and employment acts violates general non-discrimination provisions laid down in international human rights law. It will turn out that provisions on equal treatment between nationals and non-nationals in the field of social security that fit into the 'closed model', usually contain a number of qualifying conditions, such as 'lawfully staying' or 'lawfully present'. A significant part of the research in the next chapters will therefore be devoted to an examination into the exact meaning of these conditions and to the question whether asylum seekers can fulfil these conditions. The final chapter of this part of the book will integrate the results of the foregoing chapters.

4

Equal Treatment under the Refugee Convention

4.1 INTRODUCTION

THIS CHAPTER WILL examine whether asylum seekers are entitled to equal treatment with nationals with regard to access to wage-earning employment and social security under the Convention relating to the Status of Refugees of 1951 (hereafter: Refugee Convention or RC) and the Protocol relating to the Status of Refugees of 1967 (hereafter: Refugee Protocol). A separate chapter is devoted to these instruments, since they are the only international treaties that exclusively deal with the rights of refugees. The Refugee Convention and Protocol lay down important rights and obligations for persons who meet the general definition of 'refugee' provided for in these instruments, as well as for the host states.

The Refugee Convention was adopted on 28 July 1951 and entered into force on 22 April 1954.[1] The scope of the convention is restricted to persons who have fled their country as a result of 'events occurring before 1 January 1951' and contracting states may choose to restrict the convention to refugees from Europe.[2] In 1967 the Protocol relating to the Status of Refugees entered into force, following a recommendation of the Executive Committee of the UNHCR.[3] Under the protocol, states undertake to apply Articles 2 to 34 of the RC to all refugees covered by the definition of the

[1] The drafting process of the Refugee Convention was completed and the convention was signed by a United Nations Conference of Plenipotentiaries, pursuant to a resolution of the United Nations General Assembly (United Nations General Assembly Resolution 429 (V) of 14 December 1950 (fifth session)). The conference took a draft convention prepared by the Ad Hoc Committee on Refugees and Stateless Persons as the basis for its discussion, with the preamble as prepared by the Economic and Social Council and Art 1 as recommended by the General Assembly in its resolution (Goodwin-Gill and McAdam 2007, p 507).

[2] RC, Art 1(A) and (B). See on the refugee definition further s 4.2.

[3] The UNHCR subsequently submitted the draft of the protocol to the General Assembly of the United Nations. The General Assembly, in Resolution 2198 (XXI) of 16 December 1966 (twenty-first session), took note of the protocol and requested the Secretary-General 'to transmit the text of the Protocol to the States mentioned in article V thereof, with a view to enabling them to accede to the Protocol'.

convention, but without the limitation of date, and to apply the protocol without any geographic limitation.[4]

As mentioned, this chapter will examine whether asylum seekers are entitled to equal treatment with nationals with respect to eligibility for social security schemes and access to the labour market under the Refugee Convention. It will turn out that the answer to this question is to a large extent dependent on the answer to the question whether asylum seekers are 'lawfully present', 'resident' and/or 'lawfully staying' in the country in which they apply for protection. This chapter is therefore almost entirely devoted to the rather technical examination of the meaning of these qualifying conditions. After a short introduction to the Refugee Convention's personal scope, object and purpose and the provisions on access to social security and employment (sections 4.2 to 4.4), some preliminary observations about the interpretation of the terms 'lawfully in the territory', 'resident' and 'lawfully staying' will be made (section 4.5). After that, these general observations will be applied to the position of asylum seekers and it will be discussed which of the various qualifying conditions can be met by asylum seekers (sections 4.6 to 4.8). As authoritative interpretations of the Refugee Convention by an international court are not available, this chapter will pay considerable attention to legal doctrine on this matter. The question whether the Refugee Convention provides other safeguards with respect to asylum seekers' access to social security and employment, apart from provisions on equal treatment, will be examined in chapter nine.

4.2 PERSONAL SCOPE

An important preliminary question is whether asylum seekers fall under the personal scope of the Refugee Convention. In order to fall under the scope of the Refugee Convention, an alien has to meet the refugee definition laid down in Article 1 of the RC.[5]

In the first place, persons who have been considered to be refugees under earlier refugee treaties and arrangements also fall under the refugee definition of the Refugee Convention. According to Article 1(A)(1) of the RC, the term 'refugee' applies to any person who

> has been considered a refugee under the Arrangements of 12 May 1926 and 30 June 1928 or under the Conventions of 28 October 1933 and 10 February 1938, the Protocol of 14 September 1939 or the Constitution of the International Refugee Organization.

[4] Art 1(2) and (3) of the Refugee Protocol. Existing declarations restricting the Refugee Convention to events occurring in Europe, however, also apply under the protocol.

[5] See more extensively on the refugee definition Goodwin-Gill and McAdam 2007, pp 63–134; Hathaway 1991; Spijkerboer and Vermeulen 2005, pp 23–64.

The most important part of the refugee definition for contemporary purposes is laid down in Article 1(A)(2) of the RC. According to this article, the term 'refugee' applies to any person who:

> as a result of events occurring before I January 1951[6] and owing to well-founded fear of being persecuted for reasons of race, religion, nationality, membership of a particular social group or political opinion, is outside the country of his nationality and is unable, or owing to such fear, is unwilling to avail himself of the protection of that country; or who, not having a nationality and being outside the country of his former habitual residence as a result of such events, is unable or, owing to such fear, is unwilling to return to it.

From this definition it follows first of all that the Refugee Convention only applies to persons who are outside their country of origin. In addition, three important elements in this definition can be distinguished: 1) 'well-founded fear'; 2) 'of being persecuted'; and 3) 'by reasons of race, religion, nationality, membership of a particular social group or political opinion'.[7]

The 'well-founded fear requirement' is not a subjective requirement (meaning that the frame of mind of the individual person is decisive), but an objective one. Decisive is whether it is likely enough that the person concerned will become a victim of persecution if he returns to his country of origin.[8]

The second element, persecution, is difficult to define; there is no universally accepted definition of the concept of persecution.[9] In brief, it could be said that persecution means a violation of the right to life or freedom or another severe violation of human rights. Whether other violations of human rights amount to persecution depends on the individual circumstances of the case.[10] Grahl-Madsen summarizes this well by stating:

> whenever a person is faced with the likelihood of losing his life or his physical freedom for more than a 'negligible' period of time, if he should return to his home country, or is likewise threatened with other measures which, in his particular case and his special circumstances, appear as more severe than a short-term imprisonment, that person has 'well founded fear of being persecuted'.[11]

The term 'persecution' implies that there is an agent of persecution and, consequently, excludes victims of natural disasters from the refugee

[6] As has been discussed above, contracting parties to the Refugee Protocol have to apply the Refugee Convention to all refugees without this limitation of date.

[7] See for this distinction Hathaway 1991; Spijkerboer and Vermeulen 2005, p 27 with further references.

[8] Grahl-Madsen 1966, pp 173–75; Hathaway 1991, p 65; Spijkerboer and Vermeulen 2005, pp 28–29.

[9] UNHCR Handbook 1992, para 51.

[10] Hathaway 1991, pp 101–05; UNHCR Handbook 1992, paras 51–52; Spijkerboer and Vermeulen 2005, pp 32–35.

[11] Grahl-Madsen 1966, p 216.

definition. The agent of persecution is generally (a representative of) the state, but can also be (a group of) civilians if their acts are 'knowingly tolerated by the authorities, or if the authorities refuse, or prove unable, to offer effective protection'.[12]

The last element means that, in order to be a refugee, a person has to fear persecution that is connected with one of the persecution grounds: race, religion, nationality, membership of a particular social group or political opinion.[13] This requirement, also called the 'nexus requirement', does not mean that the persecution agent needs to have the *intention* to persecute *because of* a persecution ground; the definition merely requires a connection between the fear of being persecuted and a persecution ground.[14] Arguably, the persecution ground only needs to be a 'contributing cause' for the well-founded fear of persecution, and not the essential or predominant cause.[15]

In addition to this so-called 'inclusion clause' laid down in Article 1(A) of the RC, Article 1 of the RC contains cessation and exclusion clauses as well. Article 1(C) spells out six conditions under which, as an automatic legal consequence, a refugee ceases to be a refugee. These six conditions are based on the consideration that international protection should not continue to be granted where it is no longer necessary or justified.[16] The first four conditions are linked to a change in the situation of the refugee that has been brought about by himself, namely: voluntary re-availment of national protection; voluntary re-acquisition of nationality; acquisition of a new nationality; and voluntary re-establishment in the country where persecution was feared. The last two cessation clauses are linked to a change in the country where persecution was feared. These clauses state that a person is no longer a refugee if he is able to return to the country of his nationality or of his former habitual residence, because the circumstances in connection with which he has been recognized as a refugee have ceased to exist.

Article 1(D), (E) and (F) of the RC contains what are known as the exclusion clauses. According to these clauses, the Refugee Convention does not apply to persons already receiving United Nations protection or assistance (Article 1(D)), persons who are not considered to be in need of international protection (Article 1(E)) and persons who are not considered

[12] UNHCR Handbook 1992, para 65. See more extensively on agents of persecution: Grahl-Madsen 1966, pp 189–92; Hathaway 1991, pp 125–33; Spijkerboer and Vermeulen 2005, pp 35–40.

[13] See for an extensive discussion of these five grounds: UNHCR Handbook, paras 68–86; Goodwin-Gill and McAdam 2007, pp 70–90; Grahl-Madsen 1966, pp 217–53; Hathaway 1991, pp 135–88; Spijkerboer and Vermeulen 2005, pp 48–52.

[14] Spijkerboer and Vermeulen 2005, pp 52–54.

[15] Hathaway and Foster 2003; Spijkerboer and Vermeulen 2005, pp 54–55.

[16] UNHCR Handbook, para 111.

to be deserving of international protection (Article 1(F)). A person is not considered to be in need of international protection if he is 'recognized by the competent authorities of the country in which he has taken residence as having the rights and obligations which are attached to the possession of the nationality of that country'.[17] A person is not deserving international protection if

> there are serious reasons for considering that he has committed a crime against peace, a war crime, or a crime against humanity (…); that he has committed a serious non-political crime outside the country of refuge prior to his admission to that country as a refugee; or that he has been guilty of acts contrary to the purposes and principles of the United Nations.

In sum, the Refugee Convention applies to persons who have a well-founded fear of being persecuted for reasons of race, religion, nationality, membership of a particular social group or political opinion in their country of origin, and who do not fall under one of the cessation or exclusion clauses laid down in Article 1(C) to (F) of the RC. The question remains, however, whether asylum seekers, with regard to whom the authorities of the host state have not yet confirmed that they meet the definition of refugee as laid down in the Refugee Convention, fall under the personal scope of the convention.

In domestic law, the term 'refugee' or 'refugee status' is usually reserved for people who have been recognized as refugees within the meaning of the Refugee Convention by the authorities of the host state. Under international refugee law, it is, however, generally accepted that formal recognition by a state as a refugee within the meaning of the Refugee Convention is not necessary in order to fall under the scope of the convention.[18] As the UNHCR Handbook clearly states:

> A person is a refugee within the meaning of the 1951 Convention as soon as he fulfils the criteria contained in the definition. This would necessarily occur prior to the time at which his refugee status is formally determined. Recognition of his refugee status does not therefore make him a refugee but declares him to be one. He does not become a refugee because of recognition, but is recognized because he is a refugee.[19]

The recognition as refugee by the state of refuge has thus a declaratory instead of a constitutive character.[20] As a result, if an asylum seeker has a

[17] Eg ethnic Germans have the same constitutional position in Germany as 'national' Germans (Spijkerboer and Vermeulen 2005, p 25).

[18] Grahl-Madsen 1966, pp 340–41; Hathaway 2005, pp 158–59; Spijkerboer and Vermeulen 2005, p 70.

[19] UNHCR Handbook 1992, para 28.

[20] See recital 14 of the preamble to the EU Qualification Directive and recital 21 of the preamble to the Qualification Directive (recast). See also Stenberg 1989, p 124.

well-founded fear of being persecuted on one of the persecution grounds, he falls under the personal scope of the Refugee Convention, irrespective of the action taken by the host state. This does not mean, as this chapter will show, that certain articles in the Refugee Convention do not set further qualifying conditions, such as recognition by the host state or a certain period of residence in the host state, for invoking certain rights. That, however, does not alter the declaratory character of the general scope of the convention. Hence, since asylum seekers might meet the definition of refugee as laid down in the Refugee Convention and, consequently, might be entitled to some of the benefits of the convention as from the moment they arrive in the host state, they have to be treated as refugees pending the determination of their status. Otherwise, states run the risk of acting in violation of the Refugee Convention by withholding important rights from genuine refugees.[21] Accordingly, the Refugee Convention applies to (nearly) all asylum seekers.[22]

4.3 OBJECT AND PURPOSE

The object and purpose of the Refugee Convention can be determined by reference to the text of the treaty and to the preamble in particular.[23] It follows from the preamble that the object and purpose of the Refugee Convention is twofold. First of all, the Refugee Convention aims to protect the fundamental rights and freedoms of refugees in the widest possible way.[24] Hence, the preamble places the Refugee Convention in the context of international human rights law.[25] Secondly, it follows from the preamble that the convention aims to prevent unduly heavy burdens on and tension between countries by promoting international co-operation and burden sharing.[26] The solution mentioned for 'unduly heavy burdens' for contracting states is that of international co-operation. Although the protection of human rights of refugees is a primary objective of the Refugee Convention, the recognition of the possibility that the grant of asylum may place unduly heavy burdens on certain countries and the purpose of safeguarding human rights of refugees in the 'widest possible

[21] Battjes 2006, pp 493–94; Hathaway 2005, pp 156–57.

[22] 'Nearly all', because there is the (theoretical) possibility that an asylum seeker explicitly declares not to be a refugee within the meaning of the Refugee Convention, but invokes the protection of another non-*refoulement* prohibition, such as Art 3 of the ECHR.

[23] *Cf* McAdam, 'Interpretation of the 1951 Convention' in Zimmermann 2011, p 91. See also Foster, who argues that 'reference to the Preamble appears to be the predominant method of ascertaining the object and purpose of a treaty' (Foster 2007, p 42).

[24] Recitals 1 and 2 of the preamble.

[25] Alleweldt, 'Preamble 1951 Convention' in Zimmermann 2011, pp 232–33; Foster 2007, pp 42–43.

[26] Recitals 4 and 5 of the preamble.

way' (ie not entirely) means, in my opinion, that the aim of the Refugee Convention can best be summarized as that of striking a balance between the needs of refugees and those of the host state.[27]

This interpretation of the purpose of the Refugee Convention can be confirmed by its text. A balance between the needs of refugees and those of the host state seems to have been met in two important ways. Firstly, the provisions laying down substantive rights for refugees use different standards of treatment. With regard to some rights, refugees have to be treated the same as nationals;[28] most-favoured aliens;[29] or 'aliens generally',[30] while other articles lay down absolute rights for refugees.[31] Whereas the 'aliens generally' standard does not provide much extra protection for refugees, and therefore met the concern of some states that they had to treat refugees on a par with the citizens of special partner states,[32] the other standards used in the Refugee Convention provide a higher level of protection for refugees. Secondly, these provisions use different qualifying conditions. Roughly, the Refugee Convention designates four main categories of refugees for enjoying rights: refugees in the territory; refugees lawfully in the territory; refugees residing in the territory; and refugees lawfully staying in the territory. Refugees simply present in the territory,[33] regardless of their legal status, are entitled to a

[27] See also Hailbronner 2007, p 162. Alleweldt argues that such an interpretation is not supported by the wording of the convention and the drafting history, as the preamble does not say that the rights of refugees should be limited when states are confronted with unduly heavy burdens and the text of the 1951 Convention does not contain any indication to this effect (Alleweldt, 'Preamble 10 the 1951 Convention' in Zimmermann 2011, p 237). In my view, however, *interpreting* the rights laid down in the Refugee Convention on the basis of inter alia the convention's object and purpose is something different from *limiting* the rights laid down in the Refugee Convention. Even though the solution mentioned by the preamble is that of international co-operation, the recognition of possible burdens for contracting states in my view means that the needs of states should also be taken into account when interpreting the convention.

[28] Eg the right to public relief and assistance (Art 23) and the right to social security (Art 24).

[29] Eg the right to engage in wage-earning employment (Art 17).

[30] Eg the right to self-employment (Art 18) and the right to housing (Art 21).

[31] Eg the right to have free access to the courts of law (Art 16) and the right to administrative assistance (Art 25).

[32] Hathaway 2005, p 197.

[33] It is important to note that some articles of the Refugee Convention refer to refugees without further qualification (eg Art 3 on non-discrimination; Art16(1) on access to courts; Art 20 on rationing systems; Art 22(1) on elementary education; Art 33 on the prohibition of *refoulement*), while others refer to refugees in the territory (eg Art 4 on freedom of religion and Art 27 on identity papers). However, as Grahl-Madsen observes, the Refugee Convention applies to refugees within the territorial jurisdiction of contracting states and most articles formally applicable to 'all refugees' are 'meaningful only when applied to the relation between a refugee and' the country in which he finds himself' (Grahl-Madsen 1972, pp 358–59). It is generally accepted that the rights laid down in the Refugee Convention for refugees in the territory, such as the prohibition of *refoulement*, apply to refugees who apply for protection at the territorial border as well (see Hathaway 2005, p 315; Spijkerboer and Vermeulen 2005, pp 71–72 with further references).

number of basic rights, such as the right to acquisition of movable and immovable property,[34] the right to have free access to the courts of law on the territory[35] and the right to identity papers.[36] Refugees who are not merely physically present, but who are *lawfully* present in the territory, are entitled to additional rights with regard to self-employment,[37] freedom of movement[38] and protection against expulsion.[39] Some provisions in the Refugee Convention confer rights upon refugees who are *(habitually) residing* in a contracting party.[40] These provisions concern artistic rights and industrial property,[41] access to courts (including legal assistance)[42] and administrative assistance.[43] Finally, refugees who are *lawfully staying* in the territory of the host state are entitled to a number of important rights, including the right of association,[44] the right to engage in wage-earning employment, to public relief and assistance,[45] to labour laws and social security[46] and the right to be granted travel documents.[47] Hence, these conditions indicate that refugees are entitled to a wider set of rights if their ties with the host state tighten (the 'incremental system').[48] As the UNHCR states, 'there does seem to have been a conscious attempt by the drafters to match the character of the various rights in question to the degree of residence required', whereby the degree of residence required depends on 'the degree to which the rights in question carry with them financial or social responsibilities or multilateral implications for the granting State'.[49]

[34] RC, Art 13.
[35] RC, Art 16(1).
[36] RC, Art 27.
[37] RC, Art 18.
[38] RC, Art 26.
[39] RC, Art 32 RC. Protection against expulsion should be distinguished from the prohibition of *refoulement* laid down in RC, Art 33, to which all refugees are entitled.
[40] Hathaway makes a distinction between 'habitual residence' and 'residence' and treats 'habitual residence' as a condition requiring 'durable residence' and hence a longer stay than simple residence (Hathaway 2005, pp 190–92). See further on this issue s 4.7 below.
[41] RC, Art 14.
[42] RC, Art 16(2) and (3).
[43] RC, Art 25. In addition, two provisions in the convention confer rights upon refugees who have completed *three years' residence* in the country. According to RC, Art 7(2), all refugees enjoy exemption from legislative reciprocity in the territory of the contracting states after a period of three years' residence. Art 17(2)(a) provides that restrictive measures imposed on aliens or the employment of aliens for the protection of the national labour market may not be applied to a refugee who has completed three years' residence in the country. See on these provisions further ch 9.
[44] RC, Art 15.
[45] RC, Art 23.
[46] RC, Art 24.
[47] RC, Art 28.
[48] Battjes 2006, p 449; Hathaway 2005, pp 154–57; Stenberg 1989, p 89.
[49] UNHCR 1988, p 5.

4.4 EQUAL TREATMENT REGARDING WAGE-EARNING EMPLOYMENT AND SOCIAL SECURITY

The Refugee Convention contains a number of relevant provisions on equal treatment. With regard to access to wage-earning employment, Article 17(1) of the RC provides:

> The Contracting States shall accord to refugees lawfully staying in their territory the most favourable treatment accorded to nationals of a foreign country in the same circumstances, as regards the right to engage in wage-earning employment.

Hence, with respect to access to wage-earning employment, refugees are not entitled to equal treatment with nationals, but with most-favoured nationals of a foreign country. In addition, refugees are only entitled to this treatment if they are 'lawfully staying' in the territory of the host state.

Two provisions deal with the refugee's entitlement to equal treatment with regard to social security. The first one is Article 23 of the RC. This article reads:

> The Contracting States shall accord to refugees lawfully staying in their territory the same treatment with respect to public relief and assistance as is accorded to their nationals.

'Public relief and assistance' is not defined in the Refugee Convention, but it is generally accepted that these terms should be interpreted widely as encompassing a number of areas of the public or social welfare systems, including medical and hospital care.[50] Accordingly, regular social assistance schemes fall under the material scope of this provision.

The second relevant article is Article 24(1), which reads:

> 1. The Contracting States shall accord to refugees lawfully staying in their territory the same treatment as is accorded to nationals in respect of the following matters;
>   (a) (...)
>   (b) Social security (legal provisions in respect of employment injury, occupational diseases, maternity, sickness, disability, old age, death, unemployment, family responsibilities and any other contingency which, according to national laws or regulations, is covered by a social security scheme), subject to the following limitations:
>   (i) There may be appropriate arrangements for the maintenance of acquired rights and rights in course of acquisition;

[50] Grahl-Madsen 1963, commentary no 3 to Art 23; Hathaway 2005, p 810–11; Lester, 'Article 23' in Zimmermann 2011, p 1054.

(ii) National laws or regulations of the country of residence may prescribe special arrangements concerning benefits or portions of benefits which are payable wholly out of public funds, and concerning allowances paid to persons who do not fulfil the contribution conditions prescribed for the award of a normal pension.

With regard to social assistance and social insurance schemes, the convention therefore provides that refugees are entitled to the same treatment as is accorded to nationals. Both articles are provisions of equal treatment that fit into the 'closed model'; they determine that nationals and refugees are to be regarded as alike for the purpose of eligibility for social security schemes and lay down a number of qualifications and exceptions to this general rule.[51] The most important qualifying condition laid down in these provisions is that refugees are only entitled to equal treatment with nationals if they are 'lawfully staying' in the host state. For the purpose of this chapter, it is therefore necessary to examine whether asylum seekers, in other words refugees undergoing status verification procedures, can 'stay lawfully' in the territory of the host state.

4.5 INTERPRETATION OF THE VARIOUS QUALIFYING CONDITIONS

4.5.1 Introduction

As this chapter will show, in order to examine the meaning of the term 'lawfully staying', it is helpful, or even necessary, to examine the meaning of all the various qualifying conditions used in the Refugee Convention, as the interpretation of one term may be related to, or have consequences for, the interpretation of another term. In addition, these different qualifying conditions are examined thoroughly in this chapter since this can be helpful for the interpretation of other international conventions that use the same or very similar qualifying conditions.[52] The difficulty in interpreting these terms lies in the fact that there is no definition of these concepts in the Refugee Convention, nor an authoritative interpretation of these terms by an international court.[53] Moreover, at the time the Refugee Convention was drafted, individual status determination procedures had not yet come into being. The status of asylum seekers awaiting a (lengthy)

[51] See for the distinction between open and closed models of equal treatment provisions s 3.3. Since these provisions explicitly refer to refugees 'lawfully staying' in the territory, the question whether distinctions based on the immigration status of asylum seeker fall under the scope of these provisions (see s 3.5) does not have to be answered.

[52] See chs 5 and 6.

[53] The International Court of Justice can settle disputes relating to the interpretation of the Refugee Convention (RC, Art 38). Only parties to the Refugee Convention may refer disputes to the Court and to date this has not happened.

determination process was therefore not explicitly taken into account.[54] As a result, there are many different interpretations. This chapter will suggest, primarily by comparing the interpretations of three legal scholars who have written extensively on this subject (Battjes, Grahl-Madsen and Hathaway), an interpretation which is in my view most persuasive in the light of the treaty interpretation rules as laid down in the Vienna Convention on the Law of Treaties.[55]

Below, the concepts of 'refugees lawfully in the territory', 'refugees residing in the territory' and 'refugees lawfully staying in the territory' will be examined in relation to the position of asylum seekers. First, three preliminary observations with regard to the interpretation of these qualifying conditions will be made: one about deference to national law; one about the meaning of the term 'refugee'; and one about the meaning of the term 'lawful'.

4.5.2 Autonomous Meaning

The absence of a definition of the concepts of 'lawful presence', 'residence' and 'lawful stay' in the Refugee Convention could lead to the conclusion that the matter is completely left to domestic law. Battjes, for example, states: 'a refugee is "lawfully" in a state if his presence is in conformity with relevant domestic law. … Any [domestic] title to remain on a temporary (or permanent) basis makes presence "lawful" for Convention purposes'.[56] This seems at first sight an attractive and sensible interpretation. However, an important consequence of this interpretation is that states have a huge discretion in according rights to refugees. If states can under all circumstances refuse to consider a refugee to be 'lawfully present' or 'lawfully staying' in its territory, this would make the rights laid down in the Refugee Convention for these categories of refugees meaningless, which would be contrary to the object and purpose of the convention.[57] In addition, the Refugee Convention makes an explicit distinction between

[54] Dent 1998, p 16, fn 61.

[55] See s 1.7.

[56] Battjes 2006, p 451. Also the ECtHR generally states with regard to the meaning of the condition 'lawfully within the territory of the state' in Art 2 of Protocol no 4 that 'this condition refers to the domestic law of the State concerned. It is for the domestic law and organs to lay down the conditions which must be fulfilled for a person's presence in the territory to be considered "lawful"' (see, eg, *Omwenyeke v Germany* app no 44294/04 (ECtHR, 20 November 2007) (dec)).

[57] If the presence and stay of refugees is not in the process of being regularized, and as a result, these refugees are not entitled to the benefits accorded to them by the Refugee Convention, their human rights are not protected in the widest possible way. In addition, it would be contrary to the goal of international co-operation and burden sharing if member states could decide for themselves which level of protection they afford refugees.

'lawfully present' and 'lawfully staying' refugees. If states could, for example, argue that only refugees holding a residence permit are 'lawfully present' in their country, this distinction would be meaningless and it would be contrary to the 'incremental system' laid down in the Refugee Convention entailing that refugees are entitled to a wider set of rights if their ties with the host state tighten.[58]

It therefore seems unavoidable to apply some kind of an 'international' or 'autonomous' meaning to the terms 'lawfully present' and 'lawfully staying'.[59] Whereas it is undeniable that the conditions laid down in domestic law determine whether the person concerned is allowed to be present or to stay in the territory, the question which of these domestic conditions amount to 'lawful presence' or 'lawful stay' within the meaning of the Refugee Convention should be determined autonomously. For example, is a formal stay of execution of the expulsion order pending appeal procedures necessary or sufficient for presence to be 'lawful'? And what about asylum seekers who are subject to a duty to leave the country but whose expulsion order will temporarily not be enforced?[60] And asylum seekers who are allowed to remain in the territory of the host state 'for the sole purpose of the procedure'?[61] Or asylum seekers without leave to enter, who are subject to detention, but who are temporarily admitted into the country under the written authority of an immigration officer?[62] The interpretation of the concepts of 'lawful presence' and 'lawful stay' should therefore be more specific than the general observation that the matter is left to domestic law and that any (domestic) title to remain makes presence or stay lawful.

4.5.3 The Meaning of 'Refugee'

Battjes argues that some articles of the Refugee Convention only apply to refugees whose refugee status has been acknowledged or recognized, while other articles apply to unrecognized refugees as well. In his view, this recognition requirement is not implied by the term 'lawful', but by the

[58] See also Hathaway 2005, pp 177–78.
[59] See also Clark 2004, p 596 and Davy, 'Article 32' in Zimmermann 2011, pp 1304–05.
[60] See, eg, the situation of asylum seekers in the Netherlands whose asylum application has been rejected at an application centre. They have to leave the country within four weeks of the rejection of their asylum application. The expulsion order will only be enforced after this period of time (Spijkerboer 2010, p 29).
[61] See Art 7(1) of the Procedures Directive and Art 9(1) of the Procedures Directive (recast) (see ch 2).
[62] Eg the situation of some asylum seekers in the UK (see *Szoma v Secretary of State for Work and Pensions* [2005] 3 WLR 955 (HL)).

term 'refugee'.[63] This 'constitutivist view' of the term 'refugee' is implied in Articles 1C, 5, 28, 32 and 34 of the RC, according to Battjes, since reading these provisions as saying that they would also apply to unrecognized refugees would lead to unreasonable results. Other provisions do not yield indications for the 'constitutivist view', and Battjes concludes that a reading in conjunction with Articles 1A(2) and 9 of the RC, and in the light of the object and purpose of the convention, suggests that other provisions apply the term 'refugee' in the declaratory sense.[64] Hence, the term 'refugee' has two different meanings in the Refugee Convention, according to Battjes. Sometimes it means every refugee; sometimes it means 'recognized refugee' only.

Pursuant to Article 31(4) of the Vienna Convention on the Law of Treaties, a special meaning may only be given to a treaty term if it is established that the parties so intended. Since Article 1A of the RC indicates to whom, for the purposes of the convention, the term 'refugee' applies and since there is no clear indication, for example in the form of a subsequent agreement between the parties or in the preparatory work of the Refugee Convention, that the parties intended to apply a special meaning to the term 'refugee', it is at first sight not very plausible that this term has two different meanings in the Refugee Convention. Hence, persuasive arguments are necessary for this twofold interpretation of the term 'refugee'.

Battjes' observation that it would lead to unreasonable results if some articles of the Refugee Convention apply also to unrecognized refugees is closely connected to his interpretation of the terms 'lawfully in' and 'lawfully staying in'. Consequently, whether the term 'refugee' in some provisions of the Refugee Convention should mean 'recognized refugee' only will be discussed further below. It will be examined whether persuasive arguments exist to apply a different meaning to the term 'refugee' or whether the 'unreasonable results' seen by Battjes if certain articles of the convention were apply to unrecognized refugees can be solved in another way.

4.5.4 The Meaning of 'Lawful'

Two important qualifying conditions in the Refugee Convention use the word 'lawful' ('lawfully in' and 'lawfully staying in' the territory). The meaning of this term is very important in order to examine which rights laid down in the convention apply to asylum seekers. It therefore deserves some special attention.

[63] Battjes 2006, p 463.
[64] Ibid, pp 463–65.

Black's Law Dictionary defines 'lawful' as:

> Legal; warranted or authorized by the law; having the qualifications prescribed by law; not contrary to nor forbidden by the law; not illegal.[65]

Hence, the term 'lawful' can have two different meanings. It can mean not contrary to or not forbidden by the law, or it can mean authorized or warranted by the law.[66] While the former definition is negatively formulated, the latter requires some kind of positive decision. Which of the two meanings applies is dependent on the context and object and purpose of the Refugee Convention.

The context of the Refugee Convention seems to indicate that the second meaning should apply to the term 'lawfully' in the context of the Refugee Convention. Article 31 of the RC reads:

> Article 31.—Refugees unlawfully in the country of refuge
>
> 1. The Contracting States shall not impose penalties, on account of their illegal entry or presence, on refugees who, coming directly from a territory where their life or freedom was threatened in the sense of article 1, enter or are present in their territory without authorization, provided they present themselves without delay to the authorities and show good cause for their illegal entry or presence.
> 2. The Contracting States shall not apply to the movements of such refugees restrictions other than those which are necessary and such restrictions shall only be applied until their status in the country is regularized or they obtain admission into another country. The Contracting States shall allow such refugees a reasonable period and all the necessary facilities to obtain admission into another country.

According to the heading, this article applies to refugees 'unlawfully' in the country. The article itself speaks of refugees who 'enter or are present in their territory without authorization' in paragraph 1 and of refugees whose status is not 'regularized' in paragraph 2. This means that in order for a refugee to be in a country 'lawfully', his presence has to be 'authorized' or his status has to be 'regularized', both of which imply a positive action taken by the state.

In addition, it can be argued that on the basis of the object and purpose of the Refugee Convention as well, taken together with the text of

[65] Black's Law Dictionary, 6th edn. See also the definition in the Merriam-Webster Dictionary: a: being in harmony with the law; b: constituted, authorized, or established by law.

[66] *Cf* the decision of the High Court of Australia on the interpretation of the term 'lawful purpose': '[A] "lawful purpose" may mean a purpose not forbidden by law or not unlawful under the statute that enacts the term; or it can mean a purpose that is supported by a positive rule of law' (Brennan CJ, Toohey, McHugh and Gummow JJ in *Taikato v R* (1996) 186 CLR 454 (High Court of Australia, 10 October 1996)).

Article 33 of the RC, preference should be given to the second meaning of the term 'lawful'. Article 33(1) of the RC provides:

> No Contracting State shall expel or return (*refouler*) a refugee in any manner whatsoever to the frontiers of territories where his life or freedom would be threatened on account of his race, religion, nationality, membership of a particular social group or political opinion.

This article applies to all refugees, without qualification. If mere observance of this article, by prohibiting the expulsion of a refugee or tolerating his presence on the territory, would already make the presence of that refugee in the territory 'lawful', this would run counter to the carefully drafted 'incremental system' laid down in the Refugee Convention implying a difference between refugees who are simply present on the territory and refugees who are lawfully present on the territory.

Accordingly, in my view, the term 'lawfully' within the meaning of the Refugee Convention should mean authorized by a positive rule of law, and not merely not forbidden by the law.[67]

With these three preliminary observations in mind it will be examined below which qualifying conditions laid down in the Refugee Convention can be met by asylum seekers. For this purpose, the different interpretations of three legal scholars who have extensively written on this subject (Battjes, Grahl-Madsen and Hathaway) will be analysed.

4.6 REFUGEES 'LAWFULLY IN' THE TERRITORY

Refugees who are 'lawfully in'[68] the territory of a contracting state are entitled to the same treatment as is accorded to aliens generally in the same circumstances with regard to the right to engage in self-employment[69] and to the right to choose their place of residence and to move freely within its territory subject to any regulations applicable to aliens generally in the

[67] This interpretation was also accepted by the UK House of Lords in the case of *Szoma v Secretary of State for Work and Pensions* (n 62). It held that there is no reason why 'lawfully' should require 'more by way of *positive legal authorisation* for someone's presence in the United Kingdom than that they are at large here pursuant to the express written authority of an immigration officer provided for by statute' (emphasis added).

[68] Throughout this book, the term 'lawfully present' will also be used. Both terms are understood to have the same meaning.

[69] RC, Art 18. Self-employment is defined in this article as 'to engage on his own account in agriculture, industry, handicrafts and commerce and to establish commercial and industrial companies'.

same circumstances.[70] In addition, these refugees may not be expelled save on grounds of national security or public order.[71]

According to Battjes, a refugee is lawfully present if his presence is in conformity with domestic law. 'Any [domestic] title to remain on a temporary (or permanent) basis makes presence "lawful" for Convention purposes'.[72] As has been mentioned above, this absolute deference to domestic law is not in conformity with the object and purpose of the Refugee Convention and, furthermore, seems to be unworkable, given the wide variety of legal situations in which asylum seekers can find themselves. Accordingly, a more specific interpretation is needed.

Both Grahl-Madsen and Hathaway provide such an interpretation. While both of them are of the opinion that refugees are (implicitly) lawfully in the territory if states do not subject them to status verification procedures at all,[73] they have different opinions as to whether refugees that are still undergoing such procedures are lawfully present. According to Hathaway, a refugee is lawfully present as long as his admission in the territory is authorized.[74] In addition, and more importantly, Hathaway is of the opinion that all refugees undergoing refugee status verification procedures, including the time required for exhaustion of any appeals or reviews, are lawfully present, even if they have not entered the territory with authorization.[75] In his view:

> So long as a refugee has provided authorities with the information that will enable them to consider his or her entitlement to refugee status—in particular, details of personal and national identity, and the facts relied upon in support of the claim for admission—there is clearly a legal basis for the refugee's presence. The once irregularly present refugee is now lawfully present, as he or she has satisfied the administrative requirements established by the state to

[70] RC, Art 26.

[71] RC, Art 32. This article also provides procedural protection against expulsion. It provides: 'The expulsion of such a refugee shall be only in pursuance of a decision reached in accordance with due process of law. Except where compelling reasons of national security otherwise require, the refugee shall be allowed to submit evidence to clear himself, and to appeal to and be represented for the purpose before competent authority or a person or persons specially designated by the competent authority'.

[72] Battjes 2006, p 451.

[73] Grahl-Madsen 1972, pp 360–61; Hathaway 2005, pp 183–85. According to Hathaway: 'This is because while the Convention does not require states formally to determine refugee status, neither does it authorize governments to withhold rights from persons who are in fact refugees because status assessment has not taken place' (Hathaway 2005, pp 179–80). In Grahl-Madsen's view, states may be considered to be under an obligation to regularize the presence of refugees and to abstain from terminating lawful presence. If states do not fulfil these obligations, refugees may claim to be (implicitly) lawful in the territory for convention purposes (Grahl-Madsen 1972, pp 360–61).

[74] Hathaway 2005, pp 174 and 658.

[75] Ibid, p 658.

> consider which persons who arrive without authorization should nonetheless be allowed to remain there.[76]

Grahl-Madsen makes a distinction between refugees who have entered the country with authorization, refugees who have been detained at the border pending status verification and refugees who have entered or been present in the country without authorization. The first category of refugees is (always) lawfully present. He deduces from the aliens law of several contracting states to the Refugee Convention that refugees are generally authorized to enter the country

> if he [the refugee] possesses proper documentation (ie a national passport or a recognized travel document, properly visaed if required); has observed the frontier control formalities, and has not overstayed the period for which he has been allowed to stay by operation of law or by virtue of 'landing conditions', a residence permit, or any other authorization.

A refugee may also be authorized to enter the territory 'even if he does not fulfil all the said requirements, provided that the territorial authorities have dispensed with any or all of them and allowed him to stay in the territory anyway'.[77] This implies that refugees who report themselves or are apprehended at the border, are not taken into detention and are explicitly admitted into the country, are lawfully present.[78] The second category of refugees,[79] refugees who are detained at the border while their cases are being examined, is not lawfully in the territory of the detaining state, according to Grahl-Madsen.

> Whereas his more or less involuntary (continued) stay in the place of detention hardly will constitute illegal presence to the effect that it makes him liable

[76] Ibid, pp 179–80. Battjes does not agree with this interpretation. In his view, '[t]he assumption that the filing of an application for asylum entails regularisation entails assigning a special meaning to a treaty term. According to Article 31(4) VTC, this may be done only when it [is] established that the Contracting States so intended. In the absence of a clear indication to that extent, we must assume that the matter is left to domestic law' (Battjes 2006, p 451).

[77] Grahl-Madsen 1972, p 357.

[78] Grahl-Madsen: 'Similarly: an alien without a passport or recognized travel document may present himself at a frontier control point. If the authorities decide to let him enter, his presence in the territory will be as lawful as that of the next man, so long as he complies with the conditions fixed for his sojourn' (Grahl-Madsen 1972, p 348).

[79] With respect to the second and third category of refugee, Grahl-Madsen observes that Art 31 of the RC (cited above) 'seems to envisage a system whereby a refugee who has entered or been present in the territory of a Contracting State without authorization may have to pass through three stages'. The first stage concerns the period from the commencement of his illegal presence until the refugee reports himself to the authorities or is apprehended. The second stage concerns the period during which the refugee's case is being investigated. The third stage is reached when the refugee's status has been regularized or he has gained admission into a third country, whereby regularization entails 'permission to reside (establish himself) in the country' (Grahl-Madsen 1972, pp 363–64).

to penal sanctions, he will clearly be unlawfully in the territory for any other purpose.[80]

The third category of refugees, refugees who have entered or been present in the country without authorization, is not lawfully present within the meaning of the Refugee Convention while their cases are being examined. According to Grahl-Madsen, the presence of refugees who are not being detained during this stage does not truly fit into the normal categories of 'lawful' or 'unlawful' presence. Such an alien belongs to a third category: 'he would be lawfully in the territory in a strict physical sense, but not necessarily able to claim all benefits normally available to aliens (refugees, stateless persons, as the case may be) lawfully in the territory'.[81] He continues by observing that, on the one hand, such a refugee 'reminds us of the position of the lawfully entered alien who has applied for a residence permit and is allowed to remain in the country until a decision has been made'. By way of analogy, the presence of refugees who have entered or been present in the country without authorization might also be considered to be lawful pending a determination of their case. On the other hand, the permission to await the outcome of their procedure (more or less) in liberty can be seen as 'never intended to affect the alien's status', but merely to avoid needless detention.[82]

Hence, refugees undergoing status verification procedures are ipso facto lawfully present according to Hathaway, provided that they have presented the necessary information to examine their claim to the authorities. In the view of Grahl-Madsen, a distinction should be made between different categories of refugees undergoing status verification procedures. Such refugees are only lawfully present if they have entered the territory with explicit authorization. If they have entered or been present in the country without authorization, or if they are detained at the border, they are not lawfully present for convention purposes during the status verification procedure.

Both authors agree that refugees who have explicit permission to enter the territory are lawfully present. This implies that refugees who enter the territory with authorization are (immediately) lawfully present in the territory. Hence, refugees who possess the necessary documentation, ie a valid passport that is properly visaed if necessary, generally receive authorization to enter and are therefore lawfully present during the validity of the visa or the visa-free access. In addition, also the presence of refugees who do not possess the necessary documentation is positively authorized if they have presented themselves at the border and the authorities have,

[80] Grahl-Madsen 1972, p 361.
[81] Ibid, p 362.
[82] Ibid.

while they were legally authorized to do so, decided to let them enter, provided that such refugees do not violate any requirements imposed on them as a condition for their admission.[83] Accordingly, refugees who are released from border prisons to the territory will be lawfully present. Arguably, if the authorities at the border are legally authorized to decide to let a refugee enter, the presence of this refugee is authorized and therefore lawful, even if domestic law prescribes that he has not entered or has no permission to enter the country in a legal sense.[84] This would mean that an asylum seeker is lawfully present if the state deliberately allows him to (physically) enter the country, provided that he does not overstay the period for which he was admitted or violate any other condition attached to this admission.

Hathaway and Grahl-Madsen disagree, however, about the question when the presence of refugees who have entered or been present in the territory without permission becomes lawful. In other words, they disagree about the question when the status of refugees who have entered or been present in the country without permission will be 'regularized' within the meaning of the Refugee Convention.

Both authors refer to Article 31 as a basis for their interpretation. Under Article 31, refugees who enter *or* are present in the territory without authorization, ie refugees who apply for asylum after they have illegally gained entry into the territory or after their lawful presence has ended because they have, for example, overstayed their visas or violated a requirement imposed on them as a condition for their admission, are unlawfully in the country of refuge. Such refugees only become lawfully present once their status has been 'regularized' and their presence

[83] This interpretation can be confirmed by the preparatory work of the Refugee Convention. Mr Henkin (USA) stated during the forty-first meeting of the second session of the Ad Hoc Committee that 'the expression "lawfully in their territory" included persons entering a territory even for a few hours, provided that they had been duly authorized to enter' (UN Doc E/AC.32/SR.41). Also Mr Juvigny (France) stated that Belgian nationals, who needed only an identity card to spend a few hours in France, would be in France lawfully (UN Doc E/AC.32/SR.42). The Report of the Ad Hoc Committee stated that 'in any event, a Contracting State may consider that a refugee is no longer lawfully in its territory if he is in contravention of terms imposed as a condition of his admission or sojourn' (UN Doc E/AC.32/8;E/1850).

[84] In the UK, persons who are liable for detention at the border, can be temporally admitted to the country. These persons are however under statutory law 'deemed not to have entered the country'. The appellant in *Szoma v Secretary of State for Work and Pensions* (n 62) was temporally admitted. The House of Lords held that there is no reason why 'lawfully' should require 'more by way of positive legal authorisation for someone's presence in the United Kingdom than that they are at large here pursuant to the express written authority of an immigration officer provided for by statute'. Under Dutch law too, it is possible that asylum seekers whose entry has formally been refused, are nevertheless factually allowed to enter the country (see, eg, the judgment of the Administrative Jurisdiction Division of the Council of State of 29 October 2004, *JV* 2005/9).

becomes 'authorized' after all. According to Hathaway, regularization occurs when a refugee meets the requirements laid down in domestic law for entering a status determination procedure.[85] Hence, the presence of asylum seekers who present themselves without delay to the authorities and show good cause for their illegal entry or presence must be deemed lawful, even if they fail to claim refugee status immediately on arrival at the border and even if domestic law does not authorize the presence.[86] According to Grahl-Madsen however, status regularization of a refugee who is unlawfully at the territory only occurs once the authorities allow him to reside (establish himself) in the country.[87] This can only occur after status determination (see further section 4.8 below). For a number of reasons, I find Grahl-Madsen's interpretation most convincing.

Both authors refer to the preparatory work on Article 31 for the interpretation of the term 'regularization'. In my opinion, the preparatory work of the Refugee Convention contains clear indications for understanding 'regularization' in Article 31(2) as acceptance by a country of refuge for permanent settlement.[88] Even though the preparatory work is only a

[85] Hathaway 2005, p 417.

[86] Ibid, pp 175–78. Also Noll holds that any decision implying at least temporary non-removal to countries where relevant risks prevail amount to regularization within the meaning of Art 31, thereby equating it with observing the obligations stemming from Art 33 (Noll, 'Article 31' in Zimmermann 2011, pp 1272–73).

[87] Grahl-Madsen 1972, pp 363–64.

[88] In response to a Swedish amendment, the President of the Conference of Plenipotentiaries explained that the power to detain under (now) Art 31(2) would end 'when the State, after examining the appropriate files, recognized him as a bona fide refugee free from restrictions'. Mr Hoare of the UK further stated: 'The Swedish representative had understood something different to what had been intended by the Ad Hoc Committee by the use of the words "until his status in the country is regularized". Surely, for the Ad Hoc Committee that phrase had meant the acceptance by a country of a refugee for permanent settlement, and not the mere issue of documents prior to a final decision as to the duration of his stay' (Conference of Plenipotentiaries on the Status of Refugees and Stateless Persons: Summary Record of the Fourteenth Meeting, 22 November 1951, A/CONF.2/SR.14). Hathaway argues that contrary to these statements at the Conference, the Ad Hoc Committee had actually endorsed an interpretation of 'regularization' which required only that an asylum seeker makes an application for recognition of refugee status (Hathaway 2005, p 416). Even if this were to be the case, I would argue that this interpretation has been rejected by the clear interpretations offered by the Conference. In addition, the Ad Hoc Committee has also adopted language for Art 31(2) that equated 'regularization' with a decision regarding the legal admission into the country of refuge (Ad Hoc Committee on Statelessness and Related Problems, Decisions of the Committee on Statelessness and Related Problems Taken at the Meetings of 2 February 1950, UN Doc E/AC.32/L.26). According to Hathaway, this language was restored the next day to the original term of 'regularization' (Hathaway 2005, pp 416–17). I did not find any indications, however, for the assumption that this change meant that the expressed meaning of the term 'regularization' was renounced as well (the discussion rather focused on the phrase 'obtained admission to another country', see Ad Hoc Committee on Statelessness and Related Problems, first session: Summary Record of the Twenty-Fourth Meeting Held at Lake Success, New York, on Friday, 3 February 1950, at 2.30 pm, 13 February 1950, E/AC.32/SR.24).

subsidiary means of interpretation and should be used cautiously,[89] it can be used here to confirm the meaning of the term 'regularized'.

A more important argument is that the presence of refugees undergoing status verification procedures who have entered the territory without permission has not been authorized by a positive rule of law. In my view, (formal) permission to await the outcome of the asylum procedure at the territory primarily amounts to securing compliance with different prohibitions of *refoulement*[90] or with asylum seekers' right to an effective remedy.[91] Observance of these obligations is not intended to affect the legal status of the refugee and cannot therefore in itself imply that the refugee's presence is positively authorized by the law.[92] The authorities are merely confronted with the presence of the refugee on their territory as a fait accompli[93] and are generally obligated to legally prohibit their expulsion or tolerate their presence pending the status determination procedure. Issue by the authorities of a document testifying to their (temporary) permission to be present at the territory, in my view, does not alter this.[94] Such documents usually aim to confirm the identity of

[89] See s 1.7.

[90] *Cf* Battjes 2006, p 494.

[91] According to case law of the ECtHR, Art 13 of the ECHR requires in the case of an arguable claim that expulsion violates Art 3 of the said convention a remedy with automatic, de jure suspensive effect (see, eg, *Gebremedhin v France* app no 25389/05 (ECtHR, 26 April 2007), para 66; *Abdolkhani and Karimnia v Turkey* app no 30471/08 (ECtHR, 22 September 2009), paras 108 and 116). *cf* Art 7(1) of the Procedures Directive and Art 9(1) of the Procedures Directive (recast) which reads: 'Applicants shall be allowed to remain in the Member State, *for the sole purpose of the procedure,* until the determining authority has made a decision in accordance with the procedures at first instance set out in Chapter III' (emphasis added).

[92] Battjes 2006, p 494; Grahl-Madsen 1972, p 362. Also the ECtHR seems to endorse this view. With regard to a provision of Maltese law providing that an applicant shall be 'allowed to enter or remain in Malta pending a final decision of his application', the Court held that 'it may well be that what was intended was for the provision to reflect international standards to the effect that an asylum seeker may not be expelled pending an asylum claim …, without necessarily requiring that an individual be granted formal authorisation to stay or to enter the territory' (*Suso Musa v Malta* app no 42337/12 (ECtHR, 23 July 2013), para 98).

[93] *Cf* the European Court of Human Rights in eg the case of *Darren Omoregie and Others v Norway*: 'the Court does not consider that the first and second applicants, by confronting the Norwegian authorities with the first applicant's presence in the country as a *fait accompli,* were entitled to expect that any right of residence would be conferred upon him' (app no 265/07, ECtHR, 31 July 2008, para 64).

[94] According to Battjes, it does (Battjes 2006, pp 494–95). The ECtHR also seems to support this contrary view. In the case of *Omwenyeke v Germany,* the Court held that asylum seekers who are in the possession of a certificate confirming identification and temporary residence permission ('provisional residence permit') are lawfully present within the meaning of Art 2 of Protocol no 4 (on freedom of movement) as long as they comply with the conditions to which their admission and stay are subjected (app no 44294/04, ECtHR, 20 November 2007 (dec)). In the context of Art 8, the Court, however, usually refers to the stay of asylum seekers on the territory while they are allowed to await the outcome of the asylum procedure as being merely 'precarious' or 'tolerated' (see the cases of *Darren Omoregie and Others v Norway* and *Narenji Haghighi v the Netherlands*; for further references see n 141 below).

the refugee and to secure that the above-mentioned obligations are met at a practical level.[95] With respect to the permission to *enter* the territory, states have much more freedom of manoeuvre. In general, states are free, under certain conditions, to detain asylum seekers at the border and to apply (accelerated) asylum procedures at the border. Hence, even though the decision taken by the authorities at the border to admit a refugee into the territory can also be taken for the sole purpose of the determination of the refugee's claim and to avoid needless detention, this decision amounts to a deliberate authorization to legally enter and therefore to be present at the territory. As has been argued above, such a positive authorization fits in best with the text, context and object and purpose of the convention. Hence, I agree with Grahl-Madsen that the position of refugees who enter or are present in the territory without authorization, who apply for status determination and who are allowed to await the outcome of this procedure in the territory resembles the position of the lawfully-entered alien who has applied for a residence permit and is allowed to remain in the country until a decision has been made, but that these positions should nevertheless be distinguished from each other for the purpose of the interpretation of the phrase 'lawfully in the territory'.

Hathaway argues that to interpret 'regularization' in Article 31(2) of the RC as a decision on refugee status would bring Article 31(2) into conflict with Article 26 of the RC.[96] Article 26 of the RC contains the right to freedom of movement for refugees lawfully in the territory. The interpretation of the terms 'lawfully in the territory' and 'regularization' proposed here does not, however, bring these two articles into conflict. Rather, they do play 'complementary, but distinct roles in regulating the right to detain refugees'.[97] For refugees who have authorization to enter the territory, the main rule of freedom of movement in Article 26 will apply pending the status determination procedure. Refugees who enter or are present on the territory without authorization fall under the scope of Article 31(2) of the RC pending status determination, and may therefore be subjected to necessary restrictions on their freedom of movement.

Another argument for this interpretation of the concept of 'lawful presence' is that it to a large extent solves the 'unreasonable results' noted by Battjes if Article 32 of the RC were to apply to unrecognized refugees as well. If 'lawfully in the territory' is interpreted as has been argued above, a reading that Article 32 applies to unrecognized refugees as well would in my opinion not lead to unreasonable results. Article 32 provides

[95] *Cf* RC, Art 27, which requires states to issue identity papers to all refugees in their territory (whether lawfully present or not).

[96] Hathaway 2005, pp 417–18.

[97] Ibid, p 418.

important procedural and substantive protection against expulsion and applies to refugees who are lawfully in the territory. Application of Article 32 to unrecognized refugees would mean, according to Battjes, that 1) Article 33 has very little meaning alongside Article 32 and 2) the safe third-country concept, as applied widely in state practice, would be in violation of this article.[98] With respect to the overlap between Articles 32 and 33, Battjes states that '[A]rticle 33 would apply only to refugees who enter "unlawfully" (…) and then only from the moment they request asylum until the moment their presence is authorised'.[99] This is not true if 'lawfully in the territory' is interpreted as argued above. In that case, while the prohibition of *refoulement*, as laid down in Article 33 of the RC, applies to all refugees in the territory, Article 32 would only apply to refugees who have reported themselves or who are apprehended at the border, are not taken into custody and are admitted into the country. Article 32 would not apply to refugees who are being detained at the border and to refugees who have entered or been present in the country without authorization and who apply for recognition of their refugee status. In this view, Article 32 serves as a protection against, in Grahl-Madsen's words, 'untimely expulsion'[100] and does have added value next to Article 33 of the RC. With regard to the safe third-country concept, application of Article 32 to unrecognized refugees would contravene widely applied state practice according to Battjes.[101] He holds that while one could argue that the lawfulness of the refugee's presence ends at the moment when the state dismisses the asylum application on the ground that the safe third-country exception applies,[102] such an approach would deprive the guarantees of Article 32 of all meaning.[103]

For instance, if a state concludes that a lawfully present refugee poses a threat to its national security and issues an expulsion order, the lawfulness of the

[98] Battjes 2006, pp 461–62. This line of reasoning has also been adopted by the UK House of Lords. In *Szoma v Secretary of State for Work and Pensions* (62), Lord Brown, who gave the leading judgment, stated: 'The term "refugee" in Article 32(1) of the Refugee Convention can only mean someone already determined to have satisfied the Article 1 definition of that term (…). Were it otherwise, there would be no question of removing asylum seekers to safe third countries and a number of international treaties, such as the two Dublin Conventions (for determining the EU state responsible for examining applications lodged in one member state) would be unworkable' (para 24).

[99] Battjes 2006, p 462.

[100] Grahl-Madsen 1972, p 360.

[101] Davy arrives at the same conclusion, since expulsions under the safe third-country concept rarely are based on considerations of public order or national security (Davy, 'Article 32' in Zimmermann 2011, p 1324).

[102] See, eg, Hathaway 2005, p 185.

[103] Grahl-Madsen argues as well that the drafters of the convention 'obviously did not intend that the Contracting States should be able to evade their obligations under this Article by way of the simple expedient of requesting a refugee to leave the country before his time is up, and thus render his continued presence unlawful' (Grahl-Madsen 1972, p 367).

> refugee's presence ends. But we must assume that the refugee is nevertheless still 'lawfully' present for the purposes of Article 32 if, for example, the requirement that he should be allowed a 'reasonable period' to obtain admission elsewhere (Article 32(3)RC) is to have any meaning.[104]

Battjes therefore argues that Article 32 should be interpreted as applying to recognized refugees only.[105] If 'lawfully in the territory' is interpreted as proposed here, however, this would mean that states can no longer expel a refugee to a safe third country, save on grounds of national security or public order, if they have explicitly admitted him into their territory and as long as the refugee does not overstay the period for which he is admitted or violate any other condition attached to this admittance. In other situations, states can expel a refugee to a safe third country. This means that, to a large extent, state practice regarding the safe third-country concept is not in violation with Article 32 of the RC.

This implies therefore that the term 'lawfully present' as laid down in the Refugee Convention should be understood as applying only to persons who have entered the territory with authorization, and not to persons who have entered the country without authorization and who have subsequently surrendered themselves to the authorities. In the Netherlands context for example, this would mean that only asylum seekers arriving at one of the external borders, ie by air or sea, are able to become lawfully present on the territory. As there are no longer border controls at the internal borders, asylum seekers arriving over land would not be able to enter the country with authorization and, consequently, to become lawfully present. According to Edwards, such an interpretation amounts to discrimination of asylum seekers by mode of arrival, which may give rise to indirect discrimination on the ground of race or country of origin as forbidden by Article 3 of the RC.[106] What Edwards probably means is that for refugees from certain countries of origin, it will be easier to get a visa and hence to arrive by plane than for refugees from other countries of origin. However, in my view, the abandonment of internal border controls should be seen within the context of the European Union. Asylum seekers arriving over land also have the possibility to enter the territory with authorization if they apply for admission at one of the external land borders of the European Union.

The distinction between asylum seekers who apply for asylum at the border (and have thereupon been admitted into the country) and asylum seekers who apply for asylum after they have entered or been present

[104] Battjes 2006, p 462. See also Davy, 'Article 32' in Zimmermann 2011, p 1303, fn 155.

[105] Goodwin-Gill and McAdam state that the benefits of Art 32 are limited to refugees who enjoy 'resident status' in the host state (Goodwin-Gill and McAdam 2007, p 263).

[106] Edwards 'Article 18' in Zimmermann 2011, p 978.

in the country without authorization is not unfamiliar in domestic law. For example, in the United States, asylum seekers who arrive at airports or other ports of entry without valid travel documents are mandatorily detained.[107] On a discretionary, case-by-case basis, such asylum seekers may be paroled into the territory.[108] Although such a parole does not amount to an official admittance into the country, 'parolees' are eligible for state or local public benefits.[109] Asylum seekers who apply for asylum from within the country cannot be paroled and are, with a few exceptions, not eligible for public benefits.[110] In the United Kingdom as well, a distinction has been made between 'in-country applicants' and applicants who apply for asylum at a port of entry with regard to eligibility for welfare benefits.[111] Between 1999 and 2008 Australia made a distinction between refugees who arrived on the territory of Australia in an authorized fashion (eg recognized resettled refugees, refugees with a valid holiday or other visa) and refugees who arrive without authorization with respect to the kind of residence permit to which they were entitled. Only the former category of refugee was entitled to a permanent residence permit.[112] In addition, in the more general context of immigration detention, a distinction between asylum seekers applying for asylum at the (external) border and asylum seekers who are already present in the territory and apply for asylum is regularly made. Detention is usually not applied to in-country applicants, even though they may have entered the country without authorization, but is predominantly reserved for applicants at the border.[113]

[107] Such aliens are subject to 'expedited removal procedures' (8 USC § 1225 (b)(1)(A)).

[108] Asylum seekers subject to expedited removal procedures have to show a 'credible fear of persecution' (8 USC § 1225 (b)(1)(B)(v)). Pending the examination of whether such a credible fear exists, asylum seekers can only be paroled into the US if parole is required to meet a medical emergency or if it is necessary for a legitimate law enforcement objective (8 CFR § 235.3(b)(2)(iii) and (b)(4)(ii)). If credible fear of persecution is established, the criteria for parole are wider. Parole is in that case possible for urgent humanitarian reasons or significant public benefit (8 USC § 1182 (d)(5)).

[109] 8 USC § 1621 (a)(2)–(3). Aliens who are paroled into the country for less than a year are not eligible for federal public benefits (8 USC § 1611(a)). Aliens who are paroled into the country for at least one year are 'qualified aliens' and therefore eligible for federal, state and local public benefits.

[110] Asylum seekers are not 'qualified aliens' and therefore not eligible for federal, state or local public benefits (8 USC § 1611(a) and 8 USC § 1621 (a). Exceptions include emergency health care and services such as soup kitchens and short-term shelter (8 USC § 1611(b) and 8 USC § 1621(b).

[111] See s 2.2.

[112] Edwards 2003. The distinction in the Australian case was stricter, however, than the distinction proposed here, as in Australia, asylum seekers who applied for asylum at the border without authorization to enter, but who were subsequently explicitly authorized to enter the territory, were nevertheless not entitled to a permanent residence permit.

[113] Hughes and Liebaut 1998, p 17.

In summary, I agree with Grahl-Madsen that the most persuasive interpretation of the Refugee Convention entails that with regard to the question whether an asylum seeker is lawfully present, a distinction has to be made between asylum seekers who present themselves or are apprehended at the border and who have been explicitly admitted into the country thereupon, and asylum seekers who have entered or been present in the country without authorization and apply for asylum. Although the latter category is usually allowed to stay on the territory pending the determination of their asylum application,[114] only the former category of asylum seekers should in my view be considered to be 'lawfully present' within the meaning of the convention, provided that they do not violate any requirement imposed on them as a condition for entry.[115] This implies that refugees who have entered or been present in the country without authorization become lawfully present and lawfully staying in the territory at the same time. Grahl-Madsen also draws this conclusion. He states:

> A refugee covered by the provisions of Article 31 of the Refugee Convention appears to have no claim to have his status in a territory regularized at such an early time that he would become 'lawfully' present without necessarily 'lawfully staying' there.[116]

As has been argued above, whereas domestic law should determine under which conditions an alien is allowed to enter and be present in the territory or an expulsion order may be issued, the question which of these domestic conditions amount to 'lawful presence' or 'lawful stay' within the meaning of the Refugee Convention should be determined autonomously. This implies that if a refugee's presence is not in conformity with domestic law his presence might still be lawful within the meaning of the convention (eg refugees who are allowed to physically enter the territory, but whose entry is still refused in a legal sense). But also vice versa, if a refugee's presence is not unlawful or even lawful under domestic law, his presence might *not* be lawful within the meaning of the convention (eg refugees who enter or are present on the territory without authorization and apply for status determination). In Grahl-Madsen words: 'It is a fair assumption that an alien physically present is either lawfully or unlawfully within the territory. Real life is, however, not necessarily so simple'.[117]

[114] As a result of which they do fall under the more factual criterion of being 'allowed to remain on the territory' used to indicate the personal scope of EU Reception Conditions Directives (see ch 2).

[115] *Cf* the interpretation of the term 'lawfully within the territory' in the European Social Charter by Harris and Darcy. According to these authors, a person is lawfully within a party's territory 'if he has entered that territory in accordance with its laws and so long as his continued presence is in accordance with them' (Harris and Darcy 2001, p 220).

[116] Grahl-Madsen 1972, p 365.

[117] Ibid, p 359.

4.7 REFUGEES 'RESIDING' IN THE TERRITORY

As has been mentioned above, three provisions in the Refugee Convention confer rights upon refugees who are (habitually) residing in the territory of a contracting party: Article 14 on artistic rights and industrial property, Article 16(2) and (3) on access to courts (including legal assistance) and Article 25 on administrative assistance. In addition, two provisions in the Refugee Convention confer rights upon refugees who have completed *three years' residence* in the country. According to Article 7(2), all refugees enjoy exemption from legislative reciprocity in the territory of the contracting states after a period of three years' residence.[118] Article 17(2)(a) provides that restrictive measures imposed on aliens or the employment of aliens for the protection of the national labour market may not be applied to a refugee who has completed three years' residence in the country.[119]

The interpretations of the term 'residence' in the legal doctrine do not differ substantially. It is generally accepted that the term 'residence' in the Refugee Convention refers to a (factual) lapse of time, not the intent to make a prolonged sojourn.[120] The convention offers a few clues on this meaning of the term 'residence'. First, Article 28 of the RC employs the term 'lawful residence'. Hence, it can be assumed that simple 'residence'

[118] The general standard of treatment has been laid down in Art 7(1) of the RC and entails the same treatment as is accorded to aliens generally. This means that refugees are entitled, except where the Refugee Convention contains more favourable provisions, to treatment that is accorded to ordinary aliens who are not receiving any benefits based on reciprocity. After three years of residence, however, refugees are exempted from 'legislative reciprocity' according to Art 7(2). For the meaning of this provision for the position of asylum seekers see ch 9.

[119] Such restrictive measures may not be applied to refugees who have a spouse or one or more children possessing the nationality of the country of residence, either. On the meaning of this provision for the position of asylum seekers see ch 9.

[120] Battjes 2006, p 452; Grahl-Madsen 1963, commentary no 7 to Art 17; Hathaway 2005, p 756. This interpretation can be confirmed by the preparatory work to the Refugee Convention. Mr Juvigny of France pointed out during the forty-second meeting of the second session of the Ad Hoc Committee on Refugees and Stateless Persons that the expression *'résidant régulièrement'* was the result of a concession by the French delegation. The term previously used was *'résidence habituelle'*, which implied some considerable length of residence. As a concession, the French delegation had agreed to substitute the words *'résidence régulière'*, which were far less restrictive in meaning. In France, the word *'résidant'* was understood to mean 'not only a privileged resident or ordinary resident, but also a temporary resident; the word *'résident'*, which had those three connotations, was therefore very wide in meaning. Of course the three meanings did not include certain cases that were very difficult to define, such as those of refugees who might be in a certain territory for a very short period. But such cases would not, in fact, raise any problems since an examination of the various articles in which the words *'résidant régulièrement'* appeared would show that they all implied a settling down and, consequently, a certain length of residence. Mr Henkin of the USA confirmed that *'résidant régulièrement'* covered persons temporarily resident, except for a very short period (UN Doc E/AC.32/SR.42).

implies unlawful residence as well.[121] Secondly, since the Refugee Convention makes a distinction between refugees 'in' the territory of contracting states and refugees 'residing in' the territory of contracting states, it can be assumed that 'residence' implies a sojourn of a certain period of time. Further, as Battjes states, paragraph 14 of the schedule attached to the Refugee Convention distinguishes 'residence' from 'transit through' on the one hand and 'establishment' on the other hand, which implies that permanent settlement is not necessary in order to 'reside' in a country.[122] This also follows from the distinction between 'domicile' and 'residence' in Article 12 of the RC.[123]

The question remains how much time must elapse before a person is 'residing' in a country within the meaning of the Refugee Convention. Battjes refers to Grahl-Madsen's observation that 'three months seems to be almost universally accepted as the period for which an alien may remain in the country without needing a residence permit' and argues that this may imply that presence continued after the expiration of a period of three months would be 'residence'.[124] This seems to be a valid assumption.

Hathaway interprets 'habitual residence' as a condition requiring 'durable residence' and hence a longer stay than simple residence.[125] However, as the term 'residence' implies a sojourn for a certain period of time, but not a permanent sojourn, it is difficult to distinguish a sojourn for a certain period of time from 'habitual' sojourn. I will follow Battjes in his observation that the term 'habitual residence' is more restricted than the term 'residence' and is therefore used to define the state which must fulfil the obligations, or to define the relevant standard of treatment, if the refugee has a 'residence' in more than one state.[126] Whether a residence in a country qualifies as 'habitual residence' depends in my opinion on the establishment of a durable bond with the country concerned, which is dependent on various social and economic circumstances. See further chapter five on the specific meaning of the term 'habitual residence' and the difference with the term 'residence' in international social security law.

[121] *Cf* Grahl-Madsen who states that 'it seems that the term residence must be interpreted as liberally as possible, so as to include anyone who has been physically present in the country for a period of three years, irrespective of whether he has been there as a refugee, or in any other capacity, and irrespective of whether his presence has been lawful or not' (Grahl-Madsen 1963, commentary no 7 to Art 17).

[122] Battjes 2006, p 452.

[123] The term 'domicile' generally means the place where one lives permanently (see Battjes 2006, p 454 with further references).

[124] Battjes 2006, p 452. Furthermore, Battjes puts forward that European Union law also defines short-term residence as three months (Battjes 2006, p 452).

[125] Hathaway 2005, pp 190–92.

[126] Battjes 2006, pp 453–54.

For now, it suffices to conclude that asylum seekers who are (lawfully or unlawfully) present in a country for a certain amount of time, arguably three months, are entitled to the rights laid down in the Refugee Convention for refugees 'resident' in a contracting state.

4.8 REFUGEES 'LAWFULLY STAYING' IN THE TERRITORY

Many important rights laid down in the Refugee Convention have to be granted to refugees 'lawfully staying' in the territory of the contracting states, including the right to the same treatment as nationals with regard to public relief and assistance[127] and social security[128] and the right to the same treatment as most-favoured nationals of a foreign country as regards wage-earning employment.[129] While it is generally accepted that refugees who are issued a temporary or permanent residence permit are lawfully staying, opinions differ as to whether refugees undergoing status verification procedures (ie asylum seekers) can stay lawfully in the country.

Hathaway is of the opinion that refugees undergoing status verification procedures are not 'lawfully staying' in the country. In his view, the Refugee Convention does not require states formally to verify refugee status. A formal declaration of refugee status is therefore not necessary in order for a refugee to 'stay lawfully' in the territory.[130] However, if states do subject refugees to a status verification procedure, refugees awaiting the results of this procedure are not 'lawfully staying' in the country. As he states:

> [T]he purely provisional nature of such persons' presence in the host state is at odds with the Convention's reservation of these more integration-oriented rights for those who are expected to remain in the state party for a significant period of time.[131]

On the other hand, both Battjes and Grahl-Madsen are of the opinion that refugees undergoing status verification procedures who are lawfully *present* in the country will after a certain lapse of time (arguably three months) also *stay* lawfully in the country.[132] Battjes' most important argument for this interpretation is that there is no reason to suppose that the

[127] RC, Art 23.
[128] RC, Art 24(1).
[129] RC, Art 17(1).
[130] According to Hathaway, the condition of 'lawfully staying' is characterized by 'officially sanctioned, ongoing presence in a state party, whether or not there has been a formal declaration of refugee status, grant of the right of permanent residence, or establishment of domicile there' (Hathaway 2005, p 189).
[131] Hathaway 2005, p 730. See also p 159, fn 20.
[132] Battjes 2006, p 453; Grahl-Madsen 1972, p 354. See in this sense also: Lester, 'Article 23' in Zimmermann 2011, p 1053.

meaning of the term 'residence' (as a sojourn for a certain period of time, arguably three months) should not apply to the term 'lawful residence'.[133] If a refugee who is *present* in a certain country, becomes a *resident* of that country through the mere passage of time, why should a refugee who is *lawfully present* in a certain country not become a *lawful resident* of that country through the mere passage of time?

For a number of reasons I do not find this reasoning persuasive. First of all, in my view, the question as to whether someone is 'present' or 'resident' in a certain country is a question of a factual nature; the answer is dependent on factual circumstances of the person, such as the length of time he has spent in the country. This has to be distinguished from the legal question whether that residence is 'lawful'. As has been mentioned above, the qualification of 'lawful' in the Refugee Convention should mean in my view 'authorized by a positive rule of law' and not merely not forbidden by law. Whereas the (factual) residence of a lawfully present refugee undergoing a status verification procedure is obviously not forbidden by the law, it is not positively authorized either. Refugees undergoing status verification procedures who are lawfully present are authorized to await the outcome of the procedure in the country and not to take up residence there.[134] It is the status verification procedure that has to establish whether they will be authorized to reside in the country. That they should sometimes be considered to already be a resident of the country (in a factual sense) during this procedure does not alter this.

Secondly, the conclusion that asylum seekers are, under some circumstances, 'lawfully staying' in the country in which they apply for asylum is not confirmed by Conclusions from the Executive Committee

[133] As Battjes states, the English language version of the Refugee Convention uses the term 'lawfully residing' and 'lawfully staying', whereas the French language version of the convention uses the term '*résidant régulièrement*' (or '*qui résident régulièrement*') to both qualifications. Arguably, they have the same meaning (Battjes 2006, pp 452–53).

[134] *Cf* the explanatory report to Protocol no 7 of the ECHR that holds that the word 'resident' is intended to exclude from the application of the article any alien who has been admitted to the territory for a limited period *for a non-residential purpose*. This period also covers the period pending a decision on a request for a residence permit.

of the UNHCR,[135] nor by the UNHCR itself.[136] This conclusion would be contrary to national case law as well.[137] Although it can be argued that caution is needed before relying on domestic case law to interpret international treaties, it can be used to confirm a certain interpretation.[138]

Finally, this interpretation also makes it less necessary to interpret the term 'refugee' as having different meanings in different articles of the Refugee Convention, as has been argued by Battjes. It would solve the 'unreasonable result' seen by Battjes in Article of the 28 RC if this article were to apply to unrecognized refugees as well. This article lays down the obligation on contracting states to issue to refugees lawfully staying in their territory travel documents for the purpose of travel outside their territory, unless compelling reasons of national security or public order otherwise require. The issue of such a document entails obligations for other contracting states, as they must accord the rights the holder is entitled to as a refugee (simply) present in their territory. According to Battjes, '[i]f one assumes that unrecognised refugees can invoke Article 28, a contracting state would have to impose obligations on other states towards persons who are not refugees'.[139] However, if 'lawfully staying' is interpreted as excluding refugees undergoing status verification

[135] ExCom Conclusion no 93 on reception of asylum-seekers in the context of individual asylum systems recommends that '[a]sylum-seekers should have access to the appropriate governmental and non-governmental entities when they require assistance so that their basic support needs, including food, clothing, accommodation, and medical care, as well as respect for their privacy, are met'. Hence, the Executive Committee indicates that pending asylum procedures refugees are entitled only to 'basic support needs'. It is not mentioned that some asylum seekers might be entitled to the same treatment as nationals with regard to public relief and assistance, as required by Art 23 of the RC for refugees lawfully staying in the territory. Since the Executive Committee consists of representatives of the Member States of the UN, its Conclusions can be taken into account as evidence of 'subsequent agreement between the parties' within the meaning of Art 31(3)(a) of the Vienna Convention on the Law of Treaties (see further s 1.7).

[136] The UNHCR seems to indicate that persons can (only) benefit fully from the terms of the Refugee Convention (in other words: stay lawfully in the territory) if their status has been regularized 'through appropriate procedures and documentation' (UNHCR 1988, p 6).

[137] The Belgian Court of Cassation held that the equal treatment rule mentioned in Arts 23 and 24(1)(b) of the RC only applies, if necessary with retrospective effect, to persons who possess the status of refugee and are recognized as such pursuant to the applicable legislation (Hof van Cassatie 25 September 1995, S950043N; Hof van Cassatie 13 May 1996, S950118N; Hof van Cassatie 13 May 1996, S950119N). The Dutch Supreme Court held that the right to engage in wage-earning employment, as mentioned in Art 17 of the RC, only arises after the admittance into the Netherlands as a refugee (Hoge Raad 13 April 2007, ECLI:NL:HR:2007:AZ8751, para 3.4). In a case about regulations that excluded refugees undergoing status verification procedures who submit their claims for asylum otherwise than immediately upon arrival in the UK from income support, the UK Court of Appeal stated that 'no obligation arises under Art 24 of the Convention of 1951 until asylum seekers are recognised as refugees' (*R v Secretary of State for Social Security, ex p Joint Council for the Welfare of Immigrants and ex p B* [1997] 1 WLR 275 (CA)).

[138] See s 1.7.3.

[139] Battjes 2006, p 464.

procedures, then Article 28 does not apply until the status of refugee is recognized. The interpretation suggested in this chapter also solves the contradiction seen by Battjes in European Union law. According to Battjes, since only recognized refugees enjoy all Convention benefits, EU legislation interprets the term 'refugee' in the Refugee Convention as 'recognized refugee' and treats recognition of refugee status as a constituent act for enjoying Convention benefits.[140] At the same time, the preamble to the Qualification Directive explicitly states that '[t]he recognition of refugee status is a declaratory act' and European Union law acknowledges the declaratory nature of recognition of refugee status in other places as well. This contradiction does not exist if one assumes that European Union legislation sees recognition of refugee status as declaratory, and interprets the term 'lawfully staying' as not including refugees undergoing status verification procedures.

Hence, I agree with Hathaway that refugees undergoing status verification procedures do not 'stay lawfully' in the country within the meaning of the Refugee Convention.[141] This interpretation implies that refugees who have entered or been present in the country without authorization, who subsequently apply for recognition of their refugee status and are subjected to a status verification procedure, are not entitled to the benefits for refugees 'lawfully in' and 'lawfully staying in' the country. This raises the question whether contracting states are allowed to extend the procedure for a long period of time and, as such, deny refugees these important benefits. As mentioned above, after three years of (simple) residence, refugees enjoy exemption from legislative reciprocity (Article 7(2) of the RC) and restrictive measures for the protection of the labour market may no longer be applied to them (Article 17(2) of the RC). Besides providing refugees two important safeguards if a status verification procedure takes more than three years,[142] these provisions might indicate a time limit of

[140] Ibid, p 495.

[141] *Cf* the ECHR in the case of *Darren Omoregie and Others v Norway*: 'Pending his appeal to the Immigration Appeals Board against the Directorate of Immigration's rejection of his asylum request on 22 May 2002, he was granted a stay of execution of his expulsion and a temporary work permit but at no time was he granted lawful residence in Norway' (ECtHR 31 July 2008, app no 265/07, para 54). And in the case of *Useinov v the Netherlands*, the Court held: 'the Court notes that it is the applicant's submission that he was allowed to live in the Netherlands pending the proceedings on his asylum application and his subsequent application for a residence permit for compelling reasons of a humanitarian nature, i.e. a total period of just over five years. However, the Court is of the view that this cannot be equated with lawful stay where the authorities explicitly grant an alien permission to settle in their country. Therefore, the applicant's stay in the Netherlands was precarious for most of it, and illegal for the remainder' (app no 61292/00, ECtHR, 11 April 2006 (dec)). See also in this sense *Narenji Haghighi v the Netherlands* app no 38165/07 (ECtHR, 14 April 2009) (dec) and *NM and MM v United Kingdom* app nos 38851/09 and 39128/09 (ECtHR, 25 January 2011) (dec), para 74. See also Edwards, 'Article 17' in Zimmermann 2011, p 965.

[142] See further ch 10.

three years for status verification, as has been argued by Battjes.[143] This would mean that asylum seekers who are subjected to status verification procedures and who have not yet received a final decision as to their asylum application within three years after the lodging of this application would be entitled to claim the benefits laid down in the Refugee Convention for refugees 'lawfully in' and for refugees 'lawfully staying in' the territory of the host state.[144]

4.9 CONCLUDING REMARKS

This chapter shows that the Refugee Convention is very explicitly based on the 'convergence model'.[145] It grants rights to refugees on the basis of an 'incremental system', whereby legal status and passage of time are relevant factors for an accretion of rights. This chapter paid, therefore, considerable attention to the specific meaning of the qualifying conditions used in the Refugee Convention.

In my opinion, the most persuasive interpretation of the Refugee Convention entails that refugees undergoing status verification procedures do not stay lawfully in the country within the meaning of the Refugee Convention. These refugees are lawfully present if they have reported themselves or are apprehended at the border, are not taken into custody and are admitted into the country, provided that they do not violate any requirement imposed on them as a condition for their admission. Refugees who are detained at the border or who apply for recognition of their refugee status while they have entered or stayed in the country without authorization are not lawfully present for convention purposes, even though they are generally allowed to await the outcome of the status verification at the territory. These refugees only become lawfully present once a residence permit has been issued by the authorities, or, with regard to refugees detained at the border, if they are released and admitted into

143 Battjes 2006, pp 467–68.

144 *Cf* the policy that was in force in the Netherlands between 1992 and 2002 entailing that aliens who had to wait three years on a final decision on the application for a residence permit were, under certain circumstances, entitled to a residence permit (TBV 1996/15, *Stcrt* 1996, no 242, p 7). Also Edwards concludes that where status determination procedures have been subjected to long delays or suspended, asylum seekers should be considered to be de facto lawfully staying in the territory (Edwards, 'Article 17' in Zimmermann 2011, p 965).

145 See s 1.2. At the same time, elements of the 'separation model' can be detected, where the convention grants certain rights to all refugees physically present on the territory, regardless of legal status. This supports Bosniak's conclusion that also adherents of the convergence model generally argue for some separation with regard to certain rights, and that the distinction between the convergence and separation model should, therefore, not be overstated.

the country.[146] Also unlawfully present refugees however, are considered to *reside* in the country after a certain lapse of time, arguably three months. An advantage of this interpretation is that it solves to a large extent the 'unreasonable results' seen by Battjes if certain articles of the Refugee Convention apply to unrecognized refugees as well. This implies that there are no persuasive arguments to apply different meanings to the term 'refugee' in the convention.[147]

With regard to the main question of this chapter, this interpretation implies that asylum seekers are not entitled to the same treatment as nationals with respect to public relief and assistance and social security under the Refugee Convention, nor to the same treatment as most-favoured non-nationals with regard to access to wage-earning employment, as these important rights only accrue to refugees *lawfully staying* in the territory of the host states. Arguably, if asylum seekers have not yet received a final decision on their asylum application within three years after their application for asylum has been lodged, these entitlements nevertheless accrue to them.

The next chapters will examine whether asylum seekers are entitled to equal treatment with nationals in the field of social security and employment under international social security law (chapter five) and international human rights law (chapter six). Chapter nine will examine whether the Refugee Convention, apart from entitlement to equal treatment, offers other kinds of protection to asylum seekers with regard to their socioeconomic position.

[146] Under general international human rights law, the length of the detention of an alien at the border may not 'exceed that reasonably required for the purpose pursued' (*cf Saadi v United Kingdom* app no 13229/03 (ECtHR, 29 January 2008). This implies that after a certain lapse of time, states are obliged to admit refugees who are detained at the border into their territory. These refugees will then become 'lawfully present'.

[147] The text of the other articles mentioned by Battjes as presupposing status determination (Arts 1C, 5 and 34), in my view does not interfere with a declaratory understanding of the term 'refugee'. With regard to Art 1C (cessation clause), it must be kept in mind that while the Refugee Convention does not *require* states to subject refugees to status verification procedures, it does suppose that status verification *can* take place. *If* states verify the refugee status of refugees and have recognized their refugee status, then Art 1C applies. Also Battjes states that Art 1C supposes that recognition takes place, but that it does not follow that only after recognition is a refugee entitled to the benefits of the Refugee Convention (Battjes 2006, p 459). In addition, the declaratory view of the term 'refugee' only applies to Art 1A(2) of the RC. Art 1A(1) of the RC obviously assumes recognition and makes the provision laid down in Art 1C necessary. Art 34 of the RC does not lay down an obligation to naturalize refugees, but merely a duty to facilitate 'as far as possible' their assimilation and naturalization. Since states have to decide themselves whether the naturalization of a particular refugee is 'possible', it is not problematic that this article applies to unrecognized refugees as well. Finally with regard to Art 5 (on rights granted apart from the convention) I do not see why this article could not apply to unrecognized refugees as well.

5

International Social Security (Co-ordination) Law

5.1 INTRODUCTION

THE PREVIOUS CHAPTER showed that on the whole asylum seekers cannot derive a right to equal treatment with nationals in the field of social security and employment from the Refugee Convention. This chapter will examine whether asylum seekers are entitled to equal treatment with nationals under international social security law. To this end, different conventions realized within the framework of the International Labour Organization (section 5.3) and within the framework of the Council of Europe (section 5.4) will be analysed. These conventions have not been ratified by all EU Member States. However, they may be relevant sources for the interpretation of other instruments of international law discussed in this book.[1]

With respect to international social security law, a distinction is generally made between harmonizing or standard-setting instruments or provisions, on the one hand, and co-ordination instruments or provisions, on the other hand.[2] Harmonizing instruments oblige states to change the substance of their social security legislation by setting uniform or minimum standards regarding, for example, the length of qualifying periods or the amount of benefits. Such instruments therefore affect everyone covered by the national social security legislation involved. Co-ordination instruments do not aim to change the substance of national social security legislation, but are concerned with cross-border elements of social security. Co-ordination rules aim to link national social security systems in cross-border situations. Accordingly, only migrants are affected by social

[1] See s 1.6.2.

[2] *Cf* Gomez Heredero 2007, p 52; Nickless and Siedl 2004, p 11; Pennings 2010, pp 6–7, Vonk 1991, p 43. Some social security conventions deal exclusively with co-ordination or harmonization. Other social security conventions contain provisions of both kinds.

security co-ordination instruments.[3] This chapter will examine provisions laid down in social security conventions on equality of treatment between nationals and non-nationals. It is generally accepted that such provisions form part of co-ordination law, as equal treatment is one of the basic fundamental principles of this part of international social security law.[4] Hence, even though the dividing line between harmonization or co-ordination rules is sometimes difficult to draw,[5] this chapter will be mainly concerned with social security provisions that are generally assumed to form part of the field of social security co-ordination. In addition, this chapter will also pay attention to provisions on equal treatment between nationals and non-nationals in the field of social security laid down in conventions specifically aimed at the protection of migrant workers.

As this chapter will show, these provisions deal specifically with equality of treatment of non-nationals with nationals in the field of social security. In addition, these provisions generally explicitly specify a number of exceptions to the general rule of equality of treatment. This means that these provisions fit into the 'closed model', which has consequences for the methodology of the research.[6]

The title of this chapter already reveals that this chapter is concerned only with equal treatment with respect to social security. The question whether asylum seekers are entitled to equal treatment with nationals as regards access to the labour market will not be considered here, the reason being that whereas equal treatment between nationals and non-nationals is a fundamental principle of international social security (co-ordination) law, under international labour law, equality of treatment between

[3] Nickless and Siedl 2004, p 11; Pennings 2010, pp 6–7; Vonk 1991, pp 43 and 78. However, as Vonk notes, some provisions of social security co-ordination law do in fact change the substance of national legislation. eg, a prohibition of discrimination between nationals and non-nationals changes the personal scope of national social security schemes. Hence, the difference between harmonization and co-ordination might be more adequately described by reference only to the regulatory domain of the effects of the social security convention (ie only affecting 'cross-border situations' or a more general domain of national social security legislation) (Vonk 1991, p 78–80).

[4] Nickless and Siedl 2004, p 12; Pennings 2010, pp 7–11; Vonk 1991, p 1. The other issues usually dealt with by social security co-ordination law are determination of applicable legislation; maintenance of acquired rights; and export of benefits. Pieters also mentions co-operation between the social security administrations of the diverse countries as an important issue of social security co-ordination (Pieters 2006, p 126).

[5] Eg, Vonk makes a distinction between the European Convention on Social and Medical Assistance (ECSMA), on the one hand, and co-ordination instruments, on the other hand (pp 203–25), whereas Nickless and Siedl and Gomez Heredero treat the ECSMA as forming part of social security co-ordination. Nickless and Siedl note that although the European Social Charter is not specifically focused upon co-ordination, some articles included in this instrument do concern social security co-ordination (pp 89 and 91). Gomez Heredero and Schoukens, on the other hand, list the European Social Charter under harmonization instruments (Gomez Heredero 2007, p 52; Schoukens 2007).

[6] See s 3.3.

nationals and non-nationals with respect to access to the labour market does not function as a general and fundamental principle.[7]

5.2 CONTRIBUTORY, NON-CONTRIBUTORY AND SOCIAL ASSISTANCE SCHEMES

In international social security conventions a distinction is generally made between contributory schemes, non-contributory schemes and social or public assistance schemes. This section will discuss the meaning of these different terms. A general definition of the concept of social security for the purpose of this book has been provided in section 1.5.2.

A definition of the terms 'contributory' and 'non-contributory' schemes can be found in Article 1(j) of ILO Convention no 128 on Invalidity, Old-Age and Survivors' Benefits and, more implicitly, in Article 2(6)(a) of ILO Convention no 118 on Equality of Treatment.[8] The same definition can be found in Article 1(y) of the European Convention on Social Security. These definitions are generally referred to by the Committee of Experts of the ILO[9] and by the Committee of Experts for Co-ordination in the Field of Social Security of the Council of Europe.[10] According to these articles, contributory benefits are benefits the grant of which depends on direct financial participation by the persons protected or their employer or on a qualifying period of occupational activity. Hence, the financing of such benefits is primarily employment

[7] Eg, ILO Convention no 111 on Discrimination (Employment and Occupation) does not apply to discrimination on the basis of nationality (see the definition of discrimination in Art 1(1)(a)) and ILO Convention no 97 on Migration for Employment does not contain a provision on equal treatment with respect to access to the labour market. See also the conclusion of Verschueren in this regard (Verschueren 1990, pp 199–212 and 229–30). The only relevant convention seems to be the European Convention on Establishment, concluded within the framework of the Council of Europe in 1955. Art 10 of this convention reads: 'Each Contracting Party shall authorise nationals of the other Parties to engage in its territory in any gainful occupation on an equal footing with its own nationals, unless the said Contracting Party has cogent economic or social reasons for withholding the authorisation'. This provision, however, applies only to nationals of other contracting parties. The convention has been ratified by 12 states, of which only two are non-EU Member States (Norway and Turkey). The relevance of this convention for asylum seekers in the EU is therefore rather limited. See on this convention also ch 12.

[8] The ILO Committee of Experts explained in its general survey of the Reports relating to the Equality of Treatment (Social Security) Convention 1962 (no 118) that during the drafting process of the convention, a large majority of governments was clearly in favour of including a definition of non-contributory benefits. It was agreed that non-contributory benefits be defined as 'benefits which are granted independently of direct financial participation by the persons protected or their employer and of any qualifying period of occupational activity'. It was subsequently decided to delete the definition of these benefits and to replace 'non-contributory benefits' in the text of the convention itself, by the agreed definition (p 6).

[9] See, eg, the General Survey of 1989 on Social Security Protection in Old-Age, p 96, fn 4.

[10] Explanatory report to Interim agreements concerning social security schemes (para 24).

based. Non-contributory benefits are benefits the grant of which does not depend on direct financial participation by the persons protected or their employer or on a qualifying period of occupational activity. Such benefits are primarily residence based. As Nickless and Siedl note, the contribution may be made through social security payments deducted from the wages of the persons protected and/or from contributions made on a worker's behalf by that worker's employer. Some states do not require their citizens to pay distinct social security contributions. These states typically finance their social systems through income taxes, which is why reference is made to minimum periods of occupational activity.[11] However, a scheme under which entitlement to benefits depends only on residence is non-contributory, despite the fact that it is largely financed by a tax based on payrolls.[12] Hence, for the question whether a certain benefit is contributory, the relevant determining criterion is how the benefit is actually financed. It has to be considered whether that financing comes from social contributions. If not, it has to be considered whether the grant of the benefit depends on a qualifying period of occupational activity. If this is not the case, the benefit concerned is non-contributory.

A distinction that raises more difficulties in practice is the distinction between (contributory or non-contributory) social insurance schemes, on the one hand, and social or public assistance schemes, on the other hand. Social and public assistance is generally excluded from the material scope of international social security law. Hence, it is important to define the concept of social assistance clearly. Nevertheless, the term 'public or social assistance' has not been defined in any of the ILO social security conventions.[13] The European Convention on Social and Medical Assistance does contain a definition of assistance. Article 2(a)(i) defines this term as

> all assistance granted under the laws and regulations in force in any part of its territory under which persons without sufficient resources are granted means of subsistence and the care necessitated by their condition, other than non-contributory pensions and benefits paid in respect of war injuries due to foreign occupation.

[11] Nickless and Siedl 2004, p 16.

[12] ILO Committee of Experts, General Survey of 1989 on Social Security Protection in Old-Age, p 96, fn 4.

[13] The Committee of Experts notes in its general survey of the Reports relating to the Equality of Treatment (Social Security) Convention 1962 (no 118) that it was recognized during the preparatory discussions that it would be difficult to define the term 'public assistance' in a clear manner generally acceptable in an international instrument, by reason of the diversity of the conceptions which it covers in different state parties (p 12).

According to the explanatory report, the limitation is due to the fact that non-contributory pensions are social security benefits covered by the European Interim Agreement on Social Security Schemes relating to Old Age, Invalidity and Survivors. Hence, the concept of social assistance refers to the grant of means of subsistence to persons without sufficient recourses, and explicitly excludes non-contributory social insurance schemes. Since non-contributory social insurance sometimes grant minimum subsistence benefits and apply a means test as well,[14] the determining distinguishing criterion between social assistance schemes, on the one hand, and non-contributory social insurance schemes, on the other hand, seems to be the relation to one or more of the social risks laid down in social security conventions. This criterion has been developed in case law of the European Court of Justice on the interpretation of Regulation 1408/71 on social security co-ordination[15] and seems nowadays indeed to be generally accepted as the relevant distinguishing condition between social assistance and social insurance. As Nickless and Siedl for example explain, social insurance schemes protect people against one or more of the nine recognized social risks contained within the ILO Convention no 102.[16] 'Social assistance on the other hand deals purely with the social risk of need or poverty and does not require there to be any link between the reason for that need and a recognised social risk'.[17] Hence, a benefit scheme that provides a minimum income to young disabled persons and that applies a means test does show characteristics of social assistance, but should be regarded as a non-contributory social insurance scheme, as it is clearly related to the social risk of disability.

It should be noted here that in international social security law, the term 'social security' usually only refers to schemes related to one of the social risks mentioned in ILO Convention no 102. As has been mentioned in section 1.5.2, for the purpose of this book the term 'social security' also includes social assistance schemes. For schemes that do not purely deal with the social risk of need or poverty but are related to one of the

[14] Such schemes, which do show certain characteristics of social assistance as well as of social security, are generally referred to as 'mixed' schemes (Pieters 2006, p 6; Vonk 1991, p 38).

[15] CJEU 27 March 1985, Case 249/83 *Hoeckx* [1985] ECR 973 and CJEU 27 March 1985, Case 122/84 *Scrivner* [1985] ECR 1027. See further Vonk 1991, pp 333–36.

[16] ILO Convention no 102 lists the following risks to fall within the realm of 'social security': i) the need for medical care; ii) temporary incapacity for work; iii) unemployment; iv) old age; v) work accident and occupational disease; vi) the responsibility for the maintenance of children (family benefits); vii) maternity; viii) long-term incapacity for work (invalidity); and ix) death of the breadwinner (survivors' benefit). The same branches of social security are listed by ILO Convention no 118 and by the European Convention on Social Security.

[17] Nickless and Siedl 2004, p 15.

recognized social risks, the term 'social insurance' will be used. This can be represented in Figure 5.1:

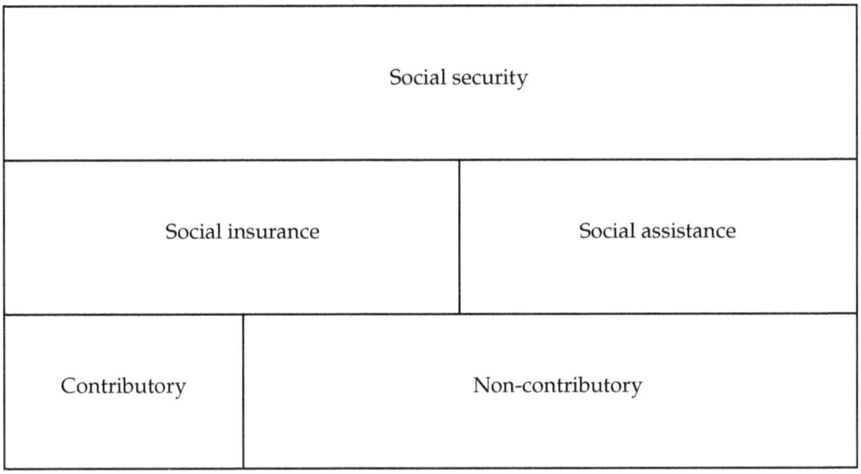

Figure 5.1: System of social security

With regard to the position of asylum seekers, the most important question is whether they are entitled to equal treatment with nationals with respect to social assistance schemes. Nevertheless, equal treatment as regards (contributory or non-contributory) social insurance schemes might also be relevant in case a social risk materializes. For example, if asylum seekers have to be granted equal treatment with nationals as regards social insurance schemes, they may be entitled to old-age pension once they reach retirement age. The following sections will therefore examine whether asylum seekers are entitled to equal treatment with nationals with respect to social insurance and social assistance schemes.

5.3 RELEVANT ILO CONVENTIONS

5.3.1 Introduction

This section will discuss a number of equal treatment provisions laid down in conventions adopted within the framework of the International Labour Organization (ILO). At the time of writing, the ILO has 185 member countries. The organization takes a leading position in setting international standards for social security among international organizations dealing with this topic.[18] The discussion in this section will be limited

[18] *Cf* Pennings 2006, p 1.

to conventions that are considered to be up to date by the ILO,[19] that are wide in scope[20] and that have been ratified by (relatively) many EU Member States. First, a provision on equal treatment in a general social security convention (Convention no 102) will be discussed. After that, the discussion will centre on a convention that specifically deals with the rights of migrant workers (Convention no 97) and one that specifically deals with equality of treatment (Convention no 118).

5.3.2 Convention no 102 on Social Security (Minimum Standards)

Introduction

Convention no 102 was adopted in 1952 and entered into force in 1955. At present, this convention has been ratified by 49 countries, of which 21 are EU Member States.[21] This convention is considered the flagship of all ILO social security conventions, as it establishes minimum standards for all nine traditional branches of social security. These branches are medical care, sickness benefit, unemployment benefit, old-age benefit, employment injury benefit, family benefit, maternity benefit, invalidity benefit and survivors' benefit.[22] Needs-based social assistance schemes that are not related to one of these nine branches do not fall under the material scope of Convention no 102.

Equal Treatment

An important provision for the purpose of this chapter is Article 68, a provision that all contracting states to the convention have to comply with.[23] This article reads:

> 1. Non-national residents shall have the same rights as national residents: Provided that special rules concerning non-nationals and nationals born outside the territory of the Member may be prescribed in respect of benefits

[19] In the 1990s the Committee on Legal Issues and International Labour Standards reconsidered all ILO conventions and made a list of those conventions the ratification of which is encouraged. This list was later adopted by the Governing Body of the ILO. These conventions are referred to as the up to date conventions (Pennings 2006, p 10).

[20] This section will not deal with ILO conventions covering only one specific branch or a limited number of branches of social security, such as the Medical Care and Sickness Benefits Convention of 1969 (no 130), the Employment Promotion and Protection against Unemployment Convention of 1988 (no 168), the Invalidity, Old-Age and Survivors' Benefits Convention of 1967 (no 128) and the Employment Injury Benefits Convention of 1964 (no 121).

[21] Ratifications are available at: www.ilo.org/dyn/normlex/en/f?p=NORMLEXPUB:11300:0::NO:11300:P11300_INSTRUMENT_ID:312247:NO.

[22] While Convention no 102 covers all nine branches, it requires that only three of these branches be ratified by state parties (Art 2 of the convention).

[23] Art 2(a)(iii) of the convention.

or portions of benefits which are payable wholly or mainly out of public funds and in respect of transitional schemes.

2. Under contributory social security schemes which protect employees, the persons protected who are nationals of another Member which has accepted the obligations of the relevant Part of the Convention shall have, under that Part, the same rights as nationals of the Member concerned: Provided that the application of this paragraph may be made subject to the existence of a bilateral or multilateral agreement providing for reciprocity.

The general rule of equal treatment laid down in this article is subject to a number of qualifications and exceptions. This provision makes two important distinctions. First, the provision distinguishes between contributory and non-contributory schemes.[24] Secondly, the provision distinguishes between general contributory schemes and contributory schemes for employees.

With respect to non-contributory schemes (or 'benefits or portions of benefits which are payable wholly or mainly out of public funds'), the second sentence of Article 68(1) provides that special rules concerning non-nationals may be prescribed. The Committee of Experts stated in its General Survey on Social Security Protection in Old-Age of 1989 that this provision 'was included to prevent possible abuses and safeguard the financial balance of non-contributory schemes'.[25] According to the Committee of Experts, the imposition of a (longer) qualifying period of residence on non-national residents or a reciprocity requirement is permitted with regard to non-contributory schemes.[26] As 'special rules' is a vague and broad term, the imposition of requirements as to the possession of a residence permit or employment authorization with regard to non-contributory benefits seems to be permitted by ILO Convention no 102.

As regards general contributory schemes, the first sentence of Article 68(1) provides that non-national residents should have the same rights as national residents. 'Resident' is defined in Article 1(1)(b) of the convention as 'a person ordinarily resident in the territory of the Member'. Accordingly, an important question to be answered in this chapter is whether asylum seekers can be considered to be 'ordinary resident' in the host state pending the asylum procedure. In that case, they are entitled to the same rights as nationals with respect to general contributory schemes. This question will be dealt with further below.

[24] Art 68(1) of the convention refers to 'benefits or portions of benefits which are payable wholly or mainly out of public funds'. This seems to include benefits the grant of which depends on qualifying periods of occupational activity—which are generally understood as contributory benefits (see s 5.2 above)—if these benefits are payable wholly or mainly out of public funds. The distinction made in art 68(1) does therefore not entirely correlate with the distinction between contributory and non-contributory benefits as defined in s 5.2 above.

[25] Committee of Experts, General Survey 1989 Social Security Protection in Old-Age, para 216.

[26] Ibid, paras 216 and 219.

With regard to contributory schemes for employees, Article 68(2) allows for equality of treatment to be limited, for the application of any part of the convention, to nationals of another contracting party which has accepted the obligations of the relevant part. Such equality of treatment may be subject to the existence of a special agreement providing for reciprocity. According to the Committee of Experts,

> the enforcement of equality of treatment thus presupposes the satisfaction of two conditions. The first condition is achieved, ipso jure, when the non-national resident is a national of another member State which has accepted the obligations arising from the relevant Part of Convention no 102. The second condition is potential in nature: equality of treatment may be made subject to the existence of a bilateral or multilateral agreement of reciprocity.[27]

Since the countries from which most asylum seekers in Europe originate have generally not ratified the convention,[28] the protection offered by Article 68(2) to asylum seekers is rather limited in scope.

Ordinarily Resident

The previous section shows that non-nationals are entitled to equal treatment with nationals with regard to general contributory social security schemes if they are 'ordinarily resident' in the state concerned. An important question is therefore whether asylum seekers can considered to be 'ordinarily resident' in the host state and if so, under which circumstances. The concept of 'ordinarily resident' or 'habitual residence' (which is generally understood to have the same meaning[29]) is a concept very often used in national and international social security and tax law as well as in private international law. In European Union law too, the concept is referred to frequently.[30] In neither of the international instruments that use the concept of 'ordinarily' or 'habitually resident' has the concept been defined. The same is probably true for national legislation using this

[27] Ibid, para 217.

[28] In 2012, Afghanistan, Syria and Russia were the three main countries of origin of asylum seekers in Europe. In 2011, these countries were Afghanistan, Russia and Pakistan and in 2010 Afghanistan, Russia and Serbia. In 2009 Afghanistan, Russia and Somalia were the three main countries and in 2008, Iraq, Russia and Somalia (source: Eurostat). Of these countries, only Serbia has ratified Convention no 102.

[29] Stone 2000; Baroness Hale of Richmond in the UK House of Lords case of *Mark v Mark* [2005] UKHL 42 (HL), para 33.

[30] See, amongst many others, eg Regulation (EC) no 883/2004 of the European Parliament and of the Council of 29 April 2004 on the coordination of social security systems [2004] OJ L166/1; Council Regulation (EU) No 1259/2010 of 20 December 2010 implementing enhanced cooperation in the area of the law applicable to divorce and legal separation [2010] OJ L343/10; Council Directive 2002/8/EC of 27 January 2003 to improve access to justice in cross-border disputes by establishing minimum common rules relating to legal aid for such disputes [2003] OJ L26/41.

term. According to Rogerson, the absence of a definition is deliberate, in order to prevent the rigidity associated with the alternative concepts of domicile and nationality.[31] Accordingly, the meaning of the term has been left to judicial interpretation. Also the explanatory report to a resolution of the Committee of Ministers of the Council of Europe on the standardization of the legal concepts of 'domicile' and of 'residence' notes that the very object of introducing the concept of 'residence' as an alternative for the concept of 'domicile' in national and international legislation was to prevent any hard-and-fast definition either in legislation or in the legal doctrine and judicial practice. Hence, while it

> is true that legislative rules and judicial decisions have also, on occasions and in certain connections, brought their influence to bear on the concept of residence; ... if the concept is to remain a flexible and adaptable instrument it seems preferable not to define residence in legal terms but to allow it to stay as factual as possible.[32]

Also national (case) law shows that the criteria for establishing ordinary residence are more of a factual than a legal nature.[33]

Generally, the concept of 'ordinary residence' should be distinguished from mere temporary or occasional residence and requires the establishment of durable ties between the individual and the territory.[34] The facts on which the establishment of such durable ties can be based vary and are assessed differently.[35] The Court of Justice of the European Union, for example, mentions as relevant facts for the establishment of 'habitual residence' with regard to eligibility for social security benefits: 'the

[31] Rogerson 2000, p 87.

[32] Explanatory report to Resolution 72(1) on the Standardisation of the Legal Concepts of 'Domicile' and of 'Residence', adopted by the Committee of Ministers of the Council of Europe on 18 January 1972 at the 206th meeting of the Ministers' Deputies, p 18. Both the resolution and the explanatory report are available at: www.coe.int/t/dghl/standardsetting/nationality/Recommendations_en.asp. According to the explanatory report, the resolution has been adopted in order to unify or harmonize these important concepts underlying all legal systems. 'This would have the advantage of facilitating the uniform interpretation of treaties among the Member States of the Council of Europe, whether or not they were concluded under the Council's auspices'.

[33] See, eg, the UK House of Lords case *R v Barnet LBC, ex p Shah (Nilish)* [1983] 1 All ER 226 (HL), and the Federal Court of Canada, Trial Division, *Perera v Canada* [1994] 2 FC 0. Dutch law provides that the place of residence has to be determined according to the circumstances (see, eg, Art 3 of the National Child Benefits Act (*Algemene Kinderbijslagwet*) and Art 3 of the National Old Age Pensions Act (*Algemene Ouderdomswet*).

[34] See rule no 9 of Resolution 72(1) (n 32); the speech of Lord Scarman of the UK House of Lords of 16 December 1982 on the 'natural and ordinary meaning' of the words 'ordinary residence' in UK statute law, *R v Barnet LBC, ex p Shah (Nilish)* (n 33); the speech of Rand J of the Supreme Court of Canada on the meaning of 'ordinarily resident', Supreme Court of Canada 16 and 17 October 1945 and 24 January 1946 *Thomson v Minister of National Revenue* [1946] CTC 51; the judgment of the Dutch Supreme Court on the meaning of resident (ingezetene), Hoge Raad 4 March 2011, ECLI:NL:HR:2011:BP6285; Pieters 2006, p 22.

[35] Explanatory report to Resolution 72(1) (n 32), pp 20–21.

person's family situation; the reasons which have led him to move; the length and continuity of his residence; the fact (where this is the case) that he is in stable employment; and his intention as it appears from all the circumstances'.[36] Hence, whether somebody should be considered to be 'ordinarily resident' in a specific state is dependent on his individual circumstances.

An important question for the purposes of this chapter is whether contracting states to ILO Convention no 102 can determine that immigration status is a decisive factor for the establishment of ordinary residence in their territory. Since the immigration status of asylum seekers is usually precarious, this would mean that asylum seekers are generally not considered to be ordinarily resident.

Resolution 72(1) of the Committee of Ministers of the Council of Europe on the Standardisation of the Legal Concepts of 'Domicile' and of 'Residence' is clear on this issue. According to rule no 7, the residence of a person does not depend upon the legal entitlement to reside.[37] In chapter four, it has been argued that the term 'residence' in the Refugee Convention applies to unlawful residence as well.

In its General Survey on Social Security Protection in Old-Age of 1989, the Committee of Experts stated, however:

> Article 1(b) of Convention No. 102 and Article 1(d) of Convention No. 128 define the term 'resident' as a person ordinarily resident in the territory of the Member.(...) As regards the question of whether the term 'resident' covers non-nationals who are not lawfully resident, which was raised by one government, it should be recalled that Article 6 of the Migration for Employment Convention (Revised), 1949 (No. 97), which lays down the principle of equal treatment in respect of social security, inter alia, applies to immigrants who are lawfully within the country's territory. This approach was upheld by the Conference in 1975, with the adoption of the Migrant Workers (Supplementary Provisions) Convention (No. 143). The Committee therefore considers that the term 'resident' is intended by Conventions Nos. 102 and 128 to be read as including only those non-nationals who are lawfully resident in the country of immigration.[38]

Hence, with reference to two other ILO conventions, the Committee of Experts holds as a general rule that the term 'resident' in ILO Convention no 102 only includes non-nationals who are *lawfully* resident in the country of immigration. In my view, this reasoning is not persuasive. First of

[36] CJEU 25 February 1999, C-90/97 Robin Swaddling [1999] ECR I-1075.

[37] See n 32. According to the explanatory report: 'According to this Rule, the residence of a person may not depend upon granting or refusal of an official authorisation. If such an authorisation is disregarded the person concerned may be liable to certain legal consequences; nevertheless, his residence should be considered as being the place where he is actually resident' (p 19).

[38] Committee of Experts, General Survey 1989 Social Security Protection in Old-Age, para 53.

all, the Migration for Employment Convention does not require 'lawful residence', but applies to immigrants 'lawfully in the territory'.[39] As chapter four shows, this is an important difference with regard to the position of asylum seekers, as their *residence* in the host state has not (yet) been positively authorized by the law, while their *presence* might, under certain circumstances, meet this test. Besides, and more importantly, the fact that another ILO convention does contain a requirement as to the lawfulness of non-nationals' presence is in my opinion not a valid argument that such a requirement should be implied into Convention no 102, which does not contain any reference to this term, which has a different, and more limited,[40] material scope and which might have different contracting parties.[41] To the contrary, the fact that the requirement as to the lawfulness of the presence has been mentioned explicitly in Convention no 97 indicates in my view that the requirement has deliberately not been used in conventions without an explicit reference to this requirement.[42] The absence of any reference to the lawfulness of the residence in Convention no 102 coupled with the general emphasis on the factual nature of the concept of ordinary residence means in my opinion that immigration status may be a relevant factor for the establishment of ordinary residence, but cannot be the decisive factor.[43]

This means that asylum seekers are 'ordinarily resident' in the sense of Convention no 102 and, accordingly, entitled to equal treatment with nationals regarding general contributory social insurance schemes if they are considered to be 'ordinarily resident' under the general test applied by domestic authorities. In applying this test, various circumstances can be relevant, but the precarious immigration status of asylum seekers, whose residence is not positively authorized by the law but generally not

[39] See s 5.3.3 below.

[40] Ibid.

[41] See for another opinion, Kapuy 2011, pp 98–99, who argues that it makes sense that the Committee of Experts strives towards a consistent application of the ILO conventions in social security. According to Kapuy, to interpret the migrant workers conventions as excluding unlawfully residing aliens from equal treatment in social security, while interpreting social security standard-setting conventions as including them would be contradictory guidance for states parties to the conventions.

[42] *Cf* Schoukens and Pieters 2004, p 8 ('but the least one can say is that the Convention makers seem to have opted for a neutral concept, and not for terms like "lawfully" or alike' (with regard to ILO Convention no 130)).

[43] *Cf* Cholewinski 2005, p 40. This interpretation finds support in national case law on the interpretation on the same term in domestic law. See, eg, the speech of Lord Scarman in the UK House of Lords case *R v Barnet LBC, ex p Shah (Nilish)* (n 33). See also Ontario Superior Court of Justice 8 May 2000 *Jenkins v Jenkins* 8 RFL (5th) 96, [2000] OJ no 1631 and the Dutch Supreme Court (Hoge Raad 4 March 2011, ECLI:NL:HR:2011:BP6285). This outcome resembles the approach adopted by Martin. He argues that in establishing a claim to membership rights for aliens, more weight should be attached to de facto community ties that the alien might have established than to the fact whether the alien has legally crossed the border or not (Martin 2001, see further s 1.2).

explicitly forbidden either, can in my opinion not be the decisive factor. Hence, domestic authorities should determine on the basis of individual circumstances whether asylum seekers are ordinarily resident on the territory. A general exclusion of asylum seekers from eligibility for general contributory social security schemes on the basis of their weak immigration status is therefore not in conformity with Convention no 102.

Summary

If asylum seekers are 'ordinarily resident' in the country, they are entitled to the same rights as nationals with regard to universal contributory social insurance schemes (social insurance schemes that protect residents) under ILO Convention no 102. In this section is has been argued that in determining whether asylum seekers are ordinarily resident, their weak immigration status cannot be the decisive factor, despite a statement of the Committee of Experts to the contrary. This means that a general exclusion of asylum seekers from universal contributory social insurance schemes is in violation of ILO Convention no 102. With regard to contributory social insurance schemes that protect employees, asylum seekers are entitled to the same rights as nationals if their country of nationality has accepted the obligations of the relevant part of Convention no 102. Usually this is not the case. Moreover, this entitlement may be made subject to the existence of a bilateral or multilateral agreement providing for reciprocity. ILO Convention no 102 does not entitle asylum seekers to equal treatment with nationals with regard to non-contributory schemes.

5.3.3 Convention no 97 on Migration for Employment (Revised)

This convention was adopted in 1949 and is entirely devoted to the labour conditions of migrants for employment. It entered into force in 1952 and has been ratified by 49 countries, 10 of which are EU Member States.[44]

'Migrant for employment' is defined in Article 11 of the Convention as 'a person who migrates from one country to another with a view to being employed otherwise than on his own account and includes any person regularly admitted as a migrant for employment'. The preparatory work of this convention clearly shows that the entire convention only

[44] Ratifications are available at: http://www.ilo.org/dyn/normlex/en/f?p=NORMLEXPUB:11300:0::NO:11300:P11300_INSTRUMENT_ID:312242:NO. The convention has been ratified by the following EU Member States: Belgium, Cyprus, France, Germany, Italy, Netherlands, Portugal, Slovenia, Spain and the United Kingdom.

applies to migrants for employment.[45] Refugees and asylum seekers do not generally migrate 'with a view to being employed' and are not generally admitted as 'migrants for employment'. However, the Committee of Experts observes that during the discussion leading to the adoption of this convention, it was pointed out that the provisions are intended to cover refugees and displaced persons, in so far as they are workers employed outside their home country.[46] This is confirmed by Article 11 of Annex II to the convention, which deals with migrants for employment who are refugees or displaced persons.[47] The terms 'refugee' and 'displaced person' are not defined in this convention, but were at the time of drafting already laid down and defined in the Constitution of the International Refugee Organization (the IRO). Under this instrument, displaced persons and refugees were defined by designating certain categories of people, such as victims of the Nazi or fascist regimes, people deported by these regimes and Spanish Republicans.[48] It can be assumed that the drafters had these categories of people in mind when discussing whether refugees and displaced persons should fall under the scope of the convention. At this period of time, international refugee protection by the IRO was primarily aimed at resettlement. When it turned out that repatriation was not possible for the large majority of refugees in Europe, the IRO tried to resettle refugees, mainly as 'manual labourers' who could contribute to post-war reconstruction. In the words of Karatani, the IRO tried 'like an international employment agency' to match the skills of refugees to the needs of each receiving country.[49] Hence, it makes sense that refugees were considered to be able to meet the definition of 'migrant for employment' and consequently, could fall under the personal scope of the Migration for Employment Convention.

A more difficult question is whether, within the current legal framework and practice of refugee protection, asylum seekers are able to meet the definition of 'migrant for employment'.[50] Do asylum seekers migrate from one country to another 'with a view to being employed otherwise

[45] International Labour Conference, 32nd session, record of proceedings, p 285 and p 582 of app XIII.

[46] Committee of Experts, General Survey 1999 Migrant Workers, para 101. According to the Reporter of the Committee on migration for employment, 'it was decided that the Convention should apply only to migrants for employment, *including, of course, refugees and displaced persons migrating for employment,* and not to migrants in general (International Labour Conference, 32nd session, record of proceedings, p 285, emphasis added).

[47] Annex II only applies to migrants for employment who are recruited under government-sponsored arrangements for group transfer.

[48] See Annex I, pt I, ss A and B of the Constitution of the International Refugee Organization.

[49] Karatani 2005, p 530.

[50] International instruments have to be interpreted and applied within the framework of the entire legal system prevailing at the time of the interpretation, see s 1.7.

than on their own account' and are they 'regularly admitted as a migrant for employment'? The phrase 'regularly admitted' seems to refer to legal entrance into the country.[51] Asylum seekers who legally enter the country are generally not admitted 'as a migrant for employment' but in order to await the outcome of their asylum procedure. Arguably, however, if they are provided with a work permit or another kind of authorization to take up employment pending this procedure, and they have legally entered the country, they are regularly admitted as a migrant for employment.[52] As the subjective and personal purpose of someone to migrate to another country cannot be tested, the requirement of migrating 'with a view to being employed' should in my view be interpreted as requiring an objective link with the national labour market. Such a condition can, for example, be fulfilled if a person applies for employment authorization. Accordingly, in my view, asylum seekers meet the definition of 'migrant for employment' and consequently fall under the personal scope of the convention if they have legally entered the country and have applied for and been provided with authorization to take up employment otherwise than on their own account.[53] Arguably, asylum seekers who have initially legally entered the country as a temporary labour migrant and who, after the expiration of their residence and employment authorization, apply for asylum and continue to work without authorization, meet the definition of 'migrant for employment' as well.

What kind of protection does this convention provide with regard to the equal treatment in social security schemes? Article 6(1) of the convention reads:

> Each Member for which this Convention is in force undertakes to apply, without discrimination in respect of nationality, race, religion or sex, to immigrants lawfully within its territory, treatment no less favourable than that which it applies to its own nationals in respect of the following matters:
>
> (...)

[51] According to the Committee of Experts, the phrase 'regularly admitted' means that 'individuals who have entered a country illegally are not covered by these provisions' (Committee of Experts, General Survey 1999 Migrant Workers, para 105). See also Kapuy 2011, pp 76–77.

[52] Kapuy argues that the requirement of regular admittance as laid down in the convention only refers to authorization to enter the country and not to authorization to take up employment in the country. Accordingly, aliens who are admitted as a temporary labour migrant and who continue to work there after the expiration of their employment authorization still meet the definition of 'migrant for employment' (Kapuy 2011, p 77). However, this situation should be distinguished from the situation of asylum seekers. In my view, asylum seekers are only regularly admitted *as a migrant for employment* if they are provided with employment authorization, since they are generally only admitted into the country in order to await the outcome of their asylum procedure.

[53] Also Böhning and Dent seem to conclude that asylum seekers can fall under the personal scope of Convention no 97 (Böhning 1991, p 707 and Dent 1998, p 27).

(b) social security (that is to say, legal provision in respect of employment injury, maternity, sickness, invalidity, old age, death, unemployment and family responsibilities, and any other contingency which, according to national laws or regulations, is covered by a social security scheme), subject to the following limitations:
  (i) there may be appropriate arrangements for the maintenance of acquired rights and rights in course of acquisition;
  (ii) national laws or regulations of immigration countries may prescribe special arrangements concerning benefits or portions of benefits which are payable wholly out of public funds, and concerning allowances paid to persons who do not fulfil the contribution conditions prescribed for the award of a normal pension;

Hence, only immigrants who are 'lawfully within' the territory are protected by this provision. Accordingly, next to the general requirement applicable to the whole convention of lawful *entrance* into the country, Article 6 requires the *presence* of the alien to be lawful. This condition is fulfilled only if the alien does not violate any of the requirements imposed on him as a condition for entry, for example as regards the length of the presence on the territory or the possibilities to work. Whereas aliens who are regularly admitted as migrants for employment and who continue to stay on the territory and to work after the expiration of their residence and work authorization still fall under the general scope of the convention, they no longer fall under the scope of Article 6. As this provision does not require immigrants to 'reside lawfully' in the country, asylum seekers might be able to meet this qualifying condition.[54] In the context of the Refugee Convention, it has been argued that asylum seekers who have legally entered the country and who do not violate a condition imposed on them as a condition for entry should be considered to be 'lawfully in' the territory of the host state.[55] Arguably, in the absence of indications pointing otherwise, this interpretation should also apply within the context of this convention. Hence, asylum seekers who have legally entered the host state; who are provided with employment authorization; and who do not

[54] Also Hathaway calls this condition of the Migration for Employment Convention 'a more relaxed standard' than the requirement of 'lawfully staying' laid down in Art 24 of the Refugee Convention (on labour legislation and social security) (Hathaway 2005, p 765, fn 178). The Committee of Experts, however, does not seem to make a distinction between 'lawfully in' and 'lawfully residing', (CEACR: Individual Observation concerning Convention no 97, Migration for Employment (Revised), 1949 France (ratification: 1954) Published: 1996). This is not very surprising, as most migrants fulfil both conditions at the same time. Yet, with regard to asylum seekers, there is a relevant difference between these two conditions.

[55] See s 4.6.

violate a condition imposed on them as a condition for their entry fall under the scope of Article 6.

In that case, contracting states should apply treatment no less favourable than that which they apply to their own nationals. The Committee of Experts observes that

> [t]he wording according to which the State must apply 'treatment no less favourable than that which it applies to its own nationals' allows the application of treatment which, although not identical, would be equivalent in its effects to that enjoyed by nationals.[56]

This seems to be a valid assumption.

There is one important exception to the requirement to grant this 'equivalent' treatment to immigrants. Special arrangements may be prescribed by national laws or regulations concerning benefits or portions of benefits which are payable wholly out of public funds and concerning allowances paid to persons who do not fulfil the contribution conditions prescribed for the award of a normal pension.[57]

Article 6 of the convention not only requires states to grant migrants for employment lawfully in the territory equivalent treatment as nationals, but it also requires granting this treatment 'without discrimination in respect of nationality, race, religion or sex'. This somewhat ambiguous wording probably means that besides treating migrants as equivalent to nationals, as a minimum standard, states should not discriminate on the basis of nationality, race, religion or sex between different categories of migrants in granting more favourable conditions to certain kinds of migrants.[58]

In comparison with Convention no 102, it turns out that the scope of Convention no 97 is wider in four respects. First, while Convention no 102 excludes from the requirement to grant non-nationals the same rights as nationals benefits which are payable wholly *or mainly* out of public funds, under Convention no 97, only benefits payable *wholly* out of public funds

[56] Committee of Experts, General Survey 1999 Migrant Workers, para 371.

[57] Such benefits will often be payable wholly out of public funds, as a result of which they are already excluded from the scope of the equal treatment provisions on the basis of the first condition laid down in Art 6(b)(ii). However, Kapuy mentions the example of Belgium, where persons not qualifying for the family allowance benefit under the relevant social insurance scheme may qualify for the family allowance of last resort for indigent parents. Both benefits are paid out of the same social insurance fund, which is financed by employers' contributions (Kapuy 2011, p 81).

[58] *Cf* the statement of the Indian member of the Permanent Migration Committee: 'In drafting a Convention and model agreement dealing with migration there were two principles to be embodied. First, that there should be no discrimination between migrants and nationals, and secondly, that there should be equality of treatment for the migrants of all States' (Report XI(2) of the International Labour Office, adopted by the Permanent Migration Committee at its third session, January 1949, p 138).

are excluded. Secondly, migrants do not have to be '(ordinarily) resident' in the country in order to be protected by Convention no 97. Thirdly, a requirement of reciprocity, which is allowed under Convention no 102 with regard to contributory employee schemes, is not allowed under Convention no 97. Fourthly, Convention no 97 also provides protection against discrimination between different categories of migrants on the basis of nationality, race, religion or sex, whereas the scope of Convention no 102 is restricted to equal treatment of non-nationals with nationals.

However, the scope of Convention no 97 is also narrower than that of Convention no 102, as Convention no 97 pays more attention to considerations of national immigration policy. First of all, the convention only applies to immigrants who have legally entered the country. Moreover, such immigrants should have legally entered the country 'as a migrant for employment' which in my opinion means that asylum seekers who are explicitly admitted into the country in order to await the outcome of the asylum procedure should have authorization to take up employment in order to fall under the personal scope of the convention. Secondly, the entitlement to treatment no less favourable than applied to nationals in the field of social security only applies to immigrants 'lawfully within' the country. In addition to this more limited personal scope of Convention no 97 as compared to Convention no 102, the material scope of the former convention is also narrower than the latter in two respects. First of all, special arrangements may be prescribed concerning allowances paid to persons who do not fulfil the contribution conditions prescribed for the award of a normal pension. Secondly, only 'equivalent' treatment has to be granted to non-nationals, instead of 'the same rights'.

With respect to the position of asylum seekers this means the following. Arguably, they fall under the personal scope of the convention and are entitled to 'equivalent' treatment as nationals with regard to social insurance schemes if they are lawfully admitted to the country, are authorized to take up employment there and do not violate one of the conditions imposed on them as a condition for lawful entry. This entitlement to equivalent treatment, however, does not apply to benefits that are payable wholly out of public funds and with regard to benefits paid to persons who do not fulfil the contribution conditions prescribed for the award of a normal pension.

5.3.4 Convention no 118 on Equality of Treatment (Social Security)

Convention no 118 on Equality of Treatment (Social Security) of 1962 is entirely devoted to equal treatment of nationals and non-nationals in the field of social security, which makes it a very relevant convention for the purpose of this chapter. This convention entered into force in 1964 and has been ratified by 37 states, seven of which are EU Member States.[59]

The most important obligation for states has been laid down in Article 3(1) of this convention, which reads:

> Each Member for which this Convention is in force shall grant within its territory to the nationals of any other Member for which the Convention is in force equality of treatment under its legislation with its own nationals, both as regards coverage and as regards the right to benefits, in respect of every branch of social security for which it has accepted the obligations of the Convention.

This obligation to grant equality of treatment to non-nationals laid down in this convention is subject to a number of qualifications and exceptions.

First of all, a contracting state may choose the branch of social security for which it accepts the obligations of this convention.[60] The branches of social security in respect of which a contracting state may accept the obligations of the convention are laid down in Article 2(1) of the convention and include:

1. medical care;
2. sickness benefit;
3. maternity benefit;
4. invalidity benefit;
5. old-age benefit;
6. survivors' benefit;
7. employment injury benefit;
8. unemployment benefit; and
9. family benefit.

Special schemes for civil servants or war victims and, more importantly for the purpose of this chapter, public assistance schemes are explicitly excluded from the scope of this convention.[61]

[59] Ratifications are available at: www.ilo.org/dyn/normlex/en/f?p=NORMLEXPUB:11300:0::NO:11300:P11300_INSTRUMENT_ID:312263:NO. The convention has been ratified by the following EU Member States: Denmark, Finland, France, Germany, Ireland, Italy and Sweden. The Netherlands had initially ratified the convention as well, but denounced it in 2004.

[60] A member state can only accept the obligations of the convention in respect of one or more branches of social security for which it has in effective operation legislation covering its own nationals within its own territory (Art 2(1) of the convention). This requirement was included in order to ensure the effective reciprocity between the nationals of Member States ratifying the Convention (Committee of Experts, General Survey of the Reports relating to the Equality of Treatment (Social Security) Convention 1962 (no 118), p 10).

[61] Art 10(2) of the convention. According to the Committee of Experts, '[t]he term "public assistance" has not been defined in the convention, since it was recognised during the preparatory discussion that it would be difficult to do so in a clear manner generally acceptable in an international instrument, by reason of the diversity of the conceptions which it covers

Contracting states therefore only have to grant equality of treatment to non-nationals with respect to the branches of social security that they have accepted. Of the EU Member States that have ratified Convention no 118, all seven states have accepted the obligations of this convention for the branches of medical care, sickness benefit and employment injury benefit. The branch of unemployment benefit has been accepted by five states; maternity benefits by four states, family benefits by three states, invalidity and survivors' benefits by two states and the branch of old-age benefit by only one state (Italy).[62]

Secondly, the requirement to provide equality of treatment to non-nationals is dependent on reciprocity. Contracting states are only under an obligation to provide equality of treatment to nationals of any other contracting state for which the convention is in force. However, Article 10(1) of the convention stipulates that the provisions of this convention apply to refugees and stateless persons without any condition of reciprocity. This means that member states to this convention should grant all refugees in their territory equality of treatment with their own nationals in respect of every branch of social security for which they have accepted the obligations of the convention. According to Article 1(g) of the convention, the term 'refugee' has the meaning assigned to it in Article 1 of the convention relating to the Status of Refugees of 28 July 1951. As has been mentioned in chapter four, the definition of refugee laid down in the 1951 Refugee Convention contains a temporal and geographic restriction; the scope of the convention is restricted to persons who have fled their country as a result of 'events occurring before 1 January 1951' and contracting states may choose to restrict the convention to refugees from Europe. Both limitations have been removed by the Protocol relating to the Status of Refugees, which entered into force in 1967 (hence after the coming into force of ILO Convention no 118). However, since conventions have to be 'interpreted and applied within the framework of the entire legal system prevailing at the time of the interpretation', the definition of 'refugee' in ILO Convention no 118 should in my opinion be interpreted as not containing the temporal and geographical limitation. Within the current legal framework, the temporal and geographic limitations to the refugee definition hardly exist, since almost all contracting states to the 1951 Refugee Convention have ratified the 1967 Refugee Protocol as well.[63] In addition,

in different member States' (Committee of Experts, General Survey of the Reports relating to the Equality of Treatment (Social Security) Convention 1962 (no 118), pp 11–12).

[62] See n 59.

[63] Besides, most states parties to ILO Convention no 118 have ratified the 1967 Refugee Protocol. Of the 37 Contracting States to ILO Convention no 118, only nine of them have not ratified the 1967 Refugee Protocol (Bangladesh, Barbados, India, Iraq, Jordan, Libyan Arab

to interpret the definition of refugee in ILO Convention no 118 otherwise would make the provision (almost) meaningless.

As has been argued in chapter four, since asylum seekers may meet the definition of refugee as laid down in the 1951 Refugee Convention (as amended by the 1967 Refugee Protocol) and, consequently, may be entitled to equality of treatment under ILO Convention no 118 as from the moment they arrive in the host state, they have to be treated as refugees pending the determination of their status. Otherwise, states run the risk of acting in violation of the convention by withholding important rights from refugees. Accordingly, (most) asylum seekers are entitled to equal treatment with nationals, both with respect to coverage and as regards the right to benefits for every branch of social security for which the host state has accepted the obligations of the convention.[64]

A third important exception to the obligation to grant equality of treatment to non-nationals has been laid down in Article 4 of the convention. This article concerns the question whether it is allowed to set residence conditions that apply to non-nationals alone. The general rule is that equality of treatment should be granted without any condition of residence. In other words, in general it is not allowed to require for non-nationals a certain period of residence in the country in order to be eligible for a benefit if such requirements do not apply to nationals as well.[65] However, contrary to this general rule, residence conditions may be applied to non-nationals alone with respect to maternity benefit, invalidity benefit, old-age benefit, survivors' benefit and unemployment benefit if the grant of these benefits does not depend either on direct financial participation by the persons protected or their employer or on a qualifying period of occupational activity (ie if it concerns non-contributory

Jamahiriya, Madagascar, Pakistan and Syrian Arab Republic). These states did not, however, ratify the 1951 Refugee Convention either.

[64] 'Most asylum seekers', because there is the (theoretical) possibility that an asylum seeker explicitly declares not to be a refugee in the sense of the Refugee Convention, but invokes the protection of another non-*refoulement* prohibition, such as ECHR, Art 3.

[65] *Cf* Committee of Experts: '[t]his does not mean, however, that benefits must in all cases be accorded to non-nationals without any condition of place of residence, but that equality of treatment of nationals and non-nationals must not be limited by a condition of residence imposed on non-nationals alone' (Committee of Experts, General Survey of the Reports relating to the Equality of Treatment (Social Security) Convention 1962 (no 118), p 22. However, Art 4(1) does contain a similar 'retortion clause' as laid down in Art 3(3). Art 4(1) provides that 'equality of treatment in respect of the benefits of a specified branch of social security may be made conditional on residence in the case of nationals of any Member the legislation of which makes the grant of benefits under that branch conditional on residence on its territory'. Nevertheless, since refugees are entitled to equality of treatment without any condition of reciprocity, these retortion clauses arguably do not apply to them.

benefits). In that case, the required period of residence on the territory may not exceed:

1. six months immediately preceding the filing of claim, for grant of maternity benefit and unemployment benefit;
2. five consecutive years immediately preceding the filing of claim, for grant of invalidity benefit, or immediately preceding death, for grant of survivors' benefit; and
3. 10 years after the age of 18, which may include five consecutive years immediately preceding the filing of claim, for grant of old-age benefit.

With regard to all contributory benefits and with regard to non-contributory benefits provided in the branches of medical care, sickness benefits, employment injury benefits and family benefits, the general rule applies, which means that no residence conditions may be applied to non-nationals alone.

The term 'residence' is defined in Article 1(e) as meaning ordinary residence. As has been argued above in section 5.3.2, this requirement generally means the establishment of durable ties between the individual and the state concerned. Accordingly, for the specific branches of social security listed above, contracting states to Convention no 118 may require non-nationals to be 'ordinarily resident' in their territory for a (limited) amount of time in order to be eligible for non-contributory social security schemes. It has been argued above that asylum seekers may, under certain circumstances, meet the ordinary resident requirement.

In brief, what does this mean for the position of asylum seekers under this Convention? Contracting states to this convention are obligated to grant them equality of treatment with their own nationals as regards every branch of social security for which they have accepted the obligations of this convention. This obligation to grant equality of treatment does not in general allow for exceptions as regards non-contributory benefits, which is an important difference with respect to Conventions nos 102 and 97, discussed above. The only exception allowed for under this convention to the general rule of equality of treatment concerns the application of (ordinary) residence conditions to non-contributory benefits in a specific number of branches of social security. Complete exclusion of asylum seekers from contributory or non-contributory social security schemes for which the host state has accepted the obligations of this convention would therefore be in violation of this convention.

However, the Committee of Experts held:

> [I]t should be borne in mind that the principle of equality of treatment implies the abolition of discrimination based on a person's nationality. Consequently, a requirement of lawful residence in the country or of lawful authorisation to be in employment does not appear to be contrary to this principle; where such conditions are imposed the difference in treatment does not appear to be

> motivated by the alien status of the persons concerned but rather by their legal position under regulations governing entry into and residence in the country, or access to employment.

This is an important statement, since this would mean that the exclusion of asylum seekers from social security schemes based on their legal status or on the absence of authorization to work would not be in violation of the convention.

As I have argued in section 3.5, there are sound reasons to treat exclusion from social security schemes on the basis of legal status or absence of employment authorization as distinctions directly based on nationality. Since such rules make eligibility for social security benefits conditional for all non-nationals, whereas nationals do fulfil the conditions ipso facto, such rules do provide for unequal treatment of non-nationals with nationals. In addition, the absence of any reference to requirements of lawful entrance, presence, residence or employment in the text of Convention no 118, whereas other ILO conventions, such as Convention no 97, do contain such requirements explicitly, forms, as I have also argued above regarding Convention no 102, a strong indication that contracting states to Convention no 118 are obliged to grant equality of treatment to non-nationals irrespective of their legal status or authorization to take up employment.

Hence, in my view, asylum seekers who find themselves on the territory of one of the contracting states to Convention no 118 are entitled to all contributory social security benefits as well as to non-contributory benefits provided in the branches of medical care, sickness benefits, employment injury benefits and family benefits without having to fulfil a qualifying condition. Asylum seekers should therefore be eligible for these benefits on the same conditions as nationals. This means that they do have to fulfil requirement as to (ordinary) residence or qualifying periods of residence or employment, but only if these conditions also apply to nationals.

5.3.5 Summary

This section shows that a number of different ILO conventions contain provisions on equality of treatment of non-nationals with nationals in the field of social security.

The obligation laid down in these conventions to provide equality of treatment to non-nationals does not, however, apply to social assistance schemes. Accordingly, asylum seekers cannot derive a right to equal treatment with nationals with regard to these schemes, the benefits of which they especially need. Another important exception laid down in these conventions concerns non-contributory schemes. With regard to this kind of social security scheme, special rules may generally be laid down in national legislation, for example as regards qualifying periods of residence on the territory.

With regard to contributory social security schemes, the ILO conventions discussed above do provide asylum seekers under certain circumstances with the right to equal treatment with nationals. Convention no 118 seems to provide asylum seekers with the most far-reaching protection. Under this convention, contracting states are obligated to grant them equality of treatment with their own nationals with respect to every branch of social security for which they have accepted the obligations of this convention, without any further qualifying condition. According to the Committee of Experts, a requirement of lawful residence in the country or of lawful authorization to be in employment does not appear to be contrary to this convention. However, it has been argued above that this reasoning is not persuasive.

Under Conventions nos 102 and 97, which both have more ratifications than Convention no 118, asylum seekers have to fulfil a qualifying condition in order to be entitled to equal treatment with nationals as regards contributory social security benefits. Under Convention no 102, this condition is 'ordinary residence' with regard to contributory schemes that protect residents. As this criterion is of a factual nature, this chapter has argued that asylum seekers are able to meet this criterion under certain individual circumstances. This means that the general exclusion of asylum seekers based on their immigration status from such schemes is not permitted by Convention no 102. With respect to employee contributory schemes, the protection offered to asylum seekers by Convention no 102 is rather limited, as the right to equal treatment is conditional upon reciprocity, which may be made subject to the existence of a bilateral or multilateral agreement providing for this reciprocity. As regards Convention no 97, asylum seekers arguably fall under the personal scope of the convention and are entitled to 'equivalent' treatment as nationals with regard to contributory social security schemes if they are lawfully admitted to the country, are authorized to take up employment there and do not violate one of the conditions imposed on them as a condition for lawful entry. As the ILO conventions specifically lay down certain exceptions to the requirement of equal treatment (for example with regard to non-contributory benefits), it can be argued that, as opposed to the opinion of the Committee of Experts, other exceptions are not allowed.

Hence, in particular with respect to contributory social security schemes, the ILO conventions do provide asylum seekers with a (conditional) right to equal treatment with nationals. Nevertheless, it is important to keep in mind that it is generally accepted that aliens may be subjected to conditions regarding the duration of their residence or employment in the country ('qualifying periods'), as long as these conditions also apply to nationals. Consequently, if asylum seekers are entitled to the same rights as nationals, this does not necessarily mean that they are immediately entitled to the granting of benefits once a social risk arises.

5.4 RELEVANT COUNCIL OF EUROPE CONVENTIONS

5.4.1 Introduction

This section will discuss provisions on equal treatment between nationals and non-nationals laid down in social security conventions that have been adopted within the framework of the Council of Europe. Section 5.4.2 will examine the European Interim Agreements on Social Security and the European Convention on Social Security. Section 5.4.3 will discuss the European Convention on Social and Medical Assistance. Since the European Code of Social Security does not contain a provision on equal treatment,[66] this instrument will not be discussed in this section. Although the European Convention on the Legal Status of Migrant Workers does contain provisions on equal treatment as regards social security and social and medical assistance, this convention will not be discussed in this section either. The reason for this is that this convention only applies to nationals of other contracting parties[67] and is therefore of only very little relevance for asylum seekers.[68] Nickless and Siedl note that in order to get a full picture of social security co-ordination law within the Council of Europe, it is necessary to include some articles of the European Social Charter in the analysis, since these articles in fact concern social security co-ordination law. I agree with this observation. Nevertheless, since the European Social Charter is generally considered to be the social counterpart to the European Convention of Human Rights, and since the supervisory mechanism of this treaty bears some resemblance to the European

[66] Art 73 merely provides that the contracting parties shall endeavour to conclude a special instrument governing questions relating to social security for foreigners and migrants, particularly with regard to equality of treatment with their own nationals and to the maintenance of acquired rights and rights in course of acquisition.

[67] Art 1 of this convention defines the term 'migrant worker' as 'a national of a Contracting Party who has been authorised by another Contracting Party to reside in its territory in order to take up paid employment'.

[68] The convention has been ratified by 11 countries, of which six are EU Member States. Non-EU Member States that have ratified the convention are: Albania, Moldova, Norway, Turkey and Ukraine. See conventions.coe.int/treaty/Commun/ChercheSig.asp?NT=093&CM=0&DF=&CL=ENG.

Convention on Human Rights, this convention will be examined in the next chapter.[69]

5.4.2 European Interim Agreements on Social Security and the European Convention on Social Security

The European Interim Agreement on Social Security Schemes relating to Old Age, Invalidity and Survivors and the European Interim Agreement on Social Security other than Schemes for Old Age, Invalidity and Survivors entered into force on 1 July 1954. Both conventions have been ratified by (the same) 21 states, 18 of which are EU Member States.[70]

The reason for developing two separate agreements was that the expectation was that some states would only be prepared to accept coordination provisions in relation to short-term benefits, such as sickness or unemployment benefits, but not to long-term benefits. However, in practice there are no states that have ratified only one of these two agreements.[71] Both agreements were originally merely intended as provisional instruments, 'pending the conclusion of a general convention based on a network of bilateral agreements'.[72] This general convention, the European Convention on Social Security, was eventually opened for signature in December 1972 and entered into force on 1 March 1979. However, despite the entry into force of this general convention, the Interim Agreements remain in force for the contracting parties that have not (yet) ratified the European Convention on Social Security. In addition, states may still choose to ratify one or both of the Interim Agreements rather than the European Convention on Social Security.[73] While both Interim Agreements have been ratified by 21 states, the European Convention on Social Security has been ratified by only eight states, seven of which are

[69] *Cf* a 1998 report of the Committee of Ministers responsible for social security of the Council of Europe: 'In the Social Charter, the rights covered by Arts 12 and 13 [on social security and social and medical assistance] are raised to the status of fundamental rights' (7th Conference of European Ministers responsible for social security, Valletta, 13–14 May 1998, Work of the Council of Europe in the social security field, Strasbourg 1998, p 34).

[70] The conventions have been ratified by the following EU Member States: Belgium, Cyprus, Czech Republic, Denmark, Estonia, France, Germany, Greece, Ireland, Italy, Latvia, Lithuania, Luxembourg, the Netherlands, Portugal, Spain, Sweden and the United Kingdom. Ratifications are available at: conventions.coe.int/treaty/Commun/QueVoulezVous.asp?NT=012&CM=0&CL=ENG and conventions.coe.int/Treaty/Commun/QueVoulezVous.asp?NT=013&CM=1&CL=ENG.

[71] Nickless and Siedl 2004, p 21.

[72] See the preamble to both agreements.

[73] Nickless and Siedl 2004, p 22.

EU Member States.[74] This section will therefore pay the most attention to the two Interim Agreements.

As the titles of the agreements suggest, the material scope of the two Interim Agreements differs. The European Interim Agreement on Social Security Schemes relating to Old Age, Invalidity and Survivors applies to social security laws and regulations which relate to:

1. benefits in respect of old age;
2. benefits in respect of invalidity, other than those awarded under an employment injury scheme; and
3. benefits payable to survivors, other than death grants or benefits awarded under an employment injury scheme.[75]

The European Interim Agreement on Social Security other than Schemes for Old Age, Invalidity and Survivors applies to all social security laws and regulations which relate to:

1. sickness, maternity and death (death grants), including medical benefits insofar as they are not subject to a needs test;
2. employment injury;
3. unemployment; and
4. family allowances.[76]

Thus, together they have the same material scope as ILO Convention no 102.[77] Both agreements expressly include schemes of contributory and non-contributory benefits and expressly exclude public assistance, special schemes for civil servants and benefits paid in respect of war injuries or injuries due to foreign occupation.[78] The Interim Agreements have an annex which contains an exhaustive list of all the national schemes to which the agreements apply. The contracting parties are obliged to notify the Secretary General of the Council of Europe of every new law or regulation of a type not included in this annex. Such notifications have to be made within three months of the date of publication of the new law or regulation.[79] At the time of making such notifications, the contracting parties may make a reservation in respect of the application of the

[74] The convention has been ratified by the following EU Member States: Austria, Belgium, Italy, Luxembourg, the Netherlands, Portugal and Spain (see conventions.coe.int/Treaty/Commun/ChercheSig.asp?NT=078&CM=1&DF=&CL=ENG. Hence, Austria is the only state that has not ratified the interim agreements as well).

[75] Art 1(1) of the European Interim Agreement on Social Security Schemes relating to Old Age, Invalidity and Survivors.

[76] Art 1(1) of the European Interim Agreement on Social Security other than Schemes for Old Age, Invalidity and Survivors.

[77] See s 5.3.2.

[78] Art 1(2) of both agreements.

[79] Art 7(2) of both agreements.

agreement to any law, regulation or agreement which is referred to in such notification.[80]

Each agreement gives effect to two main principles. The first main principle is equal treatment in each contracting party, with respect to the laws and regulations on social security, between its own nationals and the nationals of other contracting parties. The second main principle of the agreements is to extend to nationals of all contracting parties the advantages derived from bilateral or multilateral conventions on social security concluded between two or more contracting parties.[81] For the purpose of this chapter, the first principle is the most important one. This principle has been laid down in Article 2(1) of the two agreements. The first sentence of this article reads:

> Subject to the provisions of Article 9, a national of any one of the Contracting Parties shall be entitled to receive the benefits of the laws and regulations of any other of the Contracting Parties under the same conditions as if he were a national of the latter.

Hence, in order to be entitled to equal treatment, a person has to be a national of any one of the contracting parties. However, the two agreements have been supplemented by protocols extending the scope of the agreements to refugees. Both protocols are exactly the same and entered into force in October 1954. All states parties to the Interim Agreements have ratified the protocols as well. On the basis of Article 2 of both protocols, the provisions of the agreements apply to refugees under the same conditions as they apply to the nationals of the contracting parties thereto.[82] Article 1 of the two protocols stipulates that the term 'refugee' has the meaning ascribed to it in Article 1 of the 1951 Convention relating to the Status of Refugees. Hence, for the same reasons as set out above with regard to ILO Convention no 118 (see section 5.3.4), on the basis of this protocol asylum seekers are entitled to equal treatment with regard to contributory and non-contributory social security benefits under the Interim Agreements.

The right of equal treatment as laid down in the Interim Agreements is, however, not absolute. The agreements allow contracting parties to make the right to equal treatment conditional upon the requirement of

[80] Art 9(2) of both agreements.

[81] Art 3 of both agreements. The Interim Agreements do not contain rules on the maintenance of acquired rights, on the determination of the applicable legislation or on the export of benefits, but if such rules have been agreed on in other bilateral or multilateral social security conventions by two or more contracting parties, they also apply to the nationals of other contracting parties.

[82] Provided that Art 3 of the agreements applies to refugees only in cases where the contracting parties to the agreements to which that article refers have ratified the protocol or acceded thereto.

'residence', 'ordinary residence' or the completion of minimum periods of residence. The possibility of setting these conditions varies between the two agreements, between the different social risks covered and between contributory and non-contributory schemes. With regard to contributory and non-contributory benefits in respect of employment injury, contributory benefits in respect of old age and contributory benefits payable to survivors, equal treatment applies to all persons who are resident in the territory of any one of the contracting parties. With regard to the other benefits, persons are only entitled to equal treatment if they are (and continue to be) 'ordinarily resident' in the territory of the contracting party of which they claim the benefit.[83] In addition to this requirement of being ordinarily resident, the right to equal treatment with regard to benefits provided under a *non-contributory* scheme, other than benefits for employment injuries, is conditional on the completion of minimum periods of residence.[84]

Hence, asylum seekers who are 'resident' in a contracting state are entitled to equal treatment with regard to contributory and non-contributory employment injury benefits, contributory old-age benefits and contributory survivors' benefits. This raises the question under which circumstances asylum seekers are (simply) resident in the host state. In the context of the 1951 Refugee Convention, it has been argued that asylum seekers who are simply present in the host state for a relevant period of time, arguably three months, should be considered to 'reside' there (see section 4.7). Arguably, the same test applies in the context of international social security law, since both systems of law concern the provision of (non-immigration-related) rights to non-nationals. Also, the explanatory report to Resolution 72 of the Committee of Ministers of the Council of

[83] See Art 2(1) of both agreements. Only with regard to invalidity benefits is it not necessary that the person concerned continues to be 'ordinarily resident' in the territory of the contracting party of which he claims the benefit; he merely has to show that he had become ordinarily resident there before the first medical certification of the sickness responsible for the invalidity (Art 2(1)(a) of the Interim Agreement on Social Security Schemes relating to Old Age, Invalidity and Survivors). With regard to benefits claimed in respect of sickness, maternity or unemployment, persons have to continue to be ordinary resident in the country in which they claim the benefits *and* they have to show that they had become ordinarily resident before the first medical certification of the sickness, the presumed date of conception or the beginning of the unemployment (Art 2(1)(c) of the Interim Agreement on Social Security other than Schemes for Old Age, Invalidity and Survivors).

[84] With regard to non-contributory old-age, survivors and invalidity benefits, equal treatment only applies to persons who have been resident in the territory for a period in the aggregate of not less than 15 years after the age of 20 and have been ordinarily resident without interruption in that territory for at least five years immediately preceding the claim for benefit (Art 2(1)(b) of the Interim Agreement on Social Security Schemes relating to Old Age, Invalidity and Survivors). With regard to the other (short-term) non-contributory benefits, equal treatment only applies to persons who have been resident in the territory for six months (Art 2(1)(d) of the Interim Agreement on Social Security other than Schemes for Old Age, Invalidity and Survivors).

Europe convincingly argues that the term 'residence' suggests more than mere presence and notes that in almost all European countries it implies a stay of a certain length of time. The difference between habitual or ordinary residence and simple residence is, according to this report, that the former 'qualified form of residence', requires a more stable territorial link than the latter simple form of residence.[85] Since the condition 'resident' coexists in these conventions with the term 'ordinarily resident', the former condition should indeed be fulfilled more easily. Accordingly, asylum seekers who dwell in the host state for a certain period of time are 'resident' in that state and hence entitled to equal treatment with nationals with regard to contributory and non-contributory employment injury benefits, contributory old-age benefits and contributory survivors' benefits.[86] With respect to the period of time necessary to establish residence in the country some important clues can be found in the European Convention on Social and Medical Assistance, which was drawn up and signed at the same time as the European Interim Agreements on Social Security. This convention inter alia provides safeguards against repatriation for aliens who are lawfully resident in one of the contracting parties for at least five years (see further section 5.4.3 below). According to Article 13 of this convention, periods of absence of less than three months generally do not interrupt the continuity of residence, whereas periods of absence of six months or more do interrupt the continuity of residence. Arguably, *a contrario* this might imply that presence that lasts more than three months may, and presence that lasts more than six months in any case does establish residence. In addition, as has been argued in section 4.7, the period of time during which aliens are generally allowed to stay in the country on a tourist visa could be an indication for the period of time necessary for establishing a residence in the country concerned. Alternatively, the rules for registration in the population registers might be an indication for this.[87] Arguably, asylum seekers who apply for asylum at the border and are detained pending a decision on their admission into the country do not establish a residence in the country pending this procedure, independent of the length of this procedure.

Asylum seekers who are (and continue to be) 'ordinary resident' in a contracting party are entitled to equal treatment with regard to all other

[85] Explanatory report to Resolution 72 on the Standardisation of the legal concepts of 'Domicile' and of 'Residence', pp 19–21, see n 32 above.

[86] See also McLean who argues that residence is constituted by the fact of physical presence in a place that is not fleeting or transitory. The physical presence must have some degree of permanence, but it must mean no more than 'not transitory' (McClean 1962).

[87] Eg in the Netherlands, asylum seekers are only registered in the municipal population registers (*GBA*) once they have been living in an asylum seekers centre for at least six months (Art 26 of the Netherlands Act on the Municipal Population Register (*Wet gemeentelijke basisadministratie*)).

long-term and short-term social security benefits. As I have argued in section 5.3.2, the question whether asylum seekers are ordinarily resident in the host state is dependent on their individual circumstances and the ordinarily resident test that applies under the specific social security scheme. In order to be 'ordinarily resident' in a country, the establishment of durable ties between the asylum seeker and the host state should be shown. Whereas their generally weak immigration status can be a relevant factor in this regard, in my view it may not be the decisive factor. Accordingly, asylum seekers are, under certain circumstances, able to meet this criterion of ordinary residence and hence entitled to equal treatment with regard to the other social security benefits. With regard to non-contributory social security benefits, asylum seekers are, however, only entitled to equal treatment if they have fulfilled certain minimum periods of residence in the country concerned.

The European Convention on Social Security has the same material scope as the two Interim Agreements and also applies to, besides nationals of contracting parties, refugees within the meaning of Article 1 of the 1951 Convention relating to the Status of Refugees.[88] The convention affirms the principle of equal treatment between the nationals of the contracting parties (and refugees).[89] An important difference from the Interim Agreements is, however, that the right to equal treatment only applies to persons who are 'ordinarily resident' in the territory of a contracting party.[90] Just as under the Interim Agreements, the right to equal treatment with regard to non-contributory benefits may be made conditional on the fulfilment of minimum periods of residence in the country concerned.[91]

5.4.3 European Convention on Social and Medical Assistance

Introduction

The European Convention on Social and Medical Assistance (ECSMA) and its protocol entered into force on 1 July 1954, at the same time as the European Interim Agreements on Social Security. The ECSMA has been ratified by 18 countries, 15 of which are EU Member States.[92]

[88] Art 4(1) in conjunction with Art 1(o) of the convention.

[89] Art 8 of the convention.

[90] Art 8(1) in conjunction with Art 1(i) of the convention.

[91] Art 8(2) of the convention. However, Art 8(3) sets certain limitations on the possibility to subject persons to minimum periods of residence if the person concerned has been subject to the legislation of the contracting party concerned for at least one year.

[92] The convention has been ratified by the following EU Member States: Belgium, Denmark, Estonia, France, Germany, Greece, Ireland, Italy, Luxembourg, Malta, the

The previous sections showed that social assistance schemes are excluded from the material scope of all social security conventions discussed so far. The ECSMA is the only convention that deals with social assistance schemes and may therefore be very relevant for the social position of asylum seekers in Europe. The two leading principles of the ECSMA are equal treatment and non-repatriation.[93] The principle of non-repatriation entails the obligation of contracting states not to repatriate lawfully resident nationals of other contracting states on the sole ground that they are in need of social or medical assistance.[94] The principle of equal treatment will be discussed extensively below. First, the material scope of the convention will be discussed.

Material Scope

According to Article 2(a) of the ECSMA, the term 'assistance' means

> all assistance granted under the laws and regulations in force in any part of its territory under which persons without sufficient resources are granted means of subsistence and the care necessitated by their condition, other than non-contributory pensions and benefits paid in respect of war injuries due to foreign occupation.

This provision should be read in connection with the two European Interim Agreements on Social Security, as they complement each other.[95] Together, the two Interim Agreements and the ECSMA cover the full range of social security.[96] Whereas the Interim Agreements relate to (contributory or non-contributory) schemes connected to particular social risks, such as old age, invalidity and unemployment, 'social assistance' refers to schemes that are not connected to any particular social risk. 'Medical assistance' refers to medical treatment to which entitlement depends upon a needs test, as medical benefits that are not subject to such a test fall under the scope of the European Interim Agreement on Social Security other than Schemes for Old Age, Invalidity and Survivors.[97] In order to prevent uncertainty about the material scope of the convention, Article 2(b) of the ECSMA provides that the laws and regulations

Netherlands, Portugal, Spain, Sweden and the United Kingdom. See conventions.coe.int/treaty/Commun/ChercheSig.asp?NT=014&CM=0&DF=&CL=ENG.

[93] *Cf* Nickless and Siedl 2004, p 35.

[94] ECSMA, Art 6. Repatriation is not prohibited if the person concerned has not been continuously resident in the territory of that contracting party for at least five years if he entered it before attaining the age of 55 years, or for at least 10 years if he entered it after attaining that age; if the person concerned is in a fit state of health to be transported; *and* if the person concerned has no close ties in the territory in which he is resident (ECSMA, Art 7(a)).

[95] Nickless and Siedl 2004, pp 33–34.

[96] Ibid, p 26.

[97] Ibid, p 34.

in force in the territories of the contracting parties to which the present convention applies are set forth in Annex I. This annex therefore contains a list of all the schemes covered by the convention, as a result of which it plays 'a key role in identifying the undertakings of each contracting party'.[98] The contracting states are obliged to notify the Secretary General of the Council of Europe of any subsequent amendment of their laws and regulations which may affect Annex I and of any new law or regulation not already included in the Annex. At the time of making such notification a contracting party may make a reservation in respect of the application of this new law or regulation to the nationals of other contracting parties.[99] There is, however, no time limit within which such notifications have to be made.[100] An important question is therefore what the consequences are if states parties have not (yet) notified the Secretary General of a relevant amendment or new law or regulation. Under Article 1 of the ECSMA, contracting states are obliged to grant equality of treatment to nationals of other contracting parties with their own nationals with regard to (social and medical) assistance. As the list in Annex I forms no part of the definition of 'assistance' in the convention, contracting states cannot in my view absolve themselves of the obligation to grant equality of treatment by not notifying (an amendment to) an assistance scheme that falls under the scope of the definition of 'assistance' laid down in Article 2(a) of the ECSMA.[101] The list in Annex I therefore merely serves as a tool for identifying the obligations of the contracting parties and has a more 'declaratory' than a 'constitutive' character.

Equal Treatment

Article 1 of the ECSMA deals with the principle of equal treatment. It reads:

> Each of the Contracting Parties undertakes to ensure that nationals of the other Contracting Parties who are lawfully present in any part of its territory to which this Convention applies, and who are without sufficient resources, shall be entitled equally with its own nationals and on the same conditions to social and medical assistance (...) provided by the legislation in force from time to time in that part of its territory.

[98] Explanatory report to the convention.

[99] Art 16 ECSMA.

[100] Nickless and Siedl 2004, p 35. This is an important difference from the obligation to notify new schemes under the Interim Agreements, see s 5.4.2 above.

[101] *Cf* the explanatory report to the convention: 'If the Parties did not extend the application of the Convention to all relevant legislation, the treatment of nationals of other Parties would in fact no longer be equal to that of the nationals of the host State'.

This provision makes clear that with regard to social and medical assistance, nationality is not a relevant difference and lays down a number of exceptions (qualifying conditions) to the rule of equal treatment. Consequently, other, more general and open exceptions do not apply.[102] Hence, if the qualifying conditions have been met, entitlement to equal treatment exists and it is not possible to justify unequal treatment.

In order to be entitled to equal treatment with regard to social and medical assistance an alien has to fulfil the following conditions:

1. he or she must be a national of a contracting party;
2. he or she must be 'lawfully present'; and
3. he or she must be without sufficient resources.

With regard to the first condition, it should be noted that the ECSMA is accompanied by a protocol, which has been ratified by all contracting states to the ECSMA, with the exception of Malta. According to Article 2 of the protocol to the ECSMA the provisions of section I of the convention apply to refugees under the same conditions as they apply to the nationals of the contracting parties thereto. For the purposes of the protocol the term 'refugee' has the meaning ascribed to it in Article 1 of the 1951 Convention relating to the Status of Refugees.[103] This means that refugees within the meaning of Article 1 of the Refugee Convention who are lawfully present on the territory of a contracting state to both the convention and the protocol are entitled to equal treatment with nationals of that state with regard to social and medical assistance. As has been mentioned before, the definition of refugee laid down in the 1951 Refugee Convention contains a temporal and geographic restriction, which has been removed by the Protocol relating to the Status of Refugees. Although this protocol entered into force after the coming into force of the ECSMA and its protocol, the definition of refugee laid down in the latter instrument should, in my opinion, nevertheless be interpreted as not containing the temporal and geographical limitation.[104] This has also been recognized in the explanatory report.[105] Another question that needs to be answered once again,[106] is whether the term 'refugee' in the protocol to the ECSMA should be understood as including asylum seekers (ergo: refugees whose refugee status has not (yet) been recognized by the host state). According to the explanatory report, the protocol 'concerns all persons, irrespective of nationality, who have *obtained refugee status* in

[102] See s 3.3.
[103] Art 1 of the protocol.
[104] See s 5.3.4 above.
[105] Explanatory report to the European Convention on Social and Medical Assistance and the Protocol thereto, para 40.
[106] *Cf* ss 4.2 and 4.5.3.

a Contracting Party' (emphasis added). However, as has been argued in section 4.5.3, this 'constitutive view' of the recognition of refugee status with regard to the interpretation of Article 1 of the Refugee Convention is not very convincing in the light of the object and purpose and system of the Refugee Convention. The absence of a qualifying condition in the protocol to the ECSMA, while other conventions—including the Refugee Convention itself—do contain such conditions,[107] means in my view that a deliberate choice has been made to include all refugees who meet the definition of refugee as laid down in the Refugee Convention, whether the state party has recognized this already or not, within the personal scope of the ECSMA.

With regard to the requirement of 'lawful presence', a difference exists between the English and the French-language versions of the ECSMA, which are equally authoritative.[108] In the English-language version, Article 1 uses the criterion of 'lawfully *present*' and states in Article 11 that

> *residence* by an alien in the territory of any of the Contracting Parties shall be considered lawful within the meaning of this Convention so long as there is in force in his case a permit or such other permission as is required by the laws and regulations of the country concerned to reside therein.

Lawful residence is the criterion used in Article 6 of the ECSMA with regard to non-repatriation of non-nationals on the sole ground that they are in need of social or medical assistance. Hence, the definition laid down in Article 11 refers to the criterion used in Article 6, not to the condition used in Article 1. Nickless and Siedl therefore conclude that from this 'it is logical that "lawful presence" has a broader or wider meaning than "lawful residence"'.[109] However, the French-language version of the convention uses the criterion of '*séjour régulier*' in Article 1 and states in Article 11 that

> le *séjour* d'un ressortissant étranger sur le territoire de l'une des Parties contractantes est réputé régulier, au sens de la présente Convention, tant que l'intéressé possède une autorisation de séjour valable ou tout autre permis prévu par les lois et règlements du pays en question l'autorisant à séjourner sur ce territoire.

Hence, in the French-language version, the definition laid down in Article 11 of the ECSMA also applies to the criterion used in Article 1. In Article 6 of this language version, the term '*résidant en séjour régulier*' is used.

[107] See, eg, the appendix to the European Social Charter of 1961: 'Each Party will grant to refugees as defined in the Convention relating to the Status of Refugees, signed in Geneva on 28 July 1951 and in the Protocol of 31 January 1967, *and lawfully staying in its territory*, treatment as favourable as possible' (emphasis added).

[108] See the last sentence of the convention, under Art 24 and Art 33, para 1 of the Vienna Convention on the Law of Treaties.

[109] Nickless and Siedl 2004, p 35.

The explanatory report states with regard to Article 1:

> Whether or not a person's presence is lawful is determined by the Contracting Parties' laws governing the conditions of entry and the presence of foreign nationals in their respective territories, as well as any international agreements that may alter these conditions.

In addition, it states that the convention 'applies to nationals of Contracting States who are lawfully present in the territory of another Contracting State, irrespective of their length of stay'.[110] With regard to Article 11, this report states that this article 'clarifies the term "lawful" within the meaning of the Convention'. It adds to this that 'as explained with respect to Article 1, the term lawful is determined by the Contracting Parties' laws and regulations'.[111] This means that also the explanatory report seems to assume that the definition laid down in Article 11 of the ECSMA also applies to Article 1.

The most persuasive interpretation in my view is that Article 11 defines the adjective 'lawful' as used in the ECSMA.[112] For the applicability of the principle of non-repatriation, it is required that the alien *resides* (*résidant en séjour régulier*) lawfully in the territory, whereas for the applicability of the principle of equal treatment a person merely has to be lawfully *present (en séjour régulier)*, irrespective of the length of his stay.[113] This means that a person is lawfully present 'so long as there is in force in his case a permit or such other permission as is required by the laws and regulations of the country concerned' to be present therein. As a permit is not necessary, because 'such other permission' (*tout autre permis*) as is required by the laws and regulations of the country concerned makes presence lawful as well, asylum seekers might be able to fulfil this condition. That no residence permit is necessary in order to be lawfully on the territory is confirmed by Article 11(2) of the ECSMA, which holds that lawful residence will become unlawful from the date of any deportation order made out against the person concerned, unless a stay of execution is granted. On the other hand, Annex III to the convention is called: 'List of documents recognised as affording proof of residence, referred to in article 11 of the

110 Explanatory report, para 5.

111 Ibid, para 21.

112 *Cf* the French-language version of the explanatory report to Art 11: L'article 11 précise ce que signifie l'adjectif «régulier» au sens de la Convention' (para 21).

113 Support for this interpretation can also be found in a report of the European Ministers responsible for social security of the Council of Europe. As regards the ECSMA it states that 'the Convention guarantees assistance to all persons "lawfully present" in the territory of a Contracting Party; as a consequence, these persons can claim assistance when they are in need, even if they have not established their residence in the territory of this Contracting Party and are only there temporarily, for example, as tourists' (7th Conference of European Ministers responsible for social security, Valletta, 13–14 May 1998, Work of the Council of Europe in the social security field, Strasbourg 1998, p 12, cited in Minderhoud 2000, p 194).

Convention'. In this annex, most contracting states to the ECSMA have listed different kinds of residence permits. Article 11 does not, however, refer to Annex III. Article 12 of the ECSMA, on the commencement date of the period of residence, does refer to the documents listed in this annex. Annex III should therefore be interpreted as a lists of documents that supply evidence, in the absence of proof to the contrary, of the commencement date of the period of residence, which is relevant for the protection against repatriation under the convention. It is, however, not necessary to be in the possession of a document listed in Annex III in order to be 'lawfully present' on the territory and hence, to invoke the equal treatment provision.[114] Accordingly, in my opinion, in order to be 'lawfully present' within the meaning of Article 1 of the ECSMA, it is not necessary to be in the possession of a residence permit.

In chapter four, it has been argued in depth that in the context of the Refugee Convention asylum seekers who enter the territory with authorization are lawfully in the territory, provided they do not violate a condition imposed on them as a condition for entry. Asylum seekers who enter or are present on the territory without authorization are not lawfully in the territory pending the asylum procedure. Even though they are generally allowed to await the outcome of the procedure on the territory, and might even be in the possession of a document testifying to this permission, this permission has a fundamentally different character from the permission to *enter* the territory. The former permission primarily serves to comply with the prohibition of *refoulement* and with asylum seekers' right to an effective remedy and does not amount to a deliberate, positive authorization to be present on the territory.

Since the additional protocol to the ECSMA refers for the applicability of the convention to refugees to the 1951 Refugee Convention, it makes sense to adopt the same interpretation of the term 'lawfully present' under both conventions. This would mean that asylum seekers who apply for asylum at the border and who are subsequently admitted to the territory are lawfully present if they do not violate the requirements imposed on them as a condition for their entry (eg with respect to period of time for which entry is given, employment, freedom of movement, reporting duties, etc[115]). This category of asylum seeker would therefore

[114] Also, the explanatory report states that 'the documents listed in Annex III may be used as evidence of the residence' (para 21) and that 'Annex III serves to facilitate the application of the Convention, by establishing the list of documents recognised as affording proof of residence referred to in *Article 12* of the Convention' (para 51, emphasis added).

[115] To set as a requirement for lawful entry and presence that the alien concerned cannot apply for general social assistance benefits would be contrary to the object and purpose of the convention. If that were possible, contracting states would entirely undermine the safeguard for non-nationals laid down in Art 1 ECSMA and would deprive this article of any meaning.

be entitled to equal treatment with nationals as regards social and medical assistance.[116]

An important question with regard to the third condition (to be without sufficient resources) is whether the test of the resources of an alien should be the same test as applied to nationals. If it should be the same test, then this third condition seems to be superfluous, as Article 1 requires equal treatment, and application of the same conditions, as nationals. However, to interpret this condition as allowing contracting states to set a higher threshold for aliens as regards resources would undermine the object of equal treatment of the ECSMA.[117] Arguably, this third condition merely serves to assure that the convention only applies to schemes for persons without sufficient recourses and only persons without sufficient resources therefore fall under its personal scope.[118]

Analysis

The foregoing shows that asylum seekers who apply for asylum at the border and are subsequently officially admitted to the territory are lawfully present if they do not violate the requirements imposed on them as a condition for their entry. Since such asylum seekers may be refugees, they have to be treated as refugees pending the determination of their status. Otherwise, states run the risk of acting in violation of the protocol to the ECSMA by withholding important rights from refugees. As no general justification for unequal treatment is possible under Article 1 of the

[116] In 2005 the UK House of Lords arrived at the same conclusion. The asylum seeker in this case was a Polish national and temporarily admitted to the UK. This was possible under UK law for asylum seekers who applied for asylum at the border and were liable to detention, under the written authority of an immigration officer. These persons were subject to restrictions as to residence, employment and reporting to the police or an immigration officer. In this case, there was 'no suggestion that he had failed to comply with such restrictions as had been imposed upon him'. The Secretary of State's main argument was that the phrase 'lawfully present' in the relevant regulations has to be read as a whole and that lawful presence for this purpose is a status gained only by having lawfully entered the UK with leave to enter (and having subsequently remained within the terms of that leave). Not having been granted leave to enter, the appellant accordingly lacks the required immigration status and is not to be regarded as lawfully present. Lord Brown of Eaton-under-Heywood (with whom all their Lordships agreed) did not agree with this reasoning and held that there is no reason why 'lawfully' should require 'more by way of positive legal authorisation for someone's presence in the United Kingdom than that they are at large here pursuant to the express written authority of an immigration officer provided for by statute' (*Szoma v Secretary of State for Work and Pensions* [2005] 3 WLR 955 (HL)).

[117] According to the preamble, the purpose of the ECSMA is to establish for the signatory states 'the principle of equal treatment for the nationals of each of them in the application of legislation providing for social and medical assistance'.

[118] Nickless and Siedl conclude as well that the means test should be the same for aliens and nationals (Nickless and Siedl 2004, pp 35–36). The explanatory report does not mention this criterion separately. As far as I know, it has not been discussed in case law, either. This confirms the conclusion that this criterion does not have an autonomous meaning.

ECSMA, asylum seekers who are lawfully present on the territory of the contracting states are entitled to social and medical assistance equally and on the same conditions as nationals.

In state practice of many European states, asylum seekers are eligible for special assistance schemes, which provide assistance at a lower level than the assistance provided under the general social assistance scheme in the country concerned and/or provides assistance mainly in kind. In addition, qualifying conditions with respect to co-operation in the asylum procedure or presence at a reception centre usually apply. The EU Reception Conditions Directives allow for such special schemes. Directive 2013/33 even explicitly grants Member States the possibility to grant less favourable treatment to asylum seekers compared with nationals with regard to the level of social assistance. In addition, both Directives allow for benefits to be provided in kind and for reducing or withdrawing benefits on the basis of reasons connected to the asylum procedure or the presence in an accommodation centre.[119]

How does this relate to the obligation to grant asylum seekers who are lawfully present social assistance *equally and on the same conditions as nationals*? Application of the ECSMA means to me that for asylum seekers who are lawfully present on the territory, the minimum subsistence level as laid down in general social assistance schemes should be the point of reference for the quality and level of their assistance benefits. If the general assistance scheme allows for provision of benefits in kind[120] or under a separate scheme[121] for nationals, than provision of benefits in kind or provision of benefits under a separate scheme to such asylum seekers does not violate the ECSMA. If the national general assistance schemes do not contain the possibility to provide assistance entirely in kind, asylum seekers who are lawfully present on the territory should at least have the possibility to receive financial assistance in the same way as nationals. In addition, subjecting such asylum seekers to conditions that are not

[119] See ch 2.

[120] Eg, the Belgian Social Welfare Services Act, one of the two general social assistance schemes in Belgium, provides for assistance of 'material, social, medical or physiological nature' (Art 57 of the Social Welfare Services Act, *Organieke wet betreffende de Openbare Centra voor Maatschappelijk Welzijn*).

[121] Eg, in the Netherlands, the general social assistance scheme contains a clause providing that a person is no longer eligible for general social assistance if that person is eligible for another kind of welfare scheme (known as a prior ranking benefit scheme or *voorliggende voorziening*) which can considered to be sufficient and suitable for the person concerned. This clause equally applies to nationals and non-nationals. Such a prior ranking benefit scheme does not have to provide persons with exactly the same kind of assistance as under the general scheme. The decisive criterion is whether the assistance provided under the special scheme is sufficient and suitable for the person concerned.

imposed or cannot be imposed on nationals, such as conditions related to asylum procedure,[122] is not in conformity with the ECSMA.

5.4.4 Summary

The social security co-ordination conventions of the Council of Europe provide asylum seekers with some important safeguards. Although these conventions are in principle based on the idea of reciprocity, as they only apply to nationals of other contracting parties, they have been accompanied by protocols extending the protection to refugees within the meaning of the 1951 Refugee Convention. In view of the general declaratory understanding of the term 'refugee', asylum seekers also fall under the personal scope of the conventions.

An important safeguard for asylum seekers laid down in the European Interim Agreements on Social Security is that they are entitled to equal treatment with nationals as regards contributory and non-contributory benefits in respect of employment injury, contributory benefits in respect of old age and contributory benefits payable to survivors if they are resident in the territory of any one of the contracting parties. As 'residence' is dependent on the mere lapse of time, this condition can be fulfilled by asylum seekers rather easily. With regard to all other contributory and non-contributory social security benefits, asylum seekers have to show that they are 'ordinarily resident' in the country concerned. This condition is more difficult to fulfil for asylum seekers, in view of their weak immigration status, but not impossible. In addition, with respect to non-contributory benefits, asylum seekers have to fulfil certain minimum periods of residence in the country. Even though some of these conditions may be difficult to fulfil for asylum seekers, this means that a general exclusion from social security benefits on the basis of their immigration status or absence of employment authorization is not allowed under these conventions.

A very important convention for the social position of asylum seekers is the European Convention on Social and Medical Assistance, as this is the only social security co-ordination instrument that applies to social assistance schemes. This chapter shows that asylum seekers are entitled to equal treatment with nationals if they are 'lawfully present' on the territory of one of the contracting states. As has been argued before, asylum seekers can in my view only be considered to meet this condition if they

[122] *Cf* in this regard Art 4 of the Belgian Act on the reception of asylum seekers, which provides that decisions as to the provision of reception benefits may not be related to the non-compliance of asylum seekers with their procedural obligations in the asylum procedure (*Wet betreffende de opvang van asielzoekers en van bepaalde andere categorieën van vreemdelingen*).

apply for asylum at the border and are thereupon officially admitted to the territory. This category of asylum seekers is entitled under the ECSMA to equal treatment with nationals with respect to social assistance benefits, which means that the minimum subsistence level for nationals as laid down in general social assistance schemes should be the relevant standard for the quality and level of their assistance benefits. In addition, imposing conditions that do not apply to nationals, such as conditions relating to the asylum procedure, is not in conformity with the ECSMA.

5.5 CONCLUDING REMARKS

This chapter has examined whether asylum seekers are entitled to equal treatment with nationals as regards social security and social assistance benefits under relevant social security (co-ordination) conventions. No simple answer can be given to this question, as these conventions all apply different qualifying conditions.

A common aspect of social security conventions is that if they are based on reciprocity, refugees are included in the personal scope as well. In view of the declaratory understanding of the definition of refugee in the 1951 Refugee Convention, asylum seekers also fall under the personal scope of these conventions.

With respect to (contributory and non-contributory) social insurance benefits, the general conclusion can be drawn that to exclude asylum seekers entirely from eligibility on the basis of their immigration status or absence of employment authorization is not in conformity with international social security law. Generally, in order to be entitled to equal treatment in this field, asylum seekers should meet residence or ordinary residence requirements.[123] This chapter has argued that asylum seekers may, under certain circumstances, be able to meet such requirements. Accordingly, they can only be excluded from social security benefits on the basis of their individual circumstances. If they meet the (ordinary) residence requirements, they may only be subjected to the same conditions as nationals. This means for example that if they work without employment authorization and therefore do not pay social security contributions, they have to be treated the same as nationals who work in an undeclared way.[124]

[123] Even if these qualifying conditions have not been set as a condition for equal treatment, as is the case with regard to ILO Convention no 118, asylum seekers generally have to fulfil such conditions nevertheless, as nationals are subjected to such requirements as well.

[124] Such persons are generally eligible for social security and social assistance benefits, sometimes under the condition that they pay the outstanding contributions retrospectively. See (with respect to the situation in Belgium, Canada and the Netherlands) Kapuy 2011.

Only one convention applies to social assistance benefits: the European Convention on Social and Medical Assistance. This convention provides that asylum seekers who are 'lawfully present' on the territory of one of the contracting states are entitled to equal treatment with nationals as regards social and medical assistance benefits. Asylum seekers who apply for asylum at the border and are thereupon admitted to the territory should be considered to be 'lawfully present' in this regard and therefore entitled to social assistance benefits on the same conditions as nationals. Hence, contrary to eligibility for social insurance benefits, immigration status can be the decisive factor with respect to eligibility for social assistance benefits. With regard to social assistance benefits, international social security law therefore allows a larger degree of 'convergence' between the field of immigration control and the field of social policy than with regard to social insurance benefits.

In view of the qualifying condition of 'lawful presence' with regard to social assistance benefits, and the qualifying conditions of ordinary residence and fulfilling periods of residence with regard to social insurance benefits, in practice asylum seekers will only exceptionally be entitled to equal treatment with nationals. With regard to many asylum seekers in the EU, international social security law therefore does not grant the right to equal treatment with nationals in the field of social security. The next chapter will examine whether asylum seekers can derive this right from international human rights law.

6

Non-discrimination under International Human Rights Law

6.1 INTRODUCTION

THE PREVIOUS CHAPTERS have shown that under international refugee law and international social security law, asylum seekers are only exceptionally entitled to equal treatment with nationals as regards social security benefits. In order to be entitled to equal treatment with nationals, they have to meet various qualifying conditions. With respect to social assistance, they have to be 'lawfully present' in order to be entitled to the same rights as nationals. With regard to (contributory and non-contributory) social insurance benefits, they have to meet the more factual criteria of 'residence' or 'ordinary residence'. Arguably, the Refugee Convention indicates that if the asylum procedure in first instance takes more than three years, asylum seekers should de facto be considered to fulfil these conditions. With regard to access to the labour market, asylum seekers cannot derive a right to equal treatment with nationals from international refugee and social security law. In general, it is often alleged that international human rights law, with its universal scope, provides more safeguards than the 1951 Refugee Convention, which is more limited in scope.[1] The same could be expected when comparing international human rights law with international social security law. This chapter will therefore examine whether asylum seekers are entitled to equal treatment as regards social security and access to employment under international human rights law.

To this end, section 6.2 will discuss the non-discrimination provision of the International Covenant on Economic, Social and Cultural Rights; section 6.3 will discuss the non-discrimination provisions of the European Convention on Human Rights and, finally, section 6.4 will discuss provisions on equal treatment laid down in the European Social Charter (Revised). As this chapter will show, these provisions generally fit into the

[1] See, eg, Breen 2008, p 615; Cholewinski 2000, p 713; Clark and Crépeau 1999, p 400; Edwards 2005, p 299.

'open model' of non-discrimination provisions.[2] As it has been argued in chapter three, this means that these provisions are in fact rather 'empty' norms, which have to be applied and interpreted in order to acquire a specific meaning and become functional in legal contexts. The question whether asylum seekers can derive from these broadly formulated provisions an entitlement to equal treatment with nationals in the field of social security can therefore only be answered by relying on interpretations by courts or treaty-monitoring bodies. In applying and interpreting non-discrimination provisions, these bodies enjoy a large amount of freedom in deciding, for example, whether cases are comparable and whether distinctions are reasonable. In view of this large amount of room for manoeuvre for courts and treaty-monitoring bodies, it is necessary to restrict the analysis in this chapter to decisions of courts and treaty-monitoring bodies about discrimination of non-nationals in the field of social security and employment. Indeed, research has shown that the application of the principle of equal treatment is inter alia dependent on (the combination of) the ground on which the unequal treatment is based and the context within which the distinction is made.[3] Accordingly, the question whether, and to what extent, non-nationals are entitled to equal treatment with nationals in the social security system and the labour market cannot be answered by analysing jurisprudence about the discrimination of non-nationals in other areas of law or about discrimination in the social security system or labour market on the basis of other grounds than nationality or alienage.

The discussion of the various relevant provisions on non-discrimination in this chapter will follow the same structure. After a general introduction to the text and context of the convention and the relevant provisions, the question will be examined whether non-nationals in general and asylum seekers in particular fall under the personal scope of the convention.[4] Subsequently, decisions of courts and treaty-monitoring bodies on the discrimination of aliens in the field of social security and employment will be discussed.

[2] See s 3.3.

[3] Arnardóttir 2003; Gerards 2002. Also the Committee on Economic, Social and Cultural Rights held that the nature of discrimination varies according to context (General Comment no 20 on non-discrimination in economic, social and cultural rights, adopted on 2 July 2009, para 27).

[4] In the previous chapters, it was not necessary to answer this question separately, since the provisions discussed in these chapters explicitly applied to (certain categories of) aliens.

6.2 INTERNATIONAL COVENANT ON ECONOMIC, SOCIAL AND CULTURAL RIGHTS

6.2.1 Text and Context

The International Covenant on Economic, Social and Cultural Rights (ICESCR) entered into force in 1976. The ICESCR has been ratified by 161 countries, including all EU Member States.[5]

Article 2(2) of the ICESCR states:

> The States Parties to the present Covenant undertake to guarantee that the rights enunciated in the present Covenant will be exercised without discrimination of any kind as to race, colour, sex, language, religion, political or other opinion, national or social origin, property, birth or other status.

Hence, this article does not contain a general prohibition of discrimination, but has an accessory character, as it only prohibits discrimination in the exercise of the rights laid down in the ICESCR. As the covenant contains a right to work;[6] a right to social security;[7] a right to an adequate standard of living;[8] and a right to the enjoyment of the highest attainable standard of physical and mental health,[9] the prohibition of discrimination laid down in it is very relevant for the purposes of this chapter. It is generally accepted that this accessory character does not mean that one of the substantive rights laid down in the ICESCR must actually have been violated in order to claim a violation of Article 2(2). However, the field of discrimination has to fall within the ambit of one of the rights set forth in the ICESCR. For example, if a state party decides to set up a social assistance scheme, this obviously does not violate the right to an adequate standard of living within the meaning of Article 11 of the ICESCR. However, the exclusion of, for example, all Christians from this scheme, would amount to a violation of the prohibition of discrimination on the basis of religion.[10]

Article 2(2) of the ICESCR fits into the 'open model' as it does not specify exceptions to the prohibition of discrimination. Obviously, this does not mean that it is not possible to make distinctions between different

[5] See treaties.un.org/Pages/ViewDetails.aspx?src=TREATY&mtdsg_no=IV-3&chapter=4&lang=en.

[6] ICESCR, Art 6.

[7] ICESCR, Art 9.

[8] ICESCR, Art 11.

[9] ICESCR, Art 12.

[10] *Cf* Craven 1998, pp 177–81; Sepúlveda 2003, pp 380–81; Vandenhole 2005, p 22. These authors refer to similar approaches by the Human Rights Committee and, especially, by the ECtHR.

(categories of) persons.[11] The Committee on Economic, Social and Cultural Rights (the Committee) held in its General Comment on non-discrimination that differential treatment based on prohibited grounds will be viewed as discriminatory unless the justification for differentiation is reasonable and objective.[12] According to the Committee, this will

> include an assessment as to whether the aim and effects of the measures or omissions are legitimate, compatible with the nature of the covenant rights and solely for the purpose of promoting the general welfare in a democratic society. In addition, there must be a clear and reasonable relationship of proportionality between the aim sought to be realized and the measures or omissions and their effects.

These criteria bear a strong resemblance to the criteria used in Article 4 of the ICESCR; the general limitation rule of the covenant.[13] In addition, the Committee addressed one possible justification ground: unavailability of resources. In the Committee's opinion,

> a failure to remove differential treatment on the basis of a lack of available resources is not an objective and reasonable justification unless every effort has been made to use all resources that are at the State party's disposition in an effort to address and eliminate the discrimination, as a matter of priority.

Although the rights set forth in the ICESCR are subject to progressive realization and to available resources, the Committee has indicated that the prohibition of discrimination is not subject to these conditions and applies fully and immediately.[14] As Sepúlveda argues, this interpretation finds support in the specific wording used in Article 2(2) ('to guarantee') and in its position within the covenant (in Part II).[15] The rather strict justification test under Article 2(2) with regard to unavailability of resources as applied by the Committee in its General Comment on non-discrimination is convincing in this light.

Article 2(2) of the ICESCR does not use the wording 'on any ground/ of any kind *such as*'. This implies that the grounds enumerated in Article 2(2) of the ICESCR are exhaustive. However, the last-mentioned ground in

[11] This is confirmed by the fact that during the drafting of the covenant, the word 'distinction', which was originally used in Art 2(2) of the ICESCR, was replaced with the word 'discrimination', in order to indicate that some distinctions might be justified (Ramcharan 1981, pp 258–59; Sepúlveda 2003, p 383).

[12] General Comment no 20 on non-discrimination in economic, social and cultural rights, adopted on 2 July 2009, para 13.

[13] See ch 10 for an extensive discussion of this provision.

[14] General Comment no 3 on the nature of states parties obligations, adopted on 14 December 1990, para 1; General Comment no 20 on non-discrimination in economic, social and cultural rights, adopted on 2 July 2009, para 7. See also General Comment no 13 on the right to education, adopted on 8 December 1999, para 31.

[15] Sepúlveda 2003, p 396.

this article is 'other status', which can have an open-ended meaning.[16] The Committee has interpreted 'other status' broadly and held that the inclusion of 'other status' indicates that this list is not exhaustive and other grounds may be incorporated in this category.[17] Nevertheless, as Krause and Scheinin observe: '[T]he fact that many of the explicitly mentioned prohibited grounds relate to inborn characteristics or other factors beyond the free choice by the affected person, may be relevant in the interpretation of what features may count as "other status"'.[18]

6.2.2 Application to Aliens

The ICESCR does not contain an explicit reference to the personal and territorial scope. The Committee generally takes the position in its general comments that the covenant applies to 'everyone under the jurisdiction' of the contracting parties.[19] This implies that the covenant applies to aliens as well. Another indication of this can be found in Article 2(3) of the ICESCR, which states: 'Developing countries, with due regard to human rights and their national economy, may determine to what extent they would guarantee the economic rights recognized in the present Covenant to non-nationals'.

This exception for developing countries, which was laid down in the covenant in order to end the domination of certain groups of non-nationals during colonial times,[20] implies (*a contrario*) that *developed* countries should guarantee all the rights set forth in the covenant to non-nationals as well. In General Comment no 20 on non-discrimination, the Committee explicitly held that, without prejudice to the application of Article 2(3) of the ICESCR, the covenant rights apply to everyone including non-nationals, 'such as refugees, asylum-seekers, stateless persons, migrant workers and victims of international trafficking, regardless of legal status and

[16] Craven 1998, p 168; Sepúlveda 2003, p 391.

[17] General Comment no 20 on non-discrimination in economic, social and cultural rights, adopted on 2 July 2009, para 15.

[18] Krause and Scheinin 2000, p 258.

[19] See, eg, General Comment no 12 on the right to adequate food, adopted on 12 May 1999, para 14; General Comment no 14 on the highest attainable standard of health, adopted on 11 August 2000, para 12; General Comment no 18 on the right to work, adopted on 24 November 2005, para 12. In General Comment no 19 on the right to social security, adopted on 23 November 2007, para 36 the Committee stated that 'the Covenant contains no express jurisdictional limitation'. Accordingly, the Committee widened the application of the covenant to individuals outside the jurisdiction of contracting states. However, this statement was made with regard to the social security rights of non-nationals who have contributed to a social security scheme and who have subsequently left the country. Arguably, this widening of the scope of the covenant applies only in this special situation.

[20] Sepúlveda 2003, pp 414–15.

documentation'.[21] Hence, the absence of a limitation *ratione personae* in the covenant for developed countries, in combination with the approach of the Committee, indicates that the provisions of the ICESCR generally apply to everyone, including aliens, under the jurisdiction of a state party.

6.2.3 Interpretation

Since the Optional Protocol to the ICESCR only entered into force on 5 May 2013, the Committee has, at the time of writing, not yet issued views on individual complaints. It has, however, issued a number of 'general comments' relevant to the issue of equal treatment of aliens with nationals in the field of social security.

In its General Comment on non-discrimination, the Committee mentioned nationality as one of the grounds falling under the forbidden ground of discrimination of 'other status'. In general comments on substantive rights, the Committee sometimes pays separate attention to the requirement of non-discrimination and equal treatment, whereby its approach differs depending on the right at stake and (sometimes) on the category of aliens. For example, with regard to the right to water, the Committee states very clearly: 'Refugees and asylum-seekers should be granted the right to water on the same conditions as granted to nationals'.[22]

In its General Comment on the highest attainable standard of health, the Committee does not pay separate attention to the position of aliens when considering the prohibition of discrimination. It merely states in general that

> [s]tates have a special obligation to provide those who do not have sufficient means with the necessary health insurance and health-care facilities, and to prevent any discrimination *on internationally prohibited grounds* in the provision of health care and health services, especially with respect to the core obligations of the right to health.[23]

Also, in its general comments on the right to adequate food and on the right to adequate housing, the Committee does not pay attention to discrimination on the basis of nationality.[24]

[21] General Comment no 20 on non-discrimination in economic, social and cultural rights, adopted on 2 July 2009, para 30.

[22] General Comment no 15 on the right to water, adopted on 20 January 2003, para 16.

[23] General Comment no 14 on the highest attainable standard of health, adopted on 11 August 2000, para 19 (emphasis added).

[24] General Comment no 12 on the right to adequate food, adopted in 1999 and General Comment no 4 on the right to adequate housing, adopted in 1991.

In its General Comment on the right to work, the Committee does consider the principle of non-discrimination as regards non-nationals, albeit not extensively. It only states in general that this principle, 'as set out in article 2.2 of the Covenant and in article 7 of the International Convention on the Protection of the Rights of All Migrant Workers and Members of Their Families should apply in relation to employment opportunities for migrant workers and their families' and underlines in this regard 'the need for national plans of action to be devised to respect and promote such principles by all appropriate measures, legislative or otherwise'.[25] In addition, it held that states parties should refrain 'from denying or limiting equal access to decent work for all persons, especially disadvantaged and marginalized individuals and groups, including (…) migrant workers'.[26] When referring in other places to the prohibition of discrimination as regards access to the labour market, the Committee does not explicitly refer to the prohibited ground of nationality or immigration status.[27] The Committee does not define the term 'migrant worker' and does not pay attention to possible justifications for unequal treatment. The reference to the International Convention on the Protection of the Rights of All Migrant Workers and Members of Their Families (ICPRMW) might indicate that the Committee intends to adopt the same approach to equal treatment of migrant workers as under this, more specialized, convention. The principle of non-discrimination laid down in the ICPRMW only applies to the rights set forth in the convention and the ICPRMW does not entitle migrant workers to access the labour market. Arguably, then, such a right does not result from the prohibition of discrimination laid down in the ICESCR, either.

In its General Comment on the right to social security, the Committee applies the most elaborate approach to nationality discrimination. It first confirms that Article 2(2) of the ICESCR prohibits discrimination on grounds of nationality.[28] It then distinguishes between contributory and non-contributory social security schemes. The Committee defines non-contributory schemes as 'universal schemes (which provide the relevant benefit in principle to everyone who experiences a particular risk or contingency) or targeted social assistance schemes (where benefits are received by those in a situation of need)'.[29] Hence, the general comment is not restricted to social insurance schemes, but applies to the complete

[25] General Comment no 18 on the right to work, adopted on 24 November 2005, para 18.
[26] Ibid, para 23.
[27] See, eg, paras 12 and 33 of General Comment no 18.
[28] General Comment no 19 on the right to social security, adopted on 23 November 2007, para 36.
[29] Ibid, para 4.

field of social security, as understood in this book.[30] With respect to contributory schemes, the Committee merely states as a general rule that non-nationals who have contributed to the scheme should be able to benefit from that contribution or retrieve their contributions if they leave the country.[31] With regard to non-contributory schemes, the Committee states:

> Non-nationals should be able to access non-contributory schemes for income support, affordable access to health care and family support. Any restrictions, including a qualification period, must be proportionate and reasonable. All persons, irrespective of their nationality, residency or immigration status, are entitled to primary and emergency medical care.[32]

Hence, non-nationals should in general be able to access non-contributory schemes for income support, affordable access to health care and family support. However, the language of the Committee ('should be able to access') is particularly prudent. In addition, restrictions as regards access are possible, so long as they are proportionate and reasonable. With regard to primary and emergency medical care, the language of the Committee is much stronger as it clearly lays down a right ('entitled to') to it. In addition, the Committee states explicitly that entitlement should exist irrespective of immigration status.

The Committee further pays separate attention to the access of refugees and asylum seekers to non-contributory schemes. It states:

> Refugees, stateless persons and asylum-seekers, and other disadvantaged and marginalized individuals and groups, should enjoy equal treatment in access to non-contributory social security schemes, including reasonable access to health care and family support, consistent with international standards.[33]

In a footnote, the Committee explains the term 'international standards' by referring to Articles 23 and 24 of the convention relating to the Status of Refugees and the Convention relating to the Status of Stateless Persons.[34]

Hence, at first sight, the Committee seems to be of the opinion that asylum seekers should have a stronger claim to non-contributory schemes than non-nationals in general, as it pays separate attention to this category of non-nationals; as it speaks of 'other disadvantaged and marginalized individuals and groups'; as it uses the wording 'should enjoy equal treatment in access to' instead of 'should be able to access'; and as it does not refer to restrictions. However, at the same time, the Committee

[30] See ch 1 for the definition of social security for the purposes of this book.

[31] General Comment no 19 on the right to social security, adopted on 23 November 2007, para 36.

[32] Ibid, para 37.

[33] Ibid, para 38.

[34] Ibid, fn 30.

states that asylum seekers should enjoy equal treatment 'consistent with international standards', whereby it refers to Articles 23 and 24 of the Refugee Convention. It seems therefore that the prohibition of discrimination laid down in the ICESCR does not require more, in terms of rights for asylum seekers, than what has been provided for in other international standards in general and the Refugee Convention in particular. Articles 23 and 24 of the Refugee Convention prescribe that refugees should be accorded the same treatment as is accorded to nationals with regard to public relief and assistance and with regard to social security. However, these provisions only apply to refugees who are 'lawfully staying' in the host country. As has been argued in section 4.8, this qualifying condition generally cannot be met by asylum seekers. Hence, to provide refugees and asylum seekers with equal access to non-contributory schemes only once they are 'lawfully staying' in the country is consistent with 'international standards' and therefore, arguably, with the prohibition of discrimination laid down in the ICESCR as well.

6.2.4 Analysis

In its General Comment on the right to social security, the Committee has applied the general prohibition of discrimination to the position of non-nationals. Accordingly, it has applied and interpreted the 'empty' norm of non-discrimination in the context of social security, in the performance of which it has a large amount of freedom.[35] In applying this provision, the Committee distinguishes between contributory benefits and non-contributory benefits. In doing so, the Committee seems to be inspired by international social security law,[36] although it does not refer to such instruments explicitly. The Committee seems to be of the opinion that for certain distinctions between nationals and non-nationals in the field of social security, no justification is possible. This is true for the treatment of non-nationals as regards contributory social security schemes, provided that they have contributed to such schemes. The Committee has not commented upon the exclusion of non-nationals from access (and hence from the possibility to contribute) to such schemes. As regards non-contributory schemes, the general rule seems to be that distinctions between nationals and non-nationals are possible, provided that they are proportionate and reasonable. With regard to refugees and asylum seekers, such restrictions seem to be justified only if they are consistent with international standards, in particular the Refugee Convention. As the

[35] See s 3.3.
[36] See ch 5.

Refugee Convention accords the right to equal treatment with nationals only to refugees 'lawfully staying' in the territory, the exclusion of asylum seekers from non-contributory benefits schemes on the ground that they are not staying lawfully on the territory seems to be consistent with Article 2(2) of the ICESCR.

As regards access to employment, it is remarkable that the Committee does not list asylum seekers or refugees under the category of disadvantaged and marginalized groups, whereas it explicitly includes them in these groups in its General Comment on the right to social security. This raises the question whether the Committee is of the opinion that refugees and asylum seekers are not entitled to equal access to the labour market. The Committee does refer explicitly to migrant workers as regards access to the labour market. The reference to the ICPRMW might indicate, however, that the same approach with respect to access to employment should be adopted under both instruments, which would mean that migrant workers are not entitled to equal access to the labour market as nationals.

6.3 EUROPEAN CONVENTION ON HUMAN RIGHTS

6.3.1 Text and Context

The Convention for the Protection of Human Rights and Fundamental Freedoms (European Convention on Human Rights, ECHR) was opened for signature in 1950 and entered into force in 1953. The ECHR has been ratified by all Member States of the Council of Europe (and, accordingly, by all EU Member States).

Article 14 of the ECHR reads:

> The enjoyment of the rights and freedoms set forth in this Convention shall be secured without discrimination on any ground such as sex, race, colour, language, religion, political or other opinion, national or social origin, association with a national minority, property, birth or other status.

The text of this provision has a number of important implications. First of all, the words 'on any ground such as' show that the list of grounds of discrimination set out in Article 14 is 'illustrative and not exhaustive'.[37] This means that, in principle, all kinds of inequalities or distinctions may fall under the scope of this article. Nevertheless, the Court has ruled that 'Article 14 prohibits, within the ambit of the rights and freedoms guaranteed, discriminatory treatment having as its basis or reason a personal characteristic ("status") by which persons or groups of persons are

[37] This is explicitly affirmed by the Court in *Engel and Others v the Netherlands* app no 5100/71 et al (ECtHR, 8 June 1976), para 72.

distinguishable from each other'.[38] Some connection between the ground of discrimination and a characteristic of a person or a group therefore seems necessary in order for Article 14 to be applicable. However, as Gerards notes, this requirement is interpreted very broadly and is not consistently applied by the Court.[39] Indeed, the Court held that it does not have to be an innate or inherent characteristic.[40] Another relevant aspect of the ground on which the discrimination is based seems to be the extent to which this ground can be changed as a matter of choice. In the case of *Carson and Others v United Kingdom*[41] the Court held that

> ordinary residence, like domicile and nationality, is to be seen as an aspect of personal status and that the place of residence applied as a criterion for the different treatment of citizens in the grant of State pensions is a ground falling within the scope of Article 14.[42]

Nevertheless, it also held that as the place of residence is 'a characteristic which can be changed as a matter of choice', individuals do not require the same level of protection against differences in treatment based on this ground as is needed in relation to differences based on an 'inherent characteristic, such as gender or racial or ethnic origin'.[43]

Secondly, the provision does not indicate what forms of differential treatment constitute 'discrimination'. The French-language version even states '*sans distinction aucune*'. As has been argued before, to prohibit all kinds of inequalities would lead to unreasonable results.[44] This is affirmed by the Court in the *Belgian Linguistic case*, the first case on Article 14. The Court held:

> In spite of the very general wording of the French version ('sans distinction aucune'), Article 14 does not forbid every difference in treatment in the exercise of the rights and freedoms recognised. This version must be read in the light of the more restrictive text of the English version ('without discrimination'). In addition, and in particular, one would reach absurd results were one to give Article 14 an interpretation as wide as that which the French version seems to imply. One would, in effect, be led to judge as contrary to the Convention every one of the many legal or administrative provisions which do not secure

[38] *Kjeldsen, Busk Madsen and Pedersen v Denmark* app nos 5095/71; 5920/72; 5926/ (ECtHR, 7 December 1976), 2, para 56. See also *Kafkaris v Cyprus* app no 21906/04 (ECtHR, 12 February 2008), para 160.

[39] Gerards 2004a, p 10.

[40] *Clift v United Kingdom* app no 7205/07 (ECtHR, 13 July 2010), para 59.

[41] App no 42184/05 (ECtHR, 4 November 2008).

[42] Ibid, para 76.

[43] Ibid, para 80. This aspect therefore has consequences for the scope of the margin of appreciation, see further below. It is questionable whether the possibility to change the place of residence as a matter of choice also applies to refugees (see *Bah v United Kingdom* app no 56328/07 (ECtHR, 27 September 2011)).

[44] See s 3.2.

> to everyone complete equality of treatment in the enjoyment of the rights and freedoms recognised.[45]

Hence, the Court had to develop criteria on the basis of which it can be determined whether or not a given difference in treatment contravenes Article 14 of the ECHR. The Court has identified such criteria already in the *Belgian Linguistic* case. In the case of *Burden v United Kingdom* the Court summarizes these criteria as follows:

> The Court has established in its case-law that in order for an issue to arise under Article 14 there must be a difference in the treatment of persons in relevantly similar situations (…). Such a difference of treatment is discriminatory if it has no objective and reasonable justification; in other words, if it does not pursue a legitimate aim or if there is not a reasonable relationship of proportionality between the means employed and the aim sought to be realised. The Contracting State enjoys a margin of appreciation in assessing whether and to what extent differences in otherwise similar situations justify a different treatment.[46]

Thus, in order to give rise to a violation of Article 14 the following criteria have to be met:

- — persons in relevantly similar situations have to be treated differently (on the basis of a personal characteristic); and
- — no objective and reasonable justification for this difference in treatment should exist, which means:
  - — the difference in treatment does not pursue a legitimate aim; or
  - — there is not a reasonable relationship of proportionality between the means employed and the aim sought to be realized.

With regard to the first criterion, it should be noted that the Court skips this 'comparability test' in many cases,[47] while in other cases the Court only mentions this test, without applying it in substance. In addition, the Court often merges this test into the justification test by treating the discussion of analogous situations as an aspect of justification.[48] The

[45] *Belgian Linguistic* case app no 1474/62 et al (ECtHR, 23 July 1968), para 10.

[46] *Burden v United Kingdom* app no 13378/05 (ECtHR, 29 April 2008), para 60. See also *Andrejeva v Latvia* app no 55707/00 (ECtHR, 18 February 2009), para 81; *Stec and others v United Kingdom* app nos 65731/01 and 65900/01 (ECtHR, 12 April 2006), para 51.

[47] The Court often skips this test in cases of 'suspect classifications' requiring 'very weighty reasons', such as gender, nationality and sexual orientation (see further below). In these cases, comparability is apparently assumed. (Van Dijk et al 2006, p 1038, fn 36; Gerards 2004a, pp 22–23).

[48] Van Dijk et al 2006, pp 1036–39; Gerards 2004a, pp 22–26. According to Arnardóttir, while it may be argued that the comparability test and the justification test are two distinct tests, it may also be argued that the comparability test is not a distinct test, but merely a 'concrete expression of one of the viable justifications under Article 14 objective and reasonable justification test' (Arnardóttir 2003, pp 53–54). Also Schokkenbroek states that 'the question of whether or not persons or groups are in comparable situations may itself

'comparability test' is sometimes replaced by a 'test of disadvantage', which means that the Court examines whether it is sufficiently established that the applicant is actually disadvantaged by the difference in treatment.[49] If this is not the case, then the Member State does not have to give a justification for the difference in treatment.

The Court allows the states parties a margin of appreciation in assessing whether and to what extent differences in otherwise similar situations justify a different treatment. The scope of this margin will vary according to the 'circumstances, the subject matter and its background'.[50] In this respect, one of the relevant factors may be 'the existence or non-existence of common ground between the laws of the Contracting States'.[51] Other relevant factors in establishing the scope of the margin of appreciation include the ground on which the discrimination is based and the context or policy field in which the distinctions are made.[52]

Thirdly, the wording 'the enjoyment of the rights and freedoms set forth in this convention' implies that Article 14 does not have an autonomous character, but is accessory to other articles of the ECHR. It only protects against discrimination if there is a relationship with one of the substantive provisions of the convention (or of the First, Fourth, Sixth, Seventh or Thirteenth Protocol[53]). The Court has applied a flexible approach to this accessory aspect of Article 14. It usually states:

> According to the Court's established case-law, Article 14 complements the other substantive provisions of the Convention and the Protocols. It has no independent existence since it has effect solely in relation to 'the enjoyment of the rights and freedoms' safeguarded by those provisions. Although the application of Article 14 does not necessarily presuppose a breach of those provisions—and to this extent it is autonomous—there can be no room for its application unless the facts at issue fall within the ambit of one or more of the latter.[54]

require a delicate assessment (*appréciation*) of the circumstances of the case, and it may be difficult to draw the borderline between such assessments and those required under the proportionality test' (Schokkenbroek 1998, p 23). See also O'Connell 2009, pp 218–19 and 228.

[49] Van Dijk et al 2006, p 1039; Gerards 2004a, pp 26–28.

[50] *Andrejeva v Latvia* (n 46), para 82.

[51] *Rasmussen v Denmark* app no 8777/79 (ECtHR, 28 November 1984), para 40; *Petrovic v Austria* app no 20458/92 (ECtHR, 27 March 1998), para 38; *SL v Austria* app no 45330/99 (ECtHR, 9 January 2003), para 41.

[52] See s 6.3.3 below.

[53] These protocols provide that all the provisions of the convention apply to them (Art 5 of Protocol no 1; Art 6(1) of Protocol no 4; Art 6 of Protocol no 6; Art 7 of Protocol no 7 and Art 5 of Protocol no 13).

[54] *Rasmussen v Denmark* (n 51), para 29. See also (amongst others) *Abdulaziz, Cabales and Balkandali v United Kingdom* app nos 9214/80; 9473/81; 9474/81 (ECtHR, 28 May 1985), para 71; *Burden v United Kingdom* (n 46), para 58.

This means that in order for Article 14 to be applicable in a certain case, it is sufficient that the facts of the case fall within 'the ambit' of one of the substantive provisions of the ECHR and its protocols. As a breach of those provisions is not required, Article 14 has an autonomous meaning. It

> extends beyond the enjoyment of the rights and freedoms which the Convention and Protocols require each State to guarantee. It applies also to those additional rights, falling within the general scope of any Article of the Convention, for which the State has voluntarily decided to provide.[55]

The flexible approach to the accessory aspect of Article 14 is also shown by the broad interpretations by the Court of the 'general scope' of the articles of the ECHR. In the case of *Petrovic v Austria*, on alleged discrimination with regard to the granting of parental leave allowance, the Court held for example that 'by granting parental leave allowance States are able to demonstrate their respect for family life within the meaning of Article 8 of the Convention', as a result of which the allowance comes within the scope of that provision, according to the Court.[56]

On 1 April 2005, Protocol no 12 to the ECHR entered into force. It has been ratified by seven EU Member States.[57] Article 1 of this protocol reads:

> 1. The enjoyment of any right set forth by law shall be secured without discrimination on any ground such as sex, race, colour, language, religion, political or other opinion, national or social origin, association with a national minority, property, birth or other status.
> 2. No one shall be discriminated against by any public authority on any ground such as those mentioned in paragraph 1.

The most important difference from Article 14 of the ECHR is that this provision contains an autonomous prohibition of discrimination. It therefore 'affords a scope of protection which extends beyond the "enjoyment of the rights and freedoms set forth in [the] Convention".'[58]

The Court has made clear that Article 1 of Protocol no 12 extends the scope of protection not only to 'any right set forth by law', as the text of paragraph 1 might suggest, but beyond that. This follows in particular from paragraph 2, according to the Court.[59] The Court referred in this respect to the explanatory report on Article 1 of Protocol no 12, which

[55] *Stec and others v United Kingdom* app nos 65731/01/and 65900/01 (ECtHR, 6 July 2005), para 40; *Carson and others v United Kingdom* (n 41), para 70; *Andrejeva v Latvia* (n 46), para 74.

[56] App no 20458/92 (ECtHR 27, March 1998), para 29.

[57] conventions.coe.int/Treaty/Commun/ChercheSig.asp?NT=177&CM=&DF=&CL=ENG.

[58] Explanatory report to Protocol no 12, para 21.

[59] *Savez crkava 'Riječ života' and Others v Croatia* app no 7798/08 (ECtHR, 9 December 2010), para 104.

states that the scope of protection of that article concerns four categories of cases, in particular where a person is discriminated against:

i. in the enjoyment of any right specifically granted to an individual under national law;
ii. in the enjoyment of a right which may be inferred from a clear obligation of a public authority under national law, that is, where a public authority is under an obligation under national law to behave in a particular manner;
iii. by a public authority in the exercise of discretionary power (for example, granting certain subsidies);
iv. by any other act or omission by a public authority (for example, the behaviour of law enforcement officers when controlling a riot).[60]

Hence, Article 1 of Protocol no 12 is not only applicable to legislative acts, but also to all other acts and exercise of power by public authorities. According to Gerards, however, most situations mentioned in the four categories are already covered by Article 14 of the ECHR. According to her, the main difference between Article 14 of the ECHR and Article 1 of Protocol no 1 is that four categories of government behaviour have now expressly been named by the explanatory report and that the material scope is formulated more clearly in the two different paragraphs of the latter article.[61]

The meaning of the term 'discrimination' in Article 1 is intended to be identical to that in Article 14 of the ECHR, ie unjustified unequal treatment.[62] Also, the list of non-discrimination grounds is identical to that in Article 14 of the ECHR. According to the explanatory report:

> This solution was considered preferable over others, such as expressly including certain additional non-discrimination grounds (for example, physical or mental disability, sexual orientation or age), not because of a lack of awareness that such grounds have become particularly important in today's societies as compared with the time of drafting of Article 14 of the Convention, but because such an inclusion was considered unnecessary from a legal point of view since the list of non-discrimination grounds is not exhaustive, and because inclusion of any particular additional ground might give rise to unwarranted *a contrario* interpretations as regards discrimination based on grounds not so included.[63]

Accordingly, the expectation was that, with the exception of the accessory character of Article 14, the analytical approach of the Court with regard to Article 14 would be more or less the same with regard to Article 1 of Protocol no 12.[64] In December 2009 the Court delivered its first judgment

[60] Ibid.
[61] Gerards 2008b.
[62] Explanatory report to Protocol no 12, para 18.
[63] Ibid, para 20.
[64] Arnardóttir 2003, pp 40–41; Gerards 2008b.

on Article 1 of Protocol no 12.[65] This judgment confirmed the expectation with respect to the limited additional protection that Article 1 of Protocol no 12 would offer alongside the protection offered by Article 14.[66]

To conclude, this section shows that Article 14 of the ECHR and Article 1 of Protocol no 12 fit in the open model of discrimination clauses. Consequently, the Court had to come up with an interpretation of the concept of discrimination. The Court has developed an extensive analytical framework for examining complaints under this article. Below, how the Court applies this framework with regard to discrimination of aliens in the field of social security and employment will be examined. First, the question has to be answered whether Article 14 of the ECHR and Article 1 of Protocol no 12 apply to (all categories of) aliens.

6.3.2 Application to Aliens

Article 1 of the ECHR reads:

> The High Contracting Parties shall secure to everyone within their jurisdiction the rights and freedoms defined in Section I of this Convention.

The wording 'everyone within their jurisdiction' implies that all persons who are subject to the jurisdiction of a contracting state are protected by the rights laid down in the convention, irrespective of their nationality or place of residence.[67] The Court held in the case of *Banković and others v Belgium and 16 other contracting states:* 'as to the "ordinary meaning" of the relevant term in Article 1 of the convention, the Court is satisfied that, from the standpoint of public international law, the jurisdictional competence of a State is primarily territorial'.[68] The Court finds confirmation for this 'essentially territorial notion of jurisdiction' in the preparatory material of the convention.[69] Accordingly, persons on the territory of a state are 'clearly within its jurisdiction'.[70]

The term 'territory' should be interpreted broadly. The judgment of the Court in the case of *Amuur v France* shows that the ECHR is also

[65] *Sejdić and Finci v Bosnia and Herzegovina* app nos 27996/06 and 34836/06 (ECtHR, 22 December 2009).

[66] The Court held that the notions of discrimination prohibited by Art 14 and by Art 1 of Protocol no 12 are to be interpreted in the same manner (paras 55–56). In the case of *Savez crkava 'Riječ života' and Others v Croatia*, the Court did not find it necessary to examine the complaint under Art 1 of Protocol no 12, after it had already found a violation of Art 14 taken together with Art 9 of the convention ((n 59), paras 114–15).

[67] Van Dijk et al 2006, pp 13–4.

[68] *Banković and others v Belgium and 16 other contracting states* app no 52207/99 (ECtHR, 12 December 2001), para 59.

[69] Ibid, para 63.

[70] Ibid, para 68.

applicable to aliens who are refused leave to enter the territory and who are held in transit zones of airports.[71] The Court held that despite its name the international zone of Paris-Orly Airport 'does not have extraterritorial status'.[72]

Hence, the ECHR is applicable to all persons (including aliens) within or at the border of the territory of contracting states.[73]

6.3.3 Interpretation

The Court has not delivered any judgments or decisions on equal treatment of aliens and nationals as regards access to the labour market.[74] As regards access to social security benefits, the Court has delivered a number of relevant judgments on the discrimination of aliens. This section will discuss these judgments. These judgments all concern the application of Article 14; the Court has not yet delivered a judgment on the application of Article 1 of Protocol no 12 to discrimination of aliens in the field of nationality. A distinction will be made between the question of applicability of Article 14 and the question of compliance with Article 14.

Applicability of Article 14

As has been mentioned above, in order for Article 14 to be applicable, the facts of the case have to fall within 'the ambit' of one of the substantive provisions of the convention or its protocols. While neither the ECHR nor its protocols contain a right to social security, the Court has ruled that the right to social security benefits can fall within the ambit of Articles 2, 3, 8 and Article 1 of the First Protocol.

[71] *Amuur v France* app no 19776/92 (ECtHR, 25 June 1996).

[72] Ibid, para 52.

[73] The question whether the convention can under certain circumstances also be applicable to persons outside the territory of contracting states will not be discussed here. See in this regard: Spijkerboer and Vermeulen 2005, pp 81–83; Van Dijk et al 2006, pp 13–17 and, especially, Den Heijer 2012. In addition, the convention might be applicable to acts of organs of contracting states that have been committed outside their territory (see Van Dijk et al 2006, pp 19–23).

[74] The only relevant case in this regard seems to the case of *Coorplan-Jenni GESMBH and Elvir Hascic v Austria*. In this case, the applicant complained under Art 14 of the ECHR about the Austrian authorities' refusal to grant him an employment permit. The Court decided that the complaint was incompatible *ratione materiae* with the provisions of the convention, as the complaint did not fall within the ambit of Art 8, as a result of which Art 14 was not applicable. The Court held in this regard that the refusal of the work permit did not affect the possibility of the foreigner involved to pursue a professional activity to such a significant degree that there are consequential effects on the enjoyment of his right to respect for his 'private life' within the meaning of Art 8 of the ECHR (app no 10523/02, ECtHR, 24 February 2005 (dec)). See on the meaning of Art 8 of the ECHR for access to the labour market further ch 11.

The most important article with regard to the right to social security benefits is Article 1 of Protocol no 1, which guarantees the protection of property. The Court has stated that this article does not place a restriction on the state's freedom to decide whether or not to have in place any form of social security scheme, or to choose the type or amount of benefits to provide under any such scheme. But, it continued:

> If, however, a Contracting State has in force legislation providing for the payment as of right of a welfare benefit (...) that legislation must be regarded as generating a pecuniary interest falling within the ambit of Article 1 of Protocol No. 1 for persons satisfying its requirements.[75]

In the case of *Gaygusuz v Austria*, the Court ruled for the first time that the right to social security benefits falls within the scope of Article 1 of Protocol no 1.[76] This judgment did not, however, make very clear whether a link between payment of contributions and entitlement to the benefit is necessary in order for the benefit to be protected by Article 1 of the First Protocol,[77] as a result of which two distinct lines of authority can be identified in later case law.[78] The Court put an end to this ambiguity in the case of *Stec and Others v United Kingdom*, in which it held that a distinction between contributory and non-contributory benefits for the purposes of the applicability of Article 1 of Protocol no 1 is no longer justified, as the Court's approach to Article 1 of Protocol no 1 should reflect the reality of the way in which the provision of welfare is currently organized within the contracting states.[79] According to the Court, it is clear that in most states:

> Benefits are funded in a large variety of ways: some are paid for by contributions to a specific fund; some depend on a claimant's contribution record; many are paid for out of general taxation on the basis of a statutorily defined status. (...) Given the variety of funding methods, and the interlocking nature of benefits under most welfare systems, it appears increasingly artificial to hold that only benefits financed by contributions to a specific fund fall within the scope of Article 1 of Protocol No. 1. Moreover, to exclude benefits paid for out of general taxation would be to disregard the fact that many claimants under this latter type of system also contribute to its financing, through the payment of tax.[80]

[75] *Stec and others v United Kingdom* (n 55), para 54; *Andrejeva v Latvia* (n 46), para 77.

[76] *Gaygusuz v Austria* app no 17371/90 (ECtHR, 16 September 1996).

[77] While the Court first noted that the entitlement to emergency assistance was linked to the payment of contributions to the unemployment insurance fund (para 39), it subsequently stated that Art 1 of Protocol no 1 was applicable 'without it being necessary to rely solely on the link between entitlement to emergency assistance and the obligation to pay "taxes or other contributions"' (para 41). See also Vonk 2000.

[78] Kapuy 2007, p 227.

[79] *Stec and others v United Kingdom* (n 55), para 53.

[80] Ibid, para 50.

The Court continued by stating that '[w]here an individual has an assertable right under domestic law to a welfare benefit, the importance of that interest should also be reflected by holding Article 1 of Protocol no 1 to be applicable'.[81] Hence, whereas Article 1 of Protocol no 1 does not require states to develop social security schemes, if states have in place schemes providing for the payment *as of right* of a welfare benefit, Article 1 of Protocol no 1 and, consequently, Article 14 of the ECHR are applicable. It is not relevant whether (contributory or non-contributory) social security schemes in the strict sense or social assistance schemes are at stake; the relevant test is whether an assertable right to the benefit concerned exists. In such cases, Article 1 of Protocol no 1 is applicable if people are denied all or part of a particular benefit as well as if people are denied *access to* particular social security schemes.[82]

Case law shows that certain kinds of social security benefits fall under the scope of other articles of the ECHR as well. The Court has, for example, accepted that certain social security benefits that promote family life, such as child benefits or parental leave allowances, fall within the ambit of Article 8 of the ECHR.[83] Also insufficient (or denial of) public funding of health care can under certain circumstances fall under the scope of Article 8.[84] In addition,

> an issue may arise under Article 2 where it is shown that the authorities of a Contracting State put an individual's life at risk through the denial of health care which they have undertaken to make available to the population generally.[85]

Finally, the Court held that 'a complaint about a wholly insufficient amount of pension and the other social benefits may, in principle, raise an issue under Article 3 of the Convention which prohibits inhuman or degrading treatment'.[86]

Hence, Article 14 of the ECHR will generally be applicable in the case of alleged discrimination in contributory or non-contributory social insurance or social assistance schemes providing benefits as of right or with regard to discrimination in providing health care which is available to the population generally. Accordingly, even before the coming into force of

[81] Ibid, para 51.

[82] See the admissibility decision in the case of *Luczak v Poland* (app no 77782/01, ECtHR, 27 March 2007).

[83] *Petrovic v Austria* (n 51), para 29; *Niedzwiecki v Germany* app no 58453/00 (ECtHR, 25 October 2005), para 31 and *Okpisz v Germany* app no 59140/00 (ECtHR, 25 October 2005), para 32.

[84] *Pentiacova and 48 Others v Moldova* app no 14462/03 (ECtHR, 4 January 2005 (dec)).

[85] *Cyprus v Turkey* app no 25781/94 (ECtHR, 10 May 2001), para 219; *Pentiacova and 48 Others v Moldova* (n 84).

[86] *Larioshina v Russia* app no 56869/00 (ECtHR, 23 April 2002 (dec)); *Kutepov and Anikeyenko v Russia* app no 68029/01 (ECtHR, 25 October 2005), para 62.

Protocol no 12, the Court has made it possible to bring almost any claim of discrimination in the field of social security before the Court.

Compliance with Article 14

This subsection will discuss relevant case law on discrimination on grounds of nationality and immigration status as regards social security benefits.[87] Attention will also be paid to case law on discrimination on these grounds as regards social benefits closely related to social security, such as education and social housing, as these cases contain relevant observations of a general nature and explicitly refer to case law on social security benefits. The various cases discussed here will be analysed for their relevance with respect to the position of asylum seekers in more depth in section 6.3.4 below.

In the case of *Gaygusuz v Austria*[88] the Court examined for the first time a complaint of discrimination against aliens in the field of social security. This case concerned an application by a Turkish national for an allowance under the Austrian unemployment emergency assistance scheme. This application was rejected exclusively on the ground that he did not have Austrian nationality and did not fall within any of the categories exempted from that condition. The Court deals with the case in a strikingly short way.[89] After determining that Article 14 is applicable in this case (in conjunction with Article 1 of Protocol no 1), the Court holds that the ground of distinction in this case is nationality, which is covered by Article 14. The Court observes that the contracting states enjoy a certain margin of appreciation, but adds that 'very weighty reasons would have to be put forward before the Court could regard a difference of treatment based exclusively on the ground of nationality as compatible with the Convention'. The Court applies this 'very weighty reasons test' for the first time to the ground of nationality in this case, without providing any reasons for doing so. The wording 'very weighty reasons' implies that the justification put forward by contracting states must meet more stringent

[87] This subsection includes all decisions and judgments on complaints about a violation of Art 14 of the ECHR because of discrimination in the field of social security on the ground of nationality or immigration status, from the first judgment on this issue in 1996 until 1 September 2013. Cases on discrimination on other, similar grounds, such as place of residence, or on nationality discrimination in other fields, such as extradition or legal assistance, have not been taken into account (see s 6.1 for an explanation for this restriction). An indication that all relevant cases have indeed appeared in my search can be found in Dembour 2012, as she arrives at a similar list (her search was, however, not restricted to the field of social security and she does include a case on discrimination on the ground of place of residence, since the applicant argued that this was a disguised nationality criterion).

[88] *Gaygusuz v Austria* (n 76).

[89] See also Dembour 2012.

standards.[90] In assessing whether the distinction made on the basis of nationality was justifiable in this case, the Court pays considerable attention to the question of comparability of Mr Gaygusuz with Austrian nationals. In this regard, the Court finds relevant that Mr Gaygusuz was legally resident in Austria, had worked in Austria at certain times and had paid contributions to the unemployment insurance fund in the same capacity and on the same basis as Austrian nationals.[91] In addition, the Court notes that he satisfies all other statutory conditions for the award of emergency assistance. Accordingly, he was 'in a like situation to Austrian nationals as regards his entitlement thereto'.[92] Therefore, the Court concludes that the difference in treatment between Austrians and non-Austrians as regards entitlement to emergency assistance is not based on any objective and reasonable justification. Hence, the Court treats the 'comparability test' as an important, or even as the decisive element under the justification test and does not pay attention to the question whether the aim advanced by the Government to exclude non-nationals (ie that 'the State has special responsibility for its own nationals and must take care of them and provide for their essential needs'[93]) was legitimate and whether there was a reasonable relationship of proportionality between the means employed and the aim.[94] The Court only adds that the argument of the Austrian Government that Austria was not bound by any reciprocal agreement with Turkey does not stand up, as Austria 'undertook, when ratifying the Convention, to secure "to everyone within [its] jurisdiction" the rights and freedoms defined in section I of the Convention'.[95]

The case of *Koua Poirrez v France*[96] concerns the application by an Ivory Coast national for an allowance for disabled adults, which was a French non-contributory social benefit scheme. This application was refused solely on the ground that he was neither a French national nor a national of a country that had signed a reciprocity agreement in respect of the social benefit in question. The Court's assessment of the justification of this difference in treatment based on nationality is very similar to its assessment in the *Gaygusuz* case. The Court first repeats that very weighty reasons have to be put forward before it could regard a difference of treatment based exclusively on the ground of nationality as compatible with the convention.[97] It subsequently assesses the justifiability of the difference

[90] Heringa 1999, p 30; Gerards 2004a, pp 48–49. According to O'Connell, the justification put forward by the state must be 'extremely persuasive' (O'Connell 2009, p 224).

[91] *Gaygusuz v Austria* (n 76), para 46.

[92] Ibid, para 48.

[93] Ibid, para 45.

[94] *Cf* Cousins 2007, p 387.

[95] *Gaygusuz v Austria* (n 76), para 51.

[96] *Koua Poirrez v France* app no 40892/98 (ECtHR, 30 September 2003).

[97] Ibid, para 46.

of treatment by paying attention to the comparability of Mr Koua Poirrez with French nationals and nationals from countries that have signed a reciprocity agreement. Also in this case, the Court finds relevant in this regard that Mr Koua Poirrez was legally resident in France and that he satisfied all other statutory conditions entitling him to the invalidity benefit. In addition, the Court notes that he was receiving the minimum welfare benefit in France, which is not subject to the nationality condition. Accordingly, he was in a like situation to that of French nationals or nationals of a country that had signed a reciprocity agreement as regards his right to receive the benefit. The difference of treatment was therefore not based on any objective and reasonable justification. The Court repeats its statement that the argument that no reciprocal agreement had been signed with the Ivory Coast does not stand up.[98]

In the cases of *Niedzwiecki v Germany*[99] and *Okpisz v Germany*,[100] the applicants complain of discrimination in the German law on child benefits. Under that law, aliens were only entitled to child benefits if they were in the possession of an unlimited or provisional residence permit. Both applicants were Polish nationals and were only in the possession of a limited residence permit, as a result of which they were not entitled to child benefits. In both cases, the Court examines whether this distinction amounted to discrimination in the sense of Article 14 (in conjunction with Article 8) of the ECHR. The Court holds in both cases that it is not 'called upon to decide generally to what extent it is justified to make distinctions, in the field of social benefits, between holders of different categories of residence permits'.[101] Accordingly, the Court does not classify the distinctions made in the German law as distinctions between nationals and aliens, but as distinctions between holders of different categories of residence permits.[102] Subsequently, the Court reaches the conclusion, without providing any reasons, that there are not sufficient reasons justifying the different treatment with regard to child benefits of aliens who were in possession of a stable residence permit, on the one hand, and those who were not, on the other. The Court does not refer to the 'very weighty reasons test'. However, in reaching this conclusion, the Court seems to rely heavily on a decision of the German Federal Constitutional

[98] Ibid, paras 47–49.

[99] *Niedzwiecki v Germany* (n 83).

[100] *Okpisz v Germany* app no 59140/00 (n 83).

[101] Paras 33 of the *Niedzwiecki* judgment and 34 of the *Okpisz* judgment.

[102] Gerards concludes from the fact that in the *Niedzwiecki* case the Court did not mention the 'very weighty reasons test' that it is not clear whether the Court still considers nationality a suspect ground of discrimination (Gerards 2007, pp 67–68). Apparently, she finds it obvious that such distinctions should be treated as distinctions based on nationality.

Court concerning the same issue.[103] This national court did apply a 'very weighty reasons test' and found no justification for the distinction.[104]

The case of *Luczak v Poland*[105] does not concern, as do the cases discussed above, entitlement to a certain benefit, but concerns *access* to a special social security scheme. The admission of Mr Luczak, a non-Polish national, to the Polish farmers' social security scheme was refused on the sole ground that he did not have Polish nationality. He claimed that this refusal amounted to discrimination in the sense of Article 14 of the ECHR, taken in conjunction with Article 1 of Protocol no 1. With reference to the cases of *Gaygusuz* and *Koua Poirrez*, the Court first repeats that, as a general rule, very weighty reasons would have to be put forward before the Court could regard a difference of treatment based exclusively on the ground of nationality as compatible with the convention. However, the Court adds to this that 'a wide margin is usually allowed to the State under the Convention when it comes to general measures of economic or social strategy'. The Court will therefore generally respect the legislature's policy choice unless it is 'manifestly without reasonable foundation'.[106]

Before examining the possible justifications for the exclusion of the applicant from the farmers' scheme, the Court seems to apply both the 'comparability test' and the 'test of disadvantage'. The Court first states that the applicant could claim to be in a relevantly similar position to Polish nationals who applied for admission to the farmers' scheme. In this connection, 'the Court attaches importance to the fact that the applicant was permanently resident in Poland, had previously been affiliated to the general social security scheme and had contributed as a taxpayer to the funding of the farmers' scheme'.[107] The Court subsequently states in reaction to the Government's argument that the applicant nevertheless had been entitled to certain social security benefits, such as a one-off compensation payment in the event of a serious occupational injury, and that the applicant was 'undoubtedly deprived of core elements of social security cover regarding provision for sickness and invalidity'. Furthermore, the Court adds, he could not continue making his contributions towards his retirement pension.[108]

After establishing in this way that the applicant is 'relevantly comparable' to Polish nationals and that he is actually disadvantaged by the difference in treatment, the Court examines whether there is an objective

[103] See para 33 of the *Niedzwiecki* judgment and para 34 of the *Okpisz* judgment ('Like the Federal Constitutional Court').

[104] See para 24 of the *Niedzwiecki* judgment and para 18 of the *Okpisz* judgment.

[105] *Luczak v Poland* app no 77782/01 (ECtHR, 27 November 2007).

[106] Ibid, para 48.

[107] Ibid, para 49.

[108] Ibid, para 50.

and reasonable justification for the difference in treatment. Hence, unlike the above-mentioned *Gaygusuz* and *Koua Poirrez* cases, the Court does not replace the justification test by the comparability tests, but pays separate attention to it. It considers that

> the creation of a particular social security scheme for farmers that is heavily subsidised from the public purse and provides cover to those admitted to it on more favourable terms than a general scheme could be regarded as pursuing an economic or social strategy falling within the State's margin of appreciation.[109]

Hence, serving this 'general interest' is apparently a 'legitimate aim' for the difference in treatment, according to the Court. However, testing against the principle of proportionality, the Court holds that

> even where weighty reasons have been advanced for excluding an individual from the scheme, such exclusion must not leave him in a situation in which he is denied any social insurance cover, whether under a general or specific scheme, thus posing a threat to his livelihood.

According to the Court, 'to leave an employed or self-employed person bereft of any social security cover would be incompatible with current trends in social security legislation in Europe'. Probably because the applicant in this case was not denied *any* social security cover, as he was entitled to (among other things) a one-off compensation payment in the event of a serious occupational injury, the Court continues to examine the arguments advanced by the Polish Government to justify his exclusion from the farmers' scheme. The Court concludes that, 'even having regard to [its] margin of appreciation in the area of social security', the Government has 'not provided any convincing explanation of how the general interest was served by refusing the applicant's admission to the farmers' scheme'.[110]

In the case of *Andrejeva v Latvia*,[111] Ms Andrejeva complained about nationality discrimination as regards the level of her pension. She complained about the fact that the years that she had worked during the Soviet period were not taken into account, while these years would have been taken into account if she had been a Latvian citizen. The Court repeats in this case that a wide margin of appreciation is usually allowed when it comes to general measures of economic or social strategy, but also that very weighty reasons would have to be put forward before it

[109] Ibid, para 52.

[110] Ibid, paras 55–59. Particularly, the Court does not find it established that the continuation of the difference in treatment was justified because of the allegedly far-reaching and serious implications for the state's economy if the distinction were to be discontinued, as according to the Government's own estimate, the admission to the farmers' scheme of, among others, EU nationals would not generate additional budget expenditure (para 58).

[111] *Andrejeva v Latvia* (n 46).

could regard a difference of treatment based exclusively on nationality as compatible with the convention.[112] The Court does not discern such reasons in this case, even 'being mindful of the broad margin of appreciation enjoyed by the State in the field of social security'.[113] When discussing whether the distinction is in compliance with Article 14, the comparability and justification test are completely merged. First of all, the Court accepts that the protection of the country's economic system is a 'legitimate aim that is broadly compatible with the general objectives of the Convention'.[114] Subsequently, the Court examines whether there is a reasonable relationship of proportionality between this legitimate aim and the means employed in this case. In this regard, the Court notes that the applicant is lawfully resident in Latvia on a permanent basis and receives a retirement pension in respect of her years of employment in Latvia. The Court considers that Ms Andrejeva is in an objectively similar situation to Latvian citizens, as it has not been alleged that she did not satisfy the other statutory conditions entitling her to a pension in respect of all her years of employment. In addition, as she was a stateless person, Latvia is 'the only state with which she had any stable legal ties and thus the only State which, objectively, can assume responsibility for her in terms of social security'.[115] Finally, the Court repeats again that the Latvian state cannot be absolved of its responsibility under Article 14 of the ECHR on the ground that it is not or was not bound by a specific inter-state agreement on social security.[116]

In the cases of *Fawsie v Greece*[117] and *Saidoun v Greece*,[118] the applicants were recognized as political refugees in Greece and were legally resident there. They alleged that the authorities' refusal to grant them a 'large family' allowance represented discrimination on grounds of nationality. The Court repeated once again the applicability of the 'very weighty

[112] Ibid, paras 83 and 87.
[113] Ibid, para 89.
[114] Ibid, para 86.
[115] Ibid, para 88.
[116] Ibid, para 90. Another argument of the Government was that in order for the applicant to receive her full pension, she only had to become a naturalized Latvian citizen, to which she has been entitled since 1998. The Court states, however, that the prohibition of discrimination 'is meaningful only if, in each particular case, the applicant's personal situation in relation to the criteria listed in that provision is taken into account exactly as it stands. To proceed otherwise in dismissing the victim's claims on the ground that he or she could have avoided the discrimination by altering one of the factors in question—for example, by acquiring a nationality—would render Article 14 devoid of substance' (para 91). In the case of *Carson and others v United Kingdom* (n 41), the Court held, however, that the same high level of protection is not required as is needed in relation to differences based on an inherent characteristic in cases where the difference of treatment is based on a characteristic which can be changed as a matter of choice.
[117] *Fawsie v Greece* app no 40080/07 (ECtHR, 28 October 2010).
[118] *Saidoun v Greece* app no 40083/07 (ECtHR, 28 October 2010).

reasons test' with regard to distinctions based on nationality, but did not repeat the reference to the wide margin of appreciation for states in social security matters. It did not apply the comparability test and the general features of the justification test (legitimate aim and proportionality) either. With reference to changes in domestic law as regards the grant of large family allowances to certain categories of non-nationals (including recognized refugees), to a judgment of the national supreme court on this issue, and to the obligations of the state under Article 23 of the 1951 Refugee Convention, the Court held that the refusal of the benefit to recognized refugees was not reasonably justified. Another judgment that needs to be mentioned here is the case of *Ponomaryovi v Bulgaria*.[119] Even though this case does not concern social security in the strict sense, the Court makes a number of general remarks on discrimination of aliens in the field of social security. In this case two Russian nationals complained that they had been discriminated against because, unlike Bulgarian nationals and aliens having a permanent residence permit, they had been required to pay school fees to pursue their secondary education. Both applicants had been in the possession of a permanent residence permit until their 18th birthday, but did not have the money to pay the fees for an independent residence permit that they needed in order to continue residing in Bulgaria lawfully. According to the Court, the distinction as regards the obligation to pay school fees is due exclusively to their nationality and immigration status.[120] It then repeats its general principles that, on the one hand, states are usually allowed a wide margin of appreciation when it comes to general measures of economic or social strategy, but, on the other hand, that very weighty reasons would have to be put forward before the Court could regard a difference of treatment based exclusively on the ground of nationality as compatible with the convention.[121] However, it adds a general reason for applying a strict scrutiny in this case, as it 'cannot overlook the fact that, unlike some other public services (...), education is a right that enjoys direct protection under the Convention', as it is expressly enshrined in Article 2 of Protocol No. 1 to the Convention and since secondary education plays an 'ever-increasing role' in nowadays "knowledge-based" societies'.[122] The Court does not explicitly apply a comparability test and starts its justification test by observing that a state 'may have legitimate reasons for curtailing the use of resource-hungry public services—such as welfare programmes, public benefits and health care—by short term and illegal immigrants, who, as

[119] *Ponomaryovi v Bulgaria* app no 5335/05 (ECtHR, 21 June 2011).
[120] Ibid, para 50.
[121] Ibid, para 52.
[122] Ibid, paras 55–58.

a rule, do not contribute to their funding'.[123] In addition, the Court holds in general that the state may also, in certain circumstances, justifiably differentiate between different categories of aliens residing in its territory.

> For instance, the preferential treatment of nationals of Member States of the European Union—some of whom were exempted from school fees when Bulgaria acceded to the Union (...)—may be said to be based on an objective and reasonable justification, because the Union forms a special legal order, which has, moreover, established its own citizenship.[124]

In assessing the proportionality of the national measure, the Court observes that 'the applicants were not in the position of individuals arriving in the country unlawfully and then laying claim to the use of its public services'. To the contrary, the Court observes that 'the authorities had no substantive objection to their remaining in Bulgaria, and apparently never had any serious intention of deporting them'. The applicants, moreover, had taken steps to regularize their situation. Accordingly, 'any considerations relating to the need to stem or reverse the flow of illegal immigration clearly did not apply to the applicants' case'.[125] Finally, the Court attaches importance to the fact that it was not the applicants' choice to settle in Bulgaria and pursue their education there, as they arrived there with their mother at a very young age, and to the fact that the relevant law did not make provision for a possibility to request an exemption from the payment of school fees.[126] In the 'specific circumstances of the present case',[127] the Court concludes that the requirement to pay school fees on account of their nationality and immigration status violated Article 14 of the ECHR in conjunction with Article 2 of Protocol no 1.

The case of *Bah v United Kingdom*[128] does not concern social security in the strict sense either, but is nevertheless important for the purposes of this chapter as the judgment contains a number of important general observations. In this case, the applicant was refused a priority placement on a list for social housing on the basis of her son's immigration status. The applicant's minor son had conditional leave to remain in the United Kingdom, the condition being that he must not have recourse to public funds. As he was therefore considered as being 'subject to immigration control' within the meaning of relevant domestic laws, he was disregarded in the determination of whether the applicant was in priority need

[123] Ibid, para 54.

[124] Ibid. The Court refers to the cases of *Moustaquim v Belgium* app no 12313/86 (ECtHR, 18 February 1991) and *C v Belgium* app no 21794/93 (ECtHR, 7 August 1996).

[125] *Ponomaryovi v Bulgaria* (n 119), para 60.

[126] Ibid, paras 61–62.

[127] As Dembour notes, the Court adopts a very casuistic approach in this case, as opposed to the more general approach in the *Gaygusuz* case (Dembour 2012).

[128] *Bah v United Kingdom* (n 43).

for social housing. The Court finds that the facts of this case fall within the ambit of Article 8, as a result of which Article 14 is applicable.[129] The parties in this case disagreed on the relevant ground of distinction. The applicant submitted that she was discriminated against on the ground of nationality, whereas the Government contended that the basis of differential treatment was immigration status. The Court decides, without much discussion, that it was the son's 'conditional legal status, and not the fact that he was of Sierra Leonean national origin, which resulted in his mother's differential treatment under the housing legislation'.[130] Apparently, the Court does not pay attention to the fact that parents with children of British nationality could, by definition, not be subjected to this differential treatment.[131] The Court subsequently rejects the Government's argument that immigration status cannot amount to a ground of distinction for the purposes of Article 14. The fact that it is not an inherent characteristic, but rather a status conferred by law, does not preclude it from amounting to an 'other status' for the purposes of Article 14.[132] However, the specific ground of discrimination is relevant for the purposes of Article 14, as 'the nature of the status upon which differential treatment is based weighs heavily in determining the scope of the margin of appreciation'.[133] The Court observes that immigration status is subject to an element of choice. In this regard, the Court notes that while the applicant entered the country as an asylum seeker, she was not granted refugee status and cannot, therefore, be described as a person who was present in a contracting state because, as a refugee, she could not return to her country of origin. The Court therefore concludes that given the element of choice involved in immigration status, 'while differential treatment based on this ground must still be objectively and reasonably justifiable, the justification required will not be as weighty as in the case of a distinction based, for example, on nationality'.[134] The Court then proceeds to examine whether the differential treatment is objectively justified. It pays some attention to the question of comparability, but it does not consider it necessary to determine conclusively whether the applicant and her son were in an analogous situation to a relevant comparator,[135] since it concludes that the differential treatment was objectively justified anyway. In this context, the Court states that it is justifiable to differentiate between those who are in the United Kingdom unlawfully or on the condition that they

[129] Ibid, para 40.
[130] Ibid, para 44.
[131] Arguably, put this way, the differential treatment can be understood as being based on nationality, see further s 3.5.
[132] *Bah v United Kingdom* (n 43), paras 45–46.
[133] Ibid, para 47.
[134] Ibid, para 47. See for critical comments on this approach Dembour 2012.
[135] *Bah v United Kingdom* (n 43), paras 41–42.

have no recourse to public funds, and those who are not. In addition, the legislation pursued a legitimate aim according to the Court, namely allocating a scarce resource fairly between different categories of claimants.[136] The Court also finds the effect of the differential treatment not disproportionate to the legitimate aim, as the applicant and her son were never actually homeless and since there were some duties imposed by legislation for local authorities had the threat of homelessness actually manifested itself.[137]

6.3.4 Analysis

Owing to the broad interpretation of the scope of Article 1 of Protocol no 1 and other substantive articles of the convention, differences of treatment in all fields of social security, including non-contributory benefits and health care, fall under the scope of Article 14 of the ECHR.[138]

Standing case law of the Court shows that distinctions on the basis of the sole ground of nationality require 'very weighty reasons' in order to be in compliance with Article 14. This means that the justification for distinctions based on that ground must meet more stringent standards; the Court will carefully examine whether the arguments put forward by the state are of sufficient importance to justify the distinction. Gerards notes that where this test is applied the Court has almost never reached the conclusion that the difference in treatment is compatible with Article 14.[139] The Court has not given any reasons for applying this strict test in cases of alleged nationality discrimination.[140] It should be noted, however, that the very weighty reasons test has mainly been applied in cases of alleged nationality discrimination in the field of social security.[141] A convincing

[136] Ibid, para 50. Remarkably, the Government only introduced this aim before the Court. During domestic litigation on this issue, the Government justified the legislation by the need to maintain immigration control and to prevent 'benefit tourism' (see para 48).

[137] Ibid, para 51.

[138] See for a critical appraisal of this development Bossuyt 2007. As has been stated before, the same is not true with regard to differences of treatment with regard to access to the labour market (see n 74).

[139] Gerards 2004a, p 37. Consequently, she argues, the accent of the test of suspect classifications has shifted from a substantive scrutiny of the difference in treatment to the determination of the applicability of the very weighty reasons test.

[140] Dembour suggests that the Court deliberately refrains from providing any further explanation to this statement, as it touches upon a 'fundamental contradiction at the core of liberal theory and practice'. This contradiction being that liberalism is based upon and opposed to the principle of equality across nationalities at the same time (Dembour 2012). See on this contradiction also s 1.2.

[141] *Cf* the dissenting opinion of Judge Garlicki to the judgment in the case of *Carson and others v United Kingdom* (n 41): 'This Court has on several occasions found that nationality-based differentiations *in social benefits* are inherently suspect' (emphasis added). Exceptions

reason for applying a strict test in this field would be the general and widely applied principle of equal treatment between non-nationals and nationals in international social security co-ordination law.[142] As chapter five shows, provisions of equal treatment laid down in social security co-ordination law generally fit in the closed model, as a result of which only a limited number of justifications, explicitly mentioned in these provisions, apply. This would mean that the application of the 'very weighty reasons test' to nationality discrimination is not only dependent on the ground of discrimination, but also the relevant policy field. Accordingly, this test does not necessarily apply with regard to nationality discrimination in other fields. Indeed, it is often alleged that this test does not apply in the field of immigration, ie as regards distinctions made in the context of admittance and expulsion of aliens.[143] In the case of *A and others v United Kingdom*, the Court seems to confirm this view. In this case a complaint was lodged about anti-terrorism measures in the UK on the basis of which non-nationals could be subjected to indefinite detention without charge. The Court held that 'the impugned powers were not to be seen as immigration measures, *where a distinction between nationals and non-nationals would be legitimate,* but instead as concerned with national security'.[144] In the case law of the Court, the concept of 'immigration measures' therefore seems to be limited to issues of aliens' admittance into, and expulsion from, the territory.

At the same time, the Court sometimes refers to the wide margin of appreciation for states in the field of general economic or social strategy and of social security. This seems to be contradictory, if, as is submitted here, the application of the 'very weighty reasons test' to nationality discrimination is linked to the field of social security. If the cases in which the Court refers to this wide margin of appreciation are carefully examined, however, one can see that the Court very thoroughly examines the justifications put forward by the state for the difference in treatment. For example in the *Luczak* case, the Court asked the state to offer a 'convincing explanation of how the general interest was served' by refusing admission to the social security scheme concerned and paid attention to the fact that such admission would actually not generate additional budget

are the decision in the case of *Shkelzen v Germany* app no 44770/98 (ECtHR, 20 January 2000) and the case of *Rangelov v Germany* app no 5123/07 (ECtHR, 22 March 2012).

[142] *Cf* Harris et al 2009, p 590, fn 108: 'As the Commission's Report in the *Abdulaziz* case suggested, the existence of international treaties covering the particular form of discrimination may be highly influential in identifying the existence of 'suspect categories'.

[143] Arnardóttir 2003, pp 150–51, Heringa 1999, p 30, fn 7; Gerards 2004a, p 55; De Vries 2013a, pp 307–08. These statements are based on the cases of *Moustaquim v Belgium* and *C v Belgium* (n 124).

[144] *A and others v United Kingdom* app no 3455/05 (ECtHR, 19 February 2009), para 186 (emphasis added).

expenditure. This indicates a rather strict scrutiny. In the *Andrejeva* case, the Government argued that the distinction based on nationality was justified in view of the financial burden and the limited capacity of the national budget. The Court did not even examine this justification explicitly, but held, on the basis of the reasons provided above, that the reasons put forward by the state were not sufficient. In the case of *Ponomaryovi v Bulgaria,* the Court paid considerable attention to the specific circumstances of the case in order to show that certain kinds of possible justifications were not applicable in that case.[145] In addition, distinctions based on the sole ground of nationality in the field of social security have until now not been accepted by the Court as compatible with Article 14 of the ECHR. Hence, it seems that the Court applies a strict scrutiny to cases of alleged nationality discrimination in the field of social security; notwithstanding remarks about the wide margin of appreciation generally accorded to states in this field. In other words: even though states generally have a wide margin of appreciation with regard to economic and social policy measures, for example as regards the decision to set up a specific social security scheme, this wide margin of appreciation does not apply to distinctions in this field that are exclusively based on nationality.

An important question that needs to be answered is whether the 'very weighty reasons test' in cases of alleged nationality discrimination in the field of social security only applies to cases of direct nationality discrimination. The Court has not clearly expressed itself on this issue. However, the wording of the Court that very weighty reasons would have to be put forward before it could regard a difference of treatment based *exclusively* on the ground of nationality as compatible with the convention might indicate that the Court only applies the 'very weighty reasons test' to distinctions that are based directly on the ground of nationality. This would fit in with the general theory on the distinction between direct and indirect discrimination, which indicates that as regards indirect distinctions, a more lenient scrutiny applies.[146] In the *Bah v United Kingdom* case, the Court distinguishes between distinctions based on nationality and distinctions based on immigration status. Since distinctions based on immigration status in any case qualify as distinctions *indirectly* based on nationality,[147] this confirms the conclusion that the Court only applies the 'very weighty reasons test' to cases of *direct* nationality discrimination.

This, in turn, makes it important to know whether distinctions based on the lawfulness of the presence or residence of aliens or on the possession of a residence and/or work permit qualify as distinctions directly based

145 Admittedly, the Court applied a 'stricter scrutiny' in this case since the right to education is 'directly protected under the Convention', unlike other public benefits.

146 See ch 3.

147 See s 3.5.

on nationality for the purposes of Article 14 of the ECHR. As argued in chapter three, it is possible to characterize such distinctions made in the context of social security or employment as distinctions directly (albeit more covertly) based on the ground of nationality, since such distinctions are only capable of excluding non-nationals and since such distinctions make the requested benefit conditional for all non-nationals. The Court, however, has not paid attention to this kind of reasoning in the case law discussed above.[148] This case law indicates that the Court does not treat such distinctions as distinctions based on nationality. In the cases of *Niedzwiecki v Germany* and *Okpisz v Germany*, the Court did not classify requirements to be fulfilled by aliens as to the kind of residence permit they possess as distinctions between nationals and aliens, but as distinctions between holders of different categories of residence permits. In the case of *Ponomaryovi v Bulgaria*, the Court classified distinctions between, on the one hand, Bulgarian nationals and aliens having permanent residence permits and, on the other hand, other categories of aliens as distinctions being based on nationality *and* immigration status. Most explicitly, in the *Bah v United Kingdom* case, the Court characterized distinctions between persons who are and persons who are not subject to immigration control as being based on immigration status, and not on nationality.

Does this mean that the 'very weighty reasons test' does not apply to differential treatment of asylum seekers as regards social security benefits based on their immigration status? In the *Niedzwiecki* and *Okpisz* cases, the Court did apply, with reference to domestic case law, a rather strict scrutiny. In the *Ponomaryovi* case the Court even explicitly referred to the 'very weighty reasons test'. In the *Bah* case, the Court introduced the element of choice as being relevant for establishing the scope of the margin of appreciation granted to the state as regards distinctions based on immigration status. The Court explicitly paid attention to the fact that the applicant in that case was not a refugee who could not return to her country of origin. The justification required was therefore not as weighty as in cases of distinctions based on nationality. *A contrario*, this could imply that if the immigration status is not 'subject to an element of choice', as understood by the Court, such as with regard to refugees or stateless persons, the same weighty reasons are necessary as with regard

[148] In the case of *Rangelov v Germany* (n 141), a case not related to social security, the Court seems, however, to adopt this position. This case is about the preventive detention of a Bulgarian national against whom an expulsion order had been made. In view of this expulsion order, social therapy and relaxations of his detention conditions had not been offered. According to the Court, the applicant was and could only be subject to an expulsion order as a foreign national and concludes that he was treated differently compared to German nationals in a similar situation (para 95). The Court therefore applies the 'very weighty reasons test' (para 102).

to distinctions based on nationality. With respect to asylum seekers it has still to be established whether they can return to their country of origin. Only once their application has been (finally) rejected, might their status be subject to an element of choice. Before the (final) rejection of their claim, states are generally not allowed to expel asylum seekers to their countries of origin. Arguably, in line with the declaratory understanding of the term 'refugee', this means that until the (final) rejection of their asylum application, very weighty reasons are necessary for differential treatment based on their immigration status, as this status might not be subject to an element of choice.

This raises the question as to which reasons should be considered to be sufficiently weighty in order to justify unequal treatment based on nationality and/or immigration status not being subject to an element of choice. The case law discussed above does shed some light on this issue. First of all, the Court usually uses comparability terminology in the context of the justification test. In order to be in a relevant analogous situation, the Court generally attaches importance to the fact that the alien 'lawfully resides' in the country. An important question with regard to the position of asylum seekers is whether to be 'lawfully present' or even to be 'not unlawfully' present or tolerated in the territory will suffice in order to be relevantly comparable to nationals in the field of social security.[149] Even though almost every case discussed above concerns non-nationals with lawful permanent residence in the territory, the reasoning of the Court leaves room for a broader interpretation. The same is true with regard to the reference of the Court to Article 23 of the 1951 Refugee Convention in the cases of *Fawsie v Greece* and *Saidoun v Greece*[150]; with regard to refugees who lawfully reside in the country, the case law of the Court clearly indicates that a difference of treatment between them and nationals in the field of social security violates Article 14 of the ECHR, but it cannot be excluded that this article is violated with regard to other categories of refugees as well. Indeed, the *Ponomaryovi* case explicitly shows that legal permanent residence is not an absolute requirement in order to be entitled to equal treatment with nationals as regards public benefits. Rather, this case shows that it can be important whether the authorities have substantive objections to the ongoing presence of the alien concerned on their territory, whether they have any serious intentions to deport him and whether the alien concerned has taken steps to regularize his situation. The *Bah* case shows that it can be justified to distinguish between persons who are unlawfully in the territory or are there on the condition that they have no recourse to public funds and those who do not. Again,

[149] *Cf* Bossuyt 2007, pp 326–27.
[150] nn 117 and 118.

both judgments leave room for the interpretation that the legal status of asylum seekers does not stand in the way of their passing the comparability test. At least with regard to asylum seekers who have reported themselves at the border (and, therefore, have taken steps to regularize their situation) and who have explicitly been admitted into the territory (and are, therefore, lawfully present in the territory), it could be argued on the basis of this case law of the Court that their legal status is relevantly comparable to that of nationals.

Other relevant aspects in the comparability test seem to be whether the alien satisfies all other statutory conditions entitling him to the benefit in question or to access the social security scheme in question; whether the alien is, or previously has been, entitled to other kinds of benefits in the country; and whether the alien has contributed (in the case of non-contributory benefits, as a taxpayer) to the funding of the social security system. The latter requirement has been specified by the Court in the *Ponomaryovi* case, as it held that states 'may have legitimate reasons for curtailing the use of resource-hungry public services (...) by short-term and illegal immigrants, *who, as a rule, do not contribute to their funding*'. With regard to asylum seekers, who by definition have a temporary immigration status, this could mean that as long as they do not work lawfully in the country, and hence do not pay taxes or social security contributions, they are not in a relevantly analogous situation as nationals as regards eligibility for social security benefits. On the other hand, once they take up lawful employment, they can be considered to be comparable to nationals in this regard.

The question of comparability is not the only relevant factor—albeit a very important one—for determining whether distinctions made on the basis of nationality in the field of social security are justified. Next to considerations about comparability, the Court sometimes pays attention to the question whether the distinction serves a legitimate aim and/or whether the distinction bears a reasonable relationship of proportionality to this aim.

With regard to the criterion of a legitimate aim, the Court has accepted in the case of *Andrejeva v Latvia* the protection of the country's economic system as a legitimate aim for treating aliens differently from nationals in the field of social security. In the *Bah* case as well, the Court accepted 'allocating a scarce resource', ie when there is insufficient supply available to satisfy demand, as a legitimate aim for distinguishing between different categories of aliens. The background and negotiation history of the EU Directives on Reception Conditions show, however, that the distinctions allowed for by these Directives between nationals and asylum seekers with regard to social assistance do not primarily serve this aim. Rather, it appeared that the purpose of these distinctions is primarily linked to considerations of immigration policy, eg to discourage the filing of unfounded asylum claims or to facilitate the return of failed asylum seekers. The *Ponomaryovi* case indicates that the Court accepts 'considerations relating to the need to stem or reverse the flow of illegal immigration' as a legitimate aim for distinguishing between nationals and aliens in the field of public benefits. In addition, this case shows that preventing possible abuse of public benefits schemes by aliens might be a legitimate purpose for making distinctions. The Court did not, however, specify under which circumstances aliens should be considered to 'abuse' the system.

As regards the criterion of proportionality, the Court held in the *Luczak* case that even where weighty reasons have been advanced for excluding an individual from a certain social security scheme, 'such exclusion must not leave him in a situation in which he is denied any social insurance cover, whether under a general or specific scheme, thus posing a threat to his livelihood'. According to the Court, 'to leave an employed or self-employed person bereft of any social security cover would be incompatible with current trends in social security legislation in Europe'. This would mean that asylum seekers who are employed cannot entirely be excluded from social security coverage, 'even where weighty reasons have been advanced'. In the *Andrejeva* case, the Court took into account, when assessing proportionality, that the applicant was a stateless person and that Latvia was the only state with which she has any stable legal ties. This consideration could be of relevance for the situation of asylum seekers, since, pending the determination of their claim for protection, a host state that explicitly allows their presence on the territory, might be the only state with which they have any effective legal ties. Finally, it appears clearly from the judgments discussed above that states cannot be absolved of their responsibility under Article 14 of the ECHR on the ground that they are not bound by a reciprocity agreement or specific interstate agreement on social security, as states undertook by ratifying the convention to secure 'to everyone within their jurisdiction' the rights and freedoms guaranteed therein.[151] The only exception in this regard has been mentioned by the Court in the *Ponomaryovi* case, where the Court held that differential treatment between different categories of aliens residing in the territory based on nationality may under certain circumstances

[151] Strikingly, in the case of *Carson and others v United Kingdom*, the Court did accept the conclusion of bilateral social security agreements as a basis for a difference of treatment between UK nationals living in a country with which no such agreement has been concluded and UK nationals living in a country that has entered into such an agreement with the UK. According to the Court: 'it would be extraordinary if the fact of entering into bilateral arrangements in the social security sphere had the consequence of creating an obligation to confer the same advantages on all others living in all other countries. Such a conclusion would effectively undermine the right of States to enter into reciprocal agreements and their interest in so doing' ((n 41), para 89). However in this case, the ground on which the distinctions are based is place of residence, and not nationality.

be objectively justified if it is based on the 'special legal order' of the European Union.[152] So far, this possible exception has, however, not been accepted by the Court as a reasonable and objective justification in a case on discrimination on the basis of nationality in the field of social security.

In brief, this would mean that very weighty reasons have to be put forward by the state for making distinctions between asylum seekers and nationals of the host state in the field of social security benefits, the reason being that it can be argued that such reasons either qualify as distinctions based on nationality or as distinctions based on immigration status not subjected to an element of choice. Even though considerations related to immigration policy might be regarded as a legitimate aim for making such distinctions, the requirement of 'very weighty reasons' means that this justification should be considered very carefully and account should be taken of all relevant and personal circumstances of the asylum seeker concerned. Put differently, the justification put forward by the state must be 'extremely persuasive'. The case law discussed in this section has indicated a number of circumstances that should be taken into account when examining whether weighty reasons exist for making a distinction. These circumstances include the fact whether the asylum seeker contributes (as a taxpayer) to the social security system; whether the authorities have any substantive objections against the presence of the asylum seeker concerned or any intentions to deport him; whether the asylum seeker arrived unlawfully in the country and is trying to 'abuse' the social security system; and whether asylum seekers are entitled to other social security benefits or have previously been entitled thereto. In view of these circumstances and given the fact that asylum seekers might not have another state to turn to, to exclude from social security benefits asylum seekers who have been explicitly allowed access to the territory, who are lawfully employed (or otherwise contribute to the financing of the social security system) and who satisfy all other statutory conditions entitling them to the benefit would, in my opinion, be difficult to justify in view of Article 14 of the ECHR. For other categories of asylum seekers, the Court's case law indicates that very weighty reasons might be considered to be available for exclusion of general social security benefits,

[152] De Vries concludes that it could be the case that the extent to which bilateral agreements can justify a difference in treatment depends, at least partly, on the reasons why those agreements were concluded (de Vries 2013a, p 313). Indeed, this would fit in with the distinction made in Art 7 of the Refugee Conventions between 'legislative reciprocity' and 'diplomatic reciprocity'. Under this article, refugees are only exempted from 'legislative reciprocity' (if certain conditions are met) and not from 'diplomatic reciprocity'. See on the meaning of these two terms s 9.2. The European Union can be said to be based on a system of 'diplomatic reciprocity', instead of 'legislative reciprocity'. It could therefore be the case that bilateral agreements can only justify differential treatment if these agreements are based on 'diplomatic reciprocity'.

as they lack a number of important features for finding themselves in a relevantly analogous situation with nationals (eg contribution to social security system, no objections of the authorities against their presence, etc). In that case, excluding them from general social security benefits might be considered to pursue the legitimate aim of trying to stem or reverse the flow of illegal immigration and to prevent possible abuse of the welfare system.

6.4 THE EUROPEAN SOCIAL CHARTER

6.4.1 Text and Context

The European Social Charter (ESC) forms the social counterpart to the European Convention on Human Rights and deals with a number of important social and economic human rights. It entered into force in 1965. The Charter is a 'menu instrument', as contracting states should choose at least 10 articles to which they consider themselves bound.[153] From these 10 articles, states parties should choose at least five of the core Articles 1, 5, 6, 12, 13, 16 and 19.[154] In 1999 the Revised European Social Charter entered into force, which is an autonomous instrument, intended to eventually replace the ESC.[155] It amends some of the existing rights contained in the ESC and adds a number of new rights.[156] In addition, states parties should consider themselves bound by at least 16 of the articles of the Charter and they should choose at least six of the core rights, the enumeration of which has been extended by Articles 7 and 20.[157]

The European Social Charter has been ratified by 27 countries, of which 22 EU Member States.[158] The Revised European Social Charter has been ratified by 31 countries, including 18 EU Member States.[159] All EU

[153] Or 45 numbered paragraphs, see Art 20 of the Charter.

[154] These articles refer to the right to work; the right to organize; the right to bargain collectively; the right to social security; the right to social and medical assistance; the right of the family to social, legal and economic protection; and the right of migrant workers and their families to protection and assistance.

[155] Para 8 of the explanatory report to the Revised European Social Charter.

[156] Such as the right to protection in cases of termination of employment (Art 24); the right to dignity at work (Art 26); the right to protection against poverty and social exclusion (Art 30); the right to housing (Art 31); and the prohibition of discrimination (Art E).

[157] These articles contain the right of children and young persons to protection and the right to equal opportunities and equal treatment in matters of employment and occupation without discrimination on the grounds of sex.

[158] conventions.coe.int/Treaty/Commun/ChercheSig.asp?NT=035&CM=7&DF=01/07/2011&CL=ENG.

[159] conventions.coe.int/Treaty/Commun/ChercheSig.asp?NT=163&CM=7&DF=01/07/2011&CL=ENG.

Member States are party to at least one of the two instruments. Hereafter, the term 'charter' refers to both the ESC as the revised ESC, unless otherwise stated.

Two provisions contained in the Charter are of particular importance for the purpose of this chapter, namely Article 12 on the right to social security[160] and Article 13 on the right to social and medical assistance.[161] The substance of these articles has not been amended or adjusted by the revised charter. These provisions will be discussed below.

In addition, the Revised Charter contains a general prohibition of discrimination in Article E, which reads:

> The enjoyment of the rights set forth in this Charter shall be secured without discrimination on any ground such as race, colour, sex, language, religion, political or other opinion, national extraction or social origin, health, association with a national minority, birth or other status.

According to the explanatory report, this new article confirms the interpretation of the Committee of Independent Experts in respect of the Charter, ie that the non-discrimination clause in the preamble to the Charter applies to all the provisions of the Charter. The article has been based on Article 14 of the ECHR, which contains a more extensive enumeration of grounds than the preamble to the Charter.[162]

6.4.2 Application to Aliens

Text of the Charter

The personal scope of the Charter is limited. The appendix[163] to the Charter states:

> Scope of the (Revised European) Social Charter in terms of persons protected
>
> 1. Without prejudice to Article 12, paragraph 4, and Article 13, paragraph 4, the persons covered by Articles 1 to 17 and 20 to 31 include foreigners only insofar as they are nationals of other Contracting Parties lawfully resident or working regularly within the territory of the Contracting

[160] Art 12 has not been accepted by the following EU Member States: Bulgaria (para 4); Hungary (paras 2–4); Malta (paras 2 and 4b); Sweden (para 4); Latvia; and the United Kingdom (paras 2–4).

[161] Art 13 has not been accepted by the following EU Member States: Bulgaria (para 4); Cyprus (paras 1 and 4); Estonia (para 4); Lithuania (para 4); Romania (para 4); Slovakia (para 4); Slovenia (paras 1 and 4); and Poland (paras 1 and 4).

[162] Paras 135 and 136 of the explanatory report to the Revised European Social Charter.

[163] According to Art 38 of the ESC and Art N to the revised ESC, the appendix to the Charter forms an integral part of it.

> Party concerned, subject to the understanding that these articles are to be interpreted in the light of the provisions of Articles 18 and 19. This interpretation would not prejudice the extension of similar facilities to other persons by any of the Contracting Parties.

Hence, with the exception of Articles 18 and 19, an alien only falls under the scope of the Charter provisions if he is a national of one of the contracting parties and is 'lawfully resident or working regularly' within the territory of a contracting party. In the previous chapters, it has been argued in depth that asylum seekers cannot yet meet the condition of lawful residence, as they do not have a positive authorization to take up residence in the host state. Accordingly, this would mean that asylum seekers only fall under the personal scope of the Charter if they are a national of one of the contracting parties and if they are 'working regularly' in the host state. As Harris and Darcy note, the reference to interpret the provisions in lights of Article 18 is presumably intended to confirm that nationals of other contracting parties are protected by the Charter only if they have permission to work in a contracting party.[164] In my view, this also follows from the term 'regularly'. This limitation in personal scope applies 'without prejudice to Article 12, paragraph 4 and Article 13, paragraph 4' of the Charter. It is therefore necessary to examine these provisions as well.

Article 12 reads as follows:

> With a view to ensuring the effective exercise of the right to social security, the Contracting Parties undertake:
>
> 1. to establish or maintain a system of social security;
> 2. to maintain the social security system at a satisfactory level at least equal to that necessary for the ratification of the European Code of Social Security;
> 3. to endeavour to raise progressively the system of social security to a higher level;
> 4. to take steps, by the conclusion of appropriate bilateral and multilateral agreements, or by other means, and subject to the conditions laid down in such agreements, in order to ensure:
>   a. equal treatment with their own nationals of the nationals of other Contracting Parties in respect of social security rights, including the retention of benefits arising out of social security legislation, whatever movements the persons protected may undertake between the territories of the Contracting Parties;
>   b. the granting, maintenance and resumption of social security rights by such means as the accumulation of insurance or employment periods completed under the legislation of each of the Contracting Parties.

164 Harris and Darcy 2001, p 386.

Accordingly, paragraph 4 indicates that the scope of this provision is limited to nationals of other contracting parties as well. However, in order to fall under the scope of this provision, nationals of other contracting parties do not have to reside or work in the country lawfully. The personal scope of this provision is therefore broader than the general personal scope of the Charter.[165] Paragraph 4 refers to the conclusion of other bilateral and multilateral agreements and makes the right to equal treatment subject to the conditions laid down in such agreements. This paragraph does therefore not contain an autonomous right to equal treatment, as the contracting states are merely obliged to 'take steps' by concluding bi- and multilateral agreements in order to ensure this right and as this right can be made subject to various conditions laid down in such agreements, including, arguably, conditions as regards the lawfulness of the presence, residence and/or employment.[166]

Article 13 reads:

> With a view to ensuring the effective exercise of the right to social and medical assistance, the Parties undertake:
>
> 1. to ensure that any person who is without adequate resources and who is unable to secure such resources either by his own efforts or from other sources, in particular by benefits under a social security scheme, be granted adequate assistance, and, in case of sickness, the care necessitated by his condition;
> 2. to ensure that persons receiving such assistance shall not, for that reason, suffer from a diminution of their political or social rights;
> 3. to provide that everyone may receive by appropriate public or private services such advice and personal help as may be required to prevent, to remove, or to alleviate personal or family want;
> 4. to apply the provisions referred to in paragraphs 1, 2 and 3 of this article on an equal footing with their nationals to nationals of other Parties lawfully within their territories, in accordance with their obligations under the European Convention on Social and Medical Assistance, signed at Paris on 11 December 1953.

This provision as well only applies to nationals of other contracting parties. In addition, in order to fall under the scope of this provision, such nationals have to be lawfully in the territory. It is not required to *reside* or

165 *Cf* Nickless and Siedl 2004, p 91. See otherwise Krause and Scheinin 2000.

166 According to the appendix to the Charter, '[t]he words "and subject to the conditions laid down in such agreements" in the introduction to this paragraph are taken to imply *inter alia* that with regard to benefits which are available independently of any insurance contribution, a Party may require the completion of a prescribed period of residence before granting such benefits to nationals of other Parties'. This does not exclude the possibility of including other qualifying conditions in bi- and multilateral agreements.

work lawfully in the territory; mere lawful *presence* is enough to fall under the scope of this provision. Since paragraph 4 of Article 13 explicitly refers to the ECSMA, the interpretation of this term should be the same as under the ECSMA. Under the ECSMA, presence should be regarded as 'lawful' if 'there is in force in his case a permit or such other permission as is required by the laws and regulations of the country concerned' to be present therein.[167]

Just like the social security conventions with a reciprocity condition that have been discussed in chapter five, the Charter contains a provision on refugees. The appendix to the Charter states:

> Scope of the (Revised European) Social Charter in terms of persons protected
>
> 1. (...)
> 2. Each Contracting Party will grant to refugees as defined in the Convention relating to the Status of Refugees, signed at Geneva on 28th July 1951, and lawfully staying in its territory, treatment as favourable as possible, and in any case not less favourable than under the obligations accepted by the Contracting Party under the said Convention and under any other existing international instruments applicable to those refugees.

Unlike the protocols to and provisions in social security conventions on refugees discussed in chapter five, the scope of the Charter is not in general extended to refugees; they are merely granted 'treatment as favourable as possible'. In addition, this provision does not apply to all refugees as defined in Article 1 of the Refugee Convention, but only to refugees 'lawfully staying' in the territory. As asylum seekers cannot meet the condition of 'lawfully staying' in the sense of the Refugee Convention (see chapter four) and as this provision explicitly refers to the Refugee Convention, this provision does not apply to asylum seekers.

Hence, the text of the Charter clearly shows that asylum seekers who are not nationals of a contracting party to the Charter do not fall under the personal scope of the Charter. If they are nationals of one of the contracting parties, they fall under the scope of Article 12(4). This article, however, does not contain an independent right to equal treatment. They only fall under the personal scope of Article 13 on social and medical assistance if they are a national of one of the contracting parties and are 'lawfully' within the territory of another contracting party. As regards the other Charter provisions, they fall under the personal scope if they are 'working regularly' in the host state.

[167] See s 5.4.3.

Approach of the European Committee on Social Rights

The European Committee of Social Rights (ECSR) takes another approach to the limited personal scope of the Charter. In its statement of interpretation in its Conclusions 2004,[168] the ECSR held on the personal scope of the Charter:

> The Committee notes that the Parties to the Charter (in its 1961 and revised 1996 versions) have guaranteed to foreigners not covered by the Charter rights identical to or inseparable from those of the Charter by ratifying human rights treaties—in particular the European Convention of Human Rights—or by adopting domestic rules whether constitutional, legislative or otherwise without distinguishing between persons referred to explicitly in the Appendix and other non-nationals. In so doing, the Parties have undertaken these obligations.
>
> Whereas these obligations do not in principle fall within the ambit of its supervisory functions, the Committee does not exclude that the implementation of certain provisions of the Charter could in certain specific situations require complete equality of treatment between nationals and foreigners, whether or not they are nationals of member States, Party to the Charter.

So, the ECSR is of the opinion that the scope of the Charter can, with regard to 'certain provisions' and in 'certain specific situations' be extended to foreigners that are not nationals of one of the contracting parties. The committee substantiates this interpretation by referring to the scope of other human rights conventions that the states parties have ratified and of domestic rules that have been adopted by the states parties.

With regard to one specific right, the right to medical assistance, the ECSR concluded in a decision on a complaint lodged by the International Federation of Human Rights Leagues (FIDH) against France that 'legislation or practice which denies entitlement to medical assistance to foreign nationals, within the territory of a State party, even if they are there illegally, is contrary to the Charter'.[169] Apparently, the ECSR was (rather implicitly) of the opinion that illegally present foreigners fall under the personal scope of the right to medical assistance as laid down in Article 13 and, with regard to children and young persons, Article 17 of the Charter.[170] The reasoning of the ECSR on this extension of the scope of the Charter is rather thin. It starts by asserting that it interprets

[168] Conclusions 2004, Statement of Interpretation, Vol 1, s 1, Conclusion date 5 March 2004.

[169] Decision on the merits of 8 September 2004, *FIDH v France* complaint no 14/2003.

[170] Art 17 of the Charter concerns the right of children and young persons to social, legal and economic protection. It does not refer explicitly to medical assistance or health care. The ECSR notes, however, that Art 17 protects in a general manner the rights of children and young persons to care and assistance and concludes that the law and practice in France concerning children's access to medical assistance violated Art 17 (paras 36–37).

the Charter on the basis of the Vienna Convention on the Law of Treaties. The ECSR further states that it is mindful of the 'complex relationship' between the European Social Charter and the European Convention on Human Rights, as the rights laid down in the Charter are 'not ends in themselves but they complete the rights enshrined in the European Convention on Human Rights'. In addition, the ECSR holds that the Charter is 'a living instrument dedicated to certain values which inspired it: dignity, autonomy, equality and solidarity'. The Charter must therefore be interpreted so as to give life and meaning to fundamental social rights, as a result of which restrictions on rights are to be read restrictively, 'i.e. understood in such a manner as to preserve intact the essence of the right and to achieve the overall purpose of the Charter'. The restriction on the personal scope of the Charter as laid down in the appendix has a different impact on the different social rights laid down in the Charter. In this case, it impacts a right of fundamental importance to the individual, 'since it is connected to the right to life itself and goes to the very dignity of the human being'. Health care is a prerequisite for the preservation of human dignity, which is 'the fundamental value and indeed the core of positive European human rights law—whether under the European Social Charter or under the European Convention on Human Rights'.[171]

The ECSR took the same approach in its decision on the complaint lodged by Defence for Children International (DCI) against the Netherlands.[172] In this complaint, DCI alleged that Dutch law and practice that denies children unlawfully present in the territory access to adequate housing is in violation of a number of articles of the Charter, particularly Article 17 and Article 31 (on the right to housing). On the basis of more or less the same arguments as used in the case of *FIDH v France*,[173] the ECSR concludes that the restricted personal scope of the charter does not necessarily apply to every right laid down in the Charter, especially not when the protection of vulnerable groups, such as children, is at stake.[174] The ECSR adds one important argument to the arguments used in the case of *FIDH v France*. It notes that, since the UN Convention on the Rights of the Child is one of the most ratified conventions world-wide, which has been ratified by all Member States to the Council of Europe, regard must be had to this convention when interpreting the rights laid down in

[171] *FIDH v France* (n 169), paras 26–32.

[172] Decision on the merits of 20 October 2009, *DCI v the Netherlands* complaint no 47/2008.

[173] In addition to the reference to the general rule of interpretation as laid down in Art 31(1) of the Vienna Convention on the Law of Treaties in the case of *FIDH v France*, the ECSR refers in this decision explicitly to Art 31(3)(c) of this convention. This article provides that account should be taken of 'any relevant rules of international law applicable in the relations between the parties' (para 35).

[174] *DCI v the Netherlands* (n 172), paras 34–38.

the charter. In particular, the rights must be interpreted in the light of the 'internationally recognised requirement to apply the best interests of the child principle'.[175]

With regard to the question whether Article 31 (on the right to housing) applies to unlawfully present children, the ECSR makes a distinction between paragraph 1 and paragraph 2 of Article 31. Paragraph 1 concerns access to housing of an adequate standard, whereas paragraph 2 concerns the prevention and reduction of homelessness. According to the ECSR, the right to adequate housing as laid down in paragraph 1 includes a legal guarantee of security of tenancy; a temporary supply of shelter cannot be considered as adequate. To require that states provide such lasting housing to unlawfully present children would run counter the states' aliens policy objectives of encouraging persons unlawfully on their territory to return to their country of origin. Accordingly, the ECSR concludes that Article 31(1) does not apply to children unlawfully on the territory.[176] Hence, unlike the reasoning in the case of *FIDH v France*, the ECSR explicitly recognizes the interest of the state in pursuing a consistent immigration policy. With regard to paragraph 2 of Article 31, the ECSR holds that this obligation includes the introduction of immediate shelter and care for the homeless.[177] The ECSR considers that the right to shelter, just as it had considered as regards the right to health care in the case of *FIDH v France*, is closely connected to the right to life and crucial for the respect of every person's human dignity. Since growing up in the streets would leave children in a situation of outright helplessness, the ECSR concludes that children fall under the personal scope of Article 31(2), whatever their residence status.[178]

With regard to the personal scope of Article 17, the ECSR holds—with reference to its considerations on the UN Convention on the Rights of the Child and to its decision in the case of *FIDH v France*—that children fall under the personal scope of this article, whatever their residence status.[179]

These findings have been confirmed by the ECSR in its decision in the case of *Defence for Children International (DCI) v Belgium*.[180] In this case, DCI complained that even though unaccompanied foreign minors and illegally resident accompanied minors are legally entitled to

[175] Ibid, paras 28–29.
[176] Ibid, paras 41–45.
[177] In para 62 the ECSR observes that temporary housing need not be subject to the same requirements of privacy, family life and suitability as are required from more permanent forms of standard housing.
[178] *DCI v the Netherlands* (n 172), paras 46–48.
[179] Ibid, para 66.
[180] Decision on the merits of 23 October 2012, *DCI v Belgium* complaint no 69/2011.

accommodation in reception centres in Belgium, they do not have access to these centres in practice, owing to the saturation of the reception network. Again, the ECSR holds that, based on the same arguments, unlawfully present minors fall under the personal scope of Article 13 ('in particularly concerning the right to appropriate medical assistance') and Article 17. In addition, the ECSR decides that they also fall under the personal scope of Articles 7(10), 11 and the part of 16 relating to the right of families to decent housing. In this case, the ECSR, however, stresses more explicitly, the exceptional nature of the application of rights to unlawfully present migrants. It holds that since it is exceptional to apply the rights enshrined in the Charter to persons not literally included in the Charter's scope, unlawfully present migrants are not covered by all the provisions of the Charter,

> but solely by those provisions whose fundamental purpose is closely linked to the requirement to secure the most fundamental human rights and to safeguard the persons concerned by the provisions in question from serious threats to the enjoyment of those rights.[181]

As most of the economic, social and cultural measures to be taken as required by Article 30 (on the right to protection against poverty and social exclusion) are not closely related to the requirement to secure the most fundamental human rights, migrants who are unlawfully present do not fall under the personal scope of Article 30, according to the ECSR.[182]

In short, according to the ECSR, the restricted personal scope of the Charter, as laid down in the appendix and in Articles 12(4) and 13(4), does not necessarily apply to every right laid down in the Charter or in every situation. Exceptionally, the rights laid down in the Charter also apply to persons who are not literally included in the personal scope of the Charter. The ECSR has accepted that the right to medical assistance as laid down in Article 13 of the Charter applies to all *persons* on the territory, irrespective of their nationality and immigration status. Articles 7(10), 11, 17 and 31(2) apply to all *children* on the territory, irrespective of their nationality and immigration status, according to the ECSR. With regard to Article 30 on the right to protection against poverty and social exclusion and Article 31(1) on the right to adequate housing, the ECSR has not (yet) accepted an exception to the restricted personal scope of the Charter as laid down in the appendix.

[181] Ibid, para 36.
[182] Ibid, paras 145–46.

Analysis

As the decisions of the ECSR do not have binding legal force,[183] they derive their authority from the position of the ECSR in the treaty and from the persuasiveness of the argumentation in the decision,[184] or, in other words, from the power of the better argument.[185] The question is therefore whether this interpretation on the personal scope of the Charter, which is clearly contrary to the text of the Charter, is persuasive.

Article 31(1) of the Vienna Convention on the Law of Treaties, to which the ECSR itself also refers, contains the general rule of interpretation and includes literal ('ordinary meaning'), systematic ('in their context') and teleological ('in the light of its object and purpose') interpretation methods. The prevalent view is that there is no hierarchy in these methods.[186] This means that all three methods are equally important in discovering the meaning of a treaty provision. In general, interpretations of human rights conventions are often mainly or even completely based on the systematic and teleological interpretation methods, owing to the general and vague wording of human rights provisions. This does not necessarily violate the general rule of interpretation as laid down in the Vienna Convention on the Law of Treaties. However, in this case, the ECSR adopts an interpretation on the basis of systematic and teleological arguments which is, at face value, clearly contrary to the text of the Charter. Arguably, such an interpretation, which runs counter to one of the interpretation methods laid down in Article 31(1) of the Vienna Convention on the Law of Treaties, exceeds the generally wide room for manoeuvre left by that article.[187] In any case, such an interpretation puts a high onus of proof on the ECSR.[188]

However, the systematic and teleological arguments provided by the ECSR are not very convincing. With reference to Article 31(3)(c) of the Vienna Convention on the Law of Treaties, the ECSR used the systematic argument that the personal scope of the Charter must be interpreted on the basis of other international conventions, most notably the Convention on the Rights of the Child and the European Convention on Human Rights, which both have a much broader personal scope. It is, however, questionable whether Article 31(3)(c) applies where treaty provisions are in conflict. Whereas Article 31(3)(c) might be a viable principle for filling gaps left by a treaty and clarifying unclear terms, it seems to be generally

[183] See also Cullen 2009, p 75; Churchill and Khaliq 2004, p 437–40; Harris and Darcy 2001, p 376. The resolutions of the Committee of Ministers are non-binding recommendations.
[184] See s 1.7.
[185] *Cf*, about the Human Rights Committee, Noll 2005, p 563.
[186] See s 1.7.
[187] See also Buyse 2010, p 217; Mechlem 2009, p 935; Vanneste 2010, p 347.
[188] *Cf* Noll 2005, p 563.

accepted that this article does not entail that 'an extraneous treaty' can modify the applicability of the treaty under interpretation.[189]

Besides, the ECSR does not make it clear what the consequences are of the 'complex interaction' between the Charter and the ECHR for the interpretation of the personal scope of the Charter. This argument has been further elaborated upon by Mikkola.[190] The ECSR arguably relies on the same line of reasoning, albeit less clearly.[191] According to Mikkola, the material scope of the ECHR and the Charter partly overlaps, as the ECHR also includes positive obligations in the sphere of social security, housing and emergency social and medical care. The common denominators of these obligations in both the Charter as the ECHR are standards concerning the protection of dignity. As these two instruments are indivisible and interdependent, the basic standards for the right to dignity must be understood similarly. Since the personal scope of the ECHR is universal and covers all subjects under the jurisdiction of a contracting party, the Charter, as a legal instrument that supplements the ECHR, may not limit the personal scope of the ECHR. Hence, Mikkola is of the opinion that '[o]n questions of dignity and where the two treaties overlap, the limitation in the appendix to the Charter should be interpreted in a restrictive way and understood to correspond with the personal scope of the Convention'.[192]

However, whereas the personal scope of the ECHR is indeed much broader than that of the Charter, it does not mean that the positive obligations arising from the ECHR in the sphere of social welfare apply to everyone on the territory of the contracting states. With regard to the question of equal treatment of non-nationals in social security schemes, the European Court of Human Rights attaches considerable importance to the question of lawful residence or presence in the country.[193] With regard to the provision of health care, the Court held that Article 3

> does not place an obligation on the Contracting State to alleviate such disparities [between the level of treatment available in the Contracting State and in the country of origin] through the provision of free and unlimited health care to all aliens without a right to stay within its jurisdiction.[194]

Hence, also under the ECHR, the personal scope of positive obligations in the field of social security and health care is limited. In determining the scope of these positive obligations under the ECHR, the Court might as well

[189] Nele Matz-Ldick and Benn McGrady cited in Tzevelekos 2010, p 686. See also, without referring to Art 31(3)(c): Rieter 2010, p 809.

[190] Mikkola 2008, pp 37–38 and 53–54.

[191] Mikkola was one of the members of the ECSR that took the decision in the case of *FIDH v France*.

[192] Mikkola 2008, p 56.

[193] See s 6.3.3.

[194] *N v United Kingdom* app no 26565/05 (ECtHR, 27 May 2008), para 44.

take into account the scope of the obligations laid down in the Charter,[195] which will do justice to the indivisibility and interdependency of both human rights instruments as well. Hence, this systematic argument is in my view not very convincing, as it can just as well work the other way around.

The teleological argument of the ECSR that the Charter is a 'living instrument dedicated to certain values which inspired it: dignity, autonomy, equality and solidarity', as a result of which restrictions must be interpreted restrictively, in such a manner as to achieve the overall purpose of the Charter, is not very convincing, either. The ECSR does not provide any argumentation for the identification of the four values that underlie the Charter. In addition, the ECSR does not explain why it relies in this case only on the value of dignity, which is only one the four identified values. As Cullen observes, the value of 'solidarity' can possibly limit the scope of potential economic and social rights claims, as it requires a balance to be struck between individual rights and collective rights and interests. 'As a result, a claim by an individual or group that would place an excessive burden on the state to the point where it interferes with the realisation of rights of other members of the community may be rejected'.[196]

Finally, it has been argued that the general non-discrimination provision laid down in Article E of the Revised Social Charter can limit the meaning of the restricted personal scope of the Charter. As states parties may provide for more favourable treatment than provided for under the Charter in their domestic law, they can extend the personal scope of the rights laid down in the Charter. Once the personal scope of the Charter has been extended in this way, then discrimination in the application of the rights is prohibited.[197] This argument is not very persuasive, as Article E only applies to 'the rights set forth in this Charter'. Also, the explanatory report states on Article E that

> it is understood that this provision must not be interpreted so as to extend the scope *ratione personae* of the Revised Charter which is defined in the appendix to the instrument and which includes foreigners only in so far as they are nationals of other parties lawfully resident or working regularly within the territory of the Party concerned'.[198]

The ECSR has adopted the same view.[199]

[195] The Court regularly refers to the European Social Charter in its judgments. In the case of *Zehnalova and Zehnal v the Czech Republic*, the Court stated, eg, that the European Social Charter, like other international treaties, 'may provide [the Court] with a source of inspiration' (app no 38621/97, ECtHR, 14 May 2002).

[196] Cullen 2009, p 81.

[197] See Groenendijk in his case note to the decision in the case of *FIDH v France*, *JV* 2005/339.

[198] Explanatory report to the Revised European Social Charter, para 137.

[199] *DCI v the Netherlands* (n 172), para 72.

Concluding Remarks

Since the reasoning of the ECSR is not persuasive and, arguably, not in conformity with the interpretation rules as laid down in the Vienna Convention on the Law of Treaties and since no other persuasive argument exists for not applying the restricted personal scope of the Charter, the conclusion must be that asylum seekers only fall under the personal scope of the Charter if they are a national of a contracting party to the Charter. Contracting parties to the Charter include Russia, Serbia, Georgia, Turkey, Armenia, Bosnia and Herzegovina and Azerbaijan. Asylum seekers originating from these countries fall under the personal scope of Article 12(4) on the right to social security. However, as mentioned before, this article has little autonomous meaning as regards entitlement to equal treatment. They fall under the personal scope of Article 13(4) on equal treatment as regards social and medical assistance if they are 'lawfully present' on the territory of one of the contracting states. In the context of the ECSMA, it has been argued that asylum seekers are only 'lawfully present' if they apply for asylum at the border and are subsequently admitted to the territory, provided that they do not violate the requirements imposed on them as a condition for their entry.[200] Since Article 13 of the Charter explicitly refers to the ECSMA, the same interpretation of the term 'lawfully present' must be adopted under both conventions.[201] As regards the other provisions laid down in the Charter, including the general provision of non-discrimination, asylum seekers who are nationals of one of the contracting parties fall under the personal scope if they are 'working regularly' in a contracting party.

6.4.3 Interpretation

The previous section showed that asylum seekers who are a national of one of the contracting parties to the Charter can fall under the personal scope of the Charter. They only fall under the general provision on non-discrimination (Article E) if they are working regularly in the territory of one of the contracting states. This implies that this provision cannot provide any entitlement to equal treatment as regards access to the labour market.

[200] See s 5.4.3.

[201] See also Vonk 2005. Also Harris and Darcy state that a person is lawfully within a party's territory in the sense of the ESC 'if he has entered that territory in accordance with its laws and so long as his continued presence is in accordance with them' (Harris and Darcy 2001, p 220).

Asylum seekers who are nationals of one of the contracting parties fall under the personal scope of Article 13(4) of the Charter if they are lawfully present on the territory of one of the contracting parties. This raises the question how the right to equal treatment contained therein should be interpreted. To reiterate, the text of Article 13(4) of the Charter reads:

> With a view to ensuring the effective exercise of the right to social and medical assistance, the Parties undertake:
>
> (...)
>
> 4. to apply the provisions referred to in paragraphs 1, 2 and 3 of this article on an equal footing with their nationals to nationals of other Parties lawfully within their territories, in accordance with their obligations under the European Convention on Social and Medical Assistance, signed at Paris on 11 December 1953.

The appendix to the Charter provides with regard to this article:

> Governments not Parties to the European Convention on Social and Medical Assistance may ratify the Charter in respect of this paragraph provided that they grant to nationals of other Parties a treatment which is in conformity with the provisions of the said convention.

Hence, asylum seekers who fall under the personal scope of this provision are entitled to social and medical assistance 'on an equal footing' with nationals and this right should be interpreted in accordance with the ECSMA. Accordingly, as section 5.4.3 shows, such asylum seekers are entitled to social and medical assistance 'equally and on the same conditions' as nationals. This would mean that excluding them from general social assistance schemes and, instead, offering them assistance mainly in kind, at a lower level and subject to different conditions than under the general scheme is not in conformity with Article 13 of the Charter. Instead, the minimum subsistence level as laid down in general social assistance schemes should be the point of reference for the quality and level of their assistance benefits.

The ECSR has, however, adopted a different interpretation of the right to equal treatment laid down in Article 13(4) of the Charter. In the case of *FIDH v France*, the ECSR first established that non-nationals fall under the scope of the right to medical assistance as laid down in Article 13, irrespective of their nationality and immigration status (see above). Subsequently, it had to assess whether the law and practice in France concerning medical assistance for illegally residing non-nationals violated Article 13. The ECSR noted that the relevant legislation did not deprive illegal immigrants of all entitlements to medical assistance, since it did provide for state medical assistance to meet certain costs incurred by any foreign national resident in France for an uninterrupted period of more than three months and for treatment for other illegal immigrants for emergencies and life-threatening conditions.[202] It thereupon held that:

> It is true that the concept of emergencies and life threatening conditions is not sufficiently precise and that the competent body to take decisions in this field is not clearly identified. It is also true that there are numerous difficulties in the implementation in practice of the provisions applicable to illegal immigrants in France for more than 3 months and that the costs to be met by the state are narrowly defined. However given the existence of a form of medical assistance benefiting these persons, the Committee, being in doubt, considers that France does not violate Article 13 of the Revised Charter.[203]

Also in the case of *DCI v Belgium*, the ECSR concluded that the existence of 'a form of medical assistance' for unlawfully present minors meant that Article 13 was not violated by Belgium.[204]

Apparently, according to the ECSR the existence of 'a form of assistance' suffices within the context of Article 13(4) of the Charter; (formal) equal treatment between nationals and non-nationals is not necessary in order to comply with this article. In Conclusions on state reports, the ECSR has elaborated on this issue and has made a distinction between paragraph 1 and paragraph 4 of Article 13. Whereas paragraph 1 concerns the right to general social and medical assistance (to which the general limited personal scope of the Charter applies), paragraph 4 applies to 'emergency social and medical assistance' according to the ECSR (to which an extended personal scope applies). According to the ECSR, 'emergency assistance' refers to accommodation, food, emergency care and clothing; states are not required to apply the guaranteed income arrangements under their social protection systems.[205]

This would mean that providing a different kind of assistance to asylum seekers at a lower level than the assistance provided to nationals under general schemes and subject to different conditions than under the general scheme is in accordance with Article 13(4). This interpretation of Article 13(4) does not, however, find any basis in the text of the Charter. To the contrary, Article 13(4) explicitly refers to the provisions referred to in paragraphs 1–3 of Article 13 and contains the obligation for contracting states to apply *these* provisions on an equal footing with their own nationals to nationals of other contracting parties. Article 13(4) further refers to the ECSMA, which does not differentiate between general assistance and emergency assistance either. In addition, the provision of emergency

[202] *FIDH v France* (n 169), para 33.
[203] Ibid, para 34.
[204] *DCI v Belgium* (n 180), para 131.
[205] Council of Europe, *Digest of the Case Law of the European Committee of Social Rights*, 1 September 2008, p 104.

assistance arguable falls under the material scope of Articles 30 of the Charter on the right to protection against poverty and social exclusion and/or Article 31 of the Charter on the right to housing, which includes the obligation to prevent and reduce homelessness. According to the explanatory report, among the obligations subscribed to under Article 30, 'a series of measures is included, which may or may not imply financial benefits'.[206] It further notes that the article 'does not expressly mention the guarantee of minimum resources. The reason is that such protection is already provided for by Article 13'.[207] Hence, neither the text and context of Article 13(4) nor the text and context of other provisions of the Charter support the restrictive interpretation of the material scope of Article 13(4) by the ECSR. The ECSR does not provide any arguments for this restrictive interpretation and applies particularly prudent language ('being in doubt') in the decision in the case of *FIDH v France*. Presumably, this restrictive interpretation of the material scope of Art 13(4) is connected to the ECSR's extensive interpretation of the personal scope of this article. The restricted material scope then serves to prevent the placement of too heavy a burden on the contracting states.[208] According to Article 31(4) of the Vienna Convention on the Law of Treaties, a special meaning may only be given to a term if it has been established that the parties so intended. Given the absence of any indications of such an intention as regards the term 'equal footing' and as regards the reference to the ECSMA in Article 13(4) of the Charter and given the 'closed' character of the norm laid down in Article 13, which leaves not much (or even no) room for possible justifications for unequal treatment, the conclusion should in my opinion be that the reasoning of the ECSR is (again) not very persuasive.[209]

6.4.4 Summary

This section has argued that the general provision of non-discrimination laid down in Article E of the Revised Charter only applies to asylum seekers who are nationals of another contracting party and who are working regularly on the territory. The Charter therefore does not provide asylum seekers with protection against differential treatment with nationals as regards access to the labour market. To the contrary, the condition of 'working regularly' explicitly provides for such differential treatment.

206 Explanatory report to the Revised European Social Charter, para 116.
207 Ibid, para 115.
208 See also Harris and Darcy 2001, p 175.
209 See for a critical opinion on the ECSR's interpretation also Harris and Darcy 2001, pp 174–76.

As regards social security, the Charter contains two more specific provisions on equal treatment. This section has shown that Article 12(4) on the right to social security does not contain an autonomous right to equal treatment. The other non-discrimination provision of the Charter with possible relevance for asylum seekers is Article 13(4) on the right to equal treatment as regards social and medical assistance. This provision bears a close resemblance to the provisions laid down in instruments of social security co-ordination discussed in chapter five, especially with the ECSMA, to which it explicitly refers.

This section has argued that asylum seekers who are a national of one of the contracting parties of the Charter and who are lawfully present on the territory of one of the contracting parties to the Charter are entitled to social and medical assistance equally with and on the same conditions as nationals under Article 13(4) of the Charter. The ECSR has adopted a different interpretation of both the personal and the material scope of Article 13(4). Since this interpretation does not have any basis in the text of the Charter and since the ECSR has not put forward persuasive arguments for this interpretation, this interpretation has not been followed in this section.

Since Article 13(4) of the Charter explicitly refers to the ECSMA, the same interpretation of the words' lawfully present' under the ECSMA should in my view be adopted as regards Article 13(4) of the Charter. This means that asylum seekers who are a national of one of the contracting parties to the Charter, who have been explicitly allowed to enter the territory of one of the contracting parties to the Charter and who do not violate any of the conditions laid down as a condition for their entry are entitled to equal treatment with nationals as regards social and medical assistance. Providing assistance at a lower level than under general schemes and subjecting asylum seekers to different qualifying conditions from those applied to nationals is therefore in my view not in conformity with Article 13(4) of the Charter.

6.5 CONCLUDING REMARKS

This chapter shows that human rights conventions do not provide protection as regards equal access to the labour market for asylum seekers, the reason being that the principle of non-discrimination has not yet been applied to non-nationals' access to the labour market (ECHR); that the interpretation of the supervisory committee suggest that aliens are not entitled to equal access to the labour market (ICESCR); or that the general principle on non-discrimination only applies to aliens who are already 'regularly working' in the state (ESC).

Distinctions based on nationality and immigration status in the field of social security fall under the material scope of general non-discrimination provisions laid down in international human rights conventions, irrespective of whether such conventions relate to social and economic rights or civil and political rights and despite the absence of nationality and immigration status as an explicit prohibited ground of discrimination in such conventions. With the exception of the European Social Charter, the discrimination provisions discussed in this chapter all concern provisions of the 'open-model' of non-discrimination provisions, as a result of which courts and treaty-monitoring bodies enjoy a large amount of freedom in applying and interpreting these provisions. The Committee on Economic, Social and Cultural Rights and the European Court of Human Rights seem to use, albeit not explicitly, the more detailed provisions of the 'closed model' laid down in social security co-ordination law as a source of inspiration. With regard to the Committee, this is reflected in the distinction that is being made between contributory and non-contributory benefit schemes and with regard to the Court this is reflected in the application of the very weighty reasons test to nationality-based discrimination in the field of social security and in the special status awarded to refugees in this regard.

The European Court of Human Rights has provided the most extensive interpretation of the principle of non-discrimination with regard to the eligibility of non-nationals for social security benefits. In addition, the binding character of its judgments makes these interpretations most authoritative. The Court has ruled that for distinctions based exclusively on nationality in the field of social security, very weighty reasons have to be put forward, as a result of which such distinctions are generally not allowed under Article 14 of the ECHR. On the other hand, the Court has decided that distinctions based on immigration status, where this immigration status is subject to an element of choice, do not need such a strict justification. This chapter has argued that the 'very weighty reasons test' should be applied to distinctions based on the immigration status of asylum seekers, since such distinctions can be treated as distinctions based directly on nationality or, alternatively, since the immigration status of asylum seekers might not be 'subjected to an element of choice', as understood by the Court. Case law of the Court shows that for the assessment whether the reasons provided by the state are sufficiently weighty, attention should be paid to the comparability of asylum seekers with nationals. For examining whether asylum seekers are in a relevantly analogous position with nationals as regards access to and eligibility for social security benefits, their legal status is relevant, as well as the fact that they fulfil all other statutory conditions for being eligible for the benefits concerned; the fact that they have contributed to the financing of the social security system; and the fact that they have been entitled to social security benefits in the past. Accordingly, asylum seekers' individual circumstances are decisive for establishing comparability. Other factors to be taken into account for assessing whether the reasons provided by the state are sufficient weighty are the factors of a legitimate aim and proportionality. The Court has held that the need to stem or reverse the flow of illegal immigration and preventing possible abuse of public benefits schemes by aliens might be legitimate aims for making distinctions between aliens and nationals. Taking all these different factors into account, this chapter has argued that to exclude from social security benefits asylum seekers who have been explicitly allowed access to the territory, who are lawfully employed (or otherwise contribute to the financing of the social security system) and who satisfy all other statutory conditions entitling them to the benefit would be difficult to justify under Article 14 of the ECHR.

The European Social Charter is the only human rights instrument that contains a provision on equal treatment between nationals and non-nationals in the field of social security (social and medical assistance) of the closed model. This is, therefore, the only human rights instrument of which the text of the convention contains specific indications for permitted exceptions to the rule of equal treatment. Contrary to interpretations of the supervisory committee, this chapter has argued that only asylum seekers who are nationals of another contracting party and who are lawfully present on the territory of a contracting state are entitled to equal treatment with nationals as regards social and medical assistance benefits. The term 'lawfully present' should be interpreted in the same way as under the European Convention on Social and Medical Assistance (see section 5.4.3), as the text of the relevant provision of the ESC explicitly refers to this convention. As regards asylum seekers who fulfil these conditions, the minimum level of subsistence as laid down in general social assistance schemes should be the relevant standard for assessing the quality and level of their reception benefits.

The ECHR and the ESC therefore provide similar safeguards. Owing to the open character of Article 14 of the ECHR, however, the question whether asylum seekers are entitled to equal treatment with nationals as regards social security benefits is assessed on the basis of individual and factual circumstances, whereas the closed character of the relevant norm of the ESC implies that there is less room for an assessment on the basis of individual circumstances. The ECtHR has not yet delivered a judgment on equal treatment of asylum seekers as regards social security benefits. However, since it often refers to provisions of the ESC in its case law, the Court might adopt the same approach as under the ESC (without the condition of reciprocity). As this chapter shows, this would to a large extent fit with its previous case law on this issue.

An important conclusion of this chapter is that even though international human rights law may, at first sight, be based on the 'separation model', as it obliges states to grant rights to everybody under their jurisdiction, a closer look reveals that it does in fact allow for a large convergence of the state's immigration power with the material rights of aliens. International human rights law does not oblige states to grant all aliens on their territory equal treatment with nationals with regard to access to the labour market and social security schemes and allows states to make the right to equal treatment to a large extent subject to legal immigration status. This is clearly exemplified in recent case law of the ECtHR that does not require very weighty reasons for a distinction based on immigration status and that does acknowledge reasons related to immigration control as a legitimate aim for distinguishing between nationals and aliens in the field of public benefits. On the other hand, with regard to (potential) refugees, the application of the 'very weighty reasons' test to distinctions based on nationality and immigration status in the field of social security seems to indicate that the ECtHR does also, at least partially, embrace the 'separation model'. In the end, this chapter clearly shows that, indeed, the jurisdictional dispute on the proper location of the state's immigration power is a core issue with regard to the material rights of aliens.

7

Conclusions to Part II

PART II HAS examined whether instruments of international law on equal treatment and non-discrimination contain obligations for EU Member States to provide asylum seekers equal rights with nationals with respect to access to wage-earning employment and social security. In other words, it has examined whether 'equality' should be the relevant norm for assessing the quality of the reception of asylum seekers in Europe. As was found in Part I of this book, the EU Reception Conditions Directives do not require Member States to provide asylum seekers with the same access to social security schemes and to the labour market as nationals. The Directives do not deal with the access of asylum seekers to other social security benefits. As regards access to the labour market, the Directives allow for a waiting period of one year or nine months and for imposing different kinds of conditions after that year has passed. The background and legislative history of the Directives revealed that the reason for this differential treatment between asylum seekers and nationals as brought forward by states is related to their immigration powers. States argued that introducing or maintaining differential treatment in these fields mainly served to prevent the filing of unfounded asylum applications and to facilitate the expulsion of rejected asylum seekers. The purpose of Part II was therefore to examine whether this 'convergence' of the state's immigration power with the regulatory domains of social security and employment is permitted by international law, or whether states are obligated under international law to grant asylum seekers equal rights as nationals in these fields.

An important conclusion in this part is that neither international refugee law nor international labour law or international human rights law entitle asylum seekers to equal treatment with nationals as regards their access to the labour market. This means that international law does not prescribe a full separation between the sphere of immigration control, on the one hand, and the sphere of the internal labour market, on the other. States are free to determine the eligibility of asylum seekers for accessing the labour market on the basis of their immigration status.

A different conclusion can be reached with regard to social security. Even though the various instruments examined in the preceding chapters offer a mixed picture, it can be concluded that certain categories of asylum seekers are entitled to equal treatment with nationals under international law.

This conclusion cannot be reached on the basis of the Refugee Convention, however. Even though asylum seekers fall under the personal scope of this convention, the right to the same treatment as nationals with regard to social security benefits has been reserved for refugees who are 'lawfully staying' in the territory of the host state. In chapter four it has been argued that asylum seekers generally cannot fulfil this qualifying condition, since they have not yet been granted explicit permission to take up residence in the host state.

Contrary to the Refugee Convention, international social security law does provide certain categories of asylum seekers with the right to equal treatment with nationals in the field of social security. Chapter five shows that with regard to social assistance benefits, not only asylum seekers who are 'lawfully staying' on the territory, but also asylum seekers who are merely 'lawfully present' on the territory of a contracting state to the ECSMA are entitled to equal treatment with nationals. This applies to all asylum seekers independent of their nationality, since the protocol to the ECSMA extends the personal scope of the convention to all refugees. For asylum seekers who are lawfully within the territory 'equality' should therefore be the relevant standard of review for the assessment of the quality of their reception benefits. As the ECSMA explicitly refers to the Refugee Convention, the interpretation of the term 'lawfully present' should be in conformity with the Refugee Convention. As has been argued in chapter four, the most convincing interpretation of this term in the context of the Refugee Convention is in my opinion that only asylum seekers who report themselves or are apprehended at the border and who have been explicitly allowed to enter the territory of the host state are 'lawfully present'. Accordingly, this interpretation implies a distinction between asylum seekers who ask for admittance at the border and asylum seekers who cross the border without permission and apply for asylum afterwards.

With regard to social insurance benefits, not only asylum seekers who are 'lawfully staying' in the territory, but all asylum seekers who meet the more factual criteria of residence or ordinary residence are entitled to equal treatment with nationals. The obligation to grant such refugees equal treatment with nationals stems from different social security conventions at the UN and CoE level. An important consequence of the finding that fulfilment of factual criteria is decisive for the right to equal treatment in the field of social security is that a general exclusion of all asylum seekers from social insurance benefits on the basis of their legal status is not in conformity with international social security law.

Chapter six has shown that relevant human rights instruments of the Council of Europe seem at first sight to provide more safeguards than international refugee and social security law. First of all, the

European Court of Human Rights has abandoned the distinction between contributory, non-contributory and social assistance benefits. In order to be entitled to the protection of the provision on non-discrimination, the relevant test is whether the scheme concerned provides for benefits as of right; ie the benefits must not be provided on a purely discretionary basis. Secondly, the qualifying conditions used by the Court in order to establish entitlement to equal treatment for non-nationals are not as strict as those laid down in the Refugee Convention and social security conventions. While the Court attaches much importance to legal residence, its reasoning does not exclude that withholding general social security benefits from other categories of aliens would be in violation of Article 14 ECHR as well. Indeed, the Court seems to attach importance to factual criteria, such as relevant contributions to the social security system (in whatever form) and substantive objections of the government to the ongoing presence of the alien concerned on the territory. As argued in chapter six, this implies in my view that to exclude asylum seekers from general social assistance or insurance benefits if they have lawfully entered the country, continue to be lawfully present there and contribute to the financing of the social security system, for example by taking up lawful employment, would be hard to justify under Article 14 ECHR.

When this conclusion is compared to the conclusion drawn in chapter five on the entitlement of asylum seekers to equal treatment with nationals in the field of social security, it appears that the case law of the Court does not provide much extra protection to asylum seekers after all. Chapter five shows that under relevant ILO and CoE social security conventions, asylum seekers are entitled to equal treatment as regards contributory (and some kinds of) non-contributory social insurance benefits if they meet the factual criterion of (ordinary) residence. In order to fulfil this criterion, immigration status can be an important, but not the decisive factor. More important is whether the asylum seeker concerned has established links of a durable nature with the country in which he resides. This test bears close resemblance to the factual assessment of comparability as applied by the Court in its case law. In addition, under the ECSMA, asylum seekers are entitled to equal treatment as regards social and medical assistance if they are lawfully present on the territory. Hence, the protection offered by social security conventions is not limited to social insurance schemes, either. Although the ECSMA applies the qualifying condition of 'lawful presence', this condition is easier to meet than the criterion of 'lawful residence' and arguably serves as a minimum condition for entitlements under Article 14 ECHR as well. Moreover, under the ECSMA, fulfilment of the criterion of 'lawful presence' is enough in order to be entitled to equal treatment; no further aspects, such as contributions made to the financing of the social security system, are relevant. This means that in my view, Article 14 ECHR, as interpreted by the European Court of

Human Rights, hardly provides asylum seekers with more safeguards with regard to entitlement to equal treatment with nationals in the field of social security than the protection offered by international social security law. Nevertheless, given the fact that all EU Member States have ratified the ECHR, all EU Member States are now bound by similar obligations as those laid down in international social security law, whether they have ratified the social security conventions or not.

Neither does the European Social Charter (ESC) contain further-reaching state obligations as regards equal treatment in social security than those stemming from international social security law. In chapter six it has been argued, despite views of the supervisory committee to the contrary, that the personal scope of the ESC is limited and that only nationals of other contracting parties who are lawfully present on the territory are entitled to equal treatment with nationals as regards social and medical assistance. This means that, in my opinion, the protection offered by the European Social Charter is the same as the protection offered by the ECSMA, with the important exception that asylum seekers only fall under the personal scope of the ESC if they are nationals of other contracting parties.

Arguably, then, the same categories of asylum seekers are entitled to equal treatment with nationals in the field of social security under international social security law as under international human rights law. The more specialized body of international social security law might therefore have served as a source of inspiration for the interpretation of the rather open or 'empty' norms of equal treatment laid down in international human rights law.

Legal status and community ties are therefore important for being entitled to equal treatment with nationals as regards social security benefits. This means that international law does allow for a convergence of states' immigration power with the field of social security law. In contrast to the field of access to the labour market however, international law establishes certain conditions under which asylum seekers are entitled to equal treatment with nationals. In other words, as to the question how far states' sovereign immigration power may reach before they must give way to equality, international law does set some limits. An important conclusion of this part of the book is that the special status of asylum seekers is relevant in this regard. The fact that asylum seekers are potential refugees, as a result of which their immigration status is not subject to an element of choice, is an important factor for entitling them to equal treatment, both under international social security law and under international human rights law.

In brief, Part II has argued that international law does allow subjecting asylum seekers to differential treatment with nationals as regards their access to the labour market. This means that reasons related to the state's immigration power are legitimate reasons under international law for withholding asylum seekers' access to the labour market. As regards the field of social security, international law does set some limits on the reach of state's immigration power. Even though immigration status and community ties are relevant for being entitled to equal treatment, states themselves are not free to establish which conditions must be fulfilled before they grant asylum seekers equality of treatment in this field.

Part III will assess provisions of international law not devoted to equal treatment and non-discrimination as to their relevance for asylum seekers' access to the labour market and social security. How the results of Parts II and III relate to the norms laid down in the EU Reception Conditions Directives will be assessed more extensively in the concluding chapter.

Part III

Full Sovereignty?

8

Introduction to Part III

8.1 AIMS AND DELIMITATIONS

PART II HAS examined whether EU Member States are obligated under international law to grant asylum seekers equal treatment with their own nationals as regards access to social security schemes and to the labour market. To that end, it has examined provisions on equal treatment and non-discrimination laid down in international refugee law, international social security law and international human rights law. It has been seen that international law does not contain obligations for states to grant asylum seekers equal treatment with nationals as regards access to the labour market. As regards the field of social security, the research in Part II revealed that international law does contain obligations for the state to grant the same treatment as nationals for certain categories of asylum seekers. Part II concluded that asylum seekers who meet certain conditions as regards legal status and community ties should be granted access to social security benefits on the same footing and under the same conditions as nationals. In the field of social security, states themselves are therefore no longer free to establish the conditions for granting asylum seekers equality of treatment.

However, asylum seekers who do not meet the conditions stemming from international law as regards legal status and community ties, are not entitled under international law to equal treatment with nationals in the field of social security. This raises the question whether international law provides other safeguards to these categories of asylum seekers. This part will try to answer this question. It will assess provisions of international law not devoted to equal treatment and non-discrimination as to their relevance for asylum seekers' access to the labour market and social security. It will examine the extent to which the sovereign immigration power may limit the scope of the rights in these fields. Does international law 'carve out a zone of protected personhood' consisting of basic human rights?[1] If so, do such rights have any relevance for asylum seekers' access to the labour market and social security? As this relates primarily to minimum

[1] *Cf* Bosniak 2006, p 64; Da Lomba 2011.

subsistence benefits, this part will not pay much attention to social insurance benefits. It should be reiterated here that for the purposes of this book, the term 'social assistance' is not limited to financial assistance, but also includes benefits provided in kind with the purpose of providing a minimum subsistence level.[2]

As chapter two shows, the EU Reception Conditions Directives require EU Member States to provide asylum seekers with material reception benefits that (are capable of) ensur(e)(ing) a standard of living adequate for their health and their subsistence. Such benefits may be provided in kind, in vouchers or as financial allowances. Not all asylum seekers fall under the personal scope of these Directives and the Directives allow for reception conditions to be withdrawn or reduced on a number of grounds. In addition, the Directives allow Member States to link the provision of benefits to the exercise of a large amount of control. Access to the labour market may be postponed for one year or nine months and be made subject to various conditions afterwards.

These issues will be the subject of review in this part. More specifically, this part will examine whether international law, other than the provisions on non-discrimination and equal treatment discussed in Part II, contains obligations for the state to provide for minimum subsistence benefits for asylum seekers at all. If this question is answered in the positive, it will be examined whether international law provides any safeguards as to the quality of such benefits and as regards the withdrawal or reduction of such benefits. In addition to these two questions, this part of the book will examine whether asylum seekers can derive from international law an entitlement to access the labour market in the host state, albeit not on the same footing as nationals.

The research in this part will be limited to international refugee law and international human rights law. No attention will be paid here to international social security law. As has been mentioned in chapter five, international social security law can be divided into co-ordination instruments and standard-setting instruments. Co-ordination instruments typically deal with equal treatment of nationals and non-nationals, determination of applicable legislation, maintenance of acquired rights and export of benefits.[3] Accordingly, such instruments are not relevant for answering the above-mentioned questions. Standard-setting instruments generally deal with the quantitative level of social security protection in a country (minimum coverage), the qualifying conditions, the level of benefits and the periods of entitlement.[4] An important standard set by such instruments

[2] See the definition of the term 'social security' for the purposes of this book in s 1.5.2.
[3] See s 5.1.
[4] Kapuy 2011, pp 95–96 and 139.

is generally that a minimum percentage of the (working or general) population should be protected by social security schemes.[5] Accordingly, such instruments grant right of access to social security schemes only to an abstract percentage of the population, not to individuals.[6] In addition, such instruments only contain general minimum standards as regards social security schemes; they do not contain provisions on other (more minimal) kinds of protection. Such instruments are therefore not suitable either for answering the above-mentioned questions.[7]

8.2 RELEVANT CHARTER PROVISIONS

The EU Charter of Fundamental Rights (CFR) contains a number of relevant provisions for the research in this part of the book. These provisions include Article 1 on human dignity; Article 4 on the prohibition of inhuman or degrading treatment; Article 15 on the right to engage in work; Article 18 on the right to asylum; Article 34 on social security and social assistance; and Article 35 on health care. Some of these provisions are also referred to in the preambles of the EU Reception Conditions Directives (Articles 1, 4 and 18).[8] Remarkably, however, the preambles do not refer to Articles 15, 34 and 35 of the CFR, while these provisions seem at first sight very relevant for the issue of the reception of asylum seekers.

Relevant case law of the EU Court of Justice on the scope and meaning of these articles for the field of the reception of asylum seekers is (still) lacking.[9] The text of the Charter and of the explanations to the Charter indicate, however, that the scope and meaning of these articles

[5] Kapuy 2011, p 97; Schoukens and Pieters 2004, pp 5–6. See for the question whether standard-setting instruments that prescribe a minimum percentage of workers or of the population to be protected by social security legislation take irregular migrant workers into account when calculating this percentage Kapuy 2011, pp 98–100.

[6] Some standard-setting or harmonizing instruments contain prohibitions of discrimination on, for example, the ground of sex. Obviously, individuals can rely on such instruments in order to gain access to certain social security schemes.

[7] It is submitted that certain, more specific, ILO standard-setting instruments protect 'all employees' (see, eg, Convention no 121 on employment injury benefits and Convention no 183 on maternity protection (as regards all employed women)). However, at the same time, these conventions allow contracting states to exclude not further specified categories of employees. As Kapuy notes, this puts into perspective the meaning of the term 'all' (Kapuy 2011, p 97).

[8] Recital 5 of the preamble to Directive 2003/9 (reference to Arts 1 and 18) and recital 35 of the preamble to Directive 2013/33 (reference to Arts 1, 4, 6, 7, 18, 21, 24 and 47). Not all of these latter articles are relevant for the research in this part, as they are not all related to access to social security and employment.

[9] In the first and, so far, only judgment on Directive 2003/9, the CJEU did refer to Art 1 CFR, but only as an additional supportive argument. It did not explain the specific meaning and scope of that article (CJEU 27 September 2012, Case C-179/11 *Cimade and GISTI*).

can be established with reference to the ECHR, the ESC and the Refugee Convention. With regard to Article 4 of the CFR, the explanations indicate that it has the same wording as Article 3 of the ECHR and that it, by virtue of Article 52(3) of the CFR, therefore, has the same meaning and scope as this ECHR Article.[10] The explanations to Articles 15, 34 and 35 of the CFR refer to Articles 1, 12, 13, 30 and 31 of the ESC and the text of Article 18 of the CFR refers to the Refugee Convention. According to the explanations, human dignity, as referred to in Article 1 of the CFR, constitutes the basis of all fundamental rights. It is therefore likely that the rights and obligations identified in the foregoing and following chapters will provide inspiration for the interpretation of these Charter articles.[11]

What is noticeable about the text of Articles 34 and 35 of the CFR is the reference to national laws and practices. Article 52(6) of the CFR confirms once again that '[f]ull account shall be taken of national laws and practices as specified in this Charter'. According to the explanations, this reference to national laws and practices is made 'in the spirit of subsidiarity'. Arguably, this means that persons only have access to social security benefits, social services, social and housing assistance and health care if this is established by national law. Member states therefore seem to enjoy a considerable discretion in these areas. This is confirmed by one of few judgments in which the CJEU refers to Article 34 of the CFR. In the case of *Kamberaj v Italy*, the CJEU held that since Article 34(3) of the CFR refers to national law, it is for the referring court to assess whether a certain benefit falls within the scope of that article.[12] The (limited) added value of these Charter provisions could be that national law must be interpreted as much as possible in conformity with the (underlying goals of) these Charter provisions, or, in other words, Member States should as much as possible operate in the spirit of the guarantees provided by these Charter provisions.[13] This seems to be the approach of the CJEU as well. In the above-mentioned *Kamberaj* case, the Court used the purpose of Article 34(3) CFR to interpret the term 'core benefits' in a directive, while leaving it to the referring court to establish whether the benefit concerned actually fulfilled that purpose.[14]

A remarkable element of the text of Articles 15 and 34 of the CFR is the limitation in personal scope. While under Article 15(1) of the CFR 'everyone' has the right to engage in work, paragraph 2 of this article limits the right to 'seek employment in any Member State' to Union citizens and

[10] Indeed, in *NS*, the CJEU interpreted Art 4 of the CFR on the basis of case law of the ECtHR on Art 3 ECHR, notably its *MSS* judgment (see, on this judgment, ch 11).

[11] *Cf* Tooze 2003.

[12] CJEU 24 April 2012, Case C-571/10 *Kamberaj*, para 81.

[13] See also Tooze 2003, p 166.

[14] *Kamberaj* (n 12), para 92.

the entitlement to equivalent working conditions as Union citizens is limited to 'nationals of third countries who are authorised to work in the territories of the Member States' in paragraph 3. These provisions seem therefore to indicate that Article 15 of the CFR does not contain a right for third-country nationals to have access to the labour market of a Member State. Likewise, in Article 34(2), the entitlement to social security benefits and social advantages is limited to 'everyone residing and moving legally within the European Union'. The research in Part II, notably chapter four, has shown that asylum seekers generally cannot (yet) 'reside' legally in the territory. In addition, if they are undergoing an asylum procedure in a Member State, they are not 'moving' within the European Union. This entitlement does therefore not accrue to asylum seekers. The limited personal scope of these articles could also explain the omission of a reference to these articles in the preamble of the EU Reception Conditions Directives.

In the absence of a relevant body of case law of the EU Court of Justice, the above means that the Charter, at the time of writing, does not have much added value, compared to the obligations stemming from the ECHR, the ESC and the Refugee Convention, for the access of asylum seekers to the labour market and to social security and minimum subsistence benefits.

8.3 STRUCTURE OF PART III

Chapter nine will examine the substantive provisions of the Refugee Convention (as opposed to the provisions on equal treatment), chapter ten will examine the ICESCR (with an emphasis on the possibilities for justification) and chapter eleven will examine whether the ECHR contains positive obligations for the state in the socioeconomic sphere. Finally, chapter twelve will discuss Article 18 of the ESC. Chapter thirteen provides concluding remarks about the research in Part III.

9

Substantive Rights under the Refugee Convention

9.1 INTRODUCTION

IN CHAPTER FOUR it has been argued that, in my view, the most convincing interpretation of the Refugee Convention (RC) is that generally, asylum seekers are not 'lawfully staying' in the territory of the host state pending a determination of their claim to asylum. This means that the Refugee Convention does not require states to accord asylum seekers in their territory the same treatment as nationals with respect to public relief and assistance and social security,[1] nor does it require states to grant asylum seekers the most favourable treatment accorded to non-nationals as regards the right to engage in wage-earning employment.[2] This chapter will examine whether the Refugee Convention contains other obligations for contracting states with regard to the access of asylum seekers to their labour markets and social security systems.

Chapter four shows that the declaratory view of the term 'refugee' implies that recognition of refugee status is not necessary in order to fall under the personal scope of the Refugee Convention. Since asylum seekers might meet the definition of refugee as laid down in the Refugee Convention and, consequently, might be entitled to some of the benefits of the convention as from the moment they arrive in the host state, they have to be treated as refugees pending the determination of their status. Otherwise, states run the risk of acting in violation of the Refugee Convention by withholding important right from genuine refugees. This means that all asylum seekers are entitled to the benefits laid down in the Refugee Convention for refugees without further qualification.[3] In addition,

[1] See RC, Arts 23 and 24(1).

[2] See RC, Art 17(1).

[3] Hathaway notes that during the drafting process of the convention, the American representative observed that 'some of the articles did not specifically indicate to which refugees they applied. He presumed that the mention of 'refugees' without any qualifying phrase was intended to include all refugees, whether lawfully or unlawfully in the territory'. The immediate and unchallenged response of the Chairman was 'that the United States representative's presumption was correct' (Hathaway 2005, p 467, fn 861).

chapter four has argued that some categories of asylum seekers meet the qualifying condition of lawful presence as laid down in the Refugee Convention. It has been argued that the most persuasive interpretation of this condition, in view of the text, context and object and purpose of the Refugee Convention, entails that asylum seekers who present themselves to the authorities of the host state at the border, who are explicitly allowed entrance to the territory, and who do not violate any condition imposed on them as a condition for their entry are lawfully in the territory in the sense of the Refugee Convention. Hence, such asylum seekers are entitled to the benefits laid down in the convention for refugees lawfully in the territory of the host state.

This chapter will discuss the provisions of the Refugee Convention that may be of relevance for asylum seekers' access to the labour market and social security benefits, apart from entitlement to equal treatment with nationals. The following sections will discuss successively Article 7 on the general standard of treatment and exemption from reciprocity; Article 13 on movable and immovable property; Article 17 on wage-earning employment; Article 20 on rationing; Article 31(1) on exemption from penalties; and Article 33 on non-*refoulement*. The other provisions laid down in the Refugee Convention are restricted in scope to refugees lawfully staying in the territory of the host state[4] or cannot be related to asylum seekers' access to the labour market or social security benefits.

9.2 ARTICLE 7: GENERAL STANDARD OF TREATMENT AND EXEMPTION FROM RECIPROCITY

Article 7 of the RC reads:

1. Except where this Convention contains more favourable provisions, a Contracting State shall accord to refugees the same treatment as is accorded to aliens generally.
2. After a period of three years' residence, all refugees shall enjoy exemption from legislative reciprocity in the territory of the Contracting States.
3. Each Contracting State shall continue to accord to refugees the rights and benefits to which they were already entitled, in the absence of reciprocity, at the date of entry into force of this Convention for that State.
4. The Contracting States shall consider favourably the possibility of according to refugees, in the absence of reciprocity, rights and benefits beyond those to which they are entitled according to paragraphs 2 and 3, and to extending

[4] Art 19 (on access to liberal professions) and Art 21 (on housing) are relevant for the subject of this chapter, but these articles only apply to refugees lawfully staying in the territory.

exemption from reciprocity to refugees who do not fulfil the conditions provided for in paragraphs 2 and 3.

5. The provisions of paragraphs 2 and 3 apply both to the rights and benefits referred to in articles 13, 18, 19, 21 and 22 of this Convention and to rights and benefits for which this Convention does not provide.

Article 7(1) contains a general standard of treatment for refugees. It provides that, except where the convention contains more favourable provisions, states should accord refugees the same treatment as is accorded to aliens generally. The meaning of the term 'aliens generally' is not very clear. Arguably, it refers to aliens who are not entitled to benefits granted on the basis of reciprocity or on the basis of national laws instituting preferential treatment of certain groups of aliens.[5] Accordingly, Article 7(1) does not provide refugees with a very firm right, but it assures that *if* a state provides certain rights or benefits to aliens generally, then refugees are entitled to the same treatment as regards these rights or benefits. With regard to the position of asylum seekers as regards social security benefits and as regards access to the labour market, this means that excluding asylum seekers from such rights and benefits is only possible on the basis of general criteria that apply to all aliens similarly. Exclusion from benefits or from access to the labour market on the sole basis of being an asylum seeker is not in conformity with the obligation to grant refugees the same treatment as aliens generally.

More substantive protection for asylum seekers seems to be offered by Article 7(2), which provides that after a period of three years' residence, all refugees enjoy exemption from legislative reciprocity in the territory of the contracting states. Chapter four has argued that the term 'residence' in the Refugee Convention concerns physical presence for a certain amount of time, irrespective of the lawfulness of the stay. Accordingly, asylum seekers who are present on the territory of the host state for at least three years (which period is more than long enough in order to establish a residence in a given country[6]) fulfil this qualifying condition.

'Legislative reciprocity' must be distinguished from 'diplomatic reciprocity'. 'Legislative reciprocity' means a system whereby a state is prepared to grant benefits to any alien, provided that the country of nationality of the alien provides the same benefits to the citizens of the state concerned. In this system, the rule of reciprocity is a means of achieving equal rights and benefits for one's own nationals abroad. 'Diplomatic reciprocity' means a system whereby a state grants benefits only to 'preferred' nationals of states with which it has a special relationship or particularly

[5] Grahl-Madsen 1963, commentary no 2 to Art 7; Hathaway 2005, pp 197–98.

[6] Ch 4 has argued that a residence is established after being present on the territory for at least three months.

close ties, such as partner states in an economic or political union. The word 'legislative' was inserted to restrict the scope of Article 7(2), since it implies that refugees may still be excluded from rights and benefits 'which are granted for the purpose of placing nationals of particular foreign states in a privileged or favourable position', or, in other words, from rights or benefits stemming from bilateral treaties or conventions between a limited number of countries.[7] Grahl-Madsen states:

> [I]t would seem that industrial property rights, copyright, right of succession, social security benefits must nowadays be considered as subject only to legislative reciprocity. On the other hand, a right to enter a country without visa must obviously be considered as subject to diplomatic or conventional reciprocity, and the same would as a rule seem to apply to compensation for war damages and war pensions.[8]

Accordingly, Article 7(2) means that after three years of residence refugees can be subjected to diplomatic reciprocity, but no longer to legislative reciprocity. Article 7(5) specifies that the exemption from legislative reciprocity also applies to the rights laid down in the Refugee Convention that explicitly accord refugees 'treatment as favourable as possible and, in any event, not less favourable than that accorded to aliens generally'. This means that after three years of residence, refugees may not be treated as 'aliens generally', but must be exempted from legislative reciprocity.

Chapter five shows that in many social security conventions, refugees are exempted from reciprocity on the basis of an additional protocol or annex, without the qualifying condition of three years' residence in the contracting state. These conventions therefore provide more safeguards than provided for in Article 7(2) of the RC. Indeed, Article 7(4) urges contracting states to offer such further-reaching safeguards to refugees. More generally, the case law of the ECtHR implies that conditions of reciprocity are no longer allowed in the field of social security. Nevertheless, Article 7(2) of the RC might have implications for contracting states with regard to two of the social security conventions discussed in chapter five. Under ILO Convention no 102, equal treatment between nationals and non-nationals as regards contributory social security schemes that protect employees is provided on the basis of reciprocity alone. This convention has not been extended with a protocol concerning refugees. In such a case, Article of the 7(2) RC implies that refugees who reside in the host state for at least three years should have access to such schemes on the same basis as nationals, irrespective of whether their country of nationality has accepted these obligations. In addition, chapter six shows that the right

7 Grahl-Madsen 1963, commentary no 5 to Art 7. See also Hathaway 2005, pp 192–204.

8 Grahl-Madsen 1963, commentary no 5 to Art 7. See ch 12 for another example of diplomatic reciprocity.

to equal treatment with nationals as regards social and medical assistance under the ESC is reserved for asylum seekers who have the nationality of another contracting party and who are lawfully present on the territory. On the basis of Article 7(2) of the RC, *all* refugees who are resident in the territory of the host state for three years or more, irrespective of their nationality, are entitled to equal treatment with nationals with regard to social and medical assistance if they are lawfully present on the territory.[9] Hence, the same obligation already incumbent on contracting states to the ECSMA and with regard to asylum seekers who have the nationality of a contracting state to the ESC (see chapters five and six) would apply after three years of residence to all asylum seekers in all EU Member States.

9.3 ARTICLE 13: MOVABLE AND IMMOVABLE PROPERTY

Article 13 RC reads:

> The Contracting States shall accord to a refugee treatment as favourable as possible and, in any event, not less favourable than that accorded to aliens generally in the same circumstances, as regards the acquisition of movable and immovable property and other rights pertaining thereto, and to leases and other contracts relating to movable and immovable property.

As chapter six has shown, the ECtHR has ruled that social security benefits should be considered to be property rights if they are not provided on a purely discretionary basis. As Article 13 concerns the right to the 'acquisition' of property, this article is relevant for the social security position of refugees in Europe. The standard of treatment prescribed by this article is, however, rather low, since refugees are only entitled to treatment not less favourable than that accorded to aliens generally. This standard of treatment is therefore the same as the general standard of treatment laid down in Article 7 of the RC (see above). The phrase 'as favourable as possible' implies only a recommendation to the states parties: the determination of what is possible is left to the discretion of the states parties.[10] The only extra safeguard that Article 13 provides in addition to Article 7 is that it provides that refugees are entitled to the same treatment as aliens generally

[9] See ESC, Art 13. With regard to other rights laid down in the European Social Charter, the general (restricted) personal scope of the Charter still applies. This means that even though after three years of residence, asylum seekers no longer have to fulfil the condition that they are a national of a contracting state to the ESC, they still do have to be 'lawfully resident' or 'working regularly' on the territory in order to fall under the personal scope. See further ch 6. Article 18 of the ESC on the right to engage in a gainful occupation is not subjected to the restricted personal scope. This article will be discussed more extensively in ch12.

[10] Grahl-Madsen 1963, commentary part II to Art 13.

in the same circumstances. This phrase has been defined in Article 6 of the RC, which reads:

> For the purposes of this Convention, the term 'in the same circumstances' implies that any requirements (including requirements as to length and conditions of sojourn or residence) which the particular individual would have to fulfil for the enjoyment of the right in question, if he were not a refugee, must be fulfilled by him, with the exception of requirements which by their nature a refugee is incapable of fulfilling.

This article thus contains an important exception. States may not subject refugees to conditions that they are unable to fulfil. As Hathaway states: 'whatever impediments an individual refugee faces by virtue of the uprooting and dislocation associated with refugeehood should not be relied upon to deny access to rights'.[11] Grahl-Madsen mentions as an example of such conditions the requirement to produce a certificate of nationality, or the requirement to produce documentation of examinations passed and of experience gained in the country of origin.[12] Hence, Article 13 does not guarantee refugees property rights; their property rights are dependent on those accorded to aliens generally. This means that subjecting asylum seekers to conditions as regards lawfulness of residence or employment with regard to acquisition of property rights does not violate this article, provided that such conditions are generally applied to all aliens. In this regard, Article 13 does not provide any further safeguards than Article 7 of the RC. However, *if* property rights are granted to aliens generally, then refugees may not be excluded from these rights and, moreover, they may not be subjected to conditions that they are by their nature unable to fulfil. Hence, if states grant asylum seekers certain social security benefits that are considered to be property rights, they may not require asylum seekers to produce a certificate of nationality. Such a condition may be imposed on aliens generally where social security benefits are granted on the basis of reciprocity (eg under ILO Convention no 102 and under the European Social Charter).

9.4 ARTICLE 17: WAGE-EARNING EMPLOYMENT

Article 17 of the RC concerns the rights to wage-earning employment for refugees. Paragraph 1 of this article applies only to refugees who are lawfully staying in the territory and therefore not to asylum seekers. Article 17(2)

[11] Hathaway 2005, p 208.

[12] Grahl-Madsen 1963, commentary no 3 to Art 6. This does not mean, according to Grahl-Madsen, that refugees eg do not have to prove that they have passed a certain examination, but they must be allowed to prove the possession of the required degree by other means.

is, however, wider in scope and contains an important safeguard for asylum seekers. It reads:

> In any case, restrictive measures imposed on aliens or the employment of aliens for the protection of the national labour market shall not be applied to a refugee who was already exempt from them at the date of entry into force of this Convention for the Contracting State concerned, or who fulfils one of the following conditions:
>
> (a) He has completed three years' residence in the country;
> (b) He has a spouse possessing the nationality of the country of residence. A refugee may not invoke the benefit of this provision if he has abandoned his spouse;
> (c) He has one or more children possessing the nationality of the country of residence.

The benefits of this article are not reserved for refugees lawfully in or lawfully staying in the territory. Hence, asylum seekers can benefit from this provision if they have been present in the territory of the host state for at least three years (whether lawfully or not); if they marry someone with the nationality of the host state; or if they have children possessing the nationality of the host state.[13] Asylum seekers who fulfil one of these conditions cannot be subjected to 'restrictive measures imposed on aliens or the employment of aliens for the protection of the national labour market'. This means, for example, that they may not be subjected to the condition that they may only be employed if no nationals are available for the job in question.[14] On the other hand, this implies that they *can* be subjected to restrictive measures also imposed on nationals and to restrictive measures which have another purpose than protecting the national labour market, eg national security or political considerations.[15] This raises the question whether subjecting them to restrictive measures as regards access to the labour market for reasons of preventing integration into the host society or preventing a possible 'honey-pot effect' and, accordingly, an increase in the numbers of (unfounded) asylum applications is in compliance with Article 17(2). As chapter two has shown, this seems to be the main reason underlying the limited obligations under the EU Reception Conditions Directives to grant asylum seekers access to the labour market. Arguably, however, the purpose of Article 17(2) is to achieve the lifting of labour restrictions 'in favour of those refugees who have a special link with

[13] This is especially relevant for asylum seekers residing in a country where nationality is acquired in accordance with the principle of *jus soli* (meaning that children born on the territory of a country automatically acquire the nationality of that country).

[14] Weis, cited in Hathaway 2005, p 761.

[15] Hathaway 2005, pp 761–62; Grahl-Madsen 1963, commentary no 5 to Art 17.

their country of refuge'.[16] Trying to prevent the integration into the host society of refugees who fulfil one of the conditions laid down in Article 17(2), and who therefore have already established a special link with their host state, seems to be contrary to the very purpose of this article. In addition, the qualifying conditions that are necessary to fulfil in order to be entitled to the safeguard of Article 17(2) arguably serve to prevent it from becoming a pull factor for asylum seekers. Accordingly, it is submitted here that after three years of residence in the host state, or in the case of a spouse or children possessing the nationality of the host state, asylum seekers may no longer be subjected to general conditions regarding work permits that are generally imposed on aliens in order to protect the national labour market. In addition, restrictive measures specifically imposed on asylum seekers for reasons of general immigration policy (eg to discourage the filing of unfounded claims and to facilitate the expulsion of rejected asylum seekers) are not in conformity with the object and purpose of Article 17(2).

9.5 ARTICLE 20: RATIONING

Under the heading 'welfare', the Refugee Convention contains two articles that apply to all refugees without any further qualifying conditions: Article 22 on public education (which is not relevant for the subject of this book) and Article 21 on rationing systems. As has been mentioned previously, the Refugee Convention does not contain a provision on basic needs, such as the right to food, clothing and other essential products. As Hathaway notes, '[t]he one relevant concern addressed [by the RC], however, was access by refugees to essential goods not distributed on the open market'.[17] Accordingly, Article 20 provides:

> Where a rationing system exists, which applies to the population at large and regulates the general distribution of products in short supply, refugees shall be accorded the same treatment as nationals.

Grahl-Madsen observes that:

> The meaning of the phrase after the comma is intended to restrict the application of the Article to rationing of more or less essential goods for personal use, thus excluding rationing of 'commodities for commercial or industrial use, such as common or precious metals'.[18]

[16] Grahl-Madsen 1963, commentary no 5 to Art 17, referring to the origins of this provision.
[17] Hathaway 2005, p 467.
[18] Grahl-Madsen 1963, commentary no 2 to Art 20. See also Hathaway 2005, pp 467–68.

For refugees in the territory of EU Member States, this provision is not very relevant nowadays.[19]

9.6 ARTICLE 31(1): FREEDOM FROM PENALIZATION FOR ILLEGAL ENTRY

Article 31 of the RC has already been discussed rather extensively in chapter four. To reiterate, it contains a prohibition for states to impose penalties on refugees on account of their illegal entry or presence, provided they present themselves without delay to the authorities and show good cause for their illegal entry or presence.

It has been argued that measures that deny employment rights and social security benefits to asylum seekers on account of their unlawful entry or presence constitute a violation of this article.[20] According to this reasoning, denying social benefits or employment authorization amounts to the imposition of 'penalties'. In this way, the term 'penalties' is understood broadly, in conformity with the ordinary meaning of the term, as 'a loss inflicted for violation of a law'.[21] According to Hathaway, such a broad interpretation is in line with the decision taken by the drafters of the Convention to conceive Article 31 'not as a prohibition of a particular *kind of penalty,* but instead as a prohibition of penalties *imposed on a particular group of persons*'.[22]

In contrast, Grahl-Madsen notes with reference to the drafting process of the Refugee Convention, that the term 'penalties' includes

> imprisonment and fines, meted out as a punishment by a judicial or semi-judicial body and must also be construed to include measures, such as preventive detention of mentally deficient persons, which may be resorted to in lieu of punishment. On the other hand it does not include confinement or detention for the purpose of investigation or as a security measure.[23]

This indicates a rather strict interpretation of the term 'penalties'. As Hathaway notes as well, such a narrow interpretation, being limited to criminal penalties, is in line with the French-language version of Article 31, which refers to *sanctions pénales*.[24]

Goodwin-Gill states that the object and purpose of the protection envisaged by Article 31(1) is the avoidance of penalization on account of illegal entry or illegal presence. In view of this, an overly formal or restrictive

[19] As Hathaway notes, the convention was drafted when the Second World War, during which many key goods had been rationed, has just been ended (Hathaway 2005, p 467).

[20] See, eg, Cholewinski 2000, p 713 and Hathaway 2005, pp 409–12.

[21] Hathaway 2005, p 410.

[22] Ibid, p 412.

[23] Grahl-Madsen 1963, commentary no 2 to Art 31.

[24] Hathaway 2005, p 411.

approach to defining the term 'penalties' will not be appropriate, 'for otherwise the fundamental protection intended may be circumvented and the refugee's rights withdrawn at discretion'.[25]

On the basis of these different interpretations I would argue that the term 'penalties' should primarily apply to criminal sanctions, but should not necessarily be restricted to such sanctions. It might also apply to a deliberate curtailment of the rights laid down in the Refugee Convention imposed on refugees for reason of their illegal entry or presence. However, a treatment imposed on these categories of refugees specifically that is in conformity with the relevant standards of treatment laid down in the Refugee Convention should, in my view, not be seen as an imposition of a penalty. This means that a denial of access to the labour market that is in line with Article 17 or a denial or reduction of social security benefits in line with Articles 23, 24 and the other articles discussed above, is in my opinion not contrary to the safeguard of Article 31(1) of the RC, even if the denial is imposed for reasons of illegal entrance or presence.

9.7 ARTICLE 33: NON-*REFOULEMENT*

It has been argued that the complete denial of minimum subsistence benefits and the right to work violates the prohibition of *refoulement* as laid down in Article 33 of the RC, as this article prohibits the expulsion or *refoulement* of refugees 'in any manner whatsoever'.[26] According to this reasoning, refugees who suffer from serious deprivation and are therefore left with no real option but to leave would in fact be forced to leave the country.[27] Such 'repatriation under coercion' violates Article 33. According to Hathaway, the preparatory work to the convention makes clear that Article 33 was meant to avoid certain consequences (namely, return to the risk of being persecuted), whatever the nature of the actions which lead to that result.[28] However, it seems that Article 33 is violated only if return to the risk of being persecuted actually takes place.[29] If a

[25] Goodwin-Gill 2003, p 195.

[26] See, eg, Cholewinski 2000, pp 712–13; Dent 1998, p 23 with further references.

[27] Hathaway 2005, p 318.

[28] Ibid.

[29] *Cf* Hathaway who states that '[e]ven when repatriation does not in fact result, core norms of the Civil and Political Covenant already examined may be contravened by such deprivations' (Hathaway 2005, p 464), thereby implying that Art 33 is not violated if repatriation does not in fact result. See in this regard the difference between two judgments of the ECtHR on state support for asylum seekers. In the case of *Müslim v Turkey,* the Court held that the applicant's situation did not appear to be so desperate as to force to him leave Turkey because it was no longer tenable (app no 53566/99, ECtHR 26 April 2005, para 86). In the case of *MSS v Belgium and Greece,* the Court found it relevant that the applicant had tried several times to leave Greece in order to 'escape from that situation of insecurity and

refugee can survive in the country of refuge, despite an official denial of employment and any kind of state assistance—for example, with the assistance of relatives, neighbours, churches, etc—Article 33 is not violated. In addition, refugees who leave the country of refuge because they suffer from deprivation do not necessarily have to return to a country where their life and freedom would be threatened. A policy to deny asylum seekers access to employment and state-sponsored benefits therefore, in my view, does not necessarily violate Article 33.

9.8 CONCLUDING REMARKS

Chapter four has shown that the Refugee Convention does not require contracting states to provide asylum seekers with equal treatment with nationals as regards social security benefits and access to the labour market. This chapter shows that the Refugee Convention does contain a number of other obligations for contracting states with regard to asylum seekers rights in these fields. For example, contracting states may not subject asylum seekers to conditions which, by their nature, they are unable to fulfil as regards the acquisition of property rights, such as, in the European context, social security rights. More importantly, after three years of (simple) residence in the territory of a contracting state, asylum seekers should be exempted from legislative reciprocity and from restrictive measures imposed on aliens or the employment of aliens for the protection of the national labour market. The latter obligation also applies to asylum seekers who have a spouse or one or more children possessing the nationality of the country of residence. Besides providing these important obligations as regards access to the labour market and social security schemes after three years of residence, these provisions might indicate, more generally, the significance of physical presence in a given territory over a period of time for the accretion of rights.

of material and psychological want' (app no 30696/09, ECtHR 21 January 2011, para 254). Both judgments will be discussed in ch 11.

10

Justifications under the International Covenant on Economic, Social and Cultural Rights

10.1 INTRODUCTION

IN CHAPTER SIX it has already been argued that asylum seekers fall under the personal scope of the rights laid down in the International Covenant on Economic, Social and Cultural Rights (ICESCR) if they are under the jurisdiction of a state party. This means that it is the only general human rights instrument on social and economic rights that is applicable to all asylum seekers in the European Union, which at first sight would seem to make this a very relevant instrument for the purpose of this book.[1] Relevant rights laid down in the ICESCR for the purpose of this study include Article 6 on the right to work, which explicitly includes the right to the opportunity to gain a living by work, Article 11 on the right to an adequate standard of living, which explicitly includes the right to adequate food, clothing and housing, and Article 12 on the right to the enjoyment of the highest attainable standard of physical and mental health.

This chapter will examine whether state obligations with regard to the reception of asylum seekers stem from provisions of the ICESCR not related to non-discrimination. In doing so, this chapter will pay the most attention to the somewhat neglected question of permitted limitations to the rights laid down in the ICESCR, as this is, as will be argued, the relevant test with regard to the social and economic rights of asylum seekers in the European Union. Section 10.3 will discuss in detail Article 4 of the ICESCR, which contains a general limitation clause. Then, section 10.4 will apply the general findings to the situation of asylum seekers in the EU. But as a start, section 10.2 will pay attention to the nature of the rights laid down in the ICESCR.

[1] Ch 6 has shown that not all asylum seekers in Europe fall under the personal scope of the European Social Charter.

10.2 NATURE OF THE RIGHTS

Article 2, paragraph 1 of the ICESCR reads:

> Each State Party to the present Covenant undertakes to take steps, individually and through international assistance and co-operation, especially economic and technical, to the maximum of its available resources, with a view to achieving progressively the full realization of the rights recognized in the present Covenant by all appropriate means, including particularly the adoption of legislative measures.

Hence, the rights laid down in the ICESCR should be realized 'progressively' and 'to the maximum of available resources'. This is an important distinction from the general obligation on states parties laid down in Article 2 of the International Covenant on Civil and Political Rights and in Article 1 of the European Convention on Human Rights. Another difference between the ICESCR, on the one hand, and the ICCPR and ECHR, on the other hand, is the language used in the articles granting specific rights. In the former instrument, these articles generally use the wording: 'The States parties to the present Covenant recognize the right of everyone to', whereas the latter conventions generally state more absolutely that 'everyone has the right to' or that 'no one shall be subjected to'. A further difference between these conventions is the supervisory mechanism established by the convention. Whereas the ECHR provides for the establishment of a supervisory court that can issue legally binding decisions and the ICCPR provides for the establishment of a supervisory committee, the ICESCR does not establish a supervisory body, but leaves oversight to the Economic and Social Council of the United Nations.[2]

These differences can be explained, but are also caused to a large extent, by the dichotomy traditionally considered to exist between civil and political rights, on the one hand, and economic, social and cultural rights, on the other hand. The former were considered to impose only negative obligations that are of an immediate nature, non-resource-dependent and described in precise terms. The latter were held to impose only positive obligations and to be of progressive realization, highly resource-dependent and formulated in vague terms.[3] Because of this, it was often assumed that the ICESCR did not impose binding legal obligations upon states, but merely made declarations of aspirations or goals to be achieved.[4] Vierdag is usually mentioned as one of the most explicit adherents to this sceptical

[2] The Committee on Economic, Social and Cultural Rights is established by a resolution of the Economic and Social Council. See further s 1.7.

[3] Sepúlveda 2003, p 3. See also Eide 2001, p 10; International Commission of Jurists 2008, p 15; and Vandenhole 2003, p 431.

[4] Sepúlveda 2003, p 2.

view of the legal nature on the rights laid down in the ICESCR.[5] In a study on the legal nature of these rights he concludes that in the ICESCR 'the word "right" appears to be used as it often is in political programmes, viz, in a moral and hortatory sense'[6] and that, apart from some minor exceptions, the rights granted by the ICESCR 'are of such a nature as to be legally negligible'.[7] In order to reach this conclusion, Vierdag argues that he wants to reserve the term 'right' of an individual for those rights that are capable of being enforced by their bearers in courts of law.[8] Economic and social rights are not enforceable or justiciable to the extent that they are 'programmatic', ie 'lead to the adoption of programmes for the taking of measures intended to result in conditions under which what the rights promise can be enjoyed'.[9] In addition, enforceability is difficult as economic and social rights are not directed at government action that can be described or defined in terms of law. According to Vierdag, it would not be possible to determine which specific entitlements derive from economic and social rights and how limitations of economic and social rights can be legally fixed.[10]

A close reading of Vierdag's study reveals, however, that he is not completely sceptical about the legal nature of the rights laid down in the ICESCR. He submits, for example, that not all the rights laid down in the ICESCR are under all circumstances 'programmatic'. First of all, a right which would seem to be 'programmatic' in one country may be immediately enjoyed and thus enforceable in another; it can be dependent on the economic and social system of the country concerned. Secondly, whatever the socioeconomic system in any given country may be, a social right can very well be directed at the performance of a state activity that is immediately available and to that extent enforceable.[11] Vierdag mentions the example of an existing system of social security in a given country. In that case, a person whose position is such that he enjoys the right to social

[5] See, eg, Addo 1988, p 1425; Arambulo 1996, p 117; Eide 2001, p 10; Van Hoof 1984, p 98.
[6] Vierdag 1978, p 103.
[7] Ibid, p 105.
[8] Ibid, p 73.
[9] Ibid, p 83.
[10] Ibid, p 93. Contra, it can be argued that a distinction should be made between the justiciability of treaty provisions, for which the degree of concreteness is decisive, and the legally binding nature of a treaty provision, for which it is not (Van Hoof 1984, p 101). In other words, even if certain treaty provisions cannot be invoked before a court, this does not imply that these provisions are not legally binding for the state. As this book examines the provisions of international law that EU Member States should take into account when designing a reception policy for asylum seekers, the justiciability of economic and social rights is not the decisive question, but rather the content of the state obligations resulting from them. For defining this content, justiciability is, however, important, as court decisions are usually very useful in defining the content of abstract treaty provisions. Nevertheless, for the sake of clarity it is important to distinguish both aspects of treaty provisions.
[11] Vierdag 1978, p 83.

security as laid down in Article 9 of the ICESCR would be able to enforce this right in a court of law.[12] In his conclusion, Vierdag distinguishes between rights to something that is immediately available at no cost; rights to something that is immediately available which demands expenditure that can be divided, ie the funds available can be used to serve varying numbers of people, such as social security and medical care; and rights to something that is not available or of limited availability where division of what is available is not feasible ('a person is either in or out of a job, a house or a school'). Only rights of the latter category are inherently unenforceable according to Vierdag.[13] Hence, even the author generally considered to have the most sceptical view regarding the legal nature of social and economic rights sees some circumstances under which social and economic rights should be considered to be 'real rights' after all. He also submits that it is not impossible that economic, social and cultural rights will develop in such a way that they can be legally described and become a fixed legal concept.[14]

During the last decades, it is submitted, such developments have indeed taken place. They have made the traditional distinction between economic, social and cultural rights, on the one hand, and civil and political rights, on the other hand, less sharp, or even non-existent. These developments occurred both on the side of the economic, social and cultural rights and on the side of the civil and political rights.

With regard to the economic, social and cultural rights, it has already been held in legal doctrine for many years that the rights laid down in the ICESCR are not purely programmatic, vague or indeterminate, but that they impose some directly operative obligations.[15] The same opinion is held by the Committee on Economic, Social and Cultural Rights (the Committee). In its General Comment on the nature of states parties' obligations, the Committee states: 'while the Covenant provides for progressive realization and acknowledges the constraints due to the limits of available resources, it also imposes various obligations which are of immediate effect'. Of the latter obligations, the Committee mentions as examples the obligation to guarantee that relevant rights will be exercised 'without discrimination' and the obligation to 'take steps'. In addition, the Committee has held that

> a minimum core obligation to ensure the satisfaction of, at the very least, minimum essential levels of each of the rights is incumbent upon every State party. Thus, for example, a State party in which any significant number of individuals

[12] Ibid, p 86.
[13] Ibid, pp 102–03.
[14] Ibid, p 93.
[15] See, eg, Alston and Quinn 1987; Craven 1995; Eide 2001; Van Hoof 1984; Sepúlveda 2003.

is deprived of essential foodstuffs, of essential primary health care, of basic shelter and housing, or of the most basic forms of education is, prima facie, failing to discharge its obligations under the Covenant.[16]

In addition, a distinction between different types of state obligation has been developed by the legal doctrine and the Committee. The Committee distinguishes between obligations to respect, obligations to protect and obligations to fulfil. According to the Committee, the obligation to *respect* requires states to refrain from interfering directly or indirectly with the enjoyment of the right in question. The obligation to *protect* requires states to take measures that prevent third parties from interfering with the enjoyment of rights. Finally, the obligation to *fulfil* requires states to adopt appropriate legislative, administrative, budgetary, judicial, promotional and other measures towards the full realization of the right in question. The development of these different types of state obligation has contributed to reducing the supposed distinction between social, economic and cultural rights, on the one hand, and civil and political rights, on the other hand, as it has made clear that the distinction between positive and negative state obligations is too simple. It has become clear that, just like civil and political rights, economic, social and cultural rights impose obligations for the state to 'respect' and not interfere, for example with the freedom and use of resources possessed by individuals.[17]

On 10 December 2008 the General Assembly of the UN unanimously adopted the Optional Protocol to the ICESCR, which grants the Committee competence to receive and consider communications submitted by or on behalf of individuals or groups of individuals claiming to be victims of a violation of any of the economic, social and cultural rights set forth in the ICESCR.[18] This protocol has been signed so far by 45 states and ratified by 11 states. It entered into force on 5 May 2013.[19] The adoption forms another indication of the possible binding nature of the rights laid down in the ICESCR and of the absence of an inherent difference between civil and political rights, on the one hand, and economic, social and cultural rights, on the other hand.[20] Finally, domestic case law shows

[16] Committee on Economic, Social and Cultural Rights, General Comment no 3, the nature of states parties' obligations, 14 December 1990.

[17] *Cf* Eide 2001, p 25.

[18] Resolution A/RES/63/117.

[19] treaties.un.org/Pages/ViewDetails.aspx?src=TREATY&mtdsg_no=IV-3-a&chapter=4&lang=en. The only EU Member States that so far have ratified this protocol are Portugal, Spain and Slovakia.

[20] See Griffey who states that 'the Optional Protocol ended an historic imbalance in the international protection afforded 'civil and political' (CP) and 'economic, social and cultural' (ESC) rights' (Griffey 2011, p 276). Nevertheless, Vandenbogaerde and Vandenhole have identified a number of issues in the (drafting process of the) Optional Protocol that reflect the long-standing ideological prejudices against economic and social rights (Vandenbogaerde and Vandenhole 2010). One such issue is the standard of review laid down in Art 8(4) of the

that it is possible to define the content of economic and social rights and to assess whether the government has violated obligations resulting from those rights.[21]

An even more important development has taken place with regard to civil and political rights. Chapter eleven will show that according to the European Court of Human Rights' case law, the rights laid down in the European Convention on Human Rights also impose numerous positive state obligations that are resource dependent. Nevertheless, the Court is able to assess whether the state has violated these obligations. Although the scope of the positive obligation is sometimes held by the Court to be dependent on the availability of state resources, this does not mean that those obligations are not considered to be binding and of an immediate nature. In addition, the Court has to deduce these state obligations from general and not very precisely formulated provisions, such as the right to be free from torture and inhuman and degrading treatment and the right to respect for private and family life. Hence, while it was already acknowledged that economic, social and cultural rights impose obligations on the state not to interfere with existing rights of individuals, recent case law of the European Court on Human Rights shows that civil and political rights are able to impose obligations on the state to provide resources to individuals. Owing to these developments, it becomes difficult to make an abstract distinction between economic, social and cultural rights, on the one hand, and civil and political rights, on the other. While it may be true that the emphasis in civil and political rights lies more on obligations to respect and the emphasis in economic, social and cultural rights lies more on obligations to fulfil, there seems no longer to be any ground for holding that the nature, and consequently the justiciability, of economic, social and cultural rights is inherently different from the nature of civil and political rights.[22]

This chapter will therefore take as its starting point that the rights laid down in the ICESCR are not merely programmatic, vague and indeterminate, but impose some binding obligations upon states. Instead of focusing on the precise content of the state obligations under the ICESCR, this chapter will focus on a much more neglected aspect of the rights laid down in the covenant: that the ICESCR does not lay down absolute rights; but that the rights laid down in the covenant are qualified. This has often been disregarded in case law, in the work of the Committee

Optional Protocol. This article provides that the Committee should examine the 'reasonableness' of the steps taken by the state party. See further s 10.3.8 below.

[21] See the examples discussed in Coomans 2006 and International Commission of Jurists 2008.

[22] See also Vandenhole 2003, p 436. In contrast, Bossuyt still stresses the different legal characteristics of civil and social rights (see Bossuyt 2007, pp 328–29).

and in the legal doctrine. The ICESCR provides that states may impose limitations on the enjoyment of the rights if certain requirements are met. With regard to the reception of asylum seekers, it will be argued in this chapter that this is the decisive aspect of the rights laid down in the ICESCR. As Part I shows, asylum seekers' access to social security benefits and the labour market is usually not refused or reduced owing to a lack of resources, but is (explicitly and clearly) based on reasons of immigration policy. This raises the question whether it is permitted under the ICESCR to limit the social and economic rights of asylum seekers for such reasons. As the answer to this question would seem to be crucial for the existence of obligations incumbent on EU Member States under the ICESCR as regards the reception of asylum seekers, and given the relatively small amount of attention paid to this question so far in the legal doctrine, this chapter will elaborate extensively on this issue.

Interpretations of the Committee on Economic, Social and Cultural Rights are relevant in this respect. However, as has been said in chapter one, as these interpretations are not legally binding, they derive their authority from the position of the Committee in the treaty, which is not very strong in the case of the Committee on Economic, Social and Cultural Rights, and from the persuasiveness of the reasoning of the interpretation.[23]

10.3 JUSTIFICATIONS

10.3.1 Introduction

Most provisions of the ICESCR do not contain specific limitation clauses. However, the covenant does contain a general limitation clause. Article 4 of the ICESCR provides:

> The States Parties to the present Covenant recognize that, in the enjoyment of those rights provided by the State in conformity with the present Covenant, the State may subject such rights only to such limitations as are determined by law only in so far as this may be compatible with the nature of these rights and solely for the purpose of promoting the general welfare in a democratic society.

This provision has received strikingly little attention in the work of the Committee, the legal doctrine[24] or in case law. The Committee, for example, has only briefly mentioned the possibility of imposing limitations on

[23] See s 1.7.
[24] Exceptions are Alston and Quinn 1987 and Müller 2009.

the rights laid down in the Convention in four general comments.[25] As mentioned previously, with regard to the reception of asylum seekers, this provision is very relevant and therefore deserves a thorough discussion in this chapter.

10.3.2 Scope of the Limitation Provision

As Alston and Quinn note, Article 4 of the ICESCR has, like other limitation clauses in human rights treaties, both a permissive and a protective function. The permissive function authorizes states to impose limitations on the enjoyment of the rights provided for in the covenant, whereas the protective function serves to protect these rights by limiting both the purposes for which limitations may be imposed and the manner in which that may be legitimately done. Hence, the provision can be said to act 'both as a shield and as a sword'.[26] From a review of the arguments adduced for including a general limitation clause in the ICESCR in the *travaux préparatoires*, Alston and Quinn conclude that the limitation clause was meant to allow states to impose limitations where:

> (1) an unlimited interpretation of a right would lead to absurd results and would deny a state the necessary authority to enact detailed regulatory provisions; and (2) the various rights would otherwise clash with each other or with the legitimate interests of the state.[27]

According to the Committee, however, Article 4 is 'primarily intended to be protective of the rights of individuals rather than permissive of the imposition of limitations by the State'.[28] The Committee does not substantiate this view in any way. It does not explain why this protective function is more important than the permissive function and why it is necessary to depart so clearly from the text of the provision[29] and from

[25] In General Comment no 13 on the right to education (para 42); General Comment no 14 on the right to the highest attainable standard of health (paras 28–29); General Comment no17 on the right of everyone to benefit from the protection of the moral and material interests resulting from any scientific, literary or artistic production of which he is the author (paras 22–24); and General Comment no 21 on the right of everyone to take part in cultural life (para 19).

[26] Alston and Quinn 1987, p 193.

[27] Ibid, p 197.

[28] See General Comment no 13 on the right to education (para 42) and General Comment no 14 on the right to the highest attainable standard of health (para 28). This phrase is probably borrowed from para 46 of the 'Limburg principles on the implementation of the international covenant on economic, social and cultural rights', available at: www.refworld.org/docid/48abd5790.html. These principles were established unanimously by a group of experts in international law in June 1986 in Maastricht.

[29] Eg Art G of the European Social Charter (revised) reads: 'The rights and principles set forth in Part I when effectively realised, and their effective exercise as provided for in Part II,

the interpretation based on the *travaux préparatoires*. Consequently, the Committee's statement is, in my view, not very persuasive.

10.3.3 Relation to Article 2 of the ICESCR

Under Article 2 of the ICESCR, states are required to take steps 'to the maximum of their available resources'. This implies that if certain rights cannot be provided by the state owing to resource scarcity, the state has not violated the ICESCR. In other words, a resource-motivated failure to achieve the full realization of a certain right, or a resource-motivated reduction in the level of attainment of a certain right, cannot be seen as a 'limitation' on the right in question, as there is no obligation for the state to achieve the full realization if this is not possible owing to resource scarcity. Hence, resource-motivated failures to achieve the full realization of a right or resource-motivated reductions should not be dealt with in the context of Article 4. This interpretation is confirmed by the *travaux préparatoires*. As Alston and Quinn note, 'Article 4 was clearly seen by its drafters as dealing with limitations other than those that could be imposed under Article 2(1) on the grounds of limited resource availability'.[30] This reading seems also to be followed by the Committee, as it never refers to Article 4 when evaluating retrogressive measures taken owing to resource constraints.[31] As Müller concludes from the Committee's approach, states enjoy a wider discretion when they invoke resource constraints under Article 2(1) than if they impose a limitation on the basis of Article 4.[32] On the other hand, an important difference from permitted limitations under Article 4 is that for an inadequate realization within the limits of Article 2(1), the obligation for the state to take steps to (ultimately) achieve the full realization of the right in question still exists.[33]

shall not be subject to any restrictions or limitations not specified in those parts, except such as are prescribed by law and are necessary in a democratic society for the protection of the rights and freedoms of others or for the protection of public interest, national security, public health, or morals'. Hence, in contrast to Art 4 of the ICESCR, this limitation clause is formulated in negative terms (*cf* Sepúlveda 2003, p 278). In that case, it would make more sense to hold that this provision is primarily intended to be protective of the rights of individuals. As Art 4 of the ICESCR is formulated in permissive terms, such an interpretation is not very obvious.

[30] Alston and Quinn 1987, p 194.

[31] Müller 2009, p 585. However, as Müller also notes, the criteria used by the Committee to evaluate these measures, are very similar to the criteria mentioned in Art 4.

[32] Müller 2009, p 587. However, in view of the obligation laid down in Art 2(1) of achieving *progressively* the full realization of the covenant rights, as regards deliberate *retrogressive* measures based on resource constraints, the discretion of states is more limited (Sepúlveda 2003, pp 319–32).

[33] *Cf* Vlemminx 2002, p 165.

It has been argued that it would be better to use a unified standard to evaluate limitations of the rights laid down in the ICESCR, be it for reasons of resource scarcity or other reasons. Otherwise, it would be too easy for states to evade their obligations under Article 4, since it seems nearly always possible to relate limitations to resource scarcity and the notion of progressive realization under Article 2(1). In addition, it would be difficult in practice to draw a strict line between retrogressive measures that were taken because of resource constraints and limitations that are not related to scarce resources. For these reasons, the argument goes, the requirements of Article 4 should also be applied to retrogressive measures taken by states for reasons of severe resource constraints.[34]

On the other hand, it has been argued that a strict distinction between the requirements of Article 2 and Article 4 should exist. Otherwise, it is unclear how a certain situation must be legally assessed and states are able to wrongfully absolve themselves of their obligations. A disproportionate lack of supporting measures by the state, eg many people live below the poverty line, can in that case be wrongly justified under Article 4, as a result of which the obligation to take steps to improve this situation would no longer exist. According to Vlemminx, Article 4 is only relevant with regard to obligations for the state to respect rights and with regard to obligations where the performance by the state forms a necessary condition for the exercise of a certain freedom (eg procedural rights or the right for detainees to exercise family life). With regard to all other obligations for the state (eg obligations to promote or to fulfil rights, obligations to ensure a certain minimum or to make a provision for an emergency), non-compliance is caused by establishing budgetary priorities, which should be reviewed under Article 2(1) of the ICESCR.[35]

Indeed, in many cases it will be difficult to make a clear distinction between restrictions based on resource constraints and restrictions based on other reasons. Yet, as has been argued in chapter two, the background and legislative history of the EU Reception Conditions Directives reveal that the rather low standards ultimately laid down in the Directives, which were significantly less generous than the ones proposed by the European Commission, were (in any case partly) motivated by the wish of Member States to prevent possible abuse of their reception and asylum systems, for example by immigrants looking for work. Hence, restrictive and retrogressive measures taken by EU Member States with regard to the reception of asylum seekers have explicitly been based on reasons other than resource constraints. One could even ask whether it actually saves money to set up a separate welfare scheme for asylum seekers

[34] Müller 2009, pp 590–91.
[35] Vlemminx 2002, pp 150–51 and 164–66.

and to deny them access to the labour market. Indeed, Mabbett and Bolderson argue that exclusionary measures with regard to the reception of asylum seekers are administratively expensive and note that European states have been willing to 'expend substantial resources in controlling the movement and living arrangements of this group [asylum seekers], and their creation of separate and discriminatory welfare provisions'.[36] Schuster also argues that it is 'widely acknowledged that the substitution of benefits in kind is more expensive than cash benefits'.[37] Accordingly, it seems pertinent to evaluate such measures, which are permitted under the EU Reception Conditions Directives, under Article 4, and not under Article 2(1). The following sections will discuss the various conditions set by Article 4 of the ICESCR.

10.3.4 'Determined by Law'

There are very few indications regarding the interpretation of the phrase 'determined by law', as it was not discussed with any great insight or precision during the drafting of the covenant,[38] nor has it been explained by the Committee. According to the Limburg Principles, this phrase means that no limitation on the exercise of economic, social and cultural rights may be made unless provided for by national law of general application which is consistent with the ICESCR and is in force at the time the limitation is applied.[39] In addition, these principles hold that legal rules limiting the exercise of economic, social and cultural rights must be clear and accessible to everyone.[40] These conditions correspond with the requirements set in the case law of the European Court of Human Rights and in views of the Human Rights Committee on the question whether a restriction is 'determined by law' or 'prescribed by law'.[41] As there is no indication that there should be a different interpretation for this phrase used in the ICESCR, it can be assumed that the requirement of 'determined by law' is fulfilled when the limitation is defined in any form of national law of general application that is in force and that is generally accessible, foreseeable and sufficiently clear.[42]

[36] Mabbett and Bolderson 2002, p 204–206.
[37] Schuster 2000, p 123. See also Bank 2000, p 279.
[38] Alston and Quinn 1987, p 199.
[39] Limburg Principles on the Implementation of the International Covenant on Economic, Social and Cultural Rights (n 28), para 48.
[40] Ibid, para 50.
[41] Alston and Quinn 1987, pp 199–200; Müller 2009, pp 578–79.
[42] *Cf* Müller 2009, pp 578–79.

10.3.5 'Compatible with the Nature of the Rights'

A more difficult requirement to interpret is the requirement that the limitation must be 'compatible with the nature of the right(s)'. This requirement is unique among the limitation clauses of human rights treaties.[43] The Committee has never referred to this phrase directly in its general comments and from the *travaux préparatoires* it only appears that this phrase is designed to ensure 'that the problem of restrictions, and limits to their scope, should be closely studied in connexion with each of the rights proclaimed in the Covenant'.[44] Hence, this would mean that this phrase was meant to ensure that the impact of any limitation is studied with regard to each right laid down in the ICESCR individually.[45] This, however, does not answer the question how the 'nature' of a right should be established. According to the Limburg Principles, 'the restriction "compatible with the nature of these rights" requires that a limitation shall not be interpreted or applied so as to jeopardize the essence of the right concerned'.[46] This does not elucidate much either, as the question remains what should be considered to be the 'essence' of a right.

In the legal doctrine, it seems to be generally accepted that restrictions on the 'minimum core content' of a right are not compatible with the 'nature' or 'essence' of a right.[47] 'Minimum core content' or 'core minimum obligations' is an important, albeit difficult, concept in economic, social and cultural rights. It has appeared in the literature since the 1980s and has been endorsed by the Committee in General Comment no 3 on the nature of states parties' obligations in 1990. The concept tries to bridge the gap between individual rights and available resources by trying to establish the essential element(s) without which a right loses its substantive significance. If this essence of the right is not provided for by the state, then this state is violating its obligations under the ICESCR.[48] In the words of the Committee:

> [T]he Committee is of the view that a minimum core obligation to ensure the satisfaction of, at the very least, minimum essential levels of each of the rights

[43] However, in the case law of the ECtHR, the requirement can be found that limitations should not 'restrict or reduce the right in such a way or to such an extent that the very essence of the right is impaired' (see, eg, *Christine Goodwin v United Kingdom* app no 28957/95 (ECtHR, 11 July 2002), para 99; *Omar v France* app no 24767/94 (ECtHR 29 July 1998), para 34; *Demir and Baykara v Turkey* app no 34503/97 (ECtHR, 12 November 2008), para 97). The limitations clause in the EU Charter on Fundamental Rights contains the condition that a limitation must respect the essence of the right or freedom (Art 52(1)).

[44] Alston and Quinn 1987, p 201. They refer to a statement of the Chilean representative who proposed the inclusion of this requirement. This proposal was adopted by the Commission without any further discussion (Müller 2009, p 579, fn 113).

[45] Müller 2009, p 579.

[46] Limburg Principles (n 28), para 56.

[47] Griffey 2011, p 287; Müller 2009, pp 579–83; Sepúlveda 2003, pp 280–81.

[48] Chapman and Russell 2002, pp 8–9.

> is incumbent upon every State party. Thus, for example, a State party in which any significant number of individuals is deprived of essential foodstuffs, of essential primary health care, of basic shelter and housing, or of the most basic forms of education is, prima facie, failing to discharge its obligations under the Covenant. If the Covenant were to be read in such a way as not to establish such a minimum core obligation, it would be largely deprived of its raison d'être.[49]

The Committee held in this general comment that in order for a state party to be able to attribute its failure to meet at least its minimum core obligations to a lack of available resources, it must demonstrate that every effort has been made to use all resources that are at its disposition in an effort to satisfy, as a matter of priority, those minimum obligations. Hence, states can justify non-compliance with core obligations owing to a lack of resources if certain stringent conditions are met.[50] This is also the approach taken by the Committee in a more recent general comment: the General Comment on the right to social security.[51] However, in its general comments on the right to the highest attainable standard of health and on the right to water, the Committee held that a state party cannot, under any circumstances whatsoever, justify its non-compliance with core obligations.[52] The Committee does not give any explanation for this inconsistency.[53] Yet the possibility to justify non-compliance with core obligations for *other* reasons than resource scarcity is not mentioned by the Committee in any general comment. This means that the assertion that restrictions on the 'minimum core content' of a right are not compatible with the 'nature' or 'essence' of a right within the meaning of Article 4 of the convention is consistent with the work of the Committee. The question is therefore how to identify these 'core obligations'.

In its general comments, the Committee has identified core obligations for specific rights. With regard to the right to achieve the highest attainable standard of health for example, the Committee identified as minimum core obligations:

- To ensure the right of access to health facilities, goods and services on a non-discriminatory basis, especially for vulnerable or marginalized groups;
- To ensure access to the minimum essential food which is nutritionally adequate and safe, to ensure freedom from hunger to everyone;
- To ensure access to basic shelter, housing and sanitation, and an adequate supply of safe and potable water;

[49] General Comment no 3 on the nature of states parties' obligations, para 10.

[50] *Cf* Mechlem 2009, p 941.

[51] General Comment no 19 on the right to social security, para 60.

[52] General Comment no 14 on the right to the highest attainable standard of health, para 47; General Comment no 15 on the right to water, para 40.

[53] As Mechlem argues, this inconsistent and far-reaching interpretation can be very problematic (Mechlem 2009, pp 940–45).

- To provide essential drugs, as from time to time defined under the WHO Action Programme on Essential Drugs;
- To ensure equitable distribution of all health facilities, goods and services;
- To adopt and implement a national public health strategy and plan of action.[54]

The following core obligations were identified by the Committee with regard to the right to work:

(a) To ensure the right of access to employment, especially for disadvantaged and marginalized individuals and groups, permitting them to live a life of dignity;
(b) To avoid any measure that results in discrimination and unequal treatment in the private and public sectors of disadvantaged and marginalized individuals and groups or in weakening mechanisms for the protection of such individuals and groups;
(c) To adopt and implement a national employment strategy and plan of action based on and addressing the concerns of all workers on the basis of a participatory and transparent process that includes employers' and workers' organizations. Such an employment strategy and plan of action should target disadvantaged and marginalized individuals and groups in particular and include indicators and benchmarks by which progress in relation to the right to work can be measured and periodically reviewed.[55]

With regard to the right to social security, the Committee identified as core obligations:

(a) To ensure access to a social security scheme that provides a minimum essential level of benefits to all individuals and families that will enable them to acquire at least essential health care, basic shelter and housing, water and sanitation, foodstuffs, and the most basic forms of education (…);
(b) To ensure the right of access to social security systems or schemes on a non-discriminatory basis, especially for disadvantaged and marginalized individuals and groups;
(c) To respect existing social security schemes and protect them from unreasonable interference;
(d) To adopt and implement a national social security strategy and plan of action;
(e) To take targeted steps to implement social security schemes, particularly those that protect disadvantaged and marginalized individuals and groups;
(f) To monitor the extent of the realization of the right to social security.[56]

[54] General Comment no 14 on the right to the highest attainable standard of health, para 43.
[55] General Comment no 18 on the right to work, para 31.
[56] General Comment no 19 on the right to social security, para 59.

A noticeable element of these core obligations identified by the Committee is that the obligation to ensure access to different kind of goods *on a non-discriminatory basis* is mentioned several times. This is remarkable, as the prohibition of discrimination is laid down in Article 2(2) of the ICESCR and is not subjected to progressive implementation or the availability of enough resources.[57] In other words, this prohibition applies under all circumstances; it is not necessary to identify this as a core obligation of more specific rights laid down in the convention. By mentioning the obligation to ensure access on a non-discriminatory basis only a few times, the Committee seems to suggest that with regard to the other core obligations, it is not necessary for states to apply them on a non-discriminatory basis. As has just been argued, this would be an incorrect interpretation of Article 2 of the ICESCR.

Another aspect that attracts attention is the language used by the Committee. Instead of using the language of obligations to respect, protect and/or fulfil, the Committee urges states to 'ensure access to' different kinds of goods. This raises the question whether states can limit themselves to ensuring access to already existing goods or services, or whether states should, if these goods and services do not already exist, also actively provide these facilities themselves.

A final noticeable element is the amount of attention paid to vulnerable, disadvantaged and/or marginalized groups. The Committee does not define these groups, nor does it provide examples of such groups. Outside the context of core obligations, some examples can be found in the general comments. In General Comment no 14 on the right to the highest attainable standard of health, the Committee mentioned as examples of vulnerable or marginalized groups: 'ethnic minorities and indigenous populations, women, children, adolescents, older persons, persons with disabilities and persons with HIV/AIDS'.[58] In General Comment no 19 on the right to social security, small farmers and self-employed persons in the informal economy are mentioned as examples of disadvantaged and marginalized groups,[59] as well as refugees, stateless persons and asylum seekers.[60] General Comment no 4 on the right to adequate housing mentions 'homeless persons and families, those inadequately housed and without ready access to basic amenities, those living in "illegal" settlements, those subject to forced evictions and low-income groups' as examples of vulnerable and disadvantaged groups with regard to housing.[61] Hence,

[57] See General Comment no 3 on the nature of states parties' obligations, para 1. See more extensively s 6.2.1.

[58] General Comment no 14 on the right to the highest attainable standard of health, para 12.

[59] General Comment no 19 on the right to social security, para 28.

[60] Ibid, para 38.

[61] General Comment no 4 on the right to adequate housing, para 13.

the category of vulnerable, disadvantaged and/or marginalized groups is a very broad one, the meaning of which can be different depending on the right at stake. If one looks at the examples mentioned in General Comment no 14, only male adults who are not elderly persons yet and do not belong to an ethnic minority or indigenous population, nor suffer from HIV/AIDS or from a disability, do *not* fall into this category. This category therefore does not have a very distinctive character.

In brief, the Committee does give some indications regarding the 'core content' or 'nature' of the rights laid down in the ICESCR, but a lot of questions still remain. The text, context and object and purpose of the clause 'nature of the right' in Article 4 does not contain clear indications for answers to these questions, neither do the *travaux*. In my view, it is not possible to exhaustively define the nature of all the rights laid down in the covenant.[62] In addition, in view of the permissive function of Article 4, the condition should not be interpreted such that a state has in fact no possibilities to limit the rights laid down in the covenant. Consequently, the requirement in Article 4 of the ICESCR in my opinion rather implies that the state that limits the enjoyment of certain rights has the burden of proving that the limitation is compatible with the nature of the right. Put differently, the state has to show that the right in question still has some substantive significance, the scope of which can be different in different contexts. In this way, it serves both the permissive and the protective function of Article 4 of the ICESCR.

10.3.6 'For the Purpose of Promoting the General Welfare in a Democratic Society'

The last condition laid down in Article 4 is the condition that limitations may be imposed solely for the purpose of promoting the general welfare in a democratic society. A noticeable difference from limitation clauses in other human rights instruments is that there is only one legitimate purpose for which the rights laid down in the ICESCR may be limited. It can be argued therefore that there are fewer possibilities for states to limit the enjoyment of the rights laid down in the ICESCR as compared to the possibility to limit the rights laid down in other human rights conventions or that the limitation provision of the ICESCR is more restrictive than similar clauses in other human rights conventions.[63] Support for this argument can be found in the *travaux préparatoires*. During the drafting of the ICESCR, the US proposed to reproduce entirely the limitation clause

[62] *Cf* Griffey 2011, p 287.
[63] Alston and Quinn 1987, p 201; Müller 2009, p 570.

from the Universal Declaration on Human Rights. This clause provides for the possibility to impose limitations 'solely for the purpose of securing due recognition and respect for the rights and freedoms of others and of meeting the just requirements of morality, public order and the general welfare in a democratic society'.[64] This proposal was rejected as it was argued that while reasons of public order, public morals and respect for the rights and freedoms of others might justify limitations on civil and political rights, they do not seem to be relevant in the same sense with regard to limitations on economic, social and cultural rights.[65] On the other hand, it can be argued that the 'general welfare' is such a broad and vague term that it is not very difficult for states to argue that limitations imposed for reasons of public order or morality are necessary for promoting the general welfare.[66] The Committee as well is of the opinion that states can impose limitations on grounds such as national security or the preservation of public order, provided that the state can justify such a measure in relation to each of the elements identified in Article 4.[67] In addition, it can be argued that the limitation clause of the ICESCR is not more restrictive than similar clauses used in the International Covenant on Civil and Political Rights and the European Convention on Human Rights, as the latter conventions require that the limitation is 'necessary' in a democratic society for safeguarding certain interests, while Article 4 of the ICESCR merely requires that the limitation serves the purpose of 'promoting' the general welfare in a democratic society. To show that certain limitations are actually 'necessary' for safeguarding certain interests is a more difficult requirement to meet than to show that a limitation serves to 'promote' a certain interest (ie the general welfare).[68]

The meaning of the term 'general welfare' is not elaborated on in the *travaux préparatoires* or in the views of the Committee.[69] According to the Limburg Principles, this term 'shall be construed to mean furthering the well-being of the people as a whole'.[70] It has also been described as 'referring primarily to the economic and social well-being of the people and the community'.[71]

[64] Art 29(2) of the Universal Declaration.
[65] Alston and Quinn 1987, p 202; Müller 2009, pp 570–72.
[66] However, as Alston and Quinn note, '[w]hile that requirement might not be too difficult for a government to fulfil, the need to make such a case on each occasion might have a salutary impact' (Alston and Quinn 1987, p 206).
[67] General Comment no 13 on the right to education, para 42; General Comment no 14 on the right to the highest attainable standard of health, para 28.
[68] Limburg Principles (n 28) above, para 60.
[69] Müller 2009, p 573.
[70] Limburg Principles (n 28), para 52.
[71] Müller 2009, p 573, referring to EIA Daes, *The Individual's Duties to the Community and the Limitations on Human Rights and Freedoms under Article 29 of the Universal Declaration of Human*

An additional condition that a limitation on the rights laid down in the ICESCR must meet is the condition that the limitation must be imposed for the purpose of promoting the general welfare *in a democratic society*. As there is 'no single model of a democratic society',[72] this additional requirement is surrounded by uncertainty. However, it is also of vital importance, since in its absence, the limitation clause 'might very well serve the ends of dictatorship'.[73] Therefore, the decision on what constitutes 'general welfare' should be taken in the context of conditions prevailing in a democratic society. According to the Limburg Principles, a society which recognizes and respects the human rights set forth in the United Nations Charter and the Universal Declaration of Human Rights may be viewed as meeting this definition.[74] A transparent and participative decision-making process is also an important condition of such a society,[75] as well as 'pluralism, tolerance and broad-mindedness'.[76] The requirement has also been described as meaning that a decision to limit a right laid down in the ICESCR 'should be based on some consultation process (as inclusive as possible), should not be ordered unilaterally and should be subject to popular control'.[77] In any case, it can be concluded that the burden is upon a state imposing limitations to demonstrate that the limitations do not impair the democratic functioning of society.[78]

10.3.7 Additional (Inherent) Requirement of Proportionality?

Besides meeting the requirements explicitly laid down in Article 4 of the ICESCR, the Committee also requires that a limitation on a right laid

Rights. Study of the Special Rapporteur of the Sub-Commission on Prevention of Discrimination and Protection of Minorities 1983, pp 123–24.

[72] Limburg Principles (n 28), para 55.

[73] Statement by the Greek representative during the drafting process of the covenant, cited by Müller 2009, p 575.

[74] Limburg Principles (n 28), para 55.

[75] Müller 2009, p 577.

[76] According to the ECtHR, without these characteristics there is no democratic society. See, eg, *Handyside v United Kingdom* app no 5493/72 (ECtHR, 7 December 1976), para 49; *Leyla Şahin v Turkey* app no 44774/98 (ECtHR, 10 November 2005), para 108.

[77] Müller 2009, p 577, referring to OM Garibaldi, 'On the Ideological Content of Human Rights Instruments: The Clause in a Democratic Society', in T Buergenthal (ed), *Contemporary Issues in International Law: Essays in Honor of Louis B. Sohn* 1984, p 204 and Daes (n 71), p 128.

[78] *Cf* Limburg Principles (n 28), para 54. In its Advisory Opinion on the Legal Consequences of the Construction of a Wall in the Occupied Palestinian Territories, the International Court of Justice concluded that the restrictions on the economic, social and cultural rights of Palestinians living in occupied territory did not meet the conditions of being solely for the purpose of promoting the general welfare in a democratic society (ICJ Reports 2004, 131, para 136). The Court, however, did not provide any arguments for this conclusion.

down in the covenant must be proportionate, meaning that 'the least restrictive alternative must be adopted where several types of limitations are available'.[79] In its General Comment on the right to the highest attainable standard of health, the Committee related this requirement to Article 5(1) of the Convention. This article provides:

> Nothing in the present Covenant may be interpreted as implying for any State, group or person any right to engage in any activity or to perform any act aimed at the destruction of any of the rights or freedoms recognized herein, or at their limitation to a greater extent than is provided for in the present Covenant.

According to the Committee, the requirement of proportionality probably fits in with the wording 'limitation to a greater extent than is provided for' in Article 5, as this implies the possibility of imposing different kind of limitations on rights. The proportionality requirement, however, has also been held to result from the requirement that limitations must be 'compatible with the nature of the rights'[80] or from the reference to a 'democratic society' in Article 4.[81] In addition, it can be argued that proportionality must be seen as a general principle of law.[82] Hence, by adding a requirement of proportionality, the Committee seems to interpret Article 4 of the ICESCR in line with its text and context.

10.3.8 Standard of Review

The following chapter will show that the European Court of Human Rights usually allows contracting states a certain margin of appreciation. With regard to social and economic policy, the margin left to states is generally a wide one, as a result of which the protection offered by the ECHR is sometimes rather limited. This raises the question how strictly justifications brought forward by states for limitations on rights laid down in the ICESCR should be reviewed.

The Committee has held that '[e]very State has a margin of discretion in assessing which measures are most suitable to meet its specific

[79] General Comment no 14 on the right to the highest attainable standard of health, para 29; General Comment no 17 on the right of everyone to benefit from the protection of the moral and material interests resulting from any scientific, literary or artistic production of which he or she is the author, para 23; General Comment no 21 on the right of everyone to take part in cultural life, para 19.

[80] Müller 2009, p 583.

[81] Sepúlveda 2003, p 283.

[82] See, eg, Sweet and Mathews 2008.

circumstances'.[83] This finds support in the general obligation under Article 2 of the ICESCR to take steps 'by all appropriate means'.

In addition, the Optional Protocol to the ICESCR may provide some insight into this issue. The Optional Protocol to the ICESCR is unique in containing a specific standard of review for the Committee.[84] Article 8(4) of the Optional Protocol reads:

> When examining communications under the present Protocol, the Committee shall consider the reasonableness of the steps taken by the State Party in accordance with part II of the Covenant. In doing so, the Committee shall bear in mind that the State Party may adopt a range of possible policy measures for the implementation of the rights set forth in the Covenant.

Hence, this article introduces a 'reasonableness' test as the relevant standard of review. According to various authors, this test implies the same kind of judgement as the test under Article 4 of the ICESCR, as to whether a limitation is compatible with the nature of the right and whether it promotes the general welfare.[85] Indeed, it is hard to think of a measure that is considered to be compatible with the nature of a covenant right and to promote the general welfare and be proportional, but to not be considered 'reasonable'. Hence, the reasonableness test does not imply a new standard of review for the evaluation of limitations under Article 4 of the ICESCR.[86]

During the drafting process, it was discussed whether Article 8(4) should contain an explicit reference to a margin or appreciation or a margin of discretion.[87] In its statement regarding an evaluation of the obligation to take steps to the 'Maximum of available resources' under an optional protocol to the covenant, the Committee as well reiterated that 'in accordance with the practice of judicial and other quasi-judicial human rights treaty bodies, the Committee always respects the margin of appreciation of States to take steps and adopt measures most suited to their specific circumstances'.[88] The final text of Article 8(4) does not contain such an explicit reference, but the second sentence is generally

[83] See, eg, General Comment no 14 on the right to the highest attainable standard of health, para 53; General Comment no 18 on the right to work, para 37; General Comment no 19 on the right to social security, para 66.

[84] Vandenbogaerde and Vandenhole 2010, p 223.

[85] Courtis 2008, p 82; Griffey 2011, p 286. These authors also submit that the standard of reasonableness is related to the reference to 'all appropriate means' in Art 2 of the covenant.

[86] As Courtis notes more generally: 'Article 8.4 of the OP-ICESCR does not add anything that could not already be inferred from the ICESCR itself' (Courtis 2008, p 83).

[87] Griffey 2011, pp 298–300; Mahon 2008, pp 636–38; Vandenbogaerde and Vandenhole 2010, pp 223–36.

[88] Committee on Economic, Social and Cultural Rights, 'An evaluation of the obligation to take steps to the "Maximum of available resources" under an Optional Protocol to the covenant. Statement', 10 May 2007, E/C.12/2007/1.

understood as denoting the concept of a margin of appreciation.[89] Arguably therefore, also under the ICESCR, when reviewing justifications brought forward by the state for limitations on the rights laid down in the covenant, the state enjoys a certain margin of discretion.

10.4 ANALYSIS

The foregoing sections have shown that a limitation on a right laid down in the ICESCR must be defined in any form of national law of general application that is in force and that is generally accessible, foreseeable and sufficiently clear. The state imposing the limitation has the burden to show that the right in question still has some substantive significance and that the limitation serves the purpose of promoting the general welfare and does not impair the democratic functioning of society. Finally, the limitation has to meet the condition of proportionality. However, since every state has a margin of discretion in assessing which measures are most suitable to meet its specific circumstances, these various conditions should not be reviewed too strictly.

Arguably, the European Reception Conditions Directives allow for a number of possible violations of asylum seekers' rights laid down in the ICESCR. Most importantly, the Directives allow Member States to subject asylum seekers to a ban on entering the labour market for a maximum of 12 or nine months as from the start of the asylum procedure. If a first instance decision on the asylum application has been taken within 12 or nine months, Member States are allowed to refuse access to the labour market throughout the entire asylum procedure. In addition, Member States are allowed to set various requirements as a condition for entering the labour market and to give priority to other categories of aliens. A report from the Commission on the application of the Directive 2003/9 indeed shows that most EU Member States ban access to the labour market for a certain period of time—half of them for one year—and that most Member States make access to the labour market subject to the fulfilment on certain, sometimes quite restrictive, conditions.[90] Arguably, such measures imply a limitation on asylum seekers' enjoyment of the right to work, which includes 'the right of everyone to the opportunity to gain his living by work which he freely chooses or accepts'.[91] Further, the EU Reception

[89] Mahon 2008, p 638; Vandenbogaerde and Vandenhole 2010, pp 225–26.

[90] Commission of the European Communities, *Report from the Commission to the Council and to the European Parliament on the Application of Directive 20039/EC of 27 January 2003 laying down Minimum Standards for the Reception of Asylum Seekers*, COM(2007) 745 final, pp 6 and 8.

[91] Art 6, para 1 ICESCR. Craven notes that the preparatory work to the Covenant implies that Art 6 includes, 'at least, the right not to be arbitrarily deprived of work of any kind, whether remunerative or otherwise' (Craven 1998, p 197). See also Edwards 2005, p 328.

Conditions Directives allow for the reduction or complete withdrawal of reception conditions for a number of reasons related to the asylum procedure or to behaviour of the asylum seeker in accommodation centres.[92] Arguably, such restrictions imply a limitation on asylum seekers' right to an adequate standard of living for themselves and their family, including adequate food, clothing and housing[93] and the right to be free from hunger.[94] In addition, the *level* of reception benefits provided to asylum seekers may involve a limitation on the right to an *adequate* standard of living. The EU Reception Conditions Directives contain only rather vague norms on this issue and therefore allow Member States wide discretion. Arguably, such benefits could not be considered to be 'adequate' within the meaning of Article 11 of the ICESCR. However, even if it could be convincingly argued that these different measures do in fact violate the above-mentioned covenant rights, the question remains whether they fulfil the requirements laid down in Article 4 of the ICESCR, as a result of which they will be permitted. This section will try to answer this question. In view of the margin of discretion accorded to states in this regard, this section will examine whether it is possible for states to argue convincingly that certain limitations meet the conditions laid down in Article 4.

The first requirement laid down in Article 4 is that a limitation on a right laid down in the ICESCR must be determined by law, ie that it must be defined in any form of national law of general application that is in force and that is generally accessible, foreseeable and sufficiently clear. This condition will generally be fulfilled in EU Member States, as the EU Reception Conditions Directives need to be implemented in such laws as well. However, it may be the case that domestic law provides for asylum seekers' eligibility for various benefits, but that in practice, owing to, for example, a lack of capacity in reception centres, asylum seekers do not have access to these benefits.[95] Often, such a lack of capacity will be resource motivated, as a result of which it should not be reviewed under Article 4, but instead under Article 2(1). In that case, the state enjoys a wide discretion as a result of which the ICESCR will generally not be violated, provided that the state takes steps to improve the situation, in

[92] See ch 2.

[93] ICESCR, Art 11(1).

[94] ICESCR, Art 11(2).

[95] See, eg, the situation in Greece, discussed in the case of *MSS v Belgium and Greece* before the ECtHR (see ch 11). Belgium has also faced problems in accommodating all asylum seekers, in violation of domestic law. See, eg, Amnesty International, *Amnesty International Report 2010—Belgium*, 28 May 2010, available at: www.unhcr.org/refworld/docid/4c03a83ec.html; UN High Commissioner for Refugees, *Soumission du Haut Commissariat des Nations Unies pour les réfugiés (HCR) pour la compilation établie par le Haut-Commissariat aux droits de l'homme—Examen périodique universel: Belgique*, November 2010, available at: www.unhcr.org/refworld/docid/4cd8f2262.html.

order to (ultimately) achieve the full realization of the right.[96] It might, however, be difficult for a (Western) European state to argue that the lack of capacity in reception centres is resource motivated, for example in view of the country's level of development, the country's current economic situation and the absence of, for example, natural disasters or internal or international armed conflicts.[97] In that case, the practical absence of any kind of reception benefits for asylum seekers that should be provided to them under domestic law should be reviewed under Article 4. If the (temporary) unavailability of reception benefits has not been provided for by law, such a (practical) limitation is not permitted under the ICESCR.

The second condition of Article 4 is that the limitation must be compatible with the nature of the right. As has been argued above, this condition means, in my opinion, that the state has to show that the right in question, even though it has been limited, still has some substantive meaning. With regard to asylum seekers who have a restrictive and conditional access to the labour market, such as allowed for under the EU Reception Conditions Directives, it will not be difficult for states to argue that the right to work still has some substantive meaning. Likewise, with regard to asylum seekers who have at their disposal (some kind of) food, clothing and housing, which are the elements explicitly mentioned in Article 11 of the ICESCR, it will not be difficult to argue that the right to an adequate standard of living still has some substantive meaning. This might be more difficult, however, with regard to asylum seekers who are not allowed to work at all, with regard to destitute asylum seekers who are unable to dispose of food, clothing or housing and with regard to destitute asylum seekers who are denied provision of health care (reimbursement). With regard to aliens who are able to return to their country of origin or nationality, the state might be able to argue that the complete denial of the possibility to work and of state support in the case of destitution is compatible with the nature of the right to work and the right to an adequate standard of living, as such aliens can (in any case theoretically) claim protection of

[96] EU Member States facing resource constraints in realizing enough accommodation for asylum seekers can apply for a grant from the European Refugee Fund; eg, in December 2010 the Fund supported Greece in facing migration and asylum challenges, with an additional package of EUR 9.8 million for emergency needs and with teams of experts deployed in Greece to assist the country in supporting the reform of the national asylum system. The package focused on increasing the accommodation capacity, including the provision of basic services to the persons in need, setting up mobile medical units and institutional support to process asylum claims (see ec.europa.eu/home-affairs/funding/integration/EUFundingForHomeAffairs.pdf).

[97] *Cf* the criteria for reviewing states parties' claims as regards resource constraints mentioned by the Committee in its statement on the obligation to take steps to the 'Maximum of available resources' under the Optional Protocol to the covenant (n 88).

these rights in their countries of origin or nationality.[98] Asylum seekers, however, cannot return to their country of origin or nationality during their asylum procedure, as they potentially risk their life or freedom upon return. Expulsion before their asylum application has been examined is in violation of various norms of international law. With regard to this category of aliens, I therefore see no possibility for states to convincingly argue that the complete denial of state support or health care to destitute asylum seekers or an absolute prohibition to work during the entire asylum procedure is compatible with the nature of the rights laid down in the ICESCR. This would mean that such measures would not be in conformity with Article 4 of the ICESCR.

Thirdly, a limitation on a covenant right should be for the purpose of promoting the general welfare in a democratic society. A complete denial of state support or health care to destitute asylum seekers or an absolute prohibition to work already seems to founder on the requirement that a limitation must be compatible with the nature of the right. But what about asylum seekers who have restrictive and conditional access to the labour market, who receive some state support but at a level below the minimum subsistence level established under general social assistance schemes or who are only eligible for emergency health care? Arguably, such measures imply limitations on their right to work, the right to an adequate standard of living and the right to the health, respectively. The question is therefore whether it would be possible for states to argue that such limitations are for the purpose of promoting the general welfare in a democratic society. As has been mentioned previously, states generally argue that such restrictive measures serve the need to control immigration (eg to deter the lodging of (unfounded) asylum claims, to impede integration or to facilitate expulsion). Do reasons of immigration control fall within the purpose of promoting the general welfare in a democratic society and hence fulfil the third condition laid down in Article 4 of the ICESCR?

This question has been answered differently in the legal doctrine. Some authors refer to the statement of the Committee that Article 4 is primarily intended to be protective of the right of individuals and simply conclude that in the light of this statement a denial of access to the labour market does not serve the sole purpose of promoting the general welfare.[99] These authors do not examine the reasons related to immigration control put

[98] If that is not the case, expulsion of such aliens may be prohibited under Art 3 of the ECHR. As will be argued in ch 11, case law of the ECtHR implies that expulsion to dire humanitarian conditions is generally prohibited by Art 3 of the ECHR if these conditions are caused by deliberate and culpable actions of the authorities in the country of origin. If such conditions are caused by natural circumstances, such as drought or a poor economic situation, expulsion is only under very special circumstances in violation of Art 3 of the ECHR.

[99] Cholewinski 2000, pp 729–30; Edwards 2005, p 327. As has been argued above in s 10.3.2, I do not find this statement of the Committee persuasive.

forward by states for such a denial.[100] Bank does examine this reason, albeit not very thoroughly. He merely states:

> However, by virtue of Article 4 ICESCR, the state may impose restrictions on this right provided for by law for the purpose of promoting the general prosperity of democratic society. This justification will apply to restriction of immigration and therefore also to restrictions imposed on asylum seekers in order to deter immigration through the asylum procedure.[101]

Sepúlveda arrives at the opposite conclusion. She argues:

> Under article 4 ICESCR, immigration control and the eradication of abuses would not be a legitimate justification for restricting the rights set forth in the covenant. Under the obligations assumed through the ICESCR, any restriction or limitation on the rights (in this example, the welfare benefits provided to asylum seekers), must be taken solely with the purpose of promoting the 'general welfare' in a 'democratic society' and not for immigration purposes.

According to Sepúlveda, 'the State can only restrict the Covenant rights if it has economic constraints and there is a demonstrable necessity to limit the enjoyment of these rights (eg by reducing or cutting social welfare benefits to asylum seekers)'.[102] Here she seems to contradict herself, however, as she argued a few pages earlier that the limitation clause of Article 4 is not intended to deal with limitations required by inadequate resource availability.[103] This has also been argued in this chapter. Both Bank and Sepúlveda do not, however, provide any arguments as to why reasons of immigration control do or do not fit into the general aim of promoting the general welfare.

In my view, since 'general welfare' is such a broad and vague term, states will not encounter many difficulties in arguing that a limitation serves the purpose of promoting this interest, especially given the absence of a requirement of necessity and the margin of discretion left to states. In addition, the traditional sovereign power of the state to control to a certain extent the entry and stay of aliens on their territory is generally thought to be of crucial importance for the democratic functioning of the society.[104] This means that, in my opinion, states would be able to argue convincingly that pursuing a consistent and integrated

[100] Edwards merely states in general that 'it could be arguable that giving access to the labour market would itself promote the general welfare of society, enhance understanding and build confidence toward such groups, and generally contribute to their sense of self-worth and dignity' (Edwards 2005, p 327).

[101] Bank 2000, p 275.

[102] Sepúlveda 2003, pp 282–83. This is a clear example of an argument based, although not explicitly, on the 'separation model' (see s 1.2).

[103] Sepúlveda 2003, p 279.

[104] This has, for example, been argued in depth by Benhabib, see s 1.2.

immigration policy serves the purpose of promoting the general welfare in a democratic society.[105]

A final requirement that states have to fulfil in order for a limitation to be permitted under the ICESCR is the requirement of proportionality. This broad and general requirement is of course open to different kinds of interpretation. Nevertheless, it will be difficult for states to argue that an absolute ban on access to the labour market or a denial of state support or health care to destitute asylum seekers is proportionate to the aim of immigration control. However, such measures are not compatible with the nature of the rights laid down in the ICESCR either, which is another condition for imposing limitations. A more difficult question is whether providing asylum seekers with only limited and conditional access to the labour market and/or with a limited level of state support should be considered to be proportionate to the aim of immigration control. A relevant question in this regard is whether such measures are the only way to control immigration or whether less restrictive measures are available to reach the aim of immigration control.[106] At the same time it should be recalled that it is generally accepted, by member states and by the Committee, that states have a margin of discretion in assessing which measures are most suitable to meet their specific circumstances. With regard to asylum seekers, with respect to whom the state is, owing to various obligations under international law, obliged to tolerate their presence on the territory for a certain amount of time, it can be argued that the only or, at least, a very important way to control their entry and stay on the territory to a certain extent is through a limitation of their (socioeconomic) rights. According to this line of reasoning, limiting the social and economic rights of asylum seekers can be considered to be a substitute for exclusion at the border, as a result of which it is possible to argue that these limitations are not in violation of the requirement of proportionality. On the other hand, it could also be argued that once asylum seekers are present on the territory, the aim of immigration control is no longer relevant, as their removal from the territory would be contrary to various norms of international law anyway. In other words, this line of reasoning implies that even though states put forward that they are restricting the rights of asylum seekers in order to serve the aim of immigration control, this aim is not actually served by the restrictive measures. Accordingly, such measures are not proportionate. However, such a test, whether the aim put forward by the

[105] The ECtHR also holds 'immigration control' to be a legitimate aim for limiting convention rights, sometimes even without specifying which of the permitted aims explicitly laid down in the convention is at stake (see, eg, *Nnyanzi v United Kingdom* app no 21878/06 (ECtHR, 8 April 2008), para 76; *Osman v Denmark* app no 38058/09 (ECtHR, 14 June 2011), para 58).

[106] *Cf* Lu 2008, p 61.

state is actually served by the measure in question, does not seem to fit well with the margin of appreciation left to the state in deciding which measure is most suitable to meet a specific aim. To the contrary, it seems to imply a rather strict scrutiny.[107]

Hence, in my view, states are able to argue that the imposition of limitations on the provision of state support, health care or access to the labour market is *in general* proportionate to the legitimate aim of immigration control. Nevertheless, this may of course be different in view of the particular circumstances of the case.

Another relevant aspect with regard to the proportionality requirement might be the absence of a time limit during which the limitations for asylum seekers apply. As regards the provision of a limited kind of state support or health care to asylum seekers, the EU Reception Conditions Directives do not require a time limit to be applied. Since the provision of such limited assistance is linked to the status of being an asylum seeker, it lasts for an indefinite period of time. Arguably, it is more difficult for states to argue that such a limitation is proportionate if it lasts for an indefinite period of time. The introduction of a time limit might, however, as states will argue, become a pull factor for asylum seekers, which would be contrary to the aim of immigration control. Yet such a risk can be mitigated by the improvement of the asylum procedure, especially the decision periods. Hence, in my view, the absence of any time limit for limitations on state support for asylum seekers might imply that the limitation should not be considered proportionate to the aim of immigration control. As regards the length of the time limit, states obviously have a large margin of appreciation. Some indications can be found in the Refugee Convention, which would mean that after three years of (simple) residence in the host state, some accretion of rights should take place.[108]

[107] Such a test is usually not applied by the ECtHR, either (Hilbrink 2010).

[108] See chs 4 and 9. Also in state practice, the accretion of rights through the passage of time has existed with regard to asylum seekers. eg, between 1992 and 2002, a policy was in force in the Netherlands on the basis of which aliens who had to wait three years for a final decision on the application for a residence permit were, under certain circumstances, entitled to a residence permit (TBV 1996/15, *Stcrt* 1996, no 242, p 7). In Belgium, until 2007, asylum seekers' rights as regards financial assistance increased once their asylum application had been declared admissible (Bouckaert 2007, pp 534–42). As from 2007, the applicable law contains a provision making it possible that after the passage of four months, an asylum seeker can request to be transferred from large-scale accommodation to small-scale accommodation (*Wet betreffende de opvang van asielzoekers en van bepaalde andere categorieën van vreemdelingen*, Art 12). In addition, the law contains a provision making it possible for a Royal Decree to establish a time limit after which asylum seekers become eligible for a form of general financial assistance, instead of assistance in kind (Art 11). Such a Royal Decree, however, has not yet been adopted. In Germany asylum seekers were entitled to cash benefits at normal rates after one year between 1993 and 1997. The law adopted in 1997 provided that the reduced rates and in kind benefits apply during the first three years of the asylum procedure (Bank 2000, pp 279–80).

In brief, it seems to be difficult for states to argue that a limitation on the rights of asylum seekers is compatible with the ICESCR if this limitation involves subjecting asylum seekers to an absolute ban on access to the labour market or not providing any kind of state support to destitute asylum seekers. In that case, it seems to be difficult to argue that such limitations are compatible with the nature of the rights laid down in the ICESCR. As regards other, less serious, limitations, such as a restrictive and conditional access to the labour market or the provision of a limited level of state support, the ICESCR seems to leave a lot of room for manoeuvre for states. As regards such limitations, it seems not to be very difficult for states to argue that they meet the conditions laid down in Article 4 of the ICESCR. The only factor limiting this wide room for manoeuvre left to the state would, in my opinion, be the absence of any time limit for imposing such limitations on asylum seekers. In the absence of any time limit, it seems to be more difficult for states to argue that the limitation is proportional to the legitimate aim of immigration control.

10.5 CONCLUDING REMARKS

This chapter has taken as its starting point that the rights laid down in the ICESCR are not merely programmatic, vague and indeterminate, but that they impose some binding obligations upon states. In particular, Article 6 on the right to work, which explicitly includes in that right the opportunity to gain a living by work, Article 11 on the right to an adequate standard of living, which explicitly includes the right to adequate food, clothing and housing, and Article 12 on the right to the enjoyment of the highest attainable standard of physical and mental health are of relevance for the main question of this book. This chapter has extensively examined whether states may impose limitations on these rights. This is the most pertinent question as regards the position of asylum seekers in the EU, since EU Member States generally argue that the limited rights of asylum seekers as regards access to the labour market and as regards eligibility for financial state support is a necessary tool for controlling immigration. Hence, asylum seekers' limited rights in these areas are generally not based on resource constraints, but are explicitly based on other kind of policy considerations. It is submitted in this chapter that the ICESCR leaves a rather large room for manoeuvre to the states parties as regards the imposition of such limitations. Consequently, it is argued that only the complete denial of state support to destitute asylum seekers, as a result of which they are not able to dispose of (some kind of) food, clothing or housing, the complete denial of (reimbursement for) health care for destitute asylum seekers or an absolute ban on access to the labour market during the entire asylum procedure is difficult to justify under the ICESCR. If asylum seekers are able to dispose of some kind of food, clothing, housing and health care and have some kind of access to the labour market, states are in general able to argue convincingly that limitations that are imposed on asylum seekers in these fields meet the conditions laid down in Article 4 of the ICESCR. In view of the margin of discretion left to the state in this regard, this implies that such limitations are permitted under the ICESCR. Besides special individual circumstances, the only general factor that I was able to identify as being capable of limiting the large room for manoeuvre for the state is the absence of a time limit for such limitations imposed on asylum seekers.

A consequence of the broad possibilities for states to impose limitations on the rights laid down in the ICESCR is that the covenant does not seem to provide any clear and general state obligations as regards the quality or level of state support or health care to be provided to asylum seekers or with regard to providing asylum seekers access to the labour market. Nevertheless, the possibility for states to ban access to the labour market pending the entire asylum procedure or to withdraw all reception benefits for asylum seekers, which is allowed under the EU Reception Conditions Directives, seems to be hard to justify under the ICESCR.

11

Positive Obligations under the European Convention on Human Rights

11.1 INTRODUCTION

THE EUROPEAN CONVENTION on Human Rights (ECHR) does not seem at first sight to be the most obvious source for finding state obligations to provide asylum seekers with social security benefits and access to the labour market, as this instrument mainly contains civil and political rights, which were traditionally understood as containing primarily negative state obligations. However, the Court considered in as early as 1979:

> Whilst the Convention sets forth what are essentially civil and political rights, many of them have implications of a social or economic nature. The Court therefore considers, like the Commission, that the mere fact that an interpretation of the Convention may extend into the sphere of social and economic rights should not be a decisive factor against such an interpretation; there is no water-tight division separating that sphere from the field covered by the Convention.[1]

In 2008 the Court held, however, that 'although many of the rights it contains have implications of a social or economic nature, the Convention is essentially directed at the protection of civil and political rights'.[2] In addition, the Court has observed that the Convention 'does not guarantee, as such, socioeconomic rights, including the right to charge-free dwelling, the right to work, the right to free medical assistance, or the right to claim financial assistance from a State to maintain a certain level of living'.[3]

Hence, the ECHR does offer protection in the social and economic sphere, but this protection is always related to the effective enjoyment of one of the civil and political rights explicitly mentioned in the convention

[1] *Airey v Ireland* app no 6289/73 (ECtHR, 9 October 1979), para 26.
[2] *N v United Kingdom* app no 26565/05 (ECtHR, 27 May 2008), para 44.
[3] *Pancenko v Latvia* app no 40772/98 (ECtHR, 28 October 1999 (dec)).

and is therefore guaranteed in a more indirect way.[4] This chapter will examine whether the effective enjoyment of certain rights laid down in the ECHR entails an obligation for contracting states to provide asylum seekers with (some kind of) social assistance benefits or access to the labour market. As has been explained in chapter one, social assistance benefits can be provided in cash or in kind. Consequently, this chapter will examine whether states can be obligated under the ECHR to grant asylum seekers social assistance benefits in cash or in the form of food, clothing and housing in kind.

To that end, sections 11.2 to 11.4 will examine the case law on Articles 2, 3 and 8 as to its relevance for social security benefits.[5] Since the case law on social and economic interests has been most elaborately developed under Article 3 and since the Court has recently given an extensive ruling on the issue of state support for asylum seekers under Article 3,[6] the most attention will be paid to the case law on this article. Case law on Articles 2 and 8 will only be examined as to whether they provide additional safeguards for the reception of asylum seekers alongside Article 3. Section 11.5 will examine whether case law of the Court provides safeguards against the ending of social benefits or state-sponsored accommodation. In order to answer this question, case law on Article 8 of the ECHR and on Article 1 of the First Protocol to the convention will be examined. Finally, section 11.6 will examine whether a ban on access to employment violates the ECHR. The sections mentioned so far will provide a general overview and analysis of the Court's case law with respect to these issues. Section 11.7 will discuss what consequences the general conclusions drawn in sections 11.2 to 11.6 have for the obligations of the state as regards the reception of asylum seekers.

In addition to the examination of case law about general social and economic circumstances, in this chapter attention will also be paid to the case law on living conditions in detention.[7] This seems pertinent as the

[4] Brems 2007, p 138; O'Cinneide 2008, pp 586–87; Tulkens and Van Drooghenbroeck 2008, p 67; Warbrick 2007, p 241. See also *Ponomaryovi v Bulgaria* app no 5335/05 (ECtHR, 21 June 2011), para 55.

[5] See for the identification of these three articles as relevant for these kinds of state obligations also O'Cinneide 2008; Palmer 2009; and Sweeney 2008. Other articles of the ECHR that might be relevant for such state obligations include Art 14 (which has been discussed in ch 6); Art 1 of the First Protocol (which will be discussed in s 11.5) and Art 6 (which will not be discussed, as it relates only to providing support in relation to access to legal aid), see Kenna 2008 and Tulkens and Van Drooghenbroeck 2008.

[6] *MSS v Belgium and Greece* case, see s 11.2 below.

[7] Unlike the ICCPR, the ECHR does not contain a separate provision on the treatment of persons who are deprived of their freedom. Art 10(1) of the ICCPR provides: 'All persons deprived of their liberty shall be treated with humanity and with respect for the inherent dignity of the human person'. Under the ECHR, conditions of detention are generally reviewed by the court under Art 3, but occasionally also under Art 2.

situation of asylum seekers living in reception centres may to some extent be comparable to the situation of persons who are deprived of their freedom and are living in detention centres. This will be further discussed in section 11.7.

This chapter will show that European Court of Human Rights generally uses the terminology of positive and negative obligations. The distinction between positive and negative obligations is often made with regard to state obligations resulting from international human rights law. Positive obligations can be described as obligations requiring states to take the necessary measures to safeguard a right.[8] Hence, such obligations require the state to 'take action'.[9] Negative obligations are obligations requiring states to abstain from interfering with a right, or to 'refrain from action'.[10] At the same time, it is generally accepted that the distinction between negative and positive obligations is often difficult to make.[11] Acts of the state can often be characterized both as violating a positive obligation as well as violating a negative obligation[12] and some kinds of obligations impose a complex mix of both negative and positive aspects.[13] Also, the Court itself generally states: 'the boundaries between the State's positive and negative obligations under the Convention do not lend themselves to precise definition'.[14] Nevertheless, the Court sticks to the use of these terms,[15] despite the development in the field of social and economic rights of a tripartite terminology, often held more useful and appropriate,[16] distinguishing between obligations 'to protect, respect and fulfil'.[17]

8 Akandji-Kombe 2007, p 8.

9 Judge Martens in his dissenting opinion in the case of *Gül v Switzerland* app no 23218/94 (ECtHR, 19 February 1996), quoted in Mowbray 2004, p 2.

10 Ibid.

11 Akandji-Kombe 2007, pp 12–14; Battjes 2009; Sepúlveda 2003, p 171.

12 See the examples mentioned by Akandji-Kombe (Akandji-Kombe 2007, pp 12–13).

13 Sepúlveda 2003, p 171.

14 See, eg, *Gül v Switzerland* (n 9), para 38; *Verein gegen Tierfabriken Schweiz (VgT) v Switzerland (no 2)* app no 32772/02 (ECtHR, 30 June 2009), para 82.

15 *Cf* Palmer who states that 'despite the well-recognised conceptual inadequacy of the positive-negative dichotomy of rights, its pervasive influence continues to be strongly reflected in the ECtHR's jurisprudence, especially in socio-economic complaints concerning access to basic socio-economic provisions' (Palmer 2009, p 424).

16 Fredman 2006, p 500; Sepúlveda 2003, pp 171–72.

17 *Cf* Palmer 2009, p 403. In the case of *Premininy v Russia*, the Court did mention the 'obligation to respect, protect and fulfil the right of individuals not to be subjected to torture or to inhuman or degrading treatment or punishment' (app no 44973/04, ECtHR, 10 February 2011, para 85).

11.2 ARTICLE 3

11.2.1 Introduction

Article 3 of the ECHR provides:

> No one shall be subjected to torture or to inhuman or degrading treatment or punishment.

Unlike most of the substantive clauses of the ECHR, Article 3 makes no provision for exceptions and no derogation from it is permissible under Article 15 of the ECHR, even in the event of a public emergency threatening the life of the nation. Hence, the prohibition of torture and inhuman or degrading treatment or punishment is 'absolute'. The Court regularly states that 'Article 3, which prohibits in absolute terms torture and inhuman or degrading treatment or punishment, enshrines one of the fundamental values of democratic societies'.[18]

As facts do not bear the label 'torture' or 'inhuman treatment', characterization of the facts is always necessary. In a standard formulation, the Court has considered treatment to be 'inhuman' because, inter alia, it was premeditated, was applied for hours at a stretch and caused either actual bodily injury or intense physical or mental suffering. It has deemed treatment to be 'degrading' because it was such as to arouse in the victims feelings of fear, anguish and inferiority capable of humiliating and debasing them. In any event, the suffering and humiliation involved must go beyond that inevitable element of suffering or humiliation connected with a given form of legitimate treatment or punishment. The question whether the purpose of the treatment was to humiliate or debase the victim is a factor to be taken into account, but not necessarily a decisive one.[19] 'Torture' differs from inhuman treatment in the greater intensity of the suffering and in the intention with which the suffering is inflicted.[20] However, the Court does not always find it necessary to identify which type of ill-treatment has been suffered and sometimes simply concludes that Article 3 has been violated.[21]

[18] See, eg, *Ireland v United Kingdom* app no 5310/71 (ECtHR, 18 January 1978), para 162; *Soering v United Kingdom*), app no 14038/88 (ECtHR, 7 July 1989), para 88; *Saadi v Italy* app no 37201/06 (ECtHR, 28 February 2008), para 127.

[19] See, eg, *T v United Kingdom* app no 24724/94 (ECtHR, 16 December 1999), para 69; *Kudla v Poland* app no 30210/96 (ECtHR, 26 October 2000), para 92.

[20] Palmer 2007, p 69.

[21] Harris et al 2009, p 71; Palmer 2007, p 69.

The Court has ruled in this connection that ill-treatment must attain 'a minimum level of severity' if it is to fall within the scope of Article 3 of the ECHR. It held:

> The assessment of this minimum is, in the nature of things, relative; it depends on all the circumstances of the case, such as the nature and context of the treatment or punishment, the manner and method of its execution, its duration, its physical or mental effects and, in some cases, the sex, age and state of health of the victim.[22]

Hence, the threshold of seriousness set by Article 3 is not a static and absolute one: regard must be had to all the circumstances of the case and it must be considered in the light of the present-day circumstances.[23] This makes sense, as one can imagine that some ill-treatment will be more serious if it is imposed on children as opposed to adults, and that ill-treatment of a rather long duration will be more serious than ill-treatment which lasts a very short time. As Palmer observes, this relativity element does not detract from the absolute nature of Article 3.[24]

The Court has regularly held that Article 3, in addition to the primary negative obligation to refrain from inflicting serious harm on persons within their jurisdiction, also imposes a positive obligation on states to take measures designed to ensure that individuals within their jurisdiction are not subjected to torture or inhuman or degrading treatment. These measures should provide effective protection, in particular to children and other vulnerable persons, and include reasonable steps to prevent ill-treatment of which the authorities had or ought to have had knowledge.[25] The Court considered that state responsibility is engaged in this regard by a failure to take reasonably available measures which could have had a real prospect of altering the outcome or mitigating the harm

[22] See, eg, *Ireland v United Kingdom* (n 18), para 162; *Hilal v United Kingdom* app no 45276/99 (ECtHR, 6 March 2001), para 60; *Kirakosyan v Armenia* app no 31237/03 (ECtHR, 2 December 2008), para 43. This requirement means that 'a certain qualification is introduced in a norm formulated in absolute terms, which is almost inevitable in the case of the application of an abstract norm, containing subjective concepts, to concrete cases' (Van Dijk et al 2006, p 413). With reference to the drafting history of Art 3, Battjes also shows that an unequivocal or absolute prohibition of torture and inhuman and degrading treatment and punishment is possible only in abstract terms (Battjes 2009).

[23] Van Dijk et al 2006, p 412; Ovey and White 2006, p 77.

[24] Palmer 2006, p 439. See also Battjes 2009, p 613.

[25] See, eg, *Z and Others v United Kingdom* app no 29392/95 (ECtHR, 10 May 2001), para 73; *Pretty v United Kingdom* app no 2346/02 (ECtHR, 29 April 2002), paras 50–51; *E and others v United Kingdom* app no 33218/96 (ECtHR, 26 November 2002), para 88; *Mubilanzila Mayeka and Kaniki Mitunga v Belgium* app no 13178/03 (ECtHR, 12 October 2006), para 53. In the case of *L v Lithuania*, the Court held very clearly: 'Moreover, according to its established case-law, Article 3 entails a positive obligation on the part of the State to protect the individual from acute ill-treatment, whether physical or mental, whatever its source' (app no 27527/03, ECtHR, 11 September 2007, para 46).

to the applicant.[26] Such measures may imply, for instance, 'preventing any ill-treatment by public bodies or private individuals or providing improved conditions or care'.[27] In addition, the Court regularly holds that the suffering which flows from naturally occurring illness, physical or mental, may be covered by Article 3, where it is, or risks being, exacerbated by treatment, whether flowing from conditions of detention, expulsion or other measures, for which the authorities can be held responsible.[28] Hence, where the suffering flows from natural causes, an issue only arises under Article 3 if the suffering is exacerbated by treatment for which the authorities can be held responsible.

This means that in order for a state to violate its (positive) obligations under Article 3 ECHR, the relevant test is not only whether the situation complained of reaches the minimum level of severity under this article, but also whether the authorities can be held responsible for (exacerbating) the suffering.[29] This might also be implied by the term 'treatment' in Article 3 ECHR, which indicates some kind of active behaviour. Indeed, in the case of *E. and others v United Kingdom*, the Court held, without further consideration, that the sexual and physical abuse suffered by the applicants reached the threshold of inhuman and degrading treatment,[30] but it dealt more elaborately with the question whether the local authority was, or ought to have been, aware that the applicants were suffering or at risk of abuse and, if so, whether it had taken the steps reasonably available to it to protect them from that abuse.[31] In other cases, as will be shown in this section, the Court does not make such a clear distinction between the 'seriousness test' and the 'responsibility test'. Nevertheless, it will be

[26] *E and others v United Kingdom* (n 25), para 99; *Premininy v Russia* (n 17), para 84.

[27] *Pretty v United Kingdom* (n 25), para 55. Palmer divides the positive obligations under Art 3 into two broad categories: the duty to investigate alleged violations effectively, on the one hand, and the protective or deterrent duty requiring the state to protect individuals from proscribed ill-treatment emanating from state agents as well as private individuals, on the other hand (Palmer 2006, p 440). This section will focus on the latter.

[28] *Pretty v United Kingdom* (n 25), para 52; *N v United Kingdom* (n 2), para 29. In the case of *L v Lithuania*, the Court held more generally, after the above-cited consideration that Art 3 entails a positive obligation on the part of the state to protect the individual from acute ill-treatment, whatever its source, that 'if the source is a naturally occurring illness, *the treatment for which could involve the responsibility of the State* but is not forthcoming or is patently inadequate, an issue may arise under this provision' ((n 25), para 46, emphasis added).

[29] See also O'Cinneide 2008; Palmer 2006. See also Lord Brown of Eaton-Under-Heywood in the judgment of the House of Lords in the case of *Adam, Limbuela and Tesema* [2005] UKHL 66 (HL): 'It seems to me generally unhelpful to attempt to analyse obligations arising under Article 3 as negative or positive, and the state's conduct as active or passive. Time and again these are shown to be false dichotomies. The real issue in all these cases is whether the state is properly to be regarded as responsible for the harm inflicted (or threatened) upon the victim' (para 92).

[30] *E and others v United Kingdom* (n 25), para 89.

[31] Ibid, paras 92–100.

argued in this section that in these cases as well the Court, albeit more implicitly, distinguishes between these two tests.

Are there any other factors besides the threshold of seriousness and state responsibility that are relevant for the establishment of a violation of Article 3? In various cases about the expulsion of an alien, the Court has held that it is not possible to weigh the risk of ill-treatment against other (general) interests, such as the prevention of terrorism.[32] In other cases on Article 3, the Court has ruled, however, that 'inherent in the whole of the Convention is a search for a fair balance between the demands of the general interest of the community and the requirements of the protection of the individual's fundamental rights'.[33] This could indicate that a proportionality test applies as regards Article 3, which seems to be at odds with the absolute character of Article 3. On the basis of an analysis of case law of the Court, Battjes has argued that the absolute character of Article 3 does not preclude each and any form of balancing of interests. In his view, qualification under Article 3 entails, explicitly or implicitly, an assessment whether justifications for these facts apply.[34] In contrast, Palmer argues that under the Court's case law with regard to Article 3, a balancing approach is unacceptable.[35] While she does acknowledge that the (positive) duty on the state is limited by what can be reasonably expected of the state in the circumstances, she submits that this is an inevitable aspect of deciding the scope of the positive obligation, and not a proportionality test.[36]

While I agree with Palmer that many aspects of the Court's reasoning under Article 3 can be linked to the question of state responsibility or the minimum level of severity,[37] this is not always possible. The most convincing argument provided by Battjes is the *Jalloh case*. In this case, the

[32] *Chahal v United Kingdom* app no 22414/93 (ECtHR, 15 November 1996), para 80; *Saadi v Italy* (n 18), para 138.

[33] *Soering v United Kingdom* (n 18), para 89; *N v United Kingdom* (n 2), para 44. Both cases concerned expulsion of aliens. In a case on the duty of the state to conduct an effective official investigation under the 'procedural limb of Article 3', the Court considered that a fair balance should be struck between the necessity to preserve the secrecy of the data possessed by the authorities and to protect the rights of the other persons, on the one hand, and the claimant's right of effective participation in the proceedings, on the other (*Oleksiy Mykhaylovych Zakharkin v Ukraine* app no 1727/04 (ECtHR, 24 June 2010), para 72).

[34] Battjes 2009.

[35] Palmer 2006.

[36] Ibid, pp 449–50.

[37] Battjes identifies the financial burden for the state as a possible justification for ill-treatment (Battjes 2009, pp 606 and 618). In my view, it is also possible to understand observations of the Court on the financial burden for the state as forming part of the test whether the state can be held responsible. In this view, the Court uses the financial burden for the state and the difficult choices of priority that need to be taken with regard to the distribution of limited resources as reasons for holding that the state is not, as a general rule, *responsible* for providing everyone with perfect living conditions.

Court has held that in principle, Article 3 does not prohibit recourse to a forcible medical intervention that will assist in the investigation of an offence.[38] Since the aim of prosecution does not make the treatment more or less serious, such forcible medical intervention will rather easily reach the threshold of seriousness. In addition, it is very clear that the state can be held responsible for this treatment, as it directly inflicts this treatment on the applicant. Nevertheless, the Court seems to accept the interest of obtaining evidence as a possible justification for this ill-treatment. Hence, the Court seems to allow justifications for ill-treatment within the meaning of Article 3 of the ECHR. At the same time, Battjes argues that the absolute character of Article 3 is not meaningless, as it entails that the possibility to justify ill-treatment should be seen as an exception to the main rule that no justifications apply under Article 3.[39] Indeed, the research for this chapter has not revealed any factors that the Court deemed relevant for the assessment under Article 3 that cannot be linked to the question of state responsibility or the minimum level of severity.[40]

In brief, this means that I agree with Battjes that the Court's case law shows that the absolute character of Article 3 does not preclude each and any form of balancing of interests. However, I submit that this balancing can very often be understood as forming part of two broad questions: 1) can the state be held responsible for the alleged ill-treatment; and 2) does the ill-treatment reach the minimum level of severity? Only occasionally, such as in the *Jalloh* case, does the Court use argumentation that cannot be framed in terms of state responsibility or the threshold of seriousness.

This means that this section will examine whether the state can be held responsible for poor living conditions (11.2.2) and whether such living conditions can reach the threshold of seriousness set by Article 3 (11.2.3). If both questions are answered in the positive, a state obligation to provide

[38] Battjes 2009, pp 613–14.

[39] Ibid, pp 606, 618–19. In addition, the absolute character of Art 3 implies that there is no room for a margin of appreciation doctrine, which is applied with regard to the qualified rights laid down in the convention (Harris et al 2009, p 70). This means that the Court itself decides whether the minimum level of severity has been reached, whether the state can be held responsible for the ill-treatment and whether there are possible justifications for the alleged ill-treatment; this is not left to the discretion of the contracting states.

[40] In the case of *MSS v Belgium and Greece,* the Court has even indicated which circumstances cannot serve as possible justifications. It considered: 'The Court notes first of all that the States which form the external borders of the European Union are currently experiencing considerable difficulties in coping with the increasing influx of migrants and asylum seekers. (...) The Court does not underestimate the burden and pressure this situation places on the States concerned, which are all the greater in the present context of economic crisis. It is particularly aware of the difficulties involved in the reception of migrants and asylum seekers on their arrival at major international airports and of the disproportionate number of asylum seekers when compared to the capacities of some of these States. However, having regard to the absolute character of Article 3, that cannot absolve a State of its obligations under that provision' (app no 30696/09, ECtHR, 21 January 2011, para 223).

(some kind of) social assistance benefits exists. Obviously, considerable attention will be paid in this section to the *MSS v Belgium and Greece* case, in which the Court ruled on the issue of state obligations to provide support to asylum seekers under Article 3 of the ECHR. Nevertheless, in order to get the full picture, other, earlier, cases will be discussed as well.

11.2.2 State Responsibility

Sometimes the Court explicitly pays separate attention to the question whether the state can be held responsible for the alleged ill-treatment. More often however, the Court does not refer to state responsibility or uses other terms, such as the scope of the relevant obligation for the state. Nevertheless, this section will argue that it is possible to identify factors found relevant by the Court for determining whether the state can be held responsible for poor living conditions.

The state cannot as a general rule be held responsible for providing a minimum subsistence level for all persons living on its territory, according to the Court. It held:

> The Convention does not guarantee, as such, socio-economic rights, including the right to charge-free dwelling, the right to work, the right to free medical assistance, or the right to claim financial assistance from a State to maintain a certain level of living.[41]

In addition, it has also considered that

> Article 3 cannot be interpreted as obliging the High Contracting Parties to provide everyone within their jurisdiction with a home (...). Nor does Article 3 entail any general obligation to give refugees financial assistance to enable them to maintain a certain standard of living.[42]

Another general consideration made by the Court in this regard is that Article 3 does not place an obligation on the contracting state to provide free and unlimited health care to all aliens without a right to stay within its jurisdiction. According to the Court, a finding to the contrary 'would place too great a burden on the Contracting States'.[43] However, the Court has identified a number of conditions under which states can be held responsible for poor living conditions.

[41] *Pancenko v Latvia* (n 3).
[42] *MSS v Belgium and Greece* (n 40), para 249.
[43] *N v United Kingdom* (n 2), para 44.

With regard to persons in detention, the Court generally holds that the state must ensure under Article 3

> that a person is detained in conditions which are compatible with respect for his human dignity, that the manner and method of the execution of the measure do not subject him to distress or hardship of an intensity exceeding the unavoidable level of suffering inherent in detention and that, given the practical demands of imprisonment, his health and well-being are adequately secured by, among other things, providing him with the requisite medical assistance.[44]

The Court bases this responsibility of the state on the vulnerable position of persons in custody[45] by virtue of being within the control of the authorities.[46] This approach is taken by the Court in a number of different contexts, including detention on remand, following criminal conviction, pending deportation, for civil contempt, as a mentally disabled person or as an asylum seeker.[47]

In a case about the provision of expensive medication to detainees free of charge, the Court held that the state is bound to provide all medical care that its resources permit.[48] Even though unavailability of resources might therefore limit the state responsibility for detention conditions, this positively and strongly formulated rule shows that this should be considered to be an exception and that the burden of proof lies on the state.[49] In addition, state responsibility for conditions of detention might be mitigated by the actual availability of certain provisions. With regard to the availability of necessary medicines in a prison pharmacy, the Court has held for example that, in so far as the applicant was not dependent on the pharmacy's stocks, for instance where his relatives were able to procure the necessary medicines for him and he was not restricted in taking

[44] See, eg, *Kudla v Poland* (n 19), para 94; *MSS v Belgium and Greece* (n 40), para 221.

[45] *Cf Gladyshev v Russia* app no 2807/04 (ECtHR, 30 July 2009), para 51; *Isayev v Russia* app no 20756/04 (ECtHR, 22 October 2009), para 90.

[46] *Denis Vasilyev v Russia* app no 32704/04, (ECtHR, 17 December 2009), para 115; *Premininy v Russia* (n 17), para 73. In this regard, the Court also refers to the position of conscripted servicemen.

[47] See for reference to relevant case law, Harris et al 2009, p 93. With regard to detention conditions of persons detained as asylum seekers, *SD v Greece* app no 53541/07 (ECtHR, 11 June 2009), para 47. With regard to the responsibility for persons in detention, the Court does not, therefore, make a distinction between nationals and aliens. Apparently, the sovereign immigration power may have no bearing on the scope of the responsibility for conditions of detention. Hence, in this field, the Court seems to adopt complete separation.

[48] *Aleksanyan v Russia* app no 46468/06 (ECtHR, 22 December 2008), para 148.

[49] Indeed, the Court has held in a number of cases that a 'lack of resources cannot in principle justify prison conditions which are so poor as to reach the threshold of treatment contrary to Article 3 of the Convention' (see, eg, *Poltoratskiy v Ukraine* app no 38812/97 (ECtHR, 29 April 2003), para 148; *Dybeku v Albania* app no 41153/06, (ECtHR, 18 December 2007), para 50; *Iovchev v Bulgaria* app no 41211/98 (ECtHR, 2 February 2006), para 136. However, in these cases, the Court also observed that (some of the) shortcomings in the detention conditions could have been remedied even in the absence of considerable financial means, whereas the *Aleksanyan* case concerned the provision of expensive anti-retroviral drugs.

them, he may not claim to have been affected by the shortage.[50] However, this does not apply if it imposes an 'excessive financial burden' on the applicant or his relatives.[51] In addition, the Court has considered that the ability to receive additional food from relatives, or to purchase it from the prison shop, could have compensated for the applicant's dissatisfaction with the possibly monotonous diet provided by the prison canteen.[52] Accordingly, if a detainee is able to provide for adequate prison conditions himself, for example with the help of relatives, the state merely has a duty not to restrict the detainee in obtaining and using such conditions, provided that this does not impose an excessive financial burden on him or on his relatives.

State responsibility for poor living conditions can also exist outside the context of detention. In the case of *Denis Vasilyev v Russia*, the Court ruled:

> The Court reiterates its constant approach that Article 3 imposes on the State a duty to protect the physical well-being of persons who find themselves in a vulnerable position by virtue of being within the control of the authorities, such as, for instance, detainees or conscripted servicemen (…). However, given the absolute nature of the protection of Article 3, whose requirements permit of no derogation, this duty to protect cannot be said to be confined to the specific context of the military or penitentiary facilities. It also becomes relevant in other situations in which the physical well-being of individuals is dependent, to a decisive extent, on the actions by the authorities, who are legally required to take measures within the scope of their powers which might have been necessary to avoid the risk of damage to life or limb.[53]

Hence, dependency for physical well-being on state actions and legal obligations on the part of the state seem to be relevant factors for state responsibility in contexts outside detention. In this case, the applicant complained of the inadequate action taken by the police in reaction to an assault directed at him, in particular the failure to call an ambulance and the decision to carry him, while unconscious, to another place. However, this logic has also been applied by the Court to other contexts. In the case of *Budina v Russia*, the disabled applicant complained that her pension was too small for survival. The Court considered that it could not be said that the state authorities had imposed any direct ill-treatment on the applicant, but that it could not exclude that 'State responsibility could

[50] *Mirilashvili v Russia* app no 6293/04 (ECtHR, 10 July 2007 (dec)); *Grishin v Russia* app no 30983/02 (ECtHR, 15 November 2007), para 73.

[51] *Aleksanyan v Russia* (n 48), para 149. In the case of *Hummatov v Azerbaijan*, the Court even found it relevant that procuring the necessary medication could be 'quite expensive' (app nos 9852/03 and 13413/04, ECtHR, 29 November 2007, para 117).

[52] *Valašinas v Lithuania* app no 44558/98 (ECtHR, 24 July 2001), para 109.

[53] *Denis Vasilyev v Russia* (n 46), para 115.

arise for "treatment" where an applicant, in circumstances wholly dependent on State support, found herself faced with official indifference when in a situation of serious deprivation or want incompatible with human dignity'.[54]

The Court referred to this consideration in its judgment in the *MSS v Belgium and Greece* case.[55] In this case, the Court did not refer explicitly to the concept of state responsibility, but some statements of the Court should, in my view, be taken as referring (also) to the responsibility of the state. Otherwise, these considerations are difficult to understand. In addition, they fit in with the above-mentioned case law.

This case concerned the complaint of an asylum seeker from Afghanistan who travelled through Greece to Belgium, where he lodged an asylum application. On the basis of the EU Dublin Regulation, Belgium sent him back to Greece, as this was the country in which he first entered the European Union. In his complaint against Greece, the applicant alleged, inter alia, that the poor detention and living conditions for asylum seekers in Greece violated Article 3 of the ECHR. As regards the living conditions for asylum seekers outside detention, the Court recalled with reference to earlier case law that Article 3 cannot be interpreted as obliging the High Contracting Parties to provide everyone within their jurisdiction with a home and that Article 3 does not entail any general obligation to give refugees financial assistance to enable them to maintain a certain standard of living.[56] The Court referred in this regard to its judgment in the case of *Müslim v Turkey*, which also concerned a complaint of an asylum seeker about precarious living conditions in the host state. In this judgment the Court had ruled, in a strikingly short way, that it did not find anything in the documents of the case that could entail the responsibility of the state for the living conditions of the applicant.[57]

[54] *Budina v Russia* app no 45603/05 (ECtHR, 18 June 2009 (dec)).

[55] *MSS v Belgium and Greece* (n 40). Also the case of *Rahimi v Greece* concerned a complaint of an (in this case unaccompanied minor) asylum seeker about poor living conditions. In its judgment, the Court referred to its *MSS* judgment, but made less elaborate statements as regards the scope of the state obligation and the minimum level of severity. It only considered in general that the applicant had been left to his own devices after his release from prison and noted that the applicant had been emaciated and had had difficulties sleeping without lights on when he was taken into care by a NGO (app no 8687/08, ECtHR, 5 April 2011, paras 92–94). For the purpose of this chapter, this judgment is therefore less relevant.

[56] *MSS v Belgium and Greece* (n 40), para 249.

[57] *Müslim v Turkey* app no 53566/99 (ECtHR, 26 April 2005), para 86. The Court considered that the applicant did not appear to have been prevented from maintaining the standard of living which he himself had chosen on seeking refuge in Turkey. In addition, the Court held that although the situation of the applicant was difficult, it was undoubtedly no worse than that of any other citizen who was less well off than others.

In *MSS*, the Court explicitly did not depart from its judgment in *Müslim*, but held that:

> The Court is of the opinion, however, that what is at issue in the instant case cannot be considered in those terms. Unlike in the above-cited Müslim case (...), the obligation to provide accommodation and decent material conditions to impoverished asylum seekers has now entered into positive law and the Greek authorities are bound to comply with their own legislation, which transposes Community law, namely Directive 2003/9 laying down minimum standards for the reception of asylum seekers in the Member States (...). What the applicant holds against the Greek authorities in this case is that, because of their deliberate actions or omissions, it has been impossible in practice for him to avail himself of these rights and provide for his essential needs.[58]

Hence, the Court does not depart from the main rule that the state is not responsible for socioeconomic living conditions. However, state responsibility was engaged in this case, since the Greek authorities were, just as in the case of *Denis Vasilyev v Russia* (see above), legally required to provide housing and adequate living conditions to asylum seekers. This is, in my view, the most important difference from the case of *Müslim v Turkey*. Thus, the reference to Directive 2003/9 by the Court should, in my opinion, be understood as an argument for holding the Greek authorities responsible for the alleged ill-treatment. This reading is confirmed by the Court in the case of *SSH v United Kingdom* in which the Court summarizes its *MSS* judgment by stating that

> It held that the conditions in which the applicant was living reached the Article 3 threshold and found Greece to be responsible for the breach of that Article due to the inaction of the Greek authorities despite their positive obligations under both the European Reception Directive and domestic legislation regarding the provision of accommodation and decent material conditions to asylum seekers.[59]

This means that a state can be held responsible under Article 3 if it intentionally withholds certain benefits from persons while they are legally obliged to provide these benefits.

Such an intentional failure to comply with domestic legal requirements might, however, not be enough to engage responsibility, as the Court subsequently held in *MSS*:

> The Court attaches considerable importance to the applicant's status as an asylum seeker and, as such, a member of a particularly underprivileged and vulnerable population group in need of special protection (...). It notes the existence of a broad consensus at the international and European level concerning this

[58] *MSS v Belgium and Greece* (n 40), para 250.
[59] *SSH v United Kingdom* app no 60367/10 (ECtHR, 29 January 2013), para 76.

> need for special protection, as evidenced by the Geneva Convention, the remit and the activities of the UNHCR and the standards set out in the European Union Reception Directive.[60]

Accordingly, another factor relevant for state responsibility is the vulnerability of the person concerned. While this factor might also be of relevance for establishing whether the minimum level of severity has been reached, the position of this consideration in the reasoning of the Court,[61] as well as the fact that this factor has been used by the Court in earlier case law to establish state responsibility, indicates that vulnerability is also a relevant factor for the question of state responsibility. This is confirmed by the concluding holding of the Court:

> In the light of the above and in view of the obligations incumbent on the Greek authorities under the European Reception Directive (...), the Court considers that the Greek authorities have not had due regard to the applicant's vulnerability as an asylum seeker and must be held responsible, because of their inaction, for the situation in which he has found himself for several months, living in the street, with no resources or access to sanitary facilities, and without any means of providing for his essential needs.[62]

Apart from referring to the broad consensus at the international and European level, the Court does not provide any arguments as to why asylum seekers should be considered to be particularly underprivileged and vulnerable.[63] In the context of detention conditions, the Court held that the applicant, being an asylum seeker, 'was particularly vulnerable because of everything he had been through during his migration and the traumatic experiences he was likely to have endured previously'.[64] This consideration is, however, made by the Court in the context of the examination of whether the detention conditions, in view of the brief periods of detention, reached the *minimum level of severity*. Earlier case law shows, however, that vulnerability seems to be relevant for *state responsibility* if it is caused by being under the control of the authorities (as regard detainees) or by being wholly dependent on state action or support. Such factors

[60] *MSS v Belgium and Greece* (n 40), para 251.

[61] In para 252 the Court holds: 'That said, the Court must determine whether a situation of extreme material poverty can raise an issue under Article 3'. Hence, only then did the Court examine whether the situation of extreme material poverty reaches the minimum level of severity under ECHR, Art 3.

[62] Ibid, para 263.

[63] Judge Sajó states in his partly concurring and partly dissenting opinion that the concept of vulnerable groups in the Court's case law refers to groups that were historically subjected to prejudice with lasting consequences, resulting in their social exclusion. In his view, asylum seekers do not fulfil these conditions; they are not socially classified, and consequently treated, as a group.

[64] *MSS v Belgium and Greece* (n 40), para 232.

are more convincing, in my view, for holding that all asylum seekers, by definition, are in a vulnerable position (see further section 11.7 below).

It is important to note here that the Court seems to make a strict distinction between asylum seekers, on the one hand, and illegal aliens, on the other. It appears from the Court's case law that the Court does not envisage illegal aliens by definition as a vulnerable population group for which the state bears a special responsibility. For example, in *MSS*, the Court states explicitly that the applicant did not, on the face of it, have the profile of an 'illegal immigrant', but was a 'potential asylum seeker'.[65] In the *Mubilanzila Mayeka and Kaniki Mitunga v Belgium* case, which concerned the detention of an unaccompanied five-year old girl in a closed centre for adults, the Court held that the applicant was, owing to her very young age and the fact that she was unaccompanied, in an extremely vulnerable situation. According to the Court, 'it is important to bear in mind that this is the decisive factor and it takes precedence over considerations relating to the second applicant's status as an illegal immigrant'.[66] This implies that although certain categories of illegal aliens might be considered vulnerable for other reasons, such as young age, the Court does not envisage all illegal aliens as being particularly vulnerable.

Hence, the *MSS* judgment of the Court confirms earlier case law that state responsibility exists for poor living conditions for persons who are in a vulnerable position, by virtue of being in the control of the authorities or being wholly dependent on state action or support, provided that the authorities are under a (domestic) legal obligation to take care of these living conditions.[67] Accordingly, in order for state responsibility to arise with regard to poor living conditions outside the context of detention, it seems that the Court requires deliberate, and not merely negligent, conduct from the state (*cf* '*official* indifference' in the *Budina* case). In the case of *Sufi and Elmi v United Kingdom* (see further section 11.2.3 below), the Court explained that general poverty or the lack of sufficient resources to

[65] Ibid, para 225. See also *Halimi v Austria and Italy* app no 53852/11 (ECtHR, 18 June 2013 (dec)), paras 63–65.

[66] *Mubilanzila Mayeka and Kaniki Mitunga v Belgium* (n 25), para 55. In the case of *Muskhadzhiyeva and others v Belgium*, the Court held that this consideration also applies to alien children in detention who were accompanied by their parents (app no 41442/07 ECtHR, 19 January 2010, paras 56–58).

[67] See in this regard also the case of *RR v Poland* app no 27617/04 (ECtHR, 26 May 2011), in which the Court held that the failure to provide timely prenatal examinations violated Art 3. In this regard, the Court attached importance to the fact that 'there was an array of unequivocal legal provisions in force at the relevant time specifying the State's positive obligations towards pregnant women regarding their access to information about their health and that of the foetus' (para 157) and to the fact that the applicant was in a situation of great vulnerability (para 159).

deal with a naturally occurring phenomenon should not be seen as being caused by intentional acts or omissions of the state.[68]

Finally, it should be noted that both in the context of detention and in the context outside detention, the responsibility of the state can be mitigated by the behaviour of the person concerned. In the case of *Slyusarev v Russia*, the Court considered that 'in certain contexts the behaviour of the alleged victim may be taken into account in defining whether the authorities can be held responsible for the treatment complained of'. Even though the Court recalled that the general rule is that Article 3 prohibits ill-treatment irrespective of the circumstances and the victim's behaviour, it considered that this rule is not without exception. Thus, 'if a prisoner does not receive requisite medical assistance from the authorities, it may entail the State's responsibility only if he made reasonable steps to avail himself of such assistance'.[69] In the case of *O'Rourke v United Kingdom*, the applicant was evicted from his temporary accommodation, where he had been staying since his release from prison, and complained that this eviction, in consequence of which he was forced to sleep on the streets, constituted a breach of Article 3 of the ECHR. The Court did not consider that the applicant's suffering following his eviction attained the requisite level of severity to engage Article 3 but continued by observing that, 'even if it had done', he was largely responsible for his own deterioration, as he had failed to attend a night shelter and had refused two specific offers of temporary accommodation.[70] Also in the case of *Mohammed Hussein and others v the Netherlands and Italy*, the Court found the fact that the applicant never sought assistance in finding work and/or alternative accommodation a relevant factor in rejecting the complaint under Article 3.[71] In addition, if an asylum seeker voluntarily leaves a reception centre, 'it cannot be considered wrongdoing on the part of the Contracting State if the applicant was homeless and lacked access to social support and medical assistance', according to the Court.[72]

In the *MSS* case, the Greek authorities argued that the applicant's inaction, ie by not informing them of his homelessness, was the cause of his poor situation. The Court, however, considered that

> given the particular state of insecurity and vulnerability in which asylum seekers are known to live in Greece, the Court considers that the Greek authorities

[68] *Sufi and Elmi v United Kingdom* app nos 8319/07 and 11449/07 (ECtHR, 28 June 2011), paras 281–82.

[69] *Slyusarev v Russia* app no 60333/00 (ECtHR, 20 April 2010), para 37.

[70] *O'Rourke v United Kingdom* app no 39022/97 (ECtHR, 26 June 2001 (dec)). See for other self-inflicted conditions of detention, *McFeeley and others v United Kingdom* app no 8317/78 (ECtHR, 15 May 1980 (dec)). *Cf* Harris et al 2009, p 70, fn 16 and Ovey and White 2006, p 97.

[71] *Mohammed Hussein and others v the Netherlands and Italy* app no 27725/10 (ECtHR, 2 April 2013 (dec)), para 74.

[72] *Abubeker v Austria* app no 73874/11 (ECtHR, 18 June 2013 (dec)), para 59.

> should not simply have waited for the applicant to take the initiative of turning to the police headquarters to provide for his essential needs.[73]

In this regard, the Court put considerable weight on the fact that the authorities themselves had acknowledged that there were fewer than 1000 places in reception centres to accommodate tens of thousands of asylum seekers.[74] Hence, the behaviour of the individual concerned might under certain circumstances mitigate the responsibility of the state. However, if it is a well-known fact that certain individuals are homeless or live in very poor circumstances, the authorities cannot use the inaction of the person concerned as an argument for avoiding their responsibility.

11.2.3 Minimum Level of Severity

If it has been established that the state can be held responsible for poor living conditions, it must be examined whether the living conditions reach the seriousness threshold of Article 3. As has been cited before, the Court has held in this regard:

> The assessment of this minimum is, in the nature of things, relative; it depends on all the circumstances of the case, such as the nature and context of the treatment or punishment, the manner and method of its execution, its duration, its physical or mental effects and, in some cases, the sex, age and state of health of the victim.[75]

Conditions of detention have been found to reach the threshold of inhuman or degrading treatment in large numbers of cases.[76] When assessing the conditions, the Court takes into account their cumulative effect.[77] Account must be taken of 'all the circumstances, such as the size of the cell and the degree of overcrowding, sanitary conditions, opportunities for recreation and exercise, medical treatment and supervision and the prisoner's state of health'.[78] In addition, the duration of detention is a relevant factor,[79] as well as the provision of sufficient food and bed

[73] *MSS v Belgium and Greece* (n 40), para 259.

[74] Ibid, paras 258–59.

[75] Amongst (many) other cases: *Ireland v United Kingdom* (n 18), para 162; *Hilal v United Kingdom* (n 22), para 60; *Kirakosyan v Armenia* (n 22), para 43.

[76] Harris et al 2009, p 94.

[77] See, eg, *Dougoz v Greece* app no 40907/98 (ECtHR, 6 March 2001), para 46; *Kalashnikov v Russia* app no 47095/99 (ECtHR, 15 July 2002), para 95.

[78] *Assenov and others v Bulgaria* app no 24760/94 (ECtHR, 28 October 1998), para 135.

[79] See, eg, *Bakhmutskiy v Russia* app no 36932/02 (ECtHR, 25 June 2009), para 88; *Kalashnikov v Russia* (n 77), para 102; *Dougoz v Greece* (n 77), para 48.

linen.[80] The Court has even observed that 'the absence of an adequate supply of toilet paper in a prison may raise an issue under Article 3 of the Convention'.[81] Finally, when assessing particular detention conditions, the vulnerability of certain categories of detainees, such as children,[82] the mentally disabled,[83] or asylum seekers[84] has to be taken into account. With regard to children, contracting states should ensure that the amenities in detention facilities are suitable for children. The absence of baby cots, play areas and special activities for children and the use of automatic doors that are dangerous for children have, for example, been found to violate Article 3 of the ECHR.[85]

A relevant aspect of the case law in this area is the rigorous scrutiny applied by the Court.[86] For example, in the case of *Valašinas v Lithuania* the Court examined whether the temporary absence of partitions between the toilets meant that the applicant was obliged to use the toilet in the presence of another detainee and observed that bedding in the dormitory was washed and dried regularly in the prison laundry.[87] In the *Kaja v Greece* case, the Court made a fact-finding mission to the detention centre where the applicant had been held for three months pending expulsion.[88] The Court observed in this case that the conditions were acceptable for a detention of a short duration, but that the general conditions, for example the absence of a radio, TV and of any catering facilities inside the centre, were not acceptable for a detention of three months. In *Peers v Greece*, the Court observed that the applicant had to spend at least part of the evening and the entire night in his cell, which had no ventilation and which could become extremely hot. The Court went on to observe that the applicant was placed in this cell during a period of the year when temperatures have the tendency to rise considerably in Greece, even in the evening and often at night.[89]

Also with regard to the aspect of overcrowding, the Court generally examines precisely how many square metres are available per detainee. The Court has held that severe overcrowding in itself raises an issue

[80] See, eg, *Modarca v Moldova* app no 14437/05 (ECtHR, 10 May 2007); *SD v Greece* (n 47), para 51.

[81] *Valašinas v Lithuania* (n 52), para 104. In this case, the Court observed that it has not been established that the applicant was so deprived in practice. Also in the *MSS* case, the Court paid attention to the absence of soap and toilet paper ((n 40), para 230).

[82] *Mubilanzila Mayeka and Kaniki Mitunga v Belgium* (n 25), para 55; *Popov v France* app nos 39472/07 and 39474/07 (ECtHR, 19 January 2012).

[83] *Dybeku v Albania* (n 49), para 41.

[84] *MSS v Belgium and Greece* (n 40), paras 231–33.

[85] *Popov v France* (n 82).

[86] See also Arai-Yokoi 2003, p 405.

[87] *Valašinas v Lithuania* (n 52), para 104.

[88] *Kaja v Greece* app no 32927/03 (ECtHR, 27 July 2006).

[89] *Peers v Greece* app no 28524/95 (ECtHR, 19 April 2001), para 72.

under Article 3.[90] In this connection, the Court regularly observes that 'the European Committee for the Prevention of Torture and Inhuman or Degrading Treatment of Punishment ("the CPT") has set 7 m^2 per prisoner as an approximate, desirable guideline for a detention cell'.[91] However, in the case of *Valašinas v Lithuania*, the Court held that the scarce space in relative terms was compensated for by the large size in absolute terms of the dormitories, as well as the freedom of movement allowed during the day.[92] In addition, in the case of *Therani and others v Turkey*, the Court considered that suffering flowing from the fact that the applicant had been held in a dormitory with seven beds and six other people, which had completely deprived him of privacy, was not sufficient to amount to inhuman and degrading treatment contrary to Article 3 of the ECHR.[93]

Also detention of a rather short duration might reach the threshold of Article 3, provided that the conditions are particularly serious or the applicant is particularly vulnerable. Thus, if conditions are 'unfit for human habitation' owing to excessive overcrowding and a lack of orderliness and hygiene, they fall within the severity threshold of Article 3, even if the applicant is subjected to such conditions for a duration as short as two hours.[94] In addition, if an applicant is particularly vulnerable, for example because of being an asylum seeker, periods of detention of four days or a week are not considered by the Court to be insignificant.[95]

The lack of the 'requisite medical assistance' may, in itself, give rise to an issue under Article 3 as well.[96] There are numerous examples of cases where the Court has found a violation of Article 3 due to the lack of adequate medical treatment and assistance or the unavailability of the necessary medical equipment for persons in detention.[97] In general, in order to give rise to 'inhuman treatment' within the meaning of Article 3, the absence of adequate medical treatment should lead to a medical emergency or severe or prolonged pain.[98] In addition, the absence of adequate treatment can be characterized as 'degrading treatment' if it leads to

[90] See, eg, *Modarca v Moldova* (n 80), para 64; *Lyubimenko v Russia* app no 6270/06 (ECtHR, 19 March 2009), para 57.

[91] See, eg, *Kalashnikov v Russia* (n 77), para 97; *Mayzit v Russia* app no 63378/00 (ECtHR, 20 January 2005), para 39; *Kadiķis v Latvia* app no 62393/00 (ECtHR, 4 May 2006), para 52.

[92] *Valašinas v Lithuania* (n 52), paras 103 and 107.

[93] *Therani and others v Turkey* app nos 32940/08, 41626/08, 43616/08 (ECtHR, 13 April 2010), paras 88–89.

[94] Ibid, para 93.

[95] *MSS v Belgium and Greece* (n 40), para 232.

[96] See, explicitly, *Grishin v Russia* (n 50), para 72.

[97] See, eg, *Sarban v Moldova* app no 3456/05 (ECtHR, 4 October 2005); *Khudobin v Russia* app no 59696/00 (ECtHR, 26 October 2006); *Pilčić v Croatia* app no 33138/06 (ECtHR, 17 January 2008); *Paladi v Moldova* app no 39806/05 (ECtHR, 10 March 2009).

[98] *Sarban v Moldova* (n 97), para 86.

strong feelings of insecurity, stress or anxiety and physical suffering[99] According to the Court, the 'mere fact that a detainee was seen by a doctor and prescribed a certain form of treatment cannot automatically lead to the conclusion that the medical assistance was adequate'. It holds:

> The authorities must also ensure that a comprehensive record is kept concerning the detainee's state of health and the treatment he underwent while in detention (...), that the diagnoses and care are prompt and accurate (...), and that where necessitated by the nature of a medical condition, supervision is regular and systematic and involves a comprehensive therapeutic strategy aimed at curing the detainee's diseases or preventing their aggravation, rather than addressing them on a symptomatic basis.[100]

Hence, the Court has identified a number of specific and far-reaching obligations for the state with regard to the provision of medical assistance to detainees.

The denial of medical aids to detainees may violate Article 3, even if it does not affect the detainee's health. In the case of *Slyusarev v Russia*, the Court considered that the denial of the provision of glasses to the applicant was, owing to its duration of several months, serious enough to fall within the scope of Article 3 of the ECHR, 'even if having no glasses had no permanent effect on the applicant's health'.[101] The Court considered that without glasses, the applicant could not read or write normally and that the denial of glasses 'must have created a lot of distress in his everyday life, and given rise to a feeling of insecurity and helplessness'. From the case of *VD v Romania*, it appears that the denial of dentures to a detainee who could not afford one himself can also reach the seriousness threshold of Article 3.[102]

To summarize, the state should ensure that a person is detained in conditions which are compatible with respect for his human dignity and that his health and well-being are adequately secured by, among other

[99] ECtHR 26 October 2006, app no 59696/00 (*Khudobin v Russia* (n 97), para 96). *Cf* Harris et al 2009, p 97. However, the Court does not usually make a distinction between these different kinds of ill-treatment. eg, with regard to the unavailability of the necessary medical equipment, the Court has held that it may raise 'an issue under Article 3 if it has negative effects on the applicant's state of health or causes suffering of a certain intensity' (*Grishin v Russia* (n 50), para 72).

[100] *Visloguzov v Ukraine* app no 32362/02 (ECtHR, 20 May 2010), para 69 with further references.

[101] *Slyusarev v Russia* (n 69), para 36. The Court did consider that if the glasses had been returned to the applicant quickly, ie within a few days, no issue under Art 3 would have arisen (para 34).

[102] *VD v Romania* app no 7078/02 (ECtHR, 16 February 2010). Remarkably, the Court does not mention the minimum level of severity in this case. With regard to the provision of dentures free of charge to detainees see also the case of *Stojanović v Serbia* app no 34425/04 (ECtHR, 19 May 2009). In this case, the authorities eventually provided the applicant with dentures free of charge, as a result of which the application was struck from the list.

things, providing him with the requisite medical assistance. The absence of sufficient and adequate living space, sanitary products, food and medical care in detention may reach the threshold set by Article 3.

With regard to living conditions outside prisons, there is very little case law, even though the possibility that poor socioeconomic conditions might reach the threshold of Article 3 was already recognized *in abstracto* by the European Commission in 1990.[103] In the case of *Moldovan and others v Romania*, the houses of applicants were burned by police officers, as a result of which the applicants had to live in improper and overcrowded conditions. The Court held:

> It furthermore considers that the applicants' living conditions in the last ten years, in particular the severely overcrowded and unsanitary environment and its detrimental effect on the applicants' health and well-being, combined with the length of the period during which the applicants have had to live in such conditions and the general attitude of the authorities, must have caused them considerable mental suffering, thus diminishing their human dignity and arousing in them such feelings as to cause humiliation and debasement.[104]

Combined with the racial discrimination to which they had been publicly subjected, the Court found that the applicants' living conditions constituted an interference with their human dignity which, in the special circumstances of this case, amounted to 'degrading treatment' within the meaning of Article 3 of the ECHR.[105] This judgment does not make it clear, however, whether the poor living conditions of the applicants taken alone, without the 'aggravating factor' of racial discrimination, could raise an issue under Article 3.

The *O'Rourke v United Kingdom* case concerned the complaint of a homeless person who was evicted from temporary housing that had been

[103] Cassese 1991.

[104] *Moldovan and others v Romania* app nos 41138/98 and 64320/01 (ECtHR, 12 July 2005), para 110.

[105] Ibid, para 113. A similar case is that of *Tănase and others v Romania* (app no 62954/00), where the applicants, Romanian nationals of Roma origin, complained that the destruction of their homes (by villagers) had deprived them of the use of their houses and belongings, forcing them to live in very poor and cramped conditions, deprived of the basic medical and social services, of employment opportunities and schooling for their children. The applicants based their complaints (among other grounds) on Art 8, but the Court held that these facts could also raise an issue under Art 3 (ECtHR, 9 December 2003 (dec)). The Court declared the complaints admissible (ECtHR, 19 May 2005 (dec)). In 2009 the Court decided to strike the case out of the list on the basis of a unilateral declaration by the Romanian Government. In this declaration, the Government admitted that the facts of this case constituted violations of Arts 3, 6, 8, 13 and 14 ECHR and of Art 1 of Protocol no 1 to the ECHR and proposed several individual and general measures with a view to redressing the situation (ECtHR, 26 May 2009). The same thing happened in the cases of *Kalanyos and others v Romania* (app no 57884/00) and *Gergely v Romania* (app no 57885/00), in which similar complaints were lodged under (amongst others) Art 3 and which were declared admissible at 19 May 2005 and struck off the list on 26 April 2007.

offered to him after his release from prison. As a result of this eviction, he had to sleep on the street, which caused his health to deteriorate. The Court considered, however, that the applicant's suffering following his eviction did not attain the requisite level of severity to engage Article 3.[106] Apparently, homelessness does not, as such, reach the threshold of Article 3.

In the case of *Larioshina v Russia*, the applicant complained about the insufficient amount of pension and the other social benefits which she received. Although the Court held that 'in principle, it cannot substitute itself for the national authorities in assessing or reviewing the level of financial benefits available under a social assistance scheme' it continued by stating that 'a complaint about a wholly insufficient amount of pension and the other social benefits may, in principle, raise an issue under Article 3 of the Convention which prohibits inhuman or degrading treatment'. However, the Court held that it could not find an indication that the amount of the pension 'has caused such damage to her physical or mental health capable of attaining the minimum level of severity falling within the ambit of Article 3 of the Convention'.[107] Hence, in order to reach the minimum level of severity, the amount of social benefits must cause damage to some extent to the physical or mental health of the person concerned.

At the time when the applicant lodged the application the total amount of the social payments that she received was 653 Russian roubles per month. As Koch observes, 653 roubles per month was in 2001 equivalent to approximately EUR 25, which is an extremely limited amount of money. The applicant could therefore be said to be living in 'extreme poverty', namely on less than a dollar a day as the concept is understood by the World Bank.[108] This very limited amount of social benefits, however, did not reach the threshold set by Article 3 of the ECHR. The Court does not explain why this limited amount of financial means does not cause enough damage to the physical or mental health of the applicant to reach the threshold of Article 3.

In the case of *Budina v Russia*, the 61-year old and disabled applicant complained as well about the amount of her pension. She alleged that only from 2007 had her income risen above the subsistence level and in 2008 was only enough for her to pay for flat maintenance, food and hygiene items. Nevertheless, she had still been lacking funds for non-food

[106] *O'Rourke v United Kingdom* (n 70).

[107] *Larioshina v Russia* app no 56869/00 (ECtHR, 23 April 2002 (dec)). This criterion was repeated by the Court in *Kutepov and Anikeyenko v Russia* app no 68029/01 (ECtHR, 25 October 2005), para 62.

[108] Koch 2009, p 182.

goods, sanitary and cultural services, health and sanatorium treatment. In this case, the Court rephrased the relevant criterion a little by stating:

> Indeed there is no indication in the materials before the Court that the level of pension and social benefits available to the applicant have been insufficient to protect her from damage to her physical or mental health or from a situation of degradation incompatible with human dignity.[109]

Hence, this implies that *any* kind of damage to physical or mental health might reach the minimum level of severity, as well as a 'situation of degradation incompatible with human dignity'. Also in this case, however, the Court concluded that this 'high threshold' of Article 3 had not been met. The Court gave something of an explanation for this conclusion, by stating:

> [T]he applicant's income within the period in question was not high in absolute terms. However, the applicant has failed to substantiate her allegation that the lack of funds translated itself into concrete suffering. On the contrary, in her observations the applicant explained that in 2008 her pension was enough for flat maintenance, food, and hygiene items, but was not enough for clothes, non-food goods, sanitary and cultural services, health and sanatorium treatment. Of these latter items, it appears that the applicant was in fact eligible for free medical treatment. While she claimed that in practice the paperwork for sanatorium treatment was prohibitive, she has not shown that essential medical treatment has, for that reason, been rendered unavailable. Therefore even though the applicant's situation was difficult, especially from 2004 to 2007, the Court is not persuaded that in the circumstances of the present case the high threshold of Article 3 has been met.[110]

It seems therefore to be relevant that the applicant was able to provide for her most basic needs (home, food, hygiene items) and was eligible for free medical treatment. As a result, the situation of the applicant did not reach the minimum level of severity within the meaning of Article 3. The fact that a disabled woman had to live below the subsistence level for three years is apparently not serious enough. This contrasts sharply with the Court's case law on detention conditions, where living in bad conditions for only a few days has been held to reach the Article 3 threshold.

The Court ruled for the first time that poor living conditions as such reached the threshold of Article 3, outside the context of detention, in the case of *MSS v Belgium and Greece*.[111] As mentioned previously, this case concerned a complaint lodged by an asylum seeker about poor living conditions in Greece. After having established that the state could be held responsible for these living conditions in the circumstances of this

[109] *Budina v Russia* (n 54).
[110] Ibid.
[111] *MSS v Belgium and Greece* (n 40).

case (see section 11.2.2 above), the Court went on to examine whether the living conditions reached the threshold of Article 3. It held:

> It observes that the situation in which the applicant has found himself is particularly serious. He allegedly spent months living in a state of the most extreme poverty, unable to cater for his most basic needs: food, hygiene and a place to live. Added to that was the ever-present fear of being attacked and robbed and the total lack of any likelihood of his situation improving. It was to escape from that situation of insecurity and of material and psychological want that he tried several times to leave Greece.[112]

To conclude, the Court held:

> It considers that such living conditions, combined with the prolonged uncertainty in which he has remained and the total lack of any prospects of his situation improving, have attained the level of severity required to fall within the scope of Article 3 of the Convention.[113]

Hence, the Court explicitly mentions food, hygiene and a place to live as a person's most basic needs. The situation of persons who are unable to meet these basic needs for a significant period of time, coupled with the lack of any likelihood of this situation improving, apparently reaches the minimum level of severity of Article 3. The applicant in this case had to endure these poor conditions for several months.[114] As regards the lack of prospects of any improvement of his situation, the Court considered that the situation was linked to his status as an asylum seeker and to the fact that his asylum application had not yet been examined by the Greek authorities. The Court is therefore of the opinion that, 'had they examined the applicant's asylum request promptly, the Greek authorities could have substantially alleviated his suffering'.[115] Another way of alleviating the suffering is by providing asylum seekers with access to the labour market. Such access must, however, be a realistic alternative and must actually enable the person concerned to provide for his basic needs. As regards the situation in Greece, the Court observed that

> in practice access to the job market is so riddled with administrative obstacles that this cannot be considered a realistic alternative (...). In addition the applicant had personal difficulties due to his lack of command of the Greek language, the lack of any support network and the generally unfavourable economic climate.[116]

[112] Ibid, para 254.
[113] Ibid, para 263.
[114] Ibid, para 263.
[115] Ibid, para 262.
[116] Ibid, para 261.

In the *Sufi and Elmi v United Kingdom* case, the Court held, with reference to its *MSS* judgment, that the conditions in camps for refugees and internally displaced persons in Somalia were sufficiently dire as to amount to treatment reaching the threshold of Article 3. This case concerned a complaint lodged against the United Kingdom by two applicants against their expulsion to Somalia. An important aspect of this judgment, albeit less relevant for the purposes of this chapter, is that the Court confirmed that as regards complaints about *expulsion* to dire humanitarian conditions, two different 'threshold tests' exist. If the authorities of the country of *origin* can be held responsible, through intentional acts or omissions, for the poor conditions, then the general test, as identified in the *MSS* case, applies. On the other hand, if the poor conditions in the country of origin emanate from 'natural causes', such as illness, the lack of sufficient resources, poverty or drought, then expulsion will only reach the threshold in very exceptional cases on the basis of compelling grounds. This 'exceptional threshold test' was first identified by the Court in the case of *N v United Kingdom*.[117] The distinction between these two 'threshold tests' is not relevant for the purposes of this chapter, since this chapter is not concerned with *expulsion* to poor humanitarian conditions, but with the humanitarian conditions in the host state itself. The 'exceptional threshold test' does therefore not apply.

After having established in the case of *Sufi and Elmi* that the regular test applied,[118] the Court started by summarizing its approach in *MSS* as requiring 'to have regard to an applicant's ability to cater for his most basic needs, such as food, hygiene and shelter, his vulnerability to ill-treatment and the prospect of his situation improving within a reasonable time-frame'.[119] Consequently, it held that although humanitarian assistance is available in some of these camps, owing to extreme overcrowding, access to shelter, water and sanitation facilities is 'extremely limited'. In other camps, there was only very limited access to food and water, and shelter appeared to be 'an emerging problem'. Apparently, persons should not only theoretically be able to cater for their basic needs, but this possibility should be real and effective. The Court subsequently observed that the inhabitants of such camps had very little prospect of their situation improving within a reasonable timeframe, as they were either not permitted to leave, or, although permitted to leave the camps, were only

[117] *N v United Kingdom* (n 2). The distinction between the regular '*MSS* test' and the exceptional '*N* test' has been confirmed by the Court in *SHH v United Kingdom* (n 59).

[118] The Court established that the poor living conditions in the camps emanated from the situation of general violence in Somalia, which was due to direct and indirect actions of the parties to the conflict. In addition, the Court attached a lot of weight to the fact that the situation has been greatly exacerbated by al-Shabaab's refusal to permit international aid agencies to operate in the areas under its control (para 282).

[119] *Sufi and Elmi v United Kingdom* (n 68), para 283.

able to return to places in Somalia that were considered to be unsafe by the Court. Consequently, there was little prospect of their situation improving while the conflicts in Somalia continued.[120]

In the case of *Mohammed Hussein and others v the Netherlands and Italy* the Court makes clear that the existence of 'some shortcomings' in the general situation and living conditions of asylum seekers in Italy is not enough to reach the threshold of seriousness of Article 3. The Court notes in this respect that 'a detailed structure of facilities and care to provide for the needs of asylum seekers' exists in Italy and that improvements have been implemented in order to remedy some of the failings.[121] Hence, the existence of basic reception facilities for asylum seekers seems to be enough.[122]

In brief, outside the context of detention, poor living conditions will only reach the threshold of Article 3 if the (vulnerable) person concerned is unable to effectively cater for his most basic needs (ie housing, food and sanitary conditions) and therefore lives in a state of the most extreme poverty, provided that there is little prospect of any improvement of the situation within a reasonable timeframe. The mere lack of (or shortcomings in) accommodation or the inability to buy other necessary articles such as clothing is apparently not serious enough.

11.2.4 Summary

In this section it has been argued that poor living conditions can give rise to a violation of Article 3 of the ECHR if the state can be held responsible for the living conditions and if these conditions reach the minimum level of severity established by Article 3.

In order to prevent placing too great a burden on the contracting states and in view of the competing priorities as regards the states' limited resources, the Court regularly reiterates that the state is not as a general rule responsible for providing everyone in its jurisdiction with a home, a certain standard of living, medical assistance and other social benefits. However, it has identified a number of circumstances under which the state can and should be held responsible for poor living conditions. Owing to the vulnerable position of persons in custody, by virtue of being within the control of the authorities, the Court has established that the state is responsible for ensuring adequate living conditions for persons who are deprived of their liberty. Outside the context of detention, the

[120] Ibid, para 291.
[121] *Mohammed Hussein and others v the Netherlands and Italy* (n 71), para 78.
[122] See also *Mohammed Hassan and others v the Netherlands and Italy* app no 40524/10 and others (ECtHR, 28 August 2013 (dec)), para 179.

state can also be held responsible for poor living conditions. The Court then seems to demand a kind of deliberate or intentional act by the state, for example by requiring that the state, despite a (domestic) legal obligation to do so, does not provide for adequate living conditions. In addition, vulnerability of the person concerned is relevant for accepting state responsibility. Arguably, this vulnerability should stem from utter dependency on the state. The Court has explicitly acknowledged that asylum seekers are in such a vulnerable position. Exceptionally, the responsibility of the state can be mitigated by the behaviour of the person concerned, for example if the person made no reasonable steps to avail himself of the required assistance. However, if it is a well-established fact that a specific vulnerable person is subjected to very poor living conditions, then the authorities ought to be aware of this and cannot use the inaction of this person to mitigate their responsibility.

Conditions of detention have reached the required level of severity in many cases. The Court takes into account the cumulative effect of detention conditions. Relevant factors are the existence of sufficient and adequate living space, the provision of sanitary products (even toilet paper), adequate food, clean bed linen, medical care and necessary medical aids, such as glasses or dentures, the presence of a radio or TV, the temperature in the cell, etc. Especially as regards the provision of medical assistance, the Court has identified a number of detailed obligations for the state. The mere fact that a detainee is seen by a doctor is not sufficient; the authorities must also ensure that a comprehensive record of the state of health is kept, that the detainee is subjected to regular and systematic supervision and that diagnosis and care are prompt and adequate. Even detention of a rather short duration (a few hours or days) might reach the threshold of Article 3, provided that the conditions are particularly severe or the applicant is particularly vulnerable. Outside the context of detention, poor living conditions will only reach the threshold of Article 3 if the (vulnerable) person is unable to effectively cater for his most basic needs (ie housing, food and sanitary conditions) and therefore lives in a state of the most extreme poverty, provided that there is little prospect of any improvement of the situation within a reasonable timeframe. The Court has held that if the dire living conditions are linked to the status of being an asylum seeker, it should be assumed that there will be no prospect of any improvement within a reasonable timeframe.

A complaint of poor living conditions for persons in detention will therefore more easily succeed than a complaint of poor living conditions for persons who are not detained. Whereas outside detention, the complete inability of vulnerable persons to cater for the most basic necessities of life for a significant period of time emanating from intentional acts of the authorities violates Article 3 of the ECHR, a complaint about the *quality* of living conditions or the *level* of state assistance, if the basic needs are, in any way, met, will usually not succeed. Inside detention, state responsibility exists by definition. In addition, the Court not only examines whether the person concerned is able to meet his most basic needs, but also takes into account whether less basic goods are provided, such as bed linen, catering facilities, glasses, radio and TV. Hence, a complaint about the *quality* of detention conditions seems to have more chance of success. This raises the question as to which framework of review should be applied to the living conditions of asylum seekers. This will be further discussed in section 11.7 below. First, sections 11.3 and 11.4 will examine whether the Court's case law on Articles 2 and 8 of the ECHR contain more extensive state obligations as regards living conditions than its case law on Article 3.

11.3 ARTICLE 2

11.3.1 Introduction

Article 2 of the ECHR reads:

1. Everyone's right to life shall be protected by law. No one shall be deprived of his life intentionally save in the execution of a sentence of a court following his conviction of a crime for which this penalty is provided by law.
2. Deprivation of life shall not be regarded as inflicted in contravention of this article when it results from the use of force which is no more than absolutely necessary:
   (a) In defence of any person from unlawful violence;
   (b) In order to effect a lawful arrest or to prevent escape of a person lawfully detained;
   (c) In action lawfully taken for the purpose of quelling a riot or insurrection.

According to Ovey and White, it emerges from the case law of the Court that the duty to protect the right to life consists of three main aspects: 'the duty to refrain, by its agents, from unlawful killing; the duty to investigate suspicious deaths; and, in certain circumstances, a positive obligation to take steps to prevent the avoidable loss of life'.[123] This section will focus on this last aspect of the duty to protect the right to life.

In this connection, the Court generally states that the first paragraph of Article 2 'enjoins the State not only to refrain from the intentional and unlawful taking of life, but also to take appropriate steps to safeguard the lives of those within its jurisdiction'.[124] In addition, the Court held that

[123] Ovey and White 2006, p 56.

[124] See, eg, *Osman v United Kingdom* app no 23452/94 (ECtHR, 28 October 1998), para 115; *Cyprus v Turkey* app no 25781/94 (ECtHR, 10 May 2001), para 219; *Mastromatteo v Italy* app no 37703/97 (ECtHR, 24 October 2002), para 67.

'under Article 2 of the Convention, read in conjunction with Article 1, the State may be required to take certain measures in order to "secure" an effective enjoyment of the right to life'.[125] This obligation is rather extensive, as the Court held in the case of *Öneryildiz v Turkey* that the positive obligation to take appropriate steps to safeguard the lives of those within their jurisdiction 'must be construed as applying in the context of any activity, whether public or not, in which the right to life may be at stake'.[126]

This positive duty to safeguard lives 'entails above all a primary duty on the State to put in place a legislative and administrative framework designed to provide effective deterrence against threats to the right to life'.[127] In addition, the Court has held:

> [W]here lives have been lost in circumstances potentially engaging the responsibility of the State, that provision entails a duty for the State to ensure, by all means at its disposal, an adequate response—judicial or otherwise—so that the legislative and administrative framework set up to protect the right to life is properly implemented and any breaches of that right are repressed and punished.[128]

Hence, these positive obligations arising from Article 2 entail primarily obligations to *protect* and obligations to *facilitate* the right to life. The question is whether the right to life also entails positive obligations to *provide* resources, for example with regard to health care or basic necessities of life.

In *Osman v United Kingdom*, the Court held that 'it is common ground that the State's obligation in this respect extends beyond this primary duty' and that it is accepted that Article 2 of the ECHR 'may also imply in certain well-defined circumstances a positive obligation on the authorities to take preventive operational measures to protect an individual whose life is at risk from the criminal acts of another individual'.[129] In the case of *Douglas-Williams v United Kingdom*, the Court extended this obligation by stating:

> This may extend in appropriate circumstances to a positive obligation on the authorities to take preventive operational measures to protect an individual

[125] *Ergi v Turkey* app no 23818/94 (ECtHR, 28 July 1998), para 79; *Ahmet Özkan and others v Turkey* app no 21689/93 (ECtHR, 6 April 2004), para 297.

[126] *Öneryildiz v Turkey* app no 48939/99 (ECtHR, 30 November 2004), para 71. See also *Budayeva and others v Russia* app no 15339/02 et al (ECtHR, 20 March 2008), para 130 and *Ciechońska v Poland* app no 19776/04 (ECtHR, 14 June 2011), para 63. Also Harris et al observe the 'very extensive meaning that has been given to the obligation to take steps to protect the right to life' (Harris et al 2009, p 66).

[127] See, eg, *Öneryildiz v Turkey* (n 126), para 89.

[128] Ibid, para 91.

[129] *Osman v United Kingdom* (n 124), para 115.

> whose life is at risk from the criminal acts of another individual (...) or from risks to their health arising from other circumstances under the responsibility of a public authority.[130]

Hence, if a person's health is put at risk by circumstances under the responsibility of the government, a positive obligation to take measures may 'in appropriate circumstances' arise. However, the scope of this positive obligation is defined rather narrowly by the Court.[131] The Court has held:

> Bearing in mind the difficulties in policing modern societies, the unpredictability of human conduct and the operational choices which must be made in terms of priorities and resources, the scope of the positive obligation must be interpreted in a way which does not impose an impossible or disproportionate burden on the authorities.[132]

State responsibility to take preventive operational measures to protect the right to life therefore only exists if it is established that

> the authorities knew or ought to have known at the time of the existence of a real and immediate risk to the life of an identified individual and that they failed to take measures within the scope of their powers which, judged reasonably, might have been expected to avoid that risk.[133]

Hence, 'not every claimed risk to life can entail for the authorities a Convention requirement to take operational measures to prevent that risk from materialising'.[134] The question is therefore which measures can, judged reasonably, be expected of the government to avoid a 'real and immediate' risk to life. Can it be expected of the government to provide (reimbursement of the costs of) health care or basic necessities of life in order to avoid a real and immediate risk to life?

11.3.2 Health Care

With regard to the provision of health care, the Court held that 'it cannot be excluded that the acts and omissions of the authorities in the field of health care policy may in certain circumstances engage their responsibility

[130] *Douglas-Williams v United Kingdom* app no 56413/00 (ECtHR, 8 January 2002 (dec)). In the case of *Powell v United Kingdom,* the Court used more prudent language by stating that 'it cannot be excluded that the acts and omissions of the authorities in the field of health care policy may in certain circumstances engage their responsibility under the positive limb of Article 2' (app no 45305/99, ECtHR, 4 May 2000 (dec)).

[131] *Cf* Ovey and White 2006, p 63.

[132] *Renolde v France* app no 5608/05 (ECtHR, 16 October 2008), para 82; *Keenan v United Kingdom* app no 27229/95 (ECtHR, 3 April 2001), para 90; *Ciechońska v Poland* (n 126), para 64.

[133] *Douglas-Williams v United Kingdom* (n 130).

[134] *Renolde v France* (n 132), para 82; *Keenan v United Kingdom* (n 132), para 90.

under the positive limb of Article 2'.[135] With respect to the scope of the state's positive obligations in the provision of health care, the Court has held that:

> [A]n issue may arise under Article 2 where it is shown that the authorities of a contracting state put an individual's life at risk through the denial of health care which they have undertaken to make available to the population generally.[136]

Hence, with regard to the provision of health care, the case law suggests that a state will violate its positive obligation under Article 2 if:

1. the authorities deliberately deny health care which is available to the population generally;
2. an individual's life is put at a real and immediate risk as a result of that denial; and
3. the authorities knew or ought to have known of the existence of this risk to the life of the individual.

'Denial' of health care can relate to denial of access to health care as well as to denial of refunding or covering the costs of health care. In the *Nitecki v Poland* case, the Court seems to acknowledge that also denial of coverage of health care costs may raise an issue under Article 2 of the ECHR.[137]

As the scope of the positive obligation must be interpreted in a way which does not impose an impossible or disproportionate burden on the authorities, the standard of health care offered to the general public seems to be decisive.[138] As the Court held in the case of *Pentiacova and others v Moldova*:

> While it is clearly desirable that everyone should have access to a full range of medical treatment, including life-saving medical procedures and drugs, the lack of resources means that there are, unfortunately, in the Contracting States

[135] *Powell v United Kingdom* (n 130); *Nitecki v Poland* app no 65653/01 (ECtHR, 21 March 2002 (dec)); *Pentiacova and others v Moldova* app no 14462/03 (ECtHR, 4 January 2005 (dec)).

[136] *Cyprus v Turkey* (n 124), para 219; *Nitecki v Poland* (n 135); *Pentiacova and others v Moldova* (n 135); *Makuc and others v Slovenia* app no 26828/06 (ECtHR, 31 May 2007 (dec)).

[137] In this case, the applicant complained that the state refused to refund him the full price of a life-saving drug. The Court held, however, that, as the applicant had access to the standard of care offered to the public and as the greater part of the cost of the drug (70%) was refunded, 'the respondent State cannot be said, in the special circumstances of the present case, to have failed to discharge its obligations under Article 2 by not paying the remaining 30% of the drug price' (*Nitecki v Poland* (n 135)). In the case of *Scialacqua v Italy*, the Commission held that 'even assuming that Article 2 of the Convention can be interpreted as imposing on States the obligation to cover the costs of certain medical treatments or medicines that are essential in order to save lives, the Commission considers that this provision cannot be interpreted as requiring States to provide financial covering for medicines which are not listed as officially recognised medicines' (app no 34151/96, 1 July 1998).

[138] *Cf Nitecki v Poland* (n 135); *Pentiacova and others v Moldova* (n 135).

> many individuals who do not enjoy them, especially in cases of permanent and expensive treatment.[139]

In addition, for this positive obligation to arise, it is necessary that an individual's life is put at risk through the denial of health care and that the government ought to be aware of that risk. In the case of *Osman v United Kingdom*, the Court held that there must be a risk to the life of an 'identified individual'.[140] Spijkerboer observes that in the *Öneryildiz v Turkey* case the Court has accepted a positive obligation in a situation where a group of people living in an identifiable area was a risk, without being clearly identified as a number of particular individuals.[141] This case concerned the particular context of dangerous activities, more specifically the operation of waste-collection sites.[142] Also, the case of *Budayeva and Others v Russia* concerned a positive obligation towards a group of people living in an identifiable (hazardous) area.[143] The *Mastromatteo v Italy* case concerned the operation of a system of leave or relaxed custody for prisoners and posed 'a risk to life for members of the public at large rather than for one or more identified individuals'.[144] In the context of health care, the Court has not (yet) adopted a positive obligation to provide health care to a group of people or the public at large. For a positive obligation to arise in this context, it is always necessary that the life of an identified individual or of individuals is put at risk. For example, in the case of *Cyprus v Turkey*, the applicant government complained that the enclaved Greek Cypriots and Maronites were denied access to medical services. The Court held that although 'medical visits were indeed hampered' and 'in certain cases delays did occur', 'it has not been established that the lives of any patients were put in danger on account of delay in individual cases'.[145] Hence, in the context of provision of health care, a positive obligation under Article 2 only arises if a real and immediate risk exists to the life of an identified individual.

In the cases discussed so far, the Court has not found a violation of this positive obligation to provide health care in general. In the case of *Cyprus v Turkey*, in addition to the absence of the establishment of a risk to the life of an identified individual, as mentioned above, the Court considered that it had not been established that the authorities 'deliberately withheld medical treatment from the population concerned or adopted a practice

[139] *Pentiacova and others v Moldova* (n 135).
[140] *Osman v United Kingdom* (n 124), para 116. See also *Douglas-Williams v United Kingdom* (n 130).
[141] Spijkerboer 2011.
[142] *Öneryildiz v Turkey* (n 126), paras 71 and 90.
[143] *Budayeva and Others v Russia* (n 126).
[144] *Mastromatteo v Italy* (n 124), para 74.
[145] *Cyprus v Turkey* (n 124).

of delaying the processing of requests of patients to receive medical treatment in the south'.[146] In *Nitecki v Poland*, the applicants received reimbursement for a life-saving drug for the greater part of the costs (70 per cent), which was the general standard offered to the public. The authorities therefore had not violated their positive obligations under Article 2 according to the Court.[147] In the case *Pentiacova and others v Moldova*, the Court held that the applicants had not adduced any evidence that their lives have been put at risk. More specifically, they did not adduce any evidence that the cause of the death of patients was the lack of any specific drug or the lack of appropriate medical care.[148]

However, with regard to persons in detention, the positive obligation to provide health care is broader in scope. Just as for Article 3, the Court generally states in the context of Article 2 that 'persons in custody are in a vulnerable position and the authorities are under a duty to protect them'.[149] Although the conditions of detention are generally examined under Article 3,[150] the Court also stated in the context of Article 2 that the convention 'imposes an obligation on the State to protect the physical well-being of persons deprived of their liberty, for example by providing them with the requisite medical assistance'.[151] With regard to the quality and promptness of the medical care provided to persons in custody, the Court has found a number of violations of Article 2 of the ECHR. For example, in the case of *Dzieciak v Poland*, the Court held

> that the quality and promptness of the medical care provided to the applicant during his four-year pre-trial detention put his health and life in danger. In particular, the lack of cooperation and coordination between the various state authorities, the failure to transport the applicant to hospital for two scheduled operations, the lack of adequate and prompt information to the trial court on the applicant's state of health, the failure to secure him access to doctors during the final days of his life and the failure to take into account his health in the automatic extensions of his detention amounted to inadequate medical treatment and constituted a violation of the State's obligation to protect the lives of persons in custody.[152]

In the *Anguelova v Bulgaria* case, the Court concluded that the delay in the provision of the necessary medical assistance violated the state's

146 Ibid, para 219.

147 *Nitecki v Poland* (n 135).

148 *Pentiacova and others v Moldova* (n 135).

149 *Demiray v Turkey* app no 27308/95 (ECtHR, 21 November 2000), para 42; *Dzieciak v Poland* app no 77766/01 (ECtHR, 9 December 2008), para 90; *Mojsiejew v Poland* app no 11818/02 (ECtHR, 24 March 2009), para 51.

150 See s 11.2.

151 *Dzieciak v Poland* (n 149), para 91.

152 Ibid, para 101.

obligation to protect the lives of persons in custody.[153] Another aspect of the provision of adequate health care to detainees examined by the Court in the case of *Geppa v Russia* is whether there was a negligent failure to diagnose a disease.[154] As these cases illustrate, the Court generally makes very detailed statements on state obligations as regards health care for detainees. Another example may be found in the case of *Tarariyeva v Russia*.[155] With reference to the General Report from the European Committee for the Prevention of Torture and Inhuman or Degrading Treatment or Punishment (CPT) on the standards of health care in prisons, the Court held in this case that the authorities should have kept an ongoing record of Mr Tarariyev's state of health and the treatment he underwent while in detention[156] and that in the case of a prisoner returning from hospital with a known history of medical ailments, the authorities are under an obligation to ensure appropriate follow-up care independent of the initiative being taken by the prisoner.[157] In addition, the Court examined whether the prison hospital possessed the necessary facilities to perform surgical interventions successfully and to deal with post-operative complications.[158]

11.3.3 Basic Necessities of Life

A final question to be answered is whether Article 2 can also impose on the state a positive obligation to provide financial or other assistance in order to avoid a risk to life caused by (severe) destitution. This question has been examined by the Court in a number of cases. In the case of *Wasilewski v Poland*, the applicant was disabled and complained that his right to life was breached by the fact that he did not have sufficient subsistence means at his disposal. The Court held:

> Insofar as the applicant's complaints relate to his difficult financial situation, the Court recalls that neither Article 2 nor any other provision of the Convention can be interpreted as conferring on an individual a right to enjoy any given standard of living, or a right to obtain financial assistance from the State.[159]

[153] *Anguelova v Bulgaria* app no 38361/97 (ECtHR, 13 June 2002), paras 125–31.
[154] *Geppa v Russia* app no 8532/06 (ECtHR, 3 February 2011), paras 79–80.
[155] *Tarariyeva v Russia* app no 4353/03 (ECtHR, 14 December 2006).
[156] Ibid, para 76.
[157] Ibid, para 80.
[158] Ibid, para 87.
[159] *Wasilewski v Poland* app no 32734/96 (ECtHR, 20 April 1999 (dec)). The Court further observed that, 'in any event', the applicant received monthly social assistance from the social assistance authorities.

In the case of *Sokur v Ukraine*, the Court added to this consideration that 'the applicant has not shown that he suffers such destitution as to put his life at risk'.[160] The Court has repeated this line in a number of subsequent cases against Ukraine.[161] This leaves open the possibility that the state has a positive obligation to provide (some kind of) assistance if an individual suffers such severe destitution that his life is put at risk.[162] So far, the Court has not, however, found a violation of this obligation. Arguably, the same conditions apply as regards the provision of minimum subsistence benefits as those applied to the provision of health care by the Court.[163] This would mean that a positive obligation only arises if the authorities knew or ought to have known at the time of the existence of a real and immediate risk to the life of an identified individual and that they failed to take measures within the scope of their powers which, judged reasonably, might have been expected to avoid that risk. Arguably, this amounts to the same criteria as those that have more elaborately been identified by the Court under Article 3.

11.3.4 Analysis and Concluding Remarks

Case law of the Court shows that a positive obligation under Article 2 arises if a person's health is put at risk by circumstances under the responsibility of the government.[164] Hence, just as regards Article 3, the establishment of state responsibility is very important for a complaint to succeed. The provision of health care might fall under the responsibility of the government, but in order to prevent an 'impossible or disproportionate burden on the authorities', in view of the 'difficulties in policing modern societies, the unpredictability of human conduct and the operational choices which must be made in terms of priorities and resources', the Court has formulated a number of restrictive criteria for the existence of

160 *Sokur v Ukraine* app no 29439/02 (ECtHR, 26 November 2002 (dec)).

161 See, eg, *Sharko v Ukraine* app no 72686/01 (ECtHR, 19 April 2005), para 28; *Vasilenkov v Ukraine* app no 19872/02 (ECtHR, 3 May 2005), para 18; *Bukhovets v Ukraine* app no 22098/02 (ECtHR, 8 November 2005), para 15; *Tambovtsev v Ukraine* app no 20625/02 (ECtHR, 8 November 2005), para 12; *Pronina v Ukraine* app no 63566/00 (ECtHR, 10 January 2006 (dec)); *Komar and others v Ukraine* app no 36684/02 et al (ECtHR, 28 February 2006), para 19; *Kretinin v Ukraine* app no 10515/03 (ECtHR, 10 August 2006), para 14. In the case of *Kutepov and Anikeyenko v Russia*, the Court held that the applicant did not face 'any "real and immediate risk" either to his physical integrity or his life, which would warrant the application of Article 2 of the Convention', as a result of his alleged insufficient amount of old-age pension (app no 68029/01, ECtHR, 25 October 2005, para 62).

162 *Cf* Cousins 2008, p 9.

163 See Harris et al 2009, p 48.

164 *Cf* O'Cinneide, who argues that the concept of state responsibility is decisive for reviewing denial of health care under Art 2 (O'Cinneide 2008, p 590).

state responsibility in this field. According to the Court, state responsibility for the provision of (reimbursement of) health care under Article 2 only exists if:

1. the authorities deliberately deny health care which is available to the population generally;
2. an individual's life is put at a real and immediate risk as a result of that denial; and
4. the authorities knew or ought to have known of the existence of this risk to the life of the individual.

The first condition shows that the Court has chosen to apply equality as a standard of review for positive obligations in the field of health care.[165] It bears close resemblance to the conditions found relevant under Article 3 that the state can be held responsible if it deliberately does not observe domestic legal obligations. Hence, a positive obligation under Article 2 to provide medical care only exists if the state concerned has already chosen to use public resources to provide for the requested care for the public generally. The second condition means that the life of an identified individual must actually be put at risk; the mere denial or delaying of provision or reimbursement of health care is, apparently, not enough for the realization of such a risk. Also the third conditions bears resemblance with the conditions found relevant under Article 3. It has been argued that state responsibility under Article 3 can be mitigated if the person concerned did not take reasonable steps to avail himself of the necessary assistance, for example by not informing the relevant authorities as a result of which the authorities did not know of the situation. However, the Court has ruled as well that under certain circumstances the authorities 'ought to have known' of poor circumstances, even if the person concerned did not come forward.[166] Hence, the relevant conditions formulated by the Court in order for state responsibility to arise under Article 2 are very similar to the conditions found relevant under Article 3. As the scope of Article 2 is narrower than the scope of Article 3, given the necessary connection to the life of an individual, Article 2 does not provide additional safeguards with regard to complaints about poor living conditions or health care as compared to Article 3.

Just like the case law on Article 3, case law on Article 2 has adopted another approach as regards conditions of detention. Owing to the vulnerable position of detainees, the Court has held that Article 2 of the ECHR 'imposes an obligation on the State to protect the physical well-being of persons deprived of their liberty, for example by providing them

[165] Fredman 2006, p 515.
[166] See s 11.2.

with the requisite medical assistance'. In such cases, the Court uses other language than in general cases as regards denial of health care. Whereas in the latter cases the Court has formulated a number of conditions under which denial of health care might violate Article 2, in the context of detention the Court has formulated detailed legal obligations for the state as regards the provision of adequate and prompt health care. It has held in numerous cases that states acted in violation of Article 2 by not meeting these obligations. Given the identification of far-reaching obligations for the state as regards the provision of health care to detainees under Article 3 as well, again, Article 2 does not seem to provide important additional safeguards.

11.4 ARTICLE 8

11.4.1 Introduction

Article 8 of the ECHR reads:

1. Everyone has the right to respect for his private and family life, his home and his correspondence.
2. There shall be no interference by a public authority with the exercise of this right except such as is in accordance with the law and is necessary in a democratic society in the interests of national security, public safety or the economic well-being of the country, for the prevention of disorder or crime, for the protection of health or morals, or for the protection of the rights and freedoms of others.

This article places on the state the obligation to respect four different interests: private life family life, home and correspondence. As none of these interests are entirely self-explanatory and the Court has so far declined to give an exhaustive definition of them, Article 8 is potentially very wide in scope.[167] It has been described as 'one of the most open-ended' and 'one of the most dynamically interpreted' provisions of the convention.[168] The four interests protected by Article 8 are generally interpreted very broadly by the Court. For example, the Court has held that the concept of 'private life' also covers the physical and moral (or physiological) integrity of the person,[169] as well as the right to personal development and the right to establish and develop relationships with other human beings and the

[167] Harris et al 2009, p 359; Van Dijk et al 2006, p 664.

[168] Ovey and White 2006, p 241 and Feldman 1997, p 265.

[169] See, eg, *X and Y v the Netherlands* app no 8978/80 (ECtHR, 26 March 1985), para 22; *Pretty v United Kingdom* (n 25), para 61.

outside world.[170] Interference with physical integrity can also be examined under Article 3.[171] However, the threshold under Article 8 seems to be lower than under Article 3.[172] Also, if the circumstances of the case do not indicate suffering of such an intense degree as to fall within the ambit of Article 3, an issue may arise under Article 8.[173]

Unlike Article 3, and in a more extensive way than Article 2, the second paragraph of Article 8 makes provision for limitations on the right laid down in paragraph 1 if certain qualifying conditions are satisfied. Article 8 uses a similar approach to limitations as Articles 9–11 of the ECHR. The qualifying conditions are that the interference with the right must be in accordance with the law; that the aim of the interference must be legitimate in that it fits one of the expressed aims laid down in paragraph 2; and that the interference must be necessary in a democratic society. Central to this last qualifying condition is the proportionality of the interference in securing the legitimate aim.[174]

Another relevant difference between Articles 2 and 3, on the one hand, and Article 8, on the other, is the doctrine of the margin of appreciation. Whereas with regard to Articles 2 and 3, this doctrine is usually not (explicitly) used by the Court,[175] it is an important aspect of its review under Article 8. This doctrine can be described as allowing the state 'a certain measure of discretion, subject to European supervision, when it takes legislative, administrative, or judicial action in the area of a Convention right'.[176] The doctrine of the margin of appreciation mitigates to a certain extent the wide scope of Article 8. As Harris et al state with regard to the wide scope of the concept of private life:

> [T]he Court's extensive approach to the scope of private life holds out a promise of protection of individual interests which ultimately is rarely conceded by the Strasbourg authorities. The margin of appreciation allowed to states to determine what is required by 'respect' and what interferences are 'necessary in a

[170] *Pretty v United Kingdom* (n 25), para 61; *Van Kück v Germany* app no 35968/97 (ECtHR, 12 June 2003), para 69.

[171] Harris et al 2009, p 365.

[172] See, eg, *Nnyanzi v United Kingdom* app no 21878/06 (ECtHR, 8 April 2008), para 74: 'However, the Court's case-law does not exclude that treatment which does not reach the severity of Article 3 treatment may nonetheless breach Article 8 in its private-life aspect where there are sufficiently adverse effects on physical and moral integrity'.

[173] See, eg, *López Ostra v Spain* app no 16798/90 (ECtHR, 9 December 1994); *L v Lithuania* (n 25).

[174] Ovey and White 2006, p 222.

[175] With regard to Art 2, the Court has referred to the margin of appreciation in a very limited number of cases (eg, *Evans v United Kingdom* app no 6339/05 (ECtHR, 10 April 2007), para 54; *Vo v France* app no 53924/00 (ECtHR, 8 July 2004), para 82 (with regard to the issue of when the right to life begins); *Budayeva and others v Russia* (n 126), para 134 (with regard to matters where the state is required to take positive action)).

[176] Harris et al 2009, p 11.

democratic society' means that there are substantial burdens for an individual in making out his case successfully in Strasbourg even if he is able to identify his interests as falling within 'private life'.[177]

11.4.2 Negative and Positive Obligations under Article 8

The Court held in as early as 1979 that, although the object of Article 8 is essentially that of protecting the individual against arbitrary interference by the public authorities, it does not merely compel the state to abstain from such interference. In addition to this primarily negative undertaking, there may be positive obligations inherent in an effective 'respect' for family or private life.[178] Owing to the explicit and broad possibility to justify limitations on rights protected by Article 8, the distinction between positive and negative obligations seems to be more important than with regard to Articles 2 and 3. However, the Court has also held that the boundaries between the state's positive and negative obligations under Article 8 do not always lend themselves to precise definition.[179] According to established case law, whether the question is analysed in terms of a positive duty on the state—to take reasonable and appropriate measures to secure the applicant's rights under paragraph 1 of Article 8—, or in terms of an 'interference by a public authority' to be justified in accordance with paragraph 2, the applicable principles are broadly similar. The Court usually states:

> In both contexts regard must be had to the fair balance that has to be struck between the competing interests of the individual and of the community as a whole, and in any case the State enjoys a certain margin of appreciation. Furthermore, even in relation to the positive obligations flowing from the first paragraph of Article 8, in striking the required balance the aims mentioned in the second paragraph may be of a certain relevance.[180]

Consequently, the Court does not always consider it necessary to decide whether it would be more appropriate to analyse a case as one concerning a positive or a negative obligation, since the core issue is whether a fair

[177] Harris et al 2009, pp 365–66.

[178] *Marckx v Belgium* app no 6833/74 (ECtHR, 13 June 1979), para 31; *Airey v Ireland* (n 1), para 32.

[179] See, eg, *X, Y and Z v United Kingdom* app no 21830/93 (ECtHR, 22 April 1997), para 41; *Draon v France* app no 1513/03 (ECtHR, 6 October 2005), para 105.

[180] See, eg, *López Ostra v Spain* (n 173), para 51; *Armonienė v Lithuania* app no 36919/02 (ECtHR, 25 November 2008), para 37; *A, B and C v Ireland* app no 25579/05 (ECtHR, 16 December 2010), para 247.

balance was struck between the competing public and private interests involved.[181]

On the other hand, the Court has held that as regards positive obligations, the notion of 'respect' is not clear-cut, as a result of which this is an area in which the contracting parties enjoy a wide margin of appreciation in determining the steps to be taken to ensure compliance with the convention.[182] In addition, the Court has held that a state is only under a positive obligation where it has found a 'direct and immediate link' between the measures requested by an applicant, on the one hand, and his private and/or family life, on the other[183] and has emphasized the 'importance of a prudent approach to the State's positive obligations to protect private life'.[184] In the case of *Zehnalová and Zehnal v the Czech Republic*, the Court held:

> Its task here is to determine the limits to the applicability of Article 8 and the boundary between the rights set forth in the Convention and the social rights guaranteed by the European Social Charter. The Court acknowledges that the constant changes taking place in European society call for increasingly serious effort and commitment on the part of national governments in order to remedy certain shortcomings, and that the State is therefore intervening more and more in individuals' private lives. However, the sphere of State intervention and the evolutive concept of private life do not always coincide with the more limited scope of the State's positive obligations.[185]

Warbrick concludes that the tasks of the Court under Article 8(1) to decide what 'respect' requires and under Article 8(2) to decide whether an interference is justified are similar, but not identical. According to him, the 'Article 8(1) process is more favourable to the State than the Article 8(2) one'.[186] Harris et al provide a convincing explanation for this difference. They observe that under Article 8(2)

> the balance is struck between a right already established, which, formally at least, carries a special weight, and the countervailing interests which the state is seeking to protect. In reaching the balance in Article 8(1), the Court is determining

[181] See, eg, *Dickson v United Kingdom* app no 44362/04 (ECtHR, 4 December 2007), para 71; *Nolan and K v Russia* app no 2512/04 (ECtHR, 12 February 2009), para 85.

[182] *Draon v France* (n 179), para 107; *Armonienė v Lithuania* (n 180), para 38. Also Harris et al state that '[w]hile the basic test as to the proportionate balancing of interests appears the same, the margin of appreciation is clearly wider in the context of positive obligations than with respect to the state's duty not to intervene under Article 8(2)' (Harris et al 2009, pp 391–92).

[183] *Botta v Italy* app no 21439/93 (ECtHR, 24 February 1998), para 34; *Draon v France* (n 179), para 106; *Sarı and Çolak v Turkey* app nos 42596/98 and 42603/98 (ECtHR, 4 April 2006), para 34.

[184] *Karakó v Hungary* app no 39311/05 (ECtHR, 28 April 2009), para 19.

[185] *Zehnalová and Zehnal v the Czech Republic* app no 38621/97 (ECtHR, 14 May 2005 (dec)).

[186] Warbrick 1998, p 43.

> the content of the protected right. It is thus incumbent on an applicant to establish the distinctive importance of the interest to him as it can be easy for the Court to underestimate this and there is no formal weight to attach to his claim as there would be if his interest were already acknowledged as a right.[187]

In other words, with regard to negative obligations, the burden lies on the state to show that limitations meet the conditions laid down in Article 8(2), whereas with regard to positive obligations the burden lies on the applicant to show that the situation complained of falls under the scope of one of the protected interests laid down in Article 8(1).

Hence, according to the Court, it is often possible to analyse a complaint under Article 8 in terms of a positive duty for the state—to take reasonable and appropriate measures to secure the applicant's rights under paragraph 1 of Article 8—as well as in terms of an 'interference by a public authority' to be justified in accordance with paragraph 2. At the same time, however, it seems to be relevant if the Court decides to characterize a certain obligation as a positive one, as the Article 8(1) process seems to be more favourable to the state than the Article 8(2) one.

Accordingly, when discussing case law of the Court on Article 8, regard must be had to the question whether the case is analysed in terms of positive obligations or in terms of negative obligations. In addition, one cannot assume that observations made by the Court in a case that is analysed in terms of a negative obligation also apply with regard to complaints that are, as a general rule, analysed by the Court in terms of a positive obligation.

11.4.3 Case Law on Social and Economic Interests under Article 8

The Court has held in a number of cases that Article 8 does not impose a general obligation on the state to provide for financial assistance,[188] nor does it guarantee as such a right to be provided with a home,[189] a right to free medical care[190] or a right to any specific level of medical care.[191] In this regard, the Court has observed that while it is 'clearly desirable that every human being has a place where he or she can live in dignity and which he or she can call home, there are unfortunately in the Contracting

187 Harris et al 2009, p 383.

188 See, eg, *Petrovic v Austria* app no 20458/92 (ECtHR, 27 March 1998), para 26; *Müslim v Turkey* (n 57), para 85.

189 See, eg, *Chapman v United Kingdom* app no 27238/95 (ECtHR, 18 January 2001), para 99; *Codona v United Kingdom* app no 485/05 (ECtHR, 7 February 2006 (dec)); *Makuc and others v Slovenia* (n 136), para 171.

190 *Pentiacova and others v Moldova* (n 135); *Makuc and others v Slovenia* (n 136), para 177.

191 *Tysiąc v Poland* app no 5410/03 (ECtHR, 20 March 2007), para 107.

States many persons who have no home'.[192] In the same way, the Court held that while

> it is clearly desirable that everyone should have access to a full range of medical treatment, including life-saving medical procedures and drugs, the lack of resources means that there are, unfortunately, in the Contracting States many individuals who do not enjoy them, especially in cases of permanent and expensive treatment.[193]

Although Article 8 therefore does not impose a general obligation on states to provide for social and economic rights, case law of the Court nevertheless shows that, under certain circumstances, social and economic interests may fall under the scope of Article 8.[194] This case law will be discussed below, whereby a distinction will be made between case law on health care, housing and on (financial) social benefits.

Health Care

A relevant case in the area of health care is *Sentges v the Netherlands*.[195] The applicant in this case suffered from Duchenne Muscular Dystrophy, a disease characterized by progressive muscle degeneration, as a result of which he was unable to stand, walk or lift his arms, and his manual and digital functions were virtually absent. The applicant's parents requested their health insurance fund to provide him with a robotic arm, which would give him more autonomy and would enable him to perform many acts unassisted, such as drinking, making telephone calls and scratching himself. The request was rejected by the Dutch authorities. The applicant complained before the Court that this rejection violated the positive obligation for the state under Article 8 to provide him with, or pay for, this medical device. He explicitly emphasized that no general positive obligation for the state was being advocated. A distinction could be made between the entitlements of persons who are to some extent limited in the exercise of their private life and those of persons, like the applicant, who

[192] *Chapman v United Kingdom* app no 27238/95 (ECtHR, 18 January 2001), para 99; *Makuc and others v Slovenia* (n 136), para 171.

[193] *Pentiacova and others v Moldova* (n 135).

[194] An important case in this regard is the case of *Müslim v Turkey* (n 57), which concerns a complaint about financial aid to be provided to asylum seekers. This case concerned Art 3 as well as Art 8, and has therefore already been discussed above (see s 11.2). This discussion showed that this judgment is rather atypical, as it does not mention important general aspects of the Court's case law in these areas, eg the margin of appreciation doctrine and the issue of negative and positive obligations. Furthermore, the reasoning of the Court does not fit very well in the case law on Art 8, as the Court does not seem to balance different interests or to test the proportionality of the state's conduct. The observations of the Court in this case therefore seem not to be very relevant for the decision model under Art 8 with regard to social and economic circumstances, to be explored in this section.

[195] *Sentges v the Netherlands* app no 27677/02 (ECtHR, 8 July 2003 (dec)).

are not at all able to exercise their right to a private life. The Court held that Article 8 may impose such positive obligations on a state where there is a direct and immediate link between the measures sought by an applicant and the latter's private life. The Court also reiterated that Article 8 cannot be considered applicable each time an individual's everyday life is disrupted, but only in the exceptional cases where the state's failure to adopt measures interferes with that individual's right to personal development and his or her right to establish and maintain relations with other human beings and the outside world. It is thus incumbent on the individual concerned to demonstrate the existence of a special link between the situation complained of and the particular needs of his or her private life. The Court continued by stating that

> even assuming that in the present case such a special link indeed exists, regard must be had to the fair balance that has to be struck between the competing interests of the individual and of the community as a whole and to the wide margin of appreciation enjoyed by States in this respect in determining the steps to be taken to ensure compliance with the convention. This margin of appreciation is even wider when, as in the present case, the issues involve an assessment of the priorities in the context of the allocation of limited State resources.[196]

Finally, the Court observed that the applicant had access to the standard of health care offered to all persons insured under the relevant legislation in the Netherlands. The Court therefore concluded:

> The Court by no means wishes to underestimate the difficulties encountered by the applicant and appreciates the very real improvement which a robotic arm would entail for his personal autonomy and his ability to establish and develop relationships with other human beings of his choice. Nevertheless the Court is of the opinion that in the circumstances of the present case it cannot be said that the respondent State exceeded the margin of appreciation afforded to it.[197]

This case thus shows a number of important factors to be taken into account when examining whether the refusal of (funding of) medical care violates Article 8:

1. There should be a special, direct and immediate link between the provision of (funding of) medical care and the applicant's private life;
2. A fair balance has to be struck between the competing interests of the individual and of the community as a whole, in the course of which the state has a very wide margin of appreciation; and
3. When examining whether the state has exceeded this wide margin, it is relevant whether the applicant is entitled to the standard of health care offered to the general public.

[196] Ibid.
[197] Ibid.

In the *Sentges* case, the wide margin of appreciation left to the state seems to be decisive. This approach has been followed by the Court in the case of *Pentiacova and others v Moldova*, which concerned a complaint about insufficient state financing of haemodialysis.[198] Although observing that 'Article 8 is relevant to complaints about public funding to facilitate the mobility and quality of life of disabled applicants', the Court held that, as the applicants had access to the standard of health care offered to the general public, it cannot be said that the respondent state failed to strike a fair balance between the competing interests of the applicants and the community as a whole.[199]

There is no case law yet on whether the refusal of (funding of) health care that normally is offered to the general public violates Article 8 (taken alone, not in combination with Article 14).[200]

[198] *Pentiacova and others v Moldova* (n 135).

[199] In the case of *Nitecki v Poland* (n 135, discussed above in s 11.3), in which the applicant complained that the refusal to refund the full price of a life-saving drug violated Arts 2 and 8, the Court, after considering (and rejecting) the complaint under Art 2, considered that no separate issue arose under Art 8 ECHR. See also *Wiater v Poland* app no 42290/08 (ECtHR, 15 May 2012 (dec)).

[200] The only relevant case in this regard seems to be the case of *Van Kück v Germany* (n 175). This case concerned the German courts' application of the existing criteria on reimbursement of medical treatment to the applicant's claim for reimbursement of the cost of gender reassignment surgery. However, the Court emphasized that 'what matters is not the entitlement to reimbursement as such, but the impact of the court decisions on the applicant's right to respect for her sexual self-determination as one of the aspects of her right to respect for her private life' (para 78). The Court observed that in the civil proceedings against the private health insurance company, the German courts had referred the applicant to the possibility of psychotherapy as a less radical means of treating her condition; had questioned the necessity of gender reassignment for medical reasons without obtaining supplementary information on this point; had reproached the applicant with having deliberately caused her transsexuality; and had analysed her past prior to the taking of female hormones and found that she had only shown male behaviour and was thus genuinely male orientated (paras 79–81). In addition, the Court noted that the burden placed on a person to prove the medical necessity of treatment, including irreversible surgery, in one of the most intimate areas of private life, appears disproportionate (para 82). In the light of these various factors, the Court reached the conclusion that no fair balance was struck between the interests of the private health insurance company (NB: not of the community as whole), on the one side, and the interests of the individual, on the other. The Court therefore concluded that the German authorities overstepped the margin of appreciation afforded to them under para 2 of Art 8 (para 85). It is remarkable that the Court refers to para 2 of Art 8, as the applicant submitted that the German courts had failed to discharge the state's *positive* obligations (para 75). However, in view of the allegations made by the German courts, this is understandable. This judgment should be seen in the light of the particular circumstances of the case, involving gender reassignment and remarkable allegations made by German courts, and can therefore not be seen as a precedent for a broader approach to linking access to social security benefits to Art 8 (*cf* Cousins 2008, p 54).

Housing

Another area of relevant case law concerns the area of housing. In this area, a distinction should be made between complaints about evictions from homes, which are analysed by the Court within the context of negative obligations, and complaints about the failure of the state to provide adequate accommodation, which are discussed by the Court within the context of positive obligations. As has been discussed above, an examination of a complaint in terms of positive obligations seems to be more favourable to the state than an examination of a complaint in terms of a negative obligation, as a result of which observations made by the Court in the context of negative obligations cannot automatically be applied to complaints that are generally examined by the Court in terms of positive obligations. This section will therefore not discuss observations by the Court made in cases concerning evictions from homes.[201]

The Court has held that Article 8 does not guarantee a right to be provided with a home. However, it observed in the case of *Marzari v Italy* that

> a refusal of the authorities to provide assistance in this respect to an individual suffering from a severe disease might in certain circumstances raise an issue under Article 8 of the Convention because of the impact of such refusal on the private life of the individual.[202]

The applicant in this case suffered from a rare and serious illness called metabolic myopathy, as a result of which he was recognized as 100 per cent disabled. One of his complaints was that the authorities failed to provide him with accommodation adequate to his illness. The Court considered that in order for the state to be under such a positive obligation, there should be 'a direct and immediate link between the measures sought by an applicant and the latter's private life'. This requirement had been satisfied, as the Court went on to consider whether the authorities had fulfilled their positive obligation in this case. The Court observed in this respect that, in order to find a solution to the applicant's housing problem, the authorities have set up a specific Commission for the study of metabolic diseases, have requested the Commission to find an adequate apartment for the applicant, have allocated it to the applicant and are willing to carry out the further work indicated by the Commission for the study of metabolic diseases. The Court recognized that the applicant refused

[201] These cases will be discussed in s 11.5. See for another approach: O'Cinneide 2008, pp 591–92 and Palmer 2007, pp 76–79, who do not make this distinction and discuss case law concerning evictions with regard to the question to what extent the state has positive obligations to provide accommodation.

[202] *Marzari v Italy* app no 36448/97 (ECtHR, 4 May 1999 (dec)).

to accept this apartment on the ground that it was not suitable, but held that 'no positive obligation for the local authorities can be inferred from Article 8 to provide the applicant with a specific apartment'. The local authorities could therefore be considered to have discharged their positive obligations in respect of the applicant's right to respect for his private life, according to the Court.

The positive obligation for the state to provide adequate accommodation is, with reference to the *Marzari* case, confirmed by the Court in the case of *O'Rourke v United Kingdom*. However, the Court also stated in this case that this positive obligation must be limited. The Court observed that in this case

> to the extent that there was any positive obligation to accommodate the applicant when he first contacted CLBC [Camden London Borough Council, where the applicant applied for accommodation after release from prison] in early 1991, this was discharged by the provision of temporary hotel accommodation to the applicant pending the statutory inquiries into whether or not he was homeless, and thus entitled to permanent accommodation.[203]

The Court further noted that:

> To the extent that there was any positive obligation to re-accommodate the applicant following his eviction [from the hotel room], particularly in the light of the applicant's consequent health problems (see the above-mentioned Marzari case), the Court considers that this was discharged by CLBC's advice that the applicant should attend a night shelter pending a decision on permanent housing, and by its continued efforts to find suitable temporary or permanent accommodation up until the applicant's acceptance of temporary accommodation in June 1992. The Court notes in this regard the substantial role played by the applicant in obstructing his placement in suitable accommodation before that date.[204]

The limited scope of the positive obligation to house the homeless has been recalled by the Court in the case of *Codona the United Kingdom*.[205] In addition, the Court stated in this case that the obligation must be even more limited as regards an obligation to house a homeless person in a specific class of accommodation chosen by that person. This case concerned a complaint by a gypsy concerning the failure of the authorities to provide her with accommodation that she considered suitable, considering her 'cultural aversion' to living in bricks and mortar accommodation. The Court did not rule out that, in principle, Article 8 could impose a positive obligation on the authorities to provide accommodation for a homeless gypsy which is such that it facilitates their 'gypsy way of life'. However, it

[203] *O'Rourke v United Kingdom* (n 70).
[204] Ibid.
[205] *Codona v United Kingdom* (n 189).

considered that this obligation could only arise where the authorities had such accommodation at their disposal and were making a choice between offering such accommodation or accommodation which was not suitable for the cultural needs of a gypsy.

In brief, the Court has accepted a positive obligation for the state under Article 8 to accommodate homeless people, but the scope of this obligation is very limited. In addition, this positive obligation generally does not go so far as to require the authorities to house a homeless person in a specific class of accommodation chosen by that person. In order for the state to be under such a positive obligation, there should be 'a direct and immediate link between the measures sought by an applicant and the latter's private life'. Case law shows that this might for example be the case with regard to ill or disabled persons. By showing continued efforts to find suitable accommodation and/or referring the person concerned to night shelter, the authorities can discharge their positive obligation. The Court has so far not found a violation of this type of obligation.

Social Benefits

Although the Court regularly holds that Article 8 does not guarantee, as such, any right to a pension,[206] parental leave allowance,[207] or public assistance,[208] it has also held that by granting parental leave allowance or child benefits, states are able to demonstrate their respect for family life within the meaning of Article 8, as a result of which these benefits come within the scope of that provision.[209] This means that states have to provide benefits in a non-discriminatory manner within the meaning of Article 14.[210] However, this also leaves open the possibility that, under certain circumstances, the refusal of benefits violates Article 8 taken alone. Indeed, the Court held in the case of *Domenech Pardo v Spain*:

> La Cour rappelle en premier lieu que la Convention ne garantit pas, en tant que tel, le droit à pension (…). Toutefois, il n'est pas exclu que, dans certaines circonstances, le refus d'octroyer une prestation sociale, telle qu'une prestation d'orphelin, puisse poser problème sous l'angle de l'article 8 de la Convention lorsque, par exemple, un tel refus aurait pour effet de rendre impossible le développement normal de la vie familiale et privée du mineur.[211]

[206] *Domenech Pardo v Spain* app no 55996/00 (ECtHR, 3 May 2001 (dec)); *Mata Estevez v Spain* app no 56501/00 (ECtHR, 10 May 2001 (dec)).

[207] *Petrovic v Austria* (n 188), para 26.

[208] *Andersson v Sweden* app no 11776/85 (European Commission on Human Rights, 4 March 1986 (dec)).

[209] *Petrovic v Austria* (n 188), para 29; *Niedzwiecki v Germany* app no 58453/00 (ECtHR, 25 October 2005), para 31.

[210] See further s 6.3.

[211] *Domenech Pardo v Spain* (n 206).

Hence, Article 8 may be violated if the refusal of benefits makes the normal development of family or private life impossible. In the *Domenech Pardo* case, it had not been shown that the failure to backdate the orphan's pension to the date of the parent's death seriously affected the private and family life of the child.

The manner in which the state chooses to provide social benefits will generally not violate Article 8. For example, the Court did not find a violation of Article 8 where the state decided to grant public assistance in the form of day home places for children instead of financial assistance[212] or where the state decided that the costs of caring for disabled children should be borne by reliance on national solidarity, instead of leaving to the courts the task of ruling on actions under the ordinary law of liability.[213]

This means that there might be a positive obligation on the state to provide benefits if the refusal of benefits makes the normal development of family or private life impossible. However, the scope of this obligation is not (yet) fully developed in the Court's case law.

11.4.4 Asylum Seekers and Article 8

The case law on Article 8 discussed above does not involve cases on the socio-economic rights of asylum seekers. The question whether the status of asylum seeker is relevant for the scope of the positive obligation to provide benefits under Article 8 can therefore not be answered on the basis of this case law. However, as benefits are usually refused to asylum seekers for reasons of immigration control (ie to prevent abuse of the asylum system by deterring potential asylum seekers or to carry out a consistent immigration policy), the immigration status of asylum seekers may be of relevance.

With regard to family reunification cases under Article 8, the Court has paid particular attention to the (immigration) status of asylum seekers. These cases concern asylum seekers who have married a national or a lawfully staying alien during or after their asylum procedure and who are not allowed to remain in that state. They complain before the Court that the refusal by the authorities to allow them to reside in the host state violates their right to respect for their family life within the meaning of Article 8. The Court generally observes that such cases not only concern family life, but immigration as well and it has held that effective immigration

[212] *Andersson v Sweden* (n 208).

[213] *Maurice v France* app no 11810/03 (ECtHR, 6 October 2005), para 123; *Draon v France* (n 179), para 114.

control is a legitimate public aim.[214] In such cases, 'the extent of a State's obligations to admit to its territory relatives of persons residing there will vary according to the particular circumstances of the persons involved and the general interest'. Factors to be taken into account in this context include whether 'there are factors of immigration control (eg a history of breaches of immigration law) or considerations of public order weighing in favour of exclusion'.[215] Another important consideration will be 'whether family life was created at a time when the persons involved were aware that the immigration status of one of them was such that the persistence of that family life within the host state would from the outset be precarious'. If that is the case 'it is likely only to be in the most exceptional circumstances that the removal of the non-national family member will constitute a violation of Article 8'.[216] With regard to the immigration status of asylum seekers, the Court generally observes that although their presence in the country is usually tolerated pending the outcome of their asylum procedures, 'this cannot be equated with lawful stay where the authorities explicitly grant an alien permission to settle in their country'.[217] These cases should therefore be distinguished from cases concerning 'settled migrants, ie persons who have already been granted a right of residence in a host country', which are analysed by the Court in terms of a negative obligation on the state to refrain from interfering with the right to respect for family or private life. Instead, these cases are analysed by the Court in terms of a positive obligation on the state to allow an asylum seeker to reside in the country.[218]

Hence, effective immigration control is a legitimate state interest which has to be taken into account as regards complaints about Article 8. In addition, the Court attaches importance to the precarious immigration status of asylum seekers. That asylum seekers are usually allowed to remain on the territory pending their asylum procedure, which can take many years, does not mean that they have the same claim to respect for their family or private life established during that stay as aliens who explicitly have been granted the right to reside in the country. The interests of the state in

[214] *Nnyanzi v United Kingdom* (n 172), para 76.

[215] See, eg, *Useinov v the Netherlands* app no 61292/00 (ECtHR, 11 April 2006 (dec)); *M v United Kingdom* app no 25087/06 (ECtHR, 24 June 2008 (dec)); *Narenji Haghighi v the Netherlands* app no 38165/07 (ECtHR, 14 April 2009 (dec)).

[216] See, eg, *Useinov v the Netherlands* (n 215); *M v United* Kingdom (n 215); *Narenji Haghighi v the Netherlands* (n 215); *Nunez v Norway* app no 55597/09 (ECtHR, 28 June 2011), para 70.

[217] See, eg, *Useinov v the Netherlands* (n 215); *Narenji Haghighi v the Netherlands* (n 215).

[218] See, eg, *Useinov v the Netherlands* (n 215); *Narenji Haghighi v the Netherlands* (n 215). The only exception to this approach seems to be the case of *Darren Omoregie and others v Norway* app no 265/07 (ECtHR, 31 July 2008), where the Court analysed the expulsion of an asylum seeker in terms of a negative obligation.

controlling immigration are therefore usually outweighed by the individual interests of the asylum seeker.[219]

These cases, however, concern complaints about the refusal to allow an (ex-) asylum seeker to reside on the territory. The question is whether the precarious immigration status of asylum seekers and the interests of the state in controlling immigration weigh just as heavily in other contexts where the state relies on interests of immigration policy. The case of *Mubilanzila Mayeka and Kaniki Mitunga v Belgium*[220] presents an example of a complaint under Article 8 by an alien without the right to stay in another context: the context of detention. This case, which contained a complaint under Article 3 as well, concerned the detention of an unaccompanied five-year-old girl who did not dispose of the necessary documentation to enter Belgium. The Court held that this detention amounted to an interference with the applicant's family life, as she was separated from her mother as a result of the detention. This detention was in accordance with the law and pursued a legitimate aim, according to the Court. As the applicant was detained under the authorities' powers to control the entry and residence of aliens on the territory of the Belgian state, 'the decision to detain could have been in the interests of national security or the economic well-being of the country or, just as equally, for the prevention of disorder or crime'.[221] With regard to the question whether the detention was necessary in a democratic society, the Court held:

> The Convention does not guarantee, as such, any right for an alien to enter or stay on the territory of the State of which he or she is not a national (…). Furthermore, the Contracting States are under a duty to maintain public order, in particular by exercising their right, as a matter of well-established international law, to control the entry and residence of aliens. In this connection, detention in centres used for aliens awaiting deportation will be acceptable only where it is intended to enable the States to combat illegal immigration while at the same time complying with their international obligations, including those arising under the Convention for the Rights of the Child signed in New York in 1989 (and by Belgium in 1991).
>
> Furthermore, the States' interest in foiling attempts to circumvent immigration rules must not deprive aliens of the protection afforded by these conventions or deprive foreign minors, especially if unaccompanied, of the protection their

[219] An example of an exception to this general rule can be found in the case of *Nunez v Norway* (n 216). Relevant facts in this case were that the applicant's children were born in Norway, had lived all their lives in Norway and would remain in the country in order to live with their father, a settled immigrant. The Court ruled that despite the fact that the mother had re-entered Norway illegally and could not reasonably have entertained any expectation of being able to remain in the country, her expulsion would violate Art 8 in view of the children's best interest.

[220] *Mubilanzila Mayeka and Kaniki Mitunga v Belgium* (n 25).

[221] Ibid, para 79.

> status warrants. The protection of fundamental rights and the constraints imposed by a State's immigration policy must therefore be reconciled.[222]

Hence, this seems to imply that although the interests of the state in controlling immigration and combating illegal immigration are of importance in this context, they do not as a general rule outweigh the individual interests of aliens. The conclusion could therefore be drawn that the Court seems to make a distinction between cases concerning permission to enter or stay on the territory of the state, on the one hand, and cases concerning the rights of aliens in other contexts, on the other hand. With regard to the former, the Court distinguishes between 'insiders' and 'outsiders' and classifies asylum seekers as 'outsiders', as a result of which the interests of the state in controlling immigration usually prevail over the interests of the asylum seeker. With regard to the latter, the interests of the state in controlling immigration are important and should be taken into account, but do not necessarily outweigh the individual interests of aliens.

However, it is also possible to argue that the Court does not distinguish between the context of granting permission to enter or stay in the territory and other contexts concerning rights of aliens. In the case of *Müslim v Turkey,* an asylum seeker complained under Articles 3 and 8 about his poor living conditions.[223] The Government argued that the residence of the applicant was only temporarily authorized and for the sole purpose of facilitating his resettlement in a third country with the assistance of the UNHCR. The Court reiterated with regard to this complaint that the convention does not guarantee the right to enter or stay on the territory of the state for a person who is not a national of that state.[224] Hence, although the complaint did not concern access to or expulsion from the territory, the case was nevertheless placed by the Court in this context. This would mean that the 'outsiderness' of the asylum seeker prevails over the context of the case for the purpose of Article 8.[225] Still, the difference between the two cases can also be explained by the fact that the case of *Mubilanzila Mayeka and Kaniki Mitunga v Belgium* concerned a very young and unaccompanied child, whereas the *Müslim* case concerned a male adult.

[222] Ibid, para 81.

[223] *Müslim v Turkey* (n 57). See also s 11.2.

[224] Ibid, para 85.

[225] Another argument for this position would be that in the *Mubilanzila Mayeka and Kaniki Mitunga* case, the vulnerable status of the applicant as a very young and unaccompanied alien took precedence over her status as an illegal alien. The Court observed in this regard that there was no risk of the applicant's seeking to evade the supervision of the Belgian authorities, as a result of which her detention in a closed centre for adults was unnecessary (para 83). This would mean that this case, concerning a five-year-old unaccompanied minor, forms an exception to the general rule that the interests of the state in controlling immigration prevail in (all) cases concerning 'outsiders'. In other words, it is not the context of detention that is decisive in this case, but the extreme vulnerability of the alien concerned.

The limited amount of case law in this area does not make it possible to draw general conclusions about the impact of the precarious immigration status of asylum seekers and the importance of the interests of the state in controlling immigration in cases concerning the provision of benefits to asylum seekers. However, this case law does show that controlling immigration is accepted by the Court as a legitimate aim for restricting the rights of aliens under Article 8. This means that the state has an additional aim in restricting its positive obligation to provide benefits with regard to asylum seekers as compared to nationals. The question whether the interests of the state in controlling immigration as a general rule prevail over the interests of the asylum seeker in the context of providing benefits cannot be answered on the basis of this case law. However, it seems that these state interests are generally given a lot of weight by the Court.

11.4.5 Analysis and Concluding Remarks

The case law discussed in this section shows that complaints under Article 8 about the refusal of the state to provide benefits or the absence of state benefits are analysed by the Court in terms of positive obligations, which is a more favourable process for the state than the negative counterpart. In addition, the general rule laid down by the Court is that Article 8 does not guarantee social and economic rights, such as the right to financial assistance, the right to a home or the right to free medical care. However, there seems to be a (very cautious) development towards accepting that Article 8 imposes, under certain circumstances, positive obligations on the state to provide health care, housing or social benefits. The scope of these obligations is, however, very limited. In order for such an obligation to arise, there should be a 'direct and immediate link' between the measures requested of the state and the individual's private life or it should be established that the refusal of benefits makes the normal development of family or private life impossible. Since such positive obligations involve an assessment of priorities in the context of the allocation of limited state resources, the state enjoys a wide margin of appreciation in striking a fair balance between the interests of the individual and of the community as a whole. This margin is even wider with regard to complaints about the refusal to provide a specific kind or form of health care, accommodation or social benefits.

With regard to the refusal to provide benefits to asylum seekers, there is an additional factor limiting the scope of the positive obligation under Article 8. As benefits are often refused to asylum seekers with reference to the state's immigration policy, the legitimate aim of conducting effective immigration control should be taken into account. The Court does not regard asylum seekers as complete 'insiders' with regard to Article 8, which might mean that the interests of the state in controlling immigration generally prevail over the individual interests of the asylum seeker. Even if the interests of the state do not as a rule outweigh the interests of the asylum seeker, it seems that they are given a lot of weight by the Court. This would mean that the already limited scope of positive obligations under Article 8 is even more limited with regard to the provision of benefits to asylum seekers. While in the context of Article 3 the Court has ruled that asylum seekers are a vulnerable group, which is an important factor for establishing state responsibility for preventing ill-treatment, the same approach has not (yet) been adopted by the Court as regards Article 8.

All in all, the conclusion should be that Article 8 does not provide much protection with regard to the social and economic rights of asylum seekers. Although the threshold under Article 8 seems to be lower than under Article 3, the wide margin of appreciation accorded to states means a substantial burden for accepting that a certain state practice violates Article 8. Although it is possible that the refusal of benefits has such severe consequences for the private or family life that it cannot be considered proportional to the state interests, it is not very conceivable that this violation of the state's positive obligation under Article 8 will not at the same time violate the state's positive obligation under Article 3. In brief, Article 8 does not have much added value alongside Article 3 with regard to the social and economic rights of asylum seekers.

11.5 CASE LAW ABOUT ENDING ENTITLEMENT TO SOCIAL SECURITY BENEFITS AND ACCOMMODATION

11.5.1 Introduction

The previous sections have examined whether the ECHR contains obligations for the state to provide for social security benefits, whether in cash or in the form of housing, food and medical care in kind. This section will examine whether, if the state has decided to provide certain benefits to asylum seekers, the ECHR provides any safeguards against the ending or reduction of (the provision of) such benefits. To that end, case law on Article 8 (as regards the eviction from housing) and on Article 1 of the First Protocol (as regards the withdrawal or reduction of other benefits) will be discussed. Again, this section will provide a general overview and analysis of relevant case law, whereas the specific consequences for the situation of asylum seekers will be discussed in section 11.7 below.

11.5.2 Article 8

'Home' is one of the interests protected by Article 8. The concept has been interpreted broadly by the Court.[226] Whether or not a particular place constitutes a 'home' within the meaning of Article 8 depends on the factual circumstances, namely the existence of sufficient and continued links with the specific place. It is not restricted to homes that have initially been established legally, nor is ownership necessary to establish a 'home' within the meaning of Article 8.[227] Thus, in the words of the Court: 'whether a property is to be classified as a "home" is a question of fact and does not depend on the lawfulness of the occupation under domestic law'.[228]

As has been mentioned in section 11.4, complaints about evictions from homes are analysed by the Court within the context of negative obligations. This means that they have to meet the conditions laid down in paragraph 2 of Article 8, ie they have to be in accordance with the law, they have to pursue a legitimate aim and they have to be necessary in a democratic society.

An example of such a case is the case of *Chapman v United Kingdom*.[229] This case concerned a complaint by a gypsy woman against the refusal of planning permission to station caravans on her land and against various enforcement measures implemented in respect of her occupation of her land. When examining whether the interference with her right to respect for her home caused by the decisions of the planning authorities was 'necessary in a democratic society', the Court held that in this regard a margin of appreciation must, inevitably, be left to the national authorities, the scope of which will vary 'according to the nature of the Convention right in issue, its importance for the individual and the nature of the activities restricted, as well as the nature of the aim pursued by the restrictions'. In the context of planning decisions, the national authorities in principle enjoy a wide margin of appreciation. In this regard, the procedural safeguards available to the individual will be especially material in determining whether the state has remained within its margin of appreciation.[230] In addition, this judgment shows that two further circumstances are relevant

[226] Harris et al 2009, p 396.
[227] Ibid, pp 376 and 380. See also *Kryvitska and Kryvitskyy v Ukraine* app no 30856/03 (ECtHR, 2 December 2010), para 40.
[228] *Orlić v Croatia* app no 48833/07 (ECtHR, 21 June 2011), para 54.
[229] *Chapman v United Kingdom* app no 27238/95 (ECtHR, 18 January 2001). Similar cases decided on the same date and containing the same observations of the Court are *Beard v United Kingdom* app no 24882/94; *Coster v United Kingdom* app no 24876/94; *Jane Smith v United Kingdom* app no 25154/94; and *Lee v United Kingdom* app no 25289/94.
[230] *Chapman v United Kingdom* (n 229), paras 91–92.

in this regard. First of all, it is relevant whether the home was established lawfully or not. The Court held:

> If the home was lawfully established, this factor would self-evidently be something which would weigh against the legitimacy of requiring the individual to move. Conversely, if the establishment of the home in a particular place was unlawful, the position of the individual objecting to an order to move is less strong.[231]

A second relevant factor is whether alternative accommodation is available, as the Court held that if no alternative accommodation is available the interference is more serious than where such accommodation is available' and '[t]he more suitable the alternative accommodation is, the less serious is the interference constituted by moving the applicant from his or her existing accommodation'.[232]

A similar case concerning the eviction of a gypsy family from a caravan site is the case of *Connors v United Kingdom*.[233] This case differs, however, from the *Chapman* case with regard to the scope of the margin of appreciation. As a 'general principle', the Court adds in this case that the margin 'will tend to be narrower where the right at stake is crucial to the individual's effective enjoyment of intimate or key rights'. In addition, although there is authority that in spheres involving the application of social or economic policies, such as the planning or housing context, the margin of appreciation is wide, the Court stated:

> [T]his was in the context of Article 1 of Protocol No 1, not Article 8 which concerns rights of central importance to the individual's identity, self-determination, physical and moral integrity, maintenance of relationships with others and a settled and secure place in the community.

According to the Court:

> Where general social and economic policy considerations have arisen in the context of Article 8 itself, the scope of the margin of appreciation depends on the context of the case, with particular significance attaching to the extent of the intrusion into the personal sphere of the applicant.[234]

In the application of these general principles to the present case, the Court held that the interference in the present case was very serious, as the applicant and his family were evicted from the site where they had lived, with a short absence, for some 14 to 15 years, with consequent difficulties in finding a lawful alternative location for their caravans, in coping with health problems and young children and in ensuring

231 Ibid, para 102.
232 Ibid, para 103.
233 *Connors v United Kingdom* app no 66746/01 (ECtHR, 27 May 2004).
234 Ibid, para 82.

continuation in the children's education. This serious interference required, in the Court's opinion, 'particularly weighty reasons of public interest by way of justification and the margin of appreciation to be afforded to the national authorities must be regarded as correspondingly narrowed'. The Court distinguished the *Connors* case from the *Chapman* case by observing that in the latter case, it was undisputed that the applicant had breached planning law in taking up occupation of land, while in the present case, the applicant was lawfully on the site and claimed that the procedural guarantees available to other mobile home sites should equally apply to the occupation of that site by himself and his family.[235]

The Court confirmed the general principles as regards the margin of appreciation as set out in the *Connors* case in the case of *McCann v United Kingdom*,[236] which concerned an eviction of a tenant from a house owned by the City Council. The Court held that the reasoning in the *Connors* case was not to be confined only to cases involving the eviction of gypsies or cases where the applicant sought to challenge the law itself rather than its application in his particular case. As the loss of one's home 'is a most extreme form of interference with the right to respect for the home', any person at risk of an interference of this magnitude should in principle be able to have the proportionality of the measure determined by an independent tribunal in the light of the relevant principles under Article 8 of the ECHR, notwithstanding that, under domestic law, his right of occupation has come to an end.[237] The Court concluded that the lack of adequate procedural safeguards constituted a violation of Article 8.[238]

The importance of procedural safeguards even where the lawful right to occupation of the premises has come to an end has been emphasized by the Court in a number of cases.[239] The Court has held that in such cases 'an individual should in principle be able to have the proportionality of the measure determined by an independent tribunal in the light of the relevant principles of Article 8 of the Convention'.[240] Hence, in the case of *Orlić v Croatia*, the Court held that the national courts did not provide the applicant with adequate procedural safeguards by confining themselves to finding that the occupation by the applicant was without legal basis, and not undertaking any further analysis as to the proportionality of the eviction.[241] In one case, *Tuleshov and Others v Russia*, the Court itself actually considered the eviction disproportionate to the legitimate aim

235 Ibid, paras 85–86.
236 *McCann v United Kingdom* app no 19009/04 (ECtHR, 13 May 2008), para 49.
237 Ibid, para 50.
238 Ibid, para 55.
239 See *Kryvitska and Kryvitskyy v Ukraine* (n 227), para 44 with further references.
240 Ibid.
241 *Orlić v Croatia* (n 228).

pursued, by reason of the huge delay in offering alternative housing to the applicants.[242]

In short, case law of the Court shows that the most important safeguard provided by Article 8 in the case of an eviction that is provided for under domestic law is a procedural one: an individual should have the opportunity to have the proportionality of the eviction examined by an independent tribunal. When examining this proportionality, the national authorities have a wide margin of appreciation, but the availability of alternative accommodation should be an important factor.

11.5.3 Article 1 of the First Protocol

Article 1 of the First Protocol to the ECHR reads:

> Every natural or legal person is entitled to the peaceful enjoyment of his possessions. No one shall be deprived of his possessions except in the public interest and subject to the conditions provided for by law and by the general principles of international law.
>
> The preceding provisions shall not, however, in any way impair the right of a State to enforce such laws as it deems necessary to control the use of property in accordance with the general interest or to secure the payment of taxes or other contributions or penalties.

The Court has generally held that this article provides three different, but not entirely distinct rules. The first rule is that everyone is entitled to peaceful enjoyment of his or her possessions. The second rule covers deprivation of possessions and makes it subject to certain conditions. The third rule entitles contracting states to control the use of property where it is in the general interest.[243] This section will examine under which conditions the state is entitled to deprive individuals of social benefits.

The term 'possessions' is an autonomous concept and has been given a broad meaning by the Court.[244] As has been discussed in chapter six, according to the Court's case law an assertable right under domestic law to a welfare benefit should be regarded as a possession within the meaning of Article 1 of the First Protocol. The Court has held in this regard that Article 1 of the First Protocol does not create a right to acquire property. Hence:

> It places no restriction on the Contracting State's freedom to decide whether or not to have in place any form of social security scheme, or to choose the type

[242] *Tuleshov and others v Russia* app no 32718/02 (ECtHR, 24 May 2007), para 53.
[243] Van Dijk et al 2006, p 864; Harris et al 2009, p 666; White and Ovey 2010, p 478.
[244] Van Dijk et al 2006, p 865; Jacobs, White and Ovey 2010, p 481.

> or amount of benefits to provide under any such scheme (...). If, however, a Contracting State has in force legislation providing for the payment as of right of a welfare benefit—whether conditional or not on the prior payment of contributions—that legislation must be regarded as generating a proprietary interest falling within the ambit of Article 1 of Protocol No. 1 for persons satisfying its requirements.[245]

In order to establish a pecuniary right falling under the scope of Article 1 of the First Protocol, it is therefore necessary that the person concerned satisfies the various statutory conditions established by law, provided that these conditions are not discriminatory within the meaning of Article 14 of the ECHR. This means that if the person concerned does not satisfy, or ceases to satisfy, the legal conditions laid down in domestic law for the grant of social or welfare benefits, there is no interference with the rights under Article 1 of Protocol no 1.[246] Article 1 of the First Protocol therefore does not provide protection against the ending of entitlement to welfare benefits based on the ceasing of fulfilment of the relevant conditions.

However, if the relevant conditions have been changed, for example through an amendment to the relevant Act or statute, or if the fulfilment of the applicable conditions has been reassessed, Article 1 of Protocol no 1 is applicable.[247] If in such cases the amount of a benefit is reduced or discontinued, this may constitute an interference with possessions which requires justification.[248] The Court generally examines such cases in the light of the general rule of the right to peaceful enjoyment of possessions (rule no 1). In order to be compatible with this rule, an interference with property rights must strike a fair balance between the demands of the general interest of the community and the requirements of the protection of the individual's fundamental rights. Furthermore, the issue of whether a fair balance has been struck becomes relevant only once it has been established that the interference in question satisfied the requirement

[245] See, eg, *Stec and other v United Kingdom* app nos 65731/01 and 65900/01 (ECtHR, 6 July 2007 (dec)), para 54; *Andrejeva v Latvia* app no 55707/00 (ECtHR, 18 February 2009), para 77.

[246] *Cf Rasmussen v Poland* app no 38886/05 (ECtHR, 28 April 2009), para 71. See also Harris et al 2009, p 661. In the case of *Klein v Austria*, the Court seems to make an exception to this rule by holding Art 1 of Protocol no 1 applicable in a case where the person concerned was not entitled to pension benefits because he did not fulfil one relevant condition. The Court seems to attach considerable importance in this regard to the fact that affiliation to the pension scheme was compulsory as well as contributing to the scheme and to the fact that the relevant condition had in the meantime been abolished in an amendment to the relevant pension scheme (*Klein v Austria* app no 57028/00 (ECtHR, 3 March 2011)).

[247] See, eg, *Hoogendijk v the Netherlands* app no 58641/00 (ECtHR, 6 January 2005 (dec)); *Goudswaard-Van der Laans v The Netherlands* app no 75255/01 (ECtHR, 22 September 2005 (dec)); *Sali v Sweden* app no 67070/01 (ECtHR, 10 January 2006 (dec)); *Moskal v Poland* app no 10373/05 (ECtHR, 15 September 2009); *Iwaszkiewicz v Poland* app no 30614/06 (ECtHR, 26 July 2011).

[248] *Rasmussen v Poland* (n 246), para 71; *Iwaszkiewicz v Poland* (n 247).

of lawfulness and pursues aims in the public interest.[249] As regards the 'public interest requirement', the Court has ruled that the national authorities enjoy a wide margin of appreciation and the Court will respect the legislature's judgement as to what is 'in the public interest' unless that judgement is manifestly without reasonable foundation.[250] As regards the requirement of a fair balance, the Court has ruled that a fair balance will not be struck if the person concerned bears an individual and excessive burden.[251] In general, the threshold for establishing such an excessive burden is high, as a consequence of which the state is allowed a wide power to interfere with the right to peaceful enjoyment of possessions. Harris et al note that the Court has deferred extensively to the decisions of national bodies.[252] Accordingly, the Court does usually not find a violation of Article 1 of the First Protocol if social benefits are reduced as a result of amended legislation.[253] However, case law of the Court does indicate that this might be different if the benefit concerned has been entirely withdrawn and the person concerned is not eligible for other welfare benefits and therefore left without any provision at all from the social security system.[254] In addition, if fulfilment of the statutory conditions is reassessed and a mistake is discovered which has been caused by the authorities themselves, without any fault of a third party, a stricter proportionality approach must be taken in determining whether the burden borne by the person concerned was excessive.[255]

11.5.4 Concluding Remarks

This section has shown that Article 8 provides protection against eviction from a person's home. The most important safeguard provided by this article is that it should be possible to have the proportionality of the eviction examined by an independent tribunal, even if the right of occupation has come to an end under domestic law. In making this proportionality assessment, the domestic authorities have a large margin of appreciation.

249 See, eg, *Hoogendijk v the Netherlands* (n 247); *Iwaszkiewicz v Poland* (n 247).

250 *Moskal v Poland* (n 247), para 61; *Wieczorek v Poland* app no 18176/05 (ECtHR, 8 December 2009), para 59; *Iwaszkiewicz v Poland* (n 247), para 43.

251 *Iwaszkiewicz v Poland* (n 247), para 44.

252 Harris et al 2009, p 695.

253 *Cf* Brems 2007, p 155.

254 *Asmundsson v Iceland* app no 60669/00 (ECtHR, 12 October 2004) (however, in this case, the Court attributed a lot of weight as well to the fact that the vast majority of disability pensioners had continued to receive benefits at the same level as previously, whereas a small minority completely lost their entitlements); *Hoogendijk v the Netherlands* (n 247); *Iwaszkiewicz v Poland* (n 247), para 59.

255 *Moskal v Poland* (n 247).

Article 1 of the First Protocol does not provide protection against the ending of entitlement for welfare benefits if the person concerned does not satisfy, or ceases to satisfy, the legal conditions laid down in domestic law for the grant of the welfare benefits in question. However, it does provide protection if the relevant conditions are changed owing to an amendment of the applicable rules or if the fulfilment of the relevant conditions is being reassessed. Owing to the very wide margin of appreciation provided to the domestic authorities in this regard, however, a violation of Article 1 of Protocol no 1 will generally only occur if the benefit is withdrawn entirely and the person concerned is not eligible for any other welfare benefit.

11.6 CASE LAW ON ACCESS TO THE LABOUR MARKET

This section will examine whether contracting states act in violation of the ECHR if they deny asylum seekers access to their labour markets. In chapter two it has been shown that under the EU Reception Conditions Directives, Member States are allowed to ban access to the labour market for one year or nine months. After that period, access to the labour market can be made subject to various conditions. The question is how such restrictive measures relate to the ECHR.

In general, the Court has ruled that the convention does not guarantee, as such, the right to work.[256] However, in the context of Article 8, the Court has ruled that the concept of 'private life' also compromises activities of a professional or business nature, since 'it is, after all, in the course of their working lives that the majority of people have a significant, if not the greatest, opportunity of developing relationships with the outside world'.[257] In the case of *Sidabras and Džiautas v Lithuania*, the Court held, with reference to the European Social Charter and different ILO conventions, that a far-reaching ban on taking up private sector employment did affect 'private life', as a result of which Article 14 was applicable in this case.[258] With reference to this case, the Court found a violation of Article 8 in the case of *Campagnano v Italy*, where the entry of a person's name in the bankruptcy register entailed the prohibition against taking up certain kinds of employment. In finding a violation, the Court took into account that an entry in the bankruptcy register was automatic and not reviewed by courts, and that rehabilitation could only be obtained after

[256] *Jazvinsky v Slovak Republic* app no 33088/96 (ECtHR, 7 September 2000 (dec)).

[257] *Jehovah's Witnesses of Moscow v Russia* app no 302/02 (ECtHR, 10 June 2010), para 117. See also *Campagnano v Italy* app no 77955/01 (ECtHR, 23 March 2006), para 53.

[258] *Sidabras and Džiautas v Lithuania* app nos 55480/00 and 59330/00 (ECtHR, 27 July 2004), para 47.

five years.[259] Hence, a prohibition to enter certain kind of professions can under certain circumstances violate Article 8.

This raises the question whether and how this general case law applies to the context of aliens and the general requirement to obtain a work permit in order to be entitled to take up employment in the host state. In the above-mentioned case of *Müslim v Turkey*, the Court held in general that the convention does not contain the right to enter or stay in a country of which the person concerned is not a national *nor the right to work there.*[260] In the case of *Coorplan-Jenni GMBH and Hascic v Austria*, the Court recalled that the convention does not guarantee the right to work, but added to this observation:

> Nevertheless, the Court does not exclude that the refusal of a corresponding permit to a foreigner legally residing in his host state and willing to work may affect the concerned foreigner's possibility to pursue a professional activity to such a significant degree that there are consequential effects on the enjoyment of his right to respect for his 'private life' within the meaning of Article 8 of the Convention.[261]

In more recent decisions on complaints of migrants without a residence permit about the denial of the right to work, the Court has simply held that 'this does not raise an issue under Article 8 as neither this nor any other Convention provision guarantees a right to work'.[262]

Arguably therefore, even though the Court does not exclude the possibility that the denial of a work permit to a non-national violates Article 8, this possibility seems to be limited to aliens *legally residing* in the host state. This fits in well with the above-mentioned distinction made by the Court in Article 8 cases between 'settled immigrants' and immigrants who invoke the protection of Article 8 pending a precarious or merely tolerated stay in the host state.

11.7 ANALYSIS

11.7.1. Introduction

In this chapter it has been argued that Article 3 of the ECHR provides the most far-reaching protection as regards poor living conditions or inadequate health care. This conclusion applies especially to asylum seekers,

259 *Campagnano v Italy* (n 257).

260 *Müslim v Turkey* (n 57), para 85 (emphasis added).

261 *Coorplan-Jenni GMBH and Hascic v Austria* app no 10523/02 (ECtHR, 24 February 2005 (dec)).

262 *I v the Netherlands* app no 24147/11(ECtHR, 10 July 2012 (dec)), para 48 and *K v the Netherlands* app no 33403/11 (ECtHR, 25 September 2012 (dec)), para 46.

since the Court has identified them as a vulnerable category of persons for whom the state bears a special responsibility under Article 3. In addition, Article 8 and Article 1 of the First Protocol provide a few safeguards as regards the ending of entitlements to housing or social benefits. This section will discuss in more detail the consequences of the main findings in the foregoing sections for the reception of asylum seekers in EU Member States. To that end, it is necessary to make a distinction between two situations. First, section 11.7.2 will discuss under which circumstances the *complete denial* of social security benefits to asylum seekers will violate Article 3. Secondly, section 11.7.3 will discuss the consequences of the case law discussed in this chapter for the situation in which the state does provide some kind of social benefits. More specifically, this subsection will discuss under which circumstances the *poor quality* of such benefits will violate Article 3 and which safeguards apply if entitlement to such benefits *ends* or is *changed*.

As regards access to the labour market, it has been argued in the previous section that the protection offered by Article 8 in this respect only applies to aliens who are legally residing in the host state. As asylum seekers are still awaiting a decision on their request for a residence permit, they do not fulfil this requirement.[263] Consequently, this section will only pay attention to the issue of social security benefits for asylum seekers.

11.7.2 State Obligations to Provide Social Benefits

In this chapter it has been argued that being subjected to poor living conditions can violate Article 3 if it can be established that the state can be held responsible for these living conditions and if these conditions reach the minimum level of severity under Article 3. In *MSS v Belgium and Greece*, the Court has ruled that both conditions were fulfilled as regards the poor living conditions of asylum seekers in Greece. From this and other case law of the Court, it appears that the state can be held responsible for poor living conditions of vulnerable persons, such as asylum seekers, if they are caused by a deliberate or intentional act of the state. An example of such an act is the situation in which the state does not comply with a (domestic) legal obligation to provide adequate living conditions. In addition, case law shows that poor living conditions reach the severity threshold of Article 3 if the person concerned is unable to cater for his most basic needs, which include, according to the Court, housing, food

[263] See ch 4 for an extensive discussion of the rather vague nature of asylum seekers' immigration status.

and sanitary conditions. Further, there should be little prospect of any improvement of the situation within a reasonable timeframe.

Since the coming into force of Directive 2003/9, all EU Member States are under a legal obligation to provide asylum seekers with 'material reception conditions', ie housing, food and clothing.[264] This chapter shows that the adoption of this directive has as an important consequence that these states can be held responsible for providing adequate living conditions to asylum seekers, not only under EU law, but also under the ECHR. If a state does not provide reception benefits to an asylum seeker while it is under a legal obligation to do so, and if the asylum seeker is as a result of that unable to cater for his most basic needs, Article 3 of the ECHR will be violated. Given the fact that many asylum seekers are new and unfamiliar to the host state, as a result of which they will often not have access to a support network of, for example, relatives, churches or non-governmental organizations, and most asylum seekers are not allowed to work, asylum seekers who do not receive any kind of state support will often be unable to cater for their most basic needs. In addition, the Court has held that if dire living conditions are linked to the status of being an asylum seeker, the condition that there should be little prospect of any improvement of the situation within a reasonable timeframe has been met. This means that Article 3 contains an important obligation for EU Member States as regards the reception of asylum seekers.

These conclusions raise a few important questions. First of all, it raises the question whether EU Member States could also violate Article 3 by not providing reception benefits if there is no legal obligation to do so. In other words, what would be the situation if Directive 2003/9 had not been adopted and the Member States had not laid down such an obligation in domestic law? The *Müslim* case shows that states are not in general responsible under Article 3 to provide asylum seekers with a certain standard of living. Hence, state responsibility does not exist in general. Nevertheless, the Court has identified all asylum seekers as being in a vulnerable position for the purposes of Article 3. Arguably, this might indicate that general state responsibility could arise for poor living conditions of asylum seekers due to other intentional or culpable behaviour of the state, such as a lengthy ban on access to the labour market[265] and/or exclusion of eligibility for emergency support which is available for other inhabitants of the state under very special circumstances.[266]

[264] See ch 2.

[265] *Cf* the reasoning of the UK House of Lords in the *Adam, Limbuela and Tesema case* (n 29).

[266] *Cf* the Court's consideration in the *Müslim* case that the situation of the applicant was no worse than that of any other citizen who was less well off than others. Hence, in order to exclude state responsibility, the Court compared the situation of asylum seekers with that of the poorest Turkish citizens.

This latter part of the Court's approach raises the second question, namely what the Court means by the term 'asylum seekers'. Who exactly fall under this vulnerable category of persons? What is the distinguishing factor between asylum seekers and 'illegal aliens'? The case law is not clear on this point. Arguably, in order to be an asylum seeker, a person should at least have made his intention to lodge an asylum application known to the authorities; a formal lodging of an asylum application might not be necessary in order to invoke the protection of Article 3. A more difficult question is at what point of time a person who has applied for asylum turns into an 'illegal alien'. Under the Court's case law on Articles 3 and 13 of the ECHR, asylum seekers who have an arguable claim that their expulsion violates Article 3 should have access to a remedy with automatic, de jure suspensive effect.[267] In addition, the Court sometimes takes an interim measure indicating that the applicant may not be expelled pending the examination of his or her complaint by the Court. Arguably, asylum seekers whose application has been rejected but whose expulsion has been suspended by law or forbidden by the ECtHR or a domestic court in order to await the outcome of an appeal should still be considered to be an 'asylum seeker' belonging to a vulnerable category of persons. Accordingly, it can be argued that persons whose asylum application has been rejected, who have had access to an effective remedy within the meaning of Article 13 of the ECHR and whose expulsion is no longer suspended, no longer fall under this category.

As chapter two has shown, the personal scope of the EU Reception Conditions Directives is limited. It is questionable whether it already applies before an asylum application has been formally lodged and whether it applies pending a second or further domestic appeal. In addition, states have the possibility to withdraw reception benefits from asylum seekers who lodge a second or further application and the Directive do not apply to asylum seekers who lodge a complaint against their expulsion with the Court or, for example, the Human Rights Committee, once a final (domestic) decision has been taken on their application. This would mean that EU Member States do not have an obligation resulting from the EU Reception Conditions Directives as regards certain categories of asylum seekers who, arguably, do fall under the category of vulnerable persons as identified by the Court.

In brief, if an EU Member State does not provide any kind of state support to asylum seekers who are unable to cater for their most basic needs (accommodation, food, sanitary facilities) while these asylum seekers fall

[267] See, eg, *Gebremedhin v France* app no 25389/05 (ECtHR, 26 April 2007), para 66; *Abdolkhani and Karimnia v Turkey* app no 30471/08 (ECtHR 22 September 2009), paras 108 and 116.

under the personal scope of the EU Reception Conditions Directives or a similar domestic law, this situation would be in violation of Article 3 of the ECHR. If an EU Member State does not provide any kind of state support to asylum seekers who are unable to cater for their most basic needs while they have no legal obligation (domestic or resulting from EU law) to do so, this situation might still be in violation of Article 3 if it concerns asylum seekers whose expulsion has been suspended by law or forbidden by the ECtHR or a domestic court. Arguably, in that case they fall under the vulnerable category of persons identified by the Court as regards the application of Article 3, as a result of which general state responsibility can arise from other kinds of intentional state behaviour. Finally, it seems plausible that asylum seekers whose asylum application has been rejected, who have had access to an effective remedy within the meaning of Article 13 of the ECHR and whose expulsion is no longer suspended do not by definition fall under the scope of the category of vulnerable persons identified by the Court, In that case, state responsibility can only be engaged due to the individual circumstances of the case and due to other reasons of vulnerability, such as a young age.

11.7.3. State Obligations if some Kind of Social Security is Provided to Asylum Seekers

Quality of Living Conditions

Does the ECHR also contain safeguards for asylum seekers if their host state provides some kind of state support? With regard to the quality of the reception conditions, the answer to this question is to a large extent dependent on the framework of review that should be applied: the framework of review applied to persons in detention or the general framework of review. As sections 11.2 and 11.3 have shown, as regard conditions of detention, a strict framework of review applies. The Court takes into account the cumulative effect of detention conditions. Relevant factors are inter alia the existence of sufficient and adequate living space, the provision of sanitary products (even toilet paper), adequate food, clean bed linen, medical care and necessary medical aids, such as glasses or dentures, the presence of a radio or TV, the temperature in the cell, etc. On the other hand, in the general framework of review of living conditions outside detention, the relevant test seems to be whether the person concerned is able to cater for his most basic needs and whether there is any prospect of improvement of the situation within a reasonable timeframe. A complaint about, for example, a lack of toilet paper would, in my view, not raise an issue under Article 3 of the ECHR outside the context of detention.

The Court does not extensively explain why it applies another standard of review to the living conditions of detainees. As has been mentioned previously, the Court generally states that 'persons in custody are in a vulnerable position and the authorities are under a duty to protect them'. Hence, the vulnerability of detainees is apparently relevant. However, also persons outside detention can be in a specific vulnerable situation, such as severely disabled persons. As this chapter shows, the Court does not apply the more rigorous standard of review to disabled persons. Vulnerability therefore does not seem to be enough. In a few other cases, the Court seems to give a further indication, by referring to the fact that detainees are entirely under the control of the authorities.[268] Further, the Court has held that the 'applicant may be in a particularly vulnerable position when he is being held in custody with limited contacts with his family or the outside world'.[269] Hence, it seems to be decisive that the vulnerable situation of detainees is caused by the fact that they are entirely under the control of the authorities, with limited contacts with the outside world. Whereas outside the context of detention, persons might be in a vulnerable position because they are dependent on state action for their physical well-being because they cannot take care of themselves, such as, for example, severely disabled persons or children, persons who are detained are even more dependent on state action, as they are entirely under the control of the authorities and have very limited possibilities to find assistance elsewhere, eg with relatives, friends, churches or social welfare organizations. In other words, persons in detention do not have any alternative to turn to for assistance for improved living conditions.

In chapter two it has been argued that the EU Reception Conditions Directives allow Member States to implicate the social rights of asylum seekers in a system of control in various ways. In addition to the possibilities to actually detain asylum seekers, Member States are, for example, allowed to accommodate asylum seekers in large-scale reception centres, to make the provision of material reception conditions subject to the actual residence of an asylum seeker in such a centre and to withdraw reception conditions if the place of residence has been abandoned without permission or when the asylum seeker does not comply with reporting duties. In addition, the Directives permit Member States to make the enjoyment of material reception conditions subject to the behaviour of asylum seekers in the asylum procedure, as a result of which Member States are able to influence and control this behaviour. Since the Directives also allow

[268] *Slimani v France* app no 57671/00 (ECtHR, 27 July 2004), para 27; *Denis Vasilyev v Russia* (n 46), para 115; *Premininy v Russia* (n 17), para 73.

[269] *Novinskiy v Russia* app no 11982/02 (ECtHR, 10 February 2009); *Lopata v Russia* app no 72250/01 (ECtHR, 13 July 2010), para 152; *Alekseyenko v Russia* app no 41833/04 (ECtHR, 27 January 2011), para 169.

Member States to ban access to the labour market for a significant period of time, asylum seekers might be to a large extent dependent on the receipt of material reception benefits. The possibility for asylum seekers to leave the accommodation centres can therefore be rather theoretical.

Even though state control is generally a very important aspect of providing welfare,[270] I would argue that the amount of state control allowed for by the EU Reception Conditions Directives, can make the situation of asylum seekers comparable with the situation of detainees for the review of their living conditions.[271] The most important factor that distinguishes the situation of asylum seekers from other vulnerable persons who are dependent on state support is, in my opinion, the fact that the state actually can determine their place of living, from which asylum seekers have no real possibility to leave or to move to another centre of their own choosing, and can also influence to a large extent the period of time during which they have to live there.

The consequence of this reasoning is that if a European state decides to accommodate asylum seekers in reception centres, coupled with a large amount of state control, then the state is as a rule responsible for ensuring adequate living conditions in these centres. Strict obligations with regard to the quality of these living conditions have been developed in the case law of the ECtHR. The (cumulative effect of) factors such as clean and hygienic conditions, availability of clean bed linen and adequate food, an acceptable temperature, enough living space, availability of a radio or TV and adequate medical assistance should be taken into account. Especially as regards medical assistance, the authorities are under a number of important and detailed obligations. They should ensure that diagnoses and care are prompt and accurate and that a comprehensive record is kept of asylum seekers' state of health. Treatment should not just be aimed at addressing symptoms of a disease, but should be aimed at curing or preventing aggravation.

In contrast, if the state applies a reception policy that does not involve much state control, then the state seems to have more discretionary room for providing state support to asylum seekers, the quality of which is not subject to detailed obligations stemming from the ECtHR case law. If asylum seekers have any kind of accommodation, food and sanitary conditions at their disposal, the relevant test under Article 3 of the ECHR seems to have been met, as states are not obligated in general to provide asylum seekers with a certain standard of living.

270 See for an example in the UK, Larkin 2007.

271 See also Van der Horst 2004, who argues that reception centres in the Netherlands share important characteristics with other 'total institutions' such as prisons and hospitals.

End or Change of Entitlement to Reception Benefits

This chapter has also examined whether the ECHR provides safeguards for asylum seekers once entitlement to social benefits and housing ends or changes. It has been shown that Article 8 of the ECHR provides some safeguards in the case of expulsion from one's home. Given the broad interpretation of the term 'home', asylum seekers reception centres do qualify. In the case of eviction from such a centre, the most important safeguard provided by Article 8 is a procedural one; it should be possible to have the proportionality of the expulsion reviewed by an independent tribunal. This safeguard applies notwithstanding the fact that the right to live in the centre has come to an end under domestic law. The Court has provided few guidelines as regards the proportionality test and defers heavily to domestic authorities, but it seems that availability of alternative housing should be an important factor.

The EU Reception Conditions Directives only apply to asylum seekers who have not yet received a final decision on their application. Hence, once a final decision on their application has been taken, asylum seekers no longer fall under the personal scope of the Directives and are no longer entitled to the rights laid down in them, such as accommodation. Does Article 8 imply that expulsion of rejected asylum seekers from an accommodation centre is only possible if alternative housing is available? The Court has not yet ruled on this issue. However, as it has been argued in section 11.4, the Court does attach importance to the legitimate aim of effective immigration control in the context of Article 8. In addition, the Court has ruled that the precarious immigration status of asylum seekers implies that they do not have the same claim to respect for their family or private life established during that stay as aliens who explicitly have been granted the right to reside in the country. Arguably, the Court would apply the same approach as regards the establishment of a home during a precarious stay in the country. Accordingly, expulsion would only under exceptional circumstances be contrary to Article 8. This restrictive approach to the proportionality test does not, however, alter the general safeguard provided by Article 8 that it should be possible to have this proportionality examined.

Article 1 of the First Protocol to the ECHR does not provide protection against the withdrawal of social benefits if a person ceases to fulfil the relevant conditions. This means that it does not provide any safeguards against the withdrawal of reception benefits once a final decision on the asylum application has been taken. However, this article does provide protection if the relevant rules are being changed or if fulfilment of the conditions is being reassessed. In that case, a fair balance has to be struck between the general and individual interest. The national authorities have much freedom in striking this balance, but such a balance has generally not been struck if social benefits are entirely withdrawn and the person concerned is not eligible for other social benefits. Hence, if EU Member States decide to end the provision of reception benefits to asylum seekers and to withdraw the EU Reception Conditions Directives, they cannot simply withdraw all reception benefits from asylum seekers who were already receiving these benefits.

11.7.4 Concluding Remarks

This chapter shows that the adoption of the EU Reception Conditions Directives has a number of important human rights consequences. First of all, if a state intentionally does not provide asylum seekers with the benefits laid down in these Directives (or their domestic law), they can be held responsible for asylum seekers' living conditions under Article 3 of the ECHR. Secondly, by providing asylum seekers with reception benefits as of right, asylum seekers establish a home within the meaning of Article 8 and property rights within the meaning of Article 1 of the First Protocol, as a result of which interference with these rights should comply with these articles.

In addition, it has been argued in this chapter that the large amount of state control implied by the mode of provision of reception benefits might imply that a more rigorous framework of review applies to their living conditions. Again, decisions made by European states as regard the reception of asylum seekers have important consequences in the field of human rights. This conclusion is even more important as the Court does not seem to make a distinction between nationals and aliens in its case law on detention conditions. With regard to the field of conditions of detention, or, put differently, with regard to areas in which the state exercises a large degree of control over the lives of persons, the Court, therefore, seems to embrace the 'separation model'.

Finally, this chapter has shown that even apart from the choices made by European states and the adoption of the EU Reception Conditions Directives, state responsibility for asylum seekers' living conditions could arise under the ECHR. The identification by the Court of asylum seekers as a vulnerable group together with the acknowledgement of the possibility that inability to cater for one's most basic needs reaches the severity threshold of Article 3 leaves open the possibility that state responsibility for poor living conditions of asylum seekers can also exist on the basis of other kinds of intentional behaviour by the state.

12

Article 18 of the European Social Charter (Revised)

12.1 INTRODUCTION

THE EUROPEAN SOCIAL Charter (ESC)[1] is the only human rights instrument discussed in this book with an explicitly limited personal scope. This limited scope *ratione personae* has been discussed in section 6.4.2. It has been argued in that section that only nationals of other contracting parties fall under the personal scope of the ESC. The ESC provides refugees with exemption from this requirement of reciprocity, but only once they are 'lawfully staying' on the territory of contracting states. A further condition limiting the personal scope of the ESC is that, with the exception of Articles 18 and 19, and without prejudice to the articles on equal treatment in the field of social security,[2] nationals of other contracting parties only fall under the personal scope if they are lawfully residing or working regularly on the territory of a contracting party. In its decisions, the ESC's supervisory committee, the European Committee on Social Rights (ECSR), has widened this limited personal scope with regard to a number of rights. In section 6.4.2 it has been submitted, however, that the interpretations provided in these decisions are not persuasive in the light of the treaty interpretation rules of the Vienna Convention, as a result of which they should not be seen as authoritative interpretations of the ESC.

A consequence of this limited personal scope is that only a small category of asylum seekers is entitled to the rights laid down in the ESC. First, they should be a national of another contracting party or, arguably, they should have resided on the territory of a contracting party for at least three years.[3] Secondly, in order to fall under the scope of Articles 1–17 and

[1] The term 'European Social Charter' refers to both the original 1961 version and the revised 1996 version.

[2] Arts 12(4) and 13(4). Both provisions have been discussed in s 6.4.

[3] In ch 4 it has been argued that it follows from Art 7(2) of the Refugee Convention that all refugees who are (simply) residing on the territory for three years should be exempted from reciprocity conditions. See further s 12.2 below.

20–31 (with the exception of Articles 12 and 13), they have to be lawfully resident or regularly working on the territory of one of the contracting parties. Given that asylum seekers are generally not (yet) lawfully residing on the territory and given the restrictive approach as regards asylum seekers' access to legal employment in Europe, not many asylum seekers will be able to fulfil this second condition. The cumulative effect of both conditions makes it rather exceptional that asylum seekers fall under the personal scope of most charter articles. These articles will therefore not be discussed in this chapter.[4] This restriction is also based on the assumption that the standards laid down in the ESC do not contain more far-reaching obligations for the state as regards the reception of asylum seekers than those found in the previous chapters as resulting from the ECHR and ICESCR.[5]

These reasons do not, however, apply to Article 18 of the ESC, as a result of which this article merits description. This article contains the right to engage in a gainful occupation. The limited personal scope of the ESC does not (entirely) apply to this article.[6] In addition, this article merits description as it is the only provision laid down in a general human rights instrument on the right of non-nationals to have *access* to the labour market. This chapter will therefore examine the relevance of this article for the position of asylum seekers.

4 Provisions that might be relevant for asylum seekers' social security, not related to equal treatment, are, eg, Art 11 of the ESC on the right to protection of health; Art 24 of the 1996 revised ESC on the right to protection in cases of termination of employment; Art 30 of the 1996 revised ESC on the right to protection against poverty and social exclusion; and Art 31 of the 1996 revised ESC on the right to housing.

5 Just like the ICESCR, the ESC contains a general limitation clause (Art 31 of the 1961 Charter and Art G of the 1996 revised Charter). The wording of this clause suggests a stricter approach to limitations than the wording of the limitation clause in the ICESCR. The ESC clause provides that the rights 'shall not be subject to any restrictions or limitations' not specified in the ESC except such as are prescribed by law and are necessary in a democratic society for the protection of the rights and freedoms of others or for the protection of public interest, national security, public health or morals. Hence, the main rule is that the rights are not subject to restrictions and limitations and, contrary to the ICESCR, the limitation clause contains a necessity condition. On the other hand, however, the wording of relevant rights laid down in the ESC are more general and vague than the wording of similar rights in the ICESCR. eg, under the ICESCR, states parties *recognize* the right of each person to an adequate standard of living for himself and his family, including adequate food, clothing and housing, and to the continuous improvement of living conditions and the states parties must take appropriate steps to *ensure* the realization of this right (Art 11(1)). The counterpart to this provision in the ESC provides that, 'with a view to ensuring the effective exercise of the right to protection against poverty and social exclusion, the Parties undertake to take measures within the framework of an overall and co-ordinated approach to *promote* the effective access of persons who live or risk living in a situation of social exclusion or poverty, as well as their families, to, in particular, employment, housing, training, education, culture and social and medical assistance' (Art 30(1) of the 1996 revised Charter, emphasis added).

6 The same is true with regard to Art 19 of the ESC on the right of migrant workers and their families to protection and assistance. This article does not, however, contain rights related to access to the labour market or to social security.

12.2 PERSONAL SCOPE OF ARTICLE 18 OF THE ESC

Article 18 of the ESC reads:

> The right to engage in a gainful occupation in the territory of other Parties With a view to ensuring the effective exercise of the right to engage in a gainful occupation in the territory of any other Party, the Parties undertake:
>
> 1. to apply existing regulations in a spirit of liberality;
> 2. to simplify existing formalities and to reduce or abolish chancery dues and other charges payable by foreign workers or their employers;
> 3. to liberalise, individually or collectively, regulations governing the employment of foreign workers;
>
> and recognise:
>
> 4. the right of their nationals to leave the country to engage in a gainful occupation in the territories of the other Parties.

The limited personal scope of the ESC as laid down in its appendix only applies to Articles 1–17 and 20–31 of the ESC. This means that foreigners do not have to reside lawfully or work regularly in the territory of one of the contracting parties in order to fall under the personal scope of Article 18 of the ESC. The wording of Article 18 itself, however, implies that it only applies to nationals of other contracting party. This follows from the reference to 'other parties' and 'any other party' in the heading, the first sentence and paragraph 4 of the article. In addition, this is in keeping with paragraph 18 of part I of the ESC. Part I of the ESC contains a general statement of rights and principles setting out the aim of the policies of the contracting parties. Each paragraph in part I corresponds to the article of part II with the same number. Paragraph 18 reads:

> The nationals of any one of the Contracting Parties have the right to engage in any gainful occupation in the territory of any one of the others on a footing of equality with the nationals of the latter, subject to restrictions based on cogent economic or social reasons.

Harris and Darcy note that part I states objectives which may go beyond the specific terms of the obligation in the corresponding article in part II, but cannot be taken to fall below the requirements laid down in part II.[7] Consequently, since paragraph 18 of part I explicitly refers to nationals of any one of the contracting parties, Article 18 cannot be interpreted as providing protection to all non-nationals. According to Harris and Darcy, this is also evident from the *travaux préparatoires*.[8] This means that asylum seekers only fall under the personal scope of Article 18 if they are a national of another contracting party.

[7] Harris and Darcy 2001, p 204.
[8] Ibid, p 203.

In chapter nine it has been argued that Article 7(2) of the Refugee Convention requires states to exempt all refugees from legislative reciprocity after three years' residence on their territory. Since the term 'refugee' should be understood in the declaratory sense and since the term 'residence' in the Refugee Convention concerns physical presence for a certain amount of time, irrespective of the lawfulness of the stay, asylum seekers fall under the scope of this provision.[9] To reiterate, the word 'legislative' was introduced to restrict the scope of this article, as it implies that refugees may still be excluded from rights based on 'diplomatic reciprocity', ie based on a system whereby a state grants benefits only to 'preferred' nationals of states with which the state has a special relationship or particularly close ties.

Before the inclusion of this right in the ESC, the right to engage in a gainful occupation was already laid down in the European Convention on Establishment (ECE). The preamble to this convention recognizes 'the special character of the links between the member countries of the Council of Europe' and affirms 'that the rights and privileges which they grant to each other's nationals are conceded solely by virtue of the close association uniting the member countries of the Council of Europe by means of its Statute'. Hence, the ECE should not be seen as an instrument of general human rights law, but as an instrument establishing and affirming a special relationship between a number of states. The right to engage in a gainful occupation laid down in this convention should therefore be seen as a right based on 'diplomatic reciprocity'.

It can be argued, however, that with the inclusion of the right to engage in a gainful occupation in another contracting party in the ESC, a general human rights instrument, this right is no longer based on a system of 'diplomatic reciprocity', but on 'legislative reciprocity' instead. Indeed, the ESC's preamble explicitly places the ESC within the context of human rights law—by referring to 'the maintenance and further realisation of human rights and fundamental freedoms' and to 'every effort in common to improve the standard of living and to promote the social well-being of both their urban and rural populations'—and does not pay attention to the 'special links' between the Member States of the Council of Europe.

An important consequence of this interpretation is that asylum seekers can no longer be subjected to the condition of reciprocity stemming from Article 18 after three years' residence in the territory of a contracting state. Accordingly, asylum seekers fall under the personal scope of Article 18 if they are a national of one of the contracting parties, or if they have resided

[9] See more extensively ch 4.

in the territory of a contracting party for at least three years. Owing to the number of contracting parties to the ESC and the sometimes long duration of asylum procedures, a rather significant number of asylum seekers might actually fulfil this requirement.

12.3 SUBSTANTIVE MEANING OF ARTICLE 18 OF THE ESC

The first three paragraphs of Article 18 may be of relevance for the position of asylum seekers. On the basis of these paragraphs, contracting parties undertake 1) to apply existing regulations in a spirit of liberality; 2) to simplify existing formalities and to reduce or abolish chancery dues and other charges payable by foreign workers or their employers; and 3) to liberalize regulations governing the employment of foreign workers. Paragraph 1 is concerned with the application of existing rules and therefore with administrative practice rather than the law. As Harris and Darcy submit, '[a] party may comply with Article 18(1) even though it has very strict rules about the employment of aliens in law provided that these rules allow some administrative discretion and this is exercised generously'.[10] Paragraph 2 applies to formalities and dues, such as documents to be supplied for work permits, the waiting time for reply, and charges for work permits. Hence, paragraph 2 is concerned with the procedural rules governing employment of foreigners. Paragraph 3 is concerned with substantive requirements for the employment of foreigners, such as the grounds for providing a work permit or limitations upon the kind of employment permitted.[11] The procedural rules must be 'simplified' and the substantive rules must be 'liberalized'.

The ECSR has held that 'the letter and spirit of Article 18 mean that the situation of national of states bound by the ESC should gradually become as far as possible like that of nationals'.[12] According to Harris and Darcy, this is a reasonable interpretation, in light of the reference to national treatment in paragraph 18 of part I ESC.[13] On the other hand, the obligation to simplify or liberalize the rules, and not to abolish them, means that complete equal treatment with nationals is not required by Article 18. How should the obligation to simplify and liberalize the rules then be interpreted?

The ECSR has argued that the very wording of these provisions gives them a dynamic character, implying an evolution of the provisions and

[10] Harris and Darcy 2001, p 206.
[11] Ibid, p 208.
[12] Conclusions II, 31 July 1971, statement of interpretation.
[13] Harris and Darcy 2001, p 204.

of their application. Indeed, the term 'simplify' and 'liberalize' refers to a process, rather than to a certain result. However, as the ECSR has noted,

> a Contracting State cannot be required to report further progress (...), if the liberal spirit in which the existing rules are applied, the simplicity of formalities and the liberal nature of the regulations are already such that the State in question can be regarded as completely satisfying the undertakings entered into.[14]

Hence, the obligation under Article 18(2) and (3) is one of continual improvement to a certain level after which the obligation is to maintain the status quo.[15]

Article 18 of the ESC provides no indications as to when this 'liberal' level has been reached. Some clues may be found in the ECE. The appendix to the ESC states with regard to paragraph 18 of part I and Article 18 of part II that these provisions 'do not prejudice the provisions of the European Convention on Establishment'. Hence, the provisions of the ECE are not affected by Article 18 of the ESC and remain in force. In view of the explicit reference to these provisions in the appendix to the ESC, they can serve as a source of inspiration for the interpretation of Article 18 of the ESC.

Article 10 of the ECE provides that contracting parties 'shall authorise nationals of the other Parties to engage in its territory in any gainful occupation on an equal footing with its own nationals, unless the said Contracting Party has cogent economic or social reasons for withholding the authorisation'. Article 12 of the ECE provides that

> nationals of any Contracting Party lawfully residing in the territory of any other Party shall be authorised, without being made subject to the restrictions referred to in Article 10 of this Convention, to engage in any gainful occupation on an equal footing with nationals of the latter Party, provided they comply with one of the following conditions: a) they have been lawfully engaged in a gainful occupation in that territory for an uninterrupted period of five years; b) they have lawfully resided in that territory for an uninterrupted period of ten years; or c) they have been admitted to permanent residence.[16]

Hence, only nationals of contracting parties who are 'lawfully residing' are entitled to complete equal treatment with nationals, provided they fulfil another, quite restrictive, qualifying condition. As regards other nationals of contracting parties, the ECE allows states to withhold

[14] Conclusions II, 31 July 1971, statement of interpretation.

[15] Harris and Darcy 2001, p 209.

[16] This approach resembles the approach of the Refugee Convention, under which rights are granted to refugees on the basis of an 'incremental system', whereby legal status and passage of time are relevant factors for an accretion of right (see chs 4 and 9). Both conventions are clearly based on the 'convergence model', since the legal status and, consequently, the sovereign immigration power of the state is decisive for the material rights of aliens.

employment authorization on the basis of 'cogent economic or social reasons'. As these provisions remain in force, the obligation of Article 18 of the ESC to liberalize the rules does not affect the possibility for states to withhold employment authorization on the basis of cogent economic or social reasons for foreigners who are not yet lawfully resident on their territory. This also follows from paragraph 18 of part I of the ESC, which explicitly refers to restrictions based on cogent economic or social reasons.

The ECSR has argued that economic or social reasons may justify restricting the employment of aliens to specific types of jobs in certain occupational and geographical sectors, but not the obligation to remain in the employment of a specific enterprise.

> To tie an employed person to an enterprise by the threat of being obliged to leave the host country if he loses that job, in fact constitutes an infringement of the freedom of the individual such that it cannot be regarded as evidence of 'a spirit of liberality' or of liberal regulations.

Therefore, the ECSR has submitted that 'liberal' regulations

> should normally make it possible for the foreign worker gradually to have access to activities other than those he was authorised to engage in when entering the host country, and to be perfectly free to do so after a certain period of residence or of activity in his occupation.[17]

This resembles the approach taken in the ECE and seems therefore to be a reasonable interpretation.

12.4 CONCLUDING REMARKS

As the personal scope of the ESC is rather limited and the norms of the ESC presumably do not contain more far-reaching obligations for the state than those found under the ECHR and ICESCR, the ESC does not merit further description, in addition to the attention paid to it in section 6.4. This is, however, not true as regards Article 18 of the ESC. This is the only human rights provision explicitly referring to the right to engage in a gainful occupation. Asylum seekers who are a national of one of the contracting parties to the ESC or who have resided in the host state for at least three years fall under the personal scope of this article. As regards these categories of asylum seekers, the rules on access to employment should not be applied rigorously, but should leave room for some discretion. Automatic application of the rules and conditions for granting employment authorization to these categories of asylum seekers is not in conformity with the obligation of contracting parties to apply the rules in

[17] Conclusions II, 31 July 1971, statement of interpretation.

a spirit of liberality. As regards the rules themselves, contracting parties are obligated to simplify procedural aspects and liberalize substantive aspects. This means that the rules are subject to a continual obligation of improvement up to a certain level. Article 18 of the ESC does not, however, provide indications as to when the rules are simple and liberal enough. Equal treatment with nationals in this regard is not required until the foreigner is lawfully resident in the territory and the obligation to liberalize the rules does not prejudice the possibility of states to withhold employment authorization on the basis of cogent social or economic reasons.

Arguably, the possibility allowed by the EU Reception Conditions Directives for states to deny asylum seekers access to the labour market throughout the entire asylum procedure does not yet comply with the required level of liberality under Article 18 of the ESC. Consequently, as regards asylum seekers who fall under its personal scope, a liberalization of these rules is required by Article 18 of the ESC.

13

Conclusions to Part III

IN PART II it has been argued that international law requires states to grant asylum seekers equal treatment with nationals in the field of social security if they meet certain conditions with regard to their legal status and community ties. As regards access to the labour market, international law does not contain obligations for states to grant asylum seekers equal treatment with nationals. Part III has examined provisions of international refugee law and human rights law not related to equal treatment and non-discrimination as to their relevance for asylum seekers' social security and access to wage-earning employment. If states are not obligated to grant asylum seekers the same treatment as nationals, are they obligated to grant them some basic rights in these fields? Are states obligated to grant asylum seekers present on their territory a certain minimum of rights in these fields irrespective of what they decide to grant their own nationals? To what extent is the immigration status of asylum seekers relevant for the existence and scope of state obligations in this regard?

The previous chapters have shown that this issue has been dealt with most explicitly and extensively under the ECHR. This is a somewhat unexpected conclusion, as the ECHR is concerned mainly with civil and political rights. Nevertheless, the ECtHR held in as early as 1979 that many civil and political rights have implications of a social or economic nature. Recent case law of the ECtHR shows a development towards a more substantive protection of socioeconomic interests under the ECHR.

In chapter eleven it has been argued that the Court's case law on Article 3 of the ECHR contains the most far-reaching obligations for states as regards the reception of asylum seekers as compared to its case law on Articles 2 and 8 of the ECHR. The main rule, repeated by the Court in different cases, is that Article 3 of the ECHR does not contain any general obligation for the state to provide for social benefits, medical assistance, housing, etc. Nevertheless, under certain circumstances, Article 3 of the ECHR may be violated owing to poor socioeconomic conditions. In chapter eleven it has been argued that the Court's approach under Article 3 of the ECHR, as exemplified in *MSS v Belgium and Greece*, as well as in earlier and subsequent case law, should be interpreted as consisting of two distinguishable steps: the Court generally examines whether the treatment complained of reaches the minimum level of severity and whether the state can be held responsible for this treatment. In chapter eleven it was put forward that most arguments provided by the Court in its case law can be related to one of these two aspects. States are as a rule responsible for the living conditions of persons who are deprived of their freedom. Outside the context of detention, relevant factors for accepting state responsibility for poor living conditions or situations of general poverty found in the Court's case law are the vulnerability of the person concerned, caused by utter dependency on the state for decent living conditions, and the fact that the state displays deliberate and culpable behaviour, for example by not observing domestic legal obligations to provide certain benefits. In the *MSS* case, the Court identified asylum seekers as a vulnerable category of persons. This is hence a very relevant factor for accepting state responsibility for asylum seekers' living conditions. However, both in the context of detention and in the context outside detention, the responsibility of the state can be mitigated by the behaviour of the person concerned.

The adoption of Directive 2003/9 has therefore an important consequence under Article 3 of the ECHR. Since the coming into force of this directive, EU Member States have a domestic legal obligation to provide social benefits to (some categories of) asylum seekers. If a state deliberately does not comply with this obligation, it can be held responsible under Article 3 of the ECHR for the living conditions of those asylum seekers. Arguably, even if no domestic legal obligation exists to provide asylum seekers with reception benefits, the general identification of asylum seekers as a vulnerable category of persons in *MSS* implies that the state can be held responsible for their living conditions. However, some kind of deliberate or culpable state act seems to be required by the Court for accepting state responsibility; mere unavailability of resources does not seem to be enough.

As regards the minimum level of severity under Article 3 of the ECHR for poor living conditions, in chapter eleven a distinction was detected in the Court's case law between living conditions in detention and living conditions outside detention. Outside detention, the relevant test for deciding whether the minimum level of severity has been reached is whether the person concerned is able to cater for his most basic needs and whether there is prospect of any improvement of the situation within a reasonable timeframe. The Court identified accommodation, food and sanitary conditions as the most basic needs. If a person is not able to effectively cater for these needs and there is no prospect of improvement within a reasonable timeframe, the minimum level of severity has been reached. For persons who are deprived of their liberty, the Court's approach is stricter. It takes into account the cumulative effect of detention conditions. Relevant factors are inter alia: the existence of sufficient and adequate living space; the provision of sanitary products (even toilet paper), adequate food, clean bed linen, medical care and necessary medical aids, such as glasses or dentures; the presence of a radio or TV; the temperature in the cell, etc. Especially as regards medical care, the authorities are under a number of important and detailed obligations. They should ensure that diagnoses and care are prompt and accurate and that a comprehensive record is kept of asylum seekers' state of health. Treatment should not just be aimed at addressing symptoms of a disease, but should be aimed at curing or preventing aggravation. In addition, subjecting persons to poor conditions of detention can already reach the minimum level of severity if it only lasts for a couple of hours or days.

In chapter eleven, it has been submitted that even where asylum seekers are not in fact deprived of their liberty and held in closed detention centres, the accommodation in asylum seekers reception centres might be relevantly comparable to a stay in a closed detention centre. Since state authorities often decide on asylum seekers' place of living and since the degree of control applied to asylum seekers living in asylum seekers reception centres makes leaving such centres a rather theoretical possibility, it has been argued that there are sound reasons to also apply the framework of review under Article 3 of the ECHR for detention conditions to the living conditions in asylum seekers reception centres.

Accordingly, Article 3 of the ECHR, as interpreted in the case law of the Court, implies important obligations for the state. If states, in defiance of (domestic) legal obligations, do not provide some kind of support to asylum seekers who are unable to cater for their most basic needs for a significant period of time, they act in violation of Article 3 of the ECHR. Arguably, even if states are not required under domestic law to provide some benefits to asylum seekers, they can be held responsible for their inability to cater for their most basic needs if this is caused by other kinds of deliberate or intentional acts. The special status of asylum seekers is very relevant in this regard, as an important factor in accepting state responsibility is the court's identification of asylum seekers as a vulnerable group. In addition, even if the state does provide reception benefits to asylum seekers, Article 3 of the ECHR may be of relevance. If the state decides to accommodate asylum seekers in accommodation centres and decides to subject asylum seekers to a significant amount of state control, their living conditions should meet strict standards in order to comply with Article 3 of the ECHR.

If states decide to provide asylum seekers with housing in kind, as a (partial) substitute for financial social security benefits, the withdrawal of entitlement to this housing or expulsion from this housing must meet the standards of the right to respect for one's home, as laid down in Article 8 of the ECHR. In chapter eleven it has been shown that the most important safeguard in this respect is a procedural one; asylum seekers must have the possibility to have the proportionality of the expulsion reviewed by an independent tribunal. Further, if asylum seekers are entitled to reception benefits as of right, these benefits fall under the scope of the right to protection of property, as laid down in Article 1 of the First Protocol to the ECHR. This means that a change in or withdrawal of the relevant rules must meet the fair balance test as developed by the Court under this provision.

This part of the book has also paid attention to the ICESCR. This seems at first sight the most relevant source when searching for possible state obligations as regards socioeconomic rights of asylum seekers. As opposed to the ECHR, the ICESCR 'directly' guarantees social and economic rights, such as the right to an adequate standard of living and the right to the enjoyment of the highest attainable standard of health, as a result of which the additional hurdle of establishing state responsibility for poor socioeconomic conditions does not need to be taken under the ICESCR. On the other hand, the ICESCR suffers from the assumption that it does not impose binding legal obligations upon states, but merely makes declarations of aspiration or goals to be achieved. This is mainly caused by the obligation laid down in Article 2 of the ICESCR of realizing the rights laid down in the ICESCR progressively to the maximum of available resources. In chapter ten it has been argued that, owing to different developments, it is no longer tenable to hold that the nature of the rights laid down in the ICESCR is inherently different from the nature of the rights laid down in the ECHR (or ICCPR). More importantly however, the argument in chapter ten was that the identification of possible state obligations for the reception of asylum seekers in the EU is not subject to the conditions laid down in Article 2 of the ICESCR, but to the conditions laid down in the general limitations clause of Article 4 of the ICESCR. Under Article 2 of the ICESCR, states are required to take steps 'to the maximum of their available resources'. This implies that if certain rights cannot be provided by the state due to resource scarcity, the state does not violate the ICESCR. In other words, a resource-motivated failure to achieve the full realization of a certain right, or a resource-motivated reduction in the level of attainment of a certain right, cannot be seen as a 'limitation' of the right in question, as there is no obligation for the state to achieve the full realization if this is not possible owing to resource scarcity. The curtailment and introduction of certain rights of asylum seekers as regards their reception is, however, generally motivated by the EU Member States on grounds explicitly *not* related to scarcity of resources. Such measures are generally justified by reasons related to immigration control. In order to examine whether, and to what extent, state obligations as regards the reception of asylum seekers stem from the ICESCR, the most important question is therefore whether the rights laid down in the ICESCR may be limited on the basis of reasons related to immigration control. As a result, the examination to be made under the ICESCR is very similar to the examination to be made under the ECHR.

Owing to the margin of appreciation allowed for states and to the general and broad wording of the limitation clause, chapter ten has put forward the argument that states have in fact considerable latitude in imposing restrictions based on immigration control of the rights laid down in the ICESCR. However, the requirements that the limitation must be compatible with the nature of the right and that the limitation must be proportional may set some limits on this freedom of manoeuvre. As has been discussed in chapter ten, it seems difficult for states to argue that a complete denial of state support to destitute asylum seekers, as a result of which they are not able to dispose of (some kind of) food, clothing or housing, the complete denial of (reimbursement for) health care for destitute asylum seekers or an absolute ban on access to the labour market during the entire asylum procedure is compatible with the nature of the right to an adequate standard of living, the right to the enjoyment of the highest attainable standard of health or the right to work, respectively. Also, it seems hard to uphold the claim that such measures are proportional to the aim of immigration control. If asylum seekers are able to dispose of some kind of food, clothing, housing and health care and have some kind of access to the labour market, states are, in my view, generally able to argue convincingly that limitations that are nevertheless imposed on asylum seekers in these fields meet the conditions laid down in Article 4 of the ICESCR. In view of the margin of discretion left to the state in this regard, this implies that such limitations are permitted under the ICESCR.

As compared to the ECHR, the ICESCR therefore contains more far-reaching obligations for the state as regards the admittance of asylum seekers to their labour markets. Owing to the explicit acknowledgement of the right to work in the ICESCR, which includes the right of everyone to the opportunity to gain his living, a complete denial of access to employment for a category of persons that hardly has the possibility to leave the territory seems not to be compatible with the nature of this right. As regards possible obligations for the state to provide for adequate living conditions of asylum seekers, the ICESCR is not wider in scope than the ECHR. The right to an adequate standard of living laid down in the ICESCR refers to adequate food, clothing and housing, which resembles the identification of the 'most basic needs' by the ECtHR under Article 3 of the ECHR.[1] As regards the question when living conditions are so poor

[1] The ECtHR refers to food, housing and sanitary conditions as a person's most basic needs, see ch 11.

that they reach the minimum level of severity of Article 3 of the ECHR, the ECtHR seems to distinguish between the living conditions of persons in detention and the living conditions of persons outside the context of detention. The living conditions of persons in detention have to meet stricter standards. Such an approach has not (yet) been adopted under the ICESCR.[2] It would, however, be possible to make the same distinction with regard to the assessment whether a person's living standard is 'adequate' in the sense of Article 11 of the ICESCR.

Chapter nine has shown that a number of additional obligations for the state as regards the social security and employment of asylum seekers stem from the Refugee Convention. The general standard of treatment laid down in the Refugee Convention is that of 'aliens generally'. This means that, as a minimum, asylum seekers should be entitled to the same treatment as is applied to aliens who do not find themselves in a preferential position. Consequently, exclusion of asylum seekers from access to the labour market or from access to social security benefits cannot be based on the sole ground of being an asylum seeker. Such an exclusion is only possible on the basis of criteria that apply to all aliens generally. Another important obligation for states which stems from the Refugee Convention is that they may no longer subject asylum seekers to restrictive measures imposed on aliens or the employment of aliens for the protection of the national labour market if they have completed three years' residence in the country, if they have a spouse possessing the nationality of the country of residence or if they have children possessing the nationality of the country of residence. In chapter nine it has been argued that restrictive measures specifically imposed on asylum seekers who fulfil one of these conditions for reasons of general immigration policy (eg to discourage the filing of unfounded claims and to facilitate the expulsion of rejected asylum seekers) are not in conformity with this obligation. This means that states should grant asylum seekers unconditional access to their labour markets if they have resided for three years on their territory or if they have a spouse or one or more children possessing the nationality of the country of residence. As residence is a factual condition, not dependent on it being lawful, asylum seekers might be able to fulfil this condition. In addition, after three years' residence on the territory, states are also obligated under the Refugee Convention to exempt asylum seekers from legislative reciprocity.

Finally, asylum seekers who are a national of one of the contracting parties to the European Social Charter fall under the scope of Article 18 of

[2] As regards the treatment of persons in detention, the counterpart to the ICESCR, the ICCPR does, however, contain an explicit provision. Article 10(1) of the ICCPR reads: 'All persons deprived of their liberty shall be treated with humanity and with respect for the inherent dignity of the human person'.

the ESC on the right to engage in a gainful occupation. In chapter twelve it has been argued that this condition qualifies as being based on 'legislative reciprocity', as a result of which the Refugee Convention implies that asylum seekers who have resided three years on the territory should be exempted from this condition. Even though Article 18 of the ESC does not provide these asylum seekers with much substantive protection, it does set some limits on the rather large freedom of manoeuvre for states as regards the access to their labour markets. It provides that the rules on access to employment should be applied in a spirit of liberality, which means that it must be possible to make exceptions to the rules. In addition, it provides that the procedural rules should be simplified and the substantive rules should be liberalized. This 'dynamic' obligation means that states are subject to a continual obligation to improve up to a certain level. Arguably, this provision entails the obligation to work towards the abolishment of the possibility to deny access to the labour market throughout the entire asylum procedure for asylum seekers possessing the nationality of a contracting party to the ESC (or who have resided on the territory for at least three years). As has been argued above, such a complete denial seems to be in violation of the ICESCR as well. The added value of the ESC in this respect is therefore rather marginal.

In short, both the ECHR and the ICESCR impose obligations on states to ensure that asylum seekers are not left without food, housing, clothing and sanitary facilities for a significant period of time. To do so would only violate Article 3 of the ECHR if this situation can be attributed to some kind of deliberate and culpable behaviour of the state, for example by not observing (domestic) legal obligations in this regard. Likewise, it would only violate the ICESCR if it cannot be related to resource scarcity. Arguably, if states decide to accommodate asylum seekers in accommodation centres and to subject asylum seekers to a significant amount of state control, eg by making entitlement to benefits subject to actual presence in the accommodation centre and imposing obligations to report frequently at the accommodation centres, they are as a rule responsible under Article 3 of the ECHR to provide them with adequate living conditions, which have to meet the strict and detailed standards laid down in the ECtHR's case law on detention conditions.

While a complete denial of access to the labour market seems to be in violation of the right to work laid down in the ICESCR, states are not required to provide asylum seekers with unlimited and unconditional access to their labour markets under international law. It follows from the Refugee Convention, however, that an important exception should be made in this respect for asylum seekers with strong community ties, ie who have completed three years' residence in the country or who have a spouse or one or more children possessing the nationality of the country of residence. For asylum seekers who possess the nationality of one of the contracting parties to the ESC, the conditions for accessing the labour market should be applied in a spirit of liberality. The Refugee Convention implies that asylum seekers who have resided on the territory for at least three years should be exempted from this condition of reciprocity.

For the existence of most of these state obligations, the special status of being an asylum seeker is decisive. It is because of their potential refugeehood that they fall under the personal scope of the Refugee Convention and it is because of the general identification of all asylum seekers as forming part of a particular vulnerable group that the state bears a special responsibility under Article 3 of the ECHR. In addition, it seems to be easier for states to argue that restrictive measures in the socioeconomic sphere are compatible with the nature of the rights laid down in the ICESCR and are proportional to the aim of immigration control if the person concerned has another state to turn to.

While international law does not oblige states to grant all asylum seekers equality of treatment with their nationals in the field of social security and employment (see Part II), it does oblige states to provide some benefits to asylum seekers in these fields, irrespective of what they grant their own nationals. While international law therefore does not require full separation between the sovereign sphere of immigration control and the sphere of material rights, it does not allow a complete convergence, either.

14

Conclusions

14.1 INTRODUCTION

On 1 January 1954 Van Heuven Goedhart, the first United Nations High Commissioner for Refugees, said:

> The solutions of the refugee problem are not really complicated. Once a man has been driven by persecution, or fear of persecution, to leave his country of nationality and to take refuge in some other country he has a few essential demands to make. They are:
>
> — Firstly, material conditions of reception which make it possible for him to be fed, clothed and sheltered from the time of his arrival until the time when a permanent solution can be found for his difficulties;
> — secondly, the regularisation of his legal status so that he may enjoy the basic rights and freedoms in his country of asylum;
> — thirdly, the right and opportunity to work either in the country which has given him asylum or resettlement, and
> — fourthly, naturalization in the country which finally accepts him.[1]

This study has focused on the protection of the first three of these demands with regard to asylum seekers, ie persons who might qualify as refugees. It shows that the protection of these 'essential demands' for this category of potential refugees is nowadays no longer self-evident. As from the early-1990s, the protection of these demands has come under more and more pressure in Europe. When the number of spontaneously arriving asylum seekers in Europe increased, states reacted by limiting or withdrawing asylum seekers' material conditions of reception, basic social security rights and rights to work. Consequently, the question whether asylum seekers can derive entitlement to the protection of these essential demands from international law became more manifest.

[1] Speech by Dr Gerrit Jan van Heuven Goedhart, United Nations High Commissioner for Refugees, at the fourteenth session of the United Nations Economic and Social Council (ECOSOC), 1 January 1954, available at: www.unhcr.org/3ae68fb610.html.

In 2003 an important milestone was reached with regard to the reception of asylum seekers in the European Union with the adoption of Directive 2003/9. A recast of this directive was adopted in 2013: Directive 2013/33. These Directives contain a number of (minimum) obligations for EU Member States with regard to the material conditions of reception and access to the labour market for asylum seekers. According to their Treaty basis and preambles, these Directives should be in accordance with the Refugee Convention and other relevant treaties, which make international law an important and direct standard of review.

As has been indicated in the introduction, the purpose of this study was to examine which state obligations for EU Member States stem from 'relevant treaties' of international refugee law, international social security law and international human rights law on asylum seekers' access to social security and the labour market and how these obligations relate to the standards laid down in the EU Reception Conditions Directives. It has been argued in this study that even though fields of general socioeconomic policy are involved, it is possible to identify a number of binding obligations for states as regards access to their social security systems and labour markets. However, it has also been argued that the provision and curtailment of asylum seekers' rights to social security benefits and employment is primarily used as an instrument of immigration control in the EU, which is expressly allowed under the EU Reception Conditions Directives. Consequently, a relevant point in order to answer the main question of this book is to what extent this instrumental use of social law is allowed by international law. Should the sphere of immigration control be separated from the sphere of aliens' material rights? Or is some kind of convergence of both spheres allowed by international law? If so, to what extent? Does international law limit the freedom of states in this regard? This final chapter will reflect upon and summarize the answers to these questions.

Section 14.2 will reiterate a number of important aspects of the standards on social security and employment laid down in the EU Reception Conditions Directives as found in Part I of this book. Particularly, as this is relevant for an evaluation under international law, this section will discuss on different levels the degree of convergence between the sphere of immigration control and the sphere of material rights. Section 14.3 will analyse the obligations for states as regards asylum seekers' access to social security and employment that stem from international law as elucidated in parts two and three. Thus far, a distinction has been made in this book between obligations to grant equal treatment and obligations to grant other kinds of minimum protection. The conclusions on these two issues can be found in chapters seven and thirteen, respectively. Section 14.3 will discuss these different obligations together and will list a number of common and general factors relevant for the existence and scope of these obligations. Finally, section 14.4 will assess the standards laid down in the EU Reception Conditions Directives in relation to the obligations stemming from international law.

14.2 RECEPTION OF ASYLUM SEEKERS IN THE EUROPEAN UNION

14.2.1 Convergence from the Outset and in External Appearance

The need to harmonize the standards on the reception of asylum seekers in EU Member States arose in the 1990s in the context of an increasing number of asylum seekers arriving in the European Union. The European Commission urged Member States to harmonize their reception conditions for asylum seekers in order to prevent 'secondary movements' of asylum seekers, ie movements towards the Member State with the most generous conditions. In addition, the Commission noted that it is difficult to expel rejected asylum seekers who have become, owing to long asylum procedures, socially and economically integrated in the host state. Directive 2003/9 was eventually adopted in 2003 on the basis of title IV of the Treaty establishing the European Community, which dealt with visas, asylum, immigration and other policies related to the free movement of persons. The directive became one of the instruments of the Common European Asylum System, as indicated by the European Council during its meeting in Tampere in 1999. Hence, as from the outset and in external appearance, Directive 2003/9 is an instrument of EU asylum policy. The same is true for Directive 2013/33, which is adopted on the basis of title V of the Treaty on the Functioning of the European Union. The spheres of immigration or asylum policy and material rights of asylum seekers are, therefore, not separated in the European Union. To the contrary, they are integrated into one system and have the same legal basis.

14.2.2 Convergence in Official Discourse

Existing research on the reception of asylum seekers had already indicated that the rights of asylum seekers as regards social security and employment were curtailed in many European countries in order to prevent this from becoming a major pull factor for asylum seekers and in order to prevent asylum seekers' integration into the host society.[2] The examination of the negotiation process leading to the adoption of the EU Reception Conditions Directives in chapter two revealed that the standards laid down in these Directives were also for a large part based on and justified

[2] See the literature mentioned in n 6 of ch 1.

by reasons related to immigration control. This is in particular reflected in the difficult negotiations about Directive 2013/33 and the Council's unwillingness to adopt the much higher standards as were initially proposed by the Commission. Eventually, the Commission had to present a modified proposal with the explicit aim of granting Member States more latitude and better ensuring that Member States have the tools to address cases where reception rules are abused and/or become pull factors.

The state interest of exercising immigration control can point in different directions as regards the reception of asylum seekers. It can be used as a reason to *deny* (certain categories of) asylum seekers any kind of social assistance benefits in order to prevent the existence of possible pull factors for asylum seekers. It can also be used as a reason to justify the *provision of a certain kind* of assistance to asylum seekers in order to exercise control over them and facilitate expulsion if their asylum claims are rejected. An examination of the negotiation process of the EU Reception Conditions Directives shows that on the initiative of the Council, both the wider possibility to deny reception benefits and the possibility to subject asylum seekers to a certain amount of state control have been included in the Directives.

Hence, official discourse on the reception of asylum seekers in the EU is not primarily about reserving scarce resources for members of the community. The reduction of asylum seekers' rights is not only or even primarily based on the absence of community membership or, in other words, on their (precarious) immigration status. Instead, reduction and provision of rights to asylum seekers as regards social security and employment is used as a means of preventing the arrival of more asylum seekers, as a means of inciting asylum seekers to leave and as a means of facilitating the expulsion of rejected asylum seekers. This indicates a rather strong convergence of the sphere of immigration control with the sphere of asylum seekers' material rights.

14.2.3 Convergence in Standards Ultimately Adopted

The standards laid down in the EU Reception Conditions Directives on social security and employment display an intertwining with the state's immigration power with regard to the possibilities to reduce or withdraw reception benefits on the basis of the behaviour of the asylum seeker in the asylum procedure. In addition, the Directives do not require Member States to grant asylum seekers equality of treatment with nationals in these fields. Directive 2013/33 even explicitly allows Member States to grant asylum seekers less favourable treatment compared to nationals with regard to the level of material reception benefits. In addition, both Directives leave significant room for Member States to exercise control over asylum seekers and to deny asylum seekers access to the labour market. The Directives therefore do not require separating the sphere of immigration control entirely from the sphere of asylum seekers' material rights.

On the other hand, the Directives limit the freedom of manoeuvre of states in this regard. As the Directives contain a limitative list of grounds for reduction or withdrawal of reception benefits, states are no longer free to deny assistance to categories of asylum seekers of their own choosing. Moreover, even if withdrawal of reception benefits is allowed by the Directives, the Directives require Member States to justify this denial on individual grounds and to show that the denial is proportionate. Directive 2013/33 even obligates Member States to ensure a dignified standard of living for applicants in case of reduction or withdrawal of reception benefits. In addition, the Directives oblige Member States to ensure that 'material reception conditions' and necessary health care are available for asylum seekers who fall under the personal scope. 'Material reception conditions' are defined as conditions that include housing, food, clothing and a daily expenses allowance. Consequently, Member States should ensure that these basic needs of asylum seekers are catered for; eg, they cannot choose to provide asylum seekers who fall under the personal scope of the Directives with only health care and food, and not with housing.

In short, the Directives permit using the reception of asylum seekers as an instrument of immigration control, but curtail the state's freedom of manoeuvre in this regard in a number of ways.

14.3 EVALUATION OF THE STATE OBLIGATIONS STEMMING FROM INTERNATIONAL LAW

14.3.1 Introduction

Before the main question of this study will be answered in section 14.4, the results of the examination into state obligations stemming from international law will be analysed and evaluated here. Instead of repeating and summarizing the sub-conclusions to Part II and Part III, this section will take a different approach. It will list a number of relevant factors for the existence and scope of state obligations in the field of social security and employment that have been identified in this study. In this way, general tendencies can be identified and the implications of the findings outside the specific scope of this study may come to the fore.

A more detailed discussion of the various state obligations found in international law and an assessment of the standards laid down in the EU Reception Conditions Directives as to their conformity with these obligations will be provided in section 14.4.

14.3.2 Separation vs Convergence

As has been indicated in chapter one, Bosniak has convincingly argued that normative debates on the rights of aliens centre on a jurisdictional question: How far does sovereignty reach before it must give way to equality? Put differently: Which norms are supposed to govern: exclusionary norms of border control or more inclusive norms of equal human rights? If both sets of norms apply, how should they be reconciled?

Indeed, this book has shown that also in international law on the rights of aliens, jurisdictional disputes on the proper location of the state's sovereign immigration power are paramount. The extent to which the state's immigration power may converge with the material rights of aliens is inherently in a state of flux and is subject to opposite forces. As a result, questions about the specific meaning of terms like 'lawfully in the territory' or 'discrimination on the ground of nationality' are difficult to answer and lead to technical analyses and opposite views. After all, these questions are at the heart of the jurisdictional dispute.

Nevertheless, it has been shown that it is often possible to identify answers in international law to this jurisdictional question. It has been argued that international law does not require states to completely separate the field of immigration control and the field of social security and employment rights. International law does not require states to provide asylum seekers with equal access to their labour markets with their nationals. Asylum seekers' entitlement to equal treatment with nationals as regards social security is qualified. It depends on the fulfilment of different qualifying conditions as regards legal status and community ties.

The spheres of border control and social security under international law can be represented in diagram form as follows:

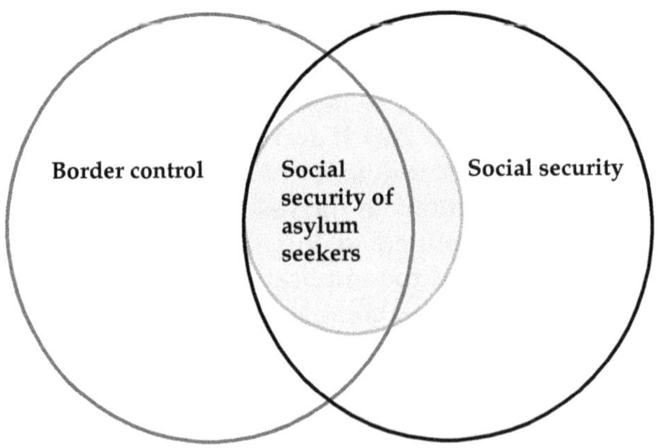

Figure 14.1: Separation and convergence under international law

This figure shows that, in my view, the sphere of immigration control and the sphere of social security are distinct but overlapping spheres under international law. As regards social security rights, states are not allowed to exclude all aliens on the basis of their sovereign immigration power. By identifying the relevant qualifying conditions for entitlement to equal treatment with nationals, international law has to a certain extent established how far the sovereign immigration power may reach before it must give way to equality. However, the proper boundaries and the extent of overlap between the different spheres are continuously challenged and therefore remain subject to change. The solutions found in international law for the jurisdictional dispute therefore have an inherently tentative character.

The following subsections will list a number of relevant factors for the existence and scope of state obligations in the field of social security and employment. Some of these factors have implications for the extent of the convergence that is allowed under international law between the state's immigration power and the material rights of asylum seekers. For example, the intensity of the convergence between the state's immigration power and the field of social security allowed for by international law may change over time. With the lapse of time, obligations of the state under international law towards asylum seekers present on their territory tend to move more towards sphere separation (see further section 14.3.7 below). While due to the tension between the sphere of immigration control and the sphere of equal human rights, the character of the specific state obligations identified in this study is inherently tentative, the factors discussed in the following subsections may have a more durable nature.

14.3.3 Relevance of the Right at Stake

This study has focused on two important rights for asylum seekers: social security and access to the labour market. It has been seen that the protection of these rights for asylum seekers differs significantly under international law. Whereas international law does provide certain categories of asylum seekers with a right to equal treatment with nationals as regards social security; it does not require states to grant any category of asylum seekers the same access to their labour markets as nationals. In addition, eligibility for certain rights under international law is dependent on whether the person concerned is allowed to work in the territory or not. As regards the regulation of access to their labour markets, states therefore have more discretion under international law than as regards the regulation of access to their social security systems. Indeed, the freedom of states to regulate access to their labour markets shows a close resemblance to the freedom of states to regulate access to their territory. Hence, the entitlement to equal treatment and, connected to that, the legitimate influence of the border on the material rights of asylum seekers, is dependent on the specific material right at stake.

On the other hand, this study demonstrates that the existence and scope of state obligations as regards asylum seekers' access to social security and employment is *not* entirely dependent on the specific human right at stake, ie whether it concerns classical human rights or civil liberties or whether is concerns social or economic human rights. Especially in the last decade, a development has taken place in the interpretations of classical human rights, such as the right to life or the right to be free from inhuman or degrading treatment, involving more and more obligations for the state of a socioeconomic nature. This study shows that for the identification of such state obligations stemming from civil and political rights, vague and general norms are being interpreted and in defining the scope of such obligations, attention is being paid to availability of resources. This bears a close resemblance to the state obligations laid down in social and economic human rights conventions. In this study it has been argued, therefore, that it is no longer tenable to hold that economic and social human rights are inherently of a different nature from civil and political rights and that economic and social rights by their very nature do not contain clear legal obligations for states. Consequently, this study underlines the indivisibility of human rights.

14.3.4 Relevance of Permitted Entry

It has been submitted in this book that in order to be eligible for certain rights, especially the right to equal treatment with nationals in the field of social assistance, it is required to be, at least, 'lawfully in' the territory of the host state. While the Refugee Convention grants this right only to refugees who are 'lawfully staying' in the territory of the host state, a condition that asylum seekers generally cannot meet, the European Convention on Social and Medical Assistance and the European Social Charter grant the right to equal treatment with nationals to asylum seekers 'lawfully present' in the territory. In addition, it can be argued that being lawfully in the territory is also a (minimum) condition for being in a relevantly comparable situation with nationals as regards social security, as required under Article 14 of the ECHR. In chapter four, it has been argued that the most persuasive interpretation of the term 'lawfully in the territory' in the Refugee Convention entails that asylum seekers can only be lawfully in the territory if they have *entered* the country lawfully, ie if they have reported themselves or are apprehended at the border and if they have explicitly been allowed to physically access the territory. Such asylum seekers continue to be lawfully in the territory if they do not violate any requirement imposed on them as a condition for entry. The status of asylum seekers who have entered the country without permission of the authorities only becomes 'regularized' within the meaning of the Refugee Convention once they are explicitly allowed to take up residence in the territory. Asylum seekers who have entered the territory without permission are therefore in general not 'lawfully in the territory' within the meaning of the Refugee Convention pending the asylum procedure, even though they might be allowed to await the outcome of this procedure on the territory. It has been argued in chapter four that this interpretation best fits the text, context and object and purpose of the Refugee Convention. In addition, chapter four has shown that a distinction with regard to asylum seekers' material rights on the basis of whether or not they have applied for asylum at the border and have thereupon been admitted to the territory can also be found in domestic law, for example in the United States and in the United Kingdom.

Owing to the *lex specialis* nature of the Refugee Convention as regards refugees' material rights and owing to explicit references in the other legal instruments to the Refugee Convention, it was contended in chapters five and six that the interpretation of the phrase 'lawfully in the territory' in the context of the Refugee Convention should also apply to such phrases in other international legal instruments. Consequently, permitted entry into the territory of the host state is relevant for entitlement to equal treatment with nationals in the field of social assistance. Asylum seekers who have entered the territory without the authorities' permission are generally not entitled to equal treatment with nationals as regards social assistance pending the determination of their asylum claim. This study shows, however, that international law does contain other safeguards for the protection of their basic subsistence needs.

14.3.5 Relevance of Being an Asylum Seeker

It is important to note here that for the existence of most state obligations identified in this book the special status of asylum seekers (as potential refugees) is decisive. This is true for state obligations to accord non-nationals the same treatment as nationals as regards social security benefits laid down in international social security law. Most of these obligations are subjected to reciprocity, but apply as well, on the basis of additional protocols, to refugees in the sense of the Refugee Convention (see chapter five). The ECtHR, when examining distinctions based on immigration status in the field of social benefits, also attaches importance to (potential) refugee status, as it argues that the immigration status of refugees is not subject to an element of choice. For (potential) refugees, therefore, it has been argued in chapter six that the ECtHR seems to require more 'weighty' reasons to justify unequal treatment with nationals based on their immigration status than for other categories of immigrants.

Not only is the obligation to grant certain categories of asylum seekers equality of treatment with nationals for a large part based on their potential refugee status but so too do the other state obligations identified in this study explicitly and, arguably, exclusively apply to asylum seekers. This is obvious for the state obligations stemming from the Refugee Convention. But again, the ECtHR also seems to find the special vulnerable status of asylum seekers decisive or at least particularly relevant for its finding in the case of *MSS v Belgium and Greece* that to leave an asylum seekers in a situation in which he is unable to cater for his most basic needs is a violation of Article 3 of the ECHR (see chapter eleven). Finally, as regards the rights laid down in the ICESCR, it has been argued in chapter ten that it is more difficult for states to argue that the complete denial of state support or the right to work to destitute asylum seekers fulfils the requirements of the covenant's general limitation clause than it is to argue that such a denial is in conformity with this clause as regards other categories of immigrants without a residence permit.

Most safeguards for asylum seekers found in this study are therefore not based on personhood alone. An important consequence of this finding is that the state obligations identified in this book do not necessarily apply to or do not necessarily have the same scope for other categories of (illegal) immigrants. It is not possible, therefore, to perceive the state obligations found in this study as general minimum norms as regards non-nationals' access to social security and employment.

14.3.6 Relevance of Availability of Resources

As has been noted above, for the evaluation of the EU Reception Conditions Directives under international law, the official *rationale* put forward by states for introducing certain standards in these Directives is important. Especially as regards the evaluation under international provisions not related to equal treatment, it has been seen to be relevant whether the policy on the reception of asylum seekers is justified on the basis of unavailability of resources or on the basis of immigration control. In general, official justifications given by the state are a relevant factor for examining compliance with international provisions on equal treatment and non-discrimination. Part II has shown, however, that provisions on equality of treatment between nationals and non-nationals in the field of social security often fit in what is known as the closed model of equal treatment provisions, as a result of which only very little or even no room exists for exceptions. As regards Article 14 of the ECHR, an 'open' provision on non-discrimination, the ECtHR has left little room for justifying unequal treatment based on nationality in the field of social security, but has held both resource scarcity and immigration control to be a legitimate aim for making distinctions. Hence, as regards the question whether asylum seekers are entitled to equal treatment with nationals as regards social security benefits, it is not relevant whether unequal treatment is based on unavailability of resources or on the state's sovereign immigration power.

This is different with regard to the question whether any (positive) state obligation to provide asylum seekers with social security benefits or access to the labour market stems from international law not devoted to equal treatment or non-discrimination. In chapter eleven it has been argued that for a positive obligation to arise in this regard from Article 3 of the ECHR, it has to be established whether the state can be held responsible for poor living conditions. The ECtHR seems to be of the opinion that states cannot in general be held responsible for poverty or for a lack of resources for dealing with naturally occurring phenomena. Hence, if states convincingly argue that denial of state support is due to the unavailability of resources, they might not be held responsible for poor living conditions under Article 3 of the ECHR. Likewise, with regard to the ICESCR, unavailability of resources is an important factor for the existence of (positive) state obligations. If states base a denial of state support on unavailability of resources, they do not have to meet the different requirements of the general limitation clause, and may still act in conformity with the ICESCR if they can show that they use all available resources to achieve the progressive realization of the right concerned (see chapter ten). To the contrary, if they explicitly do *not* refer to availability of resources, the denial of state support should meet the requirements of the covenant's general limitation clause, eg the limitation should be in conformity with the nature of the right concerned. Hence, as regards possible positive state obligations in the field of social and economic policy, states have a significant degree of discretion under international law in the case of unavailability of sufficient resources. Resource scarcity is therefore a relevant factor for the existence of positive obligations in this field.

14.3.7 Relevance of the Lapse of Time

A relevant factor for the existence and scope of state obligations stemming from international law as regards the reception of asylum seekers has been seen to be the lapse of time. In this study it has been argued that asylum seekers are entitled to equal treatment with nationals as regards social insurance benefits if they meet residence or ordinary residence requirements. Both conditions are of a factual nature. Meeting the residence test is primarily dependent on a certain lapse of time. It has been contended in chapters four and five that a person is a resident in a given territory if he dwells in the territory for a certain period of time, arguably three to six months. In order to be 'ordinarily resident' in a country, the establishment of durable ties between the person concerned and the host state should be shown. The passage of time is a relevant, albeit not decisive, factor in meeting this condition. Also in other aspects, the lapse of time has been seen to be a relevant factor for the existence and scope of state obligations. Chapters four and nine show that the Refugee Convention explicitly mentions the factual lapse of time as an eligibility condition for a number of important rights. Most relevantly, it prescribes that states may no longer subject asylum seekers to restrictive measures as regards access to wage-earning employment for the protection of the national labour market and to conditions based on legislative reciprocity if they have completed three years' residence in the country. It can even be argued that asylum seekers who have not yet received a final decision on their asylum application within three years after the lodging of their application should be considered to be eligible for the benefits laid down in the Refugee Convention for refugees 'lawfully in' and 'lawfully staying in' the territory. In addition, for a positive state obligation to arise under Article 3 of the ECHR in the socioeconomic sphere, the ECtHR generally pays attention to the duration of the ill-treatment and to the prospect of the situation improving within a reasonable timeframe (see chapter eleven). Hence, on different levels and with different consequences, the passage of time is a relevant factor for the existence and scope of state obligations to grant asylum seekers access to social security and employment.

14.3.8 Relevance of the Degree of Control Exercised over Asylum Seekers

A final factor identified in this study as being relevant for the scope of state obligations for asylum seekers' socioeconomic living conditions is the amount of control that asylum seekers are subjected to. In the context of Article 3 of the ECHR, this study has identified a different framework of review for living conditions in the context of detention than for living conditions in a context not related to detention or deprivation of freedom. Chapter eleven shows that the reason for a heightened scrutiny as regards detention conditions as brought forward by the ECtHR was that detainees are in a vulnerable position as they are entirely under the control of the authorities and have only limited contacts with the outside world. Consequently, as regards persons in detention, the Court has identified a number of detailed and far-reaching positive obligations. For example, states should ensure that detainees are entitled to enough living space, are eligible for medical aids such as glasses and dentures, are entitled to adequate food and toiletries and receive adequate and effective health care. Being subjected to poor living conditions for only a few hours or days can, under certain circumstances, already reach the threshold of seriousness in the context of detention. In the context outside detention, states should ensure that asylum seekers are able to meet their basic needs, such as accommodation, food and sanitary conditions, but the Court has not identified detailed obligations with regard to the quality of such facilities. In addition, if there is any prospect of improvement of living conditions within 'a reasonable timeframe', Article 3 of the ECHR will not be violated.

In chapter eleven, it has been argued that even where asylum seekers are not in fact deprived of their liberty and held in closed detention centres, the accommodation in asylum seekers reception centres may be relevantly comparable to a stay in a closed detention centre. Since state authorities often decide on the asylum seeker's place of living and since the high degree of control exercised over asylum seekers living in asylum seekers reception centres makes it virtually impossible to leave these centres, it has been submitted that there are sound reasons to apply the framework of review under Article 3 of the ECHR for detention conditions to the living conditions in asylum seekers reception centres as well.

This study has focused on the existence and scope of state obligations as regards social security and employment. It has therefore not examined to what extent states are allowed under international law to subject asylum seekers to a significant degree of control. However, it has identified an important consequence in the socioeconomic sphere of applying a large degree of control to asylum seekers. If states decide where asylum seekers should live, make eligibility for social benefits subject to actual residence in that specific place and impose on asylum seekers regular obligations to report there, it can be argued that these states have more far-reaching and more detailed obligations to ensure adequate living conditions under Article 3 of the ECHR than if they do not impose on asylum seekers such a large degree of control.

14.3.9 Concluding Remarks

The previous subsections have listed a number of general factors that have turned out to be of relevance for the existence and scope of state obligations under international law with regard to the access of asylum seekers to social security and employment. Some of these factors mainly influence the extent of convergence between the sphere of immigration control and the sphere of social security or employment rights allowed under international law (eg the lapse of time, permitted entry, being an asylum seeker, the specific material right at stake), whereas other factors primarily influence the existence and scope of state obligations in the socioeconomic sphere in general (eg availability of resources, degree of state control).

The relevance of the different factors identified in the previous subsections resembles the findings of Bosniak in her recent work on 'personhood rights' in the context of the US Constitution. She argues that even if rights are formally based on personhood, not all persons will necessarily receive full protection of these rights. This is caused by the fact that conceptions of personhood are often restrained as they are generally understood as requiring some kind of context to be fully actualized. Bosniak submits that there are a number of compelling reasons for requiring some kind of a context for personhood rights, a practical reason being that personhood rights can only be effectively protected if there is a sovereign body to enforce them. Personhood rights should therefore be located within the shelter of some form of collective peoplehood and/or in some specific physical place. Another reason is that personhood rights generally derive from a legal document that binds a specific political community, as a result of which such 'constitutional personhood' entails an inherently context-situated conception of personhood. The question then remains, however, when one is considered to be 'in the context'. Bosniak argues that 'being within the context' can be understood in legal-status terms, in territorial terms, or in situational terms (and argues that preference should be given to the latter). While personhood rights and human rights are distinct in a number of important ways, Bosniak submits that they nonetheless share a number of important characteristics, eg their concern with the protection of individuals from various forms of political and social harm. She assumes that the findings into the use of the concept of 'personhood' may offer insights which are also applicable to the theory on human rights, especially with regard to migrants.[3] This book shows indeed that while in international human rights law, rights generally accrue to 'everybody', one still has to be 'in the context' in legal-status terms (eg the relevance of permitted entry, being an asylum seeker), territorial terms and/or situational terms (eg the relevance of the degree of state control, the lapse of time) in order to receive full protection of these rights. In other words, sphere separation is only prescribed by international law for persons who are deemed to be 'in the context' in some kind of way.

[3] Bosniak 2011.

14.4 ASSESSMENT OF THE EU RECEPTION CONDITIONS DIRECTIVES IN RELATION TO INTERNATIONAL LAW

14.4.1 Introduction

The foregoing section has analysed the results of the examination into international law and has identified a number of general relevant factors for the existence and scope of state obligations under international law as regards asylum seekers' access to social security benefits and to the labour market. This final section will answer this study's main question by comparing the standards on social security and employment laid down in the EU Reception Conditions Directives with the obligations for states in these fields stemming from international law.

As has been noted in chapter one, the Treaty basis of the Directives explicitly states that the Directives must be in accordance with the Refugee Convention and other relevant treaties.[4] The preambles to the Directives refer to 'the full and inclusive application of the Geneva Convention relating to the Status of Refugees of 28 July 1951, as supplemented by the New York Protocol of 31 January 1967' and to Member States' consistency with 'obligations under instruments of international law to which they are party and which prohibit discrimination'.[5] As Battjes observed, by means of these statements, Member States very explicitly affirmed their anterior obligations under international law.[6] Accordingly, the standards laid down in the EU Reception Conditions Directives should be interpreted in accordance with the other relevant international treaties to which the Member States are party.[7] In addition, when a standard laid down in the EU Reception Conditions Directives conflicts with a standard stemming from international law, and conciliatory interpretation is not possible, the latter has precedence.[8] Conciliatory interpretation is often possible as regards the EU Reception Conditions Directives, as Member States have the power to introduce or maintain more favourable provisions for asylum seekers. In addition, most rules leave a large amount of discretion to the Member States.

Accordingly, this section will compare the standards on social security and access to employment laid down in the EU Reception Conditions Directives with the state obligations in these fields stemming from

[4] TFEU, Art 78, ex TEC, Art 63.

[5] The phrase 'which prohibit discrimination' is deleted in the preamble to Directive 2013/33.

[6] Battjes 2006, p 62.

[7] Ibid, p 76.

[8] See Art 30(2) of the Vienna Convention on the Law of Treaties: 'When a treaty specifies that it is subject to, or that it is not to be considered as incompatible with, an earlier or later treaty, the provisions of that other treaty prevail'. See also Battjes 2006, pp 603–04.

international law. It will examine whether the Directives allow states to act at variance with their obligations under international law and will suggest interpretations of and, if necessary, amendments to the Directives in order to assure their conformity with international law. In addition, the question will be answered whether international law contains state obligations as regards asylum seekers' rights to social security and employment that are not addressed by the EU Reception Conditions Directives.

In general, it should be noted here that, as mentioned above in section 14.2, EU Member States have not primarily referred to resource scarcity in order to justify or explain policy measures with regard to the reception of asylum seekers. To the contrary, it has been suggested in the literature that to set up separate welfare schemes for asylum seekers is actually more expensive than to provide them with access to general social security schemes (see section 10.3.3). As a result, an important factor limiting the existence and scope of state obligations in the socioeconomic field (see section 14.3.6 above) generally does not apply to the reception of asylum seekers in the European Union.

14.4.2 Access to Wage-earning Employment

As has been noted above, states have a rather large freedom of manoeuvre as regards the access of asylum seekers to the labour market under international law. The standards laid down in the Directives will therefore not easily fall short of the requirements resulting from international law. As regards access to the labour market, the Directives, however, leave the Member States a particularly large margin of discretion.

Article 11 of Directive 2003/9 allows Member States to withhold access to the labour market pending the entire asylum procedure if a decision in first instance has been delivered within a year. If a decision in first instance has not been taken within one year, Member States must grant asylum seekers access to the labour market after that year, but are allowed to impose all sorts of conditions. Article 15 of Directive 2013/33 is very similar to Article 11 of Directive 2003/9, but the relevant period is nine months instead of one year. In addition, it contains the safeguard that asylum seekers should have 'effective access' to the labour market, if no decision in first instance has been taken within nine months.

These two articles on employment are the only provisions laid down in the Directives that provide for an accretion of rights through the mere passage of time. These provisions therefore fit in well with the relevance of the lapse of time for the existence and scope of state obligations under international law. These provisions, however, do not take into account the only explicit provision of international law on asylum seekers' access to the labour market: Article 17 of the Refugee Convention. According to this article, restrictive measures for the protection of the national labour market may not be imposed on refugees who have completed three years of residence in the host state, or who have a spouse or one or more children possessing the nationality of the host state. In chapter nine it has been argued that this means that it is not permissible to impose restrictive measures on asylum seekers whose claim for refugee status has not yet been finally rejected in order to prevent a possible pull factor and/or integration into the host society if one of these conditions has been fulfilled. Where the Directives allow denying asylum seekers who fulfil one of these conditions access to the labour market and subjecting them to various restrictive conditions, the Directives allow Member States to breach their obligations under the Refugee Convention. More generally, the Directives' approval of a denial of access during the entire asylum procedure may not be in conformity with the ICESCR, as it will be difficult to argue that such a measure is in conformity with the nature of the covenant's right to work. Arguably, therefore, if the Directives should be fully in conformity with international law, the possibility to deny access throughout the entire asylum procedure should be deleted. This has in fact been proposed by the Commission in its proposal for the recast, but met with significant resistance on the part of the Member States. In addition, in order to be fully in conformity with the Refugee Convention, the Directives should stipulate that for asylum seekers who have completed three years of residence in the host state, or who have a spouse or one or more children possessing the nationality of the host state, the conditions for granting access to the labour market may no longer be aimed at the protection of the national labour market.

Chapter twelve has shown that the ESC contains a progressive obligation to liberalize the rules on access to the labour market and to simplify the procedures with regard to asylum seekers who are a national of one of the contracting parties to the ESC. Given the large number of ratifications of this instrument, a rather large number of asylum seekers in the EU actually possess the nationality of one of the contracting parties to the ESC. The rules on access to the labour market for these categories of asylum seekers are therefore subject to a continual obligation of improvement. The shortening of the period of one year to nine months in Directive 2013/33 and the safeguard to provide asylum seekers effective access to the labour market if no decision in first instance has been taken within nine months, can be seen as a (albeit rather marginal) contribution to meeting Member States' obligations under the ESC.

14.4.3 Material Benefits

Article 13(1) in conjunction with Article 2(j) of Directive 2003/9 and Article 17(1) in conjunction with Article 2(g) of Directive 2013/33 require Member States to provide asylum seekers with housing, food and clothing and a daily expenses allowance. This study shows that this is in line with and required by international law, as these 'basic needs' are also explicitly mentioned in the ICESCR and, with the exception of clothing, in the case law of the ECtHR on Article 3 of the ECHR. In addition, to deliberately and entirely deny such provisions to asylum seekers or to deliberately leave asylum seekers in a situation in which they cannot cater for these basic needs is, in general, in violation of these instruments.

As regards the level of these provisions, Article 13(2) of Directive 2003/9 requires states to ensure a standard of living adequate for the health of applicants and capable of ensuring their subsistence. Article 17(2) of Directive 2013/33 makes the obligation for Member States a bit stronger, by requiring them to ensure that material reception conditions provide an adequate standard of living for asylum seekers which guarantees their subsistence and protects their physical and mental health. In general, international law does not offer clear guidance for the interpretation of these rather general and vague norms. This study has, however, identified a number of circumstances under which international law does contain more detailed and clear standards on the quality of these benefits to be provided to asylum seekers.

In Part II, it has been argued that asylum seekers who are lawfully in the territory of the host state, ie asylum seekers who have explicit permission to enter the territory and who do not violate any requirements imposed on them as a condition for entry (see section 14.3.4 above), are entitled to equal treatment with nationals as regards social assistance schemes under international law. Most clearly, this is true for asylum seekers who are a national of one of the contracting parties to the ESC and for asylum seekers who are in the territory of one of the contracting parties to the ECSMA. In addition, chapter nine has shown that the Refugee Convention stipulates that refugees may no longer be subjected to conditions of legislative reciprocity after three years of residence in the host state. This means that all asylum seekers who have resided in a contracting party to the ESC for at least three years and who are lawfully present are entitled to equal treatment with nationals with regard to social and medical assistance under the ESC, whether they are a national of a contracting party to the ESC or not. Finally, it has been submitted in chapter six that the ECtHR seems to require 'very weighty reasons' for distinctions between nationals and asylum seekers in the field of social security. Case law of the ECtHR shows that in assessing whether such reasons exist, attention should be paid to the comparability of asylum seekers with nationals. A relevant analogous situation can be based on factual elements such as legal status, fulfilment of other statutory conditions of the benefit scheme concerned, contributions to the financing of the social security system etc. Arguments based on reciprocity are not deemed relevant in this regard by the ECtHR. There is, however, no case law yet on the distinctions between nationals and asylum seekers in social assistance schemes under Article 14 of the ECHR. In view of the more clear and detailed provisions on equal treatment with nationals in the field of social assistance in the ESC and the ECSMA and the frequent references to the ESC in the case law of the ECtHR, the ECtHR may adopt the same approach as under the ESC (without the condition of reciprocity). This would fit its previous case law on discrimination based on nationality in the field of social security.

In chapter four it has been argued that asylum seekers cannot 'stay lawfully in the territory' within the meaning of the Refugee Convention pending the asylum procedure. Asylum seekers are therefore not eligible for the benefits that accrue only to refugees lawfully staying in the territory of the host state under the Refugee Convention, such as the same treatment as is accorded to nationals with regard to social assistance and social insurance benefits. However, it has also been submitted that if states were to be allowed to extend the asylum procedure for a long period of time and, as such, deny refugees these important benefits, this would be contrary to the object and purpose of the Refugee Convention. Since the Refugee Convention attaches importance to a (factual) stay of at least three years in the territory for an accreditation of rights, it has been submitted in chapter four that this might indicate that after a (minimum) period of three years of residence in the territory, refugees should be considered to be de facto 'lawfully staying' there. Arguably, therefore, asylum seekers who have not yet received a final decision on their asylum application should after a considerable period of time, eg three years, be entitled to the same treatment as nationals with regard to social security, provided that the delay cannot be attributed to the asylum seeker.

For asylum seekers who are lawfully in the territory, therefore, equality with nationals should be the relevant standard of treatment as regards minimum subsistence benefits. Arguably, also asylum seekers who have not yet received a final decision on their asylum application within a reasonable period (eg three years) are entitled to equal treatment with nationals in this field. The level and form of social assistance benefits provided to nationals under general social assistance schemes should be the relevant benchmark for assessing the quality of the benefits provided to these sub-categories of asylum seekers. In its proposal for a recast of the Directive, the Commission initially laid down the safeguard that Member States should ensure that the total value of material reception conditions is equivalent to the amount of social assistance granted to nationals. However, this met significant resistance among Member States. Ultimately, Article 17(5) of Directive 2013/33 explicitly allows Member States to grant asylum seekers less favourable treatment compared with nationals with regard to the level of material reception benefits, in particular where material support is partially provided in kind or where the minimum subsistence level for nationals aims to ensure a standard of living higher than that prescribed under the Directive. It is submitted here that this provision is not in conformity with the requirements resulting from international law with regard to asylum seekers who are lawfully present on the territory, since this category of asylum seekers is entitled to the same level of social assistance benefits as nationals. Provision of support in kind is for this category of asylum seekers only in conformity with international law if in-kind provision is also possible with regard to (certain categories of) nationals under the general social assistance scheme.

To conclude, it can be convincingly argued that contracting states to the ECSMA, ESC and/or ECHR are obligated to grant asylum seekers who are lawfully present on their territory social assistance in the same way and on the same conditions as their own nationals. For asylum seekers who are not lawfully present, such a general obligation does arguably not exist under international law; however, it can be argued that if such asylum seekers do not receive a final decision on their asylum application within a certain considerable period of time, eg three years, an obligation to provide equal treatment with nationals arises as well on the basis of the Refugee Convention. The European Reception Conditions Directives only contain one general standard of treatment for all asylum seekers present in the territories of the Member States, which cannot be interpreted as obligating Member States to grant asylum seekers equal treatment with nationals. The Directives therefore explicitly leave room for Member States to act in violation with their obligations stemming from international law with regard to asylum seekers who are lawfully present on their territory. In order to alleviate the tension between the Directives and Member States' obligations under international law 'equality with nationals' could be included as the required level of treatment for asylum seekers who are lawfully present on the territory. In addition, the inclusion of a time limit after which all asylum seekers are eligible for equal treatment with nationals would, arguably, contribute to alleviating this tension.[9]

Further, as has been noted above, if Member States subject asylum seekers to a significant degree of state control as regards their place of living, which is allowed under the Directives, it can be argued that the general standard of treatment laid down in the Directives should be interpreted on the basis of the ECtHR's case law on detention conditions under Article 3 of the ECHR. This would mean that the living conditions of asylum seekers in accommodation centres should be subjected to a rigorous scrutiny. The (cumulative effect of) factors such as clean and hygienic conditions, availability of clean bed linen and adequate food, an acceptable temperature, enough living space, availability of a radio or TV and adequate sanitary conditions (including availability of toilet

[9] *Cf* the provision in the Belgian law on the reception of asylum seekers that stipulates that a Royal Decree can establish a time limit after which asylum seekers become eligible for general financial assistance, instead of assistance in kind (see n 108 in ch 10).

paper) should be taken into account. The general wording of the level of treatment to be accorded to asylum seekers laid down in Article 13(2) of Directive 2003/9 and Article 17(2) of Directive 2013/33, in combination with the existence of a number of additional safeguards for the provision of housing in kind in accommodation centres—including the explicit statement that accommodation centres should guarantee an adequate standard of living in Article 14(1)(b) of Directive 2003/9 and Article 18(1)(b) of Directive 2013/33—leaves room for such an interpretation.

14.4.4 Health Care

On health care, the Directives only contain one general and rather short provision. Article 15 of Directive 2003/9 determines that Member States should 'ensure that applicants receive the necessary health care which shall include, at least, emergency care and essential treatment of illness'. Article 19(1) of Directive 2013/33 adds 'serious mental disorders' to this obligation. Arguably, this obligation meets the minimum requirements under the ICESCR and under (the positive limb) of Article 2 of the ECHR (see chapters ten and eleven).

The wording 'necessary' and 'at least' indicate a rather large margin of discretion for the Member States. This study shows that international law provides some guidance as to the interpretation of this general norm. First of all, international social security law indicates that asylum seekers who are 'ordinarily resident' in the territory of the host state, should be able to access general health insurance schemes on the same footing as nationals. It has been argued in chapter five that 'ordinary residence' is a factual condition, requiring the establishment of strong social ties. Since legal status cannot be a decisive factor in meeting this test, asylum seekers may be able to establish an 'ordinary residence' in the host state under certain circumstances. Secondly, if medical assistance is subject to a needs test, asylum seekers who are lawfully in the territory are entitled to the same treatment as nationals under the ECSMA and the ESC (under the same conditions as social assistance, see further section 14.4.3 above). Under these different circumstances, equality with nationals should be the relevant standard of treatment. In that case, granting asylum seekers only 'emergency care and essential treatment of illness (and serious mental disorders)', which is allowed under the Directives, is not in conformity with international law.[10] If the Directives are supposed to be fully in line

[10] Note that the initial proposal of the Commission to lay down in the recast that asylum seekers with special needs should receive appropriate mental health care under the same conditions as nationals met with strong reservations in the Council and in the European Parliament.

with Member States' obligations under international law, they should at least stipulate that Member States should grant the categories of asylum seekers mentioned above the same access to health care insurance or medical assistance as their own nationals.

In addition, if asylum seekers live in conditions relevantly comparable to detention, the case law of the ECtHR indicates that states have far-reaching obligations to ensure their health. They should ensure that diagnoses and care are prompt and accurate and that a comprehensive record is kept of asylum seekers' state of health. Treatment should not just be aimed at addressing symptoms of a disease, but should be aimed at curing or preventing aggravation. Again, mere granting of emergency health care and essential treatment of illness would not seem to meet these requirements. Arguably, however, the specific reference to an adequate standard of living that should be guaranteed in accommodation centres according to Article 14(1)(b) of Directive 2003/9 and Article 18(1)(b) of Directive 2013/33 can be interpreted in conformity with these obligations under the ECHR if the degree of state control in such centres is relevantly similar to the degree of state control in detention centres.

14.4.5 Denial, Reduction and Withdrawal of Reception Benefits

The Directives allow Member States to reduce or withdraw reception benefits on a limited number of grounds. In addition, the Directives do not apply to asylum seekers who are not allowed to remain on the territory or once a final decision on the asylum application has been taken. How does this relate to international law? In this regard, it is important to note that this study has shown that to deliberately deny state support to destitute asylum seekers who are unable to meet their basic needs can be in violation of Article 3 of the ECHR and, arguably, of Article 11 of the ICESCR. Obviously, the possibility laid down in the Directives to withdraw reception benefits and to ask for a refund if an asylum seeker has concealed financial resources and had sufficient means to cover material benefits and health care is not in violation of these articles, as these asylum seekers are not destitute. But what about the other possibilities granted to states for reduction and withdrawal of reception benefits?

The main rule of Article 3 of the ECHR is that ill-treatment is prohibited, irrespective of the victim's behaviour. Chapter eleven has argued, however, that this rule is subject to exception. Case law of the ECtHR indicates that under certain circumstances behaviour of the person concerned can mitigate the responsibility of the state. Refusal of offered benefits in particular relieves the state of its obligations under Article 3. Arguably, therefore, to deny reception benefits to an asylum seeker who abandons the place of residence determined by the authorities, which can be taken as a refusal of offered benefits, does not violate Article 3 of the ECHR.

On the other hand, case law has made it clear that if it is a well-known fact that certain vulnerable individuals (ie asylum seekers) are homeless or live in very poor circumstances, the authorities may not use the inaction of the person concerned as an argument for circumventing their responsibility. In this light, asylum seekers' unwillingness or inability to comply with reporting duties or with requests to provide information, to appear for personal interviews concerning the asylum procedure or to claim asylum as soon as reasonably practicable after arrival, might not relieve states of their responsibility under Article 3 of the ECHR. Also the fact that an asylum seeker has already lodged an asylum claim in the same Member State does not appear to qualify as a relevant factor for mitigating the state's responsibility under Article 3 of the ECHR. Accordingly, the possibility laid down in the Directives to completely deny reception benefits on the basis of these grounds[11] seems to be at variance with Article 3 of the ECHR. Likewise, chapter ten has argued that a complete withdrawal of asylum seekers' eligibility for accommodation, food and clothing seems to violate the ICESCR, as it founders on the general limitation clause's requirement that limitations should be in conformity with the nature of the right.

To a certain extent, the complete withdrawal of reception benefits is not allowed under the Directives themselves, as they contain a number of safeguards that states have to meet in the case of reduction and withdrawal. States should take into account the special needs of vulnerable asylum seekers and the principle of proportionality.[12] Under Directive 2003/9, states should under all circumstances ensure access to emergency health care. Directive 2013/33 stipulates that states should also ensure a dignified standard of living for all applicants. This latter safeguard in particular makes conciliatory interpretation with Member States' international obligations possible.

For asylum seekers who are lawfully present and, consequently, entitled to equal treatment with nationals as regards social assistance benefits (see section 14.4.3 above), reduction and withdrawal of benefits is only possible on grounds that also apply to nationals under general social assistance schemes. Consequently, with regard to this category of asylum

[11] Under Directive 2013/33, Member States may only reduce (and not withdraw) material reception benefits if they can establish that the applicant, for no justifiable reason, has not lodged an application for international protection as soon as reasonably practicable after arrival in that Member State.

[12] In this way, the Directive is also in conformity with the procedural safeguards that apply on the basis of Art 8 of the ECHR in case of eviction from a home (see ch 11).

seekers, most possibilities allowed for under the Directives to reduce or withdraw reception benefits will probably be at variance with Member States' obligations resulting from international law, as they refer to circumstances closely connected to the status of being an asylum seeker and will therefore probably not apply to nationals.

As regards the personal scope of the Directives, it is important to note that the ECtHR has placed particular importance on the vulnerability of asylum seekers for assigning state responsibility to ensure asylum seekers' ability to meet their basic needs under Article 3 of the ECHR. The ECtHR has not provided a definition of the category of 'asylum seekers'. In chapter eleven it has been argued, however, that asylum seekers whose application has been rejected but whose expulsion has been suspended by law or forbidden by the ECtHR or a domestic court in order to await the outcome of an appeal should still be considered to be an 'asylum seeker' belonging to a vulnerable category of persons. To deliberately deny reception benefits to such asylum seekers if they are destitute would then not be in conformity with Article 3 of the ECHR. In the light of this interpretation, the terms 'allowed to remain' and 'final decision' used in the Directives to indicate their personal scope should be interpreted broadly in order to assure compliance with Article 3 of the ECHR. It has been argued in chapter two that the Directives leave room for such a broad interpretation.

14.4.6 State Obligations not Addressed by the EU Reception Conditions Directives

With respect to one field of social security, this study has revealed that international law contains obligations for states that are not addressed by the EU Reception Conditions Directives at all. While the Directives deal with asylum seekers' access to the labour market, they do not deal with asylum seekers' protection against the loss of (enough) work-related income caused by a social risk such as sickness, maternity or old age. Within the Common European Asylum System, access to social insurance benefits (as distinguished from social assistance benefits) is only addressed by the Qualification Directive, which applies to persons whose application for asylum has been granted. This study has shown, however, that also asylum seekers whose claim for recognition of their refugee status has not yet been decided may be entitled to have access to social insurance schemes on the same footing as nationals. This is dependent on meeting the (factual) requirement of ordinary residence. Accordingly, the EU Reception Conditions Directives do not address all obligations for the state as regards asylum seekers' access to social security and employment.

14.5 CONCLUDING REMARKS

Section 14.4 has provided some guidance for interpretation of norms laid down in the EU Reception Conditions Directives in order to ensure compliance with international law. In addition, section 14.4 has identified a number of shortcomings in the EU Reception Conditions Directives in relation to Member States' obligations stemming from international law that cannot be solved by conciliatory interpretation. With respect to different issues, the Directives provide for treatment that falls short of these obligations. While Directive 2013/33 alleviates some of these shortcomings (eg the safeguard that Member States should ensure a dignified standard of living for all asylum seekers in case of reduction and withdrawal of material reception benefits) compared to Directive 2003/9, it certainly does not address all of them. In view of the (minimum) nature of the standards laid down in the Directives and the discretionary room for Member States under most provisions, this does not mean that the Directives actually are *in violation of* international law. After all, the Directives allow Member States to retain or introduce more favourable provisions in order to comply with their obligations stemming from international law. However, if the standards laid down in the Directives are supposed to be fully in conformity with Member States' obligations under international law, and not to allow for treatment that falls short of these obligations, some adjustments should be made.

On a more abstract level, one could compare the general factors relevant for the existence and scope of state obligations under international law in the field of social security and employment identified in section 14.3 with the standards laid down in the EU Reception Conditions Directives. It then appears that some of these factors are reflected in the standards adopted in the Directives. For example, the Directives do provide for an (albeit arguably too limited) accretion of rights over time and leave more discretion to states in the field of access to the labour market than in the field of social security. Other factors are not taken into account. For example, the Directives do not place importance on permitted entry or on the degree of control applied to asylum seekers for establishing the scope and content of the rights of asylum seekers. Indeed, except for asylum seekers with special needs, the Directives do not distinguish between different categories of asylum seekers. Consequently, while the Directives on the whole guarantee a standard of treatment largely in conformity with international law for asylum seekers in general, this study has argued that some categories of asylum seekers are entitled to a more far-reaching protection in the light of international law.

A relevant and recurring theme of this book has been the large degree of convergence between states' immigration power and the field of social security and employment manifested in the (preparatory work for) the

EU Reception Conditions Directives and underlying domestic practice. It has been argued that while a full separation of these fields is not required, international law does set a number of limits on and attaches a number of consequences to this large degree of convergence. This outcome reflects the inherent tension between the contesting interests of equal human rights and state sovereignty. Owing to this tension, the question how far sovereignty may reach before it must give way to equality will always be contested and will produce different answers over time.

Bibliography

Addo, MK (1988) 'The Justiciability of Economic, Social and Cultural rights' 14 *Commonwealth Law Bulletin*, 1425–32.

Akandji-Kombe, JF (2007) *Positive Obligations under the European Convention on Human Rights: A Guide to the Implementation of the European Convention on Human Rights* (Strasbourg, Council of Europe).

Aleinikoff, TA (1983) 'Aliens, Due Process and 'Community Ties': A Response to Martin' 44 *University of Pittsburgh Law Review*, 237–60.

Alston, P and Quinn, G (1987) 'The Nature and Scope of State Parties' Obligations under the International Covenant on Economic, Social and Cultural Rights' 9 *Human Rights Quarterly*, 156–229.

Arai-Yokoi, Y (2003) 'Grading Scale of Degradation: Indentifying the Threshold of Degrading Treatment or Punishment under Article 3 ECHR' 21 *Netherlands Quarterly of Human Rights* 2003, 385–421.

Arambulo, K (1996) 'Drafting an Optional Protocol to the International Covenant on Economic, Social and Cultural Rights; Can an Ideal become Reality?' 2 *UC Davis Journal of International Law & Policy*, 111–36.

Arnardóttir, OM (2003) *Equality and Non-Discrimination under the European* Convention on Human Rights (The Hague, Martinus Nijhoff Publishers).

Aust, A (2007) *Modern Treaty Law and Practice* (Cambridge, Cambridge University Press).

Bank, R (2000) 'Reception Conditions for Asylum Seekers in Europe: An Analysis of Provisions in Austria, Belgium, France, Germany and the United Kingdom' 69 *Nordic Journal of International Law*, 257–88.

Barkhuysen, T and Bos, AW (2011) 'De betekenis van het Handvest van de Grondrechten van de Europese Unie voor het bestuursrecht' *JBPlus*, 3–34.

Battjes, H (2006) *European Asylum Law and International Law* (Leiden/Boston, Martinus Nijhoff Publishers).

— (2009) 'In Search for a Fair Balance. The Absolute Character of the Prohibition of Refoulement under Article 3 ECHR Reassessed' 22 *Leiden Journal of International Law*, 583–621.

— (2011) 'Straatsburgs toezicht op Unie-asielrecht. *MSS tegen België en Griekenland*', 2 *Asiel- & Migrantenrecht* 66–74.

Bell, M (2003) 'The Right to Equality and Non-Discrimination' in T Hervey and J Kenner (eds), *Economic and Social Rights under the EU Charter of Fundamental Rights. A Legal Perspective* (Oxford, Hart Publishing), 91–110.

— (2007) 'Chapter Two. Direct Discrimination' in D Schiek, L Waddington and M Bell, *Cases, Materials and Text on National, Supranational and International Non-Discrimination Law* (Oxford, Hart Publishing), 185–322.

Benhabib, S (2004) *The Rights of Others. Aliens, Residents, and Citizens* (Cambridge, Cambridge University Press).

Bloch, A and Schuster, L (2002) 'Asylum and Welfare: Contemporary Debates' 22 *Critical Social Policy*, 393–414.

Boeles, P (2005) 'Europese burgers en derdelanders: wat betekent het verbod van discriminatie naar nationaliteit sinds Amsterdam?' *Tijdschrift voor Europees en economisch recht*, 500–13.

Böhning, R (1991) 'The ILO and the New UN Convention on Migrant Workers: The Past and Future' 25 *International Migration Review*, 698–709.

Bolderson, H (2007) 'Exclusion of Vulnerable Groups from Equal Access to Social Security. The Case of Asylum Seekers in the UK' in E Riedel (ed), *Social Security as a Human Right. Drafting a General Comment on Article 9 ICESCR—Some Challenges* (Berlin Heidelberg, Springer), 129–43.

Bosniak, LS (2004) 'Human Rights, State Sovereignty and the Protection of Undocumented Migrants under the International Migrant Workers' Convention' in B Bogusz et al (eds), *Irregular Migration and Human Rights: Theoretical, European and International Perspectives* (Leiden, Martinus Nijhoff Publishers), 311–41.

— (2006) *The Citizen and the Alien. Dilemmas of Contemporary Membership* (Princeton, Princeton University Press).

— (2011) 'Human Rights within One State: Dilemmas of Personhood in Liberal Constitutional Thought' in MB Dembour and T Kelly (eds), *Are Human Rights for Migrants? Critical Reflections on the Status of Irregular Migrants in Europe and the United States* (Abingdon, Routledge), 201–21.

Bossuyt, M (2007) 'Should the Strasbourg Court Exercise more Self-restraint? On the Extension of the Jurisdiction of the European Court of Human Rights to Social Security Regulations' 28 *Human Rights Law Journal*, 321–32.

Boswell, C (2001) *Spreading the Costs of Asylum Seekers: A Critical Assessment of Dispersal Policies in Germany and the UK* (York, Anglo-German Foundation for the Study of Industrial Society).

Bouckaert, S (2007) *Documentloze vreemdelingen. Grondrechtenbescherming doorheen de Belgische en internationale rechtspraak vanaf 1985* (Antwerp/Apeldoorn, Maklu).

Breen, C (2008) 'The Policy of Direct Provision in Ireland: A Violation of Asylum Seekers' Right to an Adequate Standard of Housing' 20 *International Journal of Refugee Law*, 611–36.

Brems, E (2007) 'Indirect Protection of Social Rights by the European Court of Human Rights' in D Barak-Erez and AM Gross (eds), *Exploring Social Rights. Between Theory and Practice* (Oxford, Hart Publishing), 135–67.

Brownlie, I (2003) *Principles of Public International Law* (Oxford, Oxford University Press).

De Burca, G (2013) 'After the EU Charter of Fundamental Rights: The Court of Justice as a Human Rights Adjudicator?' 20 *Maastricht Journal of European and Comparative Law*, 168–84.

Buyse, A (2010) 'Kinderen in de kou. Gebrek aan onderdaksgarantie minderjarige illegalen schendt ESH. Europees Comité voor Sociale Rechten, 27 oktober 2009', 35 *NTM/NJCM-Bulletin*, 205–19.

Carens, JH (2005) 'On Belonging. What we Owe People who Stay' 30 *Boston Review*, 16–19.

Cassese, A (1991) 'Can the Notion of Inhuman and Degrading Treatment be Applied to Socio-Economic Conditions?' 2 *European Journal of International Law*, 141–45.

— (2005) *International Law* (Oxford, Oxford University Press).
Chapman, A and Russell, S (eds) (2002), *Core Obligations: Building a Framework for Economic, Social and Cultural Rights* (Antwerp, Oxford and New York, Intersentia).
Cholewinski, R (2000) 'Economic and Social Rights of Refugees and Asylum Seekers in Europe' 14 *Georgetown Immigration Law Journal*, 709–55.
— (2004) *Study on Obstacles to Effective Access of Irregular Migrants to Minimum Social Rights* (Strasbourg, Council of Europe Publishing).
— (2008) 'The Human and Labor Rights of Migrants: Visions of Equality' 22 *Georgetown Immigration Law Journal*, 177–219.
Churchill, RR and Khaliq, U (2004) 'The Collective Complaints System of the European Social Charter: An Effective Mechanism for Ensuring Compliance with Economic and Social Rights?' 15 *European Journal of International Law*, 417–56.
Clark, T (2004) 'Rights Based Refuge, the Potential of the 1951 Convention and the Need for Authoritative Interpretation' 16 *International Journal of Refugee law*, 584–608.
— and Crépeau, F (1999) 'Mainstreaming Refugee Rights. The 1951 Refugee Convention and International Human Rights Law' 17 *Netherlands Quarterly of Human Rights*, 389–410.
Coomans, F (ed) (2006) *Justiciability of Economic and Social Rights. Experiences from Domestic Systems* (Antwerp/Oxford, Intersentia).
Courtis, C (2008) *Commentary on the Optional Protocol to the International Covenant on Economic, Social and Cultural Rights* (Villière, Inter-American Institute of Human Rights/ International Commission of Jurists).
Cousins, M (2007) 'The *Luczak* v. Poland Judgment. Case Comment' 4 *European Journal of Social Security*, 374–88.
— (2008) *The European Convention on Human Rights and Social Security Law* (Antwerp, Intersentia).
Craven, MCR (1998) *The International Covenant on Economic, Social, and Cultural Rights. A Perspective on its Development* (Oxford, Clarendon Press).
Cullen, H (2009) 'The Collective Complaints System of the European Social Charter: Interpretative Methods of the European Committee of Social Rights' 9 *Human Rights Law Review*, 61–93.
Da Lomba, S (2011) 'Irregular Migrants and the Human Right to Health Care: a Case-Study of Health-care Provision for Irregular Migrants in France and the UK' 7 *International Journal of Law in Context*, 357–74.
Davies, G (2003) Nationality Discrimination in the European Internal Market (The Hague, Kluwer).
— (2011) 'Discrimination and Beyond in European Economic and Social Law' 18 *Maastricht Journal of European and Comparative Law*, 7–18.
De Jong, I (1990) 'De ROA en het recht op bijstand voor asielzoekers' 5 *Migrantenrecht*, 123–27.
Dembour, MB (2006) *Who Believes in Human Rights? Reflections on the European Convention* (Cambridge, Cambridge University Press).
— (2012) '*Gaygusuz* Revisited: The Limits of the European Court of Human Rights' Equality Agenda' 12 *Human Rights Law Review*, 689–721.
— and Kelly, T (2011) *Are Human Rights for Migrants? Critical Reflections on the Status of Irregular Migrants in Europe and the United States* (Abingdon, Routledge).

Den Heijer, M (2012) *Europe and Extraterritorial Asylum* (Oxford, Hart Publishing).
Dent, JA (1998) *Research Paper on the Social and Economic Rights of Non-Nationals in Europe* (London, European Council on Refugees and Exiles).
De Vries, K (2013a) *Integration at the Border. The Dutch Act on Integration Abroad and International Immigration Law* (Oxford, Hart Publishing).
— (2013b) 'Towards Integration and Equality for Third-country Nationals? Reflections on Kamberaj' 38 *European Law Review*, 248–58.
Douglas-Scott, S (2011) 'The European Union and Human Rights after the Treaty of Lisbon' 11 *Human Rights Law Review*, 645–82.
Dwyer, P and Brown, D (2005) 'Meeting Basic Needs? Forced Migrants and Welfare' 4 *Social Policy and Society*, 369–80.
Edwards, A (2003) 'Tampering with Refugee Protection: The Case of Australia' 15 *International Journal of Refugee Law*, 192–211.
— (2005) 'Human Rights, Refugees and the Right "to Enjoy" Asylum' 17 *International Journal of Refugee Law*, 293–330.
Eide, A (2001) 'Economic, Social and Cultural Rights as Human Rights' in A Eide, C Krause and A Rosas (eds), *Economic, Social and Cultural Rights. A Textbook* (Dordrecht/Boston/London, Martinus Nijhoff Publishers), 9–28.
Feldman, D (1997) 'The Developing Scope of Article 8 of the European Convention on Human Rights' 2 *European Human Rights Law Review*, 265–74.
Fiss, O (1998) 'The Immigrant as Pariah' 23 *Boston Review*, 4–7.
Fitzmaurice, G (1986) *The Law and Procedure of the International Court of Justice. Volume I* (Cambridge, Grotius Publications Limited).
Foster, M (2007) *International Refugee Law and Socio-Economic Rights. Refuge from Deprivation* (New York, Cambridge University Press).
Fox O'Mahony, L and Sweeney, A (2010) 'The Exclusion of (Failed) Asylum Seekers from Housing and Home: Towards an Oppositional Discourse' 37 *Journal of Law and Society*, 285–314.
Franssen, KAE, Larsson, FF and Slingenberg, CH (2007) 'De Opvangrichtlijn. Lacunes in de Nederlandse implementatie' 6 *Nieuwsbrief Asiel- en Vluchtelingenrecht*, 404–15.
Fredman, S (2006) 'Human Rights Transformed: Positive Duties and Positive Rights' *Public Law*, 498–520.
Geddes, A (2000) 'Denying Access. Asylum Seekers and Welfare Benefits in the UK' in M Bommes and A Geddes (eds), *Immigration and Welfare. Challenging the Borders of the Welfare State* (London/New York, Routledge), 134–47.
Gerards, JH (2002) *Rechterlijke toetsing aan het gelijkheidsbeginsel. Een rechtsvergelijkend onderzoek naar een algemeen toetsingsmodel* (The Hague, SDU Uitgevers).
— (2004a) 'The Application of Article 14 ECHR by the European Court of Human Rights' in J Niessen and I Chopin (eds), *The Development of Legal Instruments to Combat Racism in a Diverse Europe* (Leiden/Boston, Martinus Nijhoff Publishers), 3–60.
— (2004b) 'Gelijke behandeling en het EVRM. Artikel 14 EVRM: van krachteloze waarborg naar "norm met tanden?"' 29 *NJCM-Bulletin*, 176–98.
— (2007) 'Chapter One. Discrimination Grounds', in D Schiek, L Waddington and M Bell (eds), *Cases, Materials and Text on National, Supranational and International Non-Discrimination Law* (Oxford, Hart Publishing), 33–184.

— (2008a) 'Kroniek oordelen Commissie gelijke behandeling 2004-2007' 33 *NJCM-Bulletin*, 563–91.

— (2008b) 'Protocol No. 12 to the European Convention on Human Rights. Report prepared for the Commission to Propose a Comprehensive Anti-Discrimination Legislation in Norway' available at: www.regjeringen.no/nb/dep/bld/dok/nouer/2009/nou-2009-14/33.html?id=569103.

— (2011) 'Naar een "semi-open" systeem van gelijkebehandelingswetgeving?' 36 *NTM/NJCM-Bulletin*, 144–58.

Geuijen, K (1998) 'Wonen en werken in een asielzoekerscentrum' 14 *Migrantenstudies*, 261–72.

Gibney, MJ (2004) *The Ethics and Politics of Asylum. Liberal Democracy and the Response to Refugees* (Cambridge, Cambridge University Press).

Gomez Heredero, A (2007) 'Objectives and Interpretation Methods of the Conventions of the Council of Europe' in F Pennings (ed), *International Social Security Standards. Current Views and Interpretation Matters* (Antwerp/Oxford, Intersentia), 51–70.

Goodwin-Gill, GS (2003) 'Article 31 of the 1951 Convention Relating to the Status of Refugees: Non-penalization, Detention, and Protection' available at: www.unhcr.org/refworld/docid/470a33b10.html.

— and McAdam, J (2007) *The Refugee in International Law* (Oxford, Oxford University Press).

Grahl-Madsen, A (1963) *Commentary on the Refugee Convention 1951. Articles 2-11, 13-37* (Geneva, UNHCR 1997).

— (1966) *The Status of Refugees in International Law. Vol. I. Refugee Character* (Leiden, AW Sijthoff).

— (1972) *The Status of Refugees in International Law. Vol. II. Asylum, Entry and Sojourn* (Leiden, AW Sijthoff).

Griffey, B (2011) 'The "Reasonableness" Test: Assessing Violations of State Obligations under the Optional Protocol to the International Covenant on Economic, Social and Cultural Rights' 11 *Human Rights Law Review*, 275–327.

Groenendijk, K and Hampsink, R (1995) *Temporary Employment of Migrants in Europe* (Nijmegen, Katholieke Universiteit Nijmegen).

Guild, E (2004) 'Seeking Asylum: Storm Clouds between International Commitments and EU Legislative Measures' 29 *European Law Review*, 198–218.

Habermas, J (1996) *Between Facts and Norms. Contributions to a Discourse Theory of Law and Democracy* (Cambridge, MIT Press).

Hailbronner, K (2007) 'Detention of Asylum Seekers' 9 *European Journal of Migration and Law*, 159–72.

— (2008) 'Presence and Rights: A Response to Linda Bosniak' 1 *Amsterdam Law Forum*, 10–14.

Handoll, J (2004) 'Reception Conditions of Asylum Seekers' in CD Urbano de Sousa and P De Bruycker (eds), *The Emergence of a European Asylum Policy* (Brussels, Bruylant), 111–48.

— (2007) 'Directive 2003/9 on Reception Conditions of Asylum Seekers: Ensuring "Mere Subsistence" or a "Dignified Standard of Living"?' in A Baldaccini, E Guild and H Toner (eds), *Whose Freedom, Security and Justice? EU Immigration and Asylum Law and Policy* (Oxford, Hart Publishing), 195–228.

Hannum, H (1996) 'The Status of the Universal Declaration of Human Rights in National and International law' 25 *Georgia Journal of International and Comparative Law*, 287–354.

Harris, D and Darcy, J (2001) *The European Social Charter* (Ardsley, Transnational Publishers).

Harris, D et al (2009) *Harris, O'Boyle and Warbrick. Law of the European Convention on Human Rights* (Oxford, Oxford University Press).

Hart, HLA (1957) 'Positivism and the Separation of Law and Morals' 71 *Harvard Law Review*, 593–629.

— (1994) *The Concept of Law* (Oxford, Oxford University Press).

Hathaway, JC (1991) *The Law of Refugee Status* (Toronto, Butterworths).

— (2005) *The Rights of Refugees under International Law* (Cambridge, Cambridge University Press).

— and Foster, M (2003) 'The Causal Connection ("Nexus") to a Convention Ground' 15 *International Journal of Refugee Law*, 461–76.

Heringa, AW (1999) 'Standards of Review for Discrimination. The Scope of Review by the Courts' in MLP Loenen and PR Rodrigues (eds), *Non-discrimination Law: Comparative Perspectives* (The Hague, Kluwer Law International), 25–38.

Hilbrink, E (2010) 'The Proportionality Principle: Two European Perspectives. How Serving the Community Interest Ends up to be in the Individual's Best Interest' available at: dare.ubvu.vu.nl//handle/1871/15826.

Holtmaat, R (2000) 'De toekomst van gelijkheid: een agenda voor wetgeving, beleid en onderzoek op het gebied van discriminatiebestrijding en gelijke behandeling' in R Holtmaat (ed), *De toekomst van gelijkheid: de juridische en maatschappelijke inbedding van de gelijkebehandelingsnorm* (Deventer, Kluwer), 253–68.

Hublet, C (2009) 'The Scope of Article 12 of the Treaty of the European Communities *vis-à vis* Third-Country Nationals: Evolution at Last?' 15 *European Law Journal*, 757–74.

Hughes, J and Liebaut, F (eds) (1998), *Detention of Asylum Seekers in Europe: Analysis and Perspectives* (The Hague, Martinus Nijhoff Publishers).

International Commission of Jurists (2008) *Courts and the Legal Enforcement of Economic, Social and Cultural Rights* (International Commission of Jurists).

Ippolito, F (2013) 'The Contribution of the European Courts to the Common European Asylum System and its Ongoing Recast Process' *Maastricht Journal of European and Comparative Law*, 261–81.

Jansen, J (2006) *Bepaalde huisvesting. Een geschiedenis van opvang en huisvesting van immigranten in Nederland, 1945–1995* (Amsterdam, Amsterdam University Press).

Jennings, R and Watts, A (1992) *Oppenheim's International Law. Volume I* (Essex, Longman Group).

Kapuy, K (2007) 'Social Security and the European Convention on Human Rights: How an Odd Couple has Become Presentable' 9 *European Journal of Social Security*, 221–41.

— (2011) *The Social Security Position of Irregular Migrant Workers. New Insights from National Social Security Law and International Law* (Cambridge/Antwerp/Portland, Intersentia).

—, Pieters, D and Zaglmayer, B (2007) *Social Security Cases in Europe: the European Court of Human Rights* (Antwerp/Oxford, Intersentia).

Karatani, R (2005) 'How History Separated Refugee and Migrant Regimes: In Search of Their Institutional Origins' 17 *International Journal of Refugee Law*, 518–41.

Kenna, P (2008) 'Housing Rights: Positive Duties and Enforceable Rights at the European Court of Human Rights' 13 *European Human Rights Law Review*, 193–208.

Klaver, J and Tromp, E (2004) *Asielzoekers en werk. Evaluatie van de mogelijkheden van betaald werken in het kader van de Wet arbeid vreemdelingen* (The Hague, Ministerie van Sociale Zaken en Werkgelegenheid).

Koch, IE (2009) *Human Rights as Indivisible Rights. The Protection of Socio-Economic Demands under the European Convention on Human Rights* (Leiden/Boston, Martinus Nijhoff Publishers).

Krause, C and Scheinin, M (2000) 'The Right not to be Discriminated Against: the Case of Social Security' in TS Orlin, A Rosas and M Scheinin (eds), *The Jurisprudence of Human Rights Law: A Comparative Interpretive Approach* (Turku/Åbo, Institute for Human Rights/Åbo Akademi University).

Larkin, PM (2007) 'The "Criminalization" of Social Security Law: Towards a Punitive Welfare State' *Journal of Law and Society*, 295–320.

Larsson, FF (2011) *De EU-richtlijn over opvang van asielzoekers. Opvangvoorzieningen in Nederland en Frankrijk en de rechtsbescherming tegen het onthouden van opvang* (The Hague, Kluwer).

Legomsky, SH (1995) 'Immigration, Federalism, and the Welfare State' 42 *UCLA Law Review*, 1453–74.

Liedtke, M (2002) 'National Welfare and Asylum in Germany' 22 *Critical Social Policy*, 479–97.

Lillich, RB (1984) *The Human Rights of Aliens in Contemporary International Law* (Manchester, Manchester University Press).

Lu, H (2008) 'The Personal Application of the Right to Work in the Age of Migration' 26 *Netherlands Quarterly of Human Rights*, 43–77.

Mabbett, D and Bolderson, H (2002) 'Non-Discrimination, Free Movement, and Social Citizenship in Europe: Contrasting Provisions for EU Nationals and Asylum-Seekers' in R Sigg and C Behrends (eds), *Social Security in the Global Village* (New Brunswick/London, Transaction Publishers), 191–210.

MacCormick, N (2005) *Rhetoric and the Rule of Law: A Theory of Legal Reasoning* (Oxford, Oxford University Press).

McAdam, J (2007) *Complementary Protection in International Refugee Law* (Oxford, Oxford University Press).

McClean, JD (1962) 'The Meaning of Residence' 11 *International and Comparative Law Quarterly*, 1153–68.

McLachlan, CA (2005) 'The Principle of Systematic Integration and Article 31(3)(c) of the Vienna Convention' 54 *International and Comparative Law Quarterly*, 279–320.

Mahon, CA (2008) 'Progress at the Front: The Draft Optional Protocol to the International Covenant on Economic, Social and Cultural Rights' 8 *Human Rights Law Review*, 617–46.

Martin, DA (2001) 'Graduated Application of Constitutional Protections for Aliens: The Real Meaning of Zadvydas v. Davis' 2001 *Supreme Court Review*, 47–136.

Mechlem, K (2009) 'Treaty Bodies and the Interpretation of Human Rights' 42 *Vanderbilt Journal of Transnational Law*, 905–48.

Merrills, JG (1993) *The Development of International Law by the European Court of Human Rights* (New York, Manchester University Press).

Mikkola, M (2008) 'Social Human Rights of Migrants under the European Social Charter' 10 *European Journal of Social Security*, 25–59.

Minderhoud, PE (1999) 'Asylum Seekers and Access to Social Security: Recent Developments in The Netherlands, United Kingdom, Germany and Belgium' in A Bloch and C Levy (eds), *Refugees, Citizenship and Social Policy in Europe* (London, MacMillan Press), 132–48.

— (2000) 'The Dutch Lining Act and the Violation of Various International Non-Discrimination Clauses' 2 *European Journal of Migration and Law*, 185–201.

— (2003) 'Regulering van migratie door middel van sociale zekerheid' in Berghman et al (eds), *Honderd jaar sociale zekerheid in Nederland* (Delft, Eburon), 279–92.

Morris, L (2010) Asylum, Welfare and the Cosmopolitan Ideal. A Sociology of Rights (Abingdon/New York, Routledge).

Mowbray, AR (2004) *The Development of Positive Obligations under the European Convention on Human Rights by the European Court of Human Rights* (Oxford and Portland, Hart Publishing).

Müller, A (2009) 'Limitations to and Derogations from Economic, Social and Cultural Rights' 9 *Human Rights Law Review*, 557–601.

Nickless, J and Siedl, H (2004) *Co-ordination of Social Security in the Council of Europe: Short Guide* (Strasbourg, Council of Europe).

Noll, G (2000) *Negotiating Asylum. The EU Acquis, Extraterritorial Protection and the Common Market of Deflection* (The Hague/Boston/London, Martinus Nijhoff Publishers).

— (2005) 'Seeking Asylum at Embassies: A Right to Entry under International Law' 17 *International Journal of Refugee Law*, 542–73.

— (2010) 'Why Human Rights Fail to Protect Undocumented Migrants' 12 *European Journal of Migration and Law*, 241–72.

Nollkaemper, A (2005) *Kern van het internationaal publiekrecht* (The Hague, Boom Juridische uitgevers).

Noordam, FM and Vonk, GJ (2011) *Hoofdzaken sociale-zekerheidsrecht* (Deventer, Kluwer).

Nußberger, A (2007) 'Interpretation of International Social Security Standards—Problems and Prospects' in F Pennings (ed), *International Social Security Standards. Current Views and Interpretation Matters* (Antwerp/Oxford, Intersentia), 33–50.

O'Cinneide, C (2008) 'A Modest Proposal: Destitution, State Responsibility and the European Convention on Human Rights' 13 *European Human Rights Law Review*, 583–605.

O'Connell, R (2009) 'Cinderella Comes to the Ball: Art 14 and the Right to Non-discrimination in the ECHR' 29 *Legal Studies*, 211–29.

Ovey, C and White, R (2002) *Jacobs and White, The European Convention on Human Rights* (Oxford, Oxford University Press).

Palmer, E (2007) *Judicial Review, Socio-Economic Rights and the Human Rights Act* (Oxford, Hart Publishing).

— (2009) 'Protecting Socio-Economic Rights through the European Convention on Human Rights: Trends and Developments in the European Court of Human Rights' 2 *Erasmus Law Review*, 397–425.

Palmer, S (2006) 'A Wrong Turning: Article 3 ECHR and Proportionality' 65 *Cambridge Law Journal*, 438–52.

Patterson, D (1999) 'Explicating the Internal Point of View' 52 *SMU Law Review*, 67–74.

Peek, M (2010) 'Council Directive 2003/9/EC of 27 January 2003 laying down minimum standards for the reception of asylum seekers' in K Hailbronner (ed), *EU Immigration and Asylum Law. Commentary on EU Regulations and Directives* (Munich/Oxford, Beck/Hart), 871–984.

Pennings, F (ed) (2006) *Between Soft and Hard Law. The Impact of International Social Security Standards on National Social Security Law* (The Hague, Kluwer Law International).

— (2010) *European Social Security Law* (Antwerp/Oxford/Portland, Intersentia).

Pieters, D (2006) *Social Security: An Introduction to the Basic Principles* (The Hague, Kluwer Law International).

Pluymen, M (2008) *Niet toelaten betekent uitsluiten. Een rechtssociologisch onderzoek naar de rechtvaardiging en praktijk van uitsluiting van vreemdelingen van voorzieningen* (The Hague, Boom Juridische Uitgevers).

Puts, JHL (1995) *Asielzoekers tussen rijk en gemeenten. Onderhandelingen over de huisvesting van migranten* (The Hague, VNG-uitgeverij).

Ramcharan, BG (1981) 'Equality and Nondiscrimination' in L Henkin (ed), *The International Bill of Rights. The Covenant on Civil and Political Rights* (New York, Columbia University Press).

Reneman, AM (2011) 'Het Kinderrechtenverdrag krijgt tanden, Over hoe het VN Verdrag inzake de Rechten van het Kind via het EU-recht en het EVRM binnendringt in het Nederlandse vreemdelingenrecht' 2 *Asiel- en Migrantenrecht*, 349–62.

— (2012) *EU Asylum Procedures and the Rights to an Effective Remedy* (Leiden, EM Meijers Instituut 2012) (to be published by Hart Publishing).

Rieter, E (2010) 'Het EHRM en onherstelbaar letsel. De rol van internationale en regionale jurisprudentie over *interim measures* in the praktijk van het EHRM' 35 *NTM/NJCM-Bulletin*, 797–812.

Robinson, V, Andersson, R and Musterd, S (2003) *Spreading the 'Burden'? A Review of Policies to Disperse Asylum Seekers and Refugees* (Bristol, The Policy Press).

Rogers, N (2002) 'Minimum Standards for Reception' 4 *European Journal of Migration and Law*, 215–30.

Rogerson, P (2000) 'Habitual Residence: The New Domicile' 49 *International and Comparative Law Quarterly*, 86–107.

Rosenberger, S and König, A (2011) 'Welcoming the Unwelcome: The Politics of Minimum Reception Standards for Asylum Seekers in Austria' 24 *Journal of Refugee Studies*, 1–18.

Sales, R (2002) 'The Deserving and the Undeserving? Refugees, Asylum Seekers and Welfare in Britain' 22 *Critical Social Policy*, 456–78.

Sawyer, C and Turpin, P (2005) 'Neither Here nor There: Temporary Admission to the UK' 17 *International Journal of Refugee Law*, 688–728.

Schiek, D, Waddington, L and Bell, M (2007) 'Introductory Chapter. A Comparative Perspective on Non-discrimination Law' in D Schiek, L Waddington and M Bell, *Cases, Materials and Text on National, Supranationals and International Non-Discrimination Law* (Oxford, Hart Publishing), 1–32.

Schokkenbroek, J (1998) 'The Prohibition of Discrimination in Article 14 of the Convention and the Margin of Appreciation' 1 *Human Rights Law Journal*, 20–23.

Schoukens, P (2007) 'Instruments of the Council of Europe and Interpretation Problems' in F Pennings (ed), *International Social Security Standards. Current Views and Interpretation Matters* (Antwerp/Oxford, Intersentia), 71–90.

— and Pieters, D (2004) *Exploratory Report on the Access to Social Protection for Illegal Labour Migrants* (Strasbourg, Council of Europe).

Schuster, L (2000) 'A Comparative Analysis of the Asylum Policy of Seven European Governments' 13 *Journal of Refugee Studies*, 118–31.

— (2005) 'A Sledgehammer to Crack a Nut: Deportation, Detention and Dispersal in Europe' 39 *Social Policy & Administration*, 606–21.

Schwarzenberger, G (1957) *International Law. Volume I. International Law as applied by International Courts and Tribunals* (London, Stevens & Sons Limited).

Sepúlveda, MM (2003) *The Nature of the Obligations under the International Covenant on Economic, Social and Cultural Rights* (Antwerp/Oxford, Intersentia).

Shaw, MN (2003) *International Law* (Cambridge, Cambridge University Press).

Sinclair, I (1984) *The Vienna Convention on the Law of Treaties* (Manchester, Manchester University Press).

Spijkerboer, TP (2010) *De nieuwe asielprocedure—Vluchtelingenrecht* (Nijmegen, Ars Aequi).

— (2011) 'Stretching the Limits. European Maritime Border Control Policies and International Law' in M Maes, MC Foblets and Ph De Bruycker (eds), *External Dimensions of EU Migration and Asylum Law and Policy* (Brussels, Bruylant), 387–413.

— and Vermeulen, BP (2005) *Vluchtelingenrecht* (Nijmegen, Ars Aequi Libri).

Stenberg, G (1989) *Non-Expulsion and Non-Refoulement. The Prohibition against Removal of Refugees with Special Reference to Articles 32 and 33 of the 1951 Convention relating to the Status of Refugees* (Uppsala, Iustus Förlag).

Sweeney, JA (2008) 'The Human Rights of Failed Asylum Seekers in the United Kingdom' *Public Law*, 277–301.

Sweet, AS and Mathews, J (2008) 'Proportionality Balancing and Global Constitutionalism' 47 *Columbia Journal of Transnational Law*, 73–165.

Tazreiter, C (2004) *Asylum Seekers and the State. The Politics of Protection in a Security-Conscious World* (Aldershot/Burlington, Ashgate).

Tobler, C (2005) *Indirect Discrimination. A Case Study into the Development of the Legal Concept of Indirect Discrimination under EC Law* (Antwerp/Oxford, Intersentia).

Tooze, J (2003) 'Social Security and Social Assistance' in T Hervey and J Kenner (eds), *Economic and Social Rights under the EU Charter of Fundamental Rights. A Legal Perspective* (Oxford, Hart Publishing), 161–92.

Tulkens, F and Van Drooghenbroeck, S (2008) 'Armoede en mensenrechten. De bijdrage van het Europese Hof voor de Rechten van de Mens' in *Armoede, waardigheid, mensenrechten. 10 jaar samenwerkingsakkoord* (Steunpunt tot bestrijding van armoede, bestaansonzekerheid en sociale uitsluiting), 65–73.

Tzevelekos, VP (2010) 'The Use of Article 31(3)(c) of the VCLT in the Case Law of the ECtHR: An Effective Anti-fragmentation Tool or a Selective Loophole for the Reinforcement of Human Rights Teleology? Between Evolution and Systematic Integration' 31 *Michigan Journal of International Law*, 621–90.

United Nations High Commissioner for Refugees (1988) 'Lawfully Staying—a Note on Interpretation' available at: www.refworld.org/docid/42ad93304.html.

— (1992) *Handbook on Procedures and Criteria for Determining Refugee Status under the 1951 Convention and the 1967 Protocol relating to the Status of Refugees* (Geneva, UNHCR).

— (2000) 'Reception Standards for Asylum Seekers in the European Union' available at: www.refworld.org/docid/3ae6b3440.html.

— (2003) 'UNHCR Annotated Comments on Council Directive 2003/9/EC of 27 January 2003 laying down minimum standards for the reception of asylum seekers' available at: www.unhcr.org/refworld/docid/3f3770104.html.

Vanneste, F (2010) *General International Law before Human Rights Courts. Assessing the Specialty of International Human Rights Law* (Antwerp/Oxford, Intersentia).

Vandenbogaerde, A and Vandenhole, W (2010) 'The Optional Protocol to the International Covenant on Economic, Social and Cultural Rights: An Ex Ante Assessment of its Effectiveness in Light of the Drafting Process' 10 *Human Rights Law Review*, 207–37.

Vandenhole, W (2003) 'Completing the UN Complaint Mechanisms for Human Rights Violations Step by Step: Towards a Complaints Procedure to the International Covenant on Economic, Social and Cultural Rights' 21 *Netherlands Quarterly of Human Rights*, 423–62.

— (2005) *Non-Discrimination and Equality in the View of the UN Human Rights Treaty Bodies* (Antwerp/Oxford, Intersentia).

Van der Horst, H (2004) 'Living in a Reception Centre: the Search for Home in an Institutional Setting' 21 *Housing, Theory and Society*, 36–46.

Van Dijk, F et al (eds) (2006) *Theory and Practice of the European Convention on Human* Rights (Antwerp/Oxford, Intersentia).

Van Hoof, GJH (1984) 'The Legal Nature of Economic, Social and Cultural Rights: A Rebuttal of Some Traditional Views' in P Alston and K Tomaševski (eds), *The Right to Food* (Leiden, Martinus Nijhoff Publishers), 97–110.

Vierdag, EW (1973) *The Concept of Discrimination in International Law* (The Hague, Martinus Nijhoff Publishers).

— (1978) 'The Legal Nature of the Rights Granted by the International Covenant on Economic, Social and Cultural Rights, 9 *Netherlands Yearbook of International Law*, 69–105.

Vincenzi, S (2004) 'Reception Conditions for Asylum Seekers: Comments' in CD Urbano de Sousa and P De Bruycker (eds), *The Emergence of a European Asylum Policy* (Brussels, Bruylant), 157–66.

Vlemminx, F (2002) *Een nieuw profiel van de grondrechten. Een analyse van de prestatieplichten ingevolge klassieke en sociale grondrechten* (The Hague, Boom Juridische Uitgevers).

Vonk, GJ (1991) *De coördinatie van bestaansminimumuitkeringen in de Europese Gemeenschap* (Deventer, Kluwer).

— (2000) 'Social Security and the Right to Property: Gaygusuz and After' in JP Loof, H Ploeger and A van der Steur (eds), *The Right to Property, the Influence of Article I protocol No. 1 ECHR on Several Fields of Domestic Law* (Maastricht, EM Meijers Institute), 145–55.

— (2005) 'Het recht van mensen zonder papieren op minimumvoorzieningen: De invloed van internationale grondrechtverklaringen' 13 *Tijdschrift voor Sociaal Recht/Revue de Droit Social*, 589–608.

Wallace, RMM (2002) *International Law* (London, Sweet & Maxwell).

Walzer, M (1983) *Spheres of Justice. A Defense of Pluralism and Equality* (Basic Books).

Warbrick, C (1998) 'The Structure of Article 8' 3 *European Human Rights Law Review*, 32–44.

— (2007) 'Economic and Social Interests and the European Convention on Human Rights' in M Baderin and R McCorquodale (eds), *Economic, Social, and Cultural Rights in Action* (Oxford, Oxford University Press), 241–56.

Wentholt, K (1999) 'Formal and Substantive Equal Treatment: the Limitations and the Potential of the Legal Concept of Equality' in MLP Loenen and PR Rodrigues (eds), *Non-discrimination Law: Comparative Perspectives* (The Hague, Kluwer Law International), 53–64.

Westen, P (1982) 'The Empty Idea of Equality' 95 *Harvard Law Review*, 537–96.

White, RCA and Ovey, C (2010) *The European Convention on Human Rights* (New York, Oxford University Press).

Zimmermann, A (ed) (2011) *The 1951 Convention Relation to the Status of Refugees and its 1967 Protocol. A Commentary* (New York, Oxford University Press).

Zyberi, G (2008) *The Humanitarian Face of the International Court of Justice. Its Contribution to Interpreting and Developing International Human Rights and Humanitarian Law Rules and Principles* (Antwerp, Intersentia).

Index

www.ingramcontent.com/pod-product-compliance
Ingram Content Group UK Ltd.
Pitfield, Milton Keynes, MK11 3LW, UK
UKHW020131290926
15471UKWH00003B/414

9 781509 909254